# Advanced Level Business Studies

## 2nd edition

### Stephen Danks

BSc(Hons), Dip Marketing, Cert Ed.

Stephen Danks has wide experience of industry, commerce and teaching. Formerly a Head of Business Studies in a large Further Education College, he has also taught in schools.

He is currently NVQ Chief Verifier for Pitman Examinations Institute and Senior Verifier for Business Administration. He is also a former BTEC examiner, RSA examiner and City and Guilds Assessor.

DP Publications Ltd
Aldine Place
London W12 8AW
1995

## Acknowledgements

I am grateful to the following for permission to reproduce copyright material in the text.

AT & T
Commission for Racial Equality
Crown Copyright
The Daily Mail
The Department of Trade and Industry
The Employment Department
Ford Motor Company
Foreign and Commonwealth Office
Godfrey Hill
Procter & Gamble plc
Marketing Magazine
The Sunday Times

I also wish to thank all the organisations and newspapers for the use of other materials (despite every effort, I have failed to trace the copyright holders for some of the material used.)

I am also indebted to Kath Clayton who did the typing and to Catherine Tilley and Dick Chapman of DP Publications for their valuable assistance and advice.

A CIP catalogue record for this book is available from the British Library

ISBN 1 85805 112 6
Copyright S. Danks © 1995

First edition 1993
Second edition 1995

All rights reserved
No part of this publication may be reproduced, stored in a retrieval system, or transmitted in any form or by any means, electronic, mechanical, photocopying, recording, or otherwise, without the prior permission of the copyright owner.

Printed by
The Guernsey Press Co Ltd
Braye Road, Vale, Guernsey

# Preface

## Aim

The aim of this text is to provide a comprehensive text book for Business Studies courses in schools and colleges. It has been specifically written for students taking GCE Advanced Level Business Studies, but it is also suitable as an introduction to higher level courses in both business studies and management. It can also be used for teaching joint programmes of GNVQ Advanced Business (Mandatory Units) and A Level. (A text specifically written for GNVQ Advanced Business by the same author and publisher is also available.)

## Need

This text answers the need for material that:

- provides a lively and clear approach to business studies
- provides a variety of tasks and methods of assessment including
  - case studies
  - problem solving
  - data response
  - essay examination questions
  - short answer questions
  - multiple choice/completion
  - assignments
- presents business studies in a way that develops other relevant core skills and techniques such as numeracy, communication, information technology and the selection and use of relevant information.

## Approach

The text has been written in a structured form, with numbered paragraphs, summaries, self review questions and many different assessment means. Each chapter contains the following question types:

- *student-centred tasks* (answers in Lecturers' Supplement)
- *review questions* (with paragraph references to the answers in the text)
- *essay-style A Level examination questions* (half with answers in the book, half with answers in the Lecturers' Supplement)
- *short answer questions* similar to those in the A Level examinations (half with answers in the book, half with answers in the Lecturers' Supplement)
- *multiple choice/completion questions* (half with answers in the book, half with answers in the Lecturers' Supplement)
- *assignments* (answers in the Lecturers' Supplement)

## How to use the book

The book is designed to be used as a course text to support either a course with a high proportion of lecturer contact time or one that allows for less contact time and more directed self-study. For the latter type of course, students will find the numerous questions with answers allow them to test their understanding.

To help lecturers planning courses the charts on pages viii-ix map the coverage of the individual A Level board syllabuses chapter by chapter. The chapters can be tackled in any order, although Chapters 19 and 20 assume a knowledge of some principles covered earlier.

Although no previous knowledge of business studies is required to use this text, students may find it useful to refer to *A First Course in Business Studies* (S Danks, DP Publications, 1992) for additional background information.

### Lecturers' Supplement

A free Lecturers' Supplement is available on application to the Publishers in writing (on your school/college headed paper) stating the course on which the book is to be recommended, the number of students on the course, and the probable numbers of books to be purchased by them.

The Supplement contains outline answers to:

    the 300 in-text tasks

    half of the 60 essay-style questions

    half of the 60 short-answer questions

    half of the 150 multiple choice questions

    and to the 20 end of chapter assignments.

### Suggestions and criticisms

The author would welcome, via the publishers, any comments on the book. This will enable subsequent editions to be amended, if necessary, and made even more useful to students and teachers alike.

### Discrimination between the sexes

For reasons of textual fluency, you will find the words 'he/him/her' have been used throughout this book. However, in most cases the person referred to could be of either sex.

*S Danks*
*January 1995*

# Contents

**Preface** iii
**Additional Notes** vii
**Syllabus Coverage** viii

## ADVANCED BUSINESS STUDIES

*All Chapters include:*
* Self Assessment Tasks
* A Summary
* Review Questions
* Examination Practice Questions
* Multiple Choice/Completion Questions
* Assignment Activities

1. **THE BUSINESS ENVIRONMENT**   1
   *What is Business? – Development of Economic Activity – Needs and Wants – Scarcity and Choice – The Resources of Business – Profit – Economic Systems – Business Objectives – Business Functions- Management – Decision Making and Constraints – Measurement of Performance*

2. **BUSINESS ENTERPRISE**   19
   *Types of Business Organisation – Private Enterprise – Forming a Limited Company – Dissolution of Companies – Stock Exchange – Public Enterprise – Privatisation.*

3. **BUSINESS PLANNING**   41
   *Corporate Strategic Planning – SWOT Analysis – Environmental Scanning – PEST Analysis – Competitor Analysis – Corporate Gap.*

4. **THE MARKET MECHANISM**   59
   *Economics and Business – Markets – Market Prices – Demand – Elasticity of Demand – Supply – Elasticity of Supply – Theory of the Firm – Perfect Competition – Monopoly – Imperfect Competition – Oligopoly.*

5. **BUSINESS AND THE ECONOMY**   85
   *Circular Flow of Income – Unemployment – Inflation – Public Finance – Taxation – Economic Growth – Multiplier – Managing the Economy.*

6. **BUSINESS AND THE INTERNATIONAL ECONOMY**   116
   *Reasons for Trade – Absolute and Comparative Advantage – Balance of Payments – Barriers to Trade – Rate of Exchange – Fixed and Floating Exchange Rates – IMF – GATT – EFTA – EEA – European Union – International Marketing – Multi-National Companies.*

7. **MARKETING AND MARKET RESEARCH**   139
   *Marketing – Marketing Objectives – Marketing Management – Marketing Mix – Consumer, Industrial and Service Marketing – Market Research – Sampling – Desk Research – Field Research – Market Segmentation – Evaluating Market Research.*

8. **THE MARKETING MIX – PRODUCT AND PRICE**   155
   *Product Range – Product Life Cycle – Product Development – Product Withdrawal – Product Planning – Branding – Own Brands – Packaging – Product Strategy – Price – Pricing Objectives – Pricing Policies.*

9. **THE MARKETING MIX – PROMOTION AND PLACE**   172
   *Sales Promotion – Trade and Consumer Promotions – Industrial Promotions – Direct Mail – Advertising – Advertising Media – Advertising Costs – Advertising Agencies – Advertising Benefits/Criticisms – Control of Advertising – Public Relations – Personal Selling – Distribution – Wholesalers – Retailers – Distribution Decisions.*

10. **BUSINESS FINANCE**   190
    *Financial Management – Working Capital – Types of Capital – Sources of Finance – Shares and Dividends – Capital Gearing – Decision Making – Investment Appraisal – Cost-Benefit Analysis – Decision Trees – Sensitivity and Risk Analysis.*

## 11. FINANCIAL RECORD-KEEPING — 210
*Need for Accounts – Financial and Management Accounting – Auditors -Accounting Concepts – Final Accounts – Assets and Liabilities – Profit and Loss Account – Balance Sheet – Stock Valuation – Depreciation – Interpretation of Accounts – Types of Capital – Ratio Analysis – Funds Flow Statement.*

## 12. HUMAN RESOURCES IN ORGANISATIONS — 229
*People and Business – Personnel Management – Manpower Planning – Personnel Functions – Recruitment – Selection Interviews – Training – Staff Appraisal – Employment Legislation – Termination of Employment – Unfair Dismissal – Redundancy Payments – Monitoring Personnel Policy.*

## 13. ORGANISATIONAL BEHAVIOUR — 251
*Why People Work – Line and Staff Organisation – Authority – Responsibility and Delegation – Leadership – Span of Control – Organisational Culture – Organisational Management Theory.*

## 14. EMPLOYER AND EMPLOYEE RELATIONS — 267
*Motivation and Job Satisfaction – Determination of Wage Rates – Methods of Payment – Fringe Benefits – Industrial Relations – Trade Unions – Collective Bargaining – Employers Associations – Industrial Action – Joint Consultation – ACAS – The Government and Industrial Relations – Labour Turnover.*

## 15. PRODUCTION PROCESSES AND CONTROL — 282
*Production and Operations Management – Costs of Production – Product Design Strategy – Value Analysis – Purchasing – Stock Control – Organisation of Production – Productivity – Work Study – Organisation and Methods – Business Location – Economies of Scale – Size and Growth of Firms – Monopolies and Restrictive Practices.*

## 16. BUSINESS INFORMATION SYSTEMS — 310
*Types of Communication – Need for Effective Communication – Internal Communication – Business Meetings – External Communication – Telecommunications – Electronics and Information Technology – Use of Business Systems – Business Documents – Payment Documents – Banking – Security – Future Developments – Barriers to Effective Communication.*

## 17. INNOVATION AND CHANGE — 340
*Concept of Change – Internal and External Forces – Barriers to Change – Conflict – Managing Change – Innovation – Research and Development – Changing Lifestyles – Environmental Change – Recycling – Employment and Change – Community Impact.*

## 18. DATA ANALYSIS AND PRESENTATION — 362
*Introduction to Statistics – Sampling – Averages – Measures of Dispersion – Presentation of Data – Figures, Graphs, Bar Charts, Pie Charts, Diagrams – Normal Distribution – Index Numbers – Probability – Forecasting – Spreadsheets – Databases – Data Storage/Retrieval.*

## 19. MONITORING BUSINESS PERFORMANCE — 386
*Cost Control – Budgets – Budgetary Control – Standard Costing – Variance Analysis – Break-Even – Quality Control – Operational Research Techniques.*

## 20. STARTING AND RUNNING YOUR OWN BUSINESS — 404
*Why Bother – Self Assessment – Professional Advisers – Insurance – Business Planning – Marketing – Location – Legal Forms – Obtaining Finance – Accounting – Legal Basics – Taxation – Employing People – Training – Monitoring Performance.*

**BUSINESS UPDATE** — 423

**GLOSSARY** — 428

**USEFUL ADDRESSES** — 438

**OUTLINE ANSWERS** — 439

**INDEX** — 449

## Additional Notes for Students

You will find that this book contains several different types of tasks and assignments including case studies, projects and practical exercises. These are designed to encourage you to take an active part in the process of learning.

A number of the tasks require you to work outside the classroom and can be carried out either as an individual or as a member of a group. Some assignments will also require you to make oral presentations. Where possible, you are advised to make use of information technology in your studies.

### Obtaining Information

You will be asked to obtain a variety of information which will require you to use library reference books or other sources such as newspapers and journals. You will also need to contact various organisations, including local companies, to obtain information.

### Presentation and Assessment

Your work should always be well organised and neatly presented. This is particularly important if it is to form part of your coursework portfolio.

A suitable structure for research reports might be as follows:
- Title and purpose of report
- Summary of findings, including any key recommendations
- Introduction
- Body of report, that is, presentation and analysis of data collected
- Conclusions or results

As you will see in Chapter 18, graphs, pie charts, pictographs and bar charts are particularly good methods of presenting any numerical information.

Research projects are usually assessed on the quality and depth of the research, analysis of the data collected, evaluation of the findings and the final presentation.

### Keeping Up-to-date

Business studies is an exciting subject but it also changes rapidly and therefore it is often difficult to keep up-to-date. If you are to be really successful in your advanced course, it is important that you devote some time to this aspect of your studies. There are many ways of doing this but I would recommend that the following are some which you might find particularly useful to pursue on a regular basis.

- Read a quality newspaper such as the Daily Telegraph or Financial Times
- Listen and take note of news bulletins on television and radio
- Statistical data can be found in the Monthly Digest of Statistics, Annual Abstract of Statistics, Social Trends, Population Trends, and other Government publications
- Other regularly published sources of information include Bank Reviews, Company Reports, The Economist and a wide range of journals which should be available in your local library.
- Information about key trends in your area can be gathered from local press and other media reports.
- Other useful local sources include Business Enterprise Agencies, Chambers of Commerce and Trade, Careers Offices, Council Economic Development Units and Training and Enterprise Councils (TEC's).
- Many other local, regional and national organisations also publish journals and reports on economic and labour market trends including many banks, the Confederation of British Industry (CBI), Employers Associations and Trade Unions. You will find 'Economic Briefing', published by HM Treasury, and 'Labour Market and Skill Trends', 'Labour Force Survey' and 'Employment Gazette', published by the Employment Department, particularly useful.

I hope that you will enjoy using this text and wish you every success in your coursework and in obtaining your qualification.

# Coverage of Examination Topics – by chapter

## Advanced GNVQ (Vocational A Level)

**Advanced Business Studies**
Key Chapter(s) – Refer to Index for details relating to individual themes/topics

| Unit | 1 | 2 | 3 | 4 | 5 | 6 | 7 | 8 | 9 | 10 | 11 | 12 | 13 | 14 | 15 | 16 | 17 | 18 | 19 | 20 |
|---|---|---|---|---|---|---|---|---|---|---|---|---|---|---|---|---|---|---|---|---|
| Business in the economy | ■ | | ■ | ■ | ■ | ■ | | | | | | | | | ■ | | | | | |
| Business systems | | | | | | | | | | | | ■ | | | | ■ | | ■ | ■ | |
| Marketing | | | | | | | ■ | ■ | ■ | | | | | | | | | ■ | | ■ |
| Human resources | | ■ | | | | | | | | | | ■ | ■ | ■ | ■ | | | | | |
| Employment in the market economy | | | | ■ | | | | | | | | | ■ | | | | ■ | ■ | | |
| Financial transactions and monitoring | | | | | | | | | | | ■ | | | | | ■ | | | ■ | |
| Financial resources | | | | | | | | | | ■ | | | | | | | | | ■ | ■ |
| Business planning | ■ | | ■ | | | | | | | | | | | | ■ | | | | ■ | ■ |

## GCE A Level (AEB)

**Advanced Business Studies**
Key Chapter(s) – Refer to Index for details relating to individual themes/topics

| Subject content | 1 | 2 | 3 | 4 | 5 | 6 | 7 | 8 | 9 | 10 | 11 | 12 | 13 | 14 | 15 | 16 | 17 | 18 | 19 | 20 |
|---|---|---|---|---|---|---|---|---|---|---|---|---|---|---|---|---|---|---|---|---|
| Section 1 Basic business organisations and their objectives | ■ | ■ | ■ | | | | | | | | | | | | ■ | ■ | | ■ | | ■ |
| Internal factors affecting businesses in the pursuit of their objectives | | | ■ | | | | | | | | | | | | ■ | | ■ | | | |
| Section 2 Finance | | | | | | | | | | ■ | ■ | | | | | | | | ■ | |
| Section 3 Marketing | | | | | | | ■ | ■ | ■ | | | | | | | | | | | |
| Section 4 Human resources | | | | | | | | | | | | ■ | ■ | ■ | | | | | | |
| Section 5 Factors external to businesses which affect the attainment of objectives | | | | ■ | ■ | ■ | | | | | | ■ | | | | | ■ | | | |
| Section 6 The integrated nature of business decisions and objectives | ■ | | | | | | | | | | | | | | | | | | | ■ |

## GCE A Level (JMB)

**Advanced Business Studies**
Key Chapter(s) – Refer to Index for details relating to individual themes/topics

| Theme | 1 | 2 | 3 | 4 | 5 | 6 | 7 | 8 | 9 | 10 | 11 | 12 | 13 | 14 | 15 | 16 | 17 | 18 | 19 | 20 |
|---|---|---|---|---|---|---|---|---|---|---|---|---|---|---|---|---|---|---|---|---|
| The economic environment of the organisation | ■ | ■ | ■ | ■ | ■ | ■ | | | | | | | | | | | | | | |
| Operations management | | | | | | | | | | | | | | | ■ | | | | ■ | ■ |
| Accounting and finance | | | | | | | | | | ■ | ■ | | | | | | | | ■ | ■ |
| Operational research and information technology | | | | | | | | | | ■ | | | | | | ■ | | | ■ | |
| Statistics for decision making | | | | | | | ■ | | | | | | | | | | | ■ | | ■ |
| Marketing | | | | | | | | ■ | ■ | | | | | | | | | | | |
| Organisational behaviour | | | | | | | | | | | | ■ | ■ | | | | | | | |
| Employer and employee relations | | | ■ | | | | | | | | | ■ | | ■ | | | ■ | | | |

# GCE A Level (London)

**Advanced Business Studies**

Key Chapter(s) – Refer to Index for details relating to individual themes/topics

| Content | 1 | 2 | 3 | 4 | 5 | 6 | 7 | 8 | 9 | 10 | 11 | 12 | 13 | 14 | 15 | 16 | 17 | 18 | 19 | 20 |
|---|---|---|---|---|---|---|---|---|---|---|---|---|---|---|---|---|---|---|---|---|
| *Introduction: the nature and dimensions of business activity* | ■ | | | | | | | | | | | | | | | | | | | |
| *Area 1: the elements of business activity* | | | ■ | ■ | | | ■ | ■ | ■ | ■ | ■ | ■ | | ■ | | ■ | ■ | | ■ | |
| Nature of markets and market forces | | | | ■ | | | | | | | | | | | | | | | | |
| The concept and role of marketing | | | | | | | ■ | ■ | ■ | | | | | | | | | | | |
| Financial information | | | | | | | | | | | ■ | | | | | | | | ■ | |
| Sources and uses of financial resources | | | | | | | | | | ■ | | | | | | | | | | |
| Human resources | | | ■ | | | | | | | | | ■ | | ■ | | ■ | | | | |
| Non-human resources | | | ■ | | | | | | | | | | | | | ■ | ■ | | | |
| *Area 2: structure and internal organisation of businesses* | ■ | ■ | | | | | | | | | | | ■ | | ■ | ■ | | | | |
| Structure and types of business units | ■ | ■ | | | | | | | | | | | | | | | | | | |
| Organisational theories | | | | | | | | | | | | | ■ | | ■ | | | | | |
| Internal communications | | | | | | | | | | | | | | | | ■ | | | | |
| *Area 3: external influences on business activity* | ■ | | ■ | | ■ | ■ | | | | | | | | ■ | | | | | | |
| *Area 4: the management of business activity* | ■ | | | | | | | | | ■ | | | | | | | ■ | ■ | | ■ |

# GCE A Level (Cambridge)

**Advanced Business Studies**

Key Chapter(s) – Refer to Index for details relating to individual themes/topics

| Content | 1 | 2 | 3 | 4 | 5 | 6 | 7 | 8 | 9 | 10 | 11 | 12 | 13 | 14 | 15 | 16 | 17 | 18 | 19 | 20 |
|---|---|---|---|---|---|---|---|---|---|---|---|---|---|---|---|---|---|---|---|---|
| *The organisation and its environment* | ■ | ■ | | | ■ | ■ | | | | | | | ■ | | | | ■ | | | |
| The extent and nature of business units | ■ | ■ | | | | | | | | | | | | | | | | | | |
| Business structures and organisations | ■ | | | | | | | | | | | | ■ | | | | | | | |
| The national and international environment | | | | | ■ | ■ | | | | | | | | | | | ■ | | | |
| *The dynamics of business* | | | | ■ | | | ■ | ■ | ■ | ■ | ■ | ■ | ■ | ■ | ■ | | | | | |
| People in business | | | | | | | | | | | ■ | ■ | ■ | | ■ | | | | | |
| *Marketing and production* | | | | | ■ | | ■ | ■ | ■ | | | | | | ■ | | | | | ■ |
| *Finance* | | | | | | | | | | ■ | | | | | | | | | | |
| Accounting and business activity | | | | | | | | | | | ■ | | | | | | | | | |
| *Decision making in business* | ■ | | ■ | | | | ■ | | | ■ | ■ | | | | | | ■ | | | ■ |
| *Phases of decision making* | ■ | | ■ | | | | | | | | | | | | | | | | ■ | ■ |
| *Information* | | | | | | | ■ | | | | | | | | | | | ■ | | |
| *Deciding between alternatives* | | | | | | | | | | ■ | | | | | | | | | ■ | |
| *Implementation and control* | | | | | | | | | | | | ■ | | | | | | | | ■ |

# 1. The Business Environment

This Chapter provides a general introduction to the subject of business studies and is intended to provide a framework for future studies since many of the topics outlined are discussed in later chapters. Because of the integrated nature of business, many terms and concepts will recur throughout this text.

* What is Business
* Development of Economic Activity
* Needs and Wants
* Scarcity and Choice
* Key Definitions
* Organisations
* The Resources of Business
* Profit
* Production

* Economic Systems
* Business Objectives
* Business Organisations
* Business Functions
* Management
* Decision Making
* Constraints on Business
* Measurement of Performance

## What is Business?

1. The term business is used to describe all the commercial activities undertaken by the various organisations which produce and supply goods and services. Business affects nearly every part of our daily lives. Not only by supplying the food we eat, the clothes we wear and the transport we use to school, college or work, but also most of the jobs and wages which enable us to buy these goods and services.

## Development of Economic Activity

2. 
   * In primitive societies, people were **self-sufficient**, hunting, growing and making what they needed for themselves.
   * Later people began to specialise in doing what they were good at which enabled them to produce more than they needed for themselves.
   * This **division of labour** led to the development of **trade** as surplus goods were exchanged for other goods.
   * This earliest form of trade was called **barter**.
   * As the population, specialisation and technical developments increased, **money** was introduced to make the process of exchange easier.
   * This led to an increase in the quantity of goods produced and the rapid growth of trade both at home and overseas.

## Needs, Wants and Demand

3. Goods and services are produced because people need or want them. In order to survive in life, we all **need** food, clothing and shelter. These are the basic needs which must be satisfied. **Wants** on the other hand are goods and services which people seek to obtain in order to improve their standard of living, ie quality of life. When people talk about the **demand** for something, it means not just wanting it, but also being able to pay for it. That is, demand is only **effective** if it is backed by money.

## Scarcity and Choice

4. We would all like to have more or better possessions than we have now – clothes, houses, furniture, holidays etc. Our wants are unlimited, ie there is always something which we would like. However, our resources are **scarce** or limited. We only have a certain amount of money and therefore must make a **choice** of how best to spend it.

## 1. The business environment

5. The problems of scarcity and choice also apply to businesses and countries. A business must decide how to make the best use of its limited resources. Likewise a country cannot produce unlimited amounts of goods and services if its resources are limited.

6. One way of looking at this problem is to say that the cost of any choice is the next best alternative which we decide to do without. This is what economists call **opportunity cost**. For example, the cost to a teenager of going to the cinema is the compact disc which could have been bought instead; a farmer may keep cattle instead of sheep; governments may spend money on roads instead of schools or pensions.

### Task 1.1

1. Think about the problem of scarcity and choice as it affects you. List 3 goods and 3 services which you have purchased in the last week and the opportunity cost of each of those items.

2. 3 College students are faced with the following situations:

   a) Tony loses his Business Studies textbook which cost the College £9.95. He is asked to pay £5 towards the cost of replacing it.

   b) Peter earns £24 for working Saturdays on a market stall. He is picked for the College cricket team which only plays on Saturdays. He believes that a new bat will improve his play and purchases one for £20.

   c) Jasmin wants to go on a College trip to Italy which will cost £285. Her parents say she can go and they are prepared to pay.

   What is the opportunity cost:

   i) to Tony of losing his textbook?

   ii) to the local community?

   iii) to Peter of playing cricket?

   iv) to Jasmin's parents of her trip to Italy?

   v) to Jasmin?

## Some Key Definitions

7. 
- The provision of goods and services is called **production**. The people who buy them are **consumers.**
- **Goods** are tangible items which we can see and touch. For example food, drinks, make-up, motor cycles, cars and washing machines.
- **Services** are not goods but things which we use like the telephone, buses, education and entertainment.
- The term **aggregate demand** is used to describe the total expenditure of all buyers of goods and services within the economy as a whole.
- The **environment** refers to the surroundings and circumstances which affect the way in which an organisation operates.
- A **system** can be defined as a collection of inter-dependent parts organised to achieve a particular objective. The change or removal of any of these parts will affect the way in which the system operates.
- **Objectives** are the aims or goals which a business seeks to achieve. In order to check whether or not they have been achieved, they must be measurable. For example, to increase sales by 10%.
- **Management** refers to a group of people who are appointed by the owners of a company to run a business on their behalf. Their role includes determining the distribution of profits to sharehold-

ers. Managers are expected to direct the efforts of their staff towards achieving the desired objectives. Thus managers get things done through people.
- **Competition** refers to the amount of rivalry between organisations and their products or services or market. This may affect individual businesses in many ways, but in particular in terms of the prices which they can charge and quality of goods or services which they must supply in order to be competitive.

## Organisations

8. An **organisation** is a group of people who co-operate together for a common purpose. Organisations are of all types and sizes, exist everywhere and most of us belong to many of them during life as the following examples illustrate. Families, hospitals, churches, youth clubs, sports clubs, schools, colleges, libraries, charities, trade unions, political parties and businesses are all organisations. In this text we are considering the wide range of business organisations which exist today and the environment in which they operate to achieve their objectives.

9. Business organisations range in size and structure from small sole proprietors owned and run by one person, to huge national and multi-national organisations run by managers and owned by many thousands of shareholders, to industries owned and controlled by the State.

### Task 1.2
1. Make a list of all the organisations to which you belong.
2. Identify what you feel is the 'common purpose' of each organisation

10. The specific components of a business organisation can be summarised as
    - **A name** which gives it an identity e.g. Boots, Asda.
    - **People** who consist of the management and workforce and provide a range of skills, knowledge, commitment and drive.
    - **A mission and set of objectives** which are needed to define the purpose of the organisation and what it is trying to achieve.
    - **A hierarchy** with an organisational structure through which power can be exercised.
    - **A culture** and set of values which give the organisation an ethos and spirit.
    - **Communication** and information flows to enable decisions to be taken and implemented.
    - **Procedures and systems** for undertaking defined tasks.
    - **Recording systems** for reference, evidence, control and accounting purposes.
    - **A control system** to audit and influence management decisions.
    - **Specialist functions** through which tasks can be carried out.
    - **Rewards and punishments** to provide motivation and ensure compliance with objectives.
    - **A boundary** which defines the limits of the organisation.
    - **Linking mechanisms** needed to relate to other organisations.

11. All these components need to be assessed and matched together to try to achieve a harmonious whole. Complete harmonisation is, however, unlikely to be achieved because the components are always subject to change as, for example, when staff leave or new staff are appointed. In this text, we shall be considering each of these components in more detail, including the importance of each for an organisation.

### Task 1.3
Choose any business organisation which you know well or can find out about and try to identify with examples, its specific components.

*1. The business environment*

## The Resources of Business

12. In order to produce the goods and services needed to satisfy human wants, four essential resources are needed. These are also referred to as **factors of production** or *inputs*.

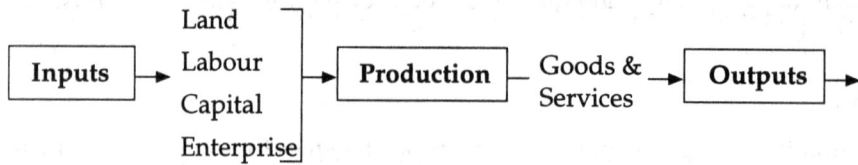

13. - **Land** consists of all natural resources and includes minerals, water, fish in the sea and land itself. Examples include Coal, Wood, North Sea Oil and Gas.
    - **Labour** refers to the physical and mental skills of people who work. It is the human resource in production whether a labourer, teacher or office worker.
    - **Capital** in its broadest sense means anything which is owned by a business and used to make production easier and more efficient. This includes buildings, machinery, equipment and vehicles.
    - **Enterprise** or the entrepreneur is someone who organises the other inputs to initiate the process of production. They risk a loss if the business fails but if successful, are rewarded by making a **profit**. Very successful examples include Tesco, ICI and Boots.

14. Clearly not all inputs are of the same quality. For example, barren hillsides will not grow crops, a clumsy person will not have the skills to produce jewellery; capital equipment may be new or worn, whilst some entrepreneurs will have more ability than others. The type and quality of inputs used will depend on the goods and services (call OUTPUTS) being produced.

## Profit

15. The difference between the total cost of running a business and the total income received by the business is the profit. The cost of the inputs include rent for land, wages for labour and interest on capital. Income comes from sales to consumers. Owners or managers will try to increase sales through good marketing (see Chapters 7, 8 and 9) and operate the business efficiently in order to reduce costs and therefore increase profits.

> ### Task 1.4
> A manufacturer of clothing has a large number of inputs.
> 1. Consider the following list and group them into Land, Labour, Capital and Enterprise.
>
>    | LABOURER | FACTORY | COMPUTER | SECRETARY |
>    |---|---|---|---|
>    | WOOL | MANAGER | PHOTOCOPIER | PENCILS |
>    | SCISSORS | COTTON | MACHINISTS | WATER |
>
> 2. Now draw up a similar list of resources for a service business such as an insurance company, transport firm or holiday tour operator or one of your own choice.

## Production

16. We all consume a wide range of goods and services in life. Therefore, people work both to produce them and also to earn the money needed to buy them. Production can be considered under three main headings – primary, secondary and tertiary industries.

- **Primary**

  This consists of all the **extractive** industries, for example coal mining, quarrying, fishing, forestry and farming. Many of these primary products form the raw materials for secondary production.

- **Secondary**

  These are the **manufacturing** and **construction** industries which change the raw materials into finished products. Example include the manufacture of chemicals, textiles and shoes, and the building of roads, houses and bridges.

- **Tertiary**

  These industries do not produce goods, but provide services. Tertiary production is often referred to as Commerce and Direct Services. The latter are personal services, not directly related to trade but needed to increase production by looking after people's health and welfare.

17. **Types of Production**

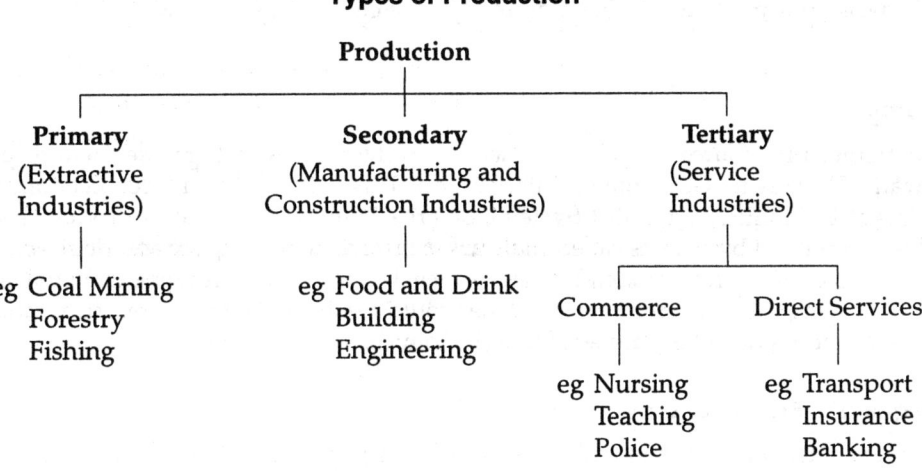

### Task 1.5

Consider the area in which you live or work. Identify by name the organisations concerned with the following types of production. List and briefly describe the products or services which they supply.

1) 2 examples of primary production.

2) At least 5 examples of secondary production.

3) Finally, at least 6 examples of tertiary production including 3 each of commercial and direct services.

4) Are any organisations involved in more than one type of production?

State which they are and in what way they are involved.

## The Economic System

18. There are 3 groups which make up what can be called the economic system of a country – individuals, business organisations and the State.

19. **Individuals** – We are all consumers of goods and services whatever our age, race or sex, free to spend our income as we choose. In addition, individuals are also important providers of capital and many also form part of the labour force needed to produce goods and services.

20. **Business Organisations** – These are the various suppliers of goods and services for consumption whether they be importers, manufacturers, processors or involved in the chain of distribution as

wholesalers or retailers. Business organisations are also consumers of raw materials and/or finished goods and services and importantly they are also employers of labour and users of capital.

21. **The State** – A variety of roles are performed by the State which includes both local and central government as well as State run industries such as the coal mines and railways. The State is also an important consumer of goods and services and a major employer.

22. But importantly, the State is also the regulating body in our society. It has the key role of devising laws which both protect individuals and organisations and also help to resolve any conflict which may take place between them. Examples include laws on Health and Safety, Consumer Protection, Employment Protection, Environmental Protection and Sunday Trading.

## Types of Economic Systems

23. All societies in the world face the basic economic problem of scarcity and choice. Because there are limited resources, it is necessary for each to decide what goods and services it is going to produce. How this decision is made will depend on the type of economic system which operates in the country.

## Free Economy

24. At one extreme, all resources could be owned by individuals who organise them to produce what people want. There is no Government intervention. This is known as a 'Free Economy', sometimes called Market Economies, Capitalist Systems or Free Enterprises. What is produced and the price charged is determined by what is called the market mechanism of supply and demand. For example, if there was no demand for wooden houses or bicycles, then an entrepreneur would not make any profit by supplying them. Therefore instead, he would use his resources to produce other goods. The USA, Canada and Japan are examples of free economies.

25. **Advantages of a Free Economy**
    - Consumers determine demand and therefore what is produced.
    - Increased competition which keeps prices down and improves efficiency and standards.
    - All members of the community are free to run businesses for profit.

26. **Disadvantages of a Free Economy**
    - Successful businesses may buy up smaller ones and control a larger share of the market. This can reduce competition and lead to higher prices.
    - Some goods and services required by the community as a whole may not be produced at all, for example, defence.
    - Pollution could increase because it may be difficult to control.

## Controlled Economy

27. At the other extreme, all resources could be owned and organised by the State. In these economies, decisions on what to produce are taken collectively by the Government on behalf of its people. Bulgaria and Cuba are examples of controlled economies, often called command, centrally planned economies or Communist states.

28. **Advantages of a Controlled Economy**
    - Resources are used to produce what the community needs which eliminates wasteful competition.
    - More equal distribution of income and wealth
    - Prevents large firms controlling markets and putting up prices.

29. **Disadvantages of a Controlled Economy**
    - Lack of competition may reduce efficiency, enterprise and innovation.
    - Central control may make it difficult to respond quickly to changes in needs and conditions

- Individuals lose their freedom of choice.

## Mixed Economy

30. Most countries in the world, including the UK, actually have what is called a mixed economy. This means that some resources and organisations are owned and controlled by the State (called the Public Sector) and others by private individuals or groups of individuals (Private Sector).

    This is more fully explained in Chapter 2.

### Task 1.6

Consider the following countries in terms of the characteristics of free, centrally planned and mixed economic systems. From what you know or can find out, place them in order from completely controlled to completely free.

| UK | USA | FRANCE | ITALY | CANADA |
| GERMANY | CUBA | AUSTRALIA | BULGARIA | CHINA |

31. We have seen so far that people demand goods and services and that they are supplied by both the private and public sector organisations. In order to pay for these goods and services, individuals work for and invest money in these organisations. This is illustrated in the following diagram.

32. 

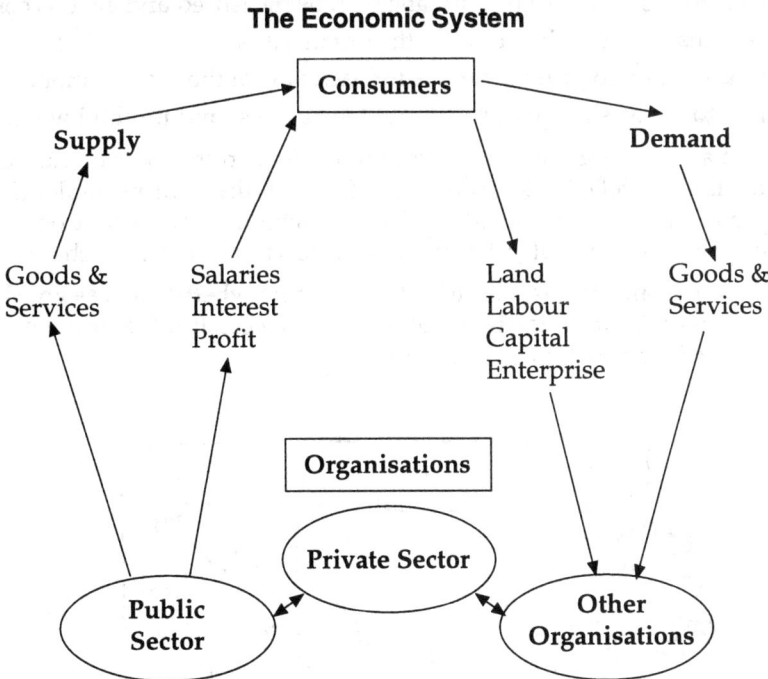

## Business Objectives

33. Business organisations are established for the purpose of achieving specific objectives and it is against these objectives that the success or failure of the organisation can be judged. The key points about objectives are that they should be quantifiable, measurable and time specific, for example, to increase profits by 5% per annum.

34. There are four questions at the root of setting objectives.

    - **What is the organisation trying to achieve?** What is important, for example, increasing the return on investment (capital employed), increasing market share or reducing bad debts?

- **How can this be done?** What methods or policies are needed, for example, increasing profit margins, improving the rate of sales growth, tighter credit control.
- **When must it be done by?** A time period should be set, for example, by the end of the next financial year.
- **How will it know that it has succeeded?** Thus a unit of measurement is required, eg 10%. This question also implies the need to monitor progress and take corrective action as necessary.

35. **Example: Setting and Achieving a Business Objective**

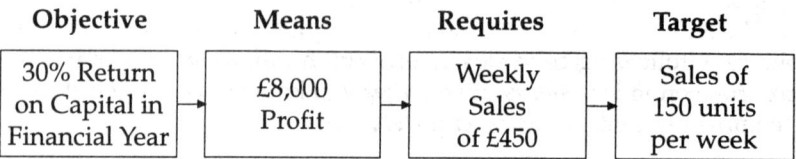

| Objective | Means | Requires | Target |
|---|---|---|---|
| 30% Return on Capital in Financial Year | £8,000 Profit | Weekly Sales of £450 | Sales of 150 units per week |

## Why Objectives are Needed

36. Objectives are needed in an organisation for a number of reasons in particular because:
    - they clarify for everyone what the business is working to achieve.
    - they aid the decision-making process and the choice of alternative strategies (courses of action).
    - they enable checks on progress and decisions on what needs to be done next.
    - they provide the means by which performance can be measured and actions controlled.
    - they provide a focus for individual roles in the organisation.
    - they can be broken down to provide targets for each part of the organisation.
    - they can be used to analyse the performance of the business and its employees.

37. It is important that an organisation's objectives are realistic in the light of market research and also achievable, particularly in relation to production. It is pointless, for example, if sales targets are 80 units daily, if production can only produce 55. It is also important that objectives are regularly reviewed to ensure that they are still relevant or realistic as circumstances change.

38. **The specific objectives of an organisation will depend upon whether it is established in the public or private sector.** However, in order for both sectors to be successful, the prime objective must always be to meet the needs of their customers or clients.

## Objectives of Private Sector Organisations

39. Organisations in the private sector are usually created to earn **maximum profits** for their owners, i.e. to achieve the best possible return on the money which they have invested in the business.

40. However, whilst this will certainly be the main aim of most businesses, some may have other objectives which they pursue, particularly in the short-term. For example, a new business may see **survival** as its main objective in its early years ie ensuring that it makes sufficient **profit** to enable it to be in a position to continue trading. This could then be followed by **consolidation** and it may be some years before it reaches a position of high profit.

41. On the other hand, established larger firms may be prepared to cut prices and accept lower profits for a short time in order to achieve the objectives of **increasing sales and market share** ie selling more of the total sales of a product or service than their competitors. In the longer term, if successful, this may enable the firm to expand its output or product range and enter a period of **growth** which will enable it to benefit from **economies of scale.**

## Objectives of Public Sector Organisations

42. Public sector organisations are created not to maximise profit but to achieve the maximum **benefit for the nation**. In order to achieve their objectives they may be involved in operating unprofitable services because it is in the public's interest to do so. For example, the provision of rail services to country areas. Another example would be keeping an uneconomic coal mine open in an area of high unemployment to prevent the loss of further jobs.

43. However, the government still expects public corporations to aim to at least 'break even' over a period of years and if possible to make sufficient profit to enable investment in new equipment to take place. Each one is set a profit target just like a commercial firm.

### Task 1.7
Consider your place of study, work or any organisation which you know well. Find out and list its main objectives.

## Business Organisation

44. In order to achieve its objectives a businesses resources must be organised and how this is done will depend upon a number of factors including the type of goods or services it supplies, the size of the market, the level of technology which it uses and the attitude and type of management which run it, all of which are discussed in this text.

45. The firms themselves also vary considerably in size and this is true even in the same industry or area of activity, for example building, retailing and farming. Hence the internal structure of a business will also vary according to its size.

### Small Firms

46. Whilst an organisation is small, one man can often control it. He is able to do all of the important jobs himself, eg ordering, accounts, VAT returns and marketing, and is very closely involved in its day-to-day running.

47. However, as a business grows, one man may be too busy to perform all the jobs which he once did and he may therefore need to take in a partner or arrange for people who work for him to take on some specialist jobs, eg accounts and ordering.

48. If a firm continues to grow, additional skills may be required and as more staff are employed further specialisation can take place.

*1. The business environment*

### Larger Organisations

49. This process of growth and specialisation may continue as a firm develops into a private or public limited company. When this happens the shareholders will elect a Board of Directors to make the policy decisions on how the business should be organised and run in order to achieve its objectives.

50.

**Organisation Chart**

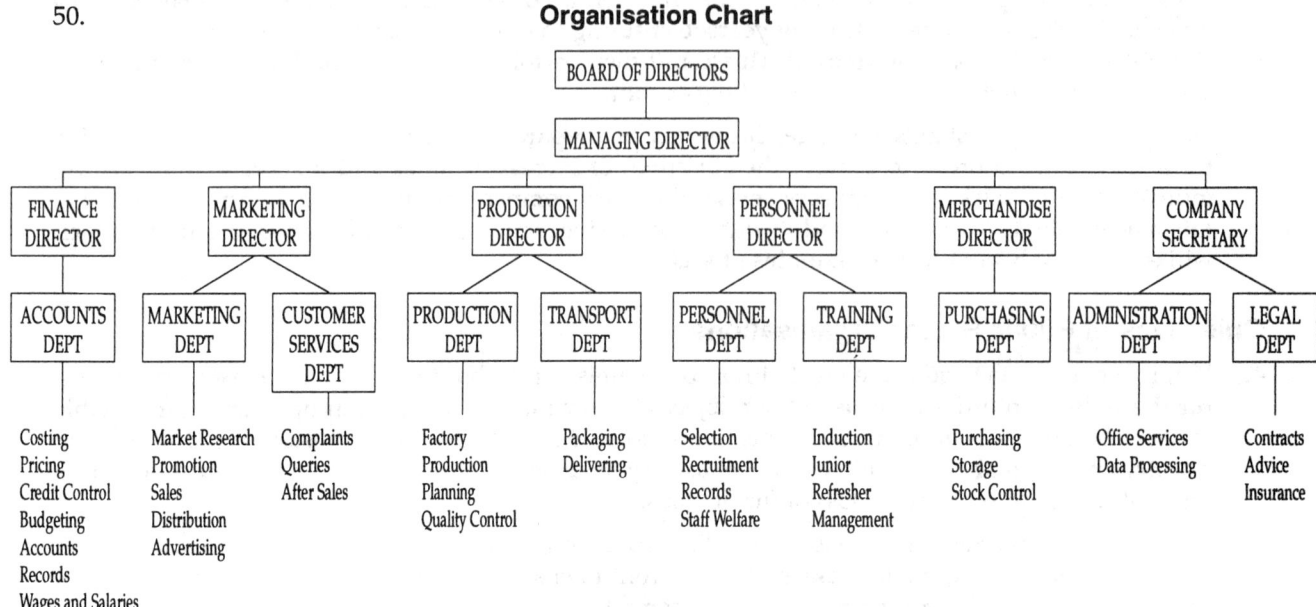

A typical organisation chart showing departments and their main functions. Businesses often use this form of diagram to illustrate positions of staff in their organisation.

### Specialist Departments

51. As shown in the organisation chart, the board will usually appoint a managing director or chief executive as head of a business. Specialist departments are often established, the actual number depending on the size of the firm, with a director in charge of each function, for example finance, production, marketing. The overall management and administration of the company involves the co-ordination of these different departments or functions of the business.

## Business Functions

52. Whatever its size, there are a number of functional areas common in all business organisations. These are personnel (or human resource management), production, purchasing, accounting and finance, marketing and administration.

Each department or functional area will then contribute to the success of the organisation by having its own specific objectives and targets based on the general objectives which have been established.

53. **Personnel.** This activity is concerned with the management of people in an organisation including recruitment, selection, training, pay, welfare, conditions of employment and negotiations with trade unions (see Chapters 12 & 14).

54. **Production.** This function deals with the making of goods or services. It includes matters relating to location of the business, the planning, co-ordination and techniques of production and quality control. It may also include product research and development. (See Chapter 15).

55. **Purchasing.** The acquisition of raw materials and other resources is the function of purchasing. It involves finding the best sources of supply, at the right price, the right quality and other factors which may be important in the organisation, like delivery times. Stock control may also be the responsibility of purchasing.

56. **Accounting and Finance.** All businesses need finance in order to start up and operate. Accountancy techniques are used to provide managers with financial control information which involves the collection, recording, presentation and analysis of data as a basis for forecasting and decision-making.

57. Other financial functions include the preparation of budgets, payment of suppliers, dealing with the payroll, calculating selling prices, credit control and the preparation of final accounts. (See Chapters 10 and 11).

58. **Marketing.** This function is concerned with a whole group of business activities (known as the **marketing mix**) which are concerned with obtaining and keeping customers. It includes market research to find out about a firm's customers, product design, pricing, sales promotion, advertising and distribution to the final customer. (See Chapters 8 & 9).

59. **Administration.** Many organisations have an administration office which provides a support service to the other functional areas. This may include reception, switchboard, typing, photocopying, secretarial and computer services.

### Task 1.8

In Task 1.7 you selected an organisation with which you are familiar.

1. Now identify its functional departments or sections and list the main services which each provides.
2. Identify the functional area associated with each of the following activities:
   a) To maintain customer goodwill, encourage existing customers to purchase more and find new customers and sales opportunities.
   b) To obtain and control supplies from various sources, at the right time, in the right quality, and at the most favourable prices.
   c) To improve relationships between the organisation and its employees at all levels.
   d) To make a better product, find improved ways of making the product, and develop new products.
   e) To record all financial transactions in order to protect assets, maintain profitability and forecast future policy from past performance.

60. In practice, functional areas cannot operate in isolation because the input of one function is often the output of another. Sales, for example, cannot operate without production, whilst production cannot operate without purchasing. They are very much linked together and must co-operate with each other to enable the organisation to achieve its objectives, hence the importance of effective management.

## Management

61. The business functions outlined above must be properly co-ordinated and managed if the organisation is to be successful. In a small business it may be the owner who is the manager, whilst in a large company, it will be the **Board of Directors.**

62. The primary task of management is to use the resources of the business efficiently and to make the right decisions in order to achieve its defined objectives.

63. Management involves 6 key tasks: planning, co-ordinating, motivating, controlling, problem solving and responding to change.
    - **Planning** to set clear business objectives and make decisions on the best use of resources to achieve them.

- **Co-ordinating** and directing activities to ensure that everyone knows what is expected of them and are working towards the agreed objectives.
- **Motivating**, delegating to and communicating with staff to encourage them to give of their best and carry out their tasks efficiently and effectively.
- **Controlling** operations and checking on progress to ensure that objectives are being achieved. Also to modify objectives if circumstances change.
- **Problem solving** – so that decisions are taken which help to resolve difficulties and enable tasks to be completed.
- **Responding to change(s)** in the environment to ensure that the organisation prospers. Good management must be dynamic and forward-looking to detect both threats to the business and opportunities for further development and respond accordingly.

### Task 1.9

#### NO ONE WANTS TO BE A BOSS!

Many junior executives are no longer reaching for the top because the incentives are not big enough, according to a recent survey.

It reveals that most companies have trouble filling senior posts, especially from inside their organisations.

This management malaise is not just in Britain but throughout Europe, according to the survey of 500 chief executives of top companies in ten European countries.

Their answers indicate that because of the demands of business life and the lack of incentives, tomorrow's executives may not be able to meet the demands of industry.

The quality of managers is improving but their jobs are getting harder and the incentive to reach the top is less than it was ten years ago.

A grim report on the survey, says: 'There is little sign of the situation improving and in the years ahead industry may well suffer from a shortage of really effective leaders.'

Chief executives in all ten countries believe the pressures on management have drastically increased in the past decade.

And there is widespread belief that the status of managers in the eyes of the community has declined.

Most top men say school-leavers are not as good as they used to be and that schools are not preparing pupils for careers in industry.

The answer, most executives believe, lies in closer liaison with educational authorities.

Read the above article and answer the following questions which are based on it.

1. Why are people no longer interested in becoming managers?
2. What consequences could this have for industry in the future?
3. If you were the Chief Executive of an organisation, what action would you consider taking to prevent your own firm suffering?

## Decision Making and Constraints

64. Each of us is involved in making decisions. Daily we have to decide what to eat, what to wear and how to organise our time. Essentially, we are faced with having to choose between **alternatives**. Similarly there is a decision-making process in organisations. It involves using the information available in order to make a choice between the various alternative ways of achieving objectives.

65. Decision making is essential to determine the future direction of an organisation. We said earlier that the prime function of management is to make the right decisions. Some of the decision making techniques available to assist managers are covered in Chapter 10.

The types of decision making can broadly be classified into strategic, tactical and operational.

### Strategic or Long-Term

66. These are decisions made by top-level management and are concerned with an organisation's overall objectives. Such corporate decisions include major capital investments, sources of finance and product and market choices.

### Tactical or Medium-Term

67. These are concerned with the best use of an organisation's resources and the management of change to achieve the agreed objectives. Such decisions are made by senior managers and would include minor capital investment, product modification and changes to marketing plans.

### Operational or Short-Term

68. These are decisions taken by departmental managers or lower level supervisors in order to put tactical plans into effect and control activities. Examples could include credit control, re-ordering of stocks and determination of delivery routes.

### Process of Decision-Making

69. The process of decision making can be summarised as follows:

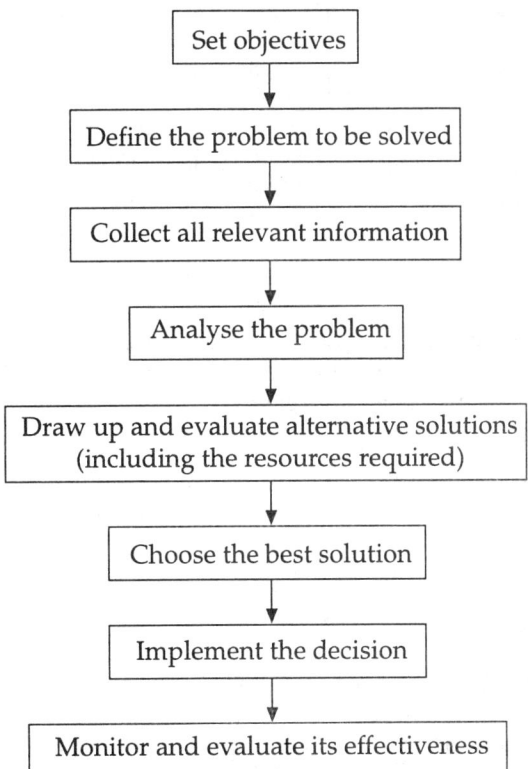

70. Not all of these processes will be needed at operational level but may be essential for tactical and strategic decision making. This is considered in more detail in Chapter 3.

## Constraints on Business

71. Throughout this text we will be considering the environmental factors or **constraints** which influence decision making in a business. A constraint is something which prevents or makes it difficult for a business to achieve 'its' objectives and therefore influences decision making. (See Chapter 3).

## 1. The business environment

72. Broadly, these fall into constraints within the organisation itself (**internal**) and those from the environment in which it operates (**external**).

73.

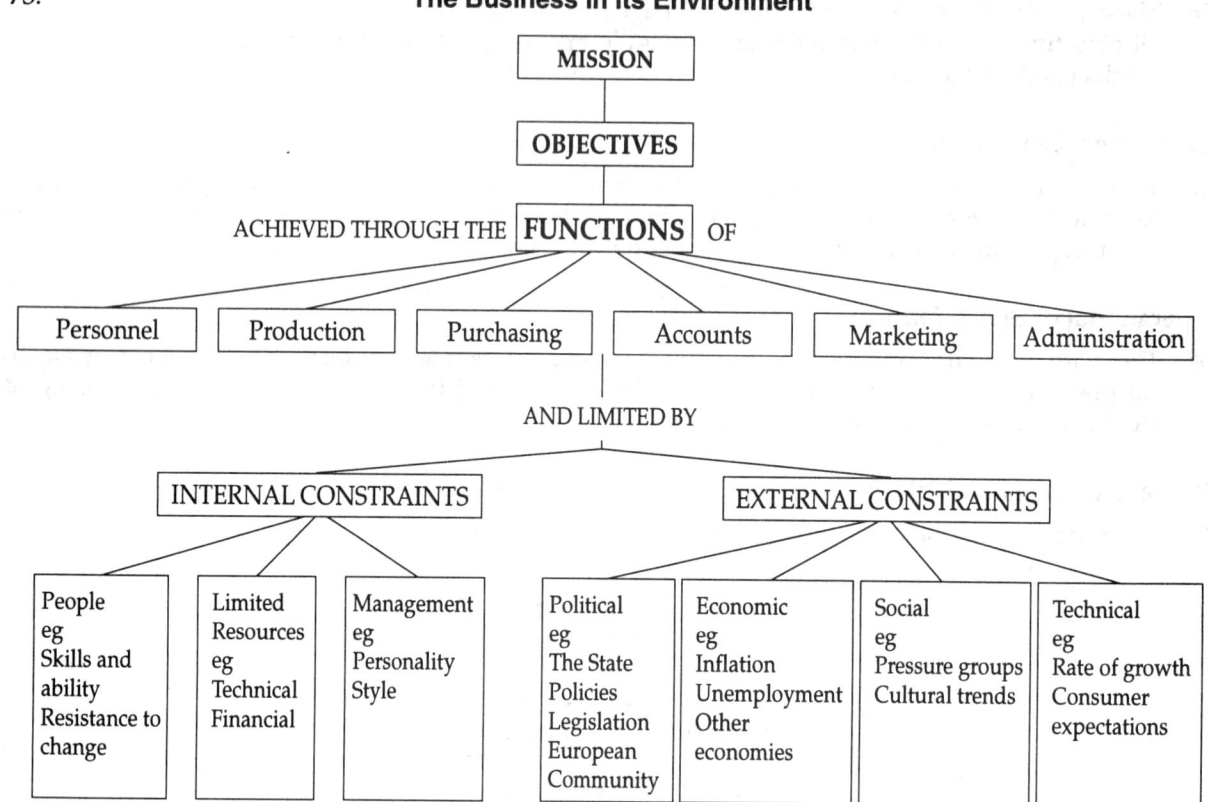

The Business in its Environment

### Task 1.10

Refer back to the information which you obtained in Tasks 1.7 and 1.8. Try to identify what might be considered as internal and external constraints and discuss how these might affect the organisation and prevent it from achieving its objectives.

**Help point:** If you have difficulty in understanding any of the terms used on the diagram above, check the index and read about them elsewhere in the text.

## Measurement of Performance

74. Traditionally an organisation can be seen in terms of a control loop which uses a range of inputs (such as labour and materials) to produce a range of outputs (goods or services). In order to achieve its objectives the management of an organisation must plan, monitor and control this process and recognise deviations from its plans in order to take corrective action as necessary. This is referred to as **Management By Objectives** (MBO)

75. **Control Loop**

⟶ INPUTS ⟶ PROCESS ⟶ OUTPUTS

ACTION ⟵ COMPARATOR ⟵ SENSOR

76. Control implies some form of quantitative measurement against which progress can be checked. The 3 fundamental aspects of performance which can and must be measured are:
    - **efficiency** which is concerned with measuring the output from given resources.
    - **economy** which involves obtaining the 'right' resources at the least cost.
    - **effectiveness** which is about producing the right outputs in the right quantities.

77. There may also be other factors which are equally important but which cannot be easily quantified. Examples might be customer satisfaction, industrial relations and staff morale.

## Summary

78. a) The term business is used to describe all the various commercial activities undertaken by organisations which produce and supply goods and services.
    b) The earliest form of trade was called barter.
    c) The division of labour or specialisation resulted in a big increase in the number of goods and services produced leading to the need for money.
    d) We all face the problem of scarcity and choice because our resources are limited.
    e) Organisations exist in all walks of life and consist of groups of people co-operating together to achieve a common purpose.
    f) Land, labour, capital and enterprise are the 4 factors or inputs required for production.
    g) Production involves primary, secondary and tertiary industries.
    h) Economic systems are made up of individuals, business organisations and the State.
    i) Business organisations set themselves specific objectives to achieve against which their success or failure can be measured.
    j) The main objective of private sector organisations is usually to achieve maximum profits.
    k) Public sector organisations also seek to make profits but their first concern is to operate for the benefit of the nation.
    l) In order to achieve its objectives, the successful running of any business, no matter how large or small, involves the co-ordination of many different functions including personnel, production, purchasing, accounts and finance, marketing and administration.
    m) Whereas in a large organisation a different department may exist to carry out each of these functions, in a small business they may all be performed by the owner or just a few people.
    n) Management involves planning, co-ordinating, motivation, control, problem-solving and responding to change.
    o) Decision making by managers to achieve objectives is influenced by both internal and external constraints.
    p) Performance must be measured to ensure that objectives are being met.

## 1. The business environment

### Review questions *(Answers can be found in the paragraphs indicated)*

1. Using 2 examples, explain the meaning of barter. (2)
2. Why does the division of labour lead to an increase in trade? (2)
3. Explain the terms scarcity, choice and opportunity-cost. (4-6)
4. Explain with examples, what you understand by an organisation. (8-9)
5. Outline the main features of business organisations. (10)
6. Briefly, describe the 4 factors of production. (12-14))
7. Distinguish between primary, secondary and tertiary production. (16)
8. Explain what you understand by an economic system. (7,18-22)
9. Outline the main features of a free economy, controlled economy and mixed economy. (23-30)
10. Why do business organisations need objectives? (33-36)
11. Outline the main objectives of private sector and public sector organisations? (38-43)
12. Describe the main functional areas in a business. (38-60)
13. Why is management needed in an organisation? (61-63)
14. Explain the difference between strategic, tactical and operational decision-making. (65-58)
15. Use examples to illustrate the difference between internal and external constraints on decision-making. (71-73)
16. How can performance be measured and controlled? (74-77)

*Asterisks indicate those questions for which there are answers in Outline Answers (page 439)*

### Essay-style questions

1.\* 'The entrepreneur is the essential factor of production'. Critically examine this statement and explain the role of the entrepreneur.
2. Why do business organisations need objectives? In what ways are the objectives for public sector and private sector organisations likely to differ?
3. Discuss the functional areas in a business organisation and the way in which they are often managed and co-ordinated.

### Short answer

1.\* With the use of an example, explain each of the following terms:
   a) Self-sufficient.
   b) Division of labour.
   c) Barter.
   d) Money
   e) Finally, explain how in the development of business and trade they are linked.
2.\* a) Identify the resources of business often referred to as the factors of production.
   b) Briefly explain each of them using examples from your own experience.
3. Distinguish between the following types of decisions in a business.
   a) Strategic.
   b) Tactical and
   c) Operational.
   d) Identify some possible constraints on decision-making.

# Multiple choice/completion

1.* A man spends £150 to have damage to his car repaired. What is the opportunity cost of this to him?
   a) £150
   b) The resources of labour and capital and the materials used in the repair.
   c) The other things he could have bought for £150.
   d) The loss in value if the car was sold without being repaired.

2.* Which is the factor of production which provides the mental and physical effort needed for the production of goods or services?
   a) Land.
   b) Labour.
   c) Capital.
   d) Enterprise.

3.* The goods and services which organisations produce in a free enterprise economy will ultimately be determined by:
   a) What they feel they can produce best.
   b) How successful they are at advertising.
   c) How consumers decide to spend their income.
   d) Decisions taken by the government.

4.* All but which of the following factors represent specific components of a business organisation?
   a) Systems.
   b) Controls.
   c) Barriers.
   d) Communication.

5. The advantages of a controlled economy would not include:
   a) Lack of competition
   b) Elimination of wasteful competition.
   c) More equal distribution of income.
   d) Use of resources for the community.

6. Which of the following statements about a business's objectives is correct?
   a) they may confuse the performance of employees.
   b) they measure performance.
   c) they provide targets for performance.
   d) they focus on the role of managers.

In each of the following questions, one or more of the responses is/are correct. Choose the appropriate letter which indicates the correct version.

   a   if 1 only is correct
   b   if 3 only is correct
   c   if 1 and 2 only are correct
   d   if 1, 2 and 3 are correct

7. Which of the following statements is/are correct?
   1. Goods and services are produced because people want them.
   2. The problems of scarcity and choice do not exist in all economies.
   3. Resources are scarce because people's wants are limited.

8. Which of the following would affect the supply of labour?
   1. Better education and training opportunities.
   2. A change in the school leaving age.
   3. An increase in unemployment.

## Assignment

This assignment is designed to recap some of the key introductory concepts in this Chapter. It will be possible to use and develop the information collected in later tasks and assignments if required.

Choose two local business organisations, one public sector, the other in the private sector. If possible, select one which provides a service and one which is involved in manufacturing. Contact each by telephone, personal visit and/or correspondence. Use the information obtained to complete the following profile for each plus any other details which you feel are important.

1. Describe the type of organisation, its location, the type of products or services which it sells, and where the demand comes from.
2. Identify the factors of production used and if possible the sources of supply.
3. State whether it is involved in primary, secondary or tertiary production.
4. Try to identify the organisational structure and functional areas in the business.
5. Identify its mission and objectives and how this is met through the organisational structure.
6. Describe the environment in which it operates and identify any internal and external constraints.
7. Finally, suggest ways in which you feel its performance could be measured.

# 2. Business Enterprise

This chapter is about the different types of business enterprises which have developed to supply the wide range of goods and services which people want to buy. It covers:

- * Private Enterprise
- * Sole Traders
- * Partnerships
- * Joint-Stock Companies
- * Private Limited Companies
- * Forming a Limited Company
- * Dissolution of Companies
- * Stock Exchange
- * Why Share Prices Fluctuate
- * Importance of Stock Exchange
- * Share Dealing in the Future
- * Control of the Stock Exchange
- * Co-operatives
- * The Franchise Business
- * Public Enterprise
- * Public Corporations
- * Government Departments
- * Local Authorities
- * Reasons for Public Ownership
- * Privatisation

## Types of Business Organisation

1. We saw in Chapter 1 that Britain has what is known as a **mixed economy** where goods and services are supplied by both private and public sector organisations.

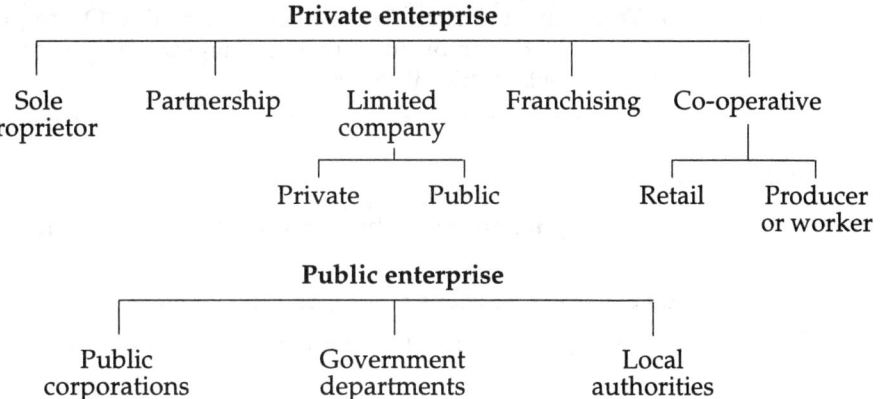

2. The **private sector or private enterprise** is the term used to describe all businesses which are owned by individuals or groups of individuals and run essentially for profit. About three-quarters of all trading in Britain is controlled by private sector organisations. The rest, known as the **public sector or public enterprise** are businesses which are owned and controlled by the Government or local authorities and run for the benefit of the country.

## Types of Private Enterprise

3. There are six main forms of business ownership in the private sector of the economy:

   - Sole Traders  } of which there are
   - Partnerships  } more than one million
   - Private Limited Companies
   - Public Limited Companies
   - Co-operatives
   - Franchising

## Sole Traders (or Proprietors)

4. The oldest, simplest and therefore most common form of business unit is the sole trader or one-person concern. This is somebody who is self-employed and who usually starts a business with capital from their savings or by borrowing from friends or a bank. **Capital** is the money which every business needs to enable it to set up and operate, for example to buy premises, equipment, stock and pay wages.

   A sole trader is not necessarily a one-person business and may have many employees or branches. However, the business is owned by only one person and it is they who receive the profits.

5. If a business operates under a name other than that of its owner(s) then under the **Business Names Act 1985** it must:

   - display in a prominent position the name of the owner(s) and a UK address where documents may be served.
   - show this information on business stationery including letters, orders, receipts, invoices and demands for payment.

6. A large number of retail outlets are owned by sole traders, for example many shoe repairers, hairdressers, cafes, laundrettes, 'corner' shops and newsagents. Other examples include many market traders, window cleaners, farmers, lorry drivers, building workers and small manufacturing concerns.

> **Task 2.1**
>
> The Department of Trade and Industry, Companies Registration Office provides guidance notes and a specimen notice on business names. Suggest why you think it could be sensible for a sole trader to obtain this information.

7. **Advantage of Sole Traders**

   - This type of business can be set up relatively easily with a small amount of capital and few legal formalities.
   - The owner is the 'boss' and can make decisions quickly about how the business is run.
   - Personal contact with customers, particularly where a business operates in a local area.
   - All profits belong to the owner.
   - Satisfaction and interest is gained from working for yourself.
   - Business affairs can be kept private except for completing tax returns.

8. **Disadvantages of the Sole Trader**

   - Unlimited Liability – this means that if the business fails and makes a loss, then the owner is responsible for all the debts incurred. Consequently, a sole trader takes the risk that they could lose all their personal possessions including their car, house and furniture.
   - May be unable to benefit from buying in bulk (large quantities) and thus be unable to offer competitive prices.
   - Expansion may be limited because the owner lacks capital and may have difficulty in borrowing.
   - Division of labour may be difficult because of the small size of the business. In a small business, the owner must do most jobs themselves.
   - Lack of continuity. If the owner dies or retires the business may go out of existence.

**Task 2.2**
1. In the area in which you live, study or work, identify as many examples as possible of sole traders. Name them and state the type of business concerned.
2. Comment on any significant features or trends.

## Partnerships

9. As the one-person business expands, it may overcome some of its disadvantages, such as lack of capital, by changing to a larger unit. For example, a plumber whose business is growing could invite one or more friends to join him to form a partnership.

10. Under the **1890 Partnership Act**, a partnership is defined as 2-20 people (10 in Banking) who agree to provide capital and work together in a business with the purpose of making a profit. More than 20 partners are allowed in the case of accountants, solicitors and members of the Stock Exchange.

11. **Advantages of Partnerships**
    - Easy to set up.
    - More capital can be brought into the business.
    - Division of labour is possible as partners may have different skills. For example, in a firm of solicitors one partner may specialise in the buying and selling of houses, another in divorce and another in criminal offences.
    - Responsibility for the control of the business is shared with more than one person. Therefore the problems of holidays, illness and long working hours are reduced.

12. **Disadvantages of Partnerships**
    - Partners have unlimited liability and are therefore personally liable for the debts of the business.
    - Disagreements among partners may cause problems.
    - Lack of capital may limit expansion.
    - There is no continuity of existence ie a partnership is dissolved (automatically ends) if one of the partners dies, resigns or becomes bankrupt.

13. People wanting to form a partnership normally draw up a legal document called a **Partnership Deed of Agreement**. This sets out the details of the partnership including the objects of the firm, how much capital each partner will provide and how profits or losses are to be shared. This Agreement is not necessary by law but is obviously very useful if a dispute arises over the terms of the partnership. If no Agreement exists then the rights and duties of the partners are determined by the **1890 Partnership Act** which states, for example, that any profits or losses must be shared equally.

14. Partnerships are usually found in the professions such as Estate Agents, Insurance Brokers, Dentists, Doctors and Accountants, although they are also found in other occupations including garage proprietors, taxi drivers, small factories and workshops, and painters and decorators. Sometimes a partner may put capital into a business but not take any active part in how it is run. In this situation they are known as **sleeping partners**.

15. Under the **1907 Partnership Act**, the **ordinary partnership** described above may be changed into a **limited partnership**. This involves at least one partner agreeing to accept unlimited liability. The number of such partnerships is quite small because limited partners are not allowed to take any active part in running a business.

### Task 2.3

K. Clayton, a successful sole proprietor in the retail trade is seeking to expand her business. She cannot decide whether or not to enter into partnership with J. Wilson. She seeks your opinion as to the potential problems and benefits of forming a partnership and asks you to advise her on what to do.

Outline your response.

## Joint Stock or Limited Companies

16. As businesses wish to expand they need more capital and in order to obtain this, they frequently become limited companies. These are business units established under the regulations of the various **Companies Acts 1948 to 1989**. Limited companies are sometimes referred to as **joint-stock** companies because the capital of the business is jointly owned by the shareholders.

17. Companies differ from sole traders and partnerships in 5 main ways:

    - **Share Capital**

      In order to raise capital, companies issue (sell) shares which means that many people are able to own a small part of the business, ie they become shareholders. This gives the company permanent capital. If a shareholder wishes to get their money back they can sell the shares but the company's capital does not change.

    - **Companies have limited liability**

      This means that should the business fail, the people who have invested their money in it cannot lose any of their personal possessions ie their liability is limited to the amount invested. It is this important feature which gives people confidence to invest in companies without the risk of losing everything.

    - **Companies are Corporate Bodies**

      That is, they **have a separate legal identity** from their owners (shareholders). This means that a company continues to exist in business even though the owners may change. Some may die, others may sell their shares but the legal existence of the company is not affected.

    - **Separation of ownership and control**

      The formation of a limited company enables people who cannot or do not want to take part in its management to still contribute capital and share any profits.

    - **Legal Control**

      Companies must by law present annual accounts to an annual general meeting to which all shareholders must be invited. The accounts must also be submitted to the Registrar of Companies.

18. As shown in the following diagram, shareholders provide the capital for the company and elect a Board of Directors to run it on their behalf. In return they are entitled to share any profits made by the firm, which is commonly called a **dividend**. The directors make the important policy decisions on how the company is to operate and may appoint managers to organise its day-to-day running. Directors also appoint a **'Company Secretary'**, who is responsible for the general administration of the company and ensuring that it meets its legal obligations. These include arranging shareholder neeetings and ensuring that the annual accounts and other returns are made on time.

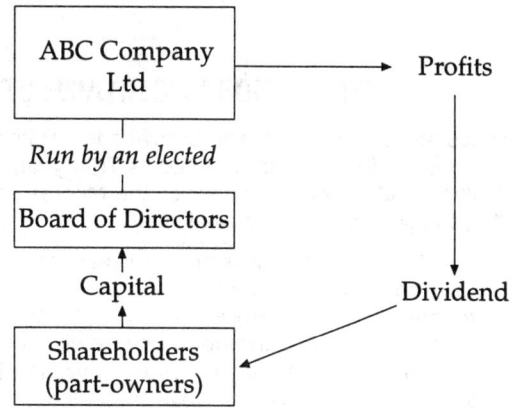

## Private Limited Companies

19. There are two types of limited company – private and public. Both must have at least two shareholders but there is no maximum.

20. The most important features of private limited companies are:
    - They are usually, but not always, small 'family' concerns.
    - The name of the company must be registered with the Registrar of Companies and it must end with the word 'Limited' (or its abbreviation Ltd), for example Travis Builders Ltd.
    - They are not allowed to offer shares to the general public.
    - Shareholders may not be able to sell their shares without the agreement of the other shareholders.

21. There are about 500,000 private limited companies in Britain, one of the largest being Littlewoods, the stores, pools and mail order firm. Other well-known examples are Famous Army Stores, Pickfords Removals and J C Bamford who specialise in making plant hire equipment. Your local Yellow Pages will include many other examples.

22. **Advantages of Private Limited Companies (Ltd)**
    - Limited liability for Shareholders.
    - Continuity of existence
    - Minimum number of shareholders is only two.
    - Greater capital potential
    - Benefits from operating on a larger scale for example bulk buying, employment of specialist staff, use of mass production techniques.

23. **Disadvantages of Private Limited Companies (Ltd)**
    - Growth may be limited by lack of capital since shares cannot be offered to the general public.
    - Transfer of shares may be limited to 'approved' new members.
    - A copy of the audited accounts must be sent to the Registrar of Companies

## 2. Business enterprise

**Task 2.4**

### LITTLEWOODS UNCERTAIN FUTURE

New challenges and uncertainties face Littlewoods – Britain's second largest private company founded in 1923 as it moves into its 70th year, determined to remain private. The football pools business, on which the Moores empire was founded, could be badly hit by the government's national lottery plans.

On the High Street the longest recession in 60 years continues. And next Spring, Sir Desmond Pitcher departs after 14 years as chief executive, during which time the annual turnover has reached £2.5 billion and profits have risen tenfold to £97m. He has brought Liverpool-based Littlewoods up-to-date improving business in all the company's core activities. The Littlewoods Organisation Ltd employs over 30,000 workers – around a third in the north west. It has three main retailing operations – high street chain stores, Index the catalogue stores, and mail order operations including Burlington and Peter Craig.

Proposals to sell off the mail order business – which has 6.5m agents – foundered earlier this year. It will now stay within the empire.

The company was also among the first to explore ventures in Russia – including two shops opened in St Petersburg last year.

Littlewoods other major interests include pools and competition partnerships operating the largest treble chance in the world. Over 5,000 people work in that pools operation, processing the eight million coupons filled in every week. But there is no doubt that the company fears the threat of a national lottery.

Read the article and answer the following questions.

1. How can Littlewoods private status be identified?
2. Which family founded the company and when?
3. What are Littlewoods' core activities?
4. What are the challenges and uncertainties faced by the company?
5. What could be the potential impact on the Company's future of these challenges and uncertainties?

## Single Member Companies

24. In 1992, new regulations came into force to allow the formation of private limited companies with only one shareholder, and to permit existing private limited companies to become single member companies. The Companies (Single Member Private Limited Companies) Regulations, which were made under the European Communities Act, implement the Twelfth Company Law Directive.

25. The regulations also provide certain safeguards. They require a single member company to ensure:

    - That the terms of certain contracts with the single member are recorded in writing.
    - That information concerning its status as a single member company is recorded in its register of members.
    - That all decisions taken by the person who is the single member acting as the company in general meetings are recorded in writing.

    Criminal penalties exist for breach of these requirements.

## Public Limited Companies (PLC)

26. Public limited companies must be registered with the Registrar of Companies, have limited liability, raise capital by issuing shares and are run by a Board of Directors elected by the shareholders. However, they are different from private companies in several important ways:

- They can advertise their shares to the general public to raise capital. To do this they must issue a **prospectus**. This is a printed document which gives details about the company (ie its history, profit record and future plans), the amount of capital it is raising and information about the share offer.
- Shares can be freely bought and sold on the Stock Exchange. (see Paragraph 36)
- The company must indicate its public status in its name by using the words 'Public Limited Company' (or its abbreviation PLC).

27. Usually a business will start as a private company and then goes 'public' at a later date in order to raise more capital to enable it to expand. To do this it must have a **nominal or authorised** share capital of at least £50,000 of which it must issue (ie sell) at least a quarter. The nominal or authorised capital is the value of the shares which the company is allowed to have. So for example, if its nominal capital is £100,000 it must issue at least £25,000 worth of shares if it wants to go public.

28. Public Limited Companies vary considerably in size from relatively small localised firms such as the world famous Caithness Glass Company based at Wick in Scotland, to very large national companies like Boots, British Telecom and Dixons, to international concerns like Shell, ICI, Ford and Unilever.

29. **Advantages of Public Limited Companies (PLC)**
    - Limited liability for shareholders.
    - Continuity of existence.
    - Easier to raise large amounts of capital and expand.
    - Shares freely transferable on the Stock Exchange.
    - Easier to borrow money ie from banks.
    - Benefits from economies of scale.

30. **Disadvantages of Public Limited Companies (PLC)**
    - Their formation requires many legal documents and may be very costly.
    - Can become very large and impersonal. People may not feel that they 'belong' to the organisation.
    - Inefficiency may result if a firm becomes very large and difficult to manage.
    - Annual accounts must be published.
    - Risk of 'take-over' bids by other companies because shares can be easily bought on the Stock Exchange.

31. **Forming a Limited Company**

    In Britain, certain legal requirements must be met before a company is allowed to begin trading and these are laid down in the various Companies Acts. Two documents must be drawn up, the **'Memorandum of Association'** and the **'Articles of Association'**.

32. The 'Memorandum of Association' gives important information about the company including:
    - The name with 'Limited' (Ltd) or 'Public Limited' (PLC) as the last word according to its status.
    - Its business address.
    - The objects of the company, for example to manufacture baked beans.
    - Details of the company's capital, for example, £250,000 divided into 250,000 Ordinary Shares of £1 each.
    - That the shareholders liability is limited.

33. The 'Articles of Association' are the **internal rules** of the company which give details of such matters as the number of directors, the voting rights of the shareholders and how profits are to be shared. The 'Memorandum' and 'Articles' must be sent to the Registrar of Companies in London. When satisfied that the prospective company has met the legal requirements, he will issue a **Certificate of Incorporation** which allows it to begin trading.

**Task 2.5**

### CADBURY CODE OF PRACTICE

Tough new guidelines about the way public companies should run themselves were published in December 1992 by the Cadbury Committee on Corporate Governance.

It recommended that

* All UK quoted companies should follow a Code of Best Practice and be required by the Stock Exchange to say in their annual reports that they are complying, and if not why not.

The main proposals were:

* Boards to have a minimum of three non-executive directors.
* Directors' service contracts not to exceed three years without shareholders' approval.
* Full disclosure of directors' total pay and those of the chairman and highest paid director, including pension scheme and stock options.
* Executive directors' pay to be decided by a sub committee made up entirely or mainly of non-executive directors.
* Clearly accepted division of responsibilities at the head of a company to prevent any individual such as the Chief Executive having unfettered power of decision.
* The board should include high calibre non-executive directors so that their views carry a significant weight in board decisions.
* Most non-executive directors should be free of any management or other tie up with the company.
* The board should establish an audit committee of at least three non-executive directors with written terms of reference.

The Code aims to improve financial reporting by providing a checklist for company shareholders which will strengthen their influence thus helping to protect their investment and also prevent another 'Robert Maxwell affair'.

Little thought, however, was given to small companies for whom 3 non-executive directors may be costly.

From the information above and your own knowledge or research, answer the following:

1. Why was a Code of Best Practice for companies needed?
2. What is the most significant proposal of the Cadbury Committee?
3. What effect, if any, do you think it will have on companies?

## Dissolution of Companies

34. As stated earlier, changes in a company's shareholders have no effect on the company or its capital. However, companies which fail to achieve their objectives and make successive losses may become insolvent (unable to pay their debts) and therefore be wound-up (liquidated). This is a legal process which can take 3 forms.

    - **Compulsory liquidation.** When a firm is unable to pay its debts, a creditor may apply to Court for a winding-up order. This can also occur if the company does not meet its statutory requirements such as failing to begin trading within one year of incorporation or not holding shareholders meetings. In this situation, a liquidator is appointed to take control of the company. This may be the Official Receiver, which is an office of the DTI.

    - **Voluntary liquidation.** Sometimes shareholders pass a 'special resolution' agreeing to dissolve a company. This may be because the company wants to merge with another or merely to discontinue trading.

- **Winding-up under supervision of the Court.** Where a company is voluntarily wound-up, the Court may still order that dissolution takes place under its supervision and in this instance may again appoint a liquidator to take control.

35. **Liquidator.** A liquidator therefore, can be appointed either by creditors, shareholders, or the Court. Their job is to sell any assets and distribute the proceeds to the Company's creditors. If there are insufficient funds to pay all creditors, then under the **Insolvency Act 1986**, preferential creditors such as the Inland Revenue, for tax due, are paid first; then ordinary creditors. Any surplus is then distributed to the shareholders.

---

**Task 2.6**

### DIRECTORS DISQUALIFIED

The DTI's Insolvency Service's network of Official Receivers are an important part of the regulatory framework protecting the public against delinquent company directors who abuse the privilege of limited liability. Over 1,000 incompetent, dishonest and negligent directors have been investigated and received disqualification orders, removing them from corporate activities.

1. Explain the 'privilege of limited liability'.
2. What does insolvency mean?
3. Why is a regulatory framework needed?
4. What does disqualification mean for a company director?

---

## The Stock Exchange

36. A company is not like a bank or building society and therefore it cannot give shareholders their money back when they ask for it because it has already been spent – on buildings, machinery, materials, wages, and all the other needs of the business. However, before buying securities investors naturally want to know that they can sell them again if they need their money back. This problem is overcome by having a Stock Market.

37. All the leading countries throughout the world except the Communist states have stock markets, for example Japan (Tokyo), USA (Wall Street, New York) and France (Paris). The UK's Stock Exchange is a highly organised financial market based in London, where over 7,000 different securities can be bought and sold, including shares in over 500 leading overseas companies.

## Share Prices

38. The price of stocks and shares varies from day to day according to the supply and demand, ie the number of people who want to sell shares and the number who want to buy. Thus if the demand for shares exceeds the supply, the price will rise. If the supply exceeds demand, the price will fall. So although you might buy a share for £1 it could go up in value if the company does well, to say £1.50. Prices may also be affected by some of the following factors.

## Some Reasons Why Share Prices Fluctuate

39. - **The recent company profit record**, rate of dividend paid and the growth prospects of the company's market(s).
    - **Rumours and announcements** of proposed take-overs and mergers or trading difficulties.
    - **Changes in Government policy,** for example restrictions on consumer spending will probably cause a fall in the share price of companies making consumer durable goods.
    - **World political and economic events** will have some effect on the shares of companies which have a large export trade, for example a recession or boom in another country.

## 2. Business enterprise

- **Changes in the rate of interest** on government securities will sometimes affect share prices. A rise in the market rate of interest might cause some 'switching' from shares to government securities.
- **Major events** such as a General Election, the Budget, or something affecting a particular company like the discovery of a new drug can all influence share prices.
- **Views of experts.** Articles by well-known financial writers can persuade people to buy or sell certain classes of shares.
- **Industrial disputes or settlements** which may affect production, sales and profits.

> **Task 2.7**
>
> The trading results of public limited companies are often reported in the financial press, ie the Financial Times and business section of the Daily Telegraph, Guardian, Times and other newspapers. Look carefully at the following article which gives a report of the results of Eagle Industries and then answer the questions which apply to it.
>
> ### EAGLES FIGHTING FINISH
>
> A much improved second half performance from computer supplies group Eagle Industries caught City pessimists by surprise yesterday and sent the shares soaring 45p to 285p. The dividend cut and poor trading figures recently announced by UK competitor Hogan had led everyone to expect another set of poor results. But Eagle has managed to maintain its unbroken profits record by the narrowest of margins and delighted shareholders by increasing the dividend for the year ending December 1993. Profits are up from £16.8 million to £18.2 million against expectations of around £15 million. A final dividend of 6p brings the total payment for the 12 months to 9p. The group has pulled back losses in the rental division from £1.6 million to almost break-even despite continuing competition from the USA. Profits in the Microchip Division have improved slightly to £8.6m and would have been better but for the recent cancellation of a large export order. Expansion in Europe has helped the maintenance division to achieve another good performance whilst profits from commercial software have moved ahead due mainly to last year's takeover of the German company Fresco.
>
> 1. Why are shareholders of Eagle Industries delighted with the results?
> 2. How have the results influenced the company share price?
> 3. What do you understand by the 'City pessimists' and why were they caught by surprise?
> 4. How has the company managed to maintain its unbroken profits record?
> 5. What information, if any, is there in the article to suggest that the company could make even higher profits in 1994?

## Economic Importance of the Stock Exchange

40.
- **It encourages people to invest** in securities because it provides a market where they can get their money back.
- **Companies can raise large amounts of money** for investment in new machinery and buildings. Firms cannot expand unless they can raise the necessary finance. Mass production could not take place, goods could not be produced as cheaply, leading to higher unemployment and a lower standard of living. Therefore ultimately our standard of living and way of life are affected by the Stock Exchange.
- **The Government can raise finance** for the nationalised industries and various essential projects by selling government bonds on the Stock Exchange. Without this finance there would be fewer and more costly state services and taxation would have to be increased to provide the funds. In recent years over 75% of new issues have been in gilt-edged securities.

- **Most people will gain from successful stock market investments** by the institutional investors, for example their pensions keep pace with the cost of living and life insurance benefits rise.
- **It provides a means of valuing companies** for takeovers and mergers because this is based on the share price.

## Share Dealing in the Future

41. 
    - It is likely that there will be share shops in the high streets of towns just like furniture, clothing or shoe shops.
    - Some banks have already begun to install dealing screens to provide customers with an over-the counter share service.
    - Building Societies are linking with brokers to offer buying and selling facilities in their branches.
    - Eventually it will be possible to buy and sell shares from home. Prices will be available on information systems like Prestel with computer links directly into the Stock Exchange dealing system.

### Task 2.8

**STILL PAPER SHARE CERTIFICATES**

The long awaited launch of Taurus, the paperless share tracking system, was finally abandoned in March 1993. It was expected to bring about the biggest change in the Stock Exchange since 'Big Bang' and put London on a par with Wall Street and Tokyo. But there are fears now that London could lose its position as a leading financial centre. Under Taurus, electronic transfer and registration of shares would have replaced the market's 30,000 paper transactions a day.

Instead of holding share certificates, shareholders would have received regular statements either from each company registrar or from their broker or bank giving a brief resume of his or her shareholdings. Taurus should have lead to more efficient settlement and reduced settlement staffing costs. But the ever increasing costs and seemingly endless technical difficulties proved too much in the end.

1. Describe the changes expected from the Taurus system.
2. Why was it abandoned?
3. What difference, if any, does it make to the UK economy?

## Control of the Stock Exchange

42. The Stock Exchange is controlled by the provisions of the **1986 Financial Services Act**. This Act was introduced to increase the protection for investors by making it an offence for any person or firm to carry out investment business unless they are authorised to do so.

43. It set up the **Securities and Investments Board** (SIB), directly accountable to Parliament, to supervise the whole operation and five **Self-Regulatory Organisations** (SROs). Each SRO sets stringent rules which member firms must follow. Investment businesses seeking authorisation can either apply direct to SIB or the appropriate SRO. They have to prove that they are 'fit and proper persons' to conduct such businesses. Investment business must also be conducted through a Recognised Investment Exchange (for example the Stock Exchange, London Metal Exchange), and each Exchange must settle its business through a Recognised Clearing House. The Settlement Service Division of the Stock Exchange is the recognised Clearing House for Stock Market transactions.

## 2. Business enterprise

44.    **Control of the Stock Exchange**

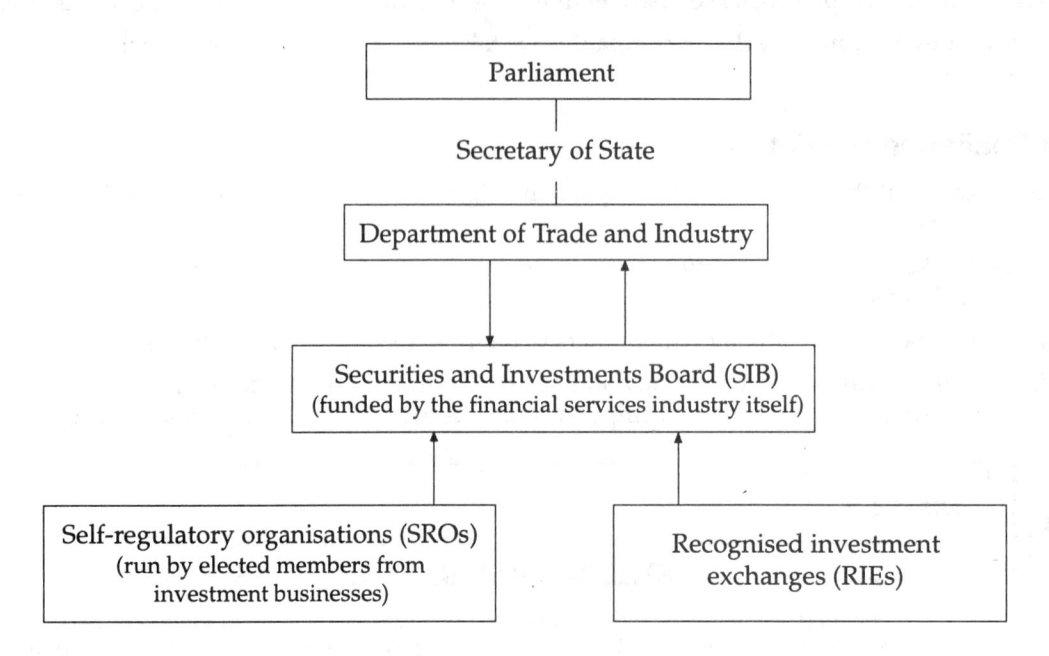

```
                    ┌──────────────┐
                    │  Parliament  │
                    └──────┬───────┘
                     Secretary of State
                    ┌──────┴─────────────────────┐
                    │ Department of Trade and Industry │
                    └──────┬─────────────────────┘
                           │         ▲
                           ▼         │
         ┌────────────────────────────────────────────┐
         │  Securities and Investments Board (SIB)    │
         │  (funded by the financial services industry itself) │
         └────────────────────────────────────────────┘
                    ▲                      ▲
         ┌──────────┴──────────┐   ┌───────┴─────────┐
         │ Self-regulatory     │   │ Recognised      │
         │ organisations (SROs)│   │ investment      │
         │ (run by elected     │   │ exchanges (RIEs)│
         │ members from        │   └─────────────────┘
         │ investment businesses)│
         └─────────────────────┘
```

45.    The SRO which regulates the Stock Exchange is called the **Securities Association.** It has the following main functions:

- To control the admission of new member firms
- To set rules for the conduct of the Exchange
- To discipline and sometimes expel members who break the rules.
- To maintain a compensation fund to pay the clients of any member firm which fails to meet its obligations.

### Task 2.9

**DTI INVESTIGATES**

In 1991 the Department of Trade & Industry inspectors handled a record 850 applications – from public, police, SIB and others – to investigate the affairs of companies. This compares with 738 in 1990 and less than 500 in 1987. In all, 18 successful trials were started by the DTI resulting in conviction of 31 individuals. Penalties included fines of up to £24,000 and 10 years prison. Ten individuals were disqualified as directors for three to 15 years.

The figures, in a DTI annual report also show that the Stock Exchange referred 11 new cases of possible insider dealing.

1. What evidence is there in the article of how companies are regulated?
2. Find out all you can about 'insider dealing' and use examples to explain what it means.

## Co-operatives

46.    A further form of business organisation is that of the co-operative. The basic idea is a large number of small separate units working together in their mutual interest to achieve economies of scale. For example, the saving from bulk buying of goods and equipment, joint advertising and the use of specialist staff. There are two basic types – retail (or consumer) co-operatives and producer (or worker) co-operatives.

47. The modern Co-operative movement began in 1844 when a group of 28 working men founded the Rochdale Equitable Pioneers Society. Its aims were to supply members with pure, wholesome food (adulteration was widespread at the time), at fair prices and return any profit as a 'dividend'. This proved so successful that the movement grew rapidly throughout the UK and abroad, gradually widening its range of products.

48. Societies do not operate under the same rules as limited companies. They are registered under the Industrial and Provident Societies Acts 1965-1975 and are responsible to the Registrar of Friendly Societies to whom they submit an Annual Return and financial statements.

49. The main features of retail co-operatives are:

    - They are owned by their customers who can become a member (or shareholder) by purchasing £1 shares.

    - They are run by a Board of Directors elected by the members.

    - Each member has only one vote regardless of how many shares they hold.

    - Each society operates independently under its own name (eg Greater Nottingham, Ipswich, Leicestershire). They are linked together through the Co-operative Union.

    - The concept of a 'dividend' ie sharing of profits with customers.

## Producer or Worker Co-operatives

50. Producer co-operatives have been most successful in agriculture for example in Denmark, New Zealand and Spain where groups of small farmers have got together to share their marketing and production facilities. This enables them to gain the maximum benefit from economies of scale and therefore to operate more efficiently.

51. Except in farming, producer co-operatives were almost non-existent in Britain until the early 1970's. At this time, the Government was faced with the problem of rising unemployment. Therefore it began to offer financial help to firms which were likely to close down and make their employees redundant (dismiss them because they were no longer needed). Worker co-operatives were formed where each employee bought shares in the firm and shared the profits. Through Co-operative Development Agencies, they also became important for the growth of small businesses.

52. There are now over 1500 Worker Co-operatives. Examples include Suma (wholefood) wholesalers, Paper Back (paper recyclers), Scott Bader (Chemicals) and Soft Solution (Computer networks).

### Task 2.10

**A STITCH IN TIME**

When a clothing firm shut down one of its factories, nine workers decided to pool £1000 of their redundancy money ... And went back into business as a workers' co-operative. Now Topstitch, at Cradley Heath, West Midlands, have won £16,000 in grants and loans to help them expand. Their former employers are also lending a hand, supplying machinery and the promise of orders.

1. From the article, identify some of the advantages of forming a workers' co-operative.
2. Can you identify any potential disadvantages?

## The Franchise Business

53. A comparatively new but growing form of business ownership in Britain is called **franchising**. Franchising involves an existing, usually well-known established company allowing someone the exclusive right to manufacture, service or sell its products in a particular area.

54. The franchise company also helps the person to set up and run the business by giving training, advice, supplying equipment and materials and assisting with the location of premises and market-

## 2. Business enterprise

ing. The company charges a royalty (fee) for its services which is usually in the form of a lump sum (eg £10,000) and a share of the profits of the business (eg 10%). Cars, petrol, printing services, certain foods and restaurants are frequently sold like this. Examples of franchises in Britain include McDonalds, Sock Shop, Dyno Rod, Holland and Barratt, Kentucky Fried Chicken and Prontoprint.

> **Task 2.11**
> 1. Re-read the paragraphs about franchising. Identify the main advantages and disadvantages of a franchise business.
> 2. Why do you feel that this type of business ownership is growing rapidly?

## Public Enterprise

55. Public sector business organisations can be divided into 3 broad categories:
    - Public Corporations or Nationalised Industries.
    - Government Departments.
    - Local Authority or Municipal Undertakings.

## Public Corporations

56. Public corporations are industries which are owned and controlled by the Government and therefore have no shareholders. To raise capital they can:
    - 'Plough' back profits.
    - Borrow from the Government.
    - Borrow from banks or
    - Issue loan stock to the public

57. When an industry which was privately owned is taken over by the Government, it is said to have been 'nationalised'. When this happens the previous owners are paid compensation.

58. Although the names may be slightly confusing, whether they are called Boards, Commissions, Councils, Authorities or Corporations, all nationalised industries are in fact public corporations, set up by an Act of Parliament and run by the government on our behalf.

59. Some examples and the year when they were nationalised are as follows:

    | Year | Name |
    |---|---|
    | 1933 | London Transport |
    | 1946 | British Coal |
    | 1946 | Bank of England |
    | 1947 | Electricity Council* |
    | 1948 | British Gas Corporation* |
    | 1948 | British Rail |
    | 1948 | National Water Council* |
    | 1954 | Atomic Energy Authority |
    | 1967 | British Steel Corporation* |

    * Now privatised (see paragraph 70)

60. Other public corporations were set up by the government in the first place. Examples of these include:

    | Year | Name |
    |---|---|
    | 1927 | British Broadcasting Corporation |
    | 1969 | The Post Office |

61. A Minister is put in charge of each industry to determine the general policy, and he appoints a Chairman and Board with responsibility for the day-to-day management. An annual report has to be prepared and submitted to the Minister who may be questioned on it by Members of Parliament. In this way, a public corporation is said to be made accountable (ie responsible) for its activities.

62. The chief aim of a public corporation is to provide an efficient public service at a price low enough to avoid making excessive profit but high enough to cover investment costs, although sometimes other priorities may be considered as being more important than making a profit. For example, some railway lines are kept open, despite the fact that they are making a loss, in order to supply some remote areas with a transport service. The Government however, believes that nationalised industries should act as commercial enterprises and has set policies accordingly.

63. Each industry is expected to achieve a 'required rate of return' on its assets currently 8 per cent in real terms before tax. The financial target set by the Government is usually supported by a series of performance aims, covering costs and, where appropriate, standards of service. External financing limits, which control the amount of finance (grants and borrowing) that a nationalised industry can raise in any financial year, are an important operating control. They are set in the light of the industry's financial target and its expected performance and investment. Any losses are financed from taxation whilst profits are used to repay loans or finance the future development of the industry. In recent years, the proportion of investment financed from internally generated funds has increased.

### Task 2.12

External scrutiny of nationalised industry efficiency is conducted by the Monopolies and Mergers Commission and where appropriate, investigations may also be undertaken by management consultants. Whilst House of Commons Select Committees, such as the Treasury and Civil Service Committee and the Public Accounts Committee, also scrutinise the industries' performance.

1. How can the efficiency of industries owned and controlled by the Government be measured?
2. Why do you think that such industries require external scrutiny?

## Government Departments

64. As well as running many industries, the government also has departments which provide a variety of services. Examples of these include the Royal Mint which supplies the country's money, Her Majesty's Stationery Office (HMSO) dealing with Government publications, the Central Office of Information which prepares Government statistics, and the Forestry Commission which controls the production and supply of timber. The Post Office was once a government department but since 1969 has been a public corporation.

## Local Authority or Municipal Undertakings

65. There are also many important services which are operated by Local Authorities for the benefit of the local community. Local Councils use money collected from rents, the council tax, business rates, government grants (revenue support grant) and by borrowing to provide services for the town. Examples include schools and nurseries for education, health clinics and hospitals, police and fire services and recreational facilities such as parks and libraries. The local authority may also receive income from trading activities. That is, many councils provide services which you pay to use, for example sports centres, entertainment facilities, public baths and cafes.

66. **Local Authorities** are managed by a combination of employed staff and councillors elected by the local people. The councillors make the policy decisions on how the town should be run and the employees implement these and carry out the day-to-day administration. The **Council Tax** which they collect, is based on the value of domestic property and the number of people living there. This was introduced in 1993 to replace the **Community Charge** (Poll Tax) which itself replaced domestic rates in 1990. The **Uniform Business Rate (UBR)** is based on the rateable values of business properties. The UBR figure is set by the government and in 1993/4 was 41.6p in the pound in England and 44p in Wales.

## Task 2.13

### COUNCIL TAX INTRODUCED

The Government predicts that in 1993 Councils will need to spend a total of just over £41.1 billion of which it will contribute £33.5 billion through grants and transitional relief. That means that the balance must be raised through the new Council Tax and business rates. Councils will be given spending targets and will be subject to 'capping' if these are exceeded. The amount of council tax to be paid per property falls into one of eight bands which relates to its value, with the standard considered to be Band D. A transitional relief scheme is being financed by the Government for 2 years to ensure no household pays no more than £3.50 a week extra when poll tax is abolished. It will only be necessary to pay more if, for example, a council exceeds its spending ceiling or assumes a tax collection rate of less than 98%. Final bills could vary widely between councils because some authorities will need to raise more cash to cover poll tax arrears and appeals against home valuations. Unlike poll tax which was a personal tax, the council tax is a property tax and more difficult for people to avoid paying. But while many large households will be better off nearly every person who lives alone will pay more. One in four households is made up of a single person. Under poll tax, they had to pay half as much as a couple sharing a house or a third as much as three adults sharing. Now they will pay three-quarters of the full bill. Many people will not have to pay full council tax or will be completely exempt. Students will not pay and if you have savings of under £6,000 and are on a low income, you may qualify for Council Tax Benefit.

It is feared that the tax could trigger a fresh fall in house prices because owners will be reluctant to 'trade up' to houses in higher bands. This is likely to depress the value of more expensive houses still further. Some prices in London and the South-East could fall by more than 4 per cent. Many councils say that they will have to make drastic cuts in services and jobs to avoid overspending and 'capping'. But the government believes that there will be no need for job losses if local authorities manage their resources sensibly and adhere to the public sector pay policy guidelines of 0-1.5 per cent.

### COUNCIL TAX IN ENGLAND

| | House Value | Transitional Relief (per wk) |
|---|---|---|
| BAND A | (less than £40,000) | £1.75 |
| BAND B | (£40,000- £52,000) | £2.00 |
| BAND C | (£52,000- £68,000) | £2.25 |
| BAND D | (£68,000- £88,000) | £2.50 |
| BAND E | (£88,000-£120,000) | £2.75 |
| BAND F | (£120,000-£160,000) | £3.00 |
| BAND G | (£160,000-£320,000) | £3.25 |
| BAND H | (over £320,000) | £3.50 |

1. Outline the key features of the new Council Tax.
2. How does it differ from the former Poll Tax?
3. Explain, with examples, the transitional relief scheme.
4. Who, if anyone, will be better-off or worse-off under the new tax?
5. What problems, if any, could the new tax lead to?

## Reasons for Public Ownership

67.
- Political – to enable the nation to share the profits of industry.
- Control of vital industries and commercial activities for example central banking and railways
- Control of monopolies – many nationalised industries are 'natural' monopolies ie they have no real competition, for example post.
- Protection of national security – eg Atomic Energy
- Capital Costs – sometimes the capital costs of setting up or modernising an industry may be too great or unprofitable for private enterprise, for example coal and docks.
- Provision of social services – which private enterprise would not wish to provide because they are unprofitable, for example railways and postal services to remote rural areas.
- Survival of unprofitable industries – which might otherwise be forced to close down, creating problems of unemployment, for example steel in the 1970's and early 1980's.

68. **Advantages of Public Ownership**
- It enables the government to plan large sections of the economy in the public interest.
- Profits belong to the nation and are therefore for everyone's benefit not just a few shareholders or individuals.
- The benefits of economies of scale can be gained from operating as a large unit.
- Reduces unnecessary and wasteful duplication of resources. For example, imagine the problems from competition if a number of companies ran the railways.
- Ensures survival of important industries.
- Provides capital investment for modernisation.
- Operates in the public interest in the provision of goods and services.

69. **Disadvantages of Public Ownership**
- Lack of competition often makes it difficult to assess their efficiency. Greater possibility of waste, over-manning and poor quality service.
- Government may delay decision-making or pursue policies which are not in the best interests of the business.
- Government interference may make it difficult for them to operate efficiently ie control of prices, or investment decisions.
- Any losses must be paid for out of taxation
- May become impersonal with lots of 'red tape'.
- National decision-making does not always work in the best interests of a local community, eg regional unemployment in the coal industry if uneconomic pits are closed.

## Privatisation

70. The reasons for the organisation and control of some industries may be based on political issues rather than just the business factors which affect it. A lot of government control of industry has taken place in periods when the Labour Party was running the country particularly from 1946-1951. However, the Conservative Party does not support public ownership to the same extent and indeed in the 1980's introduced a policy of **privatisation**. That is, it has been selling off some public corporations to the private sector as public limited companies. Recent examples of such privatisation include Cable and Wireless (1981), British Telecom (1986), British Gas (1986), British Airways (1987), Water (1989) and Electricity (1990).

71. Other forms of privatisation which the Government has introduced include:
- **Competitive Tendering or Contracting Out** whereby Private Sector firms are now invited to bid for contracts alongside local authority departments for refuse disposal, school catering and cleaning, security of council property and repairs and maintenance.

- **Deregulation** where 'traditional' state run activities are opened up to private sector competition as, for example, with long distance coaches (1980) and local bus services (1985). 'Big-bang' was another form of deregulation to promote competition among Stock Exchange members.
- **Substitution** of tax finance with a customer fee as for example, with charges for dental check-ups, eye tests and NHS prescriptions.
- **Domestic property** where over 1 million council houses were offered for sale to their occupiers at discounts of up to 60% of the 'market' price.

72. The main objectives of the privatisation programme are:
    - **To increase efficiency** by creating greater competition which provides an incentive to reduce costs.
    - **To reduce Government financing** because losses and investment would no longer come from the Government. In addition, over £30 billion has been raised from the privatisation sales.
    - **To increase customer satisfaction** because competition widens choice and company service. Waiting lists, for example, have virtually disappeared since BT's privatisation in 1984, whilst the choice of telephone products has increased.
    - **To widen share ownership**. The government saw privatisation as an opportunity to introduce the concept of share ownership to 'ordinary' individuals. Since 1979, the number of shareholders has more than trebled to over 11 million.

73. **Criticisms of Privatisation**
    - **Consumers are worse off** because in effect, they create private monopolies as with Gas, Water and Electricity. Also the removal of cross-subsidisation in some industries could mean some consumers will lose services completely or have to pay much higher charges. On the railway for example, profitable commuter routes are currently used to subsidise less busy lines.
    - **They bring major job losses** in order to increase efficiency in industries often regarded as being heavily overmanned.
    - **'Selling the Family Silver'**. Privatisation means selling the State's assets and placing them in the hands of the minority of people who can afford to purchase shares in them.

74. **Regulation of Privatised Industries**

    The privatised public utilities have monopoly characteristics and therefore the government has set up specific industry watchdogs to manage the transition and protect consumers by monitoring prices, competition and quality of service. These are OFTEL (Telecommunications), OFGAS (Gas), OFWAT (Water) and OFFER (Electricity).

75. They relied on negotiation and the government claims that consumers get a better deal from privatised utilities than when they were in the public sector with no independent regulation at all. But the watchdogs have been accused of having 'no teeth', because despite a stringent pricing formulae, based on price rises not exceeding the 'Retail Prices Index plus or minus X%' the new companies have made 'excessive' profits and give massive pay awards to their chairmen and senior executives. There have also been many thousands of complaints to the watchdogs.

76. Therefore, to extend the powers of the watchdogs, the **Competition and Service (Utilities) Act 1992** was introduced. It gives the regulators legal power:
    - to set guaranteed quality standards,
    - to arrange compensation when things go wrong.
    - to insist that consumers are kept informed about standards and performance against them.
    - to intervene in disputes.
    - to peg prices if performance targets are not met.
    - to stop unreasonable costs being passed on to consumers eg huge pay rises for bosses.

### Task 2.14

#### THE PRICE OF PURITY

Consumers has been warned that even allowing for inflation, water bills could double by the year 2000 according to the industry's watchdog OFWAT. Most of the rise will reflect the enormous cost of obeying stringent EU directives on water quality and water disposal. The water companies, under fire for making huge profits and giving massive pay rises to their bosses, claim that it is not necessary to meet the new standards which are far higher than those for food. Britain, however, could face prosecution if it does not meet the regulations. It is also argued that since 12 million people receive drinking water which is contaminated at some time with pesticides, polluters not consumers should pay the cost of cleaning it up. There are other costs connected with water management, such as preventing the pollution of rivers, cleaning up beaches and treating sewage, where again the degree of cleanliness hugely affects the costs which industry and the public must bear. Environmentalists, like Friends of the Earth, believe that the acceptance of lower standards is pandering to shareholders and overpaid water company bosses. They argue that it ignores the public good at the expense of profit. Privatisation therefore has brought the clash of interests out into the open. It has shown that water quality should not be dictated by laboratory experts but a rational consumer choice determined by balancing the social costs and benefits of water of a supremely high standard and very high bills against accepting a small risk and lower bills.

Read the article and answer the following questions.
1. Why is OFWAT warning consumers?
2. How has the water industry been affected by Britain's membership of the European Union?
3. What disadvantages or criticisms of privatisation can you identify?
4. What are the problems and issues associated with water management?
5. In what sense has privatisation brought a clash of interests out into the open?

## Methods of Privatisation

77. The government has used various methods to privatise enterprises including:
    - **Stock Exchange Flotation.** The most common method is the sale of shares direct to the public, financial institutions and foreign buyers. eg British Gas, British Steel.
    - **Sale to a single purchaser.** In some cases all the shares have been bought by a single company as for example with the Rover Group and Sealink Ferries.
    - **Management or Employee Buyout.** In the case of the National Freight Corporation, the existing workforce was given the sole right to buy the shares and own the enterprise.

## Summary

78. a) All businesses are either owned privately by individuals (or groups of individuals) or publicly by the Government.
    b) Private enterprise includes sole traders (or one-person concerns), partnerships consisting of 2-20 people, private and public limited companies, co-operatives which can be either retail or producer and franchises where people set up in business using the trade name and with the help of existing companies.
    c) All these different types of organisations need capital in order to pay for the costs of running the business. This capital is usually raised by sole traders and partnerships, from savings or borrowing from friends or a bank, whilst limited companies issue shares.

d) Shareholders own part of the business and in return for lending the capital they receive a dividend each year which is a share of any profits which the firm makes.

e) The ability of companies to raise large sums of capital has been very dependent upon limited liability. This means that if a firm is unprofitable and goes out of business then shareholders can only lose the amount of money which they have invested and not any of their personal possessions such as their house or furniture.

f) To form a limited company it is necessary for the firm to draw up a Memorandum of Association and Articles of Association giving details of the type of business and how it is to be run. These documents are sent to the Registrar of Companies who issues Certificates of Incorporation to companies who meet the legal requirements.

g) A company can be wound up either compulsorily or voluntarily. A liquidator is usually appointed.

h) The shares in a public limited company, are bought and sold on the Stock Exchange which is very important to the economy because it makes it possible for companies and the government to raise large sums of money.

i) Public sector businesses are those which are owned and controlled by the government on behalf of the nation and include: Public Corporations, Government Departments and Municipal Undertakings.

j) Public Corporations are formed by an Act of Parliament and can be set up directly by the government as with the BBC or be the result of nationalisation for example coal and railways.

k) Government Departments provide a variety of services examples of which are the Royal Mint and HMSO.

l) Municipal Undertakings are the services and trading activities provided by the local council for example schools, libraries, sports centres and entertainment facilities.

m) Reasons for public ownership include political arguments, to control vital industries, to control monopolies, protect national security, provide capital, provide social services and to ensure the survival of certain unprofitable industries.

n) In the 1980's and 1990's the Conservative Party has pursued a policy of privatisation by selling off nationalised industries.

o) Other forms of privatisation include competitive tendering, deregulation, substitutions and the sale of council houses.

**Review questions** *(Answers can be found in the paragraphs indicated)*

1. Draw a diagram to illustrate the different types of privately owned business organisations. (1)
2. Give 2 advantages and 2 disadvantages of being a sole proprietor. (7-8)
3. What is a Partnership Deed of Agreement? (12-13)
4. Explain the difference between limited and unlimited liability. (7,11,14,16)
5. Give 3 important features of private limited companies. (19-22)
6. Explain 3 features of public limited companies. (25-29)
7. Briefly explain the 2 legal documents which control the affairs of limited companies. (30-32)
8. In what ways can a company be 'wound-up'? (33)
9. List 5 factors which might affect a company's share price. (36-37)
10. Outline the importance of the Stock Exchange to the UK economy. (38-39)
11. How do producer or worker co-operatives differ from retail co-operatives? (46-52)
12. What is franchising? (53-54)
13. Give 4 examples of public corporations. (59)
14. What are the aims of a public corporation? (62-63)

15. Outline the difference between a public corporation and a Government Department. (64)
16. How does the local council get the money to pay for the services which it provides? (65-66)
17. Give 4 reasons for public ownership. (67)
18. List 3 advantages and 3 disadvantages of the public ownership of industry (68-69)
19. Explain with examples the meaning of, and reasons for, privatisation. (70-72)
20. How are privatised utilities regulated? (74-76)

*Asterisks indicate those questions for which there are answers in Outline Answers (page 439)*

## Essay-style questions

1.* 'Without limited liability it would be impossible for companies to raise large sums of capital.' Explain and comment on this statement.
2. Discuss the following statement in relation to Privatisation.

    'Free markets will ensure that the price and quality of goods and services supplied by producers and demanded by consumers will be at their most efficient levels.'
3. Britain is said to have a 'mixed economy'. Explain what this means, the reasons behind it and any recent changes or trends which are taking place.

## Short answer

1.* Write brief notes on each of the following:
    a) The Stock Exchange
    b) The Council Tax
    c) Franchising
    d) Authorised Capital

2.* You are asked to advise a friend who is considering opening a small garage specialising in repair and bodywork. He wants to know:
    a) What advantages he would gain from running his own business.
    b) What disadvantages he might face.
    c) If there are any alternative business forms he might adapt and overall which is the most suitable for someone just starting up.

3. Distinguish between the following terms and explain why and when they are needed.
    a) Memorandum of Association
    b) Articles of Association
    c) Certificate of Incorporation

## Multiple choice/completion

1.* Kentucky Fried Chicken sells the ingredients and method of production to a retail shop. This type of business arrangement is called a:
    a) Retail Co-operative
    b) Supermarket
    c) Franchise
    d) Producer Co-operative

2.* In which of the following organisations is the original owner no longer the sole decision maker?
    a) the sole proprietor
    b) the market trader
    c) the partnership
    d) the self employed gardener

## 2. Business enterprise

3.* What is normally meant by the 'division of ownership and control' in modern economies?
   a) increasing government intervention in business
   b) increasing worker participation and control
   c) owners being replaced by managers and directors
   d) growth of larger firms as a result of takeovers

4.* Public Limited Companies have all except which one of the following features?
   a) a Board of Directors elected by managers
   b) not less than 2 shareholders
   c) shares which can be bought and sold on the Stock Exchange
   d) limited liability for shareholders.

5. Which one of the following organisations operates in the public sector of the economy?
   a) W. H. Smiths
   b) Co-operative Wholesale Society
   c) British Telecom
   d) British Coal

6. Limited liability means that:
   a) a company is protected from going into liquidation
   b) all shareholders have equal liability for company debts
   c) there is a limit to the amount of debt a company can incur
   d) shareholders are not personally liable for debts but could lose their investment

*In each of the following questions, one or more of the responses is/are correct. Choose the appropriate letter which indicates the correct version.*

   A   if 1 only is correct
   B   if 3 only is correct
   C   if 1 and 2 only are correct
   D   if 1, 2 and 3 are correct

7. Which of the following is/are a form of privatisation?
   1. Sale of Council Houses to their occupiers at a discount
   2. Competitive Tendering for local authority services such as refuse disposal
   3. Reduction of tax subsidies on services such as dental health

8. Which of the following statements is/are correct?
   1. Under the 1890 Partnership Act, a partnership is defined as 2 – 50 people working together.
   2. Single member companies must issue a prospectus before trading can commence.
   3. Limited companies are sometimes referred to as joint stock companies.

---

### Assignment

Study past and current quality newspapers and business studies magazines/journals and from them collect any articles which refer to privatisation. Use these to:

1. Illustrate the benefits or advantages and
2. the criticisms or disadvantages of privatisation.
3. Analyse one of the recent privatisations such as Gas, Water or Electricity and prepare a report stating, with reasons, whether you agree or disagree with it.
4. Prepare a report on the arguments for and against a proposed privatisation like the railways or coal.
5. Finally, prepare a 5 minute presentation on your views of the likely impact on privatisation policy if there was a change of government.

# 3. Business Planning

We saw in Chapter 1 that a successful business requires a set of corporate objectives defining, for example, the market share, profit or return on investment which it is seeking to achieve within its targeted market segments.

This chapter is about the need for strategic planning in an organisation and the factors which need to be considered if the objectives of the plan are to be achieved. It covers:

* Corporate Strategic Planning
* Purpose of Corporate Planning
* Corporate Planning Framework
* Mission Statement
* Strategic Plan
* Operating Statement
* Monitoring and Evaluation
* SWOT Analysis
* Environmental Scanning
* PEST Analysis
* Political Environment
* Government Policies and Legislation
* Consumer Protection Legislation
* Economic Analysis
* Social Change
* Technological Developments
* Competitor Analysis
* Corporate Gap

## Corporate Strategic Planning

1. If an organisation is to achieve its set objectives, then clearly it must make plans and develop suitable strategies to do so. This requires a comprehensive and systematic corporate approach to planning. which takes into account the capability and resources of the organisation as a whole and the environment within which it has to operate.

2. By its very nature, corporate planning involves a long-term period of 3-5 years and often more, depending upon the type of organisation. A well formulated strategy can last several years, although the plan must be frequently reviewed and updated so that it can be modified as necessary.

## Purpose of Corporate Planning

3. Corporate planning is crucial to the success of an organisation and therefore is a key task of the Chief Executive and senior managers. It is used for a number of purposes which are essential to the organisation's survival and growth including:

- to identify all potential long-term objectives and decide which to pursue.
- to evaluate the organisation's internal resources including personnel, finance, marketing, production, purchasing and administration.
- to identify the organisation's internal strengths and weaknesses and possible external opportunities and threats which it faces. (See SWOT, paragraph 11).
- to scan the external environment within which the organisation operates in order to identify changes and trends. The ability to successfully achieve objectives will be affected by broad changes in the political, economic, social and technological environment which in turn can all have an influence on decision making. (See PEST analysis paragraph 25).
- to evaluate the present and likely future competitive situation and identify any threats. (See Competitor Analysis paragraph 62).
- to review the organisation's position in the market and identify any trends such as increasing or decreasing market share and whether or not the total market is increasing or decreasing.
- to manage and co-ordinate all activities and plans throughout the organisation.
- to establish a formal planning process with effective feedback and regular review and updating.
- to communicate with, involve and motivate all staff.

> **Task 3.1**
>
> Choosing any organisation well known to you, such as a school, college or business, identify with examples 5 key reasons why it does or should plan

## Corporate Planning Framework

4. There are certain common elements of corporate strategic planning which apply to any organisation. They are the mission statement, strategic plan, operating statement and monitoring and evaluation.

5. **The Mission Statement** – determines the nature and direction of an organisation and says what it is about.

   Based on a consideration of the environment in which the organisation operates, it should set out a clear view of the primary purpose of the organisation, its values and distinctive features and provide a rationale for its strategic plan. ICI, for example, is about chemicals and related products. MacDonalds is about hamburgers and fast food, Burtons about men's clothing and Prudential about insurance and financial services.

6. **Examples of Mission Statements**

   *Bolton College*
   'To promote, encourage and assist the enhancement of people and organisations through the provision of quality services in Education.'

   *ASDA*
   'ASDA's mission is to become the UK's leading value for money grocer with an exceptional range of fresh foods together with those clothing, home and leisure products that meet the everyday needs of our target customers.'

   *British Gas*
   'The aim of British Gas is to be a world class energy company and the leading international gas business.'

> **Task 3.2**
>
> Consider the organisation in which you work or study.
> 1. Write down what you think its mission is.
> 2. Find out what the actual mission is as determined in its strategic plan.
> 3. Now compare the two and comment on any differences.

7. **The Strategic Plan** is based on the mission statement and develops clear intentions for the organisation in terms of its major objectives and targets and a timescale by which these are expected to be achieved, often 3-5 years. Once the strategy has been determined, an organisation can then make decisions about how it is going to be achieved. This includes decisions about its products and services, the markets and customers to be served, standards of quality and the resources needed.

8. **The Operating Statement** considers each aspect of the strategic plan and determines how it is to be implemented and achieved. It is a detailed action plan which relates the short-term strategy (usually annual) to the longer-term objectives.

9. **Monitoring and Evaluation** is required to allow the organisation to review the progress towards its objectives in a regular and systematic way. It also enables it to consider the continued relevance of its broader strategy and update it as appropriate.

## 10. Strategic Planning Process

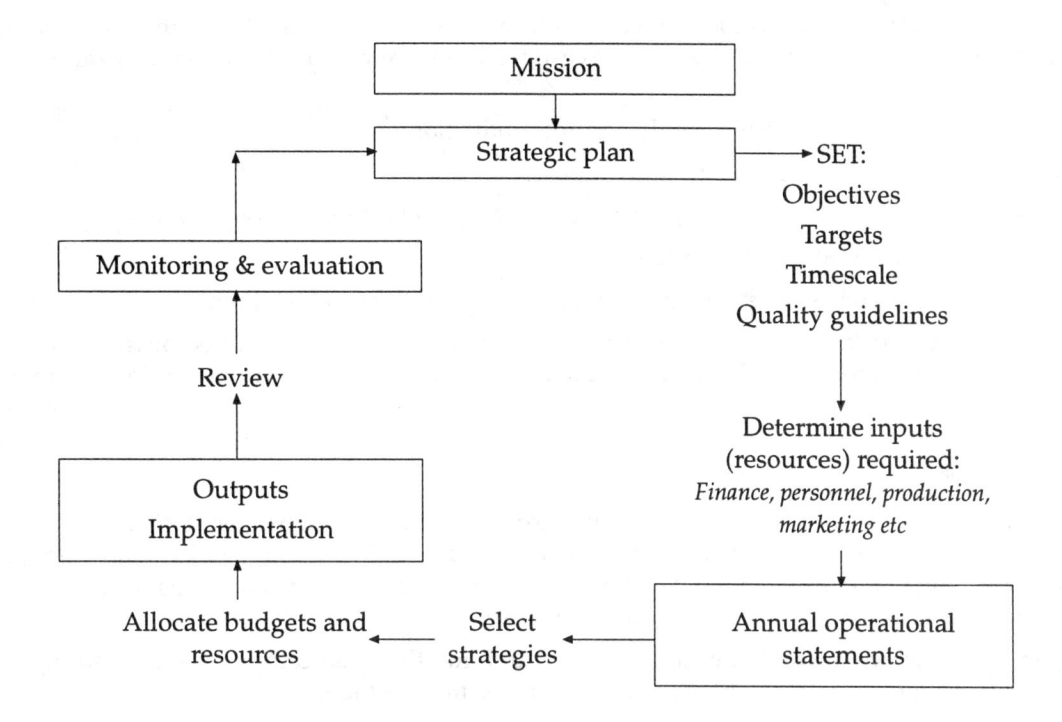

```
                    Mission
                      ↓
        → Strategic plan  →  SET:
        ↑                    Objectives
        ↑                    Targets
  Monitoring & evaluation    Timescale
        ↑                    Quality guidelines
      Review                      ↓
        ↑                   Determine inputs
     Outputs                (resources) required:
  Implementation            Finance, personnel, production,
        ↑                   marketing etc
        ↑                         ↓
  Allocate budgets and ← Select ← Annual operational
      resources         strategies    statements
```

### Task 3.3

State with reasons, how each of the following situations could affect an organisation's strategic planning.

a) A threatened strike.

b) An increase in the number of customer complaints.

c) The introduction of a new product.

d) The appointment of a new board of directors.

e) Investment in production technology.

## 11. Swot Analysis

A SWOT analysis is used to highlight an organisation's internal strengths and weaknesses, measured against its competitors, and any key external opportunities and threats. It requires management to look closely and analytically at every aspect of its operations and then develop suitable strategies to achieve the desired objectives.

It can be carried out either by line managers, although this may not always produce objective analysis, or by using external consultants.

## 12. Strengths

These are the advantageous aspects of the organisation on which its future success can be built. Examples might include:

- a well motivated, skilled workforce,
- well established products,
- a good reputation and
- modern production technology

13. **Weaknesses**

    These are the factors which could hinder the future success and potential growth of an organisation. Therefore, it is important that they are investigated and remedial action taken. Examples might include:
    - poor industrial relations which could disrupt production,
    - outdated equipment or production techniques,
    - poor quality control leading to high wastage or complaints about faulty products,
    - poor management information systems,
    - inadequate research and development and therefore limited product innovation.

14. If a strong financial position exists, then in the examples quoted it should be possible for management to implement remedies. If, however, finance itself is a weakness, then it would have to be a key priority for action.

## Opportunities

15. Usually, but not always, strengths and weaknesses relate to the organisation itself whilst opportunities come about as a result of external factors which affect it. They may be identified from planned research or just purely by chance but either way it is important that organisations seek out, recognise and grasp appropriate opportunities when they arise.

16. Organisations which fail to do this may miss out and find that their competitors are leading the way, turning opportunities into potential threats. Examples may include:
    - new market openings which could be met from existing resources,
    - opportunities for new products or services as a result of new legislation or trends, or
    - developments in technology which present opportunities for improved production techniques or administrative systems.

## Threats

17. Most threats come from outside organisations and therefore outside the control of management. Examples might be:
    - increasing competition,
    - changing technology,
    - economic factors like rises in interest rates and
    - political factors such as the introduction of new legislation.

    Nonetheless, it may be possible to overcome them. For example, controlling costs by finding alternative suppliers or substituting raw materials to reduce the effect of price increases.

18. But threats can also exist within an organisation. Examples might be:
    - an ageing workforce which resists change,
    - management complacency which can lead to an acceptance of what is happening now and therefore a failure to recognise potential opportunities and threats, or
    - a lack of financial or other management information needed for decision-making and control in an organisation.

19. One of the main reasons why Japanese manufacturers are so successful in selling goods like audio-visual equipment, cars, motor cycles and photographic equipment in both the USA and Europe is that they have been much quicker than Western companies to take advantage of technological innovation.

## Task 3.4

Choose any organisation to which you belong, such as a school, college, business, church, social or sports club.

1. Briefly explain how you fit into the organisation, for example, student, employee, treasurer, team captain.
2. Carry out a SWOT analysis on the organisation identifying at least 3-5 key factors under each heading.
3. Comment on your findings including how you think the SWOT is likely to influence the future development of the organisation.

## Environmental Scanning

20. An organisation however, does not operate in isolation but is part of the environment with which it interacts. The environment consists of a range of factors or constraints which are external to the business but which have a direct or indirect influence on its decision taking and ability to achieve its objectives. The environment can represent either or both opportunities and threats depending on the industry and the way they are managed. Therefore it is important for strategic planning that managers are aware of these factors and are alert to the impact which they can have on the organisation so that plans can be amended or abandoned accordingly.

21. One way of doing this is by means of **environmental scanning** which is a term used to describe the activities involved in the gathering, analysis and communication of information which firms need in order to keep up-to-date with changes in the business environment.

22. Consideration of the business environment is important in strategic planning because it

    - provides a base of objective data which enables more informed planning, forecasting and decision-taking.
    - enables more effective resource allocation.
    - makes an organisation aware of the changing needs and wishes of its customers.
    - provides training and development for executives thereby increasing their skills in handling problems and change and facilitating new approaches.
    - enables better understanding of government decisions and therefore effectiveness in dealing with them.
    - enables an organisation to improve its image with the public by showing that it is sensitive to its environment and responsive to it.

23. In addition, environmental scanning would include continuous monitoring of all factors which have a direct impact on an organisation including consumers, distributors, suppliers, competitors – for customers and suppliers, trade unions, government regulations, and product and process developments.

24. Information about the business environment may come from a wide variety of sources. Within an **organisation** it is available from, for example, reports, memos, meetings, management information systems, sales and technical staff, and advisory committees. Whilst sources outside the organisation include stock market reports, trade and technical journals, press reports, market research, government publications, consumer studies, suppliers, banks and trade associations.

## 3. Business planning

> **Task 3.5**
>
> From which source is an organisation most likely to find the following information:
> a) Sales trends
> b) Data on market share
> c) The organisation's objectives
> d) Customer views on the product range
> e) The current share price.

25. **Pest Analysis**

    A common way of scanning the business environment is by considering the political, economic, social and technological factors which impinge on the organisation. These are summarised on the following diagram.

26. **A Framework for Environmental Scanning**

    POLITICAL —  General level of stability
                         Party System
                         Government Policies – monetary, fiscal, industrial,
                         Economic Planning – public versus private sector control
                         Legislation
                         European Standards/Directives

    ECONOMIC — Unemployment
                         Interest Rates
                         Economic Growth
                         Taxation
                         Inflation
                         Exchange Rates

    SOCIAL — Lifestyles and Leisure Time
                         Culture
                         Demography
                         Fashion
                         Education
                         Pressure Groups
                         Environmental Issues

    TECHNOLOGICAL — New Products and Services
                         Telecommunications
                         Growth Information Technology
                         New Manufacturing Processes/Materials
                         Consumer Expectations
                         Rate of Change

## Political Environment

27. Throughout this text you will find reference to the influence of the government on organisations. The three main factors are **State ownership** which was discussed in detail in Chapter 2, and **Government policies** and **legislation.**

28. In some countries, the level of **political stability** is also a major factor which organisations need to consider. Italy, for example, frequently has changes of government whilst the economy of the former Yugoslavia was devastated by the outbreak of civil war in 1991. Third World and Middle-Eastern countries are also politically volatile.

29. The **political party** in power in a country both locally and nationally is also important because of the different policies which may be adopted. In the UK, for example, the labour party believes in a far greater level of government intervention in, and control of, the economy and business including nationalisation whilst the conservative party allows greater freedom and has carried out substantial privatisation.

---

**Task 3.6**

### INTERNATIONAL ENVIRONMENT

Cable and Wireless PLC is a major international telecommunications company which operates in highly complex and volatile markets affected by diplomacy, nationalism, politics, war, economics, high technology, intense competition and rapid innovation. Its research and development, production and pre- and after-sales service costs are enormous whilst its products are non-standard and usually tailor-made to meet the needs of large, powerful buyers. These in turn are heavily influenced by many unpredictable environmental factors such as diplomatic pressure, international funding, political loyalties and reciprocal trading which bear no direct relationship to the actual economic costs and functional benefits normally associated with the supply of telecommunications equipment.

1. Explain the meaning of PLC
2. Outline the distinguishing features of the market in which Cable and Wireless operates.
3. Why is environmental scanning important to the success of the Company.
4. Is a PEST analysis appropriate for the company?
5. What other types of information might assist the company in its strategic planning and where might it be obtained?

---

## Government Policies and Legislation

These can be summarised as follows:

30. **Control of the Economy**

    This is discussed in more detail in Chapter 5. Sufficient to note here that the Governments use of **fiscal** measures (ie taxation and public expenditure) and **monetary** measures (mainly interest rates and credit controls) can have an important impact on businesses because they affect the cost of borrowing and level of consumer expenditure (ie demand) and therefore profits.

31. **Company Legislation**

    Chapter 2 outlined the Government's control on both private and public limited companies through the Companies and Insolvency Acts.

## 32. International Trade

Chapter 6 examines the assistance given to exporters through the BOTB and ECGD. The Government also influences overseas trade through its foreign exchange and balance of payments policies, customs duties and export documentation.

## 33. Employment and Training

Chapter 12 outlines some important legislation which affects the employment of people. The Government has introduced several laws, both to protect employees and also to improve their working conditions. Training is encouraged through Government funded schemes co-ordinated by TECs.

## 34. Industrial Relations

In Chapter 14, the role of ACAS is discussed. This is a body which seeks to improve industrial relations and settle disputes quickly. The Government has also passed laws like the Trade Union Act 1984 which states that a trade union must hold a secret ballot before taking industrial action.

## 35. Location of Industry/Industrial Policy

Chapter 15 discusses the assistance given to firms to influence the location of firms. In particular, the Government provides grants, tax relief and other benefits to encourage businesses to move into or expand in the Development Areas.

## 36. Marketing and Consumer Protection

This chapter includes an outline of the various laws which exist to protect consumers. The Office of Fair Trading is responsible for consumer affairs and consumer credit, whilst the Monopolies and Mergers Commission investigates proposed mergers which may not be in the public interest. (see Chapter 15). Environmental protection legislation has also recently been introduced.

## 37. European Standards/Directives

The impact of the UK's membership of the European Union is discussed in Chapter 16. Increasingly, all UK standards and legislation will be common throughout the Community and European directives are so wide ranging that they affect all businesses to a greater or lesser extent.

### Task 3.7

#### CHICKEN CURRIE

Premier Poultry has been forced to close its plant at Ripon, with the loss of 400 jobs because of the cost of updating its processes and equipment to meet strict new EU standards. Concerned local councillors believe that Edwina Currie must share the blame because the firm never recovered from the chicken and egg salmonella scare which she started.

#### SCREEN TEST

The Intercare health products group is looking forward to January 1, 1993 when a new Brussels directive will require that anyone working at a VDU screen must have his or her eyes tested. Intercare's eyecare side now chips in with a quarter of group profits after two big recent purchases.

Read the articles and answer the questions which follow.
1. Why has Premier Poultry been forced to close?
2. Why was Intercare looking forward to January 1st 1993?
3. What do these examples illustrate about EU directives?
4. What, if anything, can firms faced with EU directives do?

## Consumer Protection Legislation

38. The vast majority of businesses are run honestly. Their goods work properly and if problems arise they offer a service to put them right with the minimum of fuss and bother. However, unfortunately, some traders are dishonest. These people will often deliberately mislead consumers about the goods or services which they provide and some even sell faulty or dangerous products. Therefore, the government has introduced several laws to protect consumers against such trades. The main legislation is briefly summarised below.

39. **Trade Descriptions Acts 1968 and 1972** make it a criminal offence to give a false or misleading description to goods, services, accommodation and facilities. This includes sale prices where the Act stipulates that goods must only be marked as reduced if they have been sold at a higher price for at least 28 consecutive days during the previous 6 months.

40. **Fair Trading Act 1973.** This set up the Office of Fair Trading (OFT) to look after consumer affairs and consumer credit. The OFT publishes information leaflets, prosecutes offenders, issues credit licences, encourages competition and fair trading, and recommends new laws.

### Task 3.8

**CDS A RIP-OFF**

Evidence is growing that compact disc prices are a 'rip-off' says the Consumers' Association.

It has found that every one of the 30 top-selling pop and classical CDs is more expensive in Britain than in the US. CDs cost just £1 to produce but are retailed at £12.99 or more – a third more in Britain than the US. But the alternative LP is becoming increasingly difficult to buy. The Office of Fair Trading decided to take no action after an investigation into claims of collusion between manufacturers and retailers to keep CD prices artificially high. They cost similar or less than an LP to produce, yet invariably they are more expensive in the shops. But a retail consultants report which agrees that CDs are expensive says it is because consumers are willing to pay more, not because of a price fixing conspiracy.

The following are based on the above article.

1. Identify the facts in the article about the price of CDs.
2. Why is the OFT concerned about the price of CDs?
3. What evidence is there to suggest that CD prices are not a 'rip-off'?
4. What possible explanation is there for the high price of CDs?
5. What effect, if any, do you feel the OFT's investigation is likely to have on the industry and who are the potential winners and losers?

41. **Consumer Credit Act 1974** requires that all businesses offering credit (eg banks, retailers) must be licensed by the OFT; borrowers must be given a written statement of the total cost of interest on any loan, known as the annual percentage rate (APR), and makes firms supplying credit jointly responsible for faulty goods with the business who sold them.

42. **Unfair Contract Terms Act 1977** prevents traders from refusing to accept responsibility for specific events by using 'small print' exclusion clauses or notices. It allows consumers to claim compensation for negligence or breach of contract, for example, if a garage scratches your car or a dry cleaner damages your clothing.

43. **Sale of Goods Act 1979** states that goods sold must be **of merchantable quality** ie a new item should work properly; **as described**, thus plastic shoes should not be called leather; and **fit for the purpose** for which they are generally used. If glue is sold to mend shoes, it must do just that. Consumers are entitled to a refund or replacement if these conditions are not fulfilled.

## 3. Business planning

44. **Weights and Measures Act 1985.** This Act makes it an offence for traders to give short weight or measure. Inspectors visit trade premises such as shops, public houses and garages to check that the scales, beer or petrol pumps used are accurate.

45. **Consumer Protection Act 1987.** This Act consolidated and enhanced previous legislation concerned with the sale of dangerous goods. Certain goods (eg bleach) must be marked with **warnings** (including symbols) and **safety advice** (eg first aid); many goods are covered by **safety regulations** including heaters, toys and nightwear and under an EU Directive on product liability, **damages** can be claimed against suppliers of defective products which cause death or injury. The Act also makes it an offence to give false or **misleading price indications.**

46. **Food and Drink Acts 1955, 1976 and 1982.** These Acts are concerned with the **hygiene, composition and labelling of food** and make it an offence to sell food which is unfit to eat.

47. **Food Safety Act 1990** requires all food handling businesses (eg manufacturers, restaurants, snackbars, shops) to take all **reasonable precautions** in the manufacture, transport, storage, preparation and sale of food; **introduce appropriate hygiene controls** and **ensure that food is safe** both chemically and microbiologically.

48. **Environmental Protection Act 1990** introduces controls on **pollution** to water/land/air covering public **nuisance** (from smoke, fumes, litter, odours, noise), **noise** where this is a risk to employees, and **waste** disposal where this can be potentially hazardous and damaging to the environment

## Economic Analysis

49. A further part of the PEST analysis involves consideration of the economic factors which affect an organisation. The general state of the economy can seriously affect the success or failure of a business because it affects purchasing power.

50. In times of recession, many people are **unemployed,** many others face the threat of redundancy and even those in employment may have less money to spend or chose to save for fear of the future. Thus, in these circumstances a firm may, for example, be forced to reduce prices, and therefore profit margins, or alter some other element of the marketing mix (see Chapter 7), just to survive. On the other hand, in times of **economic growth**, people spend more freely, business may boom and the potential for higher profits is greater.

> **Task 3.9**
>
> ### PIT LOSS
>
> British Coal is planning to close 31 of its 50 deep mines with a loss of over 30,000 jobs. This leaves only 11,000 working miners. The closures are blamed on cheaper coal imports and the move from coal to gas by privatised electricity generating companies Powergen and National Power. The move could lead to dearer electricity because although gas fired power stations are cheaper, cleaner and quicker to build, production costs are higher. Potential knock-on effects include the consequent closure of 16 power stations, the loss of jobs at BR and Road Hauliers who transport the coal and in the mining equipment industry and a social and economic decline in many communities, particularly where coal mining is the main industry
>
> The following questions are based on the above article which was written from media reports in October 1992.
>
> 1. Why are the pit closures taking place?
> 2. What are the immediate effects of the closures?
> 3. How is the economy as a whole likely to be affected?

51. Other important economic considerations include:
    - the level of **inflation** which reduces consumer purchasing power, unless wages increase proportionately, and can affect an organisation's costs, prices and profits.

- new **taxes** can affect prices and/or the distribution of income and therefore patterns of demand.
- the **rate of interest** which affects not just the cost of borrowing but also disposable income and therefore the level of consumer demand. For example, a rise in the cost of mortgages leaves consumers with less to spend.
- Where an organisation is involved in importing or exporting its raw materials or products, then **exchange rates** are important because they affect the relative cost of products and services both at home and overseas.

## Social Change

52. People's **lifestyles** have changed dramatically since the 2nd World War. Consider just the following examples:
    - changing patterns of distribution following the development of supermarkets and self-service retailing.
    - increase in car ownership and improvements in transport networks.
    - influence of the European Community.
    - growth of convenience foods – frozen, chilled, tins and packets.
    - growth in foreign holidays and other leisure and recreation activities.
    - increase in the number of working women.
    - interest in physical fitness resulting in a demand for low fat and diet foods.

    These are all social changes which influence the marketing of goods and services.

53. At the same time, **cultural changes** have also taken place which have altered the values and norms in society. An important example is the attitude to marriage and divorce, resulting in more people living together and a growth in single parent families. Attitudes towards women and ethnic minority groups in society have also changed with the movement towards equal opportunities.

54. Organisations always need to be aware of **demographic trends** such as changes in the size of the total population or working population or its distribution by age, sex or geographical location which can all affect the demand for goods and services. For example, as shown in the diagrams, the UK has an ageing population because the birth rate is low and people are living longer due to better medical facilities, food and social conditions.

55.

**Age Distribution of the Population**

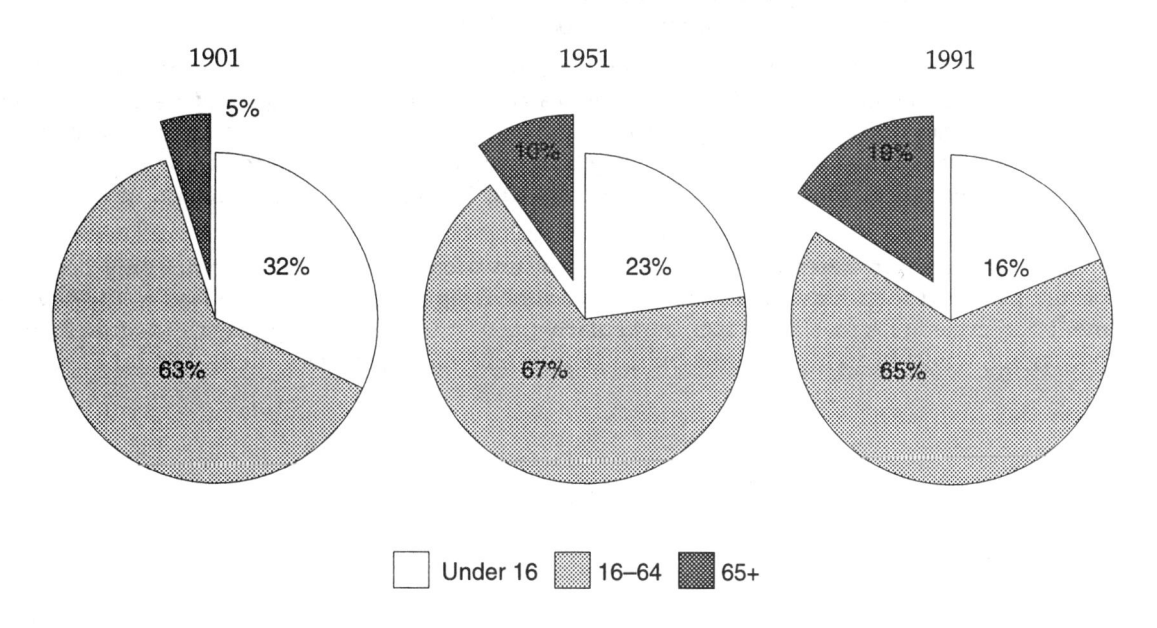

| | 1901 | 1951 | 1991 |
|---|---|---|---|
| Under 16 | 32% | 23% | 16% |
| 16–64 | 63% | 67% | 65% |
| 65+ | 5% | 10% | 19% |

56. This has a number of important affects including:
    - Changes in demand – for example less nappies, cots and prams but more retirement homes/bungalows, wheelchairs and false teeth.
    - Less mobile workforce – an older population is less able or willing to move.
    - Less progressive – an older population may lack energy, initiative and enthusiasm for new ideas and skills.
    - Increased dependence on working population – the burden of taxation to pay pensions and provide for other facilities falls on fewer people because those of working age must support the rest.
    - New market segments with spare income to spend.

> **Task 3.10**
>
> A local manufacturer specialising in the supply of school uniforms discovers the following demographic information from the latest Census results.
>
> The total population of the area has declined by 2% p.a. over the past 10 years.
>
> During the same period, the number of children aged 5-15 has declined by 15% and between 16-24 by 5% whilst the number of people aged 30-44 has increased by 20% and those aged 75 and over by 6%. These trends are expected to continue.
>
> 1. What Census was used for the information?
> 2. Which bit of information, if any, is likely to be of most importance to the manufacturer?
> 3. How are these trends likely to influence the firms business?
> 4. Is there are any other information which would help the firm?
> 5. With reasons, state what action, if any, you would recommend the firm to take.

57. Other social factors which organisations need to identify include:
    - changes in **fashion** which are particularly important with clothing and footwear. Designs, colours and styles may quickly become outdated if tastes alter.
    - **education** and in particular the general literacy level of the population. The proportion of people with a high level of training or professional qualifications is important both in terms of a potential labour force and also because education raises people's expectations.
    - a feature of the 1980's and early 1990's was the growth of organised **pressure groups** with interests in areas like consumer protection, women's rights, ethnic minorities and health education. Such groups can range in size and permanency from well-established international organisations like Greenpeace, to just a few local people getting together to campaign for a few days or weeks hoping to prevent a housing or factory development taking place, or the closure of a school or railway line.
    - concern about **environmental issues** such as conservation and pollution has not only been supported by pressure groups but also recent government legislation. It has also lead to the development of recycled or 'green' products, particularly paper, toilet rolls, paper bags and other forms of packaging, whilst firms like ICI now publish environmental objectives with its Annual Report.

### Task 3.11

#### SUGAR BABY

A baby food firm has bowed to pressure to change a £1 million advertising campaign after claims that it might be misunderstood.

The Milupa commercial shows a smiling baby and includes the line: 'All we add are the vitamins and minerals that are essential for healthy growth and development.'

But after meeting the pressure group Action and Information on Sugars, the firm agreed to make clear that sugar is also added. It is also developing a sugar-free food.

#### ANTI-ICI PROTEST

Greenpeace activists will demonstrate in Stockport tomorrow with posters saying: 'Don't buy Dulux paint until ICI stops destroying the ozone layer.' ICI says it will cease all CFC production by 1995.

#### TOP GREEN AWARD

Olives Paper of Bury, has received Europe's top award for environmental friendliness. The Blue Angel label comes from the German Ministry of the Environment for a range of 100 per cent recycled copier paper. The high-grade Continental Copier is produced from pulp made entirely of recycled paper. It is 100 per cent recyclable after use.

#### READY TO OVERTAKE

The campaign to rid Britain of leaded petrol has been remarkably successful. The use of unleaded petrol has risen from less than 1% of all road fuel in 1988 to 28 per cent in 1991, according to figures released by the Transport Department. Not counting diesel, 'green' pumps now account for 45 per cent of petrol used and are set to overtake leaded sales within 18 months.

Medical evidence shows that lead emissions can lead to stillbirths and cause handicaps and lower intelligence in children.

Taking each article in turn, discuss the implications

1. for the organisations concerned and for their customers.
2. What lessons do articles like these hold for other organisations not directly affected?
3. Now identify 2 examples of pressure groups in your area and describe the purpose of each. Find out how they are organised, their campaign methods and any evidence of success or failure.

## Technological Developments

58. We live in an age of computerised technology the rapid growth of which has made many products obsolete whilst at the same time creating opportunities for **new products and services**. For example, the growth of **telecommunications** products like the telephone, facsimile machines and satellite broadcasting and financial services like cash machines and EFTPOS. If you compare a modern hi-fi system with a 1950's record player, you will see dramatic changes whilst products like colour televisions, the Sony Walkman, battery watches, video recorders, compact discs and microwave ovens, were still being developed. The micro-chip has completely transformed the computer industry and lead to a rapid growth in **information technology** (see Chapter 16) which is beginning to alter not only products but work patterns.

59. The same is also true of industrial markets where people and heavy, bulky machinery have been replaced by robots and much smaller computer controlled **production systems,** enabling firms to

## 3. Business planning

develop new, better or cheaper products. Therefore, firms facing such change must take the opportunity to either update or replace existing products or risk losing out to competitors.

60. Technological change is also important because it raises **consumer expectations** as they expect and demand more sophisticated and innovative products not just with electronic equipment but with all products.

61. **The rate of technological change** means that it may be the most difficult environmental factor to identify, often developing very quickly and in a short space of time completely changing the character of an industry, as for example with cars. Nonetheless, an organisation must not only be aware of this but also consider the extent to which it can develop and apply new technological advancement and keep ahead of its competitors.

---

**Task 3.12**

### BLOCKED CHUNNEL

The Channel Tunnel launch date has had to be delayed again and it will not now open before Autumn 1994 – over 12 months later than originally planned.

The Anglo-French Trans-Manche Link (TML) consortium of 10 builders blamed problems over safety work on the shuttle trains which will run between Folkestone and Calais for the setback. This means operator Eurotunnel will have to ask banks and shareholders for more cash, adding to the £8.9 billion already being spent in a protracted row over construction costs. A final settlement increases the original contract price for the fixed equipment in the tunnel from £620m to £1.14bn (at 1985 prices). This will be raised mainly from a rights issue of over £500m, part of which will be taken by TML instead of cash.

At £64.50 one way for a car and its occupants, the loss of the summer's peak business will cost £70 million a month. And while independent analysts have raised estimates for the company's first year losses from £444m to £500m and predict the venture will not break even until 1999, Eurotunnel says it expects to be making £971 million by 2003. Although construction of the tunnel itself is virtually complete, a full service involving passenger and freight traffic between London, Paris and Brussels will not now be running until 1995.

1. Why has the Tunnel launch date had to be delayed?
2. What effect will this have on the Eurotunnel consortium?
3. How could this delay affect other business organisations both in the UK and Europe?

---

## Competitor Analysis

62. A business is always under potential threat from its competitors and if it gets any element of the marketing mix wrong, it could lose business. For example, if for whatever reason customers become dissatisfied with the product or the price is increased, then they may decide to switch to a competitor's product which they could then prefer to buy in future. Likewise, if a competitor has a promotional offer or customers cannot buy the product in the usual place (eg the local supermarket is out of stock) then again they may decide to switch to another product or organisation.

63. Therefore, as well as considering the general environmental factors, which to a greater or lesser extent affect all businesses in all industrial and commercial sectors, strategic analysis also requires a close study of an organisation's competitors. it needs to consider the intensity of competition, what it is based upon, whether it is likely to increase or decrease and how it can be reduced.

64. Four key factors which should be examined are:

- **The entry of major competitors into the market**
  This may represent a threat to an organisation's market share and therefore to profits. On the other hand, it may stimulate demand and lead to an overall growth in the market. If the new entrant has researched the market it could be entering into what is sees as a growth area or to seize an opportunity because current organisations are weak.

- **The exit of major competitors out of the market**
  This may assist an organisation by helping it to achieve its market share and profit targets. On the other hand, it may indicate that the market is in decline and therefore could become unprofitable in the future.

- **Availability of substitutes**
  If alternative products become available this can seriously affect a market and signal the need for action. For example, the sales of record turntables were seriously affected by the introduction of compact discs.

- **Strategic policy changes for major competitors**
  Awareness of major changes in competitors' strategies is also important. For example, the introduction of new products or heavy promotional expenditure can both affect an organisation's market share. An awareness of how they might react to your strategies is also important.

## The Corporate Gap

65. To ensure that an organisation is meeting its objectives, it needs to periodically review its progress towards them. From this, it is possible to identify any differences between the actual results and the forecasts, known as the operations or **corporate gap**.

66. Such gap analysis could indicate, for example, that the company needs to search for new products and/or new markets, or reduce costs to improve productivity. If the gap cannot be closed the organisation may have to amend its objectives.

67.

**Gap Analysis**

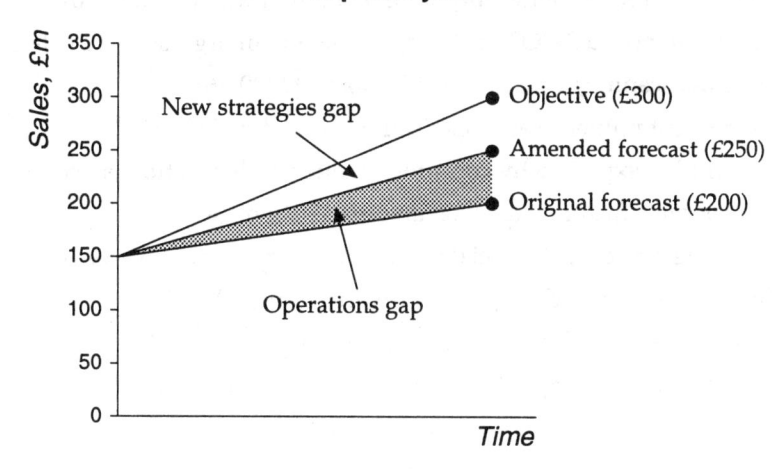

A chart with Sales (£m) on the y-axis (0 to 350) and Time on the x-axis. Three lines diverge from 150:
- Objective (£300) — top line, labelled "New strategies gap"
- Amended forecast (£250) — middle line
- Original forecast (£200) — bottom line, with "Operations gap" shaded between amended and original forecast.

## Summary

68. a) An organisation needs to plan ahead and forecast its future markets, sales revenue, costs and resources required.

   b) It is important that this takes place within a strategic planning framework which determines the nature and direction of an organisation.

   c) This involves a mission statement, strategic plan, operating statement and monitoring and evaluation.

   d) To achieve its objectives, an organisation also needs to be aware of the constraints which affect its environment.

   e) A SWOT analysis highlights the internal strengths and weaknesses measured against the competition and any key external opportunities and threats.

   f) Environmental scanning provides important planning data.

   g) A common method considers the political, economic, social and technological (PEST) factors which impinge on an organisation.

   h) Political factors include government policies and legislation.

## 3. Business planning

i) Examples of the UK Government's influence on industry and commerce include State ownership, Monetary and Fiscal policy, Company legislation, employment and training, industrial relations, location of industry, international trade, marketing, consumer protection and European directives.

j) Important consumer protection legislation includes the Trade Descriptions Acts 1968 and 1972, Fair Trading Act 1973, Consumer Credit Act 1974, Unfair Contract Terms Act 1977, Sale of Goods Act 1979, Weights and Measures Act 1985, Consumer Protection Act 1987, Food and Drugs Acts 1955, 1976 and 1982., Food Safety Act 1990 and Environmental Protection Act 1990.

k) Economic factors include unemployment, inflation and economic growth.

l) Important social trends include changing lifestyles, demography, fashion, pressure groups and environmental issues.

m) Technological developments, particularly the use of computers can quickly change an industry and consumer expectations.

n) Strategic planning also requires a consideration of the entry and exit of major competitors in the market, their policy changes and the availability of substitute products.

o) The corporate gap identifies any differences between actual results and the forecast, and indicates areas for action.

### Review Questions *(Answers can be found in the paragraphs indicated)*

1. Why is corporate planning necessary? (1-3)
2. Briefly describe the components of the corporate planning framework. (4-10)
3. Use examples to explain how a SWOT analysis can benefit an organisation. (11-19).
4. What is environmental scanning and why is it important? (20-26)
5. How can the government influence an organisation's planning? (27-37)
6. With the use of examples, explain why consumer protection legislation is necessary. (38-48)
7. In what ways do economic factors impact on an organisation? (49-51)
8. Explain what you understand by the social factors in an organisation's environment. (52-57)
9. In what ways does technological change affect organisations? (58-61)
10. What is the main threat which a business faces from competition? (62)
11. What key factors in respect of competitors should be considered? (63-64)
12. What do you understand by the corporate gap? (66-67)

*Asterisks indicate those questions for which there are answers in Outline Answers (page 439)*

### Essay-style questions

1.* 'In the 1990's population trends will reduce the number of young people entering the workforce'. How might a business organisation respond to this situation?
2. Should firms publish details of their environmental scanning?
3. 'Although the need for corporate planning in a large organisation is obvious, small businesses may regard it as an unnecessary chore.' Discuss.

### Short Answer

1.* Explain the meaning of each of the following elements of corporate strategic planning.
   a) Mission Statement
   b) Strategic plan
   c) Operating Statement
   d) Monitoring and evaluation

2.* a) Choose any 3 Acts of Parliament which have been passed to protect consumers and outline the importance of each.
   b) Identify other ways in which the State provides protection for consumers.
3. a) What do you understand by the term a 'corporate gap'.
   b) In what ways can it be useful to business organisations?

## Multiple Choice/Completion

1.* The Trade Descriptions Act 1968 requires that retailers:
   a) display notices describing their goods or services.
   b) provide accurate information about goods or services.
   c) sell goods of merchantable quality.
   d) accept responsibility for faulty products.

2.* An organisation's mission statement is used to
   a) Determine the elements of its strategic plan.
   b) Develop clear objectives and targets.
   c) Enable it to regularly review progress.
   d) Determine the nature and direction of the business.

3.* Which of the following statements about the UK is incorrect?
   a) It has an ageing population.
   b) People are living longer.
   c) Death rates are rising.
   d) Birth rates are fairly steady.

4.* Social factors which can affect an organisation and its products or services include all except
   a) trends in education.
   b) growth of pressure groups.
   c) availability of competitive products.
   d) cultural changes.

5. Modern production technology is an example in an organisation of a
   a) SWOT
   b) PEST
   c) Strength
   d) Weakness

6. Environmental scanning will not be used in an organisation to:
   a) provide a base of objective data for decision-making.
   b) make managers more aware of changing needs.
   c) enable it to take advantage of technological innovation.
   d) enable more effective planning and resource allocation.

*In each of the following questions, one or more of the responses is/are correct. Choose the appropriate letter which indicates the correct version.*

   A   if 1 only is correct
   B   if 3 only is correct
   C   if 1 and 2 only are correct
   D   if 1, 2 and 3 are correct

7. Which of the following Laws was not introduced with the specific aim of protecting consumers when they purchase goods or services.
   1. Food and Drinks Act 1982
   2. Unfair Contract Terms Act 1977
   3. Environmental Protection Act 1990

8. The Office of Fair Trading was established to fulfil which of the following functions?
    1. Encourage competition and fair trading.
    2. Enforce consumer legislation.
    3. Deal directly with consumer complaints.

> **Assignment**
>
> Using the 2 organisations which you studied in the assignment in Chapter 1, or 2 other organisations of your choice, carry out the following:
>
> 1. Research and prepare a detailed report on the external environment in which each organisation operates.
> 2. Identify any examples of each organisation reacting to its external environment.
> 3. Carry out a SWOT analysis on each organisation.
> 4. From the information collected, outline with reasons, how you think, if at all, the future strategic planning of each organisation is likely to be affected.

# 4. The Market Mechanism

This chapter introduces some important economic concepts including the significance of the market mechanism of supply and demand and theory of the firm. It covers:

* Economics and Business
* Markets
* Types of Markets
* Market Prices
* Demand
* Changes in Demand
* Elasticity of Demand
* Exceptional Demand Curves
* Supply
* Changes in Supply
* Determinants of Supply
* Elasticity of Supply
* Interaction of Supply and Demand
* Theory of the Firm
* Market Conditions
* Revenue and Costs
* Perfect Competition
* Monopoly
* Imperfect Competition
* Oligopoly

## Economics and Business

1. We saw in Chapter 3 that organisations are affected by the economic environment in which they operate. Decisions taken may be influenced by economic factors such as the level of unemployment, inflation, interest rates and taxes. Since Economics and Business Studies are very closely linked it is important to have a general understanding of some of the main principles of economic theory and how these may influence the behaviour of organisations.

2. The most widely accepted definition of economics is that of Lord Robbins 'the science which studies human behaviour as a relationship between ends and scarce means which have alternative uses.' Essentially peoples' wants (ie demands) are almost infinite but the resources needed to satisfy them are very limited. Consequently, choices must be made about how to allocate (supply) resources. Economics is the discipline which analyses these decisions and the alternatives available. In this Chapter, we shall consider a number of key aspects of economic theory.

### Task 4.1
1. List all the choices which you can remember having to make in the past week or month.
2. What type of factors influenced your final decision?
3. How, if at all, does this help your understanding of the definition of economics?

## Markets

3. A **market** is defined as any situation where buyers and sellers are brought together. It may be located in a specific place or building or merely involve the use of the telephone, fax or some other means of communication. There are many types of markets ranging from
   - you selling something to one of your friends
   - to local street markets
   - press or TV advertisements followed by telephone or postal transactions
   - highly complex financial markets dealing in millions of pounds worth of goods and services to international markets where demand can be worldwide.

4. We talk in terms of markets in, for example, tea, videos, sports cars, houses and insurance but it is not always easy to identify the limits of each. The market for cars, for example, ranges from three wheel Robin Reliants to Rolls Royces which are clearly very different.

## 4. The market mechanism

5. Therefore, a market is essentially what consumers see as offering the same goods or services even though different firms' products may vary slightly in terms of their design and specification.

## Types of Markets

6. The main types of market can be summarised as:
   - **Retailers** who sell goods and services direct to the final consumer, mainly through shops.
   - **Wholesalers** who buy goods from manufacturers for sale to retailers.
   - **Wholesale produce** markets which exist in most large towns to supply perishable goods to organisations such as shops, hotels, restaurants and schools.
   - **Commodity Exchanges** or markets where manufacturers throughout the world can buy their raw materials. London is the centre for many of these important markets including metal, diamonds and furs.
   - **Shipping and Insurance** markets. Britain is a world centre for both of these which are based on Lloyd's of London. Shipping freight services are also sold in the Baltic Exchange.
   - **Financial markets**. London again is a national and international centre for these markets, including:
     - **The Money Market** consisting of organisations like banks, discount houses and finance houses which borrow and lend money for short periods, usually up to 30 days.
     - **The Capital Market** which provides longer-term finance for the Government, businesses and individuals. It includes Institutional Investors, the Stock Exchange and Issuing Houses.
     - **The Foreign Exchange Market** which is essential for the import and export trade.

### Task 4.2
1. From the markets discussed above, identify those which supply the essential resources needed for production.
2. Name another factor market which is required for production.

## Market Prices

7. In a free economy, market prices are determined by the interaction of demand and supply. It is the market mechanism which essentially determines how resources are allocated because:
   - it enables individuals to maximise their satisfaction (utility) by choosing how they spend their income,
   - it indicates consumer demand so that producers supply what goods and services are required,
   - it encourages competition between producers leading to increasing efficiency and
   - it increases the returns to the factors of production, such as higher wages for labour and profits for entrepreneurs.

## Demand

8. When products are wanted for their own sake there is a **primary demand**, eg a video or carpet. Some products, however, have a **derived demand** due to their use as a factor of production. That is, they are wanted not for themselves, but what they go into making, eg sugar for jam, chickens for eggs, machinery and equipment to produce tins and packets. Other products are complementary, and in **joint demand** in that they are needed together. For example, petrol and cars, knives and forks, tennis balls and tennis raquets.

9. An important feature of demand is that for the great majority of products,
   - if the price falls, consumers will buy more of it;

- if it rises then they will buy less.
- Hence, the demand curve slopes downwards from left to right.

10. This is explained by the:
    - **Income effect,** essentially when prices fall, in effect real income increases and thus consumers are able to afford more; and the
    - **Substitution effect,** as prices rise, other competitive products become relatively cheaper and therefore are substituted for it.

11. The market demand for any particular product is the sum of all the individual demands. This can be shown on a **demand curve** which represents the quantity of products demanded at various price levels. Hence, the demand curve slopes downwards from left to right as shown below.

**Example of a Demand Schedule**

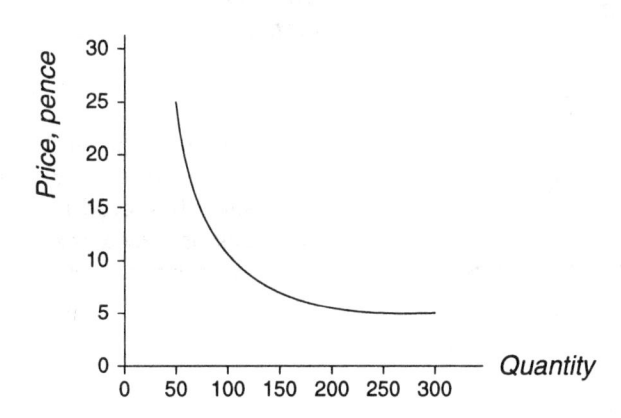

### Changes in Demand

12. However, in addition to price, demand is also influenced by many other factors including:
    - **Changes in the size and composition of the population** – for example whether it is increasing or decreasing which will affect overall demand or if it is getting younger or older, which will affect the demand for particular goods or services.
    - **Consumer income** – if people have more money to spend then this is likely to increase demand.
    - **Consumer tastes and preferences** – changes brought about by such factors as advertising or climate. For example, the latest fashion is often a reason for purchasing new clothes.
    - **Prices of complementary products** – for example to run a car you need petrol and oil and must also pay tax and insurance. A rise in the price of any of these therefore might reduce the demand for cars.
    - **New improved products** – for example the introduction of colour television led to a big fall in the demand for black and white models.
    - **Prices of substitute products** – for example an increase in the price of butter often leads to higher sales of margarine and vice versa.
    - **Taxation** – the Government can influence demand by altering either the price of goods (for example VAT) or the level of people's income (for example income tax and allowances).
    - **Legal requirements** such as the wearing of seatbelts in cars has dramatically increased the demand for them.

13. The demand curve in 11 above shows the relationship between demand and price assuming that the conditions of demand remain constant. Each time these conditions change, we get a new demand curve:

## 14. Changes in Demand

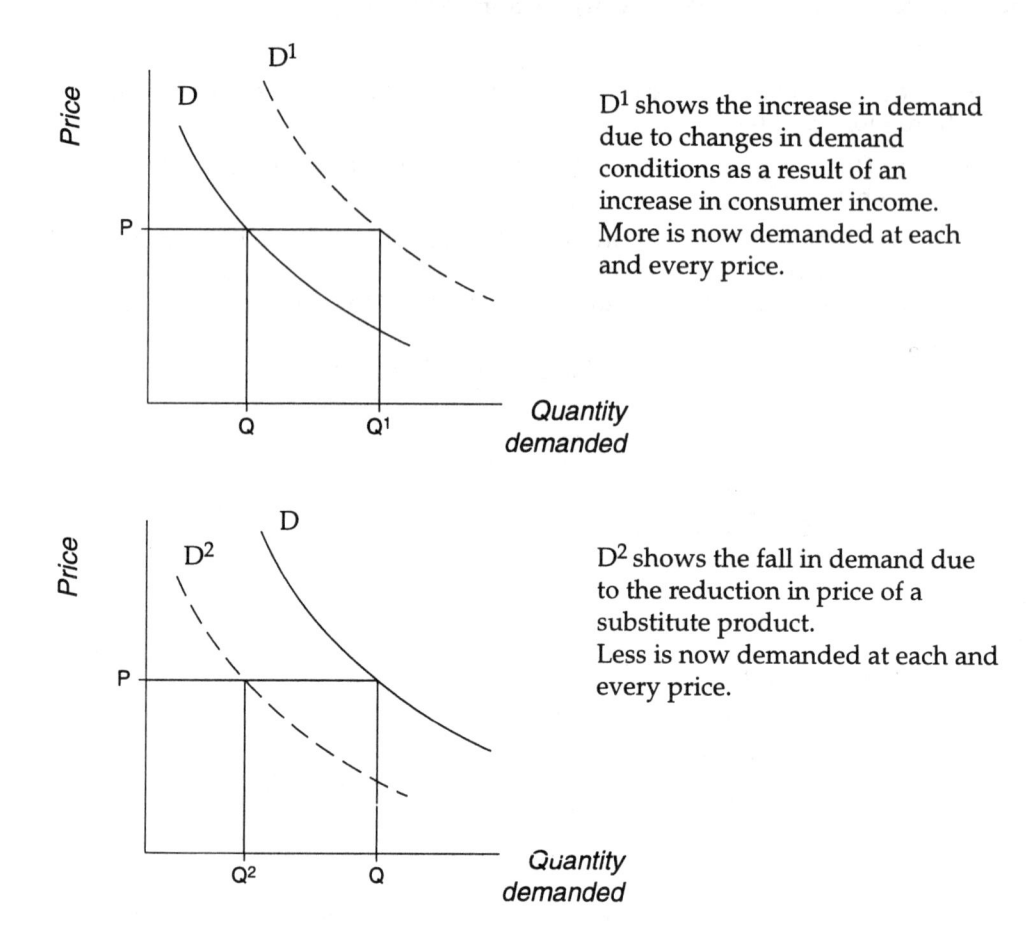

$D^1$ shows the increase in demand due to changes in demand conditions as a result of an increase in consumer income. More is now demanded at each and every price.

$D^2$ shows the fall in demand due to the reduction in price of a substitute product. Less is now demanded at each and every price.

### Task 4.3

1. Draw the demand curves and describe the changes in each of the following situations.

   a) the records of a pop group which is no longer fashionable.

   b) the sales of Levi jeans, following the introduction of new, lower priced Wrangler jeans.

   c) the reduction in the price of electricity on electrical appliances.

2. Now illustrate what would happen to demand in the following situations:

   a) an increase in the price of apples.

   b) a government subsidy on rail travel.

## Elasticity of Demand

15. The degree of responsiveness of demand to changes in demand conditions is called elasticity. There are three common forms:
    - **price elasticity** which is the effect on demand of a change in price.
    - **income elasticity** which is the effect on demand of a change in income levels and
    - **cross elasticity** which is the effect on demand of a change in the price of other goods or services.

# Price Elasticity of Demand (PED)

16. PED measures the responsiveness of demand to changes in price. It is calculated as:

$$\text{PED} = \frac{\text{\% change in quantity demanded}}{\text{\% change in price}}$$

17. If PED is greater than one, that is a small change in price causes a relatively large change in the quantity demanded, it is **elastic**. For example, if a 5% change in price causes an 8% change in demand.

18. If PED is less than one, that is a small change in price causes a relatively small change in the quantity demanded, it is **inelastic**. For example, if a 5% change in price causes a 2% change in demand.

19. If PED is equal to one, elasticity is **unitary**. That is, the proportionate change in quantity demanded is exactly the same as the proportionate change in price. Thus, for example, a 5% change in price causes a 5% change in demand.

20. Since elasticity links price and quantity demanded, it also shows the effect of changes in price and income on total revenue. This is particularly important to both businesses and government.

21. If demand is relatively elastic, a reduction in price causes total revenue to increase, whilst a price rise causes total revenue to fall. Thus price and revenue move in opposite directions.

22. If, on the other hand, demand is relatively inelastic, a reduction in price causes total revenue to fall and a price rise causes total revenue to increase. Thus price and revenue move in the same direction.

23. With unitary elasticity, total revenue stays the same at all prices. These relationships can be shown graphically as follows:

24. **Elastic Demand, Inelastic Demand and Unitary Elasticity**

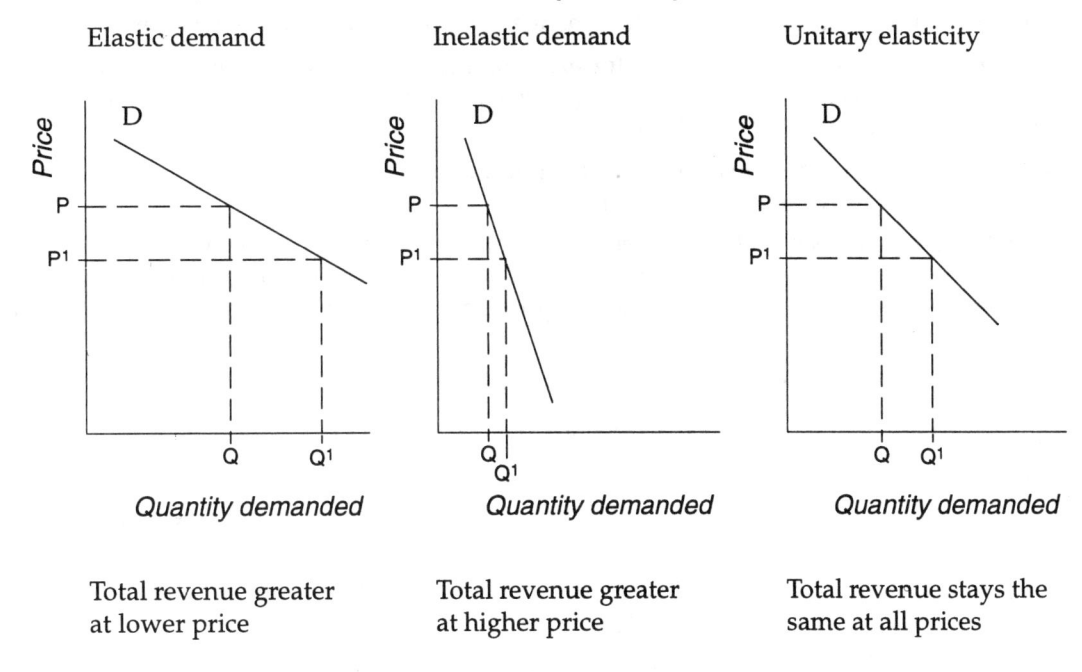

| Elastic demand | Inelastic demand | Unitary elasticity |
|---|---|---|
| Total revenue greater at lower price | Total revenue greater at higher price | Total revenue stays the same at all prices |

## 4. The market mechanism

### Task 4.4

| Demand price | Schedule quantity | Percentage change in D | Percentage change in price | Elasticity | Total revenue |
|---|---|---|---|---|---|
| a | b | c | d | c ÷ d | a x b |
| 30p | 200lb | $\frac{400-200}{200} \times 100 = 100\%$ | $\frac{30-25}{25} \times 100 = 20\%$ | 5 | 60 |
| 25p | 400lb | | | | |
| 20p | 600lb | | | | |
| 15p | 800lb | | | | |
| 10p | 1,000lb | | | | |
| 5p | 1,200lb | | | | |

1. Complete the above table which illustrates the relationship between PED and total revenue.
2. Indicate the prices at which demand is elastic, inelastic and unitary.

25. Although in reality elasticity is difficult to calculate, what is important is that businesses have an awareness of the likely effect on demand, and therefore total revenue, when proposing to alter the price of their goods or services. A misjudgement of the price sensitivity could result in both falling sales and profits.

## Factors Determining the Degree of Elasticity

26. The elasticity of any product in response to a change in price will depend upon a number of factors.
    - **The availability of substitutes.** Glass, for example has no perfect replacement and is therefore very inelastic. Likewise, cars, cigarettes and newspapers are relatively inelastic but the demand for any particular brand could be elastic.
    - **The proportion of income spent on a product.** Matches and salt, for example, are cheap to buy and therefore relatively inelastic in demand.
    - **Necessities** such as bread, milk, potatoes and clothing are inelastic, whereas **luxuries** like foreign holidays, satellite television and computers are elastic. Although you might argue that these are necessities because, where incomes are steadily rising, the luxuries of one generation become the necessities of the next.
    - **Habit forming products** such as tobacco and alcohol have a relatively inelastic demand.

### Task 4.5

1. Suggest how the following might react to a 5% rise in the price of electricity.

   A family live in a 4 bedroomed house with electric central heating. They also have an electric oven and hob. Their bills average £450 in each winter quarter and £250 in each summer quarter. Their gross income is £18,000 pa.

2. Explain, with reasons, whether you think that the demand for electricity is relatively elastic or inelastic.

## Income Elasticity of Demand (YED)

27. YED measures the responsiveness of demand to change in levels of income. It is calculated as:

$$YED = \frac{\%\text{ change in quantity demanded}}{\%\text{ change in income}}$$

28. As seen earlier, a change in income changes the demand conditions so that we get a new demand curve. if income is increased, the demand for necessities will probably not change much but the demand for luxuries is likely to increase.

29. If an increase in income produces a fall in demand, YED is negative. This is because people switch from 'inferior' to 'better' products. Examples would be, consumers buying less sausage and relatively cheap cuts of meat because they can now afford steak; or buying a car rather than using public transport.

> **Task 4.6**
>
> When John Smith had an income of £10,000 pa, he bought 4 bottles of beer per week. Following a rise in income to £12,000 pa, he now buys 5 bottles per week.
>
> 1. Calculate the elasticity of demand in this situation.
> 2. State whether or not demand is elastic.

**Cross Elasticity of Demand (XED)**

30. XED measures the responsiveness of demand to changes in the price of other products. It is calculated as:

$$XED = \frac{\% \text{ change in demand for A}}{\% \text{ change in price of B}}$$

31. If XED is positive, the products are said to be **substitutes** for each other, for example, coffee and tea, butter and margarine.

32. If XED is negative, the products are said to be **complementary** (dependent), for example, golf clubs and golf balls, cars and petrol, video recorders and video tapes.

33. If XED is zero, the products are said to be independent, and therefore have no effect on each other. The demand for food and holidays, for example, are independent.

> **Task 4.7**
>
> An increase in the price of apples from 24p to 32p caused Nina Patel to buy more pears, 3lb instead of 2lb.
>
> 1. Calculate the cross elasticity of demand in the above situation.
> 2. Is demand elastic or inelastic?

## Exceptional Demand Curves

34. There are some situations where the demand curve does not slope downwards from left to right. Examples include:
    - **price movements linked to expectations.** For example, shares bought and sold on the Stock Exchange.
    - **ostentatious products** such as diamonds, mink coats and Rolls-Royce cars, which are bought for 'snob appeal' and
    - **inferior products** (known as 'Giffen' goods) which are bought when income is very low. As income rises (or prices fall) less is bought as consumers switch to 'better' products. This is true of basic foodstuffs in underdeveloped countries.

## 4. The market mechanism

## Supply

35. This is the total amount of a particular product which suppliers are able and prepared to offer for sale, at a given price, over a period of time. For example, the supply of commodity X at a price of £2 is 4,000 units per week.

36. This can be shown on a **supply curve** which represents the quantity of products which would be supplied at various price levels. The market supply for any particular product is the sum of all the individual suppliers.

37. The key features of supply are that normally,
    - the higher the price, the greater the amount supplied because it is more profitable.
    - the lower the price, the less the supply,
    - hence the supply curve slopes upwards to the right.

38.

**Example of a supply schedule.**

| Price Per Unit (pence) | Quantity Supplied (000's per week) |
|---|---|
| 25 | 250 |
| 20 | 200 |
| 15 | 140 |
| 10 | 100 |
| 5 | 40 |

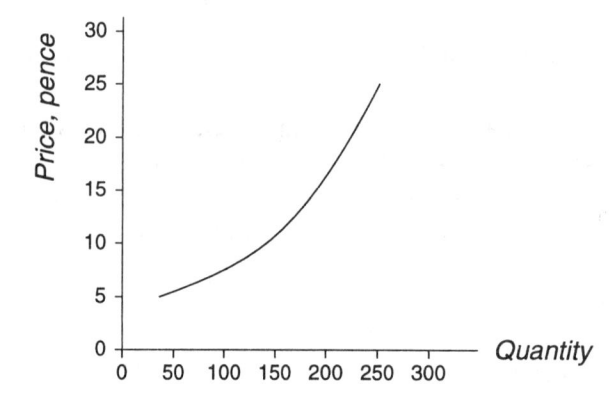

## Changes in Supply

39. The supply curve above shows the relationship between supply and the quantity supplied assuming that the conditions of supply remain constant. If the price of products changes, this is shown as a shift along the supply curve. Each time the condition of supply changes, we get a new supply curve.

40.    **Changes in Supply**

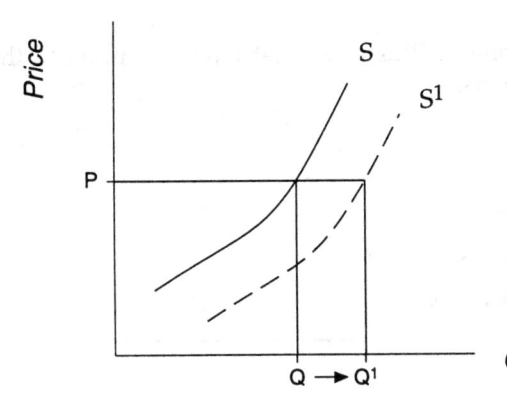

$S^1$ represents an increase in supply. More is now supplied at each and every price.

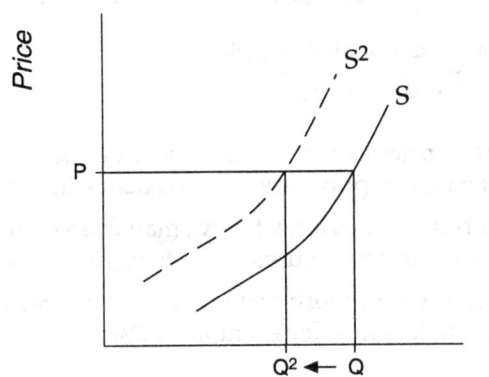

$S^2$ represents an decrease in supply. Less is now supplied at each and every price.

## Determinants of Supply

41. Factors which will cause a change in the conditions of supply include:

- **Technological progress.** If the introduction of new materials, methods or equipment improve efficiency and reduce costs, supply is likely to increase.
- **Changes in factor prices** which alter profitability if, for example, wages increase in a labour intensive industry then unless productivity also increases, supply may be reduced.
- **Government policy.** For example, when a tax is imposed on a product, it has the same effect as an increase in the costs of production. The whole supply curve moves upwards and to the left.
- **Number of Firms.** If more firms enter an industry, supply would be expected to increase and vice versa.
- **Objectives of firms.** A firm, for example, may decide to increase market share by lowering prices.
- **Legal changes.** Government legislation may increase the costs of production for manufacturers. Examples being the introduction of safety or environmental measures.

## 4. The market mechanism

### Task 4.8

XYZ is a manufacturer of confectionery. Illustrate what would happen to the supply curve in each of the following situations.

a) An increased volume of sales.

b) A fall in the price of sugar.

c) An increase in the price of sweets.

d) An agreement with unions to increase wage rates.

e) An increase in Uniform Business Rates.

## Elasticity of Supply (PES)

42. This measures the degree of responsiveness of supply to changes in price. It is calculated as:

$$PES = \frac{\% \text{ change in quantity supplied}}{\% \text{ change in price}}$$

43. If PES is greater than one, that is a small change in price causes a relatively large change in the quantity supplied, it is **elastic**. For example, if a 2% change in price causes a 5% change in supply.

44. If PES is less than one, that is a small change in price causes a relatively small change in the quantity supplied, it is **inelastic**. For example, if a 2% change in price causes a 1% change in demand.

45. If PES is equal to one, elasticity is **unitary**. That is, the proportionate change in quantity supplied is exactly the same as the proportionate change in price. Thus, for example, a 2% change in price causes a 2% change in supply.

46. This can be illustrated graphically as follows:

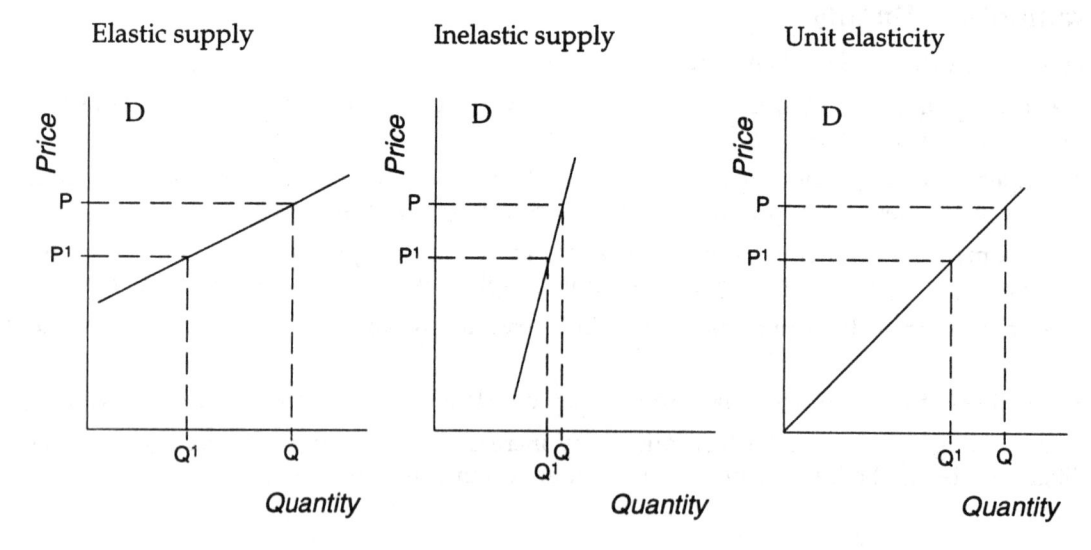

Elastic supplyInelastic supplyUnit elasticity

47. PES will depend upon the cost and flexibility of the productive resources. Supply will be elastic if production with existing capacity, can be quickly and easily expanded in response to changes in demand. Thus, for example, by overtime, employing more workers, using spare capacity or stocks. This may be possible in mass production industries such as cars, footwear and many services such as foreign holidays.

48. On the other hand, the supply of many products is inelastic. For example, it would take several years for a significant increase in the size of beef and dairy herds. Likewise, rubber trees take 5-7 years to grow, whilst the supply of many foodstuffs is governed by the acreage planted and the growing time involved. Supply will also be inelastic where the cost of entering a market are high.

## 4. The market mechanism

### Task 4.9

The following are the weekly supply schedules of 2 wheelbarrow manufacturers.

| Laurel Ltd | | Hardy Ltd | |
|---|---|---|---|
| Price, £ | Quantity | Price, £ | Quantity |
| 10 | 5 | 10 | 0 |
| 20 | 10 | 20 | 0 |
| 30 | 15 | 30 | 20 |
| 40 | 20 | 40 | 25 |
| 50 | 25 | 50 | 30 |
| 60 | 30 | 60 | 35 |

1. What is the elasticity of supply of Laurel Ltd?
2. What is the elasticity of supply between £30 & £40 of Hardy Ltd
3. What is the total supply per week of wheelbarrows at a price of £40?
4. If prices rose to £50 what would be the increase in supply?
5. Give 3 situations which would cause the supply curve for wheelbarrows to move to the right.

## Interaction of Supply and Demand

49. As shown in the following diagram, the **equilibrium price** is given by the interaction of the supply and demand curves ie 15p. At this price, the amount brought to the market by suppliers exactly matches the amount demanded by the buyers.

50.

### Interaction of Supply and Demand

| Price per Unit (pence) | Quantity Demanded | Quantity Supplied |
|---|---|---|
| 25 | 50 | 250 |
| 20 | 100 | 200 |
| 15 | 140 | 140 |
| 10 | 170 | 100 |
| 5 | 300 | 40 |

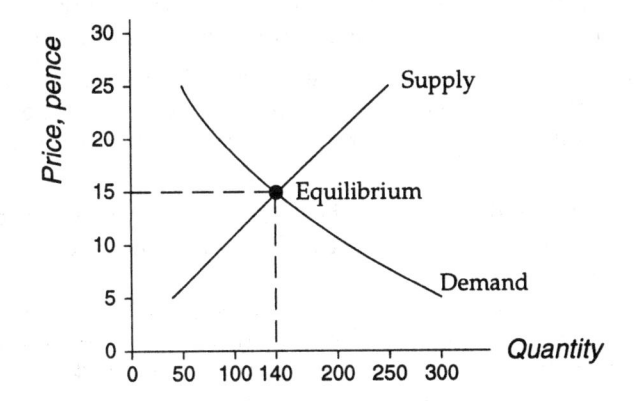

51. Above the equilibrium price, supply is greater than demand. Therefore the price must be reduced to attract more buyers. Below this price, demand is greater than supply. This will result in an increase in price.

52. This illustrates that, in theory, given a free market there is an automatic mechanism which determines price. Firms must either choose to supply at that price or leave the market. In practice, howev-

er, there are very few perfectly free markets and firms are often able to influence price because of their monopoly power or other market imperfections.

> **Task 4.10**
>
> Study the following data and answer the questions which follow:
>
> | Price, p | Quantity demanded | Quantity supplied |
> |---|---|---|
> | 25 | 350 | 40 |
> | 30 | 300 | 80 |
> | 35 | 200 | 120 |
> | 40 | 150 | 150 |
> | 45 | 120 | 300 |
> | 50 | 100 | 400 |
>
> 1. What is the equilibrium price?
> 2. If the government fixes a statutory maximum price of 35p, what will be the effect?
> 3. In what price range is demand inelastic?

## Theory of the Firm

53. The purpose of the theory of the firm is to predict the prices which firms will charge for their products and the quantity they will produce in a given period. It is useful to briefly consider this aspect of economics because it helps to provide an understanding of the importance of the market environment and how it influences the way in which firms behave.

## Market Conditions

54. The way in which the laws of supply and demand operate in any particular market will depend upon the conditions which prevail at the time.

55. The most important conditions being the:

    - **number of buyers and sellers.** The higher the number, the greater the competition and therefore the more difficult it is for any one buyer or seller to influence the price.

    - **independence of buyers or sellers.** If either group are able to collude, they may collectively be able to influence the market price.

    - **degree of product differentiation.** An important point in marketing is that a differentiated product can be sold at a price which may be slightly higher than the rest of the market.

    - **external constraints.** Prices in any market may be influenced by factors which prevent the free operation of supply and demand, for example Government intervention, such as rationing or price control; consumer preferences, to save rather than spend perhaps because of high interest rates or fear of redundancy.

56. Therefore, it is possible to identify from these market conditions a number of different competitive situations which determine how firms behave. These are usually classified as:

    - perfect competition
    - monopoly
    - imperfect competition
    - oligopoly

## Revenue and Costs

57. In order to understand the theory of the firm, it is necessary to consider both the money a firm receives from the sale of its products or services (revenue), and the expenses associated with running a business (costs) which are usually classified as fixed or variable.

58. • **Total Revenue (TR)** is simply the quantity sold multiplied by the price.
    • **Average Revenue (AR)** is the amount which a firm receives for each unit of output sold, in other words, the price. The AR and demand curve are the same thing.
    • **Marginal Revenue (MR)** is the addition to total revenue from the sale of one more unit.

## Cost Classification

59. **Fixed costs** are those costs which do not vary in direct proportion to a firm's output. They have to be paid regardless of the level of output. Even if there is no output at all, a firm will still have fixed costs which it must meet. For example rent of premises, rates, heating, lighting, insurance, postage and telephone, cost of supervision and maintenance, administration and marketing. Fixed costs are also known as **indirect costs** or **overheads** because they are not directly involved in the production of goods or services.

60. **Fixed costs and average fixed costs**

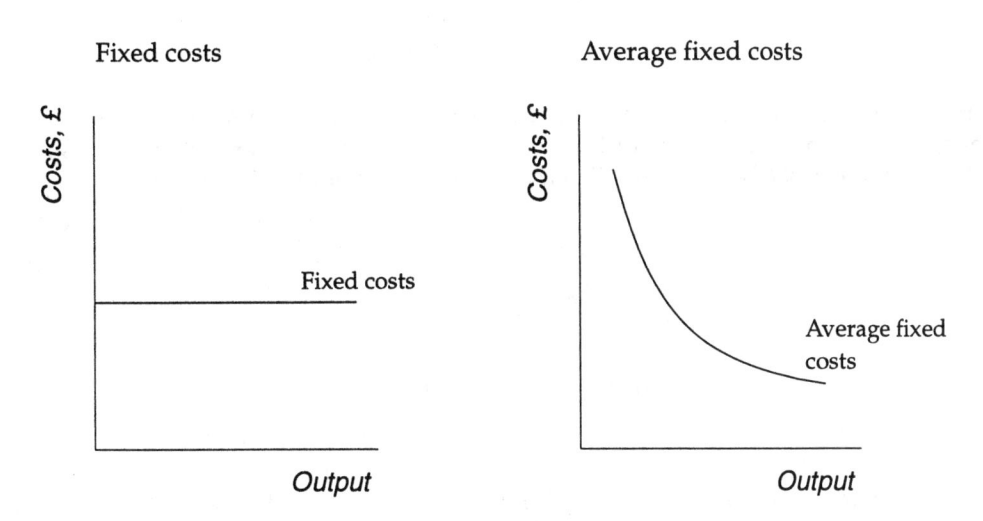

*Fixed costs* — horizontal line on graph of Costs (£) vs Output.

*Average fixed costs* — downward sloping curve on graph of Costs (£) vs Output.

61. If we know the total fixed costs then we can calculate the average fixed cost (AFC) per unit of output. For example, if 10,000 units are to be produced and fixed costs are £20,000 then:

$$\text{AFC per unit} = \frac{£20,000}{10,000} = £2 \text{ per unit}$$

Clearly the higher the output, the lower will be the average fixed cost per unit as shown in the above diagram

### Task 4.11
The total output of goods or services which a firm is able to produce is known as its capacity. If a manufacturing firm with fixed costs of £20,000 has a capacity of 10,000 pa units but is currently only producing 8,000 units p.a.
1. Name 4 fixed costs it is likely to have.
2. Indicate the significance, if any, of it operating at less than full capacity.

62. **Variable costs** or the cost of production, on the other hand, vary directly with output. For example, if a firm produces more goods, it will need additional raw materials, labour and transport. Variable costs are also known as **direct or prime costs** because they can be clearly allocated to a particular product or service. Hence we have direct-labour and direct-material costs.

## 4. The market mechanism

63.

**Costs**

*Variable costs*

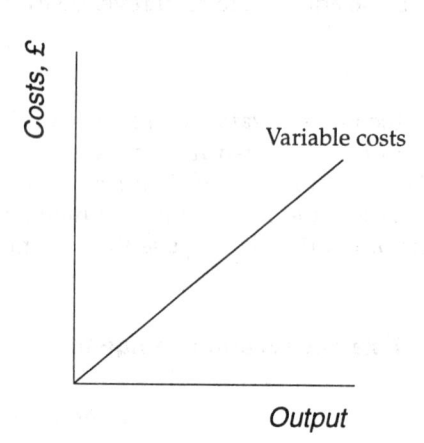

[Graph: Costs, £ (y-axis) vs Output (x-axis), showing Variable costs as a straight line from origin]

64. **Semi-Variable costs.** It is better to consider some costs as containing both a fixed and a variable element. Thus, for example, an electricity bill will include a fixed standing charge irrespective of a firm's output, but the cost of electricity will vary with the number of units produced.

65. **Example**

|  | Outputs (Units) | Costs (£) |
|---|---|---|
| High Output | 10,000 | 5,000 |
| Low Output | 5,000 | 3,000 |
| Difference | 5,000 | 2,000 |

Since each cost contains the same fixed cost if the figures are subtracted, we can calculate the variable costs needed to produce the extra units. That is, to produce an extra 5,000 units increases costs by £2,000 so the variable cost per unit is

$$\frac{£2,000}{5,000} = £0.40$$

The fixed costs for the high output can then be calculated as follows:

Variable costs = 10,000 units x 0.40p = £3600

Fixed costs = Total costs − Variable Cost = (£5,000 − £3,600) = £1400

### Task 4.12

Using the same example, calculate the fixed costs for the low level of output of 5,000 units.

66. **Stepped Fixed Costs.** These are costs which stay constant over a range of output and then suddenly increase at certain levels. Consider for example, a supervisor who can only effectively manage 10 workers. The employment of any additional staff therefore, would also require an extra supervisor, hence their salary would become a stepped fixed cost. This is shown graphically below.

67. **Stepped fixed costs**

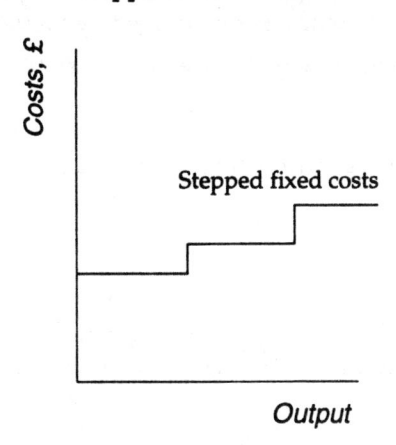

Stepped fixed costs

*[Graph showing stepped fixed costs: Costs, £ on vertical axis, Output on horizontal axis, with a stepped curve rising in discrete steps labelled "Stepped fixed costs"]*

68. **Average or Unit Costs.** The total costs of production are made up by fixed costs plus variable costs. Therefore, by dividing this figure by total output the average unit cost of each item produced can be calculated. Thus, for example, a publisher would calculate the average unit cost of producing a book, a restaurant owner the cost of a meal and a wallpaper manufacturer the cost of each roll produced.

69. These costs are particularly important because many firms use cost-plus pricing policies whereby they add a percentage profit margin to the unit cost to determine the selling price.

70. **Marginal Cost.** The extra cost (addition to total cost) of increasing output by one more unit is called the marginal cost. Since, in the short run, fixed costs do not vary with output, marginal costs (MC) are entirely marginal variable costs. As shown in the following diagram MC initially falls reflecting increasing returns to the variable-factor input, but then rises as decreasing returns set in:

71. **Marginal cost**

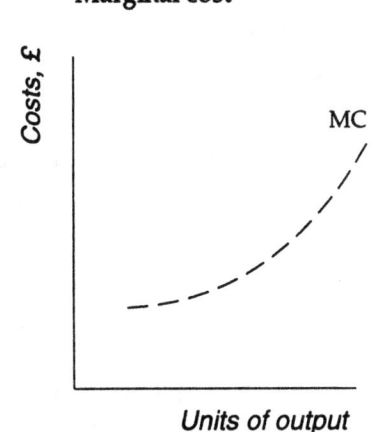

Marginal cost

*[Graph showing Marginal cost: Costs, £ on vertical axis, Units of output on horizontal axis, with a curve labelled MC that initially falls then rises]*

72. MC together with Marginal Revenue (MR), the addition to total revenue from the sale of one extra unit of output, determine the level of output at which a firm achieves its maximum profit. Since MR is, in effect the price, profit maximisation takes place at the level of output at which MC = MR. Marginal Cost or contribution pricing is discussed in Chapter 8.

## 4. The market mechanism

## Perfect Competition

73. In a perfectly competitive market:
    - each firm supplies only a small fraction of the total supply
    - each product has only one price which is determined by market forces of supply and demand and
    - each individual firm has a perfectly elastic demand curve because no matter how many units it sells it cannot change the price.

74.
**Individual Firm Under Perfect Competition**

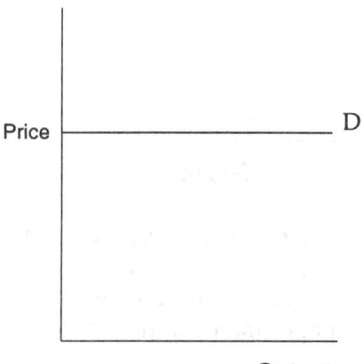

At a higher price, no demand exists and there is no incentive to sell at any lower price.

75. For this 'ideal' situation of perfect competition to exist several specific conditions are necessary:
    - **homogeneous products**, that is all sellers are offering the same product and thus there is no preference for any particular seller.
    - **many buyers and sellers** so that no individual can influence price.
    - **perfect knowledge** so that all buyers and sellers are fully aware of market conditions.
    - **freedom of entry** which requires perfect mobility of factors of production and consumers. Entrepreneurs will seek to maximise profits and must be able to move resources freely to do this.

76. In practice, these conditions are somewhat unrealistic and difficult to achieve. The nearest examples probably being the financial and commodity markets.

### Task 4.13
To what extent do the following markets meet the conditions of perfect competition?
1. Beef
2. Envelopes
3. Scissors
4. Furniture
5. Beer

77. **Output Under Perfect Competition**

In paragraph 72 we said that a firm's most profitable output is where MC=MR. The industry will be in equilibrium where all firms are producing the optimum output and earning what is called **'normal profits'**.

78. This can be shown graphically as follows:

## 4. The market mechanism

**Long-run equilibrium for the firm**

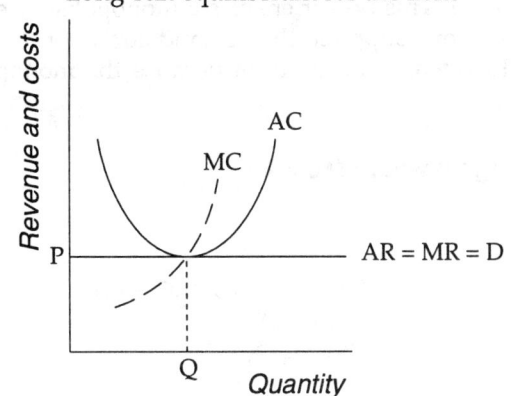

(Diagram: Revenue and costs vs Quantity; AC and MC curves with AR = MR = D horizontal line at P, tangent at minimum of AC at quantity Q.)

**Equilibrium in the industry**

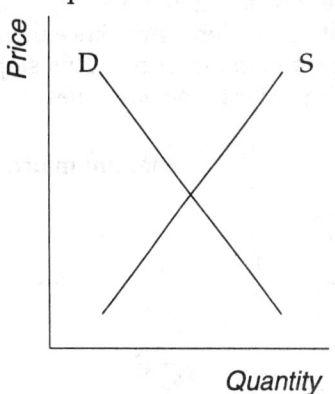

(Diagram: Price vs Quantity with demand D and supply S curves crossing.)

79. If a firm is producing at a price which exceeds AC then **'super-normal profits'** will be made as shown by the shaded area in the diagram below.

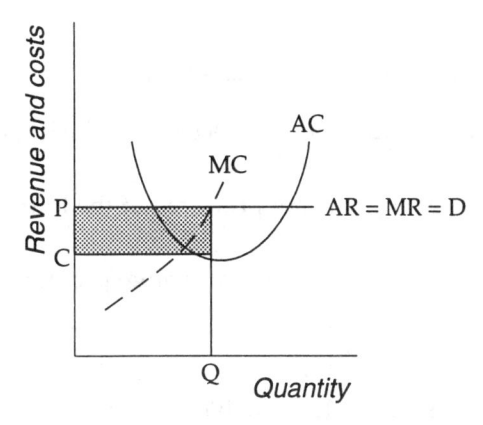

(Diagram: Revenue and costs vs Quantity; AC and MC curves with AR = MR = D horizontal line at P, shaded rectangle between P and C at quantity Q showing super-normal profits.)

80. But, under perfect competition, new firms will be attracted into the industry and total supply will therefore be increased. This will cause the price to fall until all firms are only earning normal profit.

### Task 4.14
Draw the diagram and explain what would happen to a firm whose AC exceeds the price under perfect competition.

## Monopoly

81. At the other extreme we have what is called a pure monopoly. In economic theory, this refers to a single supplier dominating a market but in practice this rarely exists. British Gas, for example, still competes with electricity and coal as a source of fuel.

82. Under UK law, a monopoly exists if either:
   - one firm accounts for 25% or more of the total supply of given goods or service or
   - two or more firms accounting for more than a 25% share of the market prevent, restrict or distort competition.

## Output Under Monopoly

84. A firm under monopoly can either determine the **price** at which its product will be sold or the quantity of **output** it is prepared to supply. It is not possible to control both because it cannot control demand.

85. For monopoly power to exist, a firm must be able to both restrict the entry of competitors and also have a product which cannot easily be substituted. This power enables a monopolist to earn super-normal profits in the long-run. Since there is only one supplier, the demand curve for the product is also the market demand curve. This slopes downwards to the right because the monopolist must reduce price in order to increase sales.

86.

**Maximum profit is again where MC = MR**

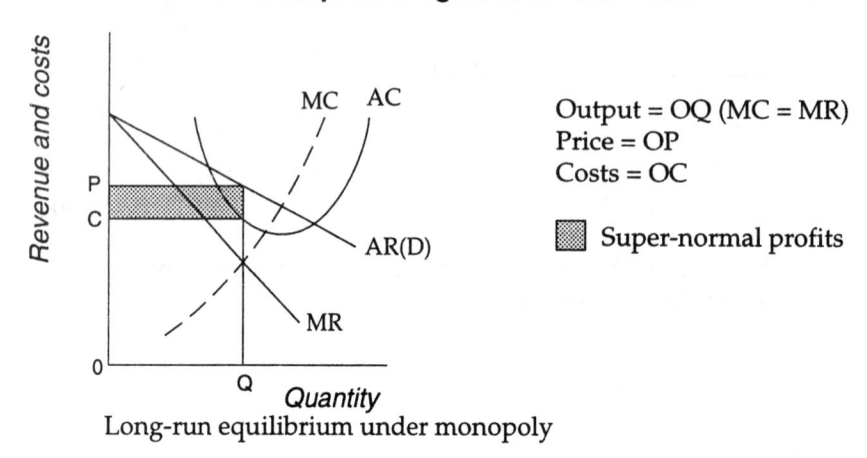

Output = OQ (MC = MR)
Price = OP
Costs = OC

▨ Super-normal profits

Long-run equilibrium under monopoly

87. Lack of competition means that under monopoly economic efficiency may be affected in two main ways:

- Costs could be higher because output is not produced at the lowest average cost. Excess capacity therefore exists and
- Price could be higher and output lower because it is more profitable for the firm.

### Task 4.15

'A monopolist sometimes finds it profitable to split a market into segments charging different prices in each for the same commodity. This is only possible where the elasticity of demand is different in each, there are no close substitutes and the market can be kept separate to prevent the product being bought only in the cheaper market. Telephone charges, for example, vary according to the time of day, whilst the railways, gas and electricity industries also discriminate in a similar way.' The above passage explains what is referred to as a discriminating monopolist.

1. Describe a discriminating monopolist in your own words.
2. Why do monopolists discriminate like this?
3. Why must the elasticity of demand be different in each market segment?
4. Which market would command the higher market price?

## Imperfect Competition

88. The more usual situation is that of imperfect, sometimes called monopolistic competition, where a large number of firms each have a small share of the market. This may be due to one of several factors which help to differentiate products including:

- branding and trade marks
- packaging
- convenience of sellers' location
- patents

89. In effect, these give each firm a small monopoly but with many close substitutes. This is very important for marketing which is discussed in detail in Chapters 7, 8 & 9.

## Output under Imperfect Competition

90. Under imperfect competition, a firm can charge a price which is different from its competitors. Sales therefore will depend on the price charged and thus the demand (AR) curve will slope downwards to the right. Output will also increase as the price falls and therefore MR is always less than AR. Maximum profit is again where MR = MC.

91. **Short-run equilibrium in imperfect competition**

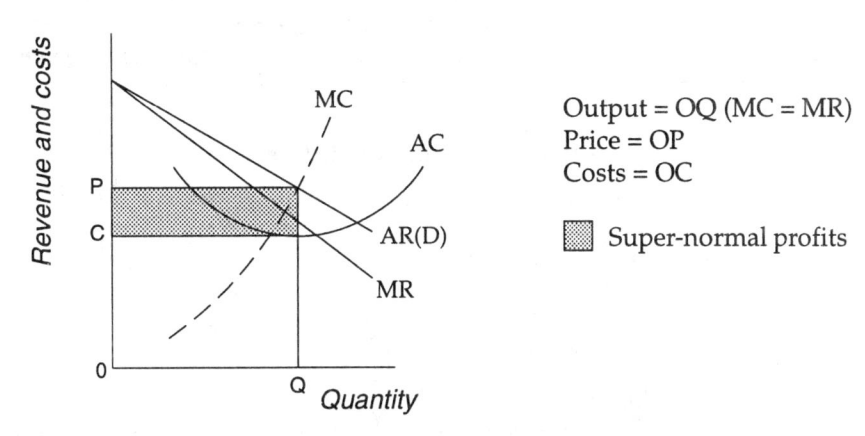

Output = OQ (MC = MR)
Price = OP
Costs = OC

▨ Super-normal profits

92. In the short-run, the number of firms is fixed and therefore individual firms can make 'super-normal' profits of PC per unit. The firm is not producing at the lowest AC because it is more profitable. Thus spare capacity exists. This will continue until more firms are attracted into the industry.

93. As new firms enter, demand will be less for individual firms at each and every price, therefore the AR curve will shift to the left. Normal profits will now be earned.

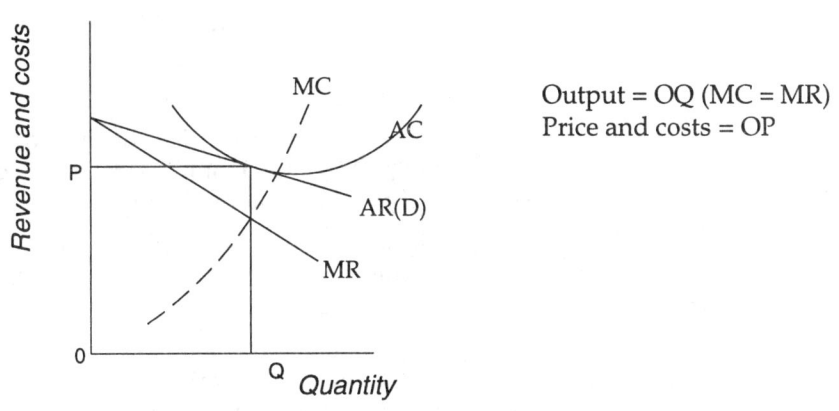

Output = OQ (MC = MR)
Price and costs = OP

Long-run equilibrium under imperfect competition

### Task 4.16

Study the market of a consumer product or service which you regularly use, such as soft drinks, bread or buses.

1. Identify the main 'brands' available locally and consider in what way(s) they are 'differentiated' from their competitors.
2. Consider also what possible substitutes exist and the extent to which this affects the price which you pay.
3. Comment on whether or not your study has affected your attitude towards the product or service which you use.

## Oligopoly

94. A particular type of imperfect competition common in the UK is that of oligopoly which refers to markets dominated by just a few large firms. Examples include cars, cigarettes, soap powders, cement, petrol and banking. These usually develop from mergers and takeovers which result in economies of scale but give monopoly power. There are usually barriers to small firms wishing to enter or grow in such a market either due to the capital investment involved or because existing firms quickly increase promotional expenditure to 'kill-off' any attempts.

95. Decisions on price and output in an oligopolistic market will depend upon the reactions of competitors who are likely to retaliate. Reduced prices, for example, are likely to be followed rather than risk losing business. On the other hand, where prices are increased, competitors are likely to prefer to try to increase market share rather than follow. This can be illustrated by the 'Kinked Demand Curve'.

96. **The Kinked Demand Curve**

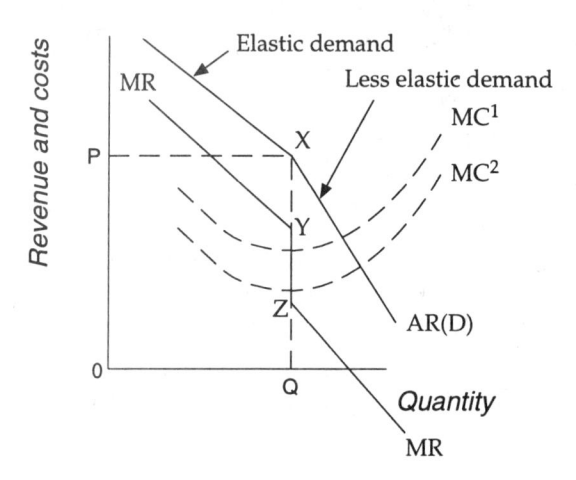

An oligopolist believes rivals will match price cuts but not price rises. Thus the demand curve is kinked at X. Price rises lead to a large loss of market share, but price cuts increase quantity only by increasing industry sales. MR is continuous at OQ. YZ = region of indeterminancy due to the sudden change in elasticity of demand. Thus MC can vary without altering price.

97. Consequently, oligopolists usually prefer non-price competition involving either **actual differences** between products such as quality, styling, reliability and after sales service; or **apparent differences** created by, for example, brand image, advertising and promotion.

98. In practice therefore, prices set by oligopolists are often very similar, particularly where products are close substitutes, as price stability is preferred to price competition. Each firm realises that any attempt to maximise its own market share may result in a price war which will only reduce total profits in the industry as a whole and thus may leave all firms worse off.

99. The pressures towards price stability can often be recognised (implicitly or explicitly) in some form of collective pricing strategy or collusion as follows:

- **Price leadership** often occurs where firms follow that of the market leader. This form of tacit collusion is a common feature of oligopolistic markets.

- **Cartels** are agreements between firms to regulate prices and/or output, thereby effectively creating a monopoly in order to increase profits, the best known example being the Organisation of Petroleum Exporting Countries (OPEC) which operates an oil cartel. Another example is where contracts are open to tender. Firms may agree to reduce competition by taking turns at offering the 'lowest' price in order to secure a regular flow of profitable work.

- **Exclusive dealing** involves a manufacturer preventing retailers from selling competitors' products as a condition of supply. For example Wall's and Mars icecream.
- **Full-line forcing** takes place when manufacturers will only supply retailers if they will sell the firms complete range of products. The costs involved thus limiting the number of suppliers a retailer can deal with.

100. All these forms of collusion are illegal in the UK under the Restrictive Practices Law because they are considered to be against the public interest. As such, they would need to be registered with the Office of Fair Trading for investigation. Most such agreements, however, are difficult to detect or prove and thus not easily prevented or controlled by legislation.

### Task 4.17

#### EU PROBE INTO STEEL CARTEL

British Steel has been accused by EU competition authorities of joining in an illegal Europe-wide cartel in steel beams for the construction industry. The UK steel-maker and at least five of its European competitors in France, Luxembourg, Spain and Germany could face fines of up to ten per cent of their annual turnover after Brussels competition authorities formally accused them of rigging markets and prices.

#### GLASS PRICE CARTEL IS UNCOVERED

A 'nationwide web of cartels on glass prices' has been uncovered, Sir Gordon Borrie, director general of fair trading said. It was a 'most serious breach of the law' and included price-fixing on window glass. The Office of Fair Trading began investigating after a building firm reported that it was 'tired of being ripped off'.

Action is expected in the Restrictive Practices Court.

#### SOAP GIANTS FACE MONOPOLY PROBE

The multi-billion pound detergent industry faces its biggest probe for more than 25 years.

A Monopolies and Mergers Commission inquiry is expected to examine the control Lever Brothers and Procter & Gamble have over the soap powders and washing-up liquids bought by every household in Britain.

The last Commission inquiry into the industry, in 1966, resulted in prices being capped for two years and cheaper 'square deal' packs. But it is felt in Whitehall that the industry continues to operate under a virtual monopoly, keeping prices artificially high, giving consumers a raw deal.

The new inquiry will examine whether Lever Brothers and Procter & Gamble prevent new competitors entering the lucrative market.

Lever Brothers spends millions promoting key brands such as Persil, Surf, Lux, Radion and Comfort. Procter & Gamble does the same for Ariel, Bold, Daz, Dreft and the newly launched Fairy Excel washing-up liquid.

From the above articles:
1. Identify the examples of potential restrictive practices.
2. Explain why the Government is concerned about them.
3. Describe the action being or likely to be taken to control them

## 4. The market mechanism

## Summary

101.
a) Economics is the study of how limited resources (supply) are allocated to satisfy human wants (demand).
b) A market is any situation where buyers and sellers come together.
c) The main types of markets are retail, wholesale, produce, commodity, shipping, insurance, financial and foreign exchange.
d) Markets with many buyers and sellers operate according to the laws of supply and demand.
e) The 2 main laws of demand are
   - the lower the price the greater the quantity demanded
   - the higher the price the lower the quantity demanded
f) Price, income and cross elasticity can be used to measure degrees of responsiveness of demand, to changes in demand conditions.
g) Exceptional demand curves are those which do not slope downwards from left to right.
h) The 2 main laws of supply are
   - the higher the price the greater the quantity supplied
   - the lower the price the lower the quantity supplied
i) The elasticity of supply measures the degree of responsiveness of supply to changes in price.
j) In a completely free market, price is determined by the interaction of demand and supply.
k) The theory of the firm shows how price and output are determined under different market conditions.
l) In economic theory, the profit maximising output is where MC=MR
m) The 2 extremes of perfect competition and monopoly rarely exist in practice.
n) Imperfect competition is more usual as a result of product differentiation.
o) An oligopoly exists in a market dominated by just a few large firms.
p) Unfair trading practices such as cartels are controlled by legislation.

## Review questions *(Answers can be found in the paragraphs indicated)*

1. Why is an understanding of economics helpful in business studies? (1-2)
2. What is a market? (3-5)
3. Briefly describe and give examples of at least 4 different types of markets. (6)
4. What is demand and what determines the shape of the demand curve? (8-11, 34)
5. What factors change the conditions of demand and how is this shown graphically? (12-14)
6. Briefly explain price elasticity of demand and its importance to firms. (15-25)
7. Distinguish between income and cross elasticity of demand. (27-33)
8. What is supply and what determines the shape of the supply curve? (35-38)
9. What factors change the conditions of supply and how is this shown graphically? (39-41)
10. Briefly explain price elasticity of supply and its significance to firms. (42-48)

11. With the use of a simple diagram, explain how prices are determined by the interaction of supply and demand. (49-52)
12. Identify the 4 key factors which determine market conditions. (53-56)
13. Distinguish between fixed and variable costs. (59-67)
14. Why are average revenue and average cost important? (58, 68-9)
15. What is the profit maximising output for a firm? (72)
16. Identify the conditions required for perfect competition. (73-75)
17. Explain how and why a firm with a monopoly can achieve super-normal profits. (81-87)
18. How is output determined under conditions of imperfect competition? (90-93)
19. Outline the distinguishing features of an oligopolistic market. (94-98)
20. Explain what you understand by collusion and why is it controlled by legislation. (99-100)

*Asterisks indicate those questions for which there are answers in Outline Answers (page 439)*

## Essay-style questions

1.\* What do you understand by elasticity of demand? Why does a business need to have some knowledge of elasticity for the goods or services which it supplies?

2. A publisher has to decide the price at which to sell a new book. He estimates that the costs incurred before publication amount to £20,000 and that variable costs amount to £2 a copy. In addition, he has agreed to pay the author royalties at a rate of 10% of sales revenue. The publisher's best estimate of the number of books he would sell at different prices is as follows:

    | Price (£) | Number Sold |
    |---|---|
    | 2.00 | 60,000 |
    | 2.50 | 40,000 |
    | 3.00 | 35,000 |
    | 3.50 | 20,000 |
    | 4.00 | 10,000 |

    a) Which of the above prices would maximise the publisher's profits?

    b) Which of the above prices would maximise the author's royalties?

    c) Publishers often allow authors to suggest the names of 50 people to whom free copies can be sent. Experience suggests that for every free copy, three further copies are ordered at the normal price. Assuming that the publisher has set a price which maximises profit without the consideration of free copies, should he try to persuade the author to suggest less than 50 people or more than 50?

    d) All the above data relates to a book published in black and white. The publisher estimates that publishing in colour would increase his variable costs by 25% and demand by 20%. How would his price be affected if he were to publish in colour instead of black and white?

3. Using diagrams where appropriate, examine the economic forces which determine the prices of:

    a) Christmas trees
    b) Stocks and shares
    c) Water

## 4. The market mechanism

### Short answer

1.* State with reasons, whether each of the following statements is true or false.
   a) The demand for bread is usually inelastic.
   b) The demand for ice-cream is highly inelastic.
   c) The supply of natural rubber is elastic.
   d) A shift in the demand curve to the right may be brought about by an increase in income.
   e) The supply of beef and hides is inter-related because they are in joint supply.

2.* A firm in a perfectly competitive market has the following schedule of average costs.

   | Output | 1 | 2 | 6 | 7 | 8 | 11 | 12 | 13 |
   |---|---|---|---|---|---|---|---|---|
   | Average Cost (£) | 36 | 30 | 17 | 15 | 13.5 | 13 | 14 | 17 |

   a) Construct the average and marginal cost curves corresponding to this data.
   b) From the curves, estimate the firm's optimum level of output and the market price necessary for this output to be supplied.

3. a) What is the main difference between the money market and the capital market?
   b) Give 3 examples of organisations which operate in each market.
   c) Why are they important to both businesses and the economy as a whole?

### Multiple choice/completion

1.* Price elasticity of demand is best defined as:
   a) The rate of response of demand to a change in supply
   b) The change in costs when output is increased by one unit.
   c) The change in consumers' tastes at different prices.
   d) The rate of response of demand to a change in price.

2.* Inelasticity of supply may be due to which **one** of the following factors:
   a) Monopoly conditions
   b) Insufficient demand
   c) Raw material shortages
   d) Highly variable demand

3.* In the traditional theory of the firm, normal profits are:
   a) Included in average costs
   b) Insufficient to keep an entrepreneur in business
   c) Negative for the marginal firm
   d) At the same level for all industries.

4.* Where a few large firms dominate a market, all but which one of the following are likely to be used to prevent new firms entering?
   a) An increase in advertising expenditure.
   b) The implementation of legal barriers
   c) The introduction of further similar but differential products
   d) Heavy short-term price-cutting

4. The market mechanism

5. If the elasticity of supply of butter is 0.5, an increase in the price to farmers from £40 to £44 per ton will increase the quality produced per week from 1,000 tons to:
   a) 2000 tons
   b) 1200 tons
   c) 1100 tons
   d) 1050 tons

6. Which of the following costs are fixed in the short-term?
   a) prime costs
   b) indirect costs
   c) semi-variable costs
   d) direct costs

*In each of the following questions, one or more of the responses is/are correct. Choose the appropriate letter which indicates the correct version.*

   A   if 1 only is correct
   B   if 3 only is correct
   C   if 1 and 2 only are correct
   D   if 1, 2 and 3 are correct

7. Which of the following is/are institutional investors?
   1. Insurance Companies
   2. Building Societies
   3. Trade Unions

8. If a monopolist wishes to discriminate, which of the following market conditions are necessary?
   1. The cost of keeping the market separate is not too great.
   2. The elasticity of demand is the same in each market.
   3. Consumers have relatively easy access to the different markets.

*4. The market mechanism*

## Assignment

1. Design a table/chart which summarises the key features of the different market structures under the following headings:
   - Number of firms.
   - Ability to influence price.
   - Barriers to entry.
   - Example(s).

2. Grabville, a small town in the West Country has 2 garages, Charlie Blacks and PRT. Both are selling petrol at the same price: unleaded at 55p per litre and leaded at 65p per litre. Charlie Black reckons that if he reduces prices, PRT will follow and between them, they will not generate much extra business. If he puts his price up, PRT would do nothing, so he would lose customers. Charlie estimates his demand schedule to be as follow:

   | Leaded price | Sales (litres per day) | Unleaded price | Sales (litres per day) |
   |---|---|---|---|
   | 75 | 50 | 75 | 100 |
   | 70 | 150 | 70 | 250 |
   | 65 | 250 | 65 | 450 |
   | 60 | 300 | 60 | 550 |
   | 55 | 350 | 55 | 600 |
   | 50 | 400 | 50 | 650 |

   a) Draw the demand curves for Charlie's business.

   b) Calculate his total revenue if he charged the following prices:

   |  | 1 | 2 | 3 |
   |---|---|---|---|
   | leaded | 65 | 70 | 75 |
   | unleaded | 55 | 60 | 65 |

   c) In what circumstances might Charlie consider increasing or reducing his prices?

   d) Charlie knows the PRT manager well and is thinking about meeting to discuss an agreement on pricing to increase profits. He is considering 70p for leaded and 60p for unleaded. What advice would you give to Charlie?

   e) Suggest ways in which Charlie could compete with PRT without getting involved in a price war.

3. Carry out some practical research into the behaviour of firms in one or more oligopolistic markets. For example, banks, building societies, large supermarket chains; soap powder, coffee, tea or cereal manufacturers, or oil companies.

   a) Select some of their products or services and compare prices in your area.

   b) Identify the main methods used to compete with each other.

   c) Comment on your findings.

# 5. Business and the Economy

In Chapter 3 we considered the many ways in which the government has an influence on all types of business organisations. In this Chapter, we are considering the intervention of the government in the economy in order to achieve its aims. It covers:

* Government and the Economy
* National Income
* Use of National Income Statistics
* Circular Flow of Income
* Keynes
* Aggregate demand and the Multiplier
* Size of the Multiplier
* Inflationary & Deflationary Gaps
* Government Macro-Economic Aims
* Fiscal Policy
* Types of Taxes
* Tax and Business
* Budget
* PSBR
* Public Expenditure
* Monetary Policy
* Monetary Sector
* Economic Growth
* Unemployment
* Inflation

## Micro-Economics

1. Much of what we consider in this text is called **micro-economics**. That is, it is concerned with the behaviour of individual consumers, firms or industries, including the allocation of scarce resources, determination of prices, supply and demand, perfect competition and monopoly and the theory of the firm. In each situation one individual, organisation or sector of the economy is considered in isolation from the rest of the economy.

## Macro-Economics

2. In this Chapter we are considering the aggregate effects of individual behaviour, what is termed **macro-economics**. That is, how the economy as a whole works including the level of real income, the level of prices, the rate of interest, the rate of saving and investment, the rate of growth, the balance of payments and the level of unemployment.

## Government and the Economy

3. The government intervenes in the running of the economy for a number of reasons and its policies and actions can and do have a major effect on business activities.

4. The main reasons for government intervention are summarised below:
   * **To manage the economy** in order to control the level of economic activity, sometimes referred to as 'demand management'. This may range from formal planning of the economy to control of the balance of payments and inflation.
   * **To provide resources for social capital** such as roads, defence, schools, hospitals and amenities which are owned collectively by the nation.
   * **To pay welfare benefits** to those who are unemployed, sick, on low incomes or retired.
   * **To control monopolies and restrictive practices** in order to increase competition and encourage efficiency in the economy, particularly where natural monopolies exist such as water, gas and electricity.
   * **To provide aid for industry** in order to tackle, for example, problems of regional unemployment or to protect firms from unfair foreign competition. It is usually given in the form of grants or other financial assistance.
   * **To provide merit goods** and services for everyone's benefit such as education, libraries and art galleries which some individuals might not otherwise be able to afford to purchase.

## 5. Business and the economy

- **To control social costs** which can occur in a free economy. For example, the sale of harmful or dangerous items like drugs or pornography, or actions which result in pollution, congestion or noise.

> **Task 5.1**
> 1. Taking the reasons for government intervention above, identify what you feel are the most important economic and social issues and state why.
> 2. Are there any issues not mentioned which you would like to see included? Again give reasons.

## National Income

5. In order to consider the government's macro-economic policies and how they affect businesses, it is important to understand how the government uses the national income to measure the level of economic activity in the economy.

6. The value of all goods and services produced by businesses in the UK each year is called the **Gross Domestic Product** (GDP). This can be expressed either:
    - **in terms of market prices** that is, what people actually pay for goods and services, or
    - **at factor cost** that it, the cost of producing goods and services, and ignoring any taxes or subsidies. This was £481,776 million in 1990.

7. GDP can also be expressed in
    - **current prices**, that is, actual prices as they exist, or
    - **constant prices**, that is, after removing the effects of inflation in order to measure the underlying growth in the economy.

8. GDP can be calculated in 3 different ways as the sum total of **income, expenditure or output**. Each method produces the same total in principle but there are slight differences. The definitive measure is therefore calculated as an average of these 3 methods. In 1990, the average of GDP at constant factor cost was 116.2 (1985 = 100) compared with 90.7 in 1980, an increase of 28% in 10 years.

9. **Table 1: Gross Domestic Product, Gross National Product and National Income**

|  | £ Million 1982 | £ Million 1992 |
|---|---|---|
| Total final expenditure | 347,343 | 745,801 |
| *less* imports of goods and services | –67,762 | –149,164 |
| Gross domestic product at market prices | 279,041 | 596,165 |
| *plus* net property income from abroad | 1,460 | 5,777 |
| Gross national product at market prices | 280,501 | 601,942 |
| *less* factor cost adjustment (taxes less subsidies) | –40,656 | –81,571 |
| Gross domestic product at factor cost | 238,385 | 514,594 |
| Net property income from abroad | 1,460 | 5,777 |
| Gross national product at factor cost | 239,845 | 520,371 |
| *less* capital consumption | –33,653 | –63,984 |
| National income (net national product at factor cost) | 206,192 | 456,387 |

*Source: United Kingdom National Accounts 1993 Edition*
*Note: Differences between totals and the sums of their component parts are due to rounding.*

See Monthly Digest of Statistics for most recent figures.

10. Table 1 shows the average estimate of GDP at both current market prices and factor cost. It also shows the:

    - **Gross National Product (GNP)** which is the total output of goods and services produced by UK businesses, plus net property income from abroad. In other words, GDP plus the output of UK owned businesses located overseas.

    - **National Income**, that is, the net national product (NNP) at factor cost. Calculated as GNP minus capital consumption. That is, an allowance for depreciation of capital equipment.

11. **Table 2: Total Final Expenditure in 1992 at Market Prices**

    |  | £ Million | per cent |
    |---|---|---|
    | Consumers' expenditure | 382,696 | 51.3 |
    | General government final consumption | 132,378 | 17.7 |
    | Gross domestic fixed capital formation | 92,892 | 12.5 |
    | Value of physical increase in stocks and work in progress | –1,992 | –0.3 |
    | Total domestic expenditure | 605,974 | 81.3 |
    | Exports of goods and services | 139,827 | 18.7 |
    | **Total final expenditure** | **745,801** | **100.00** |

    *Source: United Kingdom National Accounts 1993 Edition*
    *Note: Differences between totals and the sums of their component parts are due to rounding.*

    See Monthly Digest of Statistics for most recent figures.

12. Table 2 shows the categories of final expenditure in 1990. As can be seen, consumers' expenditure accounted for 50% of total final expenditure, whilst exports of goods and services accounted for 19%.

## Problems of Measuring Economic Activity

13. These include:

    - **Double counting**, that is, avoiding counting the same activity more than once. Components, for example, could be considered as the output of the firm selling them and the firm using them. Therefore only the value added to production by each firm is counted.

    - **Transfer payments** of income from one group to another which are not in return for the provision of factor services need to be excluded to avoid double counting. Sickness, unemployment and pension benefits are examples.

    - **Non-marketed output**. There is no allowance for work carried out at home, such as housework nor, for example, for voluntary or charity work.

    - **Black economy**. This refers to unrecorded economic activity which is often carried out by people but not declared to avoid paying tax. This will produce some inaccuracies in the accounts and is considered to represent as much as 7.5% of national income.

    - **Service industries.** Where no tangible product exists or what is produced is not sold, it is difficult to calculate 'value added'. The provision of health and education, for example. The output of these industries is therefore valued at cost.

### Task 5.2

A housewife decided to return to full-time work. Her job paid £10,000 per year having previously received a £5,000 housekeeping allowance from her husband. As a consequence, her teenage daughter agreed to give up her evening newspaper round because she was needed at home after school to look after her young brother. Her father offered to compensate her fully and increased her pocket money by £40 per month.

Calculate the increase in the family's contribution to the national income.

## Use of National Income Statistics

14. The national income data is used by the government to assist it in formulating its economic strategy. It provides a useful measure of economic activity and by calculating income per head of population, is an indicator of standards of living both at home and for international comparisons.

15. The national income accounts are presented annually in what is commonly called the 'Blue Book'. It contains a detailed analysis of the components of national income and usually shows changes over a 10 year period. The range of detailed information available includes:
    - Trends in industrial production
    - Trends in consumer expenditure
    - Changes in the distribution of income
    - **Economic growth** and the standard of living
    - International comparisons

## Circular Flow of Income

16. The main principles behind the calculation of the level of national income in the economy can be illustrated in a simple circular flow of income.

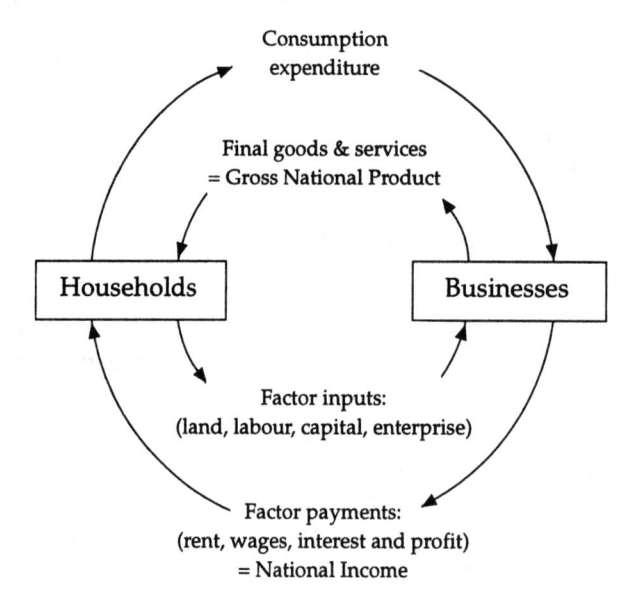

```
                    Consumption
                    expenditure
                  ↗             ↘
          Final goods & services
          = Gross National Product
                  ↓             ↑
        ┌──────────────┐   ┌──────────────┐
        │  Households  │   │  Businesses  │
        └──────────────┘   └──────────────┘
                  ↓             ↑
              Factor inputs:
          (land, labour, capital, enterprise)
                  ↘             ↗
              Factor payments:
          (rent, wages, interest and profit)
                = National Income
```

17. As shown above:
    - Businesses produce goods and services which are consumed by households.
    - Factor inputs are required for production and these are purchased by businesses from households in return for factor payments.
    - everyone in the economy belongs to a household and therefore is a consumer,
    - hence there is a circular flow of income as money flows from households to businesses and back again because all spending is someone else's income.

## Injections and Withdrawals

18. The above explanation assumes a closed economy but in practice households do not spend all their earnings in this way on goods and services.
    - part may be saved, for example in a building society or pension scheme.
    - some goes in taxation, for example, income tax and VAT.
    - part is spent on imported goods and services, for example, Japanese cars, foreign holidays.
    
    These are called **leakages** or **withdrawals** from the circular flow.

19. Likewise, not all income into a business comes from consumer spending. **Injections** into the circular flow come from:
    - **government expenditure,** for example, on defence, education, or unemployment benefits.
    - **exports,** for example, UK cars sold abroad and overseas visitors into the UK.
    - **investment** which is expenditure on capital goods such as building new factories or buying new machines to increase future wealth.

20. Investment which requires an amount of current consumption to be foregone, (that is, saved to release the resources to finance it) can be divided into:
    - **gross investment** which is the total amount of investment undertaken in an economy over a specified period of time, usually a year.
    - **net investment** which is gross investment less capital consumption. That is, investment needed to replace capital which has depreciated or been used up.

21. The level of aggregate demand in the economy at any particular time depends upon the level of leakages and injections. If they are equal, the economy is said to be in equilibrium, although this may occur at a level that is less than full employment If leakages exceed injections, there is a net outflow of money from the circular flow which would reduce the level of demand. If, on the other hand, injections are greater than leakages, this will stimulate the economy and increase demand.

22. **Injections and Withdrawals from the Circular Flow of Income**

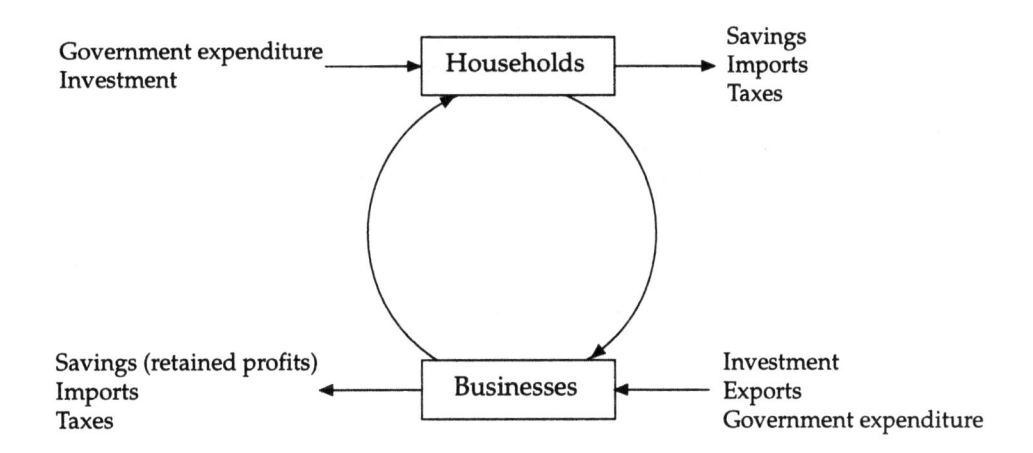

```
Government expenditure ──→ Households ──→ Savings
Investment                                 Imports
                                           Taxes

                              ↑
                              │
                              ↓

Savings (retained profits) ←── Businesses ←── Investment
Imports                                        Exports
Taxes                                          Government expenditure
```

### Task 5.3

In each of the following situations, state whether they are considered to be injections to, withdrawals from, or part of the circular flow of income

1. Widening of the M62 Motorway.
2. Insurance premiums paid by Greek ship owners to Lloyds of London.
3. Businesses retaining profits to increase their reserves.
4. The purchase of British machinery by a British manufacturer.
5. The purchase of British made consumer goods by British households.

## Keynes

23. Macro-economic thinking developed very much from the work of **John Maynard Keynes** who in 1936 published 'The General Theory of Employment, Interest and Money'. His theory dominated government thinking from the post-war period until the 1970's.

24. Prior to Keynes, the so-called **classical economists**, such as Smith, Ricardo, Mills and Say, had stated that in a free economy, the laws of supply and demand would always automatically ensure the full employment of resources provided that all savings were invested. The pressure of accumulated savings would cause interest rates to fall, thereby encouraging businesses to borrow and invest more. Whilst falling wage rates and hence, reduced production costs would encourage the employment of more workers, hence solving the problems associated with recession.

25. This thinking, however, failed completely in the depression of the 1930's where mass unemployment existed. This led Keynes to look for other explanations. He was highly critical of the government at the time which not only failed to intervene in the economy but actually made matters worse by reducing public expenditure. Keynes concentrated on the economic aggregates of National Income, Consumption, Savings and Investment to produce a general theory to explain the level of economic activity.

26. Keynes argued that:

    - the economy was not self-regulating.
    - there is no assurance that savings would accumulate during a depression and reduce interest rates because savings depend on income and with high unemployment, income is low.
    - households' consumption expenditure and savings plans are dependent on the level of national income,
    - income depends on the volume of employment and the marginal propensity to consume determines the relationship between income and consumption. The term 'propensity' meaning a psychological inclination to consume or save.
    - investment depends primarily on business confidence which would be low during a depression and therefore unlikely to increase even with low interest rates.
    - wage rates were 'rigid' and therefore unlikely to fall much in a depression and if they did, it would add to the problem by reducing income and consumption.
    - depression was caused by reduced aggregate demand and governments must intervene via fiscal policy to stimulate consumption. They should increase incomes through tax cuts or public expenditure in order to increase aggregate demand.

### Task 5.4

The following table shows consumption (C) and investment (I) at different levels of National Income (Y) in an economy.

| Y | C | I |
|---|---|---|
| 150 | 90 | 50 |
| 190 | 150 | 50 |
| 250 | 250 | 50 |
| 350 | 300 | 50 |
| 400 | 320 | 50 |

What is the equilibrium level of National Income?

## Aggregate Demand and the Multiplier

27. We have seen that aggregate demand consists of all the money which is spent on goods and services by individuals, businesses and government in a specified period, usually a year. One of the important concepts developed by Keynes (although introduced by Kahn in 1931) was that of the **multiplier** which is concerned with the effects of changes in the level of injections or withdrawals on the equilibrium level of national income.

28. The multiplier is the number by which a change in any element of aggregate demand is multiplied to give the overall effect on the level of national income. The multiplier on the level of economic

activity comes about because of the nature of the circular flow of income. Thus, for example, if the government increases expenditure on road building, incomes of firms building roads will increase. They in turn will employ more workers and buy more materials from suppliers whose income will also rise. Suppliers in turn will increase expenditure whilst all workers will spend more money in shops and other places and so on. Thus, the multiplier is a cumulative process involving successive rounds of additions to income.

### Task 5.5

Consider the likely multiplier effects of local councils deciding to reduce expenditure on house building.

## Size of the Multiplier

29. The size of the multiplier will depend upon the proportion of any extra income which is spent on consumption, that is, the marginal propensity to consume (MPC) at each successive round. The marginal propensity to save (MPS) is the proportion of any extra income which is withdrawn from the circular flow. The greater the MPS the lower is the multiplier. MPS + MPC = 1

    Thus the multiplier (K) can be calculated as:

    $$K = \frac{\text{change Y}}{\text{change I}} \quad \text{or} \quad \frac{1}{1 - \text{MPC}} \quad \text{or} \quad \frac{1}{\text{MPS}}$$

30. For example, if an increase in government investment (I) from £40 billion to £60 billion produces a change in income (Y) of £80 billion then:

    $$K = \frac{80}{20} = 4$$

    Thus, every extra £1 of investment injected into the economy will eventually produce a £4 rise in national income.

    If the MPC is ¾ then MPS = ¼ thus K = 1 ÷ ¼ = 4

31. This example pre-supposes a closed economy, in reality some of the consumption will take place on imported goods and services. Therefore any increase in government spending may not all go to assist the domestic economy unless there is also a corresponding increase in exports.

### Task 5.6

1. It has been estimated that in the UK, on average, for every £1 increase in National Income, direct tax takes 24p, indirect tax 13p, personal savings 7p, 12p is spent on imports and businesses save 17p.

    On the basis of these figures, estimate the value of the multiplier in the economy.

2. If, for every extra pound of income received, people save 10p, spend 15p on imports and have to pay 30p in taxes.

    a) What is the marginal propensity to consume home produced goods and services?

    b) What is the marginal propensity to save?

    c) What is the value of the multiplier?

## Inflationary and Deflationary Gaps

32. At any particular time, there is a level of national income which is sufficient to sustain full employment. If aggregate demand exceeds output at this level, we get an inflationary gap. That is, since out-

put cannot be increased further, the excess demand will cause prices to rise unless the government intervenes to reduce it.

33. On the other hand, if the equilibrium level of national income is below the level that generates full employment, we get a deflationary gap which may lead to unemployment. To counteract these gaps, governments can use fiscal and monetary policies to reduce or expand aggregate demand accordingly.

34. **Inflationary Gap**

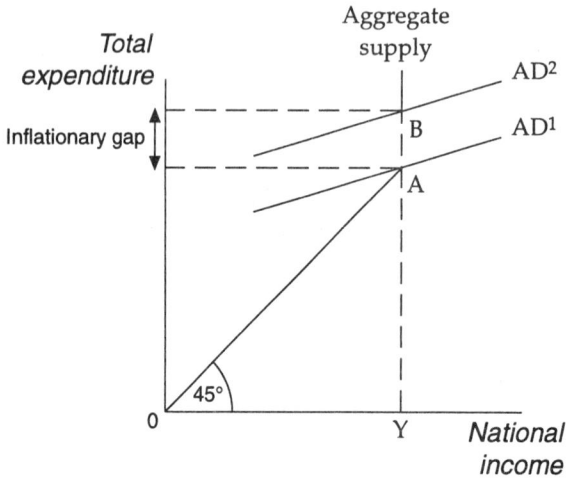

35. The full employment level of national income/output is reached at OY when the aggregate supply schedule becomes vertical. If aggregate demand was at the level indicated by $AD^1$, the economy would be operating at full employment without inflation (point A) However, if aggregate demand is at a higher level like $AD^2$, the excess demand would create an inflationary gap equal to AB.

36. **Deflationary Gap**

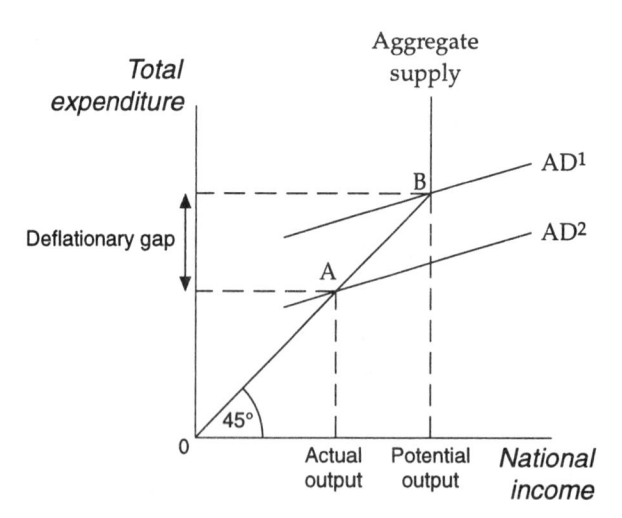

37. The full employment level of output/national income is reached at Point B on $AD^1$ when the aggregate supply schedule becomes vertical. If aggregate demand is at a lower level such as $AD^2$, then actual output will be at a where it intersects the aggregate supply schedule. At this point, there is a gap between actual and potential output.

## Government Macro-Economic Aims

38. Since Keynes, the main aims of macro-economic policy have been to achieve:
    - Economic growth and a higher standard of living. (see Paragraph 68)
    - Full employment. (see Paragraph 72)
    - Low inflation. (see Paragraph 87)
    - Balance of payments stability. This is discussed in detail in Chapter 6.

39. As already mentioned, in seeking to achieve its economic aims, the Government makes use of both **Monetary Policy** (interest rates and credit controls) and **Fiscal Policy** (Taxation and Public Expenditure). Trying to achieve these aims may cause certain conflicts. For example, a policy for growth may lead to balance of payments difficulties, whilst measures to reduce inflation may lead to unemployment.

40. The Government must also consider its social objectives. That is, issues which affect the community such as:
    - Environmental protection including noise and pollution (see Chapter 17).
    - The protection of individual's rights, for example, employment and consumer protection.
    - Democratic decision making, for example election of MP's and local councillors.
    - Freedom of opportunity and choice.
    - Conservation.
    - Fair distribution of income and wealth.

### Task 5.7

| Economic Indicators | 1980 | 1985 | 1990 |
|---|---|---|---|
| Gross domestic product (average estimate) | 323,419 | 356,083 | 416,888 |
| Exports | 88,726 | 102,208 | 123,642 |
| Imports | 80,781 | 98,866 | 139,123 |
| Consumers' expenditure | 195,825 | 217,618 | 273,304 |
| Gross domestic fixed capital formation | 53,416 | 60,353 | 79,893 |
| Percentage increase in retail prices index | 18.0 | 6.1 | 9.5 |
| Workforce in employment (000s) | n.a | 24,530 | 28,510 |
| Percentage of workforce unemployed | n.a | 10.9 | 5.8 |

*Sources: United Kingdom National Accounts 1991 Edition; Economic Trends; Employment Gazette*

£ million at 1985 market prices. n.a = not available.

See Monthly Digest of Statistics for most recent figures

a) Identify and comment on the key trends in the above data.

b) Update them with the latest available figures and identify any major changes.

c) If possible, identify the reasons for the changes identified.

## Fiscal Policy

41. The Government uses fiscal policy for a number of reasons including:
    - To finance expenditure, for example on health, education and roads.
    - To control the economy and influence the level of demand, investment, inflation, employment and economic growth.
    - To redistribute National Income and help the less well-off, for example, the unemployed.
    - To give incentives to industry to influence location and encourage production and **investment**.
    - To discourage smoking, drinking and gambling.
    - To control the import of certain goods either for Balance of Payments or other reasons.

*5. Business and the economy*

## Types of Taxes

42. There are a number of different types of taxes which the Government can use including:

- **Progressive** – a tax which takes a higher proportion of income as income rises. Income tax (1995-96) has a lower rate of 20% on the first £3,200 then a basic rate of 25% with a higher rate of 40% for people who earn more than £24,300.
- **Regressive** – a tax which takes a higher proportion of income from the poor, for example, VAT and television licences.
- **Proportional** – a tax which takes a fixed proportion of someone's income. In 1995/96 income tax was proportional for the first £24,300 of taxable income because everyone paid 25% for each £ earned.
- **Poll Tax** – This is a tax levied equally on everyone. An example is the 'Community Charge' which was replaced by the Council Tax in 1993.

## Direct and Indirect Taxes

43. Taxes are further classified as direct or indirect:

- **Direct taxes** are levied directly on the income or wealth of individuals and organisations. They are collected by the Department of Inland Revenue. The main direct taxes are income tax, corporation tax, petroleum revenue tax, inheritance tax and capital gains tax.
- **Indirect taxes** are levied on the expenditure on goods and services and therefore are paid indirectly to the tax authorities. These are collected by the Customs and Excise Department. They may be specific ie consisting of a fixed sum regardless of the value of the goods, for example, 90p per packet or pint on tobacco or alcohol or ad valorum ie a percentage of the value of the goods, for example, 10%. The main indirect taxes are Value Added Tax and Customs and Excise Duties.

44. **Direct Taxes**

- **Income Tax.** This is a progressive tax on people's income. A number of personal allowances reduce the amount of a person's taxable income. Most people pay their income tax under PAYE, whereby tax is deducted by their employer. The Government can alter the level of personal taxation by changing the rate of tax, for example, reducing the basic rate from 25% to 20% in the £ or by altering the allowances.
- **Corporation Tax.** This is a proportional tax on company profits. Companies are allowed to deduct certain expenditure as tax-free allowances from their gross profit. Tax must then be paid on the net profit remaining. The main rate is 33% with a reduced rate of 25% for small companies (those with profits below £300,000 pa). A high level of corporation tax could affect economic growth because it would leave firms with less money for investment.
- **Petroleum Revenue Tax (PRT).** Companies like BP and Shell who make profits from the production of North Sea Oil and Gas are also charged PRT at 50% but only on profits from existing fields.
- **Capital Gains Tax.** When people sell assets such as shares, works of art or land, they are liable to pay 40% capital gains tax on any profits which they make in excess of £6,000. Exemptions are granted for the sale of certain assets, such as the sale of a person's home. Tax is charged at an individual's top rate i.e. 25% or 40%.
- **Inheritance Tax.** This tax applies to transfers of personal wealth from one person to another when they die or within seven years of their death. The rate of tax is nil below a certain threshold (£154,000 in 1995/96) and 40% on anything more. Some transfers are exempt, for example those between husband and wife or involving small businesses.

45. **Indirect Taxes**

- **Value Added Tax (VAT).** VAT is levied at each stage in the production and distribution of goods and services. The final tax is paid by the consumer. The basic rate is $17\frac{1}{2}$% but some items are exempt (for example education and postal services) whilst others are zero rated, for example, most food, books, drugs and exports. The effect of VAT is to increase prices which generally reduces demand.

- **Customs and Excise Duties.** Customs duties are charged on all imported goods except those from the EU. They provide income for the Government and a measure of protection from foreign competition by increasing the price of imports. Excise duties are levied mainly on home produced goods and services including beer, wine, spirits, cigarettes, fuel and gambling.

## Other Forms of Taxation

46. These include Stamp Duty, National Insurance, Licence Duties and the Local Authority Council Tax.

    - **Stamp Duty.** This is charged at 1% on the total price of any property sold above a value of £60,000 (1995/96).
    - **National Insurance.** This is a form of direct taxation collected specifically to help finance the National Health Service and to contribute to the funds needed to provide unemployment and sickness benefits. The rate paid varies with the size of a person's income, the higher the income, the bigger the deduction. Employers must also pay National Insurance for every person employed and they contribute over 50% of the total amount. Self employed people also pay National Insurance.
    - **Licence Duties.** Television, driving and gun licences are all forms of taxation. A licence duty is also charged on all motor vehicles including cars, motor cycles, lorries and buses.
    - **Council Tax.** This is the only major tax which is not paid to the central Government. (see Chapter 2)

### Task 5.8

|                       | £      |
|-----------------------|--------|
| Income Tax            | 60,000 |
| VAT                   | 24,000 |
| Corporation Tax       | 20,000 |
| Inheritance Tax       | 5,000  |
| Capital Gains Tax     | 6,000  |
| Motor Vehicle duties  | 4,000  |
| Custom & Excise duties| 7,000  |

From the above figures, calculate:

a) the total value of direct taxes.

b) the total value of indirect taxes

c) which tax would be most effective for redistributing incomes?

d) which tax would be used to control the import of goods or services?

## Tax Implications for Business

47. Business organisations are affected by taxation in a number of ways including:

    - **Economic activity** will be reduced unless the government ploughs back money from taxation. Consumer demand depends on disposable income which is reduced by direct taxation. Thus sales and profits will be affected.
    - **Profits** are taxed thus reducing the amount available for reinvestment in the business or for distribution to shareholders.
    - **Prices** are affected which can reduce demand.
    - **Costs of Production** will increase if supplies of goods and services are taxed.

- **Supply of labour** can be affected because high taxation can act as a disincentive to work for the low paid who may be better off on unemployment benefits, whilst those in work may not be motivated by overtime or bonuses.
- **VAT registration** is a legal requirement for all firms whose turnover exceeds £46,000 (1995/96) thus involving them in extensive record-keeping and submission of VAT returns.

> **Task 5.9**
>
> Refer back to the taxes in Task 5.8.
>
> Comment on how each of these might affect a small business.

## The Budget

48. Each year, the Chancellor of the Exchequer presents a Budget to Parliament. This is a Financial Statement which gives the Government's estimated revenue and expenditure of the last financial year, and forecasts for the next year. It also gives details of any proposed tax changes. Sometimes 'mini' budgets are used at other times of the year. The Budget which in 1993 was moved from March/April to November/December, has two main functions. It enables the Government to:

- Regulate the economy by controlling the demand for goods and services.
- Redistribute income and wealth among the various sections of the community.

## Public Sector Borrowing Requirement (PSBR)

49. If the proposed revenue and expenditure are equal then the Budget is in balance. When revenue is greater than expenditure it is in **surplus**, if it is less than the Budget, it is in **deficit**. When the Budget is in deficit the Government must borrow in order to finance its expenditure. This is called the PSBR which in 1994–5 was £34.5 billion.

50.

**The PSBR and the Budget**

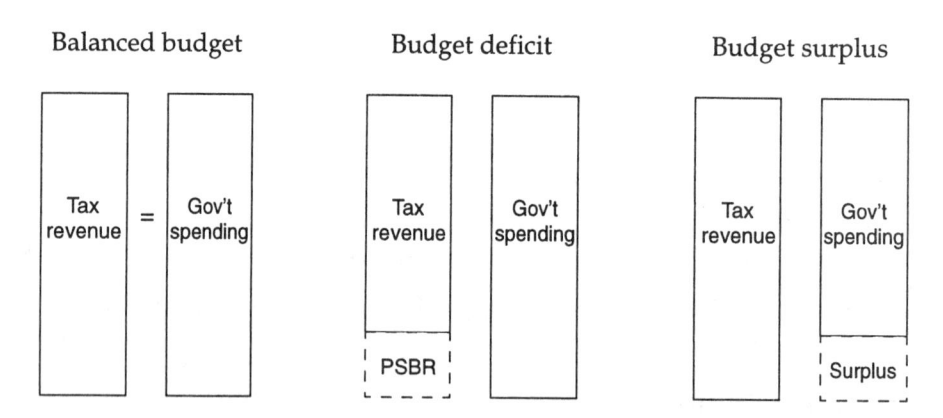

| Balanced budget | Budget deficit | Budget surplus |
|---|---|---|
| Tax revenue = Gov't spending | Tax revenue / Gov't spending (PSBR) | Tax revenue / Gov't spending (Surplus) |

51. The Government borrows by issuing Treasury Bills, Gilt-edged stock and various kinds of savings certificates in return for the money lent to it. The accumulated PSBR owed by the Government, both to people in Britain and those abroad, is called the **National Debt**. In 1993 it stood at £135 billion.

## Public Expenditure

52. This is the term used to describe the money which the Government spends for the benefit of the community as a whole. The Government uses the money which it collects in taxation to provide goods and services for the nation. Some of these are provided centrally whilst others are provided locally. As shown in the diagram opposite – total government spending in 1992 accounted for over 40% of the gross domestic product.

53. **Planned Receipts and Expenditure of Central Government 1992-93**

| Where it comes from | Pence in every £ | Where it goes[1] | Pence in every £ |
|---|---|---|---|
| Income tax | 22 | Social security | 30½ |
| National Insurance contributions | 14 | Health | 13½ |
| Value-added tax | 14 | Education and science | 12½ |
| Local authority rates and community charge | 9 | Defence | 9 |
| Excise duties | 9 | Law, order and protective services | 5½ |
| Corporation tax[2] | 6 | Transport | 4 |
| Capital taxes | 1 | Other services | 17½ |
| Interest, dividends | 2 | Debt interest | 7 |
| Petroleum revenue tax and oil royalties | ¼ | Other[3] | ½ |
| Other expenditure taxes | 4 | | |
| Borrowing | 14 | | |
| Other | 5 | | |
| **Total** | **100** | **Total** | **100** |

[1] Figures are based on Table 2.5 of the Statistical Supplement to the 1992 Autumn Statement.
[2] Including North Sea but excluding capital taxes on companies.
[3] Other accounting adjustments, privatisation proceeds and adjustment.
*Note*: Differences between totals and the sum of their component parts are due to rounding.

## Central Government Expenditure

54. The main items of Central Government expenditure are:

- Social Security and Personal Social Services – including pensions, benefits for the unemployed, sick and disabled and social security payments.
- Education and the Arts – grants to Universities, Colleges and Theatres.
- Defence – this includes the cost of keeping an army, navy and airforce at home and abroad.
- National Health Service – provision of doctors, dentists, hospitals etc.
- Debt Interest – the Government has to pay interest on the PSBR and National Debt.
- Nationalised Industries – loans to public corporations for capital expenditure.
- Trade Industry and Employment – this includes grants to industry and the cost of operating Job Centres, the Training, Education and Enterprise Directorate (TEED) and Training & Enterprise Councils (TECs).
- Environmental Services – including spending on roads, law and order, and housing.
- Grants to Local Authorities – the Government pays a 'revenue support grant' to help finance some of the services provided by local councils and also transitional relief for the new council tax.

## Local Government Expenditure

55. The main items of Local Government expenditure are:

- Education – the provision of schools is the single most important item of local authority expenditure.
- Law and Order – police and fire services.
- Roads and transport – maintenance of minor local roads. Sometimes local transport services may be subsidised or free travel passes issued.
- Housing – provision of council houses and other accommodation.

- Social Services – for example children's homes, old people's homes, home helps and social workers for those who need help.
- Environmental services – including parks, cemeteries, refuse collection and toilets etc. Also sport centres, museums, libraries and other local facilities.
- Debt interest – local councils also borrow money to finance expenditure on which interest has to be paid.

---

**Task 5.10**

### SPENDING CUTS

The Government is to impose substantial public spending cuts to stop the budget deficit ballooning from the official forecast of £28 billion in the 1992/3 financial year to almost double that amount in 1993/4.

So far, the private sector has taken all the strain of the recession. Now, without cuts in public spending, we would either get tax increases or higher borrowing.

Tax increases would reduce the incentive for people to work. Many are already caught in the unemployment trap. They have little motivation to find work because their social security benefits are worth as much as their potential after-tax pay. Higher taxes would only increase the numbers of those caught in the trap who stay at home all day watching television - demoralising for them and disastrous for the economy. Increased borrowing would be just as bad. It would cause higher interest rates and thus discourage companies from investing again. Not the way to get the wealth-producing part of our economy going.

The spending cuts on the way include pay freezes for public sector employees and tighter conditions for social security payments.

There may be industrial unrest but the Government rightly wants to preserve as much as possible of the capital spending programme although some of this will also go.

Answer the following based on the above article:

1. Why does the government need to reduce public spending?
2. Why is it doing this in preference to using other policies?
3. How could this move affect the private sector?

---

## Monetary Policy

56. The government's monetary policy is operated by the Bank of England. Essentially, it involves the control of the supply of money circulating in the economy by altering interest rates, exchange rates and the availability of credit in order to control inflation and promote economic growth.

57. Monetary policy can be used to encourage or discourage spending which in turn affects investment, the demand for goods and services, prices, employment and foreign trade. For example, if people have more money to spend (from increased wages and extra credit) then unless output increases, prices are likely to rise, leading to inflation.

## Money

58. Money which is anything generally acceptable as a means of payment, fulfils a number of important functions. It is a:
    - **Medium of exchange** which allows goods and services to be easily bought and sold.
    - **Measure of value** which is used to price goods and services.
    - **Store of value** because money can be saved for future use.
    - **Means of deferred payment**, for example, when goods are bought on credit, money is used to measure the amount owed.

59. The total supply or stock of money is currently measured in several different ways but which can be broadly defined as:

- **narrow measures** which concentrate on money as a medium of exchange.
- **broad measures** which include those assets which may be both a store of wealth and a potential medium of exchange.

60. **Definitions of Money**

- M0 the narrowest measure is the notes and coins in circulation, plus money actually held by banks (till money) and their deposits with the Bank of England.
- M2 is the money available for immediate use, that is, notes, coins and cash in banks and building society accounts.
- M4 comprises notes and coins in circulation together with all sterling deposits held with UK banks and building societies by the rest of the private sector.
- The Bank of England also publishes data for liquid assets outside M4.

## Monetary Measures

61. **Interest Rates.** A link between the Bank of England and the commercial banks is provided by the **Discount Houses.** These are banks which specialise in buying Commercial and Treasury Bills at less than their face value (at a discount) and making a profit by keeping them until they mature. They obtain their funds mainly by short-term borrowing from the banks ie 'at call or short notice' which means that they can be asked for repayment at any time which is what happens if the banks need cash to meet their obligations to customers. When this happens, it leaves the Discount Houses short of funds which they are able to borrow from the Bank which acts as **'lender of last resort'.**

62. The Bank can choose the interest rate at which it provides these funds. When it changes its official dealing rate, the commercial banks promptly follow and change their own **base rates** for lending and borrowing. This in turn affects consumer demand, investment, output and ultimately prices.

63. **The Exchange Rate.** Interest rates also affect the value of sterling in terms of foreign currencies. Generally, higher interest rates attract foreign funds into the UK and this increases the rate of exchange whilst lower interest rates have the reverse effect. To control this, the Bank manages the UK's gold and foreign currency reserves through the **Exchange Equalisation Account**. This is a fund which is used by buy and sell sterling and foreign exchange in order to 'smooth out' fluctuations in the exchange rate, known as **intervention**.

64. **Other Policy Instruments**. Other techniques used in the past by the Bank to control the economy include:

- Ceilings on the amount of bank lending.
- Special Deposits ie cash reserves which banks had to deposit with the Bank.
- Guidance on bank lending aimed at discouraging loans to consumers and
- Open-market operations ie the buying and selling of Government Securities via the Stock Exchange to influence the money supply.

### Task 5.11

Consider the likely impact on the domestic economy in each of the following situations.

1. The government increases the level of social security benefits.
2. VAT is raised from 17.5% to 25%.
3. Banks and building societies reduce the interest rates on savings accounts.
4. The value of the pound falls against other major currencies.
5. Businesses are expecting a boom in the economy.

*5. Business and the economy*

## The Monetary Sector

65. The 1979 and 1987 Banking Acts gave the Bank of England the powers to authorise and supervise all **deposit-taking institutions**. To become and remain authorised a 'bank' must have adequate capital; make provision against possible bad debts; have enough cash or liquidity to meet likely withdrawals and have fit and proper management. The aim of authorisation is to protect depositors against the risk of losing their money. If an authorised bank does fail, depositors are entitled to limited compensation from a **Deposit Protection Fund** set up under the 1987 Act and administered by the Bank but financed by contributions levied on the institutions.

66. **Monetary Sector**

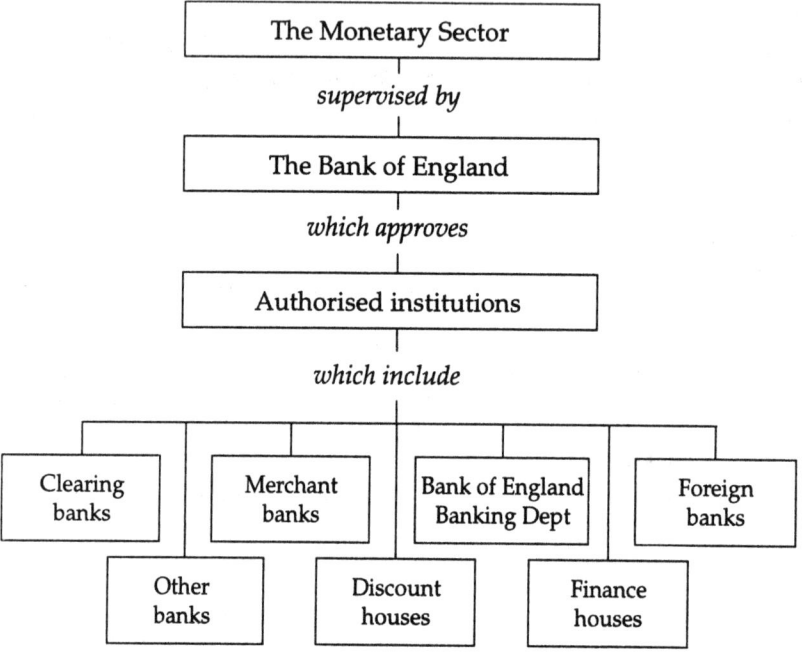

```
              The Monetary Sector
                      |
                supervised by
                      |
              The Bank of England
                      |
                which approves
                      |
              Authorised institutions
                      |
                which include
    _____|_____
    |           |              |          |
 Clearing   Merchant    Bank of England  Foreign
  banks      banks      Banking Dept     banks
       |           |            |
     Other      Discount      Finance
     banks      houses        houses
```

## Authorised Institutions

67. There are some 550 institutions authorised to accept deposits by the Bank of England. These include:

- **Clearing Banks** and commercial banks which provide a wide range of services to personal and business customers.
- **Merchant Banks** and accepting houses which provide services almost exclusively for businesses. This includes accepting Bills of Exchange, acting as issuing houses for shares, providing loans and advising on business problems.
- **Banking Department of the Bank of England** which looks after the Bank's business with the exception of the issue of notes and coins.
- **Foreign Banks** – there are over 400 operating in the UK, the largest being American and Japanese.
- **Other Banks** – these include certain banks in the Channel Islands and the Isle of Man.
- **Discount Houses** – which borrow and invest short-term.
- **Finance Houses** – these make loans for hire purchase and general consumer expenditure, usually for two to three years. They also provide short-term finance for businesses.

## Economic Growth

68. One of the main objectives of the government's macro-economic policy, economic growth is the term used for the annual rate of increase in the production of goods and services. It is measured by calculating the percentage increase in the national income.

69. Achieving economic growth depends upon a number of factors including the:
    - **quantity and quality of the factors of production.** That is, national resources, skills of the workforce, capital investment and level of enterprise.
    - **development and introduction of new technology** leading to new products, improved techniques and an increase in productivity.
    - **level of education and training.** Knowledge and skills are essential for economic growth.

70. Whether or not an economy realises its growth potential will also depend upon the level of aggregate demand which must be high enough to ensure full utilisation of its resources. The government can influence the growth rate through its economic policies which affect the level of private investment. It can also switch resources from consumption to investment in physical capital which will reduce welfare today but allow for more growth and welfare in the future.

71. Economic growth enables a country to enjoy a higher standard of living with an increasing amount of goods and services. It is sometimes argued, however, that the **social costs** of economic growth such as pollution, congestion and a hectic lifestyle often outweigh the benefits. These so called **externalities** are likely to increase as production increases unless something is done to prevent them by the government.

---

**Task 5.12**

### POST WAR RECORD

Recession has now rumbled on for 2½ years, making it the longest downturn since World War II. But the 1992 fall in gross domestic product – the value of goods and services produced in Britain – was only half as bad as Chancellor Norman Lamont's prediction. Output actually rose 0.2 pc in the last quarter, but only because of a leap in oil and gas output.

Taking out such items GDP fell 0.1 pc. The fall for the whole year was 0.5 pc.

### RECESSION CUTS DIVI

Anglo-French paper maker Arjo Wiggins Appleton is cutting its interim dividend from 3.3 pc to 2.65 pc after half-year profits fell from £135.5m to £99.1m.

Finance director Tony Issac says that 'Business and consumer confidence in the areas that affect our operations remain low', he adds. 'The outlook for the second half of the year is for a continuation, and possibly a weakening of the present difficult trading conditions.'

### PROFITS WARNING

The recession has caught up with Body Shop, the high street retailer of natural skin and hair care products.

It warned today that lower than expected sales in the UK, particularly since June, have had an adverse affect on profits.

Answer the following based on the above articles.
1. What was the level of economic growth in 1992?
2. How does recession affect businesses?
3. Is there any evidence to suggest that the recession may be nearing its end? Study current media information and compare it in your answer with the articles above.

---

## Unemployment

72. Since the depression of the 1930's and the work of Keynes, maintaining high and stable levels of employment has been an important government objective. In March 1993, Britain had over 3 million

people unemployed which is 11% of the working population. The government must therefore be aware of the affects of its policies on the creation of jobs.

73. **Unemployment 1920-1993**

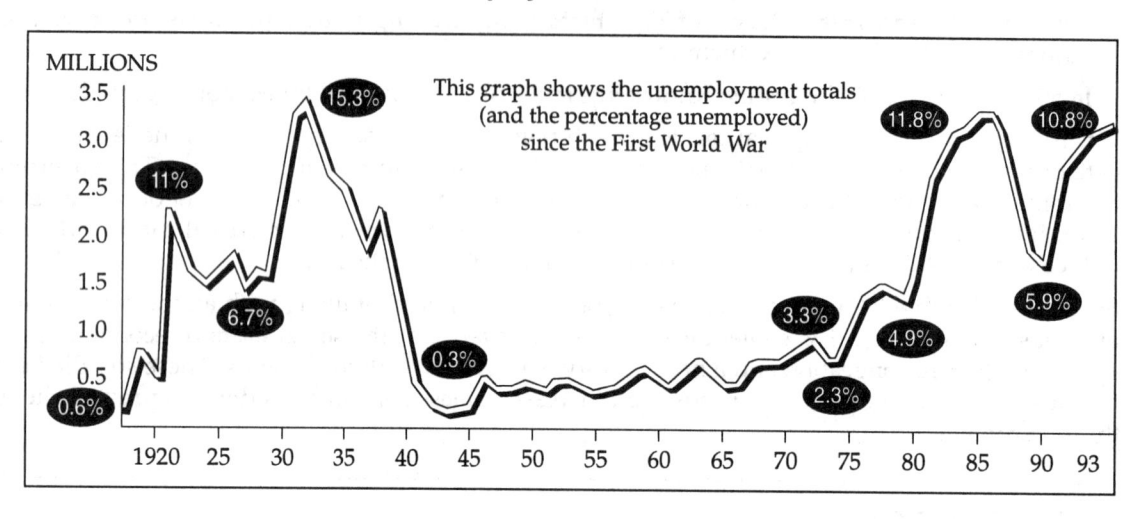

*This graph shows the unemployment totals (and the percentage unemployed) since the First World War*

[Graph showing unemployment in millions from 1920 to 1993, with annotations: 0.6%, 11%, 6.7%, 15.3%, 0.3%, 2.3%, 3.3%, 4.9%, 11.8%, 5.9%, 10.8%]

## Measuring the Level of Unemployment

74. Unemployment is a situation where people are actively seeking to obtain work but are unable to do so because there are insufficient jobs. It is officially measured by the Department of Employment as those people who are registered as unemployed and who are eligible for benefit.

75. It is believed that the official figures may well underestimate the true level of unemployment because some people

- do not register as unemployed because of pride or the nature of the benefits system.
- drop out of the jobs market when finding work is difficult. Students, for example, may decide to stay on at school or college, whilst women may stay at home.
- join government training schemes such as Youth Training or Training to Work because no jobs are available. A **Modern Apprenticeship Scheme** will replace YT from 1995–96.
- have to work short-time or part-time because full-time work is not available.

## Types of Unemployment

76. Unemployment has a variety of causes and therefore a variety of possible cures. The three main types of unemployment are summarised below.

- **Frictional** unemployment occurs as individuals move from one job to another, incurring a temporary short period of unemployment (usually less than 3 months). A small amount of frictional unemployment is a permanent feature of any economy since even under conditions of 'full employment' a degree of this type of unemployment (at around 2-3%) will be present.
- **Cyclical** or 'demand deficient' unemployment which is caused by periodic downturns in the business cycle. Industrialised market economies tend to suffer regular booms and slumps. In a slump or severe recession, business activity is low and hence less labour is required leading to rising unemployment. In the 1930's, early 1980 and early 1990's the UK suffered badly from cyclical unemployment.
- **Structural** unemployment is the result of a mismatch between the skills of the workforce and the jobs available in a given local labour market. It is common, for example, where heavy manufacturing industries have entered a phase of long term decline and new service jobs require different skills to those possessed by displaced industrial workers. Thus, unless workers are geographically or occupationally mobile, and therefore able to move to areas of expansion, they are likely to become unemployed.

77. Other types of unemployment include:
    - **Regional** unemployment which exists where the level of economic activity in certain areas is lower than the national average due to unfavourable location factors such as poor infrastructure or distance from markets. Where declining industries are concentrated in particular areas, structural and regional unemployment are closely interlinked.
    - **Real wage** unemployment which is caused when wages are at too high a level for everyone to be employed. That is, they are above market clearing levels possibly due to powerful trade unions.
    - **Seasonal** unemployment which occurs where the demand for goods and services is determined by the time of the year. The tourist and construction industries, for example, employ extra workers in the summer.
    - **Technological** unemployment which occurs when the introduction of new equipment and techniques of production replaces workers.
    - **Residual** unemployment which exists because some people who suffer from particular mental or physical handicaps are incapable of working.

78. This analysis of unemployment only provides a general guide. In reality, unemployment in any given area is likely to have not just one but a variety of causes whilst some areas are more vulnerable to the effects of structural or cyclical unemployment because of the local economic structure.

### Task 5.13

In each of the following situations, identify the type of unemployment concerned.
1. A disabled person unable to find suitable work.
2. Tourist guides unemployed in the winter months.
3. Car workers replaced by robots on the production line.
4. Young people unable to find a job at the end of their Youth Training programmes.
5. A fall in demand for cigarettes resulting in job losses at factories of the British American Tobacco company.

## Reasons for Unemployment

79. In addition to the causes identified above, it is also important to realise that unemployment can be brought about by a number of other factors, in particular the
    - **growth of the working population** that is those seeking work which has risen from 25.2 million in 1972 to 28 million in 1992.
    - **foreign competition** which has caused the decline of many manufacturing industries such as textiles and motor vehicles. For example, the import penetration ratio of vehicles which was 23% in 1972 was nearly 60% in 1992.
    - **poor industrial relations** which was a symptom of the 1980's and contributed to Britain's reputation for poor quality and unreliability thus providing opportunities for foreign competitors.

## Economic Effects of Unemployment

80. These include the:
    - **Cost to the exchequer.** It is estimated that the payment of benefit, loss of tax revenue and provision of training schemes means that it costs the government between £8,000-£10,000 per annum for each unemployed person.
    - **Waste of resources.** Unemployment means that the economy is operating below its full potential and a valuable resource is being 'lost'.
    - **Inequalities of income distribution.** Despite receiving benefits, unemployed people are still worse off financially than those in employment.

## 5. Business and the economy

### Social Effects of Unemployment

81. These include the:

- **Work ethic.** Unemployed people become demoralised and lose the will to work.
- **Loss of status.** A jobless person loses the status which a job gives.
- **Crime and vandalism.** The frustration, boredom and deprivation of unemployment often leads to mindless vandalism and increases in theft and other crimes.
- **Health.** Unemployed people experience falling living standards. This can lead to poor nutrition, depression and general ill health.

### Political Effects of Unemployment

82. Unemployment is an important political issue which can have a major effect on how people vote in local and national elections. It also influences government policies.

---

**Task 5.14**

#### £12BN DOLE MISERY

The Government is likely to spend about £12 billion on unemployment in 1993 as the nation's dole queues continue to grow.

That would cover the cost of the Channel Tunnel – the biggest and most expensive project undertaken in Britain – almost one-and-a-half times. Unemployment reached 3 million in January 1993 when the number out of work for more than a year leapt to 1,030,000, the highest total for five years. A fifth of those are between 18 and 24.

The total, which rose by 75,000 in the three months to January, has more than doubled since October 1990. Long-term unemployment is climbing everywhere but London, the South and East Anglia are worst hit.

Analysts believe unemployment will continue rising throughout the year and could peak at around 3.3m in mid-1994.

The previous jobless record was 3,124,000 reached in July 1986.

The DSS rule of thumb on unemployment benefits is that every 100,000 people joining the dole queues adds about £350m to benefit payouts.

MPs and Trade Union leaders have called for an urgent package of measures to give people the hope that comes through quality training, help to get the long-term unemployed back to work, and investment in areas like construction that will generate jobs and growth.

1. Identify the key trends in unemployment.
2. What is the cost of unemployment to the government and economy?
3. What action could be taken to alleviate the problem?

---

### Effects of Unemployment on Organisations

83. These include:

- **Reduced demand** which can result in falling sales and profits.
- **Wage rates** are forced lower because there is a large pool of labour available. This may not be the case in skills shortage areas such a high technology.
- **Trade union power** is reduced because they have less members and the threat of further job losses. Thus, it is easier for organisations to introduce change without strong resistance.

## Policies for Reducing Unemployment

### 84. Fiscal Policy

Since the Second World War governments have developed a number of standard fiscal economic policies to control unemployment based on the thinking of Keynes.

- **increased public spending** to create economic activity and expand employment via the multiplier effect.
- **reduced taxation** to increase disposable incomes in order to generate demand.
- **support for business** through investment incentives and export assistance.

### 85. Monetary Policy

Since the 1970's the monetarist approach to managing the economy has prevailed whereby interest rates are used to control the money supply. Lower rates make saving less attractive and borrowing cheaper thereby encouraging consumers to spend and businesses to invest. The increased economic activity should help to reduce unemployment.

## Direct measures

86. In addition to the main fiscal or monetary policies, governments have also introduced specific measures to combat unemployment. In particular:

- **Enterprise schemes** offering financial and tax incentives to encourage the growth of new and small businesses.
- **Education and training** to provide the skills for future employment via the 82 Training and Enterprise Councils and Employment Services. TECs are responsible for a number of schemes, including Youth Training, Community Action, Training for Work (aimed at long-term unemployed adults) and support for employers. Employment Services operate Job Centres and organise Job Clubs and the Restart Programme, which offers job search advice and training opportunities. Most schemes are usually run by approved training organisations such as FE colleges, private training providers and voluntary organisations.
- **Youth Credits** give young people who have left full-time education to join the labour market an entitlement to train to approved standards. They carry a monetary face value and can be presented to an employer or training provider in exchange for training.
- **Reducing Social Security**. The government in 1993 announced that it intends to introduce a system of 'Workfare' whereby many unemployed people will only be paid benefits if they undertake community work or training schemes. This aims to 'force' people back to work.
- **Selective Regional Assistance**. Grants and tax relief are offered in areas of high unemployment to encourage firms to locate there.
- **Reducing Trade Union Power** and therefore excessively high wages which can distort the labour market. Legislation introduced in the 1980's and 1990's included removal of the 'closed shop' and measures to reduce picketing and therefore the effectiveness of strikes.
- **Information and advice** about job hunting and opportunities is available from, for example, Job Centres, Job Clubs and the Restart Programme.
- **Ten Integrated Regional Offices** (bringing together the Departments of Transport, Trade and Industry, Employment and Environment) to co-ordinate UK and EU funds, including a **Single Regeneration Budget (SRB)**. The aim is to encourage local initiatives and partnership to overcome disadvantage and promote regeneration in employment, education and skills, economic development, housing, environment, crime prevention and aid to ethnic minorities. Local authorities, TECs and Business Leadership Teams will be key partners, together with voluntary groups, schools, police, health authorities, small firms and others.

## Inflation

87. An increase in the general level of prices in an economy over a period of time is called inflation. It is measured by the Retail Price Index (RPI) which in June 1993 showed a 1.2% increase on the previous 12 months.

## 5. Business and the economy

88.

**Inflation 1978-1992**

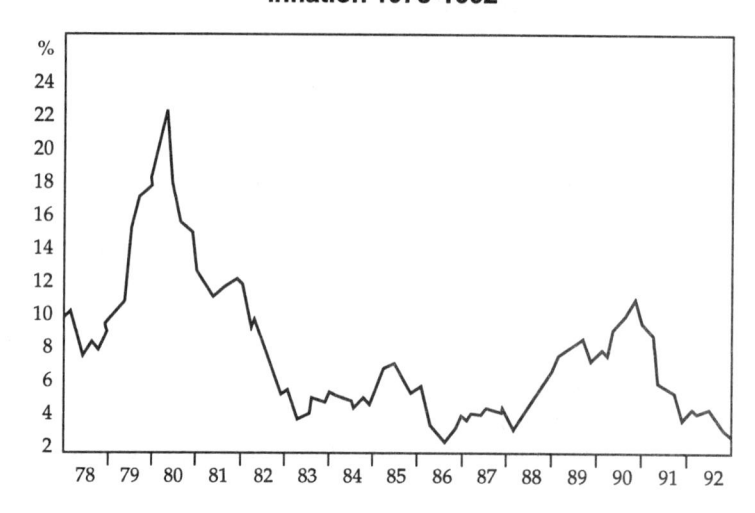

[Line graph showing inflation percentage from 1978 to 1992, with y-axis from 2% to 24%. The line starts around 10% in 1978, rises to a peak of about 22% in 1980, drops to around 4% by 1983, stays low with fluctuations through 1986-87, rises to about 10% in 1990, then declines to around 3% by 1992.]

89. The 2 extremes of inflation are:

- **Hyperinflation.** With severe inflation, prices rise rapidly and drastically. This happened, for example in 1923 in Germany and was so bad that in 1924, a completely new currency was issued.

- **Creeping inflation** is more common where the general price level rises gradually at an average rate of 2-3%. This is a situation achieved in the UK in the 1990's.

---

**Task 5.15**

### RUNAWAY TROUBLE

Inflation in Russia is running at 1,000 per cent as the price of everything from bread to vodka spirals out of control.

Some stores, especially those selling clothes and cigarettes imported from the West, now mark up prices daily rather than monthly.

And, like West Germany in the Twenties, when shoppers had to carry suitcases full of almost worthless paper money, Russians are now being forced to carry ever-larger bundles of notes to buy even basic goods.

Basic products became much more expensive after Russian President Boris Yeltsin freed price controls at the start of the year in an attempt to create an efficient, Western-style economy.

But the government is blaming the crisis on the semi-independent Central Bank for printing too much money. The average Russian now takes home around 3,500 roubles a month, which is worth less than £10 at current exchange rates. To cope with the problem of virtually worthless money, many factories have turned to giving workers food or goods instead of pay.

From the above article:

1. Identify the type of inflation which Russia is suffering from.
2. What has caused it?
3. What problems does it create for firms and individuals and how do they react?

---

## Effects of inflation

90. The control of inflation has been a main objective of economic policy in the post-war period although the approach used varies according to the beliefs of the individual governments in power. Inflation is of concern because of the effects which it can have on individual businesses and the economy as a whole.

The effects on individuals include:

- **fixed income recipients** suffer because their purchasing power is reduced, for example, shareholders of fixed interest securities, pensioners or those on benefit.
- **lenders lose** because the value of money repaid in the future is worth less than currently.
- **borrowers gain** because what they pay back is worth less.
- **'tax net'.** Inflated money wages bring more people to a taxable level of income making them worse off even though real income may actually have fallen.

91. The effects on business include:

    - **resources are diverted** into non-productive items such as antiques or works of art as savers seek to hedge against inflation.
    - **high interest rates** are needed to encourage people to save but they also add to the cost of borrowing, leading eventually to even higher prices.
    - **investment** may be discouraged by a lack of business confidence and high interest rates making a profitable return more uncertain.
    - **international trade competitiveness** is affected because exports become relatively more expensive and imports relatively cheaper. This may lead to Balance of Payments problems for the economy.
    - **rising demand.** Inflation usually occurs when demand is buoyant which might produce rising sales and profits.

## Effects on company accounts

92. In a period of rising prices, stock and fixed asset valuations based on historical cost are likely to overstate the real profit position of a firm. Therefore, in order to reflect the real progress in a business' company accounts must be adjusted to remove the effects of inflation.

93. Two common methods for overcoming this are:

    - the **current purchasing power** method which uses the retail price index to adjust calculated profits and express them in real terms.
    - the **current cost accounting** method is more detailed. Assets and depreciation are stated in the accounts at their current replacement cost values with adjustments for any specific, rather than general, price rises which have taken place in the financial year.

## Causes of inflation

94. There are two main explanations of why inflation occurs – demand pull and cost push, although in practice there is a close interaction between the two and inflation is usually considered to be **multi-causal**.

    - **Demand-pull** or 'too much money chasing too few goods'. Keynes argued that this results from excess demand when the economy is operating at full capacity which 'pulls-up' prices. Monetarists argue that demand-pull is caused by the government creating too much money in the economy making it easier for people to borrow funds which, unless supply increases, causes prices to rise.
    - **Cost-Push** inflation is attributed to higher costs of production, in particular labour, which 'push-up' prices. Strong trade unions have often been blamed for this problem. Thus, for example, if a group of workers are given a 10% wage increase and produce exactly the same output as before then, usually prices must rise to prevent profits falling. Rising import prices and falls in the value of the exchange rate also contribute to cost-push inflation.

## Expectations and inflation

95. The role of expectations can also be important in generating price rises. This is because wage claims are often excessive in anticipation of future rising prices, which then actually cause inflation as firms raise prices to cover the extra cost. This process can lead to what is called the **wage/price spiral**.

*5. Business and the economy*

## Task 5.16

### EXPECTATIONS ON INFLATION

In January 1993 the government announced that inflation had fallen to 1.7%. But does anyone really believe it? Especially if you exclude falling mortgage rates which were mainly responsible.

It means that on average, prices have gone up just under 2p in the pound since a year earlier.

That sounds unlikely; and you can produce dozens of examples of where it is not true. Except perhaps, wage packets which for one-third of the nation in the public sector, are now virtually frozen.

This is the rub. Inflation was when wages went up because prices had risen; deflation is when prices start to come down because wages have not risen. Most companies would like to put prices up. But if they try in the current recession, they cannot make the increases stick. So on items like furniture and white goods you now have 'negative inflation'. This is also seen in houses, land, property and even second-hand cars.

As for the future, what counts is 'expectations'. If you expect inflation, you will get it. People are not quite convinced that inflation is over as indeed it cannot be if the government, as suggested, puts VAT on food and newspapers, in line with other EU countries in the budget.

1. From you own experience, identify at least 6 examples of goods or services which have in the past 12 months risen in price faster than inflation.
2. What key factors are keeping prices lower?
3. How is the government controlling the cost-push element of inflation?
4. Why has 'negative inflation' come about in some markets?
5. In what ways can 'expectations' be said to influence inflation?

## Policies to control inflation

96. There are a number of policies which governments may adopt to control the level of inflation which are summarised below: It is important to realise, however, that measures of control can sometimes cause bigger problems than the inflation itself.

97. **Monetary policies**

    Higher interest rates can be used to reduce the money supply and therefore demand. However, this also raises the cost of borrowing to business which will particularly affect highly geared companies, that is, those with a high level of borrowed capital. Also, reduced demand will reduce sales and profits and thus can lead to unemployment. Higher interest rates also push up exchange rates which makes exports relatively dear.

98. Although, not favoured by the present government, it can if it chooses, issue instructions to banks to control credit by restricting the level and direction of lending for individuals and organisations. This, however, also reduces consumer demand and may affect the amount of funds available for investment.

99. **Fiscal Policy**

    Higher taxes may be introduced to reduce demand because people have less to spend and/or goods and services cost more. This, however, does not help with cost-push inflation because it puts up prices. Government expenditure on, for example, health, education and roads may also be reduced to curb demand. However, both measures could cause unemployment.

100. Alternatively, additional public expenditure may be used to expand the economy and increase output in order to match demand. This however, will depend upon the multiplier effect and could also lead to further inflation.

## Prices and incomes policies

101. Monetary and fiscal policies are indirect macro-economic policies. Alternatively the government may choose direct intervention to reduce wages and prices by 'freezing' them or restricting any rises to an agreed level, for example 3%, over a particular period of time or linking them to the Retail Price Index. Such policies may, however, be difficult to enforce, except in the public sector, other than on a voluntary basis (where unions, employers and the government agree) and may cause industrial unrest and confrontation. They may also only delay price rises and distort the market mechanism leading to factor or product shortages. Statutory policies were imposed in the mid 1960's, and late 1970's by the Labour government and in the early 1970's by the Conservatives.

102. **Price Control and Rationing**

    As a last resort, a government could introduce statutory controls on prices but this is unlikely except in a short-term emergency.

### Task 5.17

### INFLATION WORRY AS MONEY MISSES TARGET

Fears of a return to high inflation swept the City yesterday when a key money measure broke out of the Treasury's target range.

Some experts think the Government will have to postpone further cuts in interest rates until the outlook clears.

M0 – which measures the cash we all carry around with us – ended January up by 4.1 per cent compared with a year ago. The Treasury sees M0 as the most important barometer of money supply, and tries to keep it below 4 per cent.

Most economists believe a rise in money supply heralds inflationary pressure. But another measure – M4 which takes account of bank and building society deposits – seemed to be telling a different story.

In December, the latest figure available, it was rising so slowly that it fell below the Treasury's 4-8 per cent target to 3.7 per cent.

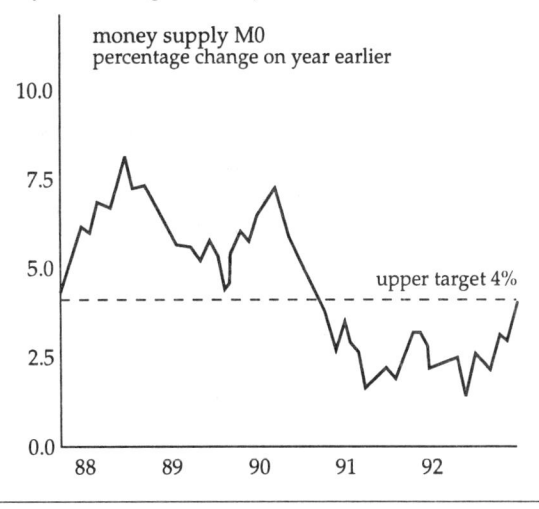

Answer the following, based on the above article.

1. Why is a return of inflation feared?
2. How can the government try to prevent this happening?

## Deflation, reflation and disinflation

103. It is important to understand three other terms in relation to inflation.

- **Deflation** which is a situation where prices are falling because supply exceeds demand. It is characterised by falling output and unemployment and occurs when action is taken which lowers prices and output below the equilibrium level of full employment. This situation existed in the UK between 1920 and 1938 when the general price level fell by almost 50%.
- **Reflation** is a deliberate expansion of the money supply undertaken to stimulate demand and investment in an economy which is under employed.
- **Disinflation** is a milder form of monetary and fiscal action taken to control rising prices.

104.     **Inflation, Deflation, Reflation and Disinflation**

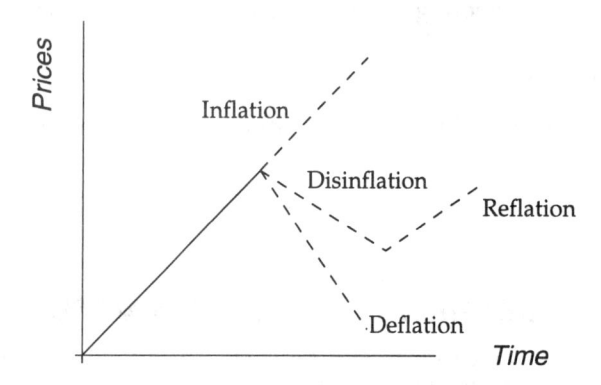

## Summary

105. a) Micro-economics is the study of individual behaviour whilst macro-economics is about the economy as a whole. The government's policies have an influence on both.

b) National income (Net National Product) measures the level of economic activity in the economy.

c) The principles behind the National Income, including injections and withdrawals, can be illustrated in a circular flow of income diagram.

d) Classical economists believed that the economy was self-regulating but this thinking failed completely in the 1930's depression.

e) Keynes argued that unemployment was caused by reduced aggregate demand which governments could boost via fiscal policies and the multiplier.

f) The size of the multiplier depends upon the proportion of any extra income which is spent on consumption.

g) If aggregate demand exceeds output at the full employment level of national income, we have an inflationary gap. If national income is below the full employment level we get a deflationary gap.

h) The main aims of macro-economic policy are economic growth, full employment, low inflation and balance of payments stability.

i) To achieve these aims, the government uses fiscal policy (taxation and public expenditure) and monetary policy (interest rates and credit controls).

j) Taxes can be direct on individuals and organisations, such as income tax and corporation tax, or indirect on the expenditure of goods and services, for example VAT and Customs and Excise duties.

k) The Budget is a statement of how the Chancellor of the Exchequer intends to raise revenue to pay for the Government's planned public expenditure.

l) The main items of expenditure are on Social Security, Health, Defence, Education and National Debt interest.

m) Economic growth is important for raising the standard of living.

n) Unemployment can be frictional, cyclical, structural, regional, real wage, seasonal, technological and residual.

o) It has important economic, social and political effects and therefore the government may use fiscal, monetary or direct measures to control it.

p) An increase in the general level of prices is called inflation and it has important effects on both individuals and businesses.

q) Inflation can be demand-pull, cost-push or multicausal.

r) Policies to control inflation can include monetary and fiscal policies, or direct measures such as a prices and incomes policy.

**Review questions** *(Answers can be found in the paragraphs indicated)*

1. Why do governments intervene in the running of the economy? (3-4)
2. How is the national income measured? (5-12)
3. Explain the circular flow of income and injections to and withdrawals from it. (16-22)
4. How did the thinking of Keynes differ from that of the classical economists? (23-26)
5. Using an example, explain the concept of the multiplier. (27-31)
6. What is the difference between an inflationary and a deflationary gap? (32-37)
7. List the main aims of government economic policy. (38,40)
8. Using examples of each, distinguish between direct and indirect taxes. (43-45)
9. In what ways are business organisations affected by taxation? (47)
10. What are the main functions of the Budget? (48)
11. Briefly explain what is meant by Public Expenditure? (52-54)
12. Describe the main measures of monetary policy. (56-64)
13. Why is economic growth important? (68-71)
14. What is unemployment and why might it be underestimated? (74-75)
15. Describe the main causes of unemployment. (76-79)
16. Distinguish between the economic, social and political effects of unemployment. (80-82)
17. How can unemployment be reduced? (84-86)
18. What is the difference between creeping and hyper-inflation? (87-89)
19. Describe the main effects of inflation on individuals and businesses. (90-93)
20. Outline the main causes of inflation and the policies to control it. (94-102)

*Asterisks indicate those questions for which there are answers in Outline Answers (page 439)*

**Essay-style questions**

1.* In recent years, the state of the British economy has been described as one of recession. Explain what this means and the social and economic factors associated with it.

2. Discuss any major national or international problem of the present time, stating what the problem is, how it arose and possible courses of action in regard to it.

3. Public Spending can be said to fall into three broad categories, those of direct expenditure on social services, transfers of income and investment to increase the production capacity of industry. Discuss the importance of each type of expenditure and the implications for economic growth.

## 5. Business and the economy

## Short answer

1.* a) Distinguish between 'injections' and 'withdrawals' in the national income accounts.
   b) Explain how a permanent change in any of these affects the equilibrium level of income in an economy.

2.* a) What is a 'progressive' tax?
   b) To what extent may each of the following taxes be described as 'progressive'?
      i) Personal income tax
      ii) Value Added Tax
      iii) Council Tax
   c) Discuss the view that 'everyone should receive exactly the same income'.

3. a) Explain what is meant by public expenditure.
   b) In what respects can public spending boost consumer demand?

## Multiple choice/completion

1.* The proportion of any extra increase in income which is spent on consumer goods and services is called the
   a) multiplier
   b) marginal propensity to save
   c) marginal propensity to consume
   d) average propensity to consume

2.* What is the value of the multiplier in an economy where the marginal propensity to consume is 2/5, marginal propensity to import is 1/10 and the level of taxation is 25p in the £.
   a) 2½
   b) 1
   c) 1⅔
   d) 2

3.* Gross domestic product at factor cost plus net property income from abroad minus capital consumption will give:
   a) Net national product at market price
   b) Net national product at factor cost
   c) Gross domestic product at market price
   d) Gross national product at factor cost

4.* The unemployment of car workers resulting from the introduction of new technology may be classed as:
   a) cyclical
   b) frictional
   c) seasonal
   d) structural

5. Which one of the following statements correctly explains an inflationary gap?
   a) Where aggregate demand is insufficient to maintain full employment.
   b) Where supply is in excess of demand.
   c) Where aggregate demand is higher than needed to maintain full employment.
   d) Where aggregate demand is just sufficient to absorb current output.

6. Which of the following measures designed to stimulate the economy is **not** a fiscal measure?
   a) Reduction in VAT
   b) Budget deficit
   c) Less credit control
   d) Lower Corporation tax

*In each of the following questions, one or more of the responses is/are correct. Choose the appropriate letter which indicates the correct version.*

    A   if 1 only is correct
    B   if 3 only is correct
    C   if 1 and 2 only are correct
    D   if 1, 2 and 3 are correct

7. The following are all potential causes of inflation. Which one(s) are possible cause(s) of cost-push inflation?

   1. increased prices of imported raw materials
   2. a budget surplus
   3. an expansion of bank credit

8. A country's economic growth is dependent upon a number of factors including which of the following?

   1. Level of investment
   2. Technological progress
   3. Skills of the workforce

## Assignment

The following data is based upon the Financial Statement and Treasury forecasts in the Budget Report 1993-4.

### SHORT-TERM ECONOMIC PROSPECTS

| % changes on previous year unless otherwise stated | 1992 | 1993 | 1994 (H1) | Av'ge errors in past f/cast[1] |
|---|---|---|---|---|
| **GDP and domestic demand at constant prices** | | | | |
| Domestic demand of which: | 1/2 | 1¼ | 3 | 1¼ |
|   Consumers' expenditure[2] | 1/4 | 1¼ | 1¾ | 1¼ |
|   General govnmnt consumption[2] | –1/4 | 1/4 | 1¼ | 1¼ |
|   Fixed investment | –3/4 | 1/2 | 2¾ | 2¾ |
|   Change in stock-building[3] | 1/2 | 1/4 | 1¼ | 1/4 |
| Exports of goods and services | 2 | 5½ | 10¼ | 1¼ |
| Imports of goods and services | 5¼ | 4¾ | 9¼ | 2 |
| GDP (average measure) | –1/2 | 1¼ | 3 | 1 |
|   Non-North Sea GDP | –1/2 | 1 | 2¼ | 1 |
|   Manufacturing output | –3/4 | 1½ | 2¾ | 1 |
| **Balance of Payments** | | | | |
| £ billion | –12 | –17½ | [4] –18½ | 4¾ |
| percent of GDP | –2 | –2¾ | –2¾ | 3/4 |
| **Inflation** | | | | |
| Retail prices index (Q4) | 3¾ | 3¾ | 3¾ | 3/4 |
| Producer output prices (Q4)[6] | 2¼ | 4 | [5] 3¼ | 3/4 |
| GDP deflator at mkt prices (fncl yr) | 3¼ | 2¾ | - | 1 |
| **Money GDP at mkt prices (fncl yr)** | | | | |
| £ billion | 599 | 628 | - | - |
| percentage change | 3¼ | 4¾ | - | 1½ |
| **PSBR (financial year)** | | | | |
| £ billion | 35 | 50 | - | 6½ |
| per cent of GDP | 5¾ | 8 | - | 1 |

[1] Average errors regardless of sign over past 10 years (apply to forecasts for 1993 or 1993-4. [2] Expenditure adjustment. [3] Percent of GDP. [4] At annual rate. [5] Q2. [6] Excluding food, drink and tobacco.

## MEDIUM-TERM TARGETS

### PUBLIC SECTOR BORROWING

| £ billion[1] | '91-2 | '92-3 | '93-4 | '94-5 | '95-6 | '96-7 | '97-8 |
|---|---|---|---|---|---|---|---|
| General govmt expenditure | 236.1 | 260 | 280 | 296 | 314 | 329 | 342 |
| Genl govmt receipts | 222.2 | 224 | 229 | 251 | 275 | 293 | 311 |
| **GGBR** | **14.0** | **36** | **51** | **45** | **40** | **36** | **31** |
| Public corporations market and overseas borrowing | −0.2 | −1 | −1 | −1 | −1 | −1 | −1 |
| **PSBR** | **13.8** | **35** | **50** | **44** | **39** | **35** | **30** |
| Money GDP | 580.4 | 599 | 628 | 671 | 716 | 756 | 792 |
| **PSBR as % of money GDP** | **2.4** | **5¾** | **8** | **6½** | **5½** | **4½** | **3¾** |

Rounded to the nearest £1 billion from 1992-3 onwards

### OUTPUT AND INFLATION

|  | 1992-3 | 1993-4 | 1994-5 | 1995-6 | 1996-7 | 1997-8 |
|---|---|---|---|---|---|---|
| General govmt expenditure | 236.1 | 260 | 280 | 296 | 314 | 329 | 342 |
| Genl govmt receipts | 222.2 | 224 | 229 | 251 | 275 | 293 | 311 |
| **GGBR** | **14.0** | **36** | **51** | **45** | **40** | **36** | **31** |
| Public corporations market and overseas borrowing | −0.2 | −1 | −1 | −1 | −1 | −1 | −1 |
| **PSBR** | **13.8** | **35** | **50** | **44** | **39** | **35** | **30** |
| Money GDP | 580.4 | 599 | 628 | 671 | 716 | 756 | 792 |
| **PSBR as % of money GDP** | **2.4** | **5¾** | **8** | **6½** | **5½** | **4½** | **3¾** |

Rounded to the nearest £1 billion from 1992-3 onwards

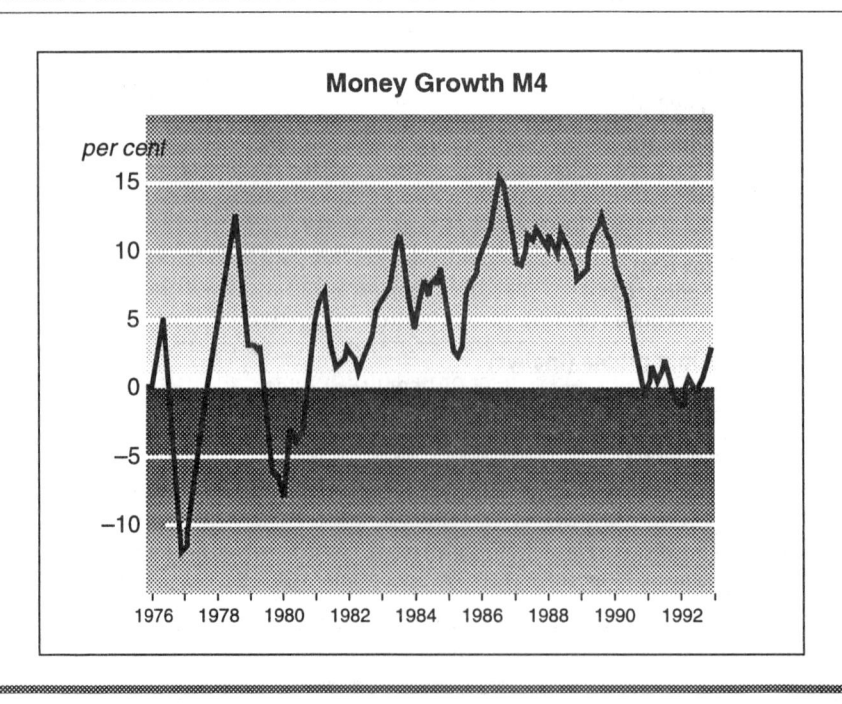

**Money Growth M4**

## 5. Business and the economy

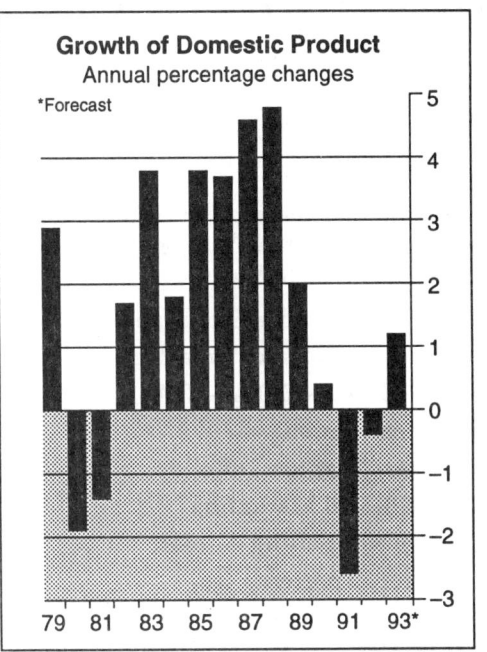

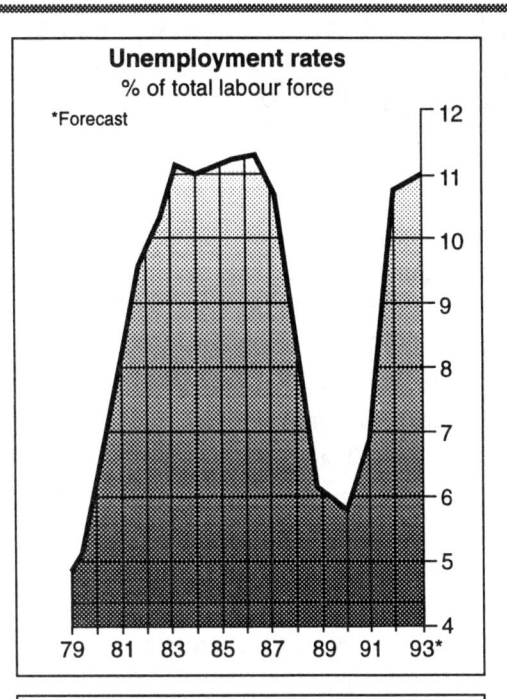

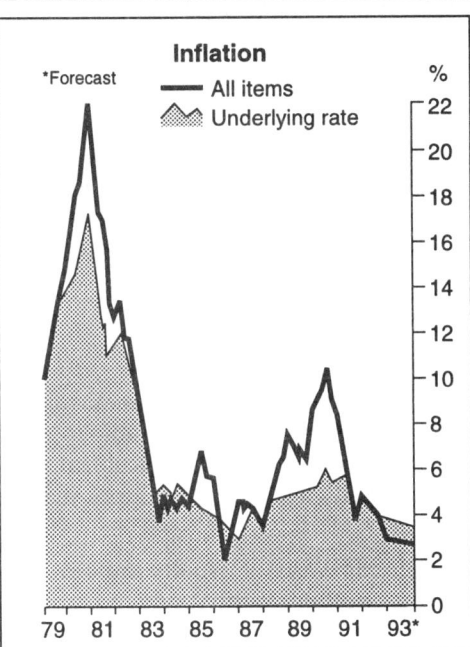

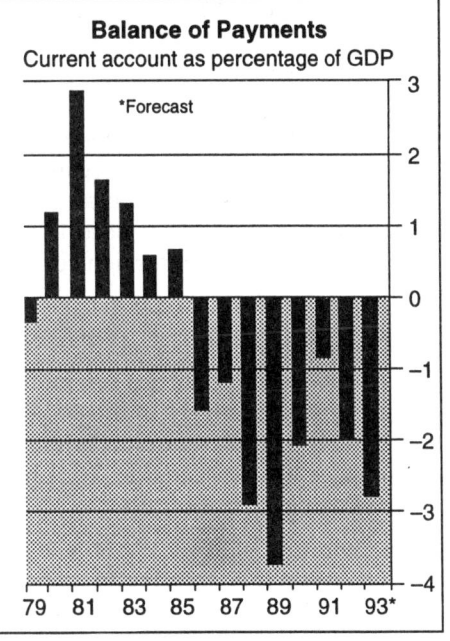

**Growth of Domestic Product**
Annual percentage changes
*Forecast

**Unemployment rates**
% of total labour force
*Forecast

**Inflation**
*Forecast
— All items
▲ Underlying rate

**Balance of Payments**
Current account as percentage of GDP
*Forecast

The Government's Medium Term Financial Strategy (MTFS) sets out its plans for achieving economic growth. This was based on low inflation within 1–4 %, interest rates dependent upon exchange rate movements and the growth of money supply confined within a monitoring range of 3–9% for M4 and a reducing PSBR. The Government believes there is no immediate prospect of unemployment falling below three million.

1. Update this information with the latest data available and identify any major changes or trends.
2. Using all the available information, devise a Budget which you think would be appropriate to our economy at the present time. List your proposals, give reasons for your decisions and outline the likely effects on the economy as a whole, in both the short and longer term.
3. Consider the likely impact of your Budget on the local economy. Use examples to illustrate the points which you make.

# 6. Business and the International Economy

In Chapter 1 we discussed the development of specialisation and the growth of trade to exchange the surplus which this provided. This chapter considers the importance of international or foreign trade both to the country as a whole and to the firms which undertake it, and includes:

- Reasons for Trade
- Absolute Advantage
- Comparative Advantage
- Benefits from Trade
- Imports and Exports
- Balance of Payments
- Barriers to Trade
- Reasons for Protection
- Tackling Balance of Payments Problems
- Rate of Exchange
- Fixed and Floating Exchange Rates
- Movement Towards Free-Trade
- IMF – GATT – EFTA – EEA
- European Union
- Overseas Markets
- International Marketing
- Methods of Selling Abroad
- Help for Exporters
- Bills of Exchange
- Multi-National Companies

## Reasons for Trade

1. All the countries of the world are dependent upon each other to a certain extent. Very few can hope to produce everything they need because every country has a different climate, physical and geographical conditions (rivers, mountains, soil etc) and resources (raw materials, machinery, labour and capital). Therefore countries need to trade with each other which explains why many goods we buy today have been made in foreign countries.

## Absolute and Comparative Advantage

2. All trade arises because countries can gain some benefit from it. It is clearly beneficial when a country has an **absolute advantage** in the production of a commodity. That is, it is able to produce something which other countries cannot. Britain, for example, cannot produce tropical fruits like bananas. Likewise, Jamaica has few facilities for producing motor vehicles and agricultural machinery. Thus both countries can gain from trade.

3. But, even if a country is physically able to produce the goods which it usually imports, it is nevertheless worthwhile for that country to import them from another country which can produce them more cheaply. Britain, for example, could grow bananas in greenhouses instead of importing them from Jamaica where they grow abundantly and cheaply. However, the cost of such production would be enormous because Britain's climate is unsuitable and therefore expensive artificial growing conditions would have to be used.

4. It is therefore better for Britain to concentrate on producing those goods which she can produce at relatively low cost such as chemicals, motor vehicles and agricultural machinery and use its surplus to pay for imported bananas and other fruits from Jamaica.

5. In this way, fewer economic resources are used because each country can concentrate on producing those goods in which it is relatively most efficient. More goods can be made at less cost enabling both countries to gain from trade. This basic reason for international trade is known as the **principal of comparative advantage**. Even if a country has an absolute advantage in all goods, the theory shows that if countries specialise according to comparative advantage then an increase in total production can be achieved.

## Task 6.1

Assuming that resources are mobile and no barriers to trade exist, consider the following situations:

1.

|  | Paper (tons) |  | Chemicals |
|---|---|---|---|
| Country A | 180 | or | 140 |
| Country B | 120 | or | 100 |

With X units of resources the production possible in two countries, A and B of products, paper and chemicals is as shown in the table above.

a) In which product does country a have an absolute advantage?
b) In which product does country B have an absolute disadvantage?
c) In which product does country a have a comparative advantage?

2.

|  | Machines |  | Cars |
|---|---|---|---|
| Country C | 200 | and | 120 |
| Country D | 150 | and | 180 |

Two countries, C and D make machines and cars. If each uses two units of resources evenly between both products, production is as shown in the table.

a) According to the theory of comparative advantage, which country should specialise in the production of machines and which in cars?
b) What will be the increase in total production of machines and cars if specialisation does take place?

## Benefits from Trade

These include:

6. • **Higher standard of living.** International trade is very important to a country because it enables it to have a higher standard of living. Trade widens the choice of goods in the shops because countries can buy foods, raw materials and finished goods which they cannot produce themselves.

   • **Economies of Scale.** Also, each country can concentrate on producing those goods which it can grow or make most easily and therefore this often means that they are cheaper due to economies of scale.

   • **International co-operation.** Trade also helps to develop International understanding and closer political and economic ties. The European Union, for example, was a logical development from the trading links which already existed in Europe.

## Imports and Exports

7. The goods and services bought from abroad are called **imports** and those sold abroad **exports**. As shown in the following diagram the UK's main imports are food, raw materials and manufactured goods. The main exports are manufactured goods including machinery, vehicles and chemicals.

## 6. Business and the international economy

**8. UK imports and exports 1992**

|  | Exports (fob) £m | per cent | Imports (cif) £m | per cent |
|---|---:|---:|---:|---:|
| **Non-manufactures** | 17,561 | 16.2 | 25,503 | 20.3 |
| Food, beverages and tobacco | 8,713 | 8.0 | 13,426 | 10.7 |
| Basic materials | 1,965 | 1.8 | 5,092 | 4.0 |
| Fuels | 6,881 | 6.4 | 6,985 | 5.5 |
| **Manufactures** | 88,672 | 81.9 | 98,729 | 78.4 |
| Semi-manufactures | 30,484 | 28.1 | 32,339 | 25.7 |
| *of which:* chemicals | 14,996 | 13.8 | 11,615 | 9.2 |
| textiles | 2,456 | 2.3 | 3,944 | 3.1 |
| iron and steel | 3,007 | 2.8 | 2,524 | 2.0 |
| non-ferrous metals | 1,753 | 1.6 | 2,591 | 2.1 |
| metal manufactures | 2,211 | 2.0 | 2,571 | 2.0 |
| other | 6,061 | 5.6 | 9,095 | 7.2 |
| Finished manufactures | 58,188 | 53.7 | 66,389 | 52.7 |
| *of which:* machinery | 30,690 | 28.3 | 31,801 | 25.3 |
| road vehicles | 8,895 | 8.2 | 12,121 | 9.6 |
| clothing and footwear | 2,427 | 2.2 | 5,633 | 4.5 |
| scientific instruments & photographic apparatus | 4,455 | 4.1 | 4,255 | 3.4 |
| other | 11,721 | 10.8 | 12,579 | 10.0 |
| Miscellaneous | 2,065 | 1.9 | 1,661 | 1.3 |
| **TOTAL** | 108,298 | 100.0 | 125,896 | 100.0 |

SOURCE: *Monthly Review of External Trade Statistics*
Table is on an overseas trade basis.
cif = cost, insurance and freight, that is, including shipping, insurance and other expenses incurred in the delivery of goods as far as their place of importation in Britain.

Differences between totals and the sums of other components are due to rounding. See Monthly Digest of Statistics for most recent figures

### Balance of Payments

9. A nation must keep an account of its financial dealings with the rest of the world. This is called the **Balance of Payments.** It is a record of all the money which flows into or out of a country and it is rather like a bank account. If the account does not balance then the government may need to borrow money, repay loans or use its gold and foreign currency reserves to solve the problem.

10. The Balance of Payments which is published monthly is made up from three accounts.

    - The **Balance of Trade** or **visible balance.** This is the difference in the value of all the actual goods which are imported and exported.

    - The **Balance on Current Account**. This includes the visible balance and also the invisible items of trade, that is services such as transport, banking, tourism and insurance which are not physically taken in and out of the country.

    - The **Transactions in External Assets and Liabilities.** This lists all the lending to, borrowing from, and investment between countries, trade credit and any other capital flows.

11. A **balancing item** is also shown which includes any errors and omissions which occur in compiling the accounts.

12. Adding together the totals on the Current Account and External Assets and Liabilities Account plus the balancing item, gives the **balance for official financing.**

13. **Britain's balance of payments 1988-1992**

|  | £m 1988 | £m 1989 | £m 1990 | £m 1991 | £m 1992 |
|---|---|---|---|---|---|
| Current account |  |  |  |  |  |
| Visible trade balance | −21,480 | −24,683 | −18,809 | −10,284 | −13,406 |
| Invisible transactions balance | 4,863 | 2,171 | 541 | 2,632 | 4,786 |
| Current balance | −16,617 | −22,512 | −18,268 | −7,652 | −8,620 |
| Financial account |  |  |  |  |  |
| Transactions in assets and liabilities |  |  |  |  |  |
| British external assets | −58,458 | −90,089 | −82,187 | −18,925 | −84,976 |
| British external liabilities | 68,812 | 109,503 | 93,148 | 24,652 | 93,295 |
| Balancing item | 6,265 | 3,097 | 7,308 | 924 | 301 |

*Source: United Kingdom Balance of Payments 1993 Edition.*

Differences between totals and the sums of their component parts are due to rounding. See Monthly Digest of Statistics for most recent figures.

14. The ideal situation for any country is to pay for its imports by the value of goods and services which it sells abroad. Traditionally, Britain has for many years had great difficulty in doing this and usually has a deficit on its Balance of Trade. However, this has always been reduced by a surplus on invisible trade but still, in recent times, leaving a deficit on the Current Account. This can be seen in the figures above.

### Task 6.2

The following article is based on newspaper reports

#### TRADE BALANCE DIVES INTO RED

According to Department of Trade and Industry figures, in May Britain had its second worst Current Account deficit on record at £561 million. This was despite a £600 million net contribution from invisibles like banking, insurance and tourism. The visible trade gap doubled between April and May as the bill for imports leapt by £375 million to £7,450 million while export earnings fell £282 million to £6,290 million.

Demand for foreign goods rose by seven per cent across the board, with purchases of capital equipment and intermediate goods rising as fast as imports of consumer goods.

However, since the country is now growing faster than almost any other major economy in the world, it is hardly surprising that we are buying more from others than they are prepared to buy from us.

The set-back for exports reflects sluggish world demand but may also have something to do with the 5% rise in the price of sterling since the beginning of the year. Even so, exports are still running at levels 6.5% higher than a year ago.

The following are based on the information in the article.

1. How much was the deficit on the Current Account and how is it calculated?
2. What was the net contribution from invisible trade?
3. Calculate the size of the visible trade deficit in May.
4. Give 3 examples of invisible items.
5. Explain why 'invisibles' are vital to Britain's trade.
6. Explain fully and in your own words why Britain is importing more than she is exporting.

*6. Business and the international economy*

## Barriers to Trade

15. Despite the benefits which trade brings, a country may still decide to restrict it by imposing protective measures such as:
    - **Tariffs** (or customs duties) which are put on imported goods in order to make them more expensive.
    - **Quotas** which are physical restrictions on the amount of particular goods which can be imported into a country.

16. Tariffs and quotas are usually placed on imported goods which are already produced in the UK. This protects the home market and encourages us to 'Buy British'. They may also be placed on goods that we cannot produce ourselves but wish to restrict for one reason or another. (see paragraph 18).

17. Other methods of protection which a country might use include:
    - **Embargoes** – this is the complete banning of trade between one country and another.
    - **Subsidies** – a government may provide finance to enable home goods to be sold at a lower price and thus reduce the demand for imports.
    - **Exchange controls** – a country may decide to restrict the supply of foreign currency thus reducing the volume of imports which can be purchased.

## Reasons for Protection

18. There are five main reasons why a country may decide to impose barriers to trade:
    - **To reduce unemployment** – imported goods might result in job losses in some industries.
    - **To prevent dumping** – this takes place when surplus foreign goods are sold abroad at a lower price than in the home market. This creates unfair competition.
    - **To provide for self sufficiency** – a country might wish to protect industries in case of war.
    - **To protect 'Infant' industries** – young industries may need protection from foreign competition to enable them to develop and grow.
    - **To correct Balance of Payment problems** – a country may want to reduce imports in order to correct a trade deficit.

---

### Task 6.3

#### EXPORT TONIC

Sales of British medicines abroad earned a record £1.2 billion in 1992 – almost £14,000 for every worker in the drugs industry.

Figures from the Association of the British Pharmaceutical Industry reveal that output rose by 6.8 per cent – a marked contrast to a fall in UK manufacturing as a whole Nationally the industry employed over 87,000 people up by 23 per cent since 1970 One in five is a scientist or technician involved in research and development. A record £1.2 billion was invested in such work last year. An ABPI spokesman says: 'A lot of the success of the industry is in its international competitiveness. The foundations are laid in the amount of money companies are prepared to invest in research and development. That means we are able to compete with the Japanese the Americans and Europeans.'

#### CHINA CONTRACT

GEC Alsthom is close to winning a £290m contract to fit out the Shajiao C power station in southern China. A letter of intent with the project managers has already been signed, and detailed negotiations on the contract terms are in progress. If GEC is successful, it could mark the start of several weeks of big orders for UK companies.

*continued...*

> **Task 6.3** continued
>
> ### AIRBUS ORDER
>
> The four-nation Airbus consortium of which Britain is a member, has won a £300 million order for six ultra-long range A340-200 passenger jets. Up to 300 UK companies will gain some £60 million from the contract with Philippine Airlines, announced at the Farnborough Air Show.
>
> ### JOBS WASTELAND
>
> An MP claims that so many manufacturing jobs have been lost that Britain can no longer produce the goods its population needs. Lawrence Cunliffe says his Leigh constituency has seen thousands of jobs go in recent years in the mining, textile and engineering sectors. 'Even in the depth of the recession we are still running an enormous trade deficit because imported goods are taking the place of home-made products in our shops, at a terrible price for employment'. The collapsing pound may make these imports dearer, but the damage has already been done. Mills, heavy engineering factories and collieries cannot be reopened quickly – industrial vandalism takes decades to repair.' Over the last 13 years, 2.4m manufacturing jobs have been lost throughout the country, leaving just 4.6m he said. 'All over, local factories which used to be landmarks are lying derelict and skilled workers are thrown on the scrapheap at an early age.'
>
> ### TOURIST ATTRACTIONS
>
> A recent study shows that the Japanese see in us a combination of solemnity, propriety and long traditions, which they feel builds a character similar to their own. Their admiration has seen the number of big-spending UK visitors from Japan climb from 132,000 in 1978 to some 600,000 in 1992 – spending £300 million.
>
> From the above news extracts:
>
> 1. Identify examples of visible and invisible exports.
> 2. What arguments are there to support the idea of free trade?
> 3. Are there any arguments in favour of protection?
> 4. Comment on any key factors which are or may be considered important for the development of trade.

## Tackling Balance of Payments Problems

19. If a Balance of Payments deficit persists then, in addition to the measures of protection already mentioned the government can also consider:

    - **Measures to stimulate exports.** The ongoing help for exporters is outlined in paragraph 70 but the government could also choose to introduce specific measures to assist exporters such as tax relief or encouraging banks to provide cheap loans.

    - **Deflation of the economy.** A government may choose to increase interest rates, increase taxation, reduce public expenditure or introduce a credit squeeze in order to reduce demand in the economy and consequently the level of imports. This could work but may result in unemployment due to falling demand.

    - **Devaluation of the pound.** Another measure is to allow the value of the pound to depreciate in value against other currencies thereby making exports cheaper and imports dearer. This can work but could also lead to domestic inflation.

## Rate of Exchange

20. Since the Balance of Payments is a record of the **total currency flow** into or out of a country a further term which must be understood is the rate of exchange. This expresses the value of the pound in terms of other currencies used by the countries with which we trade. For example £1 = 197 (Spanish) pesetas or £1 = 1.48 (American) dollars. If you have had a holiday abroad you will have bought foreign currency yourself to spend whilst away. Similarly, businessmen must also buy foreign currency to pay for imports or investments, whilst at the same time, customers abroad buy pounds to pay for the goods and services which we export to them.

21. Thus we have both a demand for foreign currency and a supply of it. At the equilibrium exchange rate the two will balance out. The equilibrium is linked to the Balance of Payments because in a deficit situation, less domestic currency is required causing it to depreciate.

22.

**The Dollar/Pound Exchange Rate**

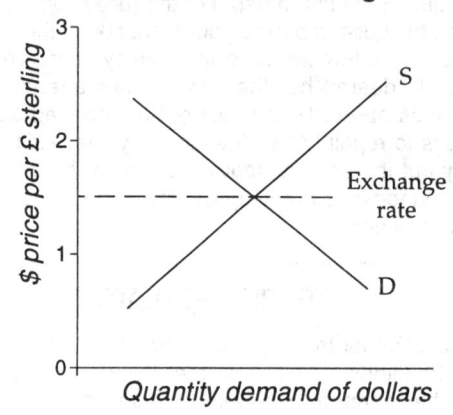

23. In the above graph, for example, the demand curve (D) for £'s is downward-sloping, which means that if the £ falls in value, British goods and services will become cheaper for Americans to buy. This will produce an increase in demand for them and therefore also more £'s.

24. The supply curve (S) of £'s is upward-sloping, which means that as the dollar price of the £ rises, USA goods and services become cheaper in Britain, causing an increase in demand for them. Hence the supply of £'s offered also increases to pay for them. The equilibrium rate of exchange between the two currencies is determined by the interaction of demand and supply, in this case, £1=$1.50.

## Fixed and Floating Exchange Rates

25. How the price will respond to this trading pressure will depend on whether the exchange rate is floating or fixed.

26. Under a **floating exchange rate** the exchange rate is allowed to vary until supply and demand is in equilibrium. In a completely free market, this is called '**clean floating**'.

27. Under a **fixed exchange rate,** the government will intervene in currency markets to keep the price fixed by buying or selling its foreign exchange reserves or by borrowing abroad.

28. In order to help promote trade after the Second World War under the **Bretton Woods** agreement, countries agreed to fix their exchange rates to the US dollar. The pound, for example, was fixed at £1 = $2.80. This system was supervised by the IMF but abandoned in 1973 since when most of the world's currencies have been floating. But this has led to a system called '**dirty floating**' whereby governments still intervene to try and stabilise the system by buying and selling currency.

## Importance of the Rate of Exchange

29. Movements in exchange rates can have important effects on business profitability for a number of reasons:
    - They can affect the costs of imported raw materials making it difficult to forecast costs of production.

- They can also influence the selling price of imported goods and services.
- Profit margins on exports can increase or decrease substantially if the value of currencies change between the contract and delivery date.
- If exports are priced in foreign currencies, sales could be lost if the relative values change.
- They can increase the risk of investing in overseas assets, such as foreign government bonds, shares in foreign companies or buildings and land, because future returns are subject to exchange rate fluctuations.

> **Task 6.4**
>
> Munir Shortt Ltd, a Manchester based import/export company has asked you to advise it on contracts which it has negotiated with 2 of its main overseas customers.
>
> The first contract signed in June was for the export of £20,000 worth of china tea sets to the USA. The buyer agreed to pay $30,000 at the time when the exchange rate was £1 = $1.50. The order was duly delivered and paid for in October as agreed. At this time the exchange rate was £1=$1.42
>
> The second contract, signed in July, involved the import of 10,000 electronic games from Japan at a price of £10 each payable in yen. In July the exchange rate was £1=200yen. Delivery took place in November, and payment in December at which time the exchange rate was £1=190yen.
>
> You have been asked to:
>
> 1. explain in each situation how the firm was affected, if at all, by the change in the exchange rates.
> 2. outline the potential advantages and disadvantages to the company of negotiating its contract in sterling or in a foreign currency.
> 3. Using information from the Financial Times or other quality newspapers, plot the value of the dollar and yen against the pound over a 3-6 month period and comment on the relative values including reasons for any significant fluctuations and whether or not this information is useful to the company.

## Movement Towards Free Trade

30. Despite these many barriers recognition of the economic importance of **Free Trade** has been clearly illustrated since the end of the second World War. Nations throughout the world have been involved in negotiations in an attempt to reduce trade barriers and make trade easier. The result of these negotiations is shown by the International Monetary Fund (IMF) 1944, the General Agreement on Tariffs and Trade (GATT) 1948, the formation of the European Free Trade Area (EFTA) in 1959, the European Economic Community in 1957 (now called the European Union but still sometimes referred to as the European Community or EC), and the European Economic Area (EEA) in 1993 (see Task 5.7).

31. **IMF**. Most of the countries of the Western World are members of this organisation. Each member pays a contribution to the Fund (25% in gold and 75% in its own currency). The main aim is to encourage trade by using the Fund to provide short-term loans to members with a Balance of Payments deficit. It also wants to see stable (fixed) exchange rates.

32. **GATT** was established with the aim of helping to increase world trade by reducing tariffs and other barriers. It now has nearly 120 members and since 1947 has completed 7 rounds of multi-national trade agreements. The eighth, the Uruguay Round, was launched in 1986, and concluded in 1993.

33. Initially GATT was very successful but since the recession of the early 1970's what is often referred to as the 'new protectionism' has emerged. That is, trade is not restricted by tariffs but by 'hidden' controls such as import licensing, domestic price subsidies and technical specifications all of which create unfair competition. The latest agreement will replace GATT with a tougher policing body, the **World Trade Organisation**.

## 6. Business and the international economy

34. **EFTA** was formed to abolish tariffs on manufactured goods between its members who are Austria, Finland, Iceland, Norway, Sweden and Switzerland. Members are allowed to impose whatever restrictions they choose on non-member countries.

35. **The European Union**

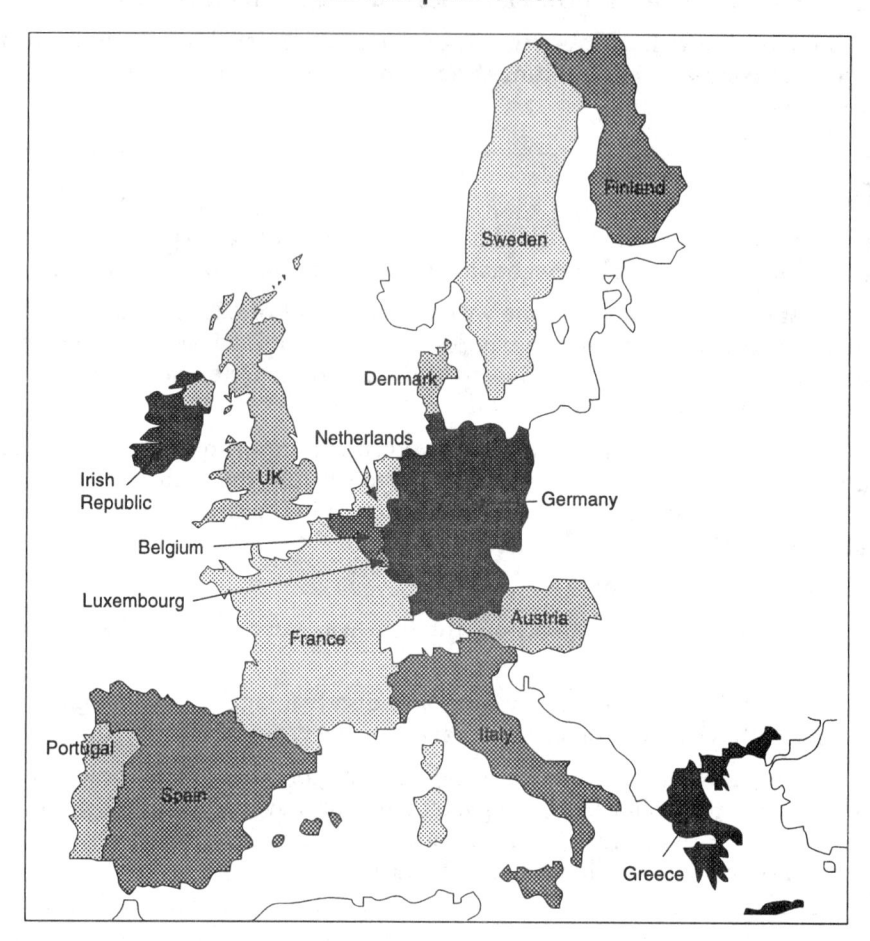

36. **EU.** The EU or Common Market was originally formed by the Treaty of Rome in 1957 by **Belgium, France, Italy, Luxembourg, the Netherlands and West Germany.** The UK, Eire and Denmark joined on 1 January 1973 followed by Greece in 1981, Portugal and Spain in 1986 and Austria, Finland and Sweden are to join in 1995. The Community now has a total population of over 380 million.

37. The EU is a **customs union** in that it has:
    - abolished virtually all tariffs between the member countries and
    - established a common external tariff on all imported goods.

    Britain applies the common customs tariff to all countries which do not belong to, or have any special arrangement with, the EU.

38. In addition to the removal of physical trade barriers the Community also aims to encourage the free movement of services, capital and people. The **Single European Act 1986** set an implementation date for this of 1st January 1993. Ultimately, European political and monetary union is planned with a single currency, a Federal Central Bank and one Central Parliament.

39. **European Monetary System (EMS)**

    The EMS was set up in March 1979 with 3 aims:
    - to stabilise currency fluctuations between EU countries
    - to help keep down interest rates and
    - to control inflation

40. The EMS consists of 4 main elements:

- **European Currency Unit (ECU)**

    The ECU is a hypothetical exchange rate, based on a basket of EU currencies. It is used to value EU transactions, government bonds, travellers cheques and even mortgages.

- **Exchange Rate Mechanism (ERM)**

    The ERM is a system of semi-fixed exchange rates within agreed bands. It limits how far member currencies can fluctuate against the ECU and between each other before intervention is demanded. Initially movements of 2.25% either way were allowed, although sterling and the peseta had a 6% band. In August 1993 the band was widened to 15% either way. If exchange rates look likely to break these guidelines, the 2 countries involved are obliged to buy or sell currency to push it up or down.

- **European Monetary Co-operation Fund (EMCF)**

    The Co-operation Fund is used by EU Central Banks, including the Bank of England, for borrowing to balance their books after intervening in the foreign exchange markets to adjust supply and demand.

- **The Very-Short-Term Finance Facility (VSTF)**

    The VSTF gives ERM members unlimited credit facilities in their own currency. This can be used to finance intervention when currencies reach their ERM margins.

### Task 6.5

#### BLACK WEDNESDAY

On Wednesday 16 September 1992 the pound plunged through its ERM floor level of 2.7780 pfennigs. This despite massive intervention, estimated at over £10bn, by the Bank of England to try to prevent it.

In a sensational day, minimum lending rate was increased by 2% in the morning, its biggest jump for seven years. There were fears about the impact of the higher cost of borrowing on mortgages, expansion, jobs, pay and prices. But this rise did not stop the pound falling even further despite buying by the German Bundesbank to try to support it.

Three hours later, it was announced that the lending rate would be increased again by a further 3% to 15% from Thursday morning. This helped to steady the pound only slightly and as it continued to struggle, there were rumours of a further 5% rise to maintain its value. Share prices plunged initially but recovered later. Sterling closed the day at 2.7528 Dm – more than two pfennigs below its ERM floor. Later that evening Chancellor Norman Lamont announced both the suspension of Britain's membership of the ERM, and that interest rates would remain at 12%.

Thus the pound was allowed to float downwards to find its own level, effectively being devalued on what was regarded as the wildest and most expensive day ever seen on the foreign exchange market.

This made it possible for the Government to reduce interest rates substantially in the following months which was essential in order to try to revitalise the economy.

Answer the following which are based on the above article.

1. Explain the link between interest rates and exchange rates.
2. Why do high interest rates cause concern?
3. Why do share prices react to such situations.
4. Why did the Central Banks intervene in the foreign exchange market?
5. In what sense could membership of the ERM be said to have prevented economic recovery?

## Organisation of the European Union

41. As shown in the following diagram there are 5 main institutions responsible for the functioning of the European Union – the Council of Ministers, the European Commission, the European Parliament, the Court of Justice and the Court of Auditors.

42. **European Decision-Making**

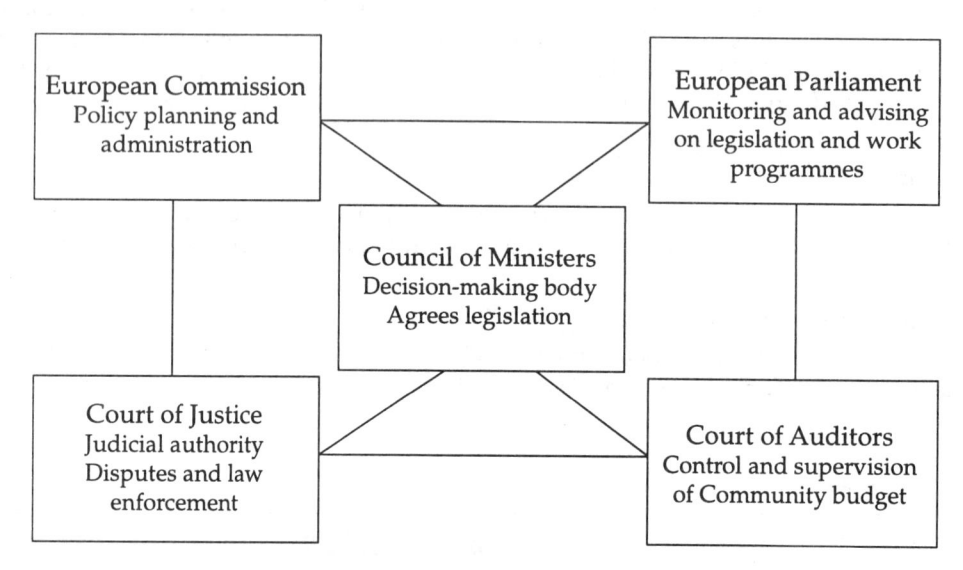

```
┌─────────────────────┐                    ┌─────────────────────┐
│ European Commission │                    │ European Parliament │
│ Policy planning and │                    │ Monitoring and      │
│ administration      │                    │ advising on         │
│                     │                    │ legislation and     │
│                     │                    │ work programmes     │
└─────────────────────┘                    └─────────────────────┘
            \         /                   \          /
             \       /                     \        /
              ┌─────────────────────┐
              │ Council of Ministers│
              │ Decision-making body│
              │ Agrees legislation  │
              └─────────────────────┘
             /       \                     /        \
            /         \                   /          \
┌─────────────────────┐                    ┌─────────────────────┐
│ Court of Justice    │                    │ Court of Auditors   │
│ Judicial authority  │                    │ Control and         │
│ Disputes and law    │                    │ supervision of      │
│ enforcement         │                    │ Community budget    │
└─────────────────────┘                    └─────────────────────┘
```

43. **The Council of Ministers** is the decision-making body with at least one Minister appointed by each member country. Decisions are made on proposals submitted to it by the Commission. On matters of major importance, the Council can only act on a unanimous vote. That is, all countries have a power of 'veto' which they can use to prevent a decision being taken. The Presidency of the Council, which rotates round member states every 6 months, was last held by the UK from July-December 1992.

44. **The European Commission**, based in Brussels, is the Community's planning and day-to-day administrative agency which proposes policies and legislation and executes decisions. It is led by 17 commissioners appointed by member states, to act in the interests of the whole community, each with responsibility for a particular policy area. The Commission is divided into 23 administrative departments called Directorate Generals (DG's). Each DG is in charge of a specific policy area such as energy, agriculture, competition and transport.

45. **The European Parliament** meets once a month usually in Strasbourg (France). Member states elect representatives according to their population. Of the 518 Euro MP's, Britain has 81 (England 66, Scotland 8, Wales 4, Norther Ireland 3). The Parliament debates all major aspects of policy and influences the proposals made by the Commission. It also examines and approves the EU budget.

46. **The European Court of Justice** exists to ensure that EU laws are observed by member states and to deal with any disputes. It is based in Luxembourg. The Court consists of 13 judges whose decisions, which are made by majority vote, are binding on all community institutions, governments, companies and individuals.

47. **The Court of Auditors** based in Luxembourg supervises the operation of the Community budget and is responsible for examining the accounts of all community revenue and expenditure. It helps to counteract waste and fraud.

48. **Other EU Bodies** include:

    - **European Investment Bank (EIB).** Contributions from member states are used to make loans and help finance projects in the less developed areas of the Community or to support projects of common interest to several members such as the Channel Tunnel.

    - **Economic and Social Committee** is an advisory body which must be consulted by the Commission on proposals relating to these matters.

- **European Regional Development Fund.** This is the largest of the EU's structural funds, intended to help redress the principal regional imbalances. Its budget in 1991-2 was £4,686 million, 10 per cent of which was allocated to Britain.
- **European Social Fund.** This provides help for re-training the unemployed.
- **European Agricultural Guidance and Guarantee Fund.** This operates the Common Agricultural Policy (CAP) which determines the price and distribution of food produce.

## EU Budget

49. All members pay a contribution to a common fund to cover the costs of running the EU. The amounts paid by each member vary as does the amount of benefit which each receives.

### Task 6.6

Read the following extract from 'Britain in Europe' published by the Foreign and Commonwealth Office in 1992 and answer the questions which follow.

> The Community's activities have to be financed by contributions from its member countries. In 1992 the Community plans to spend about £50 billion (about 3.5% of total central government expenditure in all EU member states). Some of this money (about £2.5 billion in 1992) is spent on aid to Eastern Europe and the developing world, but most of it is spent within the Community. At present, just over half goes on the Common Agricultral Policy (CAP) and about a quarter on aid to EU regions with particular problems.
>
> All member states receive some money back from the Community budget as well as paying in. But the amount they get back varies. Countries with large farming sectors, or with many poorer regions, tend to receive more money than they pay in. Some countries, including the UK, Germany and France, are net contributors to the budget, paying in more than they receive. When we joined the Community we paid more than our fair share of the budget, but since 1984 we have received an annual rebate in which the Community pays some of our contribution back to us: we will retain this rebate in full in the future. Our net contribution for 1992, after all receipts from the Community, and after we have had our rebate, is expected to be around £1.7 billion. By comparison, the UK defence budget is £24.18 billion and the budget of the Scottish Office is £12.15 billion.

1. What was the planned expenditure in the Community in 1992?
2. Where is most of the budget spent, and which countries benefit most?
3. How much did Britain contribute to the Community in 1992.
4. In what ways, if any, could the extract be said to suggest that the cost of the Community is a good investment for the UK?
5. Update the figures with the latest available and comment on any significant changes.

## Types of EU Legislation

50. Nearly 300 measures have been proposed within the Single European market programme. A basic knowledge of the different types of legislation is therefore useful for a broader understanding of the European business environment.

51. **Directives** are binding instructions to Member States to achieve a specified legislative result by a given deadline. Member States are allowed to determine how best to achieve this, taking into account its own circumstances, existing law, and enforcement methods. Directives can apply to all or only to specified Member States.

52. Three examples of directives follow:

- **The Directive for Minimum Health and Safety Requirements for the Workplace,** which came into effect on 1st January 1993, sets down general health and safety criteria for workplaces and covers specific issues such as emergency exists, fire detection, ventilation and stability of structures (see Chapter 12).
- **The General Product Safety Directive** must be implemented by Member States from June 1994. It aims to ensure that all products (new, used or reconditioned) marketed in the Community are safe for consumers. Manufacturers are made responsible for supplying safe products and ensuring that their products can be traced.
  - **The Language Instruction Directive** implemented from 1st January 1993 requires companies exporting machinery in the Community to ensure that instruction manuals are available in the language of the country where it is to be used.

53. **Regulations** are laws which are directly applicable in **all** Member States, rather like an Act of Parliament. Regulations tend to be technical and used to deal with particular activities in areas such as agriculture and transport. Council Regulation 2137/85 introduced the European Economic Interest Grouping (EEIG) designed to facilitate cross-border collaboration and joint ventures between European Companies.

54. **Decisions** are addressed to particular parties – Member States, companies or individuals on whom they are binding. Many EU Decisions relate to cases of unfair competition.

55. In 1991, for example, the Commission decided that several leading European airlines were charging excessively high fares on European routes. The Decision was notified to the Member States concerned who were required to take steps to ensure a more balanced relationship between air fares and costs. As a consequence of this Decision, flights in Europe should be cheaper from 1993 onwards following agreement between Member States on a new formula for fixing fares on scheduled air routes.

56. **Recommendations and Opinions** merely state the view of the European institution that issues them and urge action for change. However, they are not legally binding.

## Benefits of EU Membership

57. As a result of the end to customs control and the many changes brought about by the UK's membership of the European Union, it is argued that it has and will continue to bring many benefits to us all including:
    - Political stability thus lessening the risk of war.
    - Prosperity from increased trade and investment
    - Wider choice of goods and services.
    - Higher quality food based on European Standards.
    - Less lead pollution.
    - A better protected ozone layer.
    - More opportunities for living and working in Europe, with wider recognition of qualifications.
    - More health benefits when travelling in Europe.
    - More competition leading to lower prices, eg cheaper air fares.
    - More jobs as business opportunities grow.

## Impact of Membership On Business

58. In addition, businesses will benefit from:
    - New market opportunities with all member states.
    - Free movement of goods between member states.
    - Economies of scale from increased output.
    - Access to new sources of finance in European countries.
    - Cheaper raw materials due to competition.
    - Greater efficiency and innovation in response to competition.

59. Against this however, businesses also face some potential disadvantages including:
- Additional costs to implement EU directives such as those for Health & Safety and Product Standards and Labelling.
- Increased competition from EU firms.
- Complex VAT returns for registered businesses trading in the EU where imports/exports exceed £120,000 with penalties for non-compliance.
- Other VAT requirements such as the need to:
    - Quote the customer's VAT number on each invoice.
    - Provide a quarterly return showing the total sales to each registered customer.
    - Be able to give a full description of the goods and their price.

## Task 6.7

### EUROPEAN ECONOMIC AREA (EEA)

January 1st 1993 was not only the date for completion of the single market programme but also that originally proposed for the creation of the European Economic Area (EEA).

The (EEA) is made up of all European Union states and the countries of EFTA (European Free Trade Association: Austria, Finland, Iceland, Norway, Sweden and Switzerland) together with Liechtenstein. Switzerland did not join the EEA following a referendum.

The agreement does not grant automatic EU membership to the countries, although Austria, Finland, Sweden and Switzerland have already applied. Norway is expected to follow. In effect, most Community legislation, including the four freedoms – movement of goods, services, capital and people, now extends to all 18 countries making up the EEA.

The EEA is a market of some 380 million consumers and offers tremendous scope for specialisation, growth and prosperity.

EFTA is the Community's main trading partner, with Community states supplying over 60% of EFTA imports and taking more than 58% of its exports in 1990. Trade between the two groups of countries is concentrated on manufactured goods, which represent 85% of total EFTA imports. The aim of the EEA is to strengthen trade and economic relations between the European Union and EFTA countries.

The EEA opens up the affluent markets of the EFTA states to EU countries and widens the scope of the single European market by promoting trade between the two groups of countries. Britain currently exports goods and services worth about £8 billion to the members of the EFTA but it is estimated that as trade and tariff barriers come down in those countries, Britain's gross domestic product could be boosted by up to two per cent. British fishermen will also be allowed to catch more cod off northern Norway.

The EEA also creates the world's largest trading alliance – bigger than the US and Japan combined. It is estimated that the EU and EFTA together account for 43% of world trade. As part of the deal, the EFTA nations will contribute more than £1 billion to a special fund to help develop the poorer regions of Spain, Portugal and Greece.

The two blocs will also set up a joint ministerial council to provide consultation on new legislation, but without voting rights, and a joint court to settle disputes.

It also reduces the likelihood of the Community turning into an exclusive, bureaucratic, European fortress surrounded by tariffs and barriers erected against competition from the outside world. It also takes it nearer to Britain's goal of an outward-looking, confederal Europe of nations. This deal should also help hasten the inclusion in the free trade zone of the newly-liberated countries of the old Soviet bloc.

> Answer the following questions which are based on the above article.
> 1. Why was the 1st January 1993 an important date?
> 2. Who are the members of the EEA?
> 3. Why is the EEA being formed, and how will it operate?
> 4. What benefits arise from its formation?
> 5. How will Britain in particular benefit from its formation?
> 6. What future trade development could now take place?

## Other Overseas Markets

60. Although EU, EFTA and the EEA represent Britain's major trading partners, there are several other important overseas markets, particularly in terms of their purchasing power and growth potential. Broadly, these can be grouped as Western Industrialised, Third World, New Industrialised, Eastern Bloc and Oil Exporters.

61. **Western Industrial Economies** are the advanced, wealthy nations of Western Europe, North America, Japan and Australia. These countries have sought to promote free trade agreements and trade is now well developed between them.

62. **Third World or Developing Countries** are those whose level of economic development is not yet sufficiently advanced to generate the savings necessary to finance industrialised investment programmes. About 70% of the world's population live in developing countries which include Africa (except the Republic of South Africa), Asia (except Japan) the Soviet Republics and Central and Latin America (except Argentina, the Caribbean and Pacific Islands).

63. The criteria usually used to distinguish developing countries include low levels per head of population of

    - National income
    - Net average per capita income
    - Energy available and literacy
    - They also tend to face problems of over-population, poverty, disease and a heavy dependency on one or a small number of products.
    - They earn foreign currency mainly from primary production (usually agriculture) and have to rely to a large extent on international aid for capital investment and technical knowledge.
    - Consequently, their effective demand for imports is limited.

64. **Oil Exporting Countries** such as the Gulf States of Iraq and Kuwait are extremely wealthy, although it is not usually evenly distributed amongst the population. Hence they tend to provide markets for luxury items and arms rather than general consumer goods.

65. **Newly industrialising countries** are developing countries which have moved away from reliance on primary production and established manufacturing capabilities as part of a long-term programme of industrialisation. Examples include Brazil, Mexico, Hong Kong and Taiwan. They represent a potential opportunity for exporters, although trade barriers often make it difficult. But they can also be a threat often regarded as offering unfair competition because they use low-cost labour to produce relatively inexpensive goods such as textiles, shoes and electrical goods which have lead to declining home industries and heavy unemployment.

66. **Eastern Bloc or Communist Economies** have experienced considerable change in recent years. Communism involves a centrally planned economy where strategic decisions concerning production, distribution and trade are taken by the government as opposed to the price system of a free market economy. True communism still exists in a few countries like Bulgaria and Romania but many former communist states such as China, the former USSR, East Germany, Poland, Hungary and Czechoslovakia are now introducing market economies. These will present new and major opportunities for exporters throughout the 1990's.

## Task 6.8

**Geographical Distribution of Trade 1990**

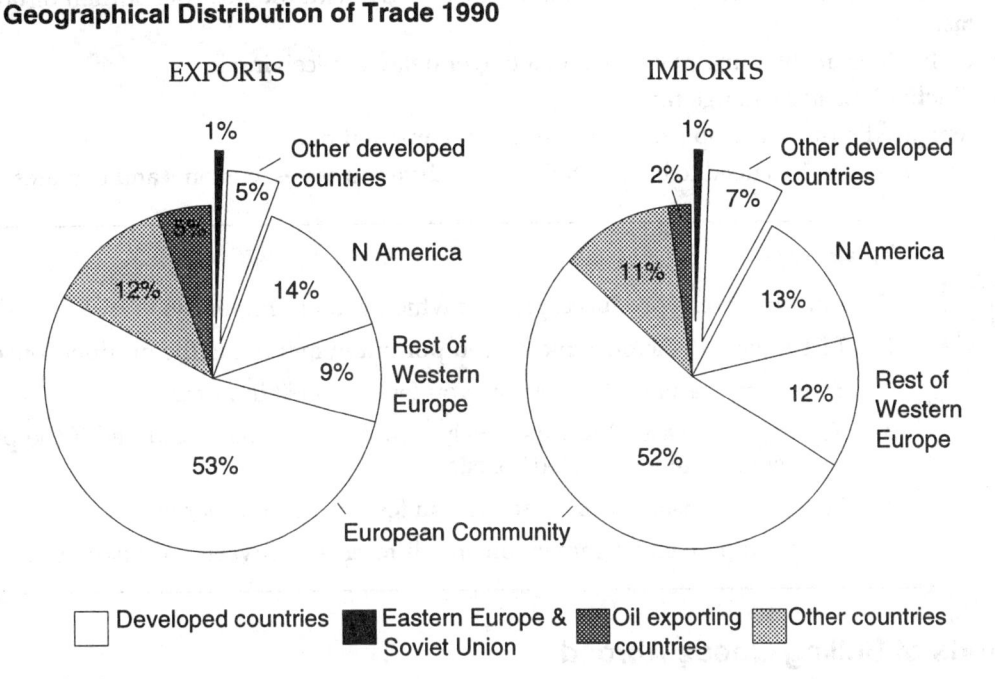

EXPORTS

- 1%
- Other developed countries 5%
- 5%
- 12%
- N America 14%
- 9% Rest of Western Europe
- 53% European Community

IMPORTS

- 1%
- 2%
- Other developed countries 7%
- 11%
- N America 13%
- 12% Rest of Western Europe
- 52%

Legend: ☐ Developed countries  ■ Eastern Europe & Soviet Union  ▓ Oil exporting countries  ▒ Other countries

Consider the above pie charts and the following facts about the geographical distribution of Britain's trade.

- In 1970 trade with developed countries accounted for 73% of exports and a similar proportion of imports.
- In 1970 non-oil developing countries accounted for 17% of exports and 15% of imports.
- In 1972 around 1/3 of trade was with the 11 countries which now make up the European Union.
- In 1990 non-oil developing countries accounted for 13% of exports and 12% of imports.

1. Identify from the above the key trends in Britain's distribution of trade.
2. From your knowledge of and research into overseas markets, comment, with reasons on trends since 1990, and likely future trends.

## International Marketing

67. The world population explosion, plus the movement towards free trade and demand for higher standards of living has lead to increased opportunities for exporters. We have already outlined the benefits arising from foreign trade which for individual companies could also include the following:

    - An opportunity to increase or maintain sales when the domestic market is stagnant or shrinking.
    - The chance to benefit from economies of scale achieved through higher levels of output/sales.
    - Possibility of obtaining government advice and financial backing.
    - Possibility of charging different prices in overseas markets.

68. On the other hand, exporters face a number of problems which increase the risks involved in business. Some of these also exist in home trade but require special attention when sending goods overseas. The difficulty of obtaining market information and political or economic uncertainty abroad can increase these problems, examples of which include:

    - Customer remoteness making good communications important.

- Different languages and cultures.
- Supplying a suitable product, for example with foreign measurements and safety standards.
- Import regulations will be different in every country with the possible burden of tariffs and quotas.
- Difficulties in obtaining payment and a longer delay in receiving it.
- Fluctuations in exchange rates.
- Increased costs of transport, insurance and documentation.
- Products/services need to be adapted to meet different tastes, customs and climates.

> **Task 6.9**
>
> Consider any home produced product which you use regularly.
> 1. List at least 10 factors which are important in marketing the product concerned.
> 2. State with reasons which factors you feel are most important.
> 3. Try to list at least 10 factors which would need to be considered if the product was to be successfully marketed abroad.
> 4. State, with reasons, which factors you feel are most important.
> 5. Now compare and comment on any differences between your two lists.

## Methods of Selling Goods Abroad

69. A firm can sell goods abroad in a number of different ways including:
    - **Direct sales from UK** – this would involve running an export sales department and probably mean sending representatives abroad to meet foreign buyers.
    - **Foreign distributors** sometimes goods can be sold in bulk to foreign buyers who will sell and distribute them in that country.
    - **Overseas agents** – these may be appointed abroad to represent the firm and sell goods on its behalf. They are usually paid a commission on sales for the work which they do.
    - **Export houses** – these are specialist organisations which can assist a firm in three main ways:
        - They act as merchants buying a company's products and selling them overseas on their own account.
        - They act as agents responsible for handling all or part of a firm's overseas sales. For example, promotion, transport, distribution.
        - They act as agents for foreign buyers making contact with UK firms who can supply the goods required.
    - **Overseas Subsidiaries** – instead of exporting, a firm may choose to set up its own factory in a foreign country. (See Multi-national companies, paragraph 78).
    - **Licencing Agreement** – alternatively a firm may decide to allow a foreign producer to manufacture its goods under licence. In return the licencing firm receives a special royalty payment. Coca-Cola is sold world-wide on this basis.

## Help for Exporters

70. In order to reduce the risks associated with exporting and in order to encourage trade, help is supplied by the Department of Trade and Industry, Consular Officials, Chambers of Commerce, the Confederation of British Industry and banks.

## Department of Trade and Industry (DTI)

71. This government department runs the British Overseas Trade Board (BOTB) which aims to promote trade. It offers a wide range of advice and services for exporters. The Head Office is in London and it operates in England through seven regional offices. The Northern Ireland Department of Economic

Development, Welsh Office Industry Department and Industry Department for Scotland all assist exporters in their respective areas.

72. **BOTB Services for Exporters** include:
    - Assessment of overseas markets for potential exporters
    - Help with market research
    - Organisation of and/or support for overseas trade fairs and exhibitions
    - Information on trade restrictions and regulations abroad
    - Issue of export licences where required

## Export Credits Guarantee Department (ECGD)

73. The ECGD is a separate department within the DTI which provides insurance cover for exporters. It will also guarantee loans and overdrafts taken out to finance exports. The main risks insured against are:
    - That the buyer does not pay
    - That a government may take action which prevents payment, for example exchange control
    - That a government may cancel an export licence
    - The possible effects of war
    - Rises in costs and currency fluctuations

## Consular Officials

74. These are UK diplomats appointed by the government who are based in Embassies in most countries throughout the world. They can give advice and assistance to exporters and also help with import documentation.

75. **Other sources of help include:**
    - **Chambers of Commerce** which can often provide information about overseas markets and help with export procedures and documentation.
    - **Confederation of British Industry (CBI)** which provides up-to-date information about export opportunities.
    - **Banks** which provide information and advice, short and long-term loans and special facilities for dealing with payments from abroad including the discounting of Bills of Exchange.

> **Task 6.10**
> Carry out an investigation and then prepare a brief report on the assistance available locally for firms who wish to engage in overseas trade.

## Bills of Exchange

76. Bills of Exchange are widely used for payment in foreign trade. The exporter (seller) makes out the Bill requiring the importer (buyer) to pay a stated sum of money on demand OR at some agreed future date (usually three months). The buyer then signs (to accept) the Bill and returns it to the seller. If the exporter requires money immediately, he can then sell the Bill to a bank. To make a profit, banks buy Bills at a discount, ie less than their face value.

## 6. Business and the international economy

76. **Bill of Exchange**

```
No 490        £2,000              LONDON   20 June 199.
       At 3 months after date pay to my order the sum of
                    TWO THOUSAND pounds.

          Value received Drawn-under-Credit No. T4175
                 against the purchase of goods.

  To:  San Ching                        FOR: FRANK JONES
  41 Colonial Ave, HONG KONG
                                              (Signature)
```

The Bank might discount the above Bill by buying it for £1,800. It will then receive £2,000 when it becomes due for payment on 20 September.

## Multi-National Companies

78. A multi-national company is one which owns and controls business operations outside the country in which it is based. They are in effect holding companies with shares in many individual overseas subsidiaries each of which is subject to the company law of the country in which it is located.

79. Multi-nationals are very large and well known companies many of whom are based in the USA. Examples include: Ford, General Motors, IBM and the world's largest EXXON (Esso). The major European multi-nationals are Philips, Shell, Nestle and Unilever; whilst BP, ICI and Lonrho have their headquarters in the UK. Japanese multi-nationals include Toyota, Mitsubishi, Nissan and Hitachi.

## Importance of Multi-Nationals

80. Multi-national companies are growing very rapidly and represent a significant source of industrial investment in countries throughout the world. Therefore their sheer size and wealth make them extremely important and influential in a number of different ways.

81. These include:

- **Levels of employment**. Multi-nationals are very large employers thus they can have a major impact on an economy when they open or close factories.

- **Political power**. Governments will not want to deliberately offend companies who may choose to withdraw investment and go elsewhere. South Africa, for example, suffered badly after 1986 when Coca-Cola and IBM withdrew from the country. Governments often offer very attractive terms to try to influence a multi-national in its choice of location.

- **Foreign exchange**. The need for large volumes of foreign currency means that multi-nationals are also involved heavily in the exchange rate market.

- **Tariff barriers**. To avoid the impact of trade tariffs or quota controls, multi-nationals set up subsidiaries or give franchises to other companies. Another recent trend has been to set up joint ventures with home producers, as for example with car manufacturers Honda and Rover.

- **Transfer pricing**. Multi-nationals are able to take advantage of the tax systems of the countries in which they operate. This involves deliberately making a small profit in countries with high taxation and transferring the price of inputs so that the greater part of the profit is made in countries with low taxation.

## Summary

82. a) International or foreign trade is the buying and selling of goods and services between different countries throughout the world.

   b) The basic reason for international trade is known as the principle of Comparative Cost or Comparative Advantage.

   c) Specialisation and trade results in a higher standard of living, economies of scale and international co-operation.

   d) Goods and services bought from abroad are called imports and those sold abroad, exports.

   e) The main UK imports are food, raw materials and manufactured goods.

   f) The main exports are manufactured goods including machinery, vehicles and chemicals.

   g) Invisible imports and exports include banking, insurance, tourism, transport, loans and investments and other services.

   h) The Balance of Payments Account consists of:

      i) Visible exports – visible imports = Balance of Trade

      ii) Balance of Trade + invisible balance = Current Balance

      iii) Current Balance + external assets and liabilities + balancing item = Total Currency Flow

      iv) Total Currency Flow = Balance for Official Financing

   i) Protective measures include tariffs, quotas, embargoes, subsidies and exchange control.

   j) A country may restrict trade to prevent unemployment and dumping, remain self-sufficient, to protect 'infant' industries or to solve its Balance of Payments problems.

   k) The rate of exchange which can be floating or fixed, expresses the value of the pound in terms of other currencies.

   l) Free Trade is encouraged by the IMF, GATT, EFTA, EU and more recently the EEA.

   m) The Single Market EU is Britain's largest trading partner and continues through its directives, regulations, decisions and recommendations and opinions to have a major impact on businesses and individuals.

   n) Its main institutions are the Council of Ministers, European Commission, European Parliament, Court of Justice and Court of Auditors.

   o) Other important trading areas are the Western industrialised, Third World, New industrialised, Eastern Bloc and Oil exporters.

   p) Exporters face many additional trading problems including language and market differences, transport and packaging, documentation, insurance, import regulations, obtaining payment and fluctuations in exchange rates.

   q) A firm can sell goods abroad itself or through foreign distributors, agents, export houses, overseas subsidiaries or by licencing agreements.

   r) Exporters can obtain help from the BOTB, ECGD, Consul Officials, Chambers of Commerce, CBI and banks.

   s) Bills of Exchange are widely used for payment in foreign trade.

   t) Multi-national companies have subsidiaries in many countries and are particularly predominant in the oil and car industries.

## Review questions *(Answers can be found in the paragraphs indicated)*

1. Explain the difference between absolute advantage and comparative advantage in International Trade. (2-5)

2. List 3 benefits from trade. (6)

## 6. Business and the international economy

3. Give 4 examples of goods which the UK imports and 4 which it exports. (7-8)
4. What is the Balance of Payments and how is it calculated and financed? (9-14)
5. Briefly explain 4 methods of protection. (15-17)
6. Give 4 reasons why a country might use protection measures. (18-19)
7. What determines the rate of exchange? (20-24)
8. Explain the difference between fixed and floating exchange rates. (25-28)
9. Give brief details of 3 attempts to promote 'free trade' since 1945. (30-34)
10. How is the European Union organised? (35-49)
11. Briefly distinguish between the different types of EU legislation. (50-56)
12. Identify the other main overseas markets. (60-66)
13. What factors are likely to cause problems in International Trade? (68)
14. Name 5 ways in which a firm can sell its goods abroad. (69)
15. What sources of help are available to firms in the export trade? (70-74)
16. What is a Bill of Exchange and how does it assist exporters? (76-77)
17. What are multi-national companies? (78-79)
18. Why are they important? (80-81)

*Asterisks indicate those questions for which there are answers in Outline Answers (page 439)*

### Essay-style questions

1.* a) Discuss the likely impact of the Single European Market on the UK economy.
   b) How is this affected by the formation of the European Economic Area?
2. How do changes in the exchange rate affect the trading position of a country?
3. What are the advantages and disadvantages to developing nations of trying to attract investment from multi-national companies?

### Short answer

1.* Explain how the following are calculated
   a) The Balance of Trade
   b) Invisible earnings
   c) The Balance of Payments

2.* Describe the role of the following in assisting foreign trade.
   a) An import agent
   b) A broker
   c) An export merchant

3. a) Complete the following table by filling in the missing trade figures for (a) (b) (c) (d) and (e).

|  | a | b | c | d | e |
|---|---|---|---|---|---|
| Visible exports | 400 | 400 | 200 | 450 | 211 |
| Visible imports |  | 100 | 350 | 400 |  |
| Balance of trade | +100 |  |  |  | −3 |
| Invisible exports | 325 | 150 | 50 | 100 |  |
| Invisible imports | 500 | 140 | 60 | 190 | 109 |
| Balance of payments | −175 −75 |  |  |  | +34 |

b) Comment on any trends in the figures (a) – (e) which represent monthly periods.

# 6. Business and the international economy

## Multiple choice/completion

1.* International trade arises when countries specialise in producing those goods:
   a) In which they have a comparative advantage.
   b) Which are protected by tariffs and quotas.
   c) Which are cheap to produce.
   d) Which they cannot obtain from abroad.

2.* What does it mean if the pound has appreciated against other currencies?
   a) It is worth less.
   b) It is worth the same.
   c) It is worth more.
   d) It is worth proportionally less.

3.* Which of the following situations would be likely to cause other countries to retaliate?
   a) Deflation in the economy.
   b) The Government imposing import duties.
   c) Increasing wholesale prices in the home country.
   d) Privatisation of more of the nation's wealth.

4.* Which of the following is concerned with stabilising exchange rates and providing international liquidity:
   a) IMF
   b) EFTA
   c) GATT
   d) EU

5. Which of the following statements is **NOT** true?
   a) The ECGD will provide insurance cover for exporters.
   b) The BOTB aims to help exporters and promote trade.
   c) The government will provide long-term loans for exporters.
   d) The ECGD will guarantee loans and overdrafts for exporters.

6. The balance of trade is:
   a) The balance on current account.
   b) The difference in value between the import and export of goods.
   c) The difference in value between income from abroad and expenditure abroad.
   d) The difference in volume between the import and export of goods.

*In each of the following questions, one or more of the responses is/are correct. Choose the appropriate letter which indicates the correct version.*

   A   if 1 only is correct
   B   if 2 only is correct
   C   if 1 and 2 are correct
   D   if 1, 2 and 3 are correct

7. Despite the advantages of specialisation arising from the law of comparative costs, many countries 'protect' their trade and industry. Which of the following are reasons why:
   1) To correct a long-term balance of payments deficit
   2) To help maintain the level of employment in particular industries.
   3) To prevent some goods entering the country for medical, moral or political reasons.

8. Which of the following are 'invisible' items in the balance of payments?
   1) Tourism
   2) Insurance
   3) Oil

## Assignment

### Treaty of Maastricht

In December 1991 leaders of the 12 member states met to agree a new Treaty on European Union, including political, economic and monetary co-operation.

The Maastricht Treaty builds on the original Treaty of Rome in 1957 and Single European Act of 1987. The main aims are summarised below.

- the establishment of monetary union (a single European currency by 1999 for all those countries meeting certain economic criteria)
- European citizenship (enabling people to live, travel and vote freely in any EU country)
- a greater co-operation on defence and security policy
- formal commitments for the protection of the health, safety and economic interests of consumers
- more powers for the European Parliament
- an increase in status for the Court of Auditors to tighten budgetary control
- the creation of a Cohesion Fund by the end of 1993 to help reduce the disparities between Community regions by financing environment and transport projects in poorer regions;
- the establishment of a Committee of the Regions to help shape regional policy;
- trans-European networks in transport, telecommunications and energy infra-structures;
- an enhanced role in consumer protection, public health, environment, culture and energy policy;
- initiatives in education, vocational training and youth policy;
- the creation of an EU ombudsman to investigate cases of maladministration by the Community's institutions.

The Maastricht Treaty has been signed by representatives of the 12 EU countries and ratified by all the national parliaments. This process of ratification was completed in Britain in August 1993.

The agreement at Maastricht is a major landmark in the development of the European Union. You are asked therefore to carry out research and prepare a report (word processed if possible) which considers in detail:

1. What the Maastricht Treaty means for Britain.
2. The Social Chapter (or Social Charter of Fundamental Social Rights for Workers) and why Britain opted out.
3. Includes a collection of newspaper articles to support the points in your report.
4. Explains the principle of 'subsidiarity' and why it is included in the Treaty.

# 7. Marketing & Market Research

The next 3 chapters are about the marketing activities of organisations. This chapter is about the collection and analysis of market information and covers:

* Marketing Defined
* Marketing Objectives
* Marketing Management
* Marketing Mix
* Consumer, Industrial and Services Marketing
* Market Research
* Sampling
* Desk Research
* Field Research
* Market Segmentation
* Evaluating Market Research

## Marketing Defined

1. The term **marketing** is used to describe a whole group of business activities which are concerned with obtaining and keeping customers. The Chartered Institute of Marketing defines it as 'The management process which indentifies, anticipates and supplies customer requirements efficiently and profitably.' The aim of good marketing is that firms should identify, by **market research**, the goods and services which consumers want and then produce and sell them at a profit.

2. A marketing orientated business therefore puts the consumer first. Instead of saying 'we only make two colours and sizes of paint (or paper, or pipes or whatever) – take it or leave it'; they now ask consumers what colours they require and in what sizes and then produce them. Operating this way – trying to discover and meet consumer needs – does not remove the risks of business but it greatly reduces them thus improving a firm's choices of selling more and making a profit.

## Marketing Objectives

3. In Chapter one we considered the overall objectives of business organisations and how these are achieved through the planning and co-ordination of its functional activities. Each functional area has its own set of objectives which for marketing are usually based on sales. Specific targets are usually set so that performance can be measured. Targets also serve to motivate individuals in the organisation.

4. The marketing objectives in any particular year or trading period would typically include some or all of the following:

   * **Sales revenue** eg to achieve a turnover of £50,000
   * **Unit sales** eg to sell 8,000 units
   * **Profit** eg to earn an overall level of 10%
   * **Market share** ie to increase business by attracting sales from competitors.
   * **Rate of growth** of all or any of the above, eg to increase market share by 5%.
   * **Market Penetration** i.e to find new markets or new parts of existing markets.
   * **Quality assurance** ie to provide standards for customers eg 24-hour delivery, money-back guarantees.

## 7. Marketing and market research

5.

**Examples of Market Share**

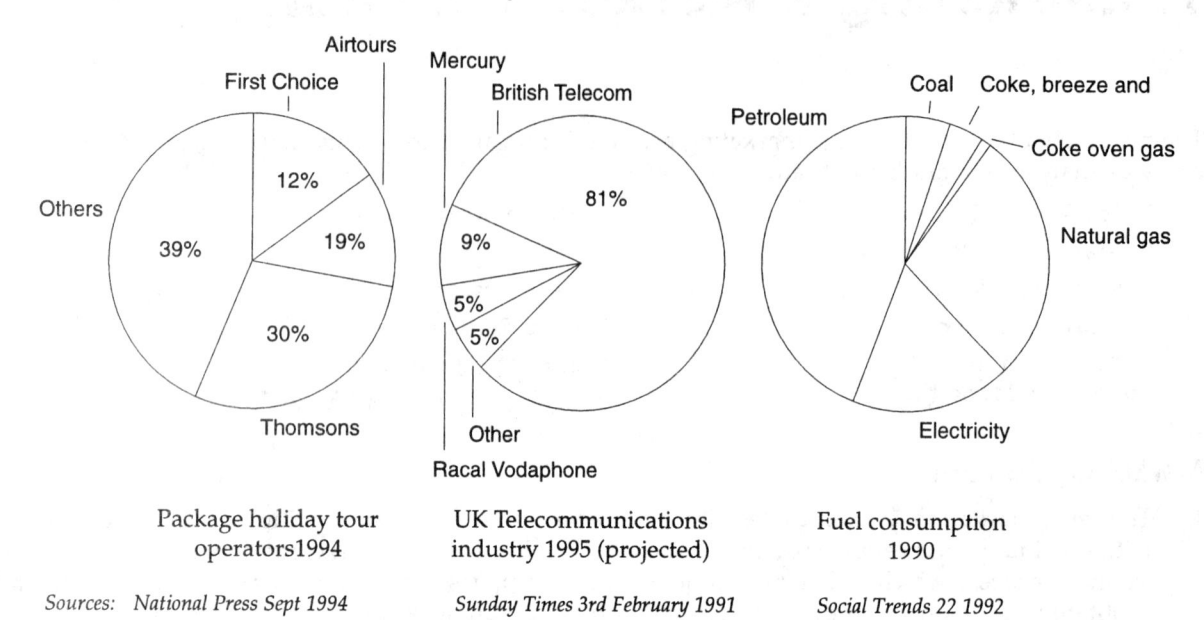

*Package holiday tour operators 1994*
- First Choice 12%
- Airtours 19%
- Thomsons 30%
- Others 39%

*UK Telecommunications industry 1995 (projected)*
- Mercury 9%
- British Telecom 81%
- Racal Vodaphone 5%
- Other 5%

*Fuel consumption 1990*
- Coal
- Coke, breeze and
- Coke oven gas
- Petroleum
- Natural gas
- Electricity

Sources: National Press Sept 1994 · Sunday Times 3rd February 1991 · Social Trends 22 1992

6. Some marketing objectives are more difficult to quantify but nonetheless important in helping an organisation to achieve its overall objectives. This would be the case, for example, if a firm wanted to develop its **corporate image**, that is, the way in which it is seen as a whole rather than by the individual products or services which it sells. Consider, for example, the low-cost image of Kwik-Save compared with the more up-market image of Sainsburys. Important in this is the **corporate identity** which is usually established through the use of logos which appear on letter headings, in advertising, on promotional materials, on vehicles and staff uniforms. The image projected can have an important influence on an organisation's sales.

---

### Task 7.1

A small manufacturer of cosmetics is seeking to increase its turnover and profit.

a) Consider the following marketing objectives and advise the company as to which you feel it would be best to pursue.

To improve customer service

To launch a new product

To Improve distribution

To identify new markets

b) Explain how each of these objectives can best be measured

---

## Marketing Management

7. The organisation of marketing activities will vary from firm to firm. Large organisations usually have a specialist department with functional managers possibly covering market research, product development, advertising, sales and distribution. On the other hand, in smaller concerns, marketing may be just one of the many responsibilities of the owner, a partner, or director.

## Marketing Mix

8. The main activities involved in marketing a product or service are known as the 4 P's of the marketing mix, that is, product, price, promotion and place, any or all of which may be altered in order to increase sales. These activities are briefly outlined below and considered in more detail in Chapters 8 and 9.

9. **Marketing Mix**

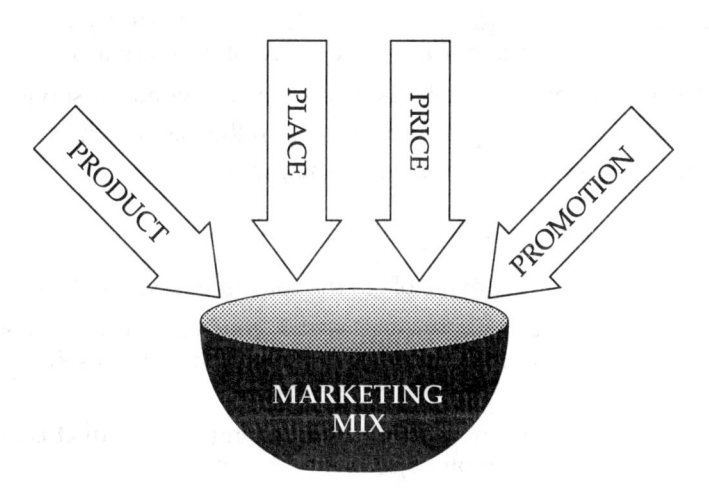

*[Diagram: Four arrows labelled PRODUCT, PLACE, PRICE, PROMOTION pointing into a bowl labelled MARKETING MIX]*

10. **Product**

    Using the findings from market research firms can develop products to satisfy consumer needs, introduce new products or improve existing ones. This involves considering the design, quality and technical specifications of products such as materials and features, the **product mix** (range) offered and how they are packaged.

11. Appearance factors such as the size(s), shape(s), colour(s), label(s) and brand name of a product are all very important in attracting customers, as might be guarantees and after-sales service, depending on the product. (see Chapter 8)

12. **Marketing a Product**

    *[Diagram: A bottle of SUPER COLA! with labels:]*
    - 'Handy' shape
    - Brand name
    - Attractive label
    - Convenient size (500ml)

## Price

13. Deciding how much to charge for goods or services is also very important and will be linked to the overall marketing objectives. A price must be set which:

    - is competitive and attractive to customers so that they will buy the goods, and
    - covers the cost of production and provides a profit for the firm.

    The price may also be affected by discounts, credit facilities, special promotions and pricing psychology, for example £1.99 sounds a lot cheaper than £2.03. (see Chapter 8)

## Promotion

14. This includes sales promotion, advertising, public relations and personal selling which together are often referred to as 'marketing communications'. The aim of promotion is:

    - to tell potential customers about the benefits of a company's goods or services.
    - remind existing customers that the products are still on the market, and
    - encourage both groups to buy or use them. (see Chapter 9)

## Place

15. This is about how products are made available to the consumer and involves:

    - choosing the channels of distribution through which goods or services are sold. A manufacturer, for example, may use wholesalers or retailers or he may decide to sell his goods direct to consumers.
    - ensure that they are available when required. If, for example, a product is out of stock, then sales may be lost to competitors. (see Chapter 9)

> **Task 7.2**
>
> The following is an example of how the 4 P's of the marketing mix can be illustrated in the marketing of video recorders.
>
> What facilities and services does the consumer require? (the product), for example remote control, 7 day timer, 12 month's guarantee.
>
> How much is the consumer prepared to pay and what profit does the manufacturer require? (the price), for example £399.
>
> How and when should the manufacturer inform potential customers about his product? (the promotion), for example television and newspaper advertising.
>
> Where and how should the recorders be offered for sale? (the place), for example shops, mail order.
>
> Produce your own example for any product or service with which you are familiar.

16. If a firm is to be successful in providing what consumers want at a profit then it is important that its market research and the 4 P's are carefully planned and co-ordinated to achieve this. The particular mix used at any time will vary depending upon the type of goods or services and the circumstances. Fashion clothing, for example, is always changing and therefore will require considerable product development and promotion. On the other hand, manufacturers of some goods such as basic foodstuffs like tea and sugar will be more concerned with price and place, i.e. making the goods available to consumers at the right price. Whilst an increase in competition might mean that a firm must alter its prices or increase its promotion if it is to avoid a fall in sales.

17. The balance between an organisation's long, medium and short-term objectives will also affect the relative emphasis on the marketing mix. Lower prices, for example, may be used to increase market share but will also reduce profit levels and could cause competitors to retaliate. Thus this may only be suitable in the very short-term. In the longer-term it may be more profitable to develop new products or enter new markets e.g. selling overseas.

> **Task 7.3**
>
> a) Select 3 supermarket companies and
>
> b) any other 3 companies well known to you.
>
> For each company, state, with reasons, where you feel the emphasis on the marketing mix is placed.

## Different Types of Marketing

There are three broad categories into which marketing can be divided – consumer, industrial and services.

18. **Consumer Marketing**

    Where products are sold directly to the general public mainly through the retail trade, e.g. shops. This includes:
    - **Consumer Goods** such as food and cosmetics, ie, items which are bought frequently and are relatively cheap.
    - **Consumer Durables** such as cars, furniture and washing machines which are expected to last several years and are relatively expensive to buy.

19. **Industrial Marketing**

    Industrial products are those sold to companies and manufacturers who use them to produce other goods and services. They can be consumer or durable and range in price from a few pence to thousands or even millions of pounds. Examples include nuts and bolts, raw materials, machinery, equipment and office supplies.

20. **Marketing in Service Industries**

    Services such as banking, insurance, plant hire, office cleaning, maintenance and repair, travel and transport can include either consumer or industrial marketing. Banks, for example, advertise their services to both the general public and businesses whilst garages repair cars owned by both individuals and companies.

21. **Types of Marketing**

    **Consumer Goods**

    Tea, Shirt, Computer, Car

    **Industrial Marketing**

    Packaging, Chemicals, Timber

    **Marketing in Service Industries**

    Insurance, Shipping, Restaurants

*7. Marketing and market research*

> **Task 7.4**
> Give at least 5 other examples for each of consumer, industrial and service products. Identify those which are sold to both business organisations and the general public.

## Market Research

22. A firm which finds out about the people who buy, or may buy, its products is far more likely to be successful in selling them. This information can be used to improve the way in which goods and services are marketed. Market research is used to find this out and to provide information about past, current and future trends. It is now seen as essential by most successful companies.

23. **Market Research** involves collecting, recording and analysing information about products or markets, in order to improve decision-taking.

    - The more a firm can find out about the people who use, buy or may buy their products, the easier it becomes both to produce what they want and then to persuade them to buy.
    - This could include information about consumers age, sex, occupations, habits, likes and dislikes, where they live, which newspapers they read or when they watch television, which can all be used to improve the way in which goods and services are marketed.

24. Market Research then is used to find the answers to a number of questions. For example:
    a) Who might buy a product? – anyone, teenagers, parents.
    b) Who actually buys it? – most childrens' toys are bought by adults.
    c) Who uses it? – a lot of mens clothing is actually purchased by women.
    d) How often do they buy it? – weekly, monthly.
    e) Why do they buy it? – like smell, colour, sound, quality or shape.
    f) How did they find out about it? – TV, newspapers, friends.
    g) Where did they buy it from? – supermarket, mail order catalogue.
    h) Who are the main competitors and why? – location, price, quality, promotion, image.

25. Based on this type of information, it is possible for firms to **forecast** (estimate) the likely sales of their products or services. They can then make the important marketing decisions which are necessary to achieve these sales including:

    - What and how much to produce
    - What price to charge
    - The best place to advertise
    - Which method of distribution to use

## Sampling

26. Except in some small industrial markets, it is not usually possible to ask all consumers (called the **population** or total market) what they think about a particular product or service. The time and cost involved would be too great. Therefore, market research surveys usually select a 'representative' cross section, or **sample** of people and question them.

27. A carefully chosen sample should produce very similar results to asking everyone, although it has to be recognised that a certain amount of **bias** may exist. That is, any research may be distorted by a number of factors, for example samples which are poorly selected or too small or questionnaires with complex interview questions or whose responses might be misinterpreted. If bias takes place then the accuracy and reliability of the information collected will be reduced.

## Probability Samples

28. The two main types of sample are known as probability and non-probability samples. The main type of probability sample is called random sampling which can be simple, systematic or stratified.

29. **Simple Random Sampling** means that every member of the population has an equal chance of being selected. Names and addresses for example, may be chosen at random from the electoral register and then visited for the interview. A slight variation to this is **systematic random sampling** which involves selecting every nth item or person, for example every 10th name in a telephone directory.

30. **Stratified random sampling** divides the population into groups (called strata) by, for example, age, sex, occupation or social class to provide a more representative cross-section of the whole. Each selected sub-group is then randomly sampled.

31. A major problem with random sampling is that only those selected are interviewed which often involves 'calling back' to complete them.

## Non-Probability Samples

32. These are samples where there is no way of estimating the probability of any particular item being included. This has the advantage of being cheaper and more convenient than probability samples.

33. **Quota Sampling** involves the interviewer in selecting a given number of the population who fulfil certain criteria such as age and sex. These are often used for street interviews when, for example, the quota may be to interview 25 males and 25 females in each of the following age groups: 15-24, 25-40, and 41-50.

34. **Purposive Sampling** involves deliberately biasing a sample depending on the market being investigated. Thus, for example, a manufacturer launching a new drug would want to discover doctors' likely reactions to it whilst a textbook publisher would seek teachers' opinions of a proposed book.

35. **Cluster Sampling** is often used to reduce the costs of interviewing such as travelling and involves selecting a random group which is concentrated in a particular area or region rather than individual respondents. Thus, for example, just a few streets or a particular town could be chosen.

### Task 7.5

A national manufacturer of washing machines is planning to develop a new model to compliment its current range. It believes from an analysis of the sales of its existing products that the likely market is females in the 30-45 age group. To confirm this view it plans to obtain further information by carrying out a market research survey.

a) Suggest, with reasons, the type of sample which should be used to give the most accurate forecast of the potential market for the new product.

b) Indicate how changes in the age distribution of the population might influence its future strategies.

## Market Research Methods

36. Most market research uses **quantitative** techniques to discover **how many** consumers are in a particular market, eg the total number of car owners and/or **qualitative** techniques to discover **why** consumers behave in certain ways, eg why they buy one make or model of car in preference to another. Market research information can be obtained in two ways – using Desk Research or Field Research.

37. **Desk Research** or secondary data involves studying **existing information** which can be found either:

    - internally – within an organisation ie a firm's own records, for example sales, stock or accounting records, customer complaints and salesmen's reports OR

    - externally – outside an organisation ie published by someone else, for example by banks, newspapers, Trade Associations, governments, professional bodies and Chambers of Commerce.

## 7. Marketing and market research

> **Task 7.6**
>
> Look in the reference section of a library and try to identify at least 5 potential sources of secondary data for a firm which is considering producing a new leisure product aimed at the 16-25 age group.
>
> State how each source will assist the firm in its decision-taking.

38. **Field Research** or primary data involves the collection of **new information** which could be about a firm's market, products, advertising, promotion, pricing, distribution or competition. Eight common methods of field research include the use of questionnaires, consumer panels, test marketing, discussion groups, opinion polls, retail audits, observation and motivational research.

39. **Questionnaires** consist of a number of questions which are used to ask the opinions of existing or potential consumers. You or your parents for example, may have been stopped in the street and interviewed about a particular product or asked which television programmes you watch. Sometimes these **surveys** are also carried out on the telephone, by post, or in a person's home. Companies may also buy into an **omnibus survey** requesting specific questions to be asked in a survey which covers several (often unrelated) topics together.

> **Task 7.7**
>
> Questionnaires will only be successful if they are well designed with relevant, unambiguous, easy to understand questions which can be quickly answered.
>
> Discuss other possible advantages and disadvantages of using questionnaires. Consider the differences between personal interviews, telephone and postal surveys in terms of time, cost, speed, accuracy, ease of use, accessibility of sample, interview bias and potential response rate. Present your answer in the form of a simple chart or diagram.

40. **Consumer Panels** are another method of field research. They involve the selection of groups of consumers who are either questioned about their **reactions to** new or existing **products**; asked to **record details** of their spending over a period of time or to participate in **user tests** where they try a particular product and say what they think about it.

41. The success of consumer panels, however, depends very much upon the personality, enthusiasm and reliability of the people involved. Since they can be quite time-consuming it is likely that they will not appeal to certain groups of the population and therefore may not be truly representative of the whole population.

42. **Test Marketing** is sometimes used by manufacturers to gauge consumer reaction to a new product or promotion in a particular town or area before deciding whether or not to market it nationwide.

    Manufacturers of mass produced consumer goods for example, tea, coffee and cereals often base tests on ITV regions such as: Border, Yorkshire or Ulster.

    Although this is a relatively expensive form of research, it is more thorough and reliable than simply asking people what they might buy. However, the 'sample' area may not be truly representative of the total population and the results of a successful test launch may not necessarily be repeated nationally. Test marketing also means that competitors get to know about the product, advertisement or promotional idea and therefore may decide to develop something similar.

43. **Discussion groups** are sometimes used whereby a number of existing or potential consumers are brought together and asked to give their opinions of a particular product or service. Someone from the research organisation involved usually chairs the group in order to structure the discussion.

44. **Opinion polls** are used for a quick check on people's views or awareness of particular issues. They normally involve just a few (sometimes only 3 or 4) questions. A business may use these, for example, to gauge quickly the impact of a particular advertising campaign or product improvement.

## Task 7.8

Test marketing may also be carried out in other ways as the following news extract illustrates.

---

### TROLLEY FOLLY

It was supposed to be the answer to a shopper's prayer, but the five-wheeled trolley invented by Sainsburys to cut accidents in the aisles is now consigned to the scrapheap.

An extra wheel fixed to one side of a traditional trolley to increase stability and aid steering drove customers round the bend when it went on trial at the firm's store in Somerford, near Christchurch, Dorset.

The store turned into an obstacle course, and a book for shoppers' comments was soon filled with angry complaints.

Sainsburys which has 317 stores, bowed to public pressure and halted the trial only six days after it had begun.

One disgruntled shopper said 'It's hard to believe anything could be worse than the trolleys we're used to, but this one was almost impossible to manoeuvre. I found that whenever I moved, it wouldn't. Going round corners was a nightmare, and I'm sure I hit other shoppers with it. When I first went into the store, I thought I'd got a duff trolley until someone said they were all like that.'

A spokesman for Sainsburys said: 'We would never introduce equipment which would prove unpopular with the majority of our customers. We frequently carry out trials of different types of equipment as part of our policy to offer the best new technology and service to customers.'

---

In your own words, briefly outline the reasons for the research taking place and what benefits the firm gained from the trial.

---

45. **Retail Audits** involve the use of sample surveys to analyse market trends. They are usually carried out by specialist research organisations who then sell the information to firms in the industry.

46. **Observation** involves monitoring consumer behaviour, particularly in supermarkets to study how people actually shop. This information is then used in the design of store layouts and use of shelf space, both of which can have a major impact on sales. Firms considering opening a new store may also use this technique to determine whether or not a particular location is likely to be busy.

47. **Motivational Research** involves the use of psychological techniques, including in-depth interviews and word association tests, to determine why particular products are purchased, or not. Often consumers themselves do not really know why they buy particular products.

## Market Research Agencies

48. We have seen that a firm can carry out its own market research, particularly where secondary data is required. When primary data is required, however, it is usual to engage the expertise of a specialist market research company, many of whom also produce and sell regular research reports.

49. Some well-known examples of commercial research organsations include:

    *A.C. Neilsen* – who specialise in retail audits.

    *Gallup* – famous for its political opinion polls and the weekly 'pop' charts.

    *Audits of Great Britain* (AGB) – which uses consumer diaries to provide information on household expenditure.

    *Audit Bureau of Circulation* (ABC) – which provides information on newspapers and other media circulation.

    *Joint Industrial Committee On Television Audience Research* (JICTAR) – which produces weekly television viewing figures.

    *Mintel* – which produces a monthly journal containing reports on various consumer markets such as bread and insurance.

## Market Segmentation

50. In order to market successfully, a firm needs to know what the total potential market is for its particular products or services and then try to identify the various **segments** or parts within it. The total UK market for footwear for example, includes mens, ladies and children of all ages. A footwear manufacturer can therefore decide to carry out the activities necessary to supply the whole market or instead to target particular segments of it such as ladies or children only. The market can, however, be further sub-divided for example, children's' shoes include boys and girls and different ages such as the under 5's and 5-15. There are also many different types and qualities of footwear ranging from slippers to trainers to work shoes and specialist shoes such as those worn by dancers or footballers.

51. Thus, unless a market is either very small or dominated by one brand, it is unlikely that a particular product will be bought by everyone. Therefore, a manufacturer will usually select one or more specific market segments and devise a marketing mix which will appeal to those segments.

> **Task 7.9**
>
> How many market segments can you identify for each of the following products?
>
> a) Potatoes    b) Computers    c) Central Heating    d) Oil    e) Paint

## Market Characteristics

52. Through research, markets can be analysed and classified according to the key factors which influence buyers' behaviour. The following classifications are considered below: demographic, geographical, geo-demographic, ethnic and religious influences, behavioural factors, life-styles and national characteristics; all of which are of significance for marketing.

53. **Demographic** classification is important in providing basic information about buyers and consumers. For example, many products such as nappies, 'pop' music and retirement homes are clearly aimed at specific **age groups**, whilst others like newspapers and cars are targeted at different **socio-economic groups** (usually based on income and occupation). The **number of households** is important in determining the potential market for products such as the number who own fridges or washing machines, whilst the **size of households** can affect the demand for types of housing and family used items such as carpets and furniture.

54. **Geographical** classification considers the physical location of consumers for example, urban or rural. Particular regions of the country also often have distinct purchasing patterns which can have important marketing implications for advertising, promotion and product development.

55. **Geo-demographic** is the classification of small areas according to the characteristics of their inhabitants such as age, race and social class. It links purchasing power to where people live.

56. **Ethnic and religious** classifications identify the characteristics of groups which represent distinct markets or parts of markets for certain goods and services. Many ethnic groups, for example, prefer brighter colours which could be important for packaging, whilst Jews, Asians and West Indians all have their own diet, retail outlets, entertainment facilities, communication media (eg own language newspapers) and culture.

57. **Behavioural** classifications cover product usage, such as the frequency of purchase and brand loyalty, and the differences between regular users and occasional users.

58. **Life-style** classifications attempt to determine the personality traits of consumers covering likes, dislikes, attitudes, opinions and interests. From this, for example, it may be found that a particular product only appeals to people who are introverts or extroverts.

59. **National** classifications. Although a product or service may be successful in the UK, it may require modification if it is to be sold in other countries. Thus firms who target this market segment must research it thoroughly in order to identify any factors which may influence its market-strategy. This could include for example, social, political and cultural differences; legislation, particularly that affecting consumer protection, health and safety and advertising; religious influences and the level

of technological development. Firms planning to enter the Single European Market will need to be aware of some of these factors.

### Task 7.10

#### SIMPLY CORNFLAKES

Kelloggs Cornflakes were launched over 70 years ago with an excellent and really innovative product with wide appeal. Over the years, heavy advertising expenditure, plus product and packaging updating have made and kept the brand successful.

Since the 1970's, however, there have been dramatic changes in the breakfast cereal market. This is illustrated, for example, by the fact that in 1979 there were 84 brands with a turnover of over £1m, whilst today there are more than 150. Thus many new and successful products have emerged to segment the cereal market. Faced with this development, Kelloggs has consistently spent more on advertising cornflakes than any other product (over £7.5 million in 1988-9 out of a total expenditure of almost £50m). It has also launched new 'added-value' products like Raisin-Splitz, Toppas, Smacks and Pop Tarts to appeal to new consumer groups wanting something different. Through market research, the success of cornflakes has also been re-assessed and the product relaunched in the 1990's as having something 'simple' in a market full of complex products. Thus today, cornflakes is re-emerging as a reliable old friend, targetted at the same customer with slogans like 'Have you forgotton how good they taste', and clearly re-establishing its own market niche.

The following questions are based on the above article:

1. Why have Kelloggs Cornflakes been so successful for over 70 years?
2. How has the product been affected by market segmentation?
3. What action has the company taken to re-establish the brand?
4. What do you understand by a 'Market Niche'?
5. What evidence, if any, is there to suggest that it could continue to be successful in the future?

### 60. Evaluating market research

The value of market research information will usually be measured in terms of the increased sales or profits which result from the application of the results. Ultimately, it is only worthwhile if this value exceeds the cost of the research. Thus, for example, take a company with current sales of 100,000 units at a profit of £5 per unit. The advertising manager believes from £5,000 spent on research that a switch from poster to radio advertising will increase sales by 2 – 5% for the same level of expenditure. If we assume a 2% increase this equals £10,000 (£2,000 x 5) minus the cost leaving an extra profit of £5,000.

### 61. Classification of Consumers By Socio-Economic Groups

| Social grade | Social status | Occupation of head of household | Approx % of total pop |
|---|---|---|---|
| A | Upper middle class | Higher managerial, administrative or professional | 3 |
| B | Middle class | Middle managerial, administrative or professional | 12 |
| $C^1$ | Lower middle class | Supervisory, clerical or junior managerial | 23 |
| $C^2$ | Skilled working class | Skilled manual workers | 32% |
| D | Working class | Semi and unskilled manual workers | 20% |
| E | Those at subsistence level | State pensioners, casual or lowest grade workers | 10% |

## 7. Marketing and market research

62. **Socio-economic** classifications are shown in the table on page 149. The basis being that consumers spending is related to social class, which is determined largely by the head of the household's income and occupation. Although still widely used, particularly by advertising media, classifications such as geo-demographic, which take account of other factors are now considered to be more accurate.

> **Task 7.11**
>
> 1. Using the information in the table showing socio-economic groups, plus the information below on magazine readership, select the most appropriate publication in which to advertise the products a-e. Give reasons for your choice of publication.
>    a) Lager
>    b) A new DIY product
>    c) Luxury holidays
>    d) A foodmixer
>    e) Male cosmetics
> 2. What additional information would you have found useful in completing this task?

63. **Readership of the most popular magazines: by sex and age, 1971 and 1990**

|  | % adults reading each mag in 1990 | | | % of each age group reading each mag in 1990 | | | | Readership (m) | | Readers per copy |
|---|---|---|---|---|---|---|---|---|---|---|
|  | Male | Female | All adult | 15-24 | 25-44 | 45-64 | 65 + | 1971 | 1990 | 1990 |
| **General magazines** | | | | | | | | | | |
| Radio Times | 18 | 19 | 19 | 20 | 20 | 18 | 17 | 9.5 | 8.5 | 2.9 |
| TV Times | 18 | 19 | 19 | 21 | 19 | 18 | 15 | 9.9 | 8.4 | 3.0 |
| Readers Digest | 14 | 13 | 13 | 8 | 13 | 17 | 14 | 9.2 | 6.1 | 3.9 |
| What Car? | 7 | 1 | 4 | 6 | 5 | 3 | 1 |  | 1.8 | 12.2 |
| National Geographic | 5 | 3 | 4 | 4 | 4 | 4 | 2 | 1.1 | 1.7 |  |
| Exchange and Mart | 5 | 2 | 3 | 5 | 4 | 3 | 1 |  | 1.5 | 8.2 |
| **Women's magazines** | | | | | | | | | | |
| Woman's Own | 3 | 16 | 10 | 10 | 11 | 9 | 8 | 7.2 | 4.3 | 4.2 |
| Bella | 3 | 15 | 10 | 12 | 11 | 8 | 6 |  | 4.3 |  |
| Woman's Weekly | 2 | 11 | 7 | 4 | 5 | 9 | 10 | 4.7 | 3.1 | 2.6 |
| Woman | 2 | 11 | 7 | 6 | 8 | 6 | 5 | 8.0 | 3.0 | 3.2 |
| Best | 2 | 11 | 6 | 9 | 8 | 5 | 3 |  | 2.9 | 3.1 |
| Prima | 2 | 10 | 6 | 7 | 8 | 5 | 2 |  | 2.6 | 3.0 |

*Source: Social Trends 22, Reproduced by kind permission of the Controller of HMSO. 1992*

## Summary

64. a) Marketing is concerned with the way in which a business operates and includes all aspects of selling goods and services from initial market research to distribution to the final consumer.

    b) An organisation's marketing objectives may include specific targets for growth in sales, profit and market share.

    c) The marketing activities of the 4P's – product, price, promotion and place are together known as the marketing mix.

    d) The three main types are Consumer Marketing, Industrial Marketing and Marketing in Service Industries.

e) Market research is used to provide information to firms about consumers which can be obtained through desk or field research.

f) Desk research involves the analysis of existing data.

g) Field research is based on a 'sample' of consumers and uses questionnaires, consumer panels, test marketing, retail audits, observation and motivational research.

h) Probability sampling uses simple, systematic or stratified random sampling.

i) Non-probability techniques include quota, purposive and cluster sampling.

j) Market segmentation identifies consumer characteristics according to demographic, geographical, geo-demographic, ethnic, religious, behavioural, life-styles and, where appropriate, national classifications.

## Review questions *(Answers can be found in the paragraph indicated)*

1. What is marketing? (1-2)
2. Give examples of some typical marketing objectives. (3-6)
3. Name the 4 elements of the marketing mix. (8-17)
4. Explain, using examples, the 3 different types of marketing. (18-21)
5. What is market research and why do firms use it? (22-25)
6. Why is sampling used in market research and in what ways can it become biased? (26-27)
7. Briefly, explain 3 types of probability sampling. (28-31)
8. Describe 3 different types of non-probability sampling techniques. (32-35)
9. Explain the difference between desk research and field research. (36-38)
10. Briefly, describe 4 different methods of field research. (39-47)
11. Explain the meaning of market segmentation. (50-52).
12. Describe 4 ways in which markets can be classified. (53-59)

*Asterisks indicate those questions for which there are answers in Outline Answers (page 439)*

## Essay-style questions

1.* A firm is considering exporting its range of consumer products. Explain how and why it might use marketing research to inform its decision-making.

2. A toy manufacturer is about to launch a new product aimed at the 2 – 6 age group. It is expected to appeal to a mass-market and likely to retail at about £10. Discuss how market research could be used by the firm to assist it in developing a marketing strategy.

3. 'Markets can be classified according to the key factors which influence buyers' behaviour'.

   Discuss this statement and then explain why market segmentation is important for the successful marketing of a firm's products or services?

## Short answer

1.* a) What do you understand by the marketing activities of an organisation?
   b) In what ways could marketing activities affect the profitability of a business?

2.* Write brief notes and use examples to explain each of the following terms:
   a) Consumer marketing
   b) Industrial marketing
   c) Services marketing

3. Briefly describe the sampling techniques you would use to carry out the following survey requirements. Give reasons for your choice of technique.
   a) to gather opinions about a new commercial television channel.

b) to assess the attitude to health foods among housewives.
c) to discuss the reactions of newsagents to stocking a new fishing magazine.

## Multiple choice/completion

1.\* Marketing is best defined as:
   a) Advertising and promotion
   b) Market research
   c) Choosing distribution channels
   d) An activity including all of the above.

2.\* Which of the following would provide secondary data in respect of a firm's sales?
   a) An analysis of orders.
   b) A retail audit
   c) Test marketing
   d) The use of consumer panels

3.\* Which of the following is a probability sample?
   a) Quota sampling
   b) Purposive sampling
   c) Random sampling
   d) Cluster sampling

4.\* Market segmentation is used
   a) To find the total potential market for a product.
   b) Where products are sold directly to the public.
   c) For the collection and analysis of market information.
   d) To sub-divide markets into parts for targetting.

5. Test marketing is sometimes used by manufacturers to:
   a) Guage consumer reaction to new products or promotions.
   b) Provide information on household expenditure
   c) Determine the personality and opinions of potential consumers.
   d) Identify distinct markets for goods or services.

6. Which of the following market research agencies provides weekly information on television viewing figures?
   a) GALLUP
   b) JICTAR
   c) ABC
   d) AGB

*In each of the following questions, one or more of the responses is/are correct. Choose the appropriate letter which indicates the correct version.*

   A  if 1 only is correct
   B  if 3 only is correct
   C  if 1 and 2 only are correct
   D  if 1, 2 and 3 are correct

7  Which of the following statements is/are true?
   1. Desk research involves the analysis of existing data.
   2. Product, Primary, Promotion and Price are the 4 P's of the marketing mix.
   3. Motivational research involves the use of retail audits.

8. Which of the following is/are an advantage of using cluster sampling of a population?
   1. It reduces the cost of interviewing such as travelling.
   2. Every member has an equal chance of being selected.
   3. Interviewers can select anyone who fulfils certain criteria.

## Assignment

You are asked to carry out some research into an area of interest related to your school, college or place of work. This will give you practical experience of field research, including constructing a simple questionnaire, selecting and interviewing a sample, analysing the results, presenting them in the form of a short report and discussing the limitations of your research.

### Tasks

1. **Decide on the topic to be investigated.**

   It could be why a particular product sells well, or what people think about your school/college/works magazine/newsletter, meals service or working conditions.

2. **Design a questionnaire**

   a. *Information required.* It is necessary to decide what questions you want to ask, and then to write them carefully in a clear and logical way. (It is recommended that your questionnaire is fairly brief, consisting of not more than 10-15 questions). The following example may help.

   **Crisp Survey**   *Circle the answer

   1. When did you last buy a packet of crisps?

      * Today         * Yesterday         * Within the last week

      * Within the last month            * Over a month ago

   2. Which brand of crisps did you buy?
   3. Why did you buy that particular brand?
   4. Which flavour did you buy?
   5. How did you rate the taste of the crisps?

      * Very good   * Good   * Fair   * Not very good   * Poor

   6. Would you buy the same brand again?       *Yes/No
   7. Would you buy the same flavour again?     *Yes/No
   8. What is your favourite flavour of crisps?

   b. *Question content.* It is possible to use different styles of questions. The example illustrates **closed** questions which require a simple *yes* or *no* response, those which give a choice of answers and those which leave the answer **open-ended**. The latter may give more information but be different and time consuming to analyse.

   c. You could also use a **prompt card** which lists items (eg brands of crisps) to help respondents, and/or **skips** which tell them to ignore irrelevant questions.

   d. *Electronic monitoring.* Developments in information technology have already influenced the design of questionnaires so that nowadays answers are coded for rapid analysis. In future the anticipated growth of interactive view data systems such as cable television and voice recognition computers is likely to lead to further electronic monitoring which could dramatically change the methods and speed with which much market research is carried out. Consider whether you can use it in your research.

3. **Select a Sample**
   a. When your questionnaire is ready, the next task is to select the type and number of people that you wish to interview. For example, if you are attending a college with 1,000 students, then you might decide to ask the opinions of 1 in every 20 students, ie 50 altogether. You could break this sample down further into various categories by interviewing 25 male and 25 female students and by dividing these into different age groups. Remember, if your sample is to be representative of all of the students you will need to select the people you interview very carefully.
   b. You will need to reproduce sufficient copies (and spares) of your questionnaire to cover the total number required.

4. **Carry out the interviewing**

   Once the sample has been selected you can begin the interviews. If it is a group assignment, each person should interview a small number of people, perhaps ten.5. **Analyse the results**

   Again, working as a group, it will be necessary to count the answers to each question. When completed, the results can be presented in the form of tables, charts and diagrams. These are often much easier to understand than a long written description.

6. **Present a report**

   Each group member should now present their own report of the survey, word processed if possible.

   This should contain full details of each person's contribution to the assignment in addition to a summary of the work of the other group members. It should also give details of the problems involved in carrying out the research.

   A suitable structure might be as follows:
   a) Title and purpose of report
   b) Introduction
   c) Body of report, ie presentation and analysis of data collected.
   d) Summary of findings including the value of the information discovered.
   e) Any conclusions or recommendations based on the findings.

7. **Discuss** the findings and limitations of your research and what changes you feel could be made to improve the reliability of the survey.

8. **Finally**, if you used information technology, comment on how it helped with your research. Alternatively consider how it would have assisted you.

# 8. The Marketing Mix – Product and Price

In Chapter 7 we considered the use of market research to find out which goods and services people want. In the next 2 chapters, we look in detail at the four elements of the marketing mix which are used to sell them. This chapter covers product and price and includes:

* Product Range
* Product Life Cycle
* Product Development
* Product Withdrawal
* Product Planning
* Branding
* Own Brands
* Packaging
* Product Strategy
* Price
* Pricing Objectives
* Pricing Policies

1. **Product Range**

    In order to be successful a firm must produce a product which satisfies consumer needs. The product must have appeal to consumers and serve the purpose for which it is intended. Most firms actually produce not just one but usually a range of related products in order to spread the risks associated with business.

2. This has several advantages including the following:
    - **a contribution to profits** from successful products if sales of other products fall.
    - **economies of scale** can be gained by using the same method of production to produce larger quantities.
    - **advertising and selling costs can be spread,** for example one advertisement could be used to promote several lines; a sales representative could handle the full product range.
    - **distribution costs** can be reduced if the products can be transported together.

3. **Product Life Cycle**

    Just as we are born, grow up, mature and eventually become old and die, so the sales of many products have a similar life cycle. This involves six important stages which are illustrated below:
    - **Development** – with the help of market research new products are designed. This is the most risky and expensive stage where the costs of research and technical development are incurred but no sales revenue is being earned.
    - **Introduction** – once it has been developed, the product is advertised and brought to the market for sale.
    - **Growth** – if the product is successful sales and the profit contribution will increase rapidly.
    - **Maturity** – once established in a market the sales of a product do not grow so rapidly. A main reason for this is likely to be increased competition as other firms introduce similar products.
    - **Saturation** – in time sales stop increasing, leading to
    - **Decline** – eventually competition and other new products are likely to result in falling sales and profits. If this continues, the product may be withdrawn from the market.

## 8. The marketing mix – product and price

4. **Stages in the Product Life Cycle**

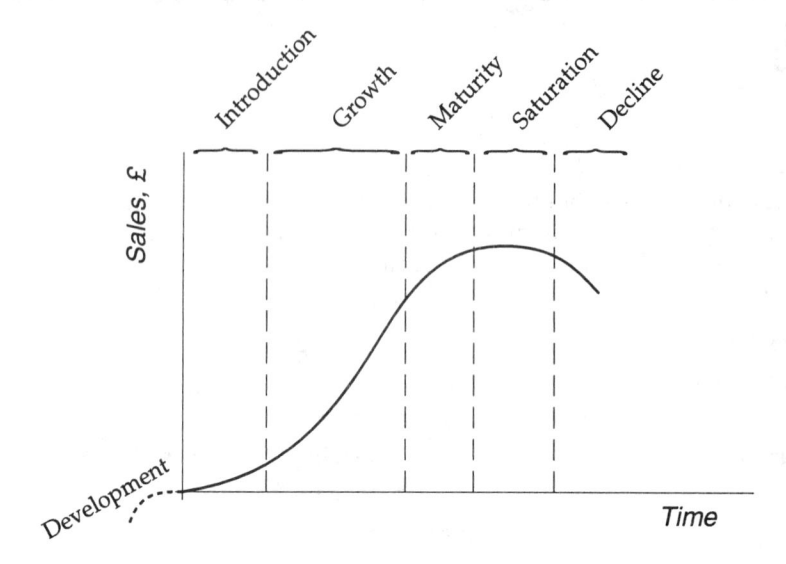

*[Diagram: Sales (£) vs Time curve showing stages – Development, Introduction, Growth, Maturity, Saturation, Decline]*

5. Changing consumer tastes and expectations, developments in new technology and the introduction of new and improved products can all affect the length of a life cycle which clearly will not be the same for all products.

---

**Task 8.1**

1) Draw a diagram to show the product life cycle over a 5 year period for a seasonal product the sales of which are growing.

2) Compare the life cycle of any three 'new' products with which you are familiar, perhaps a compact disc, car or soft drink. Discuss, giving reasons, the time which each is likely to take to complete the various stages of its product life cycle.

---

6. **Cash Flow and the Product Life Cycle**

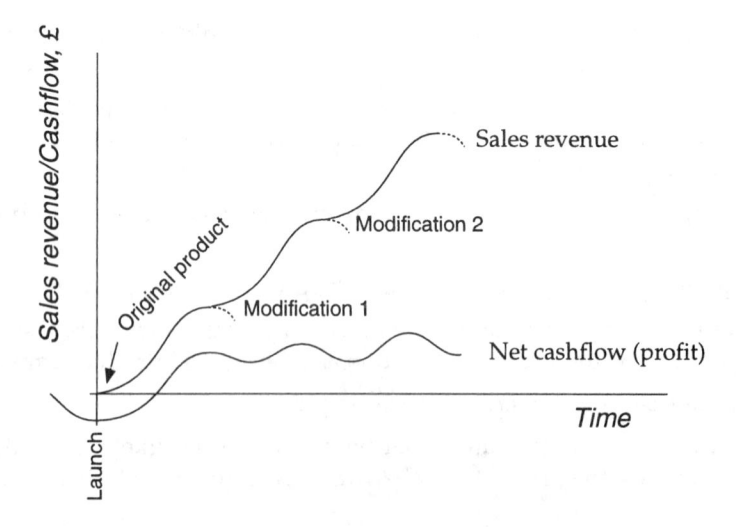

*[Diagram: Sales revenue/Cashflow (£) vs Time showing Launch, Original product, Modification 1, Modification 2, Sales revenue, Net cashflow (profit)]*

7. As the above diagram shows in the early stages of a product's life, the net cash flow is initially negative. This is due partly to the costs of developing and promoting the product but also because the full benefits from economies of scale are not gained at lower levels of production. The dotted line indicates the effects on sales revenue if the product life cycle is not extended.

8. **Extending the Product Life Cycle**

An organisation with a range of products is likely to have them at different stages of the life cycle. It needs to recognise this because of the implications for the rest of the marketing mix. Also, because it is possible to extend the life of an established product beyond the maturity stage by means of an **extension strategy**. This needs to be based on carefully planned marketing and production decisions and could involve strategies for any or all of the following.

- **More frequent use** of the product eg sales of Mars confectionery products in the Summer were increased by 'Cool Em' in the fridge advertising; frozen turkeys are now sold throughout the year and not just at Christmas.
- **Finding new uses or markets** for the product eg Johnsons baby powder promoted to adults; electric shavers for ladies; exporting Scotch Whisky; shampoo for different hair types.
- **Modifying the product** to retain its consumer appeal. This may involve changing its physical appearance, image or ingredients and relaunching it in new packaging on a regular basis, often with heavy promotional expenditure. For example, new styling or accessories such as central locking or electronic windows on cars, introducing new shoes and clothes as existing ones go out of fashion.
- **Technical developments** for example, new packaging techniques can also bring about new market opportunities like the use of plastic bottles and wax cartons for milk, fruit juices and wine; ring-pull cans for beers and soft drinks.

Likewise, the growth in the home freezer market and consequently frozen food means that many products such as meats can now be sold both fresh and frozen, whilst ice cream can be sold in larger quantities.

- **Wider product range**. It may also be possible for a firm to introduce associated products or variations to its present range. Examples include diet (Pepsi), slimline (Schweppes Tonic Water) and low-fat (Ambrosia 'light' Creamed Rice) versions of main brands; new flavours (Shreddies – Coco and Frosted); new sizes (Kleenex tissues pocket pack) and simplicity to create wider appeal (Shredded Wheat 'Byte Size').

### Task 8.2

Ask yourself why products like Coca-Cola, Persil, Whiskas, Dairy Milk, Weetabix and Heinz baked beans have been so successful as market leaders for so many years, whilst others fail.

1. Identify at least 2 competitors for each of the products mentioned. Study and compare the marketing activities used.
2. Choose any 3 of the above or 3 examples of your own and briefly outline why you feel they have been so successful in extending the product life cycle.

9. **Product Development**

Although a product life cycle can be extended, for a firm to remain successful innovation is essential. New products must be developed which cater for changing markets as consumers demand new and better quality products. As sales of one product decline it must be replaced by a new one if the firm is to survive and keep ahead of its competitors.

10. As shown in the following example, Proctor and Gamble Limited have regularly introduced new fabric washing products, particularly during the 1980's. Some other examples of recent successful new products include Body Shop, Red Rock Cider, Plax, Lucozade Sport, Mars Ice-Cream snacks, Radion Micro and Persil washing up liquid. Against this, however, it has to be recognised that an incredible 95% of new advertised grocery brands have failed in the past 10 years, whilst many of the top brands like Kodak, Del Monte and Campbells have been around since the 1920's.

*8. The marketing mix – product and price*

## 11. Proctor & Gamble Limited Retail Fabric Washing Products

(with dates of national introduction)

| | | | |
|---|---|---|---|
| Dreft | 1937 | Daz Automatic Liquid | 1988 |
| Tide | 1950 | Fairy Automatic | 1989 |
| Daz | 1953 | Fairy Automatic Liquid | 1989 |
| Fairy Snow | 1957 | Bold Liquid | 1989 |
| Ariel | 1969 | Ariel Ultra | 1989 |
| Bold | 1972 | Daz Ultra | 1990 |
| Daz Automatic | 1979 | Bold Ultra | 1990 |
| Ariel Automatic | 1981 | Fairy Ultra | 1990 |
| Dreft Automatic | 1984 | Ariel Ultra Liquid | 1992 |
| Ariel Automatic Liquid | 1986 | Ariel Color | 1992 |
| Ariel Rapide | 1988 | | |

## 12. Product Withdrawal

When sales of a particular product or service do decline, a firm will need to determine whether this is

- **temporary** due, for example, to circumstances such as economic recession, the weather or new competition. The sales of ice cream, for example, would suffer in a bad summer.
- **capable of being reversed** by changing the marketing mix, perhaps the price or methods of distribution.
- **due to obsolesence** brought about by new technology which makes the product out-of-date. A recent example being the Sony Betamax VCR system which was replaced by VHS.
- **permanent and irreversible** making it necessary to withdraw it from the market. Launderettes, for example, were very successful until quite recently. However, the increase in the number of people buying their own automatic washing machines is now forcing many launderettes to close down.

13. In the short-term if sales are expected to recover, a firm may allow **cross-subsidisation.** This means it will retain it in the product range using profits from other products to cover any losses. However, a product which is not selling well may become relatively expensive to produce due to reduced economies of scale from lower production runs. Therefore if volume continues to decline, the product may be withdrawn (see Chapter 15).

---

**Task 8.3**

### LYMESWOLD IS OFF

Lymeswold, which in 1982 became the first new British cheese for 200 years, is being discontinued because of falling sales. The soft mould cheese was initially so popular that Dairy Crest build a new creamery at Aston, Cheshire, to cope with demand. But sales slipped and a relaunch failed to win back customers. The plant will close this week with a loss of 38 staff.

1. Why do you think that well-known products like Lymeswold Cheese and the Sinclair C5 electric vehicle have turned out to be unsuccessful?

2. Can you think of any other products or services which have been withdrawn from sale in recent years?

Try to identify at least 3 and consider what you feel are the likely reasons for their failure.

## Branding

14. Nowadays many goods are mass-produced, standard in nature with few, if any, real differences between competing rivals in terms of value and performance. Therefore, most products are given **brand names** or trade marks to differentiate between them. These names are usually registered so that they cannot be used by anyone else. Branding is used in consumer, industrial and service markets.

15. Branding enables manufacturers to advertise the **characteristics** and **qualities** of their products and build **brand loyalty**. Thus, for example, when consumers go into a shop, they do not just buy butter or coffee but look for Anchor, Lurpak, Nescafe, Maxwell House or some other favourite brand. This also affects **price elasticity** because consumer loyalty makes brands less susceptible to falling sales following a price increase. (See Chapter 4)

16. **Consumer Brands**

    Based on grocery outlets. Source: Neilsen. *All figures in millions.*

    | The Top Six Brands 1992 | | Top Six Fizzy Drinks 1992 | |
    |---|---|---|---|
    | 1 Coco-Cola | Over £400 | 1 Coca-Cola | Over £400 |
    | 2 Persil | £235 – £240 | 2 Pepsi Cola | £130 – £135 |
    | 3 Ariel | £230 – £235 | 3 Lucozade | £85 – £90 |
    | 4 Andrex toilet tissue | £185 – £190 | 4 Tango | £65 – £70 |
    | 5 Nescafé | £185 – £190 | 5 Schweppes mixers | £50 – £55 |
    | 6 Pampers | £170 – £175 | 6 Lilt | £35 – £40 |

    | Top Six Sweets 1992 | | Top Six Snacks 1992 | |
    |---|---|---|---|
    | 1 Kit Kat | Over £105 | 1 Walkers Crisps | Over £170 |
    | 2 Mars Bar | £85 – £90 | 2 Golden Wonder | £60 – £65 |
    | 3 Cadbury'sDairy Milk | £60 – £65 | 3 Hula Hoops | £55 – £60 |
    | 4 Roses | £55 – £60 | 4 Quavers | £30 – £35 |
    | 5 Twix | £55 – £60 | 5 Skips | £25 – £30 |
    | 6 Snickers | £55 – £60 | 6 KP Peanuts | £20 – £25 |

17. Branding can also be used to project a product 'image' that is an association of ideas which suggest that a product possesses particular characterisitics or qualities. 'Limmits', for example, suggests control as in a calorie controlled diet, whilst 'Gas Miser' conveys an image of economical heating.

### Task 8.4

1) What image is created by the following brand names?

    a) **Colour match** toilet rolls

    b) **Kwik-fit** car exhausts

    c) **Bonus Print** photographic developers

    d) **Tender Care** baby lotion

    e) **Pronto-print** printers

2) Identify 5 other products or services whose name promotes an 'image' and state what that image is.

18. Some firms sell their products under a **'family'** brand name such as Kelloggs, Heinz, McVities, Fisons and Amstrad, thus increasing the cost-effectiveness of advertising and promotion. This is known as **brand stretching**. This can also produce the **'halo effect'** as successful promotion of one brand often encourages the purchase of others in the 'family' range. Whilst on the other hand disappointment with one product may discourage the purchase of others.

19. **Multiple branding** sometimes called **product segmentation** is another technique which is widely used by, among others, pet food suppliers Spillers (eg Bonus, Choice, Champ, Kenomeat) and Pedigree (eg Chum, Bounce, Chappie, Pal) and soap powder giants Unilever (eg Persil, Surf, Radion, Comfort) and Proctor & Gamble (eg Daz, Tide, Bold, Ariel). This involves selling broadly similar products under a **variety of brand names** in order to achieve sales in a number of **market segments**. It also **creates competition** within an organisation between the various brand managers.

### Task 8.5

1. Make a list of as many different brands as possible of tea, television sets, paint and cars.
2. From your list, identify any examples of multiple-branding and/or brand stretching.

20. **Own Brands**

    Many retailers also sell goods which are specially made for them under their **own brand** name, which in many cases are a cheaper version of the well known brand. Examples include St Michael (Marks & Spencer), Boots, Tesco and Winfield (Woolworths).

21. Own brands are becoming **increasingly important** in attracting business because they are cheaper than famous brands (due to lower advertising and promotional costs); create store identity (through packaging) and customer loyalty (if you like ASDA's yoghurts you can only buy them from ASDA). They also offer higher profit margins than manufacturers' brands and enable retailers to control quality, prices and stock levels.

### Task 8.6

1) Referring back to Task 7.5, how many examples of 'own brands' can you identify for tea, television sets, paint and cars?

2) Why do you think that manufacturers of branded goods are prepared to produce similar products which retailers then sell at a lower price? The following news extract provides part of the answer.

#### BEATING THE RECESSION

The home market for Scotch Whisky represents only about 15% of total sales and exports were up by 6% in the first half of 1992.

Invergordon Distillers Group exports went up even faster, by 14%.

It even increased home sales by 6%.

The secret is in supplies to supermarkets of own brand whiskies.

A 12% rise in sales to Tesco and Safeway is highly visible.

## Packaging

23. An important part of branding is the use of packaging. Originally introduced to protect goods, packaging is now used to develop a **brands image** by making it distinct and easily recognisable. It is often an integral part of a product designed to add to its appeal through the use of colour, shape, size and logos all of which can have a significant effect on sales.

24. **Product differentiation** through packaging has become a vital aspect of consumer marketing since the development of self-service stores and impulse purchasing and is particularly important for successful advertising and sales promotion. In fact, with many products, the cost of packaging often

represents a very high proportion of the total price as, for example, with boxes of chocolates and Easter eggs.

25. **Product Strategy**

   In Chapter 7 we discussed the importance of setting market objectives such as increasing sales or market share. An organisation will usually achieve these objectives through the range of products which it offers to its chosen market segments. The product strategy which it adopts will essentially depend not just on the position of these products in their life cycle, but also the market forces which affect them including the type of consumer.

26. **Products and Market Forces**

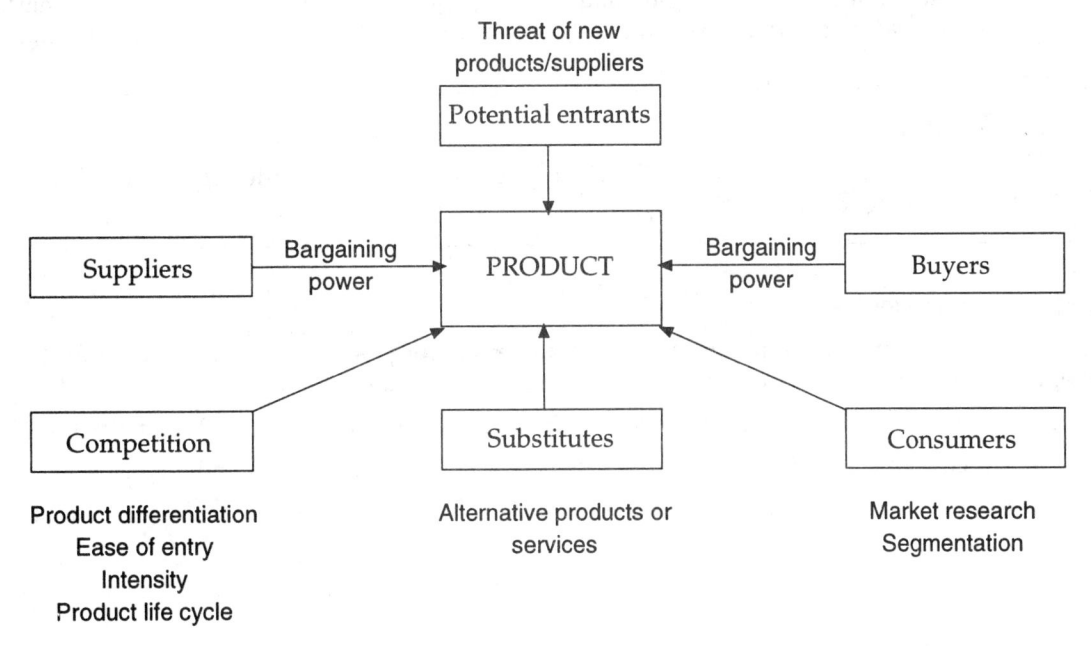

```
                        Threat of new
                        products/suppliers
                        ┌──────────────────┐
                        │ Potential entrants│
                        └──────────────────┘
                                 │
                                 ▼
   ┌──────────┐  Bargaining  ┌─────────┐  Bargaining  ┌────────┐
   │ Suppliers│─── power ───▶│ PRODUCT │◀─── power ───│ Buyers │
   └──────────┘              └─────────┘              └────────┘
                              ▲  ▲  ▲
             ┌────────────┐   │  │  │   ┌────────────┐
             │ Competition│───┘  │  └───│ Consumers  │
             └────────────┘  ┌───┴────┐ └────────────┘
                             │Substitutes│
                             └──────────┘

   Product differentiation   Alternative products or   Market research
   Ease of entry             services                  Segmentation
   Intensity
   Product life cycle
```

27. As shown in the diagram which is based on the model developed by Porter, there are a number of market forces which need to be considered in determining a product strategy. These include existing competition, potential for new entrants, availability of substitutes, power of suppliers, power of buyers and consumer analysis

28. **Existing Competition.** This may depend, for example, on the amount of product differentiation and therefore segmentation in a market. Thus, products like Coca-Cola and Heinz Baked Beans have created their own market segments. Other factors include the product maturity and ease of entry into the market which is considered below.

29. **Potential for New Entrants.** This is likely to depend on the existence of barriers, for example, high initial investment costs as with oil exploration or chemicals; government barriers like import tariffs; access to distribution channels such as wholesalers and large retailers, and again product differentiation. All of these factors make it difficult for new firms to enter an industry. Some markets, however, may be relatively inexpensive and easy to enter. For example, building trades, catering, nurseries, printing and retailing.

30. **Availability of Substitute Products.** This depends on whether or not there are other products which can perform the same function. Examples include butter and margarine; artificial sweeteners and sugar; savings accounts offered by banks and building societies.

31. **Power of Suppliers.** An organisation is dependent upon other businesses for the supply of goods and services which it uses. The power of these suppliers will usually depend on the actual number of firms involved. Some industries like British Telecom and Mercury for the supply of telephone services are dominated by a small number of very large and powerful firms. In this situation, lack of competition could cause potential problems. For example, if material costs are increased it could

force a business to either raise prices or accept a lower profit and thus possibly reduced investment whilst labour problems or a delay in delivery could affect production. It could also lead to the possible threat of the business being taken over the supplier. In the 1960's and 1970's large companies such as General Motors and British Leyland chose this vertical integration as a way of controlling supplies and obtaining a larger share of the added value. In more competitive industries, the power of suppliers is of less concern to organisations.

32. **Power of Buyers.** Some sectors like the retail trades are dominated by a small number of very powerful buyers like Sainsburys, Tesco and Marks and Spencer. They may choose to takeover a supplier or if dissatisfied, stop buying from them with possible disastrous consequences for the firm. They can also negotiate large discounts which can squeeze a firm's profit margins.

33. **Consumer Analysis.** This requires the use of market research to ensure that the companies existing products and new product developments are meeting the changing need of final consumers. It can also involve identifying customer segmentation so that products can be more effectively marketed. Thus, different strategies may be needed to sell the same product to different consumer groups.

> **Task 8.7**
>
> Choose any **two** products with which you are familiar and identify the market forces which affect them.

### 34. Competitive strategies

In most markets there will be a number of products jockeying for position. According to Porter there are 3 competitive strategies which a firm can use to achieve success in an industry.

- To produce **low-cost** products or services with wide appeal as with Ford or Vauxhall cars.
- To produce high-cost but **differentiated** products or services such as Mercedes cars.
- To **focus** products on a particular market niche, which is too small to attract bigger companies, as with Rolls Royce cars.

35.

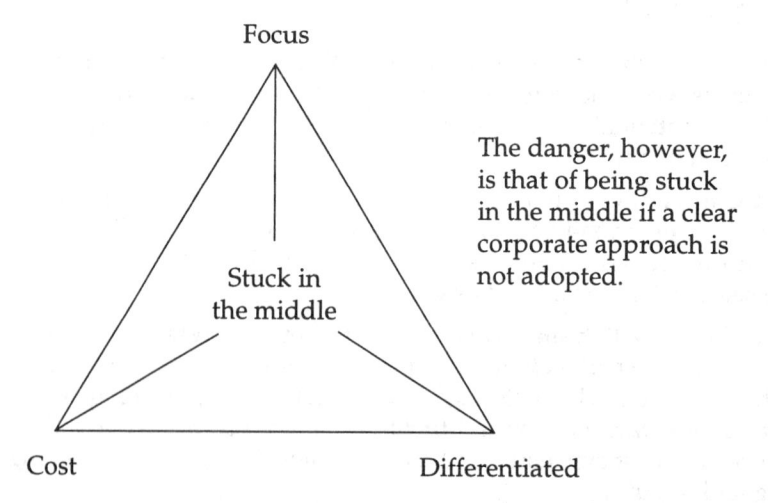

```
                Focus
                  /\
                 /  \
                /    \
               /      \
              /        \
             /  Stuck in \         The danger, however,
            /  the middle \        is that of being stuck
           /      /\       \       in the middle if a clear
          /      /  \       \      corporate approach is
         /_____/_____\     not adopted.
        Cost            Differentiated
```

## Market Analysis

36. Two major techniques used to analyse the product and market options available to organisations are the Boston Matrix developed by the Boston Consulting Group and the Ansoff Matrix, developed by Igor Ansoff.

# Boston Matrix

37. This is a way of representing a firms product range in terms of market share and market growth. It uses a simple log scale according to a product's ability to generate income.

38. **Boston Matrix**

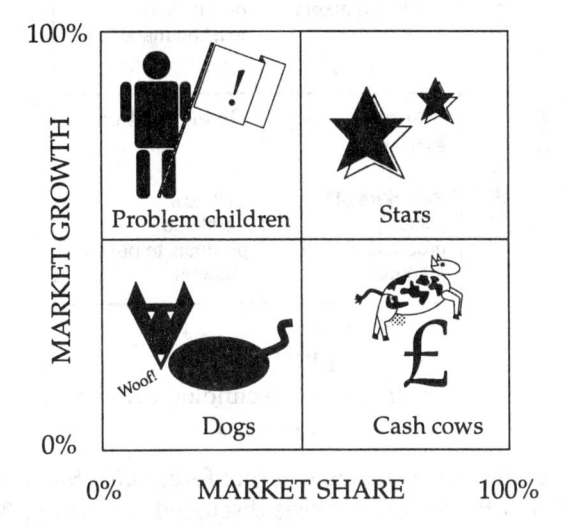

    (Matrix diagram: vertical axis MARKET GROWTH 0%–100%, horizontal axis MARKET SHARE 0%–100%. Top-left: Problem children. Top-right: Stars. Bottom-left: Dogs. Bottom-right: Cash cows.)

39. The matrix uses four categories of product:
    - **Stars** are very profitable products with high market share and a high growth rate. They are usually at the early stages of the product life cycle.
    - **Cash Cows** are established products which require little advertising. They have a high market share but low growth. These products generate a lot of cash and are usually 'milked' to help finance other products.
    - **Dogs** have low market share and a low growth rate. They have little potential for development and should therefore be withdrawn from sale.
    - **Problem Children** are products which are under achieving and therefore have an uncertain future. They have a high growth rate but only small market share. Therefore with a cash injection they may become stars but equally without it, could end up as dogs.

40. It is important for a firm to have a balanced product portfolio across the Boston Matrix. Cash generated from cash cows should be used to help the development of problem children and thereby help to ensure the future survival of the business.

41. **Ansoff Matrix**

    Ansoff considered marketing objectives as being about products and markets and explained his matrix as follows:
    - **Product Development** is the selling of new products in existing markets. Recent examples include Mars Ice Cream Snacks and Persil Washing-Up Liquid.
    - **Market Penetration** is the objective of increasing the sales of existing products in existing markets. That is, increasing market share or setting higher sales targets.
    - **Market Extension** involves increasing the sales of existing products but in new markets. Thus identifying a new age group or geographical area to which products can be sold.
    - **Diversification** involves selling new unrelated products in new markets. An example is Pedigree Petfoods which is a subsidiary of Mars.

42. **Ansoff Matrix**

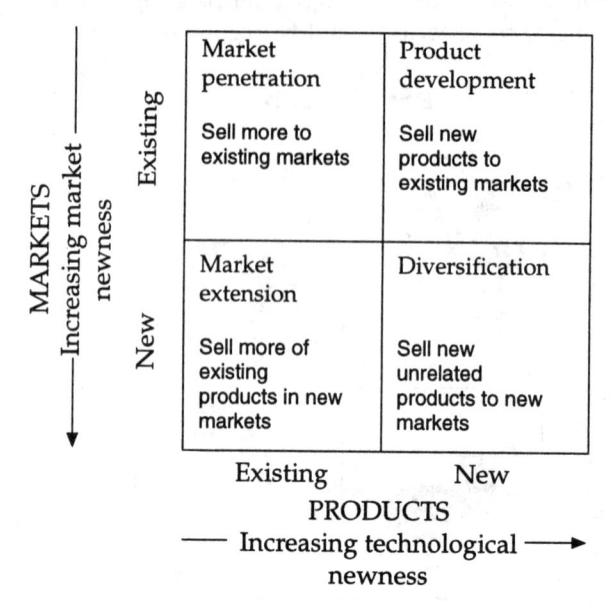

|  | Existing Products | New Products |
|---|---|---|
| **Existing Markets** | Market penetration — Sell more to existing markets | Product development — Sell new products to existing markets |
| **New Markets** | Market extension — Sell more of existing products in new markets | Diversification — Sell new unrelated products to new markets |

MARKETS — Increasing market newness (↓)
PRODUCTS — Increasing technological newness (→)

43. Thus, by examining the product life cycle, the external forces affecting a market and by using techniques like Boston, Ansoff and the SWOT analysis discussed in Chapter 3, an organisation can consider the many product options available to it. In respect of any particular product, this could include for example, decisions on whether to consolidate, expand, change its quality, features or performance, change the product mix or alter the branding. The product strategy will then provide a focus for the future direction of the organisation.

### Task 8.8

#### A LIGHTER MARS

The Mars bar was launched in this country in 1932 by American-born Forrest Mars. Using £25,000 borrowed from his chocolate magnate father, he set up a one-room factory in Slough, Berkshire. In his first year he sold two million bars at two old pence – less than 1p – each.

His family now controls 41 factories and has the world's fifth largest private fortune, estimated at £8 billion.

The business is now run by Forrest Jnr, John and Jacqueline Mars Vogel. Yet they still clock in and earn punctuality bonuses like every other Mars worker.

For 60 years Mars has helped us to 'work, rest and play' and is currently Britain's favourite chocolate bar, with annual sales of £55 million. But fierce competition in the 1990's has caused its market share to slip from 16 to 12.5 per cent which is why it is being given what its makers term 'image refreshment' involving a complete change of recipe and a multi-million pound relaunch. Out goes the traditional combination of 'glucose, milk and thick, thick chocolate'; replaced by a lighter, chewier and less malty-tasting confection. Out too goes the old advertising slogan in favour of 'Now there's more to a Mars'. Fronting the £5 million campaign, which is focused particularly on the teenage market, will be TV and radio presenter Danny Baker. A company spokesman explained that 'Major consumers of chocolate confectionery are teenagers and young adults, and we want to keep the product in the forefront of their minds'.

continued...

## Task 8.8 continued

If anyone can pull it off, Mars can. Many in the industry predicted that the firm would come unstuck when it renamed its Marathon bar Snickers two years ago. In fact, sales increased. Even so, the latest move is 'incredibly risky', according to Alan Mitchell of Marketing magazine. Pointing to the change of the recipe of Coca-Cola, which turned into a multi- million dollar flop in the US a few years ago, he warned: People's tastes are generally conservative. The new bar is very different in texture and taste, bringing a real danger that lovers of the traditional Mars will turn against it. The fact that the revamped product carries 15 more calories than the old one could also hurt sales, Mr Mitchell said.

Both bars have 452 calories per 100 grammes, but the replacement is bigger for the same price - 24p – so has 294 calories.

'People are turning away from big, sugary, gungey bars which are perceived as being unhealthy', said Mr Mitchell. 'That partly explains the Mars bar's drop in market share.

'Any company selling chocolate confectionery has to be wary of the health lobby, and Mars has had problems in this area in the past'.

In June 1992, the company won the right to keep its 'work, rest and play' slogan after the food watchdog Action on Information on Sugars complained to the Independent Television Commission that it was not medically justifiable.

The following are based on the case study.
1. Where would you place Mars bars on the Boston and Ansoff Matrixes?
2. What is 'new' about the new Mars bar?
3. What risks are associated with the relaunch of Mars bars?
4. Identify the examples of both the successful and unsuccessful relaunching of other well-known brands.
5. How and why will the new product be promoted?

## Price

44. The price of a product or service is another important part of the marketing mix. To maximise sales and profits, a firm will seek to fix a price which suits the market so that it is judged by customers to be reasonable and offering value in the circumstances prevailing at the time. This will be based on a combination of factors including the firm's objectives, the market in which it is operating, the type of product and the expected life span of the product.

45. Thus, for example, with new products, consumers are often initially prepared to pay a higher price. Likewise, quality products must be sold at a price which reflects that quality. The prices of commodities such as gold, sugar and wheat move up and down in response to changes in supply and demand, whilst a market trader selling fresh fruit and vegetables will often lower prices at the end of the day to clear stock. Insurance premium are calculated from the risk involved; products differentiated by branding such as Heinz baked beans may well sell at a price higher than that of rivals. These examples merely serve to illustrate the vast diversity of markets and products and the importance of pricing in the marketing mix.

## Pricing Objectives

46. If an organisation is to maximise its sales and profit potential it must have sound pricing strategies which support its marketing and corporate objectives. Clearly pricing objectives will not be the same for all business but commonly they will include the following:

- **Profitability** a key objective could be to set the price which increases the overall profitability of the business.

## 8. The marketing mix – product and price

- **Rate of return** – a firm may seek to obtain a specified return on its investment (capital employed) eg at least 10% or 20% pa.
- **Growth** – a price must be set which provides a steady profit over a period of years to enable the firm to survive and grow.
- **Competition** – the price charged should be competitive and attractive to customers. It can also be used to beat rivals in a price war or to discourage new firms from entering the market. In recent years many retail firms like Do-It-All and Currys have offered price promises like, 'never knowingly undersold'.
- **Market Share** – a price must be set which enables a firm to at least maintain its market share. Whilst lower prices may be used in an attempt to increase sales and market share by a quantifyable amount eg 10,000 or 10%.

### Task 8.9

**PRUDENTIAL CUSTOMERS PAY THE PRICE**

Around 30,000 motorists have deserted the Pru and gone elsewhere. Following rises in motor premiums of 8% in January, 6% in March and 5% in August with further increases expected.

The increase in premiums meant that the company was getting roughly the same income from policies despite having fewer policyholders but this demonstrates the difficult balance which the company faces between providing profits for its shareholders without upsetting its policyholders.

So far, shareholders are winning hands down. Shares in the Prudential jumped 6p to 236p yesterday after a 46pc jump in half time pre-tax profits to £249m. The dividend is lifted 7.9pc to 4.1p. But the profit increases owed much to large rises in premiums on motor and household insurance policies, turning a loss of £23m last time into a profit of £3m.

Some city experts believe that the Pru only stays in the car insurance business to allow its sales force the chance to sell savings plans to customers. Profits from its life operation rose 5pc to almost £200m, helped by a 6pc rise in new annual premiums and a 56pc jump in single premiums which the company says reflects the benefit of reorganising its direct sales force.

Nonetheless, policyholders face the prospect of a cut in bonus rates for the third year running.

1. What is the difficult balance which the Prudential faces?
2. Why did the company need to put up its prices and what effects did it have?
3. Explain the statement that 'so far the shareholders are winning hands down':
4. What type of pricing policy do you think the Company has adopted?

47. **Pricing Policies**

There are a number of different pricing policies or strategies which a firm amy adopt in order to achieve its pricing objectives. These include: skim, penetration, mixed, differential, absorption, promotional, marginal-cost, negotiable, single and market pricing.

48. **Skim Pricing** uses high prices to obtain a high profit and quick recovery of the research and development costs in the early stages of a product's life before competition intensifies. This is useful for products with a short life cycle such as 'pop' records and fashion items. Computers, videos, toys and compact discs provide other examples of 'new' products where consumers are often prepared to pay a high price.

49. **Penetration Pricing** is the use of lower than normal prices to increase market share. It is also used to establish a new product in a market which is expected to have a long-life and potential for growth. Consumer products are often introduced in this way.

50. **Mixed Pricing** is a policy which initially uses skim pricing and then, as competition increases, price cutting, sometimes even below cost, to penetrate the market, increase market share and eliminate competition.

51. **Skim, Penetration and Mixed Pricing**

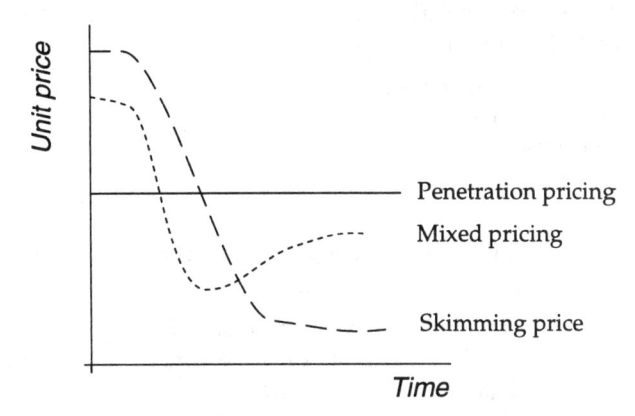

    (graph: Unit price vs Time showing Penetration pricing, Mixed pricing, and Skimming price curves)

52. **Differential Pricing** is the use of different prices for the same product when it is sold in different locations or market segments. Large buyers for example, often receive quantity discounts, whilst small buyers or those located in remote areas may be charged a higher price to cover the additional distribution costs. Telephone, gas and electricity are sold at different prices to domestic and industrial consumers and the price charged also depends on the time of day used.

53. **Absorption (cost-plus or full-cost) Pricing** involves calculating the cost of producing each unit of output and then adding a fixed percentage profit mark-up to give the price eg cost per unit £10, percentage mark-up 20%, price £10 + 2 = £12. Relatively slow selling items such as furniture are usually given a high mark-up whilst fast turnover items like foodstuffs in supermarkets are given a lower mark-up.

54. **Promotional Pricing** involves the use of lower than normal prices either to launch a new product or to periodically boost the sales of existing products. Supermarkets for example, have regular special offers and sometimes use **'loss leaders'** where everyday goods like tea and sugar are sold at less than cost to attract customers into the store.

55. **Marginal Cost (or contribution) Pricing** is sometimes used when a firm has some spare capacity which it wishes to use without diverting away from its regular business. Essentially, a firm incurs fixed costs such as rent, light and heat whether or not it is operating at full capacity. These costs are covered by the firm's regular products. Therefore sometimes a firm is prepared to accept additional business provided that the marginal (ie additional) revenue covers the marginal costs (ie materials and labour) involved and makes at least some contribution to the fixed costs which represents the profit. Market traders, for example, use this method when clearing fresh produce at the end of the day. Another example is the 'last minute' holiday bargains offered by package tour operators.

56. **Negotiable (or Variable) Pricing** is common in industrial markets and the building trade. The price is individually calculated to take account of costs, demand and any specific customer requirements. Customers may obtain estimates from a number of suppliers before placing an order, although factors other than price, such as quality and delivery may also be important.

57. **Single (or range) Pricing** involves a policy of charging one price to everyone. Examples include standard fares on bus or tube routes and publishers who often have a range of books at one price.

58. **Market Pricing.** In Chapter 4 we considered how prices can be determined by the interaction of demand and supply. The seller has little control over the price in this situation which is likely to fluctuate daily. Examples include commodity markets such as gold, silver, wheat and wool, and the Stock Exchange.

## 8. The marketing mix – product and price

59. **Sealed-bid pricing** is widely used in public sector markets whereby suppliers are invited to tender (offer a fixed price) for the supply of specified goods or services such as building work, furniture, catering or cleaning. Tenders must normally be submitted by a specified date in a sealed envelope. The contract is then usually awarded to the lowest bidder. A business will calculate a tender price based on its own costs and an analysis from knowledge and experience of competitors' likely bids.

> **Task 8.10**
>
> 1. Discuss the pricing objectives and market factors which are likely to influence the price of the following products and services:
>    a) Package Holidays to Spain
>    b) Inter-City Rail Fares
>    c) Dishwashers
>    d) Tinned Dog Food
>    e) Petrol
> 2. Is it possible to identify the typical pricing policies in each type of market?

60. As shown in Chapters 5 and 6, the price of a product or service may also be influenced by other factors. Examples include changes in interest rates or government policy and for imports or exports trading agreements, tariffs, barriers and customs duties.

> **Task 8.11**
>
> Glazeaway, a small local manufacturer of double glazing, which uses full-cost pricing, is facing increasing competition from both national companies and also a new company Bestglaze, which has recently commenced trading in the area. Bestglaze is using a number of price promotions to establish itself in the local market.
>
> From your knowledge of pricing policies:
>
> 1. Explain to Glazeway's owner the thinking behind the pricing policy of Bestglaze.
> 2. Advise Glazeway on a possible alternative to its current pricing policy.

## Summary

61. a) Successful firms produce products which satisfy consumer needs.
    b) Most products have a life cycle of sales covering their development, introduction, growth, maturity, saturation and decline.
    c) With careful planning and development, this life cycle can be extended.
    d) Products whose sales continue to decline over a period of time are likely to be withdrawn from the market.
    e) Innovation and new product development are essential if a firm is to remain successful.
    f) Branding is used by manufacturers and retailers to differentiate products and promote customer loyalty.
    g) Packaging is important not just to protect products but also to develop brand identity.
    h) A firm will usually achieve its objectives through its range of products
    i) A product strategy can be developed following analysis of the range and the market forces which affect it.
    j) The Boston and Ansoff Matrixes can be used to help analyse the various options available.
    k) Sound pricing strategies are important in order to maximise sales and profits.
    l) Pricing objectives may be related to a rate of return, growth, competition or market share.

m) Pricing policies include skim, penetration, mixed, differential, absorption, promotional, marginal-cost, negotiable, single and market.

## Review questions *(Answers can be found in the paragraphs indicated)*

1. What advantages are there to a firm of having a product range rather than a single product? (1-2)
2. Briefly describe the stages of the product life cycle. (3-4)
3. Outline the relationship between cash flow and the product life cycle. (6-7)
4. What can a firm do to extend the life cycle of a product? (8)
5. Outline the importance of product development and give at least 2 examples of recent successful new products. (9-11)
6. In what circumstances might a firm choose cross-subsidisation rather than product withdrawal? (12-13)
7. Why are brand names used in marketing? (14-17, 20-21)
8. Explain the difference between 'family brands' and 'multiple brands'. (18-19)
9. Why is packaging an important part of branding? (23-24)
10. Why does a firm need a product strategy? (25)
11. What factors will influence a firm's product strategy? (26-34)
12. Briefly describe the Boston and Ansoff Matrixes. (36-42)
13. Using examples, explain the key factors which a firm will need to consider when pricing its products. (44-45)
14. Distinguish between pricing objectives and pricing policies. (46-47)
15. Describe four pricing policies which a firm amy choose to adopt. (48-59)

*Asterisks indicate those questions for which there are answers in Outline Answers (page 439)*

## Essay-style questions

1.* Discuss the view that marketing is wasteful because good products should sell themselves.
2. Two major techniques used to analyse the product and market options available to organisations are the Boston Matrix and the Ansoff Matrix. Describe and discuss the usefulness of each of these techniques.
3. Outline some potential pricing objectives for an organisation and the policies which may be used to achieve them.

## Short answer

1.* a) Explain, with the aid of a diagram, the concept of a product life-cycle.
    b) What can firms do to extend this cycle?
2.* a) With the use of examples, explain what is meant be a brand's 'image'.
    b) How can packaging be used to develop such an image.
3. a) What is a product strategy?
   b) What factors would be taken into account by a firm preparing a product strategy?

## 8. The marketing mix – product and price

**Multiple choice/completion**

1.* Which of the following is an example of 'own label' branding of video tapes:
   a) BUSH
   b) MEMOREX
   c) DIXONS
   d) FUJI

2.* Goods deliberately sold for little or no profit to attract business are called:
   a) Impulse purchases
   b) Loss leaders
   c) Special price offers
   d) Premium offers

3.* Which of the following would not be used to extend the life of a product?
   a) Finding new uses or markets
   b) Modifying the product to retain consumer appeal
   c) Extending the range with associated products
   d) Introducing new technological developments to replace it

4.* Skim pricing is best defined as charging:
   a) different market prices for the same product
   b) higher initial prices before competition intensifies
   c) lower than normal prices to increase market share
   d) lower than normal prices to boost sales

5. The packaging of Easter Eggs is an important part of product development for the following reasons except
   a) It is not part of branding
   b) It aids advertising and promotion
   c) It represents a high proportion of price
   d) It is necessary for protection

6. A product can be said to have reached the maturity stage in the product life cycle when
   a) sales are only increasing slowly
   b) sales are increasing rapidly
   c) sales are falling
   d) sales have stopped rising

*In each of the following questions, one or more of the response(s) is/are correct. Choose the appropriate letter which indicates the correct version.*

   A  if 1 only is correct
   B  if 3 only is correct
   C  if 1 and 2 only are correct
   D  if 1, 2 and 3 are correct

7. Which of the following is/are likely to be a pricing objective for a business?
   1. To increase market share
   2. To achieve a specified return on investment
   3. To follow the lead of competitors

8. Which of the following statements is/are correct according to the Boston Matrix analysis?
   1. Cash cows are established products which require little advertising.
   2. Dogs have low market share and a low growth rate.
   3. Problem children are products with an uncertain future.

## 8. The marketing mix – product and price

## Assignment

### BUBBLE BURSTS AFTER 32 YEARS

Now hands that do dishes can feel soft as your face ... with mild green Fairy Excel. No, it's not an adman's slip-up. It's the end of an era for a household brand name.

Procter and Gamble, who make Fairy Liquid, the country's best-selling washing-up product, are withdrawing it from sale after 32 years. It is being replaced by new Fairy Excel in a dramatic attempt by the company to see off a challenge from Persil Liquid, made by rivals Lever Brothers.

The two giants have been locked in combat ever since Persil's TV campaign launch in August 1990.

Fairy – ranked 29th in the list of products most bought by shoppers – has long relied on claims, backed up on screen by established stars like Nanette Newman in recent years, Barbara Murray in the late Seventies and Tony Blackburn in the early Eighties.

By 1990, it had captured about 44 per cent of the £110 million market but dropped two or three points by 1992.

Fairy Excel will be sold in new 'dumpy' bottles and launched with a £10 million TV campaign supported by a nationwide issue of money-off coupons.

Procter & Gamble have been very careful in that the bottle still uses the name Fairy very prominently. Marketers spend millions trying to buy public recognition. 'No-one wants to pour that down the drain, especially with a market leader' said a spokesman, who also claimed that the name change was purely the result of an improvement in the liquid's formula. 'The new product's grease-cutting action is sufficiently marked to merit the change to one of the best-known brand names in the country'.

The battle between Fairy and Persil, which now has about 18 per cent of the market, has seen a succession of price cuts and special promotions. Fairy's boast of being the best was challenged by Persil's makers in September 1990. The ITV Commission stunned Procter & Gamble by upholding a claim that Persil was better, provoking the launch of a 'stronger formula' Fairy Liquid.

After a series of hearings, the Commission finally ruled that neither product could say it was the best, though both could claim to be 'unbeatable'. Procter & Gamble promptly launched a campaign claiming Fairy was longer-lasting.

Fairy Excel is Procter & Gamble's answer to this ruling.

The story may not end there, however, it is already rumoured that Persil Liquid will soon be relaunching.

The above article is based on newspaper reports in August 1992.

1. Explain, with examples, the following terms which are used in the article.
    a) Household brand name.
    b) TV campaign
    c) Launch and relaunch
    d) Market and Market Leader
    e) ITV Commission

2. How had the Fairy Liquid brand managed to achieve the position of market leader?

3. Why did the 'bubble burst' after 32 years?

4. Identify the key factors of the launch of new Fairy Excel.

5. Describe and discuss the current competitive position in the market for washing-up liquids. Comment on how you feel it might develop in the future.

# 9. The Marketing Mix – Promotion and Place

In Chapter 8 we considered two elements of the marketing mix namely, product and price. This chapter covers the other two elements of promotion and place and includes:

- * Sales Promotion
- * Trade and Consumer Promotions
- * Industrial Promotions
- * Direct Mail
- * Advertising
- * Advertising Media
- * Advertising Costs
- * Advertising Agencies
- * Advertising Benefits/Criticisms
- * Control of Advertising
- * Public Relations
- * Personal Selling
- * Distribution
- * Wholesalers
- * Retailers
- * Distribution Decisions

## Promotion

1. A third element of the marketing mix is promotion or the **'communications mix'** which is an essential part of modern business activities. It comprises sales promotion, advertising, public relations (PR) and personal selling. Promotion focuses on the distinctive feature(s) of a product called the **unique selling point** (USP). The basic aim of the promotion then is to communicate information to customers and potential users about the products or services on offer and eventually to persuade them to buy.

2. **Sales Promotion**

   Sales promotion involves many carefully planned events and activities which take place throughout the year to attract customers. With consumer goods and services promotional activities basically fall into three groups covering trade promotions, consumer promotions and in-store displays.

3. **Trade Promotions**

   These are aimed at distributors (retailers and wholesalers) to persuade them to stock a firm's products. Examples include:

   - **competitions** offering prizes such as televisions and holidays.
   - **special discounts** usually for buying large quantities
   - **bonuses** such as free extra packets per case.
   - **cash incentives** like money back in return for proofs of purchase.

4. **Consumer Promotions**

   These are used to create interest and tempt potential customers to make a purchase. Examples include:

   - **free gifts** like underfelt or fitting with carpets.
   - **special price offers** such as 'sales' and the regular monthly promotions run by supermarkets.
   - **loss-leaders** where certain items like bread or sugar are sold at below cost to attract customers.
   - **free samples** either given out in-store or distributed door-to-door.
   - **competitions** offering holidays, cars and other prizes.
   - **personality promotions** where famous people like actors and footballers are used to open or visit stores.

- **coupons** offering money off.
- **premium offers** where goods like soft toys are offered at special prices in return for proofs of purchase.
- **credit cards** are often issued by large retailers like Debenhams and Dixons in an attempt to increase sales.
- **credit facilities** offered at low-cost or interest free can be as important as price with some products such as cars and electrical appliances.

5. **In-Store Displays**

   Displays or demonstrations are used to attract potential customers at the **point-of-sale**, that is, where they make their purchases. These are usually supported by related point-of-sale materials such as posters, banners, placards and showcards and often linked to some other promotional offer like a special price for maximum impact.

   > **Task 9.1**
   > 1) Visit 3 local retailers and in each try to identify at least 4 examples of consumer and/or trade promotions. Alternatively you could list as many examples as possible of consumer promotions which have been purchased in your household during the last month.
   > 2) Try to identify the USP for each product.

6. **Industrial Promotions**

   Modified versions of some consumer promotions may also be suitable for industrial goods depending on the type of product.

   Examples include:

   - **seminars and demonstrations** to illustrate the features and benefits of products.
   - **catalogues**, technical and other promotional leaflets.
   - **trade shows and exhibitions** like the Business to Business Exhibition and Automotive Trade Show.
   - **free training** which is popular with computer sales.
   - **credit terms** using special low interest finance may be a big incentive with expensive items.

   > **Task 9.2**
   > Which types of sales promotion would you recommend in each of the following situations?
   > 1) An educational publisher promoting a new textbook.
   > 2) A company launching a new ice-cream product.
   > 3) A manufacturer of industrial safety equipment.
   > 4) The launch of a new automatic washing machine.

7. **Direct Mail**

   A rapidly growing form of promotional activity in both consumer and industrial markets involves the use of **direct mail** communication. This mail can be sent either by door-to-door distribution (mail drops) or more commonly through the post (mail shots).

8. Mail shots are often referred to as 'junk mail' but despite this they are often successful and cost-effective because they can be used to target particular market segments. Firms use market research

and computer databases to obtain and record information about existing and potential consumers. Then, by carefully analysing this data, they can more accurately target mail shots thus increasing the potential response rate.

> **Task 9.3**
>
> Read the following news item and complete the tasks which follow:
>
> ### THE BUYERS WHO CAN'T RESIST JUNK
>
> Junk mail may be seen as a nuisance by many people – but it sells.
>
> More than a quarter of adults who receive it go on to buy goods and services offered, a report by market analysts Key Note reveals. Over half of the items that land on the country's doormats are received unsolicited. Direct mail accounts for almost 20 per cent, free newspapers another 18 per cent and leaflets and coupons a further 16 per cent.
>
> Junk mail is ditched unopened by 44 per cent of adults and eight per cent have asked to be taken off a mailing list. But the study shows that 26 per cent use it for purchases.
>
> 1) Define 'junk mail'.
> 2) Identify the examples given of junk mail.
> 3) How much junk mail is never read?
> 4) What evidence is there of the success of junk mail?
> 5) How might this information be of value to business organisations?

## Advertising

9. Over £7,700 million was spent on advertising in 1993 and it is an essential part of any business if firms are not to lose out to their competitors. The largest advertising expenditure is on food, retail and mail order services, financial services, cars, drink, household goods and leisure equipment. It is through advertising that sales promotions are communicated to existing and potential customers.

   Advertising is also used by other organisations such as charities wishing to raise funds and the government to put across messages to the public, eg 'don't drink and drive!'.

10. **Consumer Advertising**

    Advertising is used by firms to **inform** potential customers about goods and services which they sell. This may include details of new lines, special offers or features, support seasonal, national or local events or coincide with a manufacturers promotion.

    However, the main object of advertising is to increase sales by **persuading** people to buy a certain brand of goods or buy at a particular shop.

    Advertising is also frequently used to raise **awareness** by keeping the name of a product or store before the public in order to maintain sales.

11. **Two Parts to Consumer Advertising**

    - Advertising by **stores** who want to persuade as many customers as possible into their shops to make purchases, for example, MFI, Dixons, and ASDA.
    - A massive volume of advertising is carried out by **manufacturers** to encourage consumers to buy their products. For example Kelloggs, Wrangler, Phillips, and Nike.

    Some firms such as BP and ICI also use **corporate advertising** where the image of the organisation rather than its products are promoted, although clearly this can have the spin-off of extra sales.

*9. The marketing mix – promotion and place*

> **Task 9.4**
> Make a list of advertisements shown on television and the number of times each is shown in one evening (or within a particular period of time).
> Consider and compare:
> 1) the time at which each is shown.
> 2) the age or type of person at which each is aimed ie target group.
> 3) Whether they are of national, or purely local interest.
> 4) What 'gimmick', if any, is used to catch people's attention.
> 5) Whether it is a retailer or manufacturer advertising.
> 6) Any examples of corporate advertising.
> 7) Any other interesting features.
> 8) Draw conclusions from your findings.

## Advertising Media

12. The term media is given to the various methods which firms can use to advertise their goods and services. If a firm wants its advertising to be seen throughout the country, then it may well use the **mass media** such as television and newspapers which can very quickly reach millions of people everywhere.

13. Media have both **quantitative** characteristics, basically the **cost** and **coverage** (number of people likely to see or hear it), and **qualitative** characteristics. The latter includes

    - the **usage** of the media; for example a daily newspaper is often quickly thrown away whilst a magazine may be kept for several days or weeks. Also
    - the **creative scope**, that is, the opportunities for audio or visual effects from television and cinema compared with newspapers and magazines;
    - the **vehicle effect** or how an audience perceives the media, for example the *Times* as representing quality and social class compared with the *Sun*; and
    - the **user-friendliness** or how easy or difficult the media is to buy, schedule, control and evaluate. A TV advertisement for example, can often only be booked or cancelled many months in advance, whilst newspaper advertisements can be placed within a few days.

14. **Main Advertising Media**

    Some key features of various media can be summarised as follows:

    - **Newspapers and magazines.** Printed media which represents a cheap way of reaching millions of people. Can be local or national, and targetted to cater for particular groups or special interests, eg *Financial Times, Womans Own, Gardeners Weekly*. Trade magazines, for example, the *Grocer, National Newsagent, Nursing Times* and *Computer News* may be used by manufacturers to inform potential customers about new products or special promotions.
    - **Television.** More expensive but offers colour, sound and movement to catch attention. Can demonstrate product features and benefits. A very powerful local and national media, difficult to target accurately, but reaches vast audiences which vary with channel and time.
    - **Cinema.** Some 75% of total audiences are in the 16-34 age group. Accurate targetting possible. With 'captive' audience in relaxed atmosphere. But advertisement may only be seen once.
    - **Commercial Radio.** Popular with local business as a relatively cheap form of advertising. Portable but audio only. 'Spots' can be repeated.
    - **Outdoor Advertising.** Includes large hoardings along main roads, posters on buses and shop windows and neon signs which are lit up at night. Cheap but sites vary in size, visibility and impact.

- **Catalogues, circulars and leaflets.** Often handed out in shopping centres, at exhibitions or sent by direct mail. Relatively cheap and may be used for general distribution or specific targetting.

> **Task 9.5**
>
> Collect three advertisements from three different publications aimed at a particular target group.
> 1. Say where they were published.
> 2. Identify the target group at which they were aimed.
> 3. State whether or not you think they are likely to be effective, giving reasons for your views.
> 4. Compare and contrast your findings with those from Task 9.4.

15. **Other Methods of Advertising**

    These include the advertising on beer mats, sandwich boards, bags and wrapping paper, the back of bus tickets, names on key rings, pens and calendars, the use of the Yellow Pages telephone directory and sponsorship where businesses support special events to gain publicity and/or promote an associated product image. Carling in football and Powergen ITV weather are well known examples.

## Choosing Advertising Media

16. Where firms advertise will depend on the cost involved, the type of goods or services being promoted, the size of the firm, the market aimed at, the results expected and the budget available. The aim is to find the most effective combination of media at the lowest cost and with the most persuasive message possible.

17. Since advertising is expensive, to be effective it must be done where the maximum number of potential customers can see it, and be done well to attract the greatest number of buyers. When choosing a media, advertisers will always take into account the type of people they wish to reach, for example will they be male, female, young, old, rich or poor? It is the type of people who are likely to buy the product which determines how an advertisement is designed and where it is to be placed.

## Advertising Costs

18. This depends on the media used and the size, or length of the advertisement. As a general rule, the bigger or longer the advertisement, the more it will cost. But the cost also depends upon the number of people who are likely to see it. For example, a television advertisement is most expensive at peak viewing times because the potential audience is greater; a full page in a national newspaper costs considerably more than a full page in a local newspaper because the larger circulation means that more people will read it.

19. **Some Typical Examples of Advertising Costs**

    | | |
    |---|---|
    | Regional Television | £12,000 for 10 seconds (peak viewing) |
    | Local Radio | £250 for 30 seconds |
    | National Daily Newspaper | (10cm x 2 columns) £2,500 per day |
    | Local Evening Newspaper | (10cm x 2 columns) £200 per evening |
    | Local 'Free' Newspaper | (10cm x 2 columns) £100 per issue |
    | Oracle | £1,000 per page per week |
    | Stands at Major Exhibition | £1,000 per day |
    | Panel on side of Bus | £70 per space per month |

    *NB* Rates vary depending on size/time/position/frequency of advertisement

20. Up-to-date information on the unit costs and size of audiences or circulation of all the main media (press TV, cinema, radio and outdoor) is published monthly in the British Rate and Data (BRAD).

21. **Expenditure On Advertising**

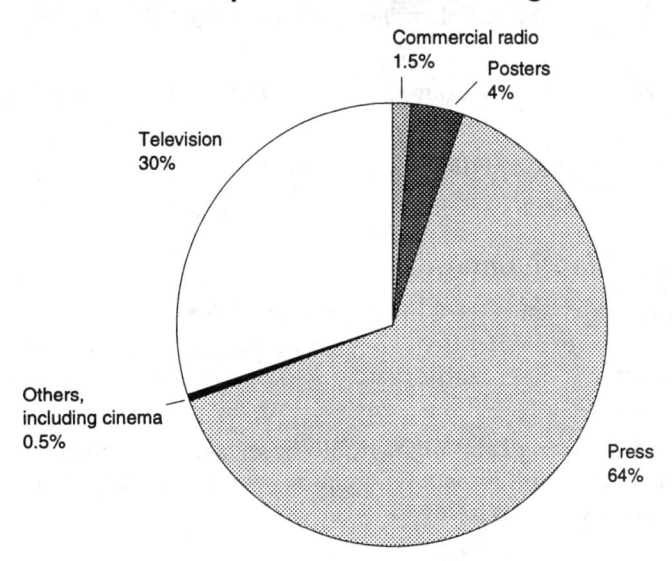

- Commercial radio 1.5%
- Posters 4%
- Television 30%
- Others, including cinema 0.5%
- Press 64%

### Task 9.6

Which method(s) of advertising and promotion would you consider to be the most suitable and effective for each of the following. Be specific and give reasons for your answer.

a. A small local newspaper
b. A multiple shoe retailer
c. A large mail order company
d. A bank
e. A teenage magazine
f. To attract foreign tourists to your area
g. To introduce a new toothpaste
h. To sell a second-hand bicycle
i. To promote a school charity concert
j. To sell Rolls-Royce cars

## Advertising Agencies

22. Firms can either arrange their own advertising or instead may use an advertising agency, for example Saachi and Saachi, J.Walter Thompson. These are specialist firms who employ experts to find the most effective way of advertising. An agency will plan and carry out an advertising campaign for clients for which they usually charge a fee. This involves the firm in **below-the-line** expenditure.

23. Alternatively, they may operate on an **above-the-line** basis, where their main income comes from commission received in the form of a discount from the media concerned. The firm may only have to pay for artwork or other specialist services.

24. Press, radio, TV, cinema and outdoor advertising media all offer agency discounts. In practice, a campaign will often involve both above and below-the-line expenditure.

25. Agencies carry out five main functions:

- **Market Research** is used to discover information on which to base the advertising. The success of a campaign can also be monitored through research.

- **Media Planning** – which involves selecting the most suitable media and booking it. For example, the time on television or space in the press.

- **Creating the Advertisement** – ie designing the advertisement and writing what is called the copy often with 'catchy' slogans. For example, 'The answer's yes at TSB', 'Mr Kipling makes exceedingly good cakes.'

- **Producing the advertisement** – for example making a film for television or drawing an illustration for the press.

- **Account Management** – agencies will look after a firms advertising budget and advise them on future campaigns.

## Measuring Advertising Effectiveness

26. To be successful, advertising must be cost effective, that is, it must bring in greater revenue than it costs. The advertising message, media, frequency and duration plus the other elements of the marketing mix must be carefully chosen and organised to produce the maximum impact and desired increase in sales at least cost.

27. The effectiveness of an advertising campaign should be measured against the objectives it was trying to achieve and therefore the full impact may not be easy to calculate. Typically, this is evaluated in terms of increased sales revenue as follows:

$$\frac{\text{Proportionate change in sales volume}}{\text{Proportionate change in promotional expenditure}}$$

28. For example, if from market research a firm discovers that 25% of the market is aware of a product and 10% have tried it, an advertising campaign might be launched with the objective of increasing these figures to 50% and 20% within 6 months. The success of such a campaign could only be measured using market research techniques. Other objectives, however, such as increasing consumer awareness, pack recognition, brand image, or raising a firm's public profile may also be important but much more difficult to measure against objective criteria. Therefore, market research techniques such as questionnaires, consumer panels and psychological testing may be used for evaluation (see Chapter 7).

29. Other methods used include 'keyed' (coded) advertisements in the press so that the response from particular newspapers or magazines can be identified, whilst with direct mail, the percentage response rate can be used as a measure. It must be remembered however, that increased sales may not necessarily come about immediately but could be spread over several months after the end of a campaign.

### Task 9.7

John Cronin and Nina Patel have recently started a small Greengrocery business on the outskirts of a large town. They have budgeted £750 to cover both advertising and sales promotion for 12 months.

1) Advise them on how best to spend it using at least 3 different methods of each.

2) With reasons, say whether or not you would recommend them to use an advertising agency.

3) How would you suggest that they measure the success of their campaign?

## Benefits of advertising

30. - Consumers receive **information** about new and exciting products, enabling them to make comparisons.

- If firms sell more then mass production is possible. Producing larger quantities is cheaper and therefore leads to **lower prices.**
- Advertising promotes **competition** between firms and this results in lower prices and better quality products.
- Advertising **pays for ITV and Commercial Radio,** and keeps down the cost of **newspapers and magazines.**
- It can help to reduce sales fluctuations thus **aiding production planning.**

## Criticisms of Advertising

31  It is often argued that advertising is both **immoral** and **wasteful of resources** because:
- Initially it can lead to **higher prices,** for example if a product costs 10p to make and 2p to advertise, then this will mean a higher selling price.
- People may be persuaded to **buy goods which they cannot afford** and do not really want.
- Some products may be **harmful,** for example medicines, alcohol and tobacco. The advertising of cigarettes on television was banned in 1965 because it was felt that they were harmful to health.
- Advertising **can make people dissatisfied** by appealing to their ambitions, desires and emotions. For example, 'keeping up with Jones's, success with the opposite sex, or in a job; it encourages greed, or an easier life with more leisure.
- Advertising may lead us to believe that we can **only achieve** these **by buying a particular product.**
- It can be used to maintain **monopoly power** and prevent entry of rival products.
- It is used by **charities and under-developed countries** whose resources could be put to better use.

## The Control of Advertising

32. Manufacturers and retailers cannot say anything they like in **advertisements,** otherwise this might lead to all sorts of misleading claims to entice customers. Therefore advertising is carefully controlled to protect consumers. This control takes two forms, voluntary control consisting of a list of rules drawn up by the industry itself and which advertisers have agreed to follow, and legal control enforced by laws passed by the government.

33. **Voluntary Control**

    **The Advertising Standards Authority (ASA)** This is a self-regulating body, financed by the industry. It issues the 'British Code of Advertising Practice' which is a list of guidelines aimed at ensuring that all advertising is 'legal, decent, honest and truthful', monitors advertisements and investigates complaints.

34. **Legal Control**

    **The Broadcasting Act (1990).** This was introduced to provide for the regulation of both independent television (ITV) and radio. It set up an **ITV Commission** which controls the issue of licences and generally regulates ITV including local cable and satellite services. The Commission has a Code of Practice which includes advertising standards and methods. It also has the power to investigate complaints and ban advertisements which do not comply with the Code. A **Radio Authority** was also set up to issue licences and oversee all independent radio services again including advertising.

35. **The Trade Descriptions Act (1968).** This aims to ensure that traders tell the truth about goods and services. The descriptions used in advertisements must be accurate and truthful. If the law is broken, offenders may be fined or imprisoned. Altogether about 60 laws have been passed which affect advertising in some way.

36. **The Consumer Credit Act (1974).** This states that advertisements for goods sold on credit must include the cash price, the credit price and the true rate of interest.

*9. The marketing mix – promotion and place*

> **Task 9.8**
>
> ### DIY STORE FINED
> Texas Homecare was fined £2,400 with £1,000 costs by St Albans magistrates after being found guilty of eight charges of overcharging under the Trade Descriptions Act. The case was brought by Hertfordshire Trading Standards Department.
>
> ### MFI FINED OVER PRICES 'CON'
> The furniture giant MFI has been ordered to pay nearly £27,000 in fines and costs for misleading customers during sales promotions. The company was convicted of breaching consumer protection laws following an inquiry by trading standards officers. Swansea magistrates heard the firm made false claims of huge discounts at a store at Llansamlet and issued misleading sales literature and newspaper adverts.
>
> 1. Why do consumers need protection from unfair trading practices?
> 2. What legal protection is currently available?
> 3. How do the above news reports illustrate the enforcement of the law?

## Public Relations

37. In order to create goodwill, an organisation will often deliberately try to ensure that the public is kept informed about its trading and other activities. This is called **public relations** (PR) which can be defined as **the planned and sustained action to establish and maintain mutual understanding between an organisation and its public.**

38. The 'public' is very wide ranging and depending on the organisation could include not just existing and potential customers, but also suppliers, distributors, shareholders, trade unions, financiers such as banks, local and central government departments, pressure groups, employees and the general public.

39. PR should be used as an integral part of the 'Communications mix' and targetted at a wide range of media, most typically this will be newspapers, magazines, TV and radio. It is a highly specialist function, usually handled by a PR consultant or senior marketing personnel, which involves issuing regular 'press' releases, adapted for the chosen media, about the organisation's activities, products and employees. For example, the opening of a new shop or factory or a change of management. This has the added advantage that it is 'published' free of charge.

40. An organisation may use PR for a number of reasons, some examples of which are outlined below:

    - To develop a **corporate image** and reputation by making sure that the public has a favourable impression of the organisation and knows about its strengths and achievements.
    - To **offset bad publicity** in a positive and constructive way.
    - To show that the organisation is a **leader** or innovator in its area of business eg reporting the latest advances in research or new product development which may be important in attracting employees and customers.
    - To inform the public that the organisation is **socially responsible** and concerned about the interests of its customers and the community, eg support for charity events, environmental protection.
    - To inform the public about **proposed actions** and policies, and possibly influence pressure groups, particularly where this may affect the social or physical environment. eg if plans to build a new factory are likely to produce major objections.
    - To foster **good relations** with all levels of staff in an organisation. Good PR can enhance an employees sense of pride and commitment to an organisation and hence their level of performance.

## Task 9.9

### SHARE STATEMENT

The board of construction group M J Gleeson says it considers a fall in the company's share price is nothing more than a 'market adjustment' since it has out performed the sector for 12 months.

### KEEP IN TOUCH PLEASE!

Tourists should have a contact point when they go abroad in case of urgent messages, and should register with the British consulate if away more than a few months, the Red Cross advises.

### COUNDON SHOP TOP

Master butcher Geoffrey Saunders, manager of Dewhurst, Coundon, Coventry, and his staff are celebrating success in a national Best Kept Shop competition. Geoffrey and his team are Coventry district winners in the Dewhurst Group's Best Kept Shop competition, open to 1,400 shops throughout England, Scotland and Wales.

1. From the above examples of PR, identify the target 'public(s)'.
2. Collect 5 other examples of PR from a selection of local and national newspapers.
3. From these, identify what you feel is the main purpose of each 'story' and which members of the 'public' it is aimed at and/or most likely to influence.

41. A possible problem with PR is that, although the organisation submits the 'story' it has no control over the final content of the communication as this is determined by the editor of the media concerned. Nonetheless, this form of PR is very cheap and important in promoting a business and its products or services.

42. A further important aspect of PR is customer relations which in large organisations is often the responsibility of a separate department. Customer dissatisfaction must be dealt with promptly both to protect an organisation's reputation and to prevent the loss of future business.

43. PR can also be developed in other ways including the production of house magazines, loan videos about the organisation and its products and factory visits. The advantage of these methods is that although there is a cost involved, the organisation can actually control the PR content and invite direct feedback from the 'users'.

## Task 9.10

1) Which of the following would represent PR for a local company?

   a) Sponsorship of a hospital Summer Fete.
   b) An advertisement in the national press.
   c) Use of direct mail to launch a new product.
   d) Factory visits for organised groups
   e) A promotional video for use in schools

2. For the organisation in which you work or study, suggest with reasons, the three most appropriate methods of PR.

## Promotional Budgets

44. There are a number of different ways of determining the amount to be spent on the various forms of promotion including advertising and PR.

    The following methods are amongst those commonly used.

    - A percentage of last year's sales volume.
    - A percentage of next year's planned turnover.
    - With regard to the level of expenditure by competitors.
    - The allocation of an arbitrary sum.
    - Considering the objectives to be achieved and the cost of doing this.

    It is this latter method which would seem to be most logical and sensible although it may be more complex to work out.

## Personal Selling

45. Personal selling offers a two-way means of communication. By meeting customers 'face-to-face', sales staff can present the benefits of and, if appropriate, demonstrate an organisation's products or services. They can also deal with any queries and overcome objections which is particularly important with complex or expensive products. The most difficult task is to 'close-the-sale' having obtained an order.

46. Therefore, to increase the potential success of personal selling, it is usually supported by advertising, sales promotion and PR. These create awareness and develop interest and together, all four should form an integrated promotional plan.

47. Personal selling is widely used in **consumer markets** for both goods and services as the following examples show:

    Van deliveries eg milk, bread, coal.
    Double glazing, encylopaedias        } These are often sold direct
    Financial services eg insurance, pensions   to consumers' homes
    Retail outlets, eg clothing, footwear, cars
    Exhibitions eg Ideal Home, Motor Show.

48. It is also used by manufacturers whose sales representatives call on wholesalers and retailers. Nowadays, the power of mass advertising has reduced the need for selling in consumer markets and turned many company representatives into 'order-takers'. Consequently, some firms now telephone customers for orders to reduce selling costs.

49. Personal selling is particularly suited to **industrial markets** where products such as machinery, aircraft, chemicals and plastics and services like cleaning and maintenance are very specialised and may require modification or individual design to suit specific needs. Negotiations on technical specifications, finance, delivery and installation may be of paramount importance and require considerable selling skills.

## Sales Targets

50. Personal selling is a relatively expensive form of promotion and therefore an organisation must ensure that it is carried out in a cost-effective way. Therefore in order to achieve this, sales staff are usually set specific targets to achieve, such as a particular level of sales revenue (eg £2000); number of unit sales per week or month (eg 100) or a target ratio of orders to calls (eg 1:5) depending on the product or service. They are then often rewarded with commission, bonuses or prizes if these targets are met or exceeded.

### Task 9.11

Explain from your knowledge of advertising and personal selling why you agree or disagree with the statement 'Mass advertising often reduces the need for actual selling and consequently many company representatives have essentially become just 'order-takers'.

## Place – the Role of Distribution

51. A further element of the marketing mix is concerned with distribution. That is, the physical process of getting goods from manufacturers to consumers. Distribution involves the storage, transport and handling of goods which together can represent a significant element of a firm's costs.

52. **Distribution Objectives**

    The objectives of distribution are to get the right quantity, in the right place, at the right time and in the right condition. By right means what is right for the consumer. A supermarket customer, for example, looking for a $\frac{1}{2}$lb pack of a particular brand of butter will expect to find it. If it is out-of-stock then they are likely to purchase another brand. Thus, if distribution fails, all the other elements of the marketing mix will have been in vain.

53. **Chain of Distribution**

    In industrial markets there is often a direct link between the manufacturer and customer but in consumer markets, distribution more commonly involves the use of wholesalers and retailers as shown in the following diagram.

**The Chain of Distribution**

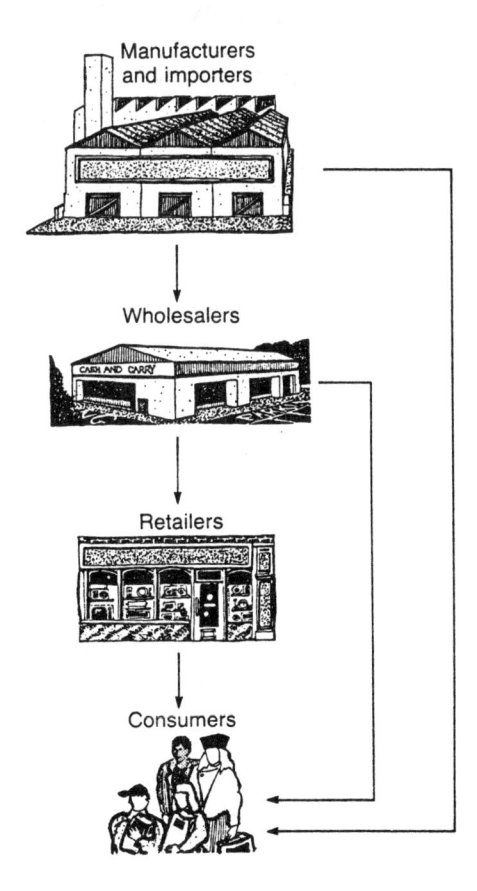

Manufacturers and importers
↓
Wholesalers
↓
Retailers
↓
Consumers

## Wholesalers

54. Wholesalers are often described as **middlemen** because they are the middle link in the chain of distribution. They buy goods in bulk from manufacturers and then sell them in smaller quantities to retailers. The goods are stored in a warehouse until required.

55. There are four main types of wholesalers:

    - **Traditional wholesalers** collect orders from retailers, deliver the goods and allow trade credit, eg W H Smith (newspapers and magazines)

    - **Cash and carry wholesalers** are rather like supermarket warehouses where retailers go to buy their goods and pay cash at the exit, eg Booker, Nurdin and Peacock.

    - **Voluntary or symbol groups** consist of a number of independent retailers who join together with a local wholesaler to enable him to buy in bulk from manufacturers. This leads to lower prices and it helps them to compete with bigger organisations. Sometimes a number of voluntary groups join together throughout the country to form voluntary chains, for example, Mace, Spar and VG.

    - **Co-operative Wholesale Society (CWS)** is the largest wholesaler in the UK and supplies goods for co-operative retail societies.

56. Several factors have led to a general decline in the number of wholesalers in particular improved transport and communications which make restocking easier and the development of large retail organisations who buy direct from manufacturers.

57. Despite this, wholesalers are still very important in the distribution of certain products, for example, newspapers and electrical items. Wholesalers also serve the needs of independent retailers, particularly in the grocery, fish, fruit and vegetable and clothing trades. When the wholesaler is eliminated someone else has to do the work. Large retailers, for example, who buy direct from manufacturers have to provide their own financing and storage for the goods.

58. It should be noted that 'middlemen' may be called merchants, agents, brokers, factors or wholesalers depending on which type of trade they work in. Examples include Corn Merchant, Insurance Agent, Stockbroker, Coal Factor and Cash and Carry Wholesaler. Thus some 'middlemen' make a profit by selling actual goods whilst others are paid commission or a fee for the work they do. Agents never actually own the goods or services which they sell but are paid for negotiating a sale, eg Estate Agents who sell houses.

### Task 9.12

The number of customers served by wholesalers has fallen considerably in recent years. Modern shopping centres are becoming increasingly dominated by large retailers who now buy direct from manufacturers and receive quantity discounts. Whilst some manufacturers, like Boots, sell direct to their own retail outlets. Cash and Carry Wholesalers have therefore developed in response to the need for independent retailers to be able to buy cheaper in order to compete with large retailers. But, although it has been possible to pass on the savings from transport costs to retailers, at the same time, they have lost the traditional facilities of delivery and credit on their purchases.

Answer the following questions which are based on the above article:

1. Who are a wholesalers customers?
2. In what sense have large retailers caused a decline in wholesaling?
3. How have some wholesalers adapted to this decline?
4. Why are the goods purchased by small independent retailers more expensive than those of large retailers?
5. What main advantage does a retailer gain from using a cash and carry wholesaler?
6. What services does a retailer give up in order to gain this advantage?

## Retailers

59. The retail trade is referred to as the last link in the chain of distribution because it brings goods and services to the final consumer.

60. There are many different types of **retailers** each of which provides particular services for consumers.
    - **Independent traders** offer personal counter service but their prices are often higher than other shops.
    - **Self-service stores** are often independent but frequently join group wholesalers, like Spar, to enable them to compete with larger shops.
    - **Supermarkets** offer cut prices and a wider choice of goods. eg ASDA, Tesco.
    - **Superstores and hypermarkets** are very large supermarkets usually located away from town centres, which sell a vast range of merchandise. eg Carrefour.
    - **Department stores** are found in the centre of large towns and cities and offer a large range of goods and have facilities such as toilets and restaurants. eg Debenhams, Harrods.
    - **Multiple retailers** (those with more than 10 branches) specialise in selling a wide variety of one particular type of merchandise. eg Burtons, Dixons.
    - **Variety chain stores** are multiples which sell a variety of goods. eg Woolworth, British Home Stores.
    - **Discount stores** concentrate on selling durable household goods at cut prices. eg Comet, Argos.
    - **Co-operative stores** are best known for the dividend which they give to customers.

61. There are also many methods of retailing **without using shops** including markets, mail order, mobile 'shops', door-to-door selling, party selling, automatic vending machines and trade fairs and exhibitions.

### Task 9.13

1. Suggest with reasons, the most appropriate distribution channel(s) for each of the following products:
    a) the sale of Asda's own brand tomato sauce
    b) the sale of paperback books
    c) the sale of industrial machinery
    d) the export of whisky to Europe
    e) the import of bananas from Jamaica
2. Outline the possible channels of distribution for each of the following services:
    a) package holidays abroad
    b) car insurance
    c) plumbing
    d) theatre tickets
    e) bank loan

## Distribution Management

62. Distribution is expensive and a firm must take decisions in respect of a number of important issues in order to achieve its overall objective of getting goods or services to final consumers.

63. These decisions include:
    - **Distribution chain**, for example, whether to sell direct or via wholesalers and retailers. If wholesalers are used it must consider how to ensure that its products are 'pushed'. Thus advertising and sales promotion may be needed so that customer demand 'pulls' the products and forces retailers to stock them. This is particularly important with the launch of a new product.

## 9. The marketing mix – promotion and place

- **Method of transport** such as whether to move goods by road, rail, sea or air. In addition, whether to have its own fleet of 'vehicles' or contract out. Efficient journey planning to reduce costs is also important.
- **Market Penetration**, for example, whether a firm's objective is to have the product stocked by all retail outlets or just selected ones such as chemists or supermarkets.
- **Location of warehouses** near to major transport routes may be important. Alternatively a firm may choose to have production facilities in several locations to reduce warehousing and transport costs.
- **Communication methods** like telephone or fax may be important for ordering and restocking products.
- **Type of packaging** used which may depend on the method of transport chosen.
- **Promotional policy.** Distribution can also be used as an important part of a firm's promotion. Thus, for example, fast cheap or free same day delivery, linked to telephone or fax ordering could give a firm an important competitive edge.

### Task 9.14

A car accessory company has recently developed a new technically advanced car polish. It has decided to sell this by mail order and through a selected number of specialist retail outlets.

1) Outline the main distribution factors which the management must consider.
2) Discuss the possible implications for the other elements of the marketing mix.

## Summary

64. a) Promotion involves all the activities used by businesses to maintain and increase sales and comprises sales promotion, advertising, PR and personal selling.
    b) Sales promotion covers trade promotions, consumer promotions and in-store displays to assist purchase at the point of sale.
    c) Some methods of sales promotion include reduced price offers, competitions, free gifts, trade fairs and exhibitions, coupons and low-cost credit facilities.
    d) A rapidly growing form of promotional activity is the use of direct mail.
    e) Advertising is used to inform potential customers about goods and services and to persuade them to buy.
    f) Advertising media includes press, television, cinema, commercial radio, outdoor advertising, catalogues, circulars and leaflets.
    g) Other methods may include names on carrier bags, key rings, pens, 'Yellow Pages' and sponsorship.
    h) Because advertising is a very specialised business, firms frequently use an advertising agency to carry out campaigns for them.
    i) There is both voluntary and legal control of what can be said or shown in advertisements.
    j) PR is used by organisations to keep their 'public' informed and to create goodwill and a favourable selling climate.
    k) Personal selling is widely used in both consumer and industrial markets and sales staff usually have to achieve targets.
    l) Distribution is the process of getting goods and services to the final consumer which may involve wholesalers and retailers or direct selling.
    m) There are many different types of retailers each providing particular services for consumers.
    n) There are also many methods of retailing without shops, including markets and mail order.

## Review questions *(Answers can be found in the paragraphs indicated)*

1) What do you understand by sales promotion? (1-2)
2) Distinguish between trade promotions, consumer promotions, and in-store displays. (3-5)
3) With examples, explain what you understand by direct mail. (7-8)
4) What are the main purposes of advertising? (9-10)
5) Name 10 different advertising media including two examples of mass media. (12-15)
6) Outline the main factors which a business should consider when choosing advertising media. (16-20)
7) How can the effectiveness of advertising be measured? (26-28)
8) Is advertising harmful or does it benefit consumers? (30-31)
9) In which 2 ways are consumers protected from false or misleading advertising? (32-36)
10) Explain with examples, what you understand by public relations. (37-43)
11) Outline the various methods of determining promotional budgets. (44)
12) Why is personal selling used in some markets and not others? (45-47)
13) Why are wholesalers generally less important today than they used to be? (53-57)
14) Identify the key features of 4 different types of retail outlets. (59-60)
15) List 8 methods of retailing without shops. (61)
16) Identify at least 5 factors which need to be considered in distribution management. (62-63)

*Asterisks indicate those questions for which there are answers in Outline Answers (page 439)*

## Essay-style questions

1.* Advertisers frequently have to choose between different advertising media. What are the main media and what factors have to be taken into account when making a choice? What media research is available to assist them?

2. Retailers often complain that promotional offers such as free gifts, coupons and competitions have become a nuisance to them. Discuss this comment and the advantages of promotional activity to retailers and manufacturers.

3. A recent newspaper article was strongly critical of the effects of advertising on society. Write a response to refute this view and include in it an outline of what you consider to be the benefits of advertising.

## Short answer

1.* a) What is the role of an advertising agency?
   b) On what basis do they charge for their services?
   c) State, briefly, with reasons, whether or not you would advise a business organisation to use such an agency.

2.* Give the full names and explain the purposes of each of the following commonly used abbreviations.
   a) USP
   b) PR
   c) BRAD
   d) ASA

3. Distinguish between
   a) 'above-the-line' and
   b) 'below-the-line' advertising expenditure
   c) What is the significance of each for advertisers and advertising agencies?

## 9. The marketing mix – promotion and place

**Multiple choice/completion**

1.* Which of the following is most useful to indicate to a firm that an advertising campaign has been successful?
   a) More people made enquiries about its products.
   b) A decision was made to move to larger premises
   c) Its buyers were contacted by more sales representatives
   d) More products were bought by its customers.

2. A manufacturer of plumbing supplies is most likely to advertise
   a) On television
   b) In cinemas
   c) In trade newspapers
   d) In national newspapers

3.* Which of the following statements is incorrect?
   a) A multiple is a retail group with 10 or more branches.
   b) Spar is an example of a voluntary chain.
   c) British Home Stores is a department store.
   d) Mail order is becoming more popular.

4.* Which of the following advertising media would be most appropriate for a sole trader opening a DIY store in a large town.
   a) Trade magazine
   b) Local newspaper
   c) Sunday newspaper
   d) Television

5. Direct mail advertising is often described as all but which one of the following?
   a) 'junk mail'
   b) mail drops
   c) mail shot
   d) trade mail

6. An education publisher promoting a new textbook is likely to use all except which one of the following?
   a) Catalogues
   b) Personality promotions
   c) Exhibitions
   d) Free samples

*In each of the following questions, one or more of the response(s) is/are correct. Choose the appropriate letter which indicates the correct version.*

   A  if 1 only is correct
   B  if 3 only is correct
   C  if 1 and 2 only are correct
   D  if 1, 2 and 3 are correct

7. Which of the following is/are reasons for the use of public relations.
   1) To promote the corporate image
   2) To give details of future developments
   3) To promote bad publicity

8. 'Middlemen' have different names depending upon the type of trade in which they work. Which of the following is/are middlemen?
   1. Insurance Agents
   2. Cash and Carry Wholesalers
   3. Stockbrokers.

## Assignment

# THINGS YOU DIDN'T KNOW ABOUT...

# BISTO

Bisto was created by Cerebos in 1910, to simplify gravy making.

**The initial appeal lay in its time saving: Bisto Browns, Seasons and Thickens In One – hence the anagram.**

It wasn't until 1919 that an inspired piece of marketing transformed the product's future. Cartoonist Will Owen created the Bisto Kids and the "Ah! Bisto" slogan.

Such was the popularity of the "Bisto Kids" that cinema audiences in the 30s were treated to a 20-minute animated film entitled The New Adventures of the Bisto Kids, which was screened as suppport to the main feature.

**Bisto became invaluable during the Second World War, when women used it to paint their legs, as an alternative to "American Tan" nylons.**

The Bisto kids have undergone some changes since their early days. They were even known to sport flared trousers during the 70s.

**Bisto's parent company Cerebos was sold to Ranks Hovis McDougall, in 1971.**

Bisto gravy granules were launched in 1979.

**Bisto's share of the £150m meat extract market, currently stands at 39% (Source: AGB Superpanel).**

RHM's marketing budget in support of the Bisto brand, is set to top £7.5m for this year.

**Independent research conducted on behalf of RHM, shows that 37% of home-made shepherd pies are made using Bisto as a "pour in" ingredient.**

Bisto Fuller Flavour Gravy Granules was launched last year, following extensive research.

RHM is currently involved in a massive sampling exercise through door to door distributor, The Leaflet Company. Mini packs of Fuller Flavour Gravy granules are being delivered to one million UK households, each with a "10p-off coupon".

**1075 tonnes of Bisto were sold during the four weeks leading up to Easter, last year – that's the same weight as 215 African male elephants.**

Spontaneous awareness for the Bisto brands stands at 93%.

Bisto Original Gravy Powder and Traditional Gravy Granules are currently carrying on-pack promotions for celebrity cookery books endorsed by the NSPCC charity.

*Reproduced by kind permission of Marketing Magazine*

1. From the above information about Bisto identify the examples of:
   a) market research
   b) the original and alternative uses of the product.
   c) product development.
   d) market share.
   e) brand identification.
   f) promotional activities.
   g) consumer awareness.
   h) the promotional budget.
   i) it's unique selling proposition.

2) Comment on the marketing strategies used to extend the product life cycle and keep Bisto a successful brand.

3) How might the information in the article be of use to a competitor?

# 10. Business Finance

This chapter is about the need for capital in a business, how it is obtained and how it is used and covers:

- * Need for Capital
- * Sources of Business Finance
- * Cost of Borrowing
- * Advantages and Disadvantages of Borrowing
- * Company Finance
- * Types of Securities
- * Methods of Share Issue
- * Shares and Dividends
- * Shareholder Ratios
- * Capital Gearing
- * Decision-Making Techniques
- * Investment Appraisal
- * Payback Technique
- * Average Rate of Return
- * Discounted Cash Flow
- * Net Present Value
- * Internal Rate of Return
- * Cost-Benefit Analysis
- * Decision Trees

## Need for Capital

1. **Capital** is vital to the running of a business. It includes everything that is used in a business from the money invested to set it up to the equipment purchased to help run it. A window cleaner for example needs to buy a ladder, bucket and wash leather. A retailer needs shop premises and a stock of goods to sell, whilst a manufacturer needs a factory, machinery and raw materials as well as money to pay expenses like wages, advertising, heat, light and transport before he can make and sell anything. If the business is successful more capital may be needed for a variety of reasons. For example it may be expanding and therefore needs to buy new premises or equipment. Or it may need to modernise its equipment and perhaps introduce computers or other forms of new technology in order to increase efficiency.

2. Within this short introduction we have identified three key types of capital:

   - **Venture capital** which is needed to start a business venture or enterprise.
   - **Investment capital** which is used to finance the purchase of new equipment.
   - **Working capital** which is the finance used in the day-to-day running of a business.

## Sources of Business Finance

3. If a business wishes to raise finance there are a number of sources from which this might come:

   - **The public.** As we saw in Chapter 2 in a small firm, most of the capital required is provided by the businessman himself, possibly with the help of his family and friends or by borrowing from a bank. Whilst in companies finance can be obtained by issuing debentures, shares or borrowing.
   - **'Ploughed back' or retained profits.** An existing business might be able to make sufficient profits to enable it to provide its own additional finance.
   - **The Government.** Frequently it is possible for a business to obtain grants or loans from the DTI, TECs or other government agencies, particularly in areas where unemployment is high.
   - **Financial Institutions.** Capital may also be obtained by borrowing from banks, insurance companies, building societies and other financial institutions. These offer business mortgages (eg for premises), short, medium and long-term loans usually at different rates of interest to those for personal borrowing. Banks may also provide short-term borrowing in the form of an overdraft. This allows customers to withdraw more than they have in their current account, up to an agreed limit.
   - **Factoring Companies.** When a firm sells goods it will invoice the customer and may have to wait several weeks or even months before it is paid. An alternative to this is to sell the invoices to a factor for less than the full amount. This service has developed in recent years and is usually provid-

ed by banks or finance companies. A factor purchases the invoiced debts of a business, usually paying up to 80% of their value depending on the risk involved. The firm therefore gets its money immediately leaving the factor to collect the amount outstanding and deal with any possible bad debts. For example, a business has invoices outstanding for £1,000. It sells these to a factor and receives £800 for them.

- **Trade Credit.** Some traders build up credit with their suppliers in order to give them additional capital, particularly in the short-term. That is they buy goods and pay for them some weeks later by which time they may have already received the money for selling them.

- **Leasing or renting of equipment.** Leasing enables firms to acquire expensive up-to-date equipment without the large amounts of capital needed to buy it. Just as your family might rent a television set so a business can obtain goods in this way by paying an annual rental fee which includes maintenance. It is quite common for firms to lease major items like office equipment, machinery and company vehicles rather than buying them outright.

- **Finance Companies.** It may be possible for a business to purchase some items like furniture, equipment and cars on credit rather than paying for them immediately. The firm will pay a deposit and pay the balance outstanding by monthly instalments over a period of 2-5 years thus spreading the cost. Specialist companies (often subsidiaries of banks) often provide the finance on **hire purchase (HP)**. With HP, the goods remain the property of the finance company until all payments have been made. With credit sales the goods belong to the purchaser immediately.

- **Venture Capital Companies.** For example 3i Group PLC. These meet the need for capital when funds are not readily available from traditional sources such as banks or the stock market. They provide finance in excess of £100,000 to small and medium companies in return for an equity stake in the business. Many of these companies are subsidiaries of other financial institutions including banks, insurance companies and pension funds.

- **Loans by Organisations.** A number of other organisations offer loans to businesses for example, Local Authorities seeking to attract industry into an area, and Finance for Industry (FFI), set up in 1973, which provides loans through its two subsidiaries, the Industrial and Commercial Finance Corporation (ICFC) and the Finance Corporation for Industry (FCI).

4. It is important to recognise that trade credit, leasing and hire purchase do not actually increase the amount of money coming into a business. Instead they enable a firm to have the use of additional capital without needing to lay out large amounts of cash. The difference between borrowed money and venture capital should also be understood. The former is usually secured on property or other assets and involves repayments of capital and interest, whilst the latter is unsecured and rewarded by dividends and capital gain from the sale of the equity if the company is successful and goes 'public'.

### Task 10.1

From the above sources of business finance, with examples:

1. Identify those which are most suitable for
    a) Long-term borrowing (5-20+ years)
    b) Medium-term borrowing (1-5 years)
    c) Short-term borrowing (less than 1 year)
2. Distinguish between the internally generated and externally generated sources of finance.

## Cost of Borrowing

5. A loan is a fixed sum of money lent for a stated period of time, such as 2 years. The charge made for providing a loan is called interest which is calculated as a percentage of the amount borrowed. Interest may be calculated as simple or compound.

## 10. Business finance

6. **Simple interest** is calculated on the original sum (called the principal) only using the following formula:

$$I = P \times \frac{R}{100} \times N$$

where  I = simple interest
P = Principal
R = % rate of interest
N = Time period

7. **Example**

|  | £ |  |
|---|---:|---|
| Loan | 1,500 | for 4 years |
| 10% Interest | 600 | £150 pa × 4 |
| Total Cost | 2,100 |  |

Repayments £43.75 per month (2100 ÷ 48)

8. **Compound interest** is calculated on the original principal plus all interest earned so far which is added to it. The formula used is

$$A = P\left(1 + \frac{R}{100}\right)^n$$

Where  A = compound sum
P = Principal
R = % rate of interest
n = time period

Thus, for example, a £100 loan earning 10% compound interest p.a. would accumulate to £110 at the end of a year and £121 at the end of 2 years and so on.

$$\text{ie} \quad 121 = 100\left(1 + \frac{10}{100}\right)^2$$

9. **Example**

Loan £1,500 borrowed at 10% compound interest for 4 yrs

|  | £ |
|---|---:|
| YEAR 1 PRINCIPAL | 1500 |
| end year 1 interest 10% | 150 |
| YEAR 2 PRINCIPAL | 1650 |
| end year 2 interest 10% | 165 |
| YEAR 3 PRINCIPAL | 1815 |
| end year 3 interest 10% | 181.50 |
| YEAR 4 PRINCIPAL | 1996.50 |
| end year 4 interest 10% | 199.65 |
| TOTAL PAID BACK | 2196.15 |

Repayments £45.75 per month (2196.15 ÷ 48)

### Task 10.2

What is the total amount repaid and the monthly repayment on the following loans.

1. A principal of £1,000 over 3 years with a simple interest of 9%.
2. A principal of £750 over 4 years with a compound interest of 8%.

## Advantages and Disadvantages of Borrowing

10. There are a number of factors which a business must consider when deciding whether or not to borrow money.

    - It provides a **source of capital** to finance business development and growth.
    - It requires a **regular outlay** in order to make the repayments.
    - **Collateral** (security) may be required by lenders so that if the business becomes bankrupt, the loan is repaid from the sale of the asset. A mortgage, for example, is secured on premises.
    - **Assets may be 'tied-up'** if they are used as security which may create difficulties if they need to be sold.
    - A **higher rate of interest** is usually payable **on unsecured loans** because of the greater risk involved.
    - **Further interest rate increases** add to the cost of borrowing. This could **cause problems** if it leaves the business with insufficient funds to pay off other debts.
    - Investment decisions will depend on the **cost** of borrowing **relative** to the **anticipated rate of return** eg a 10% interest rate requires a profit of at least 10% to cover it.

## Company Finance

11. When a limited company is formed, the Board of Directors must decide how much capital is needed to finance the trading operations. This capital is then divided up into smaller equal parts called shares. Each share therefore represents a small part of the business and these are then sold to raise the money required to trade. Shares normally carry some voting rights which enables their holders to have a say in how the company is run, but this varies according to the type of share.

## Types of Securities

12. A security is simply a written or printed document acknowledging the investment of money. People who purchase securities are call **investors** and they can put their money into either stocks or shares. Generally speaking stocks are loans which carry a fixed rate of interest, whilst the return on shares varies. There are a number of different types of company securities, the most common being preference shares, ordinary shares and debentures.

13. **Methods of Share Issue**

    A public limited company can issue shares in a number of ways.

    - **Offer by prospectus.** This is a direct approach to the public which is usually handled by a specialist issuing house such as a merchant bank. The shares are sold at a fixed offer price.
    - **Offer for sale.** Sometimes a company will sell its entire share issue to an issuing house which then sells them to the public at a slightly higher price to cover fees and expenses.
    - **Offer by tender.** Rather than fixing the price in advance, companies sometimes issue shares to the public by inviting them to state a price at which they are prepared to buy them, subject usually to a set minimum. The issue price is then fixed according to demand and anyone offering less than this receives no shares.
    - **Placing.** A large number of share issues are 'placed' by the issuing house with a selected group of its own clients, usually large financial institutions, rather than the general public.

- **Rights Issue.** Sometimes existing shareholders are offered the 'right' to buy additional shares in the company at a discount to the market price.
- **Bonus Issue.** Shares are sometimes issued free to existing shareholders in proportion to their holdings, eg. 1 bonus for every 10 held. This makes shares more marketable by reducing their market price.
- **Scrip Issue.** Sometimes instead of paying a cash dividend, a company offers shareholders a choice of receiving it in the form of extra shares, thus keeping the money in the business.

**Task 10.3**

### ALLIED RIGHTS OUT

The food and drinks group Allied-Lyons has ruled out a rights issue in order to cut borrowing of nearly £2bn, which represents about 66 per cent of share-holders' funds.

It will only tap investors for cash if it makes a major acquisition. Although a move is not imminent.

### IT ASDA BE RIGHT

Asda, the fourth largest supermarket group, said 94 per cent of its £347m rights issue had been taken up by shareholders. The money raised will be used to cut debts to around £100m and to speed up the refitting of some stores for £2m each and relocation of some other poor performers at £12-£20m a time. Two years ago, Asda faced debts of nearly £1 billion. It is already investing £130m a year but still losing market share to new openings by Sainsbury, Tesco and Safeway.

### BURTON RIGHT ON

Burton Group, which includes Top Shop, Debenhams and Dorothy Perkins, has had a 90 per cent take-up for its £163m rights issue.

Burton, which recently said that 20,000 full-time jobs were to go and 3,000 part-time staff hired instead, will use some of the cash to cut borrowings to around £160m.

### BIG RIGHTS AHEAD

Recent successful rights issues include Asda the supermarket chain (£347m), High Street fashion group Burton (£163m) Trafalgar House (£204m) and Commercial Union (£438m). Kingfisher is also asking for £313m to buy French electrical retailer Darty.

The stock market rise has encouraged companies to raise new capital, support recession hit balance sheets and make acquisitions. But some are raising extra funds now because they are worried that the Government's heavy borrowing programme for 1993/4 will drain funds out of the market and lead to a cash shortage.

1. Explain what is meant by a rights issue.
2. Why do companies need to raise such funds?
3. What factors can determine the timing of such issues?

## Shares and Dividends

14. Investors who purchase shares in a company stand to profit in two ways:
    - Firstly, the shares in a successful company are likely to rise in price, thereby offering a **capital gain**.
    - Secondly, they receive a share of the company's profits called a **dividend**.

15. Most companies pay a dividend twice a year, an **interim** (for the first 6 months of their financial year) and a **final** (at the end). A dividend is declared as a percentage of the nominal (face) value of a share, for example, a 5% dividend would pay 5p on every £1 share in the company Thus a shareholder with 1,000 shares would receive £50.

16. The size of the dividend is dependent upon the amount of profit made and how much the directors decide to retain in the company before distributing the balance to shareholders. The Directors, however, will only declare a dividend if they judge that the Company has made sufficient profit to be able to do so.

---

**Task 10.4**

### MOWLEM PROFITS PLUNGE

John Mowlem today became the latest group to expose the dire state of the construction industry as it crashed £9.9m into the red, reversing a £7m profit. The interim dividend is slashed from 5.67p to 2p a share.

On the positive side, the company says borrowings have fallen and will continue dropping thanks to the £17.6m sale of its US scaffolding business. It is also closing its Canadian operation. The Board has focused its attention on reducing costs in all areas, the disposal of non-core assets and businesses, cash control within all companies and the maintenance of its strong and cash-positive contracting business.

Core businesses of contracting, housing and equipment hire in the UK all made operating profits, but less than in the previous two half-years. The group, which built and operates London City Airport, had a £2.5m loss on this business.

1. Identify Mowlem's core business.
2. What difficulties is the company experiencing and how are shareholders being affected?
3. How are the directors reacting to the current situation?

---

## Preference Shares

17. These are so called because they receive a fixed dividend which is paid before all other classes of shareholders. The dividend is expressed as a fixed % on the nominal (original) value of the share, for example 8% £1 Preference Shares, means that the dividend is 8p per share p.a. Preference shareholders do not usually have any voting rights.

18. There are several types of preference shares which are as follows:

   - **Cumulative Preference Shares.** If there is insufficient profit to pay the dividend in one year, then this will be made up in later years. For example, 1993 no profit, therefore no dividend on 8% £1 Preference Shares, then in 1994 if there is sufficient profit the dividend will be 16p per share.

   - **Non-cumulative Preference Shares.** These are exactly the same as cumulative, but without the right to receive any arrears of dividend. Dividends are paid out of current year profits only, therefore no profit means no dividend.

   - **Redeemable Preference Shares.** These shares are issued for a specified period and the company agrees to repay the capital at some future date, for example 10,000 £1 Preference Shares, Redeemable 1998 means that the company must repay this capital in 1998.

   - **Participating Preference Shares.** In addition to the fixed dividend, these shares receive an additional dividend depending on the company's profits.

## Ordinary Shares

19. These are by far the most common type of share. Once the preference shareholders have been paid, then the directors of the company decide how much of the profits to keep in reserve (ie money

which is kept for future expansion or against a 'rainy day') and how much to pay as a dividend on the ordinary shares. Ordinary shareholders usually have voting rights and they also carry the greatest risk because profits and therefore the dividends may fluctuate considerably from year to year. These shares are often referred to as **'equities'** because they participate equally in the profits of the company.

## Debentures

20. These are not shares in a company but long-term loans. They are issued in £100 units and secured against property or other assets. Debenture holders receive a fixed rate of interest, which must be paid whether the company makes a profit or not, and usually have a guaranteed repayment date.

## Shareholder Ratios

21. In paragraph 15 we saw that a 5% dividend would produce an income of £50 for a shareholder with 1,000 £1 shares. However, because shares can increase or decrease in value, it is more meaningful to use various ratios in order to assess the return on shares.

22. **Dividend Yield**

    The yield is the percentage return on the price paid for shares and is calculated as follows:

    $$\text{Yield} = \frac{\text{Nominal value of share}}{\text{Cost or market price of share}} \times \% \text{ dividend}$$

    Thus if the current market value is £1.50 then:

    $$\text{Yield} = \frac{100}{150} \times 5 = 3.3\%$$

    Generally, lower yields reflect a secure business with growth potential, whilst higher yields suggest riskier investments.

23. **Dividend Cover**

    This is a measure of the number of times a company's earnings cover the dividend payments on its shares. It is calculated as:

    $$\frac{\text{Net profit, after tax}}{\text{Declared dividend on ordinary shares}}$$

24. For example, a company makes a profit of £500,000 and has a tax liability of £200,000. The dividend on preference shares is £50,000 leaving earnings of £250,000 available for distribution. If a dividend amounting to a total of £50,000 is declared on its 100,000 ordinary shares, then it is said to be covered 5 times, i.e.

    $$\frac{250,000}{50,000}$$

25. Dividends can, however, exceed earnings, as for example when a company maintains its dividend despite sharply reduced profits. In this situation, the dividend is uncovered. Sometimes firms deliberately retain profits for future expansion, giving a higher cover. However, a high cover often implies a low yield especially with a quality share whose price may be at a premium to the market.

26. **Earnings per share (EPS)**

    This expresses in money terms, the relationship between profits and the number of issued ordinary shares.

$$\text{EPS} = \frac{\text{Net profit after tax}}{\text{Number ordinary shares}}$$

In the previous example:

$$\text{EPS} = \frac{250{,}000}{100{,}000} = 2.5\text{p}$$

This figure is useful because it is the denominator of the price earnings ratio which is one of the most widely used investment statistics.

27. **Price/earnings ratio (P/E ratio)**

    This is the share price divided by the earnings per share.

    $$\text{P/E ratio} = \frac{\text{Market price per share}}{\text{Earnings per share}}$$

    Thus a share with a market price of £1.50 and an EPS of 5p would have a P/E ratio of 30:

    $$\frac{150}{5} = 30$$

28. Shares of companies with a good profits record tend to have a high P/E ratio and probably usually a low yield. On the other hand, companies with poor profits records will usually have a low P/E ratio.

29. Thus, a share selling at 75p with a P/E ratio of 10 would be less profitable than one selling at 75p with a P/E ratio of 5. Hence, when deciding whether or not to buy a particular share, the P/E ratio can be compared with that of similar companies to determine which is potentially the better buy.

### Task 10.5

Detailed information about share prices are shown daily in the Financial Times and quality newspapers like the Guardian, Independent and Daily Telegraph.

Using these sources:

1. Select 6 shares from each of any 2 sectors, eg Banks, Chemicals or Food Retailing and identify the current market prices, yield and P/E ratio for each share.
2. Comment on your findings and identify which of your chosen shares in each sector you feel represent the best value.

## Capital Gearing

30. One of the indicators which may be used to evaluate the financial health and stability of an organisation is its loan gearing. This is simply a measure of the degree to which a business is financed by loans rather than equity capital. Often banks and other lenders will insist that a business applying for a loan puts up a proportion of what is needed as an indicator of its financial stability. In a company, capital gearing refers to the relationship between the amount of fixed interest borrowing (including preference shares and debentures) and equity investment (ordinary shares).

31. Two gearing ratios can be calculated from a company's balance sheet: Capital (CGR) or Income (IGR)

    $$\text{CGR} = \frac{\text{Gross borrowing}}{\text{Equity investment}} \times 100$$

The IGR shows the relationship between interest charges and profit and is calculated as follows:

$$IGR = \frac{\text{Interest charges}}{\text{Profit before interest and tax}} \times 100$$

> **Task 10.6**
>
> Obtain copies of the annual reports of two public limited companies. From the accounting information given, calculate the CGR and IGR for 2 years and comment on any possible reasons for changes in the ratios.

32. An organisation with a high proportion of fixed interest securities is said to be **highly geared** because it is committed to making substantial interest payments. This may be beneficial to ordinary shareholders when the company is enjoying buoyant trading and high profits, but detrimental in poor trading. On the other hand, companies with **low gearing** may be unable to pay large dividends because profits are distributed to numerous shareholders and therefore the shares may prove unattractive to investors.

33. Hence there needs to be a balance between the two gears. Overall gearing will depend on a variety of factors such as the asset structure of the firm, the risk associated with the business, the growth rate of future sales and the effect of taxation on dividends.

34. The gearing adopted by an organisation will reflect its changing balance sheet structure as it develops. Expansion may be financed by issuing additional ordinary shares which reduces capital gearing rather than by borrowing which increases it.

> **Task 10.7**
>
> **Capital Gearing**
>
> | | Firm X | Firm Y |
> |---|---|---|
> | Ordinary Shares | £ 9,000 | 5,000 |
> | Fixed interest loans | 1,000 | 5,000 |
> | Total capital employed | 10,000 | 10,000 |
> | *Year 1* | | |
> | Trading profit | 1,500 | 1,500 |
> | Less loan interest (at 10%) | 100 | 500 |
> | Net Profit | 1,400 | 1,000 |
> | Return to shareholders | 1,400 | 1,000 |
> | | 10,000 | 5,000 |
> | *Year 2* | | |
> | Trading profit | 700 | 700 |
> | Less loan interest (at 10%) | 100 | 500 |
> | Net profit | 600 | 200 |
> | Return to shareholders: | 600 | 200 |
> | | 10,000 | 5,000 |
>
> From the above information:
> 1. Identify how each of the companies are geared.
> 2. Calculate the returns on capital employed in each year.
> 3. State which company's gearing you feel is most beneficial to its shareholders.

## Decision-Making Techniques

35. Decision-making in an organisation involves making choices between future uncertain alternatives in order to achieve objectives. It is therefore an essential part of management and control but decisions are not always straightforward and easy to take. However, there are many management techniques which can be used to assist in this process and whilst it is useful for managers to have at least some knowledge of them, they will usually employ specialists or bring in consultants to apply them.

36. The most common techniques used include:

    - **Investment Appraisal and Decision Theory** which are used to assist in making capital expenditure decisions. These are discussed in detail in this Chapter.
    - **Work Study and Organisation and Methods** which are concerned with finding the most efficient way of organising work. (see Chapters 13 & 15).
    - **Operational Research** or statistical techniques used for production planning and control (see Chapter 19).
    - **Cost Accounting and Contribution Analysis** which determine the effects of individual products on overall profitability, assist with pricing decisions and provide a basis for cost control (see Chapter 11).
    - **Network Analysis** techniques for planning and co-ordinating complex projects in which timing is important. (see Chapter 15)

## Investment Appraisal

37. Capital investment is essential in any organisation providing the key to its future development and growth. There are a number of situations when an organisation will need to make investment decisions but particularly when it is considering the possibilities of any of the following.

    - **replacing existing tangible assets** such as plant, buildings and equipment which are old, and unreliable or technically outdated.
    - **introducing new tangible assets** possibly in order to increase production, improve quality or reduce administrative or production costs due to financial constraints.
    - **purchasing modern 'state-of-the-art' equipment** in order to operate more efficiently and keep up with or overtake competitors.
    - **internal expansion** by acquiring new premises, launching a new product(s) or increasing research and development.
    - **external expansion** involving another organisation such as a merger or joint venture (see Chapter 15).

38. In making investment decisions, it is important for managers to consider the various ways of achieving the desired objectives, to assess whether or not the benefits or return expected from the investment will outweigh the costs involved and then to choose between several uncertain alternatives. In order to do this, it is necessary to compare the immediate cash outlay with the income which the investment is expected to generate over a period of time.

39. There are a number of techniques which can be used for this, the most common of which are payback, average rate of return and discounted cash flow (DCF). The latter can be calculated using either net present value (NPV) or internal rate of return (IRR).

## Payback Techniques

40. This is the simplest method of investment appraisal and therefore widely used particularly by smaller businesses. The payback is the time required, usually in years, to recoup the cost of an investment. It is calculated by estimating the projects net cash inflow and comparing it with the cash outflow, including the initial investment cost. In comparing projects, the one with the shortest payback period would be chosen.

41. For example, a manufacturer is considering investing £200,000 in a new machine which is expected to last for 8 years and increase the company's cash flow (net of operating costs) by £50,000 per year over its life.

    Thus the total cash flow = 8 × £50,000 = £400,000

    against a cost of £200,000

    $$\text{Therefore the payback period} = \frac{£200,000}{£50,000} = 4 \text{ years}$$

42. This method of appraisal is useful for short-term investment or in situations of rapid obsolescence such as fashion items or computer technology. It ignores, however, net cashflow over the full life of a project. It also does not take into account the rate of return compared to the market rate of interest and therefore whether or not the money might be better invested elsewhere.

### Task 10.8

1. Calculate the payback period for an investment costing £15,000 which is expected to increase net cashflow by £2,500 p.a.
2. Compare this with an alternative investment costing £25,000 but expected to increase net cashflow by £4,000 p.a.
3. State, with reasons, which, if any, you feel is the better investment.

## Average Rate of Return (ARR)

43. The ARR is calculated by expressing the average expected profits (over the life of an asset) after depreciation, as a percentage of the capital invested. This method is also known as the Return on Capital Employed.

44. **Example**

    A new machine costs £35,000 and is expected to have a life of 7 years and generate a profit of £800 per year. If the **residual value** of the machine (value at the end of its life) is £7,000 then the cost of the machine can be calculated as:

    $$\frac{35,000 - 7,000}{7} = £4,000 \text{ per year}$$

    $$\text{Therefore the ARR} = \frac{800}{4,000} = 20\%$$

45. This method is simple to calculate but has several disadvantages for investment decision-taking.
    - It ignores the timing of cash flow. All money is treated as being of equal value irrespective of when it is received.
    - It uses profit as a measure of return but in accounting terms this is not the same as cash flows into and out of a business.
    - There is no one universally accepted method of calculating ARR

## Task 10.9

1. In what way does the ARR method overcome one of the defects of the payback technique?

2. Calculate the ARR and recommend which, if any, of the the following projects should be selected. Each requires an initial investment of £28,000 with an estimated residual value of £3,000. The two columns of figures represent the estimated annual net profits over the life of the projects.

|  |  | Project A | Project B |
|---|---|---|---|
| Year | 1 | 3,500 | 5,000 |
|  | 2 | 5,000 | 6,000 |
|  | 3 | 4,500 | 3,500 |
|  | 4 | 4,000 | 2,000 |
|  | 5 | 3,000 | 1,000 |
| Total |  | £20,000 | £17,500 |

## Discounted Cash Flow (DCF)

46. DCF is a widely used method of investment appraisal because it takes account of the time value of money. For example, £1,000 available now is worth more than £1,000 which we cannot have for 1, 2, 3 years and so on. Therefore it uses a test discount rate to convert future cash flows into current day values. The two main DCF methods are net present value (NPV) and internal rate of return (IRR).

47. **Net Present Value (NPV)**

NPV involves 6 basic steps:

- **Determining the economic life of the investment.** ie the number of years that the investment is expected to continue in use, eg 5 years for computer equipment, 25 years for a building.

- **Identifying the relevant cash flows** into and out of the business resulting from the investment. Cash flows such as the cost of new equipment, operational savings and the resale of old equipment, are estimated before tax and after allowing for inflation, in each year of the economic life.

- **Deciding on the discount rate to be used** which should be the minimum rate of return required for capital investment eg 15% pa.

- **Specifying the compounding frequency** ie, when cash actually flows into the business for reinvestment, which in practice most firms assume occurs at the year-end.

- **Calculating the NPV** ie the total value of each of the investments cash flows at today's prices. The process used to calculate this is called discounting. If the NPV is positive, a project is acceptable, if negative it is unacceptable. Discount tables are available to speed calculations (see paragraph 50)

- **Evaluating the NPV against competing alternatives** ie there may be a number of proposals to compare against before deciding which to choose. For example, upgrading the existing system, choosing some other system or continuing with the present system.

## 48. Example

*Image PLC – Purchase of a Computer System*

|  | Year 1 £000 | Year 2 £000 | Year 3 £000 | Year 4 £000 | Year 5 £000 |
|---|---|---|---|---|---|
| Purchase equipment | (25) | | | | |
| Installation & Training | (6) | | | | |
| Sale of old equipment | 5 | | | | |
| Net operational savings | | 4 | 5 | 7 | 8 |
| Salvage value in 5 yrs | | | | | 8 |
| Total cash in/(out) | (26) | 4 | 5 | 7 | 16 |
| Discount factor* | 0.833 | 0.694 | 0.579 | 0.482 | 0.402 |
| Net present value | (21,658) | 3,332 | 2,639 | 3,374 | 6,432 |

Therefore the total net present value of the investment is the sum of today values

= (£21,658) – £15,777 = – £5,881

*The discount factor is based on the discount rate of 20% and is calculated using the formula

$$\frac{1}{(1.20)^n}$$

where n is the year, eg

$$\frac{1}{(1.20)^4} = 0.482$$

## 49.

Although NPV is a valuable technique, it is nonetheless only a method of forecasting based on assumptions about such factors as inflation, markets, the competition and funding costs. There may also be other factors to consider in investment appraisal which cannot be easily quantified, such as the company's strategy.

## 50. Present Value Factors

**Present value of £1 at compound interest: $(1 + r)^{-n}$**
**Rate of discount (r)**

| Years (n) | 1% | 2% | 4% | 6% | 8% | 10% | 12% | 14% | 15% | 16% | 18% | 20% | 22% | 24% | 25% | 26% | 28% | 30% |
|---|---|---|---|---|---|---|---|---|---|---|---|---|---|---|---|---|---|---|
| 1 | 0.990 | 0.980 | 0.962 | 0.943 | 0.926 | 0.909 | 0.893 | 0.877 | 0.870 | 0.862 | 0.847 | 0.833 | 0.820 | 0.806 | 0.800 | 0.794 | 0.781 | 0.769 |
| 2 | 0.980 | 0.961 | 0.925 | 0.890 | 0.857 | 0.826 | 0.797 | 0.769 | 0.756 | 0.743 | 0.718 | 0.694 | 0.672 | 0.650 | 0.640 | 0.630 | 0.610 | 0.592 |
| 3 | 0.971 | 0.942 | 0.889 | 0.840 | 0.794 | 0.751 | 0.712 | 0.675 | 0.658 | 0.641 | 0.609 | 0.579 | 0.551 | 0.524 | 0.512 | 0.500 | 0.477 | 0.455 |
| 4 | 0.961 | 0.924 | 0.855 | 0.792 | 0.735 | 0.683 | 0.636 | 0.592 | 0.572 | 0.552 | 0.516 | 0.482 | 0.451 | 0.423 | 0.410 | 0.397 | 0.373 | 0.350 |
| 5 | 0.951 | 0.906 | 0.822 | 0.747 | 0.681 | 0.621 | 0.567 | 0.519 | 0.497 | 0.476 | 0.437 | 0.402 | 0.370 | 0.341 | 0.328 | 0.315 | 0.291 | 0.269 |
| 6 | 0.942 | 0.888 | 0.790 | 0.705 | 0.630 | 0.564 | 0.507 | 0.456 | 0.432 | 0.410 | 0.370 | 0.335 | 0.303 | 0.275 | 0.262 | 0.250 | 0.227 | 0.207 |
| 7 | 0.933 | 0.871 | 0.760 | 0.665 | 0.583 | 0.513 | 0.452 | 0.400 | 0.376 | 0.354 | 0.314 | 0.279 | 0.249 | 0.222 | 0.210 | 0.198 | 0.178 | 0.159 |
| 8 | 0.923 | 0.853 | 0.731 | 0.627 | 0.540 | 0.467 | 0.404 | 0.351 | 0.327 | 0.305 | 0.266 | 0.233 | 0.204 | 0.179 | 0.168 | 0.157 | 0.139 | 0.123 |
| 9 | 0.914 | 0.837 | 0.703 | 0.592 | 0.500 | 0.424 | 0.361 | 0.308 | 0.284 | 0.263 | 0.225 | 0.194 | 0.167 | 0.144 | 0.134 | 0.125 | 0.108 | 0.094 |
| 10 | 0.905 | 0.820 | 0.676 | 0.558 | 0.463 | 0.386 | 0.322 | 0.270 | 0.247 | 0.227 | 0.191 | 0.162 | 0.137 | 0.116 | 0.107 | 0.099 | 0.085 | 0.075 |
| 11 | 0.0896 | 0.804 | 0.650 | 0.527 | 0.429 | 0.350 | 0.287 | 0.237 | 0.215 | 0.195 | 0.162 | 0.135 | 0.112 | 0.094 | 0.086 | 0.079 | 0.066 | 0.056 |
| 12 | 0.887 | 0.788 | 0.625 | 0.497 | 0.397 | 0.319 | 0.257 | 0.208 | 0.187 | 0.168 | 0.137 | 0.112 | 0.192 | 0.076 | 0.069 | 0.062 | 0.052 | 0.043 |
| 13 | 0.879 | 0.773 | 0.601 | 0.469 | 0.368 | 0.290 | 0.229 | 0.182 | 0.163 | 0.145 | 0.116 | 0.093 | 0.075 | 0.061 | 0.055 | 0.050 | 0.040 | 0.033 |
| 14 | 0.870 | 0.758 | 0.577 | 0.442 | 0.340 | 0.263 | 0.205 | 0.160 | 0.141 | 0.125 | 0.099 | 0.178 | 0.062 | 0.049 | 0.044 | 0.039 | 0.032 | 0.025 |
| 15 | 0.861 | 0.743 | 0.555 | 0.417 | 0.315 | 0.239 | 0.183 | 0.140 | 0.123 | 0.108 | 0.084 | 0.065 | 0.051 | 0.040 | 0.035 | 0.031 | 0.025 | 0.020 |
| 16 | 0.853 | 0.728 | 0.534 | 0.394 | 0.292 | 0.218 | 0.163 | 0.123 | 0.107 | 0.093 | 0.071 | 0.054 | 0.042 | 0.032 | 0.028 | 0.025 | 0.019 | 0.015 |
| 17 | 0.855 | 0.714 | 0.513 | 0.371 | 0.270 | 0.198 | 0.146 | 0.108 | 0.093 | 0.080 | 0.060 | 0.045 | 0.034 | 0.026 | 0.023 | 0.020 | 0.015 | 0.012 |
| 18 | 0.836 | 0.700 | 0.494 | 0.350 | 0.250 | 0.180 | 0.130 | 0.095 | 0.081 | 0.069 | 0.051 | 0.038 | 0.028 | 0.021 | 0.018 | 0.016 | 0.012 | 0.009 |
| 19 | 0.828 | 0.686 | 0.475 | 0.331 | 0.232 | 0.164 | 0.116 | 0.083 | 0.070 | 0.060 | 0.043 | 0.031 | 0.023 | 0.017 | 0.014 | 0.012 | 0.009 | 0.007 |
| 20 | 0.820 | 0.675 | 0.456 | 0.312 | 0.215 | 0.149 | 0.104 | 0.073 | 0.061 | 0.051 | 0.037 | 0.026 | 0.019 | 0.014 | 0.012 | 0.010 | 0.007 | 0.005 |
| 21 | 0.811 | 0.660 | 0.439 | 0.294 | 0.199 | 0.135 | 0.093 | 0.064 | 0.053 | 0.044 | 0.031 | 0.022 | 0.015 | 0.011 | 0.009 | 0.008 | 0.006 | 0.004 |
| 22 | 0.803 | 0.647 | 0.422 | 0.278 | 0.184 | 0.123 | 0.083 | 0.056 | 0.046 | 0.038 | 0.026 | 0.018 | 0.013 | 0.009 | 0.007 | 0.006 | 0.004 | 0.003 |
| 23 | 0.795 | 0.634 | 0.406 | 0.262 | 0.170 | 0.112 | 0.074 | 0.049 | 0.040 | 0.033 | 0.022 | 0.015 | 0.010 | 0.007 | 0.006 | 0.005 | 0.003 | 0.002 |
| 24 | 0.788 | 0.622 | 0.390 | 0.247 | 0.158 | 0.102 | 0.066 | 0.043 | 0.035 | 0.028 | 0.019 | 0.011 | 0.008 | 0.006 | 0.005 | 0.004 | 0.003 | 0.002 |
| 25 | 0.780 | 0.610 | 0.375 | 0.233 | 0.146 | 0.092 | 0.059 | 0.038 | 0.030 | 0.024 | 0.016 | 0.010 | 0.007 | 0.005 | 0.004 | 0.003 | 0.002 | 0.001 |

## Internal Rate of Return (IRR)

51. IRR is a DCF alternative to NPV which uses percentages rather than values. IRR is the rate of interest, which when used to discount the cash flows of a proposed investment, reduces the NPV to zero. At this point, the sum of the NPV is exactly equal to the capital cost of the project. A certain amount of trial and error is involved in calculating this. A project is only worthwhile if the IRR is greater than the market rate of interest which has to be paid to borrow the funds needed to finance it. For example, if the IRR is 15% and market rate is 12%, then the project is worthwhile.

52. This can be shown graphically as follows:

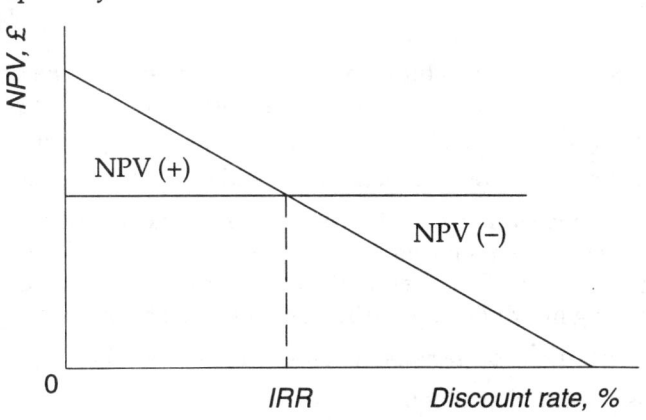

## Cost-Benefit Analysis

53. The investment appraisal techniques of payback, average rate of return and discounted cash flow (NPV and IRR) are widely used in the private sector. In the public sector, one of the most important techniques is cost-benefit analysis (CBA) which is used to evaluate large-scale investment projects such as the construction of new railway lines, motorways and airports. CBA seeks to estimate the NPV of such projects by discounting the total social costs and benefits or affects on the community against the private (economic) costs.

54. For example, the building of a new motorway could involve some or all of the following costs and benefits.

    COSTS: Pollution from exhaust fumes; noise from increased traffic; loss of countryside; loss of business on the existing route; economic costs of construction, maintenance and repairs.

    BENEFITS: By-passing towns and villages; faster travel; greater convenience; extra jobs for road maintenance and in garages for parts and servicing; a more mobile workforce; increase in Government revenue from the tax on petrol sales.

## Principles of Cost-Benefit Analysis

55. The main principles of CBA are:
    - identifying which costs and benefits to include.
    - deciding how to value them in relation to the estimated life of the project.
    - determining the rate at which costs and benefits are to be discounted in order to calculate the NPV.
    - considering the relevant constraints such as the budget available or influence of pressure groups.
    - evaluation, so that only if benefits exceed costs is it worth proceeding with the project.

56. It is important to realise that there is always uncertainty surrounding estimates of future costs and benefits associated with a project and this must be allowed for and considered against potential changes in such factors as project life and interest rates.

## Task 10.10

1. Consider the potential costs and benefits of building either a major new car park, superstore or other development in a town or city near to where you live or work.
2. What difficulties can you foresee in putting a monetary value on the factors which you have identified.

## Decision Trees

57. A tree diagram (named after its branching appearance) aids decision making by illustrating possible alternative courses of action and their economic consequences or outcomes over a period.

58. In an **Algorithmic Diagram** this may involve simple 'YES' or 'NO' alternatives depending on the choice made until the branch route taken leads to an end destination (decision).

59. A more useful type of decision tree, however, uses statistical probability. Here, the alternative branches lead to expected events based on the likely frequency of them occurring in the future which is predicted from historical facts and/or by assumption. The expected value of an event is the probability of it occurring multiplied by the benefit which the business can expect if it happens.

60. Managers using this technique for decision making will use the following process:
    - Identify the courses of action available.
    - Identify the possible outcomes of the action.
    - Determine the probabilities for each outcome.
    - Calculate the expected value of each outcome.
    - Select the course of action with the highest value.

61. **Example**

    A firm wishes to undertake a new marketing campaign with the aim of increasing sales and market share. It is considering two possible approaches.

    CAMPAIGN A at a cost of £100,000

    CAMPAIGN B at a cost of £150,000

    Expected value at node 2 = 0.7 (70,000) + 0.3 (30,000)

    Expected value at node 3 = 0.6 (90,000) + 0.4 (60,000)

    Therefore the expected values of **A** are     0.7 × £100,000 = +70,000
    
    0.3 × −£30,000 = −10,000
    
    +60,000

    Therefore the expected values of **B** are     0.6 × £90,000 = +£54,000
    
    0.4 × −£60,000 = −£24,000
    
    +£30,000

    In this situation, Campaign **A** would be chosen

    This is shown on a decision tree diagram below.

62.     **Basic Structure of a Decision Tree**

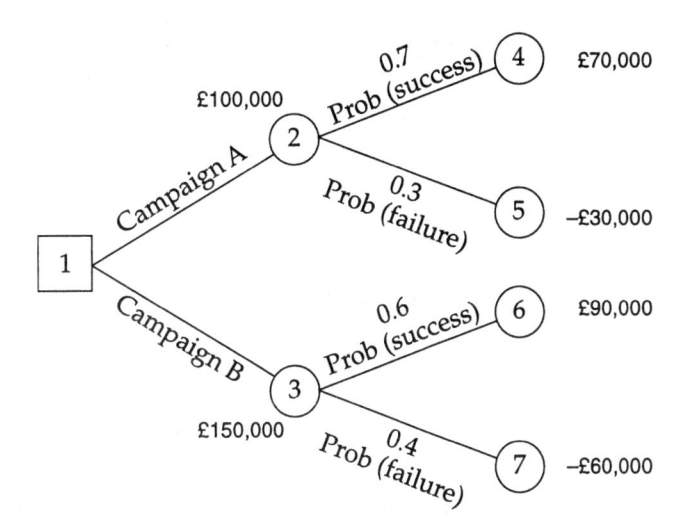

```
                    0.7
              Prob (success) ──(4)  £70,000
         £100,000  ┌──────────
              ┌─(2)
     Campaign A   └──────────
                  Prob (failure) ──(5)  −£30,000
                    0.3
   [1]
                    0.6
     Campaign B    Prob (success) ──(6)  £90,000
              ┌─(3)
         £150,000  └──────────
                  Prob (failure) ──(7)  −£60,000
                    0.4
```

The figure at the right hand side of each branch is the expected pay-off as a result of certain action.

63. **NB**

- **Squares** indicate where management decisions must be made.
- **Circles** represent the probable outcomes of a particular decision.
- **Decimals** show the probability of an event occurring.
- **£ Values** represent the income to the business if that event occurs.
- **The total probability** always adds up to 1.0
- **The expected value** at one mode is the starting point for calculating the expected value for the next node.
- **Costs** must be deducted from the expected values at each node.

64. The above is a relatively simple tree with only 2 alternatives and 2 outcomes in each case. Other trees can have many more branches and complications. Sometimes an indication may also be given of the maximum, middle and minimum effects that could result with the likely repercussions of each carried forward to the next step.

> **Task 10.11**
>
> Gwen Harris is thinking of opening a shop. She knows that success will depend largely on consumer spending which in turn is influenced by the state of the economy. Gwen has been advised that their is a 0.5 probability of a future boom which she estimates would enable her to make a £50,000 profit. However, there is a 2 in 1 chance of a recession, the financial consequences of which would probably be a loss of £36,000. You are asked to assist Gwen by drawing a decision tree and advising her on whether or not to proceed with the project.

## Sensitivity and Risk Analysis

65. Investment appraisals are based on forecasts and assumptions about the future which clearly are uncertain. Therefore, in order to consider all the possibilities, businesses often use a **sensitivity analysis**.

66. This involves making a range of what/if assumptions – from the optimistic to the pessimistic – about possible alternative factors. In particular, the costs and time involved to assess how they would impact on the overall benefits from the proposed investment.

67. For particularly large or risky projects a **risk analysis** may be necessary to assess the likelihood of particular events occuring. If, for example, heavy borrowing is involved then clearly assumptions about interest rates are crucial. Likewise, the purchase or sale of large assets may be affected by changes in market conditions. Thus, in these situations, a more detailed consideration of the financial risks involved is essential.

## Summary

68. a) Capital is vital in any business for starting up, day-to-day operation and expansion or modernisation.

b) A business can obtain capital by borrowing from the public, using retained profits, government grants and loans, borrowing from the financial institutions or venture capital companies, factoring, extended trade credit, leasing of equipment or by buying items on hire purchase.

c) The cost of borrowing is calculated by using either simple or compound interest rates.

d) Whilst borrowing provides a source of capital, it also involves a regular outlay, collateral, the 'tying-up' of assets and an increase in costs if interest rates rise.

e) A public limited company can raise capital by issuing shares on which it pays a dividend out of any profits.

f) Shares can be issued by prospectus, offer for sale, tender, placing, rights issue or bonus issue.

g) The success of a company can be evaluated from the dividend yield, dividend cover, earnings per share, and the price/earnings ratio.

h) Capital gearing provides a measure of the degree to which a business is financed by loans rather than equity capital.

i) A range of decision making techniques are available to assist managers including investment appraisal, decision theory, workstudy, organisation and methods, operational research, cost accounting, contribution analysis and network analysis.

j) Capital investment is essential for the development and growth of organisations and is worth pursuing if the expected return exceeds the costs involved.

k) The payback technique is the simplest method of investment appraisal. Other techniques include the average rate of return and discounted cash flow (DCF).

l) DCF takes account of the time value of money and uses a discount rate to convert future cash flows into current day values.

m) Net present value (NPV) and internal rate of return (IRR) are the 2 main methods of DCF.

n) NPV uses monetary values and IRR percentage returns.

o) In the public sector cost-benefit analysis is used for investment appraisal which considers the effect of an investment project on a community.

p) Decision tree diagrams can be used to illustrate possible alternative courses of action and their outcomes over a period.

**Review questions** *(answers can be found in the paragraphs indicated)*

1. List the main sources of capital available to a business.(2-4).
2. With the use of examples, explain the difference between simple and compound interest .(5-9)
3. Outline some of the main advantages and disadvantages associated with borrowing. (10)
4. Identify ways in which a public limited company can issue shares. (13)
5. Why do investors put their money into shares? (14)
6. Distinguish between preference shares, ordinary shares and debentures. (15-17)
7. Briefly explain at least 3 shareholder ratios and why they are used. (21-29).

8. What is capital gearing and why is it important in a company? (30-34)
9. Why is capital investment essential for the growth and development of organisations? (37)
10. What key criteria is used to determine whether or not capital investment is worthwhile? (38).
11. Distinguish between the payback and average rate of return techniques of investment appraisal. (39-45).
12. How is the net present value method of discounted cash flow calculated? (46-49)
13. Explain how the internal rate of return differs from the net present value. (51-52).
14. With the use of examples explain cost-benefit analysis. (49-56).
15. Why are decision trees a useful tool for managers? (57-64)

*Asterisks indicate those questions for which there are answers in Outline Answers (page 439)*

## Essay-style questions

1.* In what ways can small firms obtain capital if they want to become larger?
2. Discuss the various methods of share issue available to a public limited company and the situations in which each might be used.
3. What techniques are available to assist a business which is considering an expansion programme involving major capital investment?

## Short answer

1.* Distinguish between the following types of preference shares.
   a) Cumulative
   b) Non-cumulative
   c) Redeemable
   d) Participating

2.* Explain with the use of examples, the difference between the following shareholder ratios.
   a) Dividend yield
   b) Dividend cover
   c) Earnings per share
   d) Price/earnings ratio

3. a) What is meant by capital gearing?
   b) Why is it important to shareholders in a company?

## Multiple choice/completion

1.* Which of the following, according to British company law, must always be paid first.
   a) dividends to ordinary shareholders.
   b) dividends to deferred shareholders.
   c) dividends to preference shareholders.
   d) fixed interest to debenture holders.

2.* Factoring can be defined as:
   a) the selling of invoices to raise cash.
   b) the collection of bad debts.
   c) a business grant or loan from the government.
   d) the borrowing of money from a venture capital company.

## 10. Business finance

3.* The monthly repayments on a 5 year £5,000 loan on which simple interest is charged at 8% will be:
   a) £120.00
   b) £114.25
   c) £129.15
   d) £118.75

4.* Which of the following methods of share issue is only available to existing shareholders in a company?
   a) Placing
   b) Offer by tender
   c) Rights issue
   d) Offer for sale

5. The shares in a particular company have a nominal value of 25p and a current market value of 130p. It has recently announced a dividend of 3p per share. The yield is:
   a) 2.3%
   b) 6.2%
   c) 12%
   d) 15.6%

6. Which of the following techniques would be used to calculate the discounted cash flow on a proposed investment?
   a) Payback
   b) Cost benefit analysis
   c) Net present value
   d) Average rate of return

*In each of the following questions, one or more of the responses is/are correct. Choose the appropriate letter which indicates the correct version.*

   A   if 1 only is correct
   B   if 3 only is correct
   C   if 1 and 2 only are correct
   D   if 1, 2 and 3 are correct

7. On which of the following securities is a fixed rate of dividend paid?
   1. Preference shares
   2. Debentures
   3. Equities

8. Which of the following methods of finance do not actually increase the amount of cash in a business?
   1. Equipment leasing
   2. Trade credit
   3. Retained profits

## Assignment

Woodway Industries PLC which makes instruments for the scientific and chemical industries was founded in 1975 when it was heralded as having one of Europe's most advanced manufacturing plants.

In the past 3 years, however, it has faced increasing market pressure due to problems with quality and uncompetitive prices and it is now facing new tighter EU technical specifications.

The Board has recognised the need to invest in new equipment and the Production Director has identified two potential alternatives either of which would overcome Woodway's current difficulties.

**Alternative 1.**

A replacement of the existing equipment with its technically advanced modern equivalent. This would cost £3 million but is expected to increase efficiency by 10%.

This investment should produce additional profits over the next 5 years, of £1m per annum, starting in 1993, with a corresponding increase from any further sales (eg a 40% increase in sales would produce a £1.4 million profit).

**Alternative 2.**

The latest 'Flexible Manufacturing System' with integrated computer controlled machines. This, however, would involve a major investment of £22 million and increase annual production by 50% more units than Woodway's is currently selling.

The Production Director estimates that additional profits for the next 5 years from this investment would be as follows:

| (£m) | 1993 | 1994 | 1995 | 1996 | 1997 |
|---|---|---|---|---|---|
| Sales increase by 50% | 10 | 15 | 20 | 20 | 20 |
| Sales increase by 20% | 4 | 6 | 8 | 8 | 8 |
| No sales increase | 1 | 3 | 4 | 4 | 4 |

In the present economic climate, it is estimated that investment in new machinery would result in a 30% chance of sales increasing by 50%, a 50% chance of sales increasing by 20% and a 20% chance that sales will not increase at all.

The Production Manager would like you to prepare on his behalf an evaluation of the 2 alternatives using the sales forecasts given and the Board's requirement for a 20% discount rate.

In your report, you are asked to include the following:

1. An outline of the Company's current problems and why investment is needed.
2. Potential sources of funding for the investment.
3. Calculations of the net present value of each of the two alternatives.
4. A decision tree to analyse the viability of the two alternatives.
5. To identify any other factors/problems which the company may face if it makes the investment and which therefore could influence the Board's decision.
6. To make a recommendation to the Board on the basis of your evaluation.

# 11. Financial Record-Keeping

This Chapter is about financial record-keeping in a business and the use and analysis of trading accounts. It includes:

* Need for Accounts
* Financial and Management Accounting
* Auditors
* Accounting Concepts
* Double entry book-keeping
* Ratio Analysis
* Trading and Profit and Loss
* Balance Sheet
* Assets
* Liabilities
* Stock Valuation
* Depreciation
* Interpretation of Accounts
* Types of Capital
* Final Accounts
* Performance Ratios
* Liquidity Ratios
* Funds Flow Statement

## Need for Accounts

1. All organisations need to keep records of their financial transactions whether they are profit-making businesses or non-profit making charities and Local Authorities. These financial records are called accounts and there are a number of reasons why they must be kept.

    - To **record financial transactions** called book-keeping. It is important to record sales and purchases and to keep track of money owed to and by the business and thus determine its assets and liabilities and whether it is trading at a profit or a loss. Computers are now widely used in business for this purpose.

    - To **provide management information** as a basis for decision-taking and control and thus to assist in planning to meet business objectives.

    - To **provide information for owners and shareholders.** Company directors and managers are entrusted to act honestly and efficiently and are accountable to shareholders for results.

    - To determine liability for **tax** e.g. corporation tax, value added tax.

    - The Companies Act 1985 and European **legislation** make it a requirement for companies to disclose accounting and other information about the business.

    - **Business evaluation.** Customers, suppliers, employers, creditors, potential lenders and prospective investors are all parties likely to be interested in an organisation's accounts to enable them to assess the likely business risks and/or potential profitability.

> **Task 11.1**
> 1. Identify which of the above reasons for keeping accounts apply to the organisation in which you are working or studying.
> 2. State which, if any, do not apply and say why.

## Financial and Management Accounting

2. Accountants are used to ensure that statutory records of business transactions are maintained and that accounting conventions, principles and practices are adhered to. It is necessary to distinguish between 2 different types of accounting – financial and management.

3. **Financial accountants** are essentially concerned with ensuring that a businesses accounts are a true and fair record of its financial transactions, as required by law.

4. They are responsible for:
   - planning, monitoring and controlling all financial and accounting systems.
   - the preparation of periodic and annual accounts, including the profit and loss accounts and balance sheet.
   - safeguarding the assets of the business and
   - maintaining an assets register.
5. **Management accountants** on the other hand are not covered by legislation but are concerned with the statistical analysis of accounts to ensure that managers are supplied with the information they need to assist them in making decisions in order to achieve objectives.
6. This could include:
   - cash flow analysis,
   - cost accounting,
   - preparation of budgets and
   - the evaluation of projects including the application of discounted cash flow (see Chapter 10).
7. Management accountants also provide variance and control ratios relating to liquidity, utilisation of resources and overhead expenditure (which is discussed later in this Chapter).

### Task 11.2

Look at a selection of advertisements for financial and management accountants in both the local and national press.

From these, identify which key skills are being sought by the organisations concerned and the responsibilities involved in each type of accounting.

## Auditors

8. Whilst an organisation's own accountants prepare the financial statements, independent assessment is carried out by auditors of which there are 2 categories – internal and external.
9. **Internal Auditors** are company employees who are responsible for carrying out impartial monitoring of accounting and other systems and procedures thereby providing information and advice for management. They present audit reports with recommendations direct to appropriate senior management.
10. **External Auditors** are independent of the company and appointed to examine the accounts and business records at the end of the financial year to ensure that they represent a true and fair view of the profits, losses, assets and liabilities. External auditors' reports by law must be attached to a company's published accounts. Guidelines on standards are issued by the Auditing Practices Board.

## Accounting Concepts

11. To ensure consistency in the way accounts are prepared an independent organisation, the Accounting Standards Board issues **Statements of Standard Accounting Practice**, on which the keeping of financial records is based. The published accounts of a company must by law comply with these concepts which are summarised below.
12. 'Going-concern'. A Balance Sheet is prepared on the basis that a business will continue to operate in the future i.e. as a going-concern.
13. 'Accruals' of Realisation. The Profit and Loss Account must take account of any outstanding debts which have not yet been paid and payments received which do not appertain to the current financial year i.e. transactions must be recorded for the trading period to which they relate and not in the period where the money is paid or received.
14. 'Consistency'. Methods used must be consistent to enable accounts to be compared both over a period of time and between other organisations.

## 11. Financial record-keeping

15. **'Prudence'** or conservation. Accounts should reflect the least favourable position in a business. So, for example, projected income should not be over-estimated, whilst anticipated expenditure should take the likely maximum.

16. **Separate business entity.** A set of accounts should always be treated from the business' viewpoint and not the owners, regardless of the legal entity. In a limited company, the business is a separate legal entity but with sole traders and partnerships there is possible confusion between personal and business finances.

17. **Money-measurement.** All accounts are shown in money terms and include only aspects of the business which can be expressed in this way.

18. **Stability of cost.** Assets in the Balance Sheet are valued at their cost price.

19. **'Verification'.** All statements in the accounts should be based on verifiable evidence, i.e. can be proved to be true.

20. **Double-Entry book-keeping**

    This essentially means that all items (invoices, credit notes, etc) are entered as both a debit (which represents an expense or asset) and a credit (which represents income or a liability) in the books of original entry. So for example, if a business buys £2,000 of stock on credit, this will increase both the stock and creditors. If, on the other hand, the stock was purchased for cash, it would increase stock but reduce the cash balance.

21. The books of original entry which are used include the:
    - **Cash-book** in which receipts and payments are recorded, ie cash, cheques etc.
    - **Sales Day Book or Sales Journal** in which all sales on credit are recorded.
    - **Purchases Day Book or Purchases Journal** in which all sales on credit are recorded.
    - **Journal(s)** which are used for all other credit transactions, for example the purchase or sale of assets such as equipment or buildings or liabilities such as bank loans.
    - **Ledger Accounts.** Entries in all the other books of account are posted (transferred) to the Ledger, hence the system of double-entry.

> **Task 11.3**
>
> Mary Cox is a sole trader who owns a small 'corner shop' where she sells mainly groceries and fresh foods. At present she does her own book-keeping.
>
> Explain to Mary:
> 1. Why she should keep the business accounts separate from her own personal finances.
> 2. Why she should be aware of basic accounting concepts.
> 3. How an accountant could assist with her accounts.

## Final Accounts

22. At the end of each financial period, any business needs to know whether or not it has made a profit. To provide this information, final accounts are prepared from the accounting records, the accuracy of which are checked by providing a **'Trial Balance'**. From this we get the Trading and Profit and Loss Account which shows the gross and net profit (or loss) for the period concerned, usually a year.

    The trial balance is not part of the double entry book-keeping system. It is a summary of all the balances in the ledger accounts and cash book at the end of the financial period, which may be monthly, quarterly, six-monthly or annually. Public Limited Companies, for example, publish accounts twice a year. Although it provides a useful check it does not necessarily mean that the accounts are accurate and indeed it may not actually balance, due, for example, to mistakes in addition, entries being missed, the wrong accounts being debited or credited, or the wrong balances being brought forward from the previous financial period.

23. **Example**

**Best Buy Stores**

**Trading and Profit and Loss Account for the year ending 31 December 19..**

|  | £ | £ | £ |
|---|---:|---:|---:|
| **Sales** |  |  | 15,400 |
| **Cost of sales:** |  |  |  |
| Opening Stock (1st Jan) |  | 5,000 |  |
| Add Purchases |  | 4,800 |  |
|  |  | 9,800 |  |
| Less Closing Stock (31 Dec) |  | 4,600 | 5,200 |
| **GROSS PROFIT** |  |  | 10,200 |
|  |  |  |  |
| **Less Overheads:** |  |  |  |
| **Administration** |  |  |  |
| Wages | 3,800 |  |  |
| Lighting & heat | 500 |  |  |
| Rates | 810 |  |  |
| Insurance | 150 |  |  |
| Stationery | 35 | 5,295 |  |
| **Finance** |  |  |  |
| Interest on loan | 100 | 100 |  |
| **Selling** |  |  |  |
| Advertising | 100 |  |  |
| Transport | 200 | 300 | 5,695 |
| **NET PROFIT** |  |  | 4,505 |

### Task 11.4

From the following information, prepare a trading and profit and loss account for the business of Trevor Jones.

| Stock at 1st July £2,410 | Purchases £18,000 | Sales £29,550 |
| Wages £8,420 | Postage £120 | Rent and Rates £1,160 |
| Transport £490 | Insurance £220 | Stationery £80 |
| Lighting and Heat £590 | Stock at 30 June £2,500 | |

## Balance Sheet – 'Statement of Affairs'

24. In addition to calculating the gross and net profit, a Balance Sheet must also be prepared which shows the financial position of the business at that particular time. A balance sheet consists of two lists – one of the **Assets** (things possessed or owned by a business) and the other the **Liabilities** (anything owed by a business). That is, it shows the sources of funds in a business and the uses to which those funds have been put.

*11. Financial record-keeping*

25. **Example**

### Balance Sheet of J Taylor's – Sole Trader as at 30 June 199...

| | | |
|---|---:|---:|
| **Fixed Assets** | | |
| Premises | 14,800 | |
| Fixtures & Fittings (8,000 less depreciation 800) | 7,200 | |
| Motor Vehicles (6000 less depreciation 1000) | 5,000 | |
| | | 27,000 |
| **Current Assets** | | |
| Debtors | 3,500 | |
| Stock | 7,000 | |
| Cash | 500 | |
| | 11,000 | |
| **Less Current Liabilities** | | |
| Bank Overdraft | 2,000 | |
| Creditors | 2,000 | |
| Unpaid expenses | 1,000 | |
| | 5,000 | |
| **Working Capital** | | 6,000 |
| **Net Assets** | | 33,000 |
| | | |
| *Financed By* | | |
| **Capital** | | 26,000 |
| ADD Net Profit | | 5,000 |
| **Long Term Liabilities** | | |
| Bank Loan | | 2,000 |
| | | 33,000 |

26. It is important to note the following in respect of accounts.

  - A **Debtor** is someone who owes money to a business, for example for goods which they have bought.

  - A **Creditor** is someone to whom a business owes money, for example a supplier from whom raw materials have been bought.

  - On a balance sheet, the assets must always be equal to the liabilities.

  - The final accounts and balance sheet of a large company or other organisation are much more complex than the simple example of J Taylor but the basic information and presentation is essentially the same.

## Assets

27. **Assets** are of two main types, fixed or current.

  - **Current Assets** (or circulating capital) are those which are constantly changing from day-to-day for example stock of goods, debts, cash and bank balances.

  - **Fixed Assets** (or fixed capital) are those which remain the same over a period of time and are held for use in the business rather than for resale. Fixed assets can be **tangible**, for example: land, buildings, fittings, furniture, equipment and vehicles; or **intangible**, for example: goodwill, copyrights, patents and trademarks.

28. **Tangible Assets**

Land and buildings may be freehold or leasehold. **Freehold** means that they belong totally to the business owner and **leasehold** that they are owned by someone else but used by the business for which rent is paid.

29. **Intangible Assets**

- **Goodwill** is the difference between the value of a business's tangible assets and its market price and thus can only really be accurately valued when a business is sold. Essentially, it represents the value of the existing customer base in a business.
- **Copyrights** are covered by the 1956 Copyright Act. They have the effect of granting to the owner automatic legal protection against their work being copied, for example: records, books, videos, computer software and advertisements.
- **Patents** give inventors of products or processes the right to have sole use for a specified number of years, if they register them with the Patents Office under the 1977 Patents Act.
- **Trademarks** are brand names given to products to distinguish them from others. They are registered as copyright by firms to prevent them from being used by anyone else, which is important for marketing. (see Chapter 8)

30. **Liquidity**

Fixed Assets are usually shown on a Balance Sheet in order of liquidity with the least liquid first. That is, the asset which is most difficult to turn into cash without loss of value if the business went bankrupt or into liquidation. The most liquid asset, that is, cash itself, is shown last.

## Liabilities

31. **Liabilities** are also of two main types:
    - **Fixed Liabilities** such as capital and long-term loans which remain the same over long periods.
    - **Current Liabilities** such as creditors, bank overdrafts, and short-term loans which change from day-to-day

### Task 11.5

From the following information, compile Trading and Profit and Loss Accounts and a Balance Sheet for the year ended 31 December 199..

| | | | | | |
|---|---|---|---|---|---|
| Opening Stock | £13,500 | Purchases | £40,000 | Overheads | £8,000 |
| Premises | £50,000 | Vans | £12,000 | Debtors | £3,200 |
| Capital | £75,000 | Closing Stock | £9,500 | Cash-in-hand | £300 |
| Sales | £60,000 | Cash at Bank | £13,000 | Loans | £1,000 |
| Creditors | £4,000 | | | | |

## Stock Valuation

32. Where, at the end of a trading period, a firm has stocks of raw materials, components, work-in-progress or finished goods, then they must be valued for accounting purposes. Invariably this is done using one of the following methods – FIFO, LIFO, Replacement Price, Standard Price or Average Cost System (AVCO).

33. **First-In, First Out (FIFO)**

This method assumes that goods are withdrawn from stock in the order in which they are received. Thus the cost of goods sold is based on the cost of the oldest stock, whilst the closing stock value is based on the prices of the most recent purchases. FIFO is acceptable to the Inland Revenue for tax

## 11. Financial record-keeping

purposes because costs are related to those actually incurred and the closing stock value is close to the current market price.

### 34. Last-In, First Out (LIFO)

This method assumes that the most recently bought stock is used first. Therefore the cost of goods sold is based on the cost of the most recent purchases, whilst the closing stock is valued on the cost of the oldest goods available. LIFO is unacceptable for tax purposes because it understates the profitability of a business. However, this does not prevent a firm from choosing this method for its own internal use.

### 35. Example

| FIFO | | LIFO | |
|---|---|---|---|
| Sales (1,000 × £25) | 25,000 | Sales (1,000 × £25) | 25,000 |
| Cost of goods sold: | | Cost of goods sold: | |
| 500 × £15 = £7,500 | | 1,000 × £17 | 17,000 |
| 500 × £17 = £8,500 | | | |
| | 16,000 | | |
| PROFIT | 9,000 | PROFIT | 8,000 |
| Closing Stock (200 × £17) | 3,400 | Closing Stock (200 × £15) | 3,000 |

In the above example, under FIFO the cost of goods sold is based on those actually incurred, ie 500 at £15 and 500 at £17, whilst the closing stock of 200 is valued at its replacement cost of £17. On the other hand, using LIFO, the cost of goods sold is valued at its current cost of £17, whilst the closing stock of 200 is valued at £15 which is what it cost when purchased.

### 35. Replacement Price Method

This method is also unacceptable for tax purposes because it values all stock at the current cost of replacement rather than at actual cost.

### 36. Average Cost System (AVCO)

This is the simplest method of valuing stock acceptable for tax purposes. The total value of stock bought in a period is divided by the number of items purchased to give the value of each unit, thus smoothing out price fluctuations.

### 37. Example

| Value of stock bought on | 1st January | £5,000 (500 × £10) |
|---|---|---|
| | 1st March | £7,000 (500 × £14) |
| | 1st May | £7,200 (600 × £12) |

Therefore the total cost of stock bought is £19,200 and the value of each unit

$$= \frac{19,200}{1,600}$$

therefore average cost per unit = £12.00

Thus, if the stock level at the end of the trading period is 400 its valuation = 400 × £12 = £4,800.

### 39. Standard Price Method

This method uses a pre-determined standard price to value stock. Thus, although it eliminates price fluctuations, it does not use actual costs.

## Task 11.6

1. Using the following information from a book retailer, calculate the value of the stock sold on 30 March using the methods of FIFO, LIFO and AVCO.
2. Comment on the effect which each method would have on a firm's gross profit.

| Date | Details | Unit Cost | Total Stock | Valuation |
|---|---|---|---|---|
| 1st March | Bought 50 | £1.50 | 50 | £75.00 |
| 10 March | Sold 10 | | | |
| 20 March | New delivery | £2.00 | | |
| (Price change) | Bought 20 | | | |
| 30 March | Sold 50 | | | |

## Depreciation

40. The Balance Sheet shows the value of a business's assets at a particular point in time, i.e. how much each asset would be worth if it was sold for cash. Each year some fixed assets lose value due to wear and tear. For example, a two year old car will be worth less than a new one. Therefore in its accounts, a business will make an allowance (deducted as an expense in the Profit and Loss Accounts) for this called depreciation.

41. In T Taylor's Balance Sheet, the fixtures and fittings are estimated to depreciate (lose value) by £800 each year, whilst the motor vehicles depreciate by £1,000 each year. Eventually these will need to be replaced. The depreciation allowance saved each year can therefore be used to purchase new items. The figure for depreciation is usually calculated by using either the straight line or reducing instalment methods.

42. **Calculation of Depreciation**

    Using the **'Straight line'** or equal instalment method, the cost of the asset is divided by the length of time it is expected to be used before needing replacement.

    ### Example

    A machine costing £10,000 and expected to last 5 years would depreciate by £2,000 p.a.

    Sometimes this formula is modified slightly by allowing for a resale or scrap value at the end of the period.

43. The **Reducing instalment** method is calculated by assuming that an asset depreciates by the same percentage each year.

    ### Example

    A machine costing £10,000 with a 20% annual rate of depreciation

    | Year 1 | Cost | 10,000 | |
    |---|---|---|---|
    | Year 2 | Worth | 8,000 | |
    | Year 3 | Worth | 6,400 | |
    | Year 4 | Worth | 5,120 | etc |

The method chosen will depend on decisions which best suit the financial needs of the business.

## Task 11.7

Which method of depreciation allowance would you recommend as being most appropriate for a new computer system costing £15,000?

Show possible comparative depreciation methods over a 5 year period and give reasons for the method chosen.

## Interpretation of Final Accounts

44. By examining the figures in the Trading Profit and Loss Account, and in particular the Balance Sheet, it is possible to discover the financial strengths and weaknesses of a business. They provide a summary of all the important financial facts and thus it is possible to see, for example, the amount and types of capital in the business, the net profit and how much is owed to the bank and other creditors.

## Types of Capital

45. The assets in the Balance Sheet show how a business's capital has been spent for example to buy premises, stock or vehicles. It is also possible to calculate the capital owned, capital employed and working capital.

46. **Capital owned** is a measure of the value or net worth of a business.

    CAPITAL OWNED = TOTAL ASSETS – CURRENT LIABILITIES

47. But this may not be all the capital in a business since money may be borrowed from a bank or goods bought on credit, in other words, someone else's capital may also be used. On the other hand, a business may also be owed money by its debtors. Therefore the actual **capital employed** that is used in a business may be slightly different from what is owned.

    CAPITAL EMPLOYED = TOTAL ASSETS – DEBTORS

48. **Working capital** is the money which a business must have available to meet its day-to-day expenses such as staff wages, purchasing of stock and other overheads.

    WORKING CAPITAL = CURRENT ASSETS – CURRENT LIABILITIES

49. Working capital is essential to ensure that a firm can operate efficiently and remain **solvent** i.e. in a position to pay its expenses. If a business is **insolvent** it means that the current assets are less than the current liabilities and thus it cannot pay its debts in full. For example, if current assets were £10,000 and current liabilities £12,000, then the firm would not have sufficient working capital to carry on the business.

50. In the short-term it may be possible to solve this problem by borrowing or extending credit, but if it continues for any length of time, the business may be forced to close down. In the case of an individual this is called **bankruptcy** or in the case of a company **liquidation**. (See Chapter 2.)

## Task 11.8

1. From the following information, draw up the Balance Sheet as at 31 March 199.. for ABC Ltd.
2. From it, identify the figures for capital owned, capital employed and working capital.

| | | |
|---|---|---|
| Creditors £15,200 | Debtors £11,000 | Stock £1,600 |
| Land £14,000 | Machinery £15,000 | Depreciation £3,000 |
| Bank £12,000 | Cash £1,200 | Capital £40,600 |
| 10-year loan £14,000 | Premises £18,000 | |

## Ratio Analysis

51. Simple statistics, however, are by themselves of limited value and therefore ratio analysis is used to assess the performance, profitability and solvency of a business. The use of ratios enables more meaningful comparisons to be made between companies of different sizes, the same company over a period of time and between several companies in an industry.

52. The key accounting ratios are:
    - **Performance ratios,** including the return on capital employed, assessment of profitability and turnover of capital, which measure a business's level of activity and efficiency.
    - **Liquidity ratios** including the current ratio and acid test which indicates a business's ability to pay its debts.
    - **Investment (or shareholder) ratios** which measure the returns on capital investment. These are covered in Chapter 10.
    - **Capital gearing ratios** which measure how assets are financed are also covered in Chapter 10.

## Performance Ratios

53. There are a number of ratios which can be used to assess the performance and efficiency of a business. Three which we shall consider here are the return on capital employed (or prime ratio), profit on turnover and turnover of capital.

54. **Return on Capital Employed**

    Investors in a business will obviously wish to see a return on their money which is assessed by determining the return on capital employed (ROCE).

    $$\text{This is calculated as } \frac{\text{Net profit}}{\text{Capital employed}} \times 100$$

    Thus, for example, if we compare a company with capital of £30,000 and profits in Year 1 of £5,000 and in Year 2 £6,600

    $$\text{ROCE in year 1} = \frac{£5,000}{£30,000} \times 100 = 19\% \text{ approx}$$

    $$\text{ROCE in year 2} = \frac{£6,600}{£30,000} \times 100 = 22\%$$

    So, for every £100 invested in the business, in Year 1 £19 was earned in profit, and Year 2, £22.

55. These would probably be considered as satisfactory returns on capital, but if the return was less than about 10% then it would not be very good because it would be possible to invest money elsewhere, say in a building society and earn a similar rate of return but without the risks involved by investing in a business.

56. **Profit on Turnover (or Profit-Margin Ratio)**

    In order to compare a firm's profits with both previous years and those of other businesses, it is usual to calculate it in percentage terms. The profit margin is used to measure the return on turnover in a business and can be calculated on either gross or net profit.

## 11. Financial record-keeping

**57. Example 1**

Turnover = £120,000
Gross Profit = £30,000
Net profit = £12,000

$$\% \text{ profit} = \frac{\text{Gross profit} \times 100}{\text{Turnover}} = \frac{30,000}{120,000} \times 100 = 25\%$$

That is for every £100 of sales £25 has been earned as gross profit.

OR

$$\% \text{ profit} = \frac{\text{Net profit} \times 100}{\text{Turnover}} = \frac{12,000}{120,000} \times 100 = 10\%$$

**58. Example 2**

|  | Year 1 £ | Year 2 £ |
|---|---|---|
| Turnover | 400,000 | 600,000 |
| Gross Profit | 100,000 | 120,000 |
| Net Profit | 50,000 | 66,000 |

If we compare the 2 years, at first glance, it would seem that most profit was made in year 2 but this does not take account of inflation or the quantity of goods sold and therefore we use a percentage comparison.

**Gross Profit to Turnover**

$$\text{Year 1} = \frac{100,000}{400,000} \times 100 = 25\%$$

$$\text{Year 2} = \frac{120,000}{600,000} \times 100 = 20\%$$

Thus the firm actually made less gross profit in Year 2.

**Net Profit to Turnover**

$$\text{Year 1} = \frac{50,000}{400,000} \times 100 = 12\tfrac{1}{2}\%$$

$$\text{Year 2} = \frac{66,000}{600,000} \times 100 = 11\%$$

From these calculations it can be seen that in year 1 for every £100 worth of goods sold, the cost was £75, the overheads £12.50 leaving £12.50 profit. Whilst in year 2 the cost was £80, the overheads £9 leaving £11 profit.

59. By calculating the percentage profit on turnover, a business can compare its trading results with previous years to see what progress is being made and to take action where needed. For example, they may indicate improved efficiency and better buying or inefficiency, higher overheads and overmanning (ie too many staff employed).

## 60. Capital Turnover

This is used to measure the extent to which an organisation has utilised its capital to achieve its sales. Any investment in capital should lead to an increase in sales which is calculated as turnover of capital rather than as a percentage. The higher the turnover of capital, the better the capital has been used.

$$\text{CAPITAL TURNOVER} = \frac{\text{SALES REVENUE}}{\text{CAPITAL EMPLOYED}}$$

Thus a company with capital of £250,000 and sales of £1 million would have a turnover of capital of 4.

---

**Task 11.9**

The return on capital, profit on turnover and capital turnover are all inter-related.

1. Calculate each ratio from the following information to show this relationship.

    ABC Company has capital employed of £400,000

    Sales of £800,000 and a net profit of £50,000

2. Comment on your findings

---

## Other Performance Ratios

61. Other important measures of the efficiency of a business include the rate of turnover, creditors ratio and debtors ratio.

## 62. Rate of Turnover

Turnover is the value of sales over a period of time. The ratio of turnover or stockturn is a measure of how quickly those goods are sold (turned over). It can be measured in two different ways.

$$1. \quad \frac{\text{Value of total sales}}{\text{Average stock at selling price}} \qquad 2. \quad \frac{\text{Cost of goods sold}}{\text{Average stock at cost price}}$$

Thus if a business has annual sales of £24,000 and the average stock at selling price is valued at £2,000, then the rate of turnover, using method 1 is 12 times per year. In other words the stock is turned over about once a month.

63. There are several ways of calculating the average stock, but one of the most popular is as follows:

$$\frac{\text{Stock at the beginning of the year} + \text{stock at the end of the year}}{2}$$

Thus if we have £20,000 of stock at the beginning of the year and £16,000 at the end then our average stock is

$$\frac{20{,}000 + 16{,}000}{2} = £18{,}000$$

That is, at any particular time in the year the business would probably have about £18,000 worth of goods in stock. This is important because stock has to be financed and therefore ties up capital. On the other hand, too little stock might lead to lost sales.

64. The rate of turnover depends very much upon the type of business, since where fresh food is sold such as meat, fish and vegetables, stock must be turned over and replaced quickly. As a result, the

business will have a high rate of stock turn, whereas a television, carpet or furniture trader might have goods in stock for several weeks or even months and therefore have a low rate of stockturn.

65. The rate of turnover in a business can usually be increased in two ways:
    - By **cutting prices** so that customers will buy more or,
    - By **increasing the amount of advertising** and sales promotion to attract more customers.

> ### Task 11.10
> Stock turnover is important to a business because of the costs of storage, finance and because high stock levels can cause liquidity problems if goods prove difficult to sell. Supermarket retailers like Tesco expect stock to turnover every 10-20 days, whilst manufacturing companies like British Steel would expect it to be nearer 90-100 days.
> 1. Identify the importance of stock turnover to a business.
> 2. Explain, with reasons, why you would expect Tesco and British Steel to have widely differing stock turnovers.

66. **Creditors Ratio (Average Payment Period)**

This indicates the average time taken by a business to pay its debts. It is important because it can indicate that a firm is having difficulty paying its debts which may eventually create problems with its suppliers. It is calculated as:

$$\text{Average payment period} = \frac{\text{Average trade creditors}}{\text{Total credit purchases}} \times 365$$

Up to 30 days is the normal period allowed by suppliers to pay for credit puchases.

67. **Debtors Ratio (Average Collection Period)**

This indicates the average time taken to collect payments for goods sold. It is important because it is a measure of a firm's credit control and can draw attention to potential bad debts. It is calculated as:

$$\text{Average collection period} = \frac{\text{Average trade debtors}}{\text{Total credit sales}} \times 365$$

If a firm does not collect money owed to it efficiently, it may well experience cash flow difficulties and find itself unable to pay its own debts. It it allows 30 days credit it must try to ensure that payment is made during this period.

## Other Performance Indicators

68. Depending on the business, there are many other figures which may be used to measure performance. Even though some are less sophisticated than those discussed so far, nonetheless they can still be of assistance to managers, for example:
    - Average overtime payments per employee can influence costs.
    - Time taken to produce a quantity of products, eg number of cars per man/hour may prove a useful measure of efficiency.
    - Customers per thousand population may indicate market penetration.
    - Advertising costs per unit of sales may indicate value for money.
    - Total output per employee may be useful in manufacturing industries.
    - Turnover per square metre of floor or shelf space is commonly used in retailing outlets.

## Liquidity Ratios

69. Sometimes working capital is a misleading measure of a firm's ability to meet its immediate debts and liquid capital is used instead. Liquidity refers to those assets which are available as cash or can be easily converted into cash, for example bank balances and debtors. The current and acid test are two **liquidity ratios** frequently used:

70. **Current (or Working Capital) Ratio = Current Assets:Current Liabilities**

    For example, a business with current assets of £15,000 and current liabilities of £10,000 would have a current ratio of 15,00:10,000 or 1.5:1. A ratio of 2:1 is generally considered as about ideal. A ratio of less than 1:1 would mean that a firm could not meet its immediate debts because current liabilities exceed current assets. Whilst a ratio of more than 2:1 means that too much capital is being tied up in stock or debtors are taking a long time to pay.

71. The current ratio calculation uses all current assets which includes stock but stock is not always easy to convert into cash, therefore the **Acid Test Ratio or Quick Ratio** is usually considered to be a better measure of liquidity.

    Acid Test Ratio = Current Assets less Stock : Current Liabilities

    This measures whether a business can meet its short-term liabilities without having to sell more or reduce its stock levels. Some assets are usually financed by borrowing which incurs interest charges. Consequently, if sales (and therefore revenue) fall, this may affect a firm's liquidity position.

72. For example, a company with current assets of £15,000, stock of £7,000 and current liabilities of £10,000 would have an acid test ratio of:

    15,000 – 7,000:10,000 = 4:5

    Thus it would have a problem if all creditors demanded to be paid at the same time. A ratio of 1 : 1 is ideal because a business can then meet its objectives without having to sell off stock, possibly at a discount, to obtain cash quickly.

### Task 11.11

From the following statement, identify some potential advantages and disadvantages of using ratio analysis to assess a company's investment potential.

'Ratio analysis is a technique which may be used to assist management decision-taking or to provide information about a company for shareholders, potential investors, banks, suppliers and customers. But whilst it enables a company's financial performance to be assessed and is useful to indicate trends over a period of time, it is not without its limitations. Since final accounts are prepared at a particular point in time ratios may not reflect the 'normal' situation in a business. Also, because companies can record information and value assets in different ways, comparisons may be imprecise.

'Ratio analysis also ignores non-quantitative data about products and developments which may be equally important when assessing a company's growth potential.'

## Cash Flow Statement

73. In addition to the Profit and Loss Accounts and Balance Sheet, a Cash Flow Statement is also prepared which shows the movement of cash in five key categories. The aim is that it is possible to see at a glance how and why cash flow has changed during a trading period and whether or not a company is generating cash as well as making a profit. This information is presented in a standard format and replaces the Funds Flow or Statement of Source and Application of Funds used previously.

## 11. Financial record-keeping

76. **Example**

Cash Flow Statement

for the 12 months ending 31 July 199..

|  | Current year 199x £m | Previous year 199y £m |
|---|---|---|
| Net cash flow from operating activities | 135.0 | 132.6 |
| **Returns on investment and servicing of finance** | | |
| Interest received | 3 | |
| Interest paid | (6.2) | |
| Dividends paid | (4) | |
| Net cash outflow from returns on investment and servicing of finance | (7.2) | (8.3) |
| **Taxation** | | |
| Corporation tax paid | (4.7) | (9.5) |
| **Investing activities** | | |
| Purchase of tangible fixed assets | (31.9) | (17.6) |
| Fixed asset investment | (8.2) | (5.4) |
| Sale of plant and machinery | 5.1 | 2.9 |
| Net cash outflow from investing activities | (35.0) | (20.3) |
| **Movements in cash and cash equivalents** | 88.1 | 94.5 |

75. In the example we can see that:

   ❏ The cash flow is healthy and rising at £135m.

   ❏ £7.2 million was used for interest and dividends.

   ❏ Corporation tax used up £4.7 million.

   ❏ A further £35 million was used in new investments.

   ❏ The overall cash balance fell by £6.4 million.

76. Fortunately this company is in a strong cash flow position. If this had not been the case then it would have been necessary to secure additional finance from loans and or the issue of extra shares in order to pay for its investments.

77. 3 other terms which are commonly used in accounting are the

   - **Appropriation account** which shows how the dividends in a company are distributed between the various types of shareholder or in a partnership, the distribution of profit between the partners.

   - **Manufacturing account.** A wholesaler or retailer sells finished goods which in the accounts are shown as purchases. Where a business is engaged in manufacturing, the cost is calculated and then transferred to the Trading Account instead of purchases. The elements involved are prime costs, factory overheads and work-in-progress which together give the cost of goods manufactured.

   - **Value Added Statement.** This is used to indicate the difference between the cost of goods and services purchased in a business and the sales revenue. It indicates how much value has been added by the business itself. Whilst profit is the wealth which a business creates for its owners, value added is shared between the people who create it, for example, wages to staff. Thus value added includes profit.

## Summary

78. a)   All organisations whether profit-making or non-profit making need to keep a record of their financial transactions.

b) Financial accountants are used to ensure that a business's accounts are a true and fair record as required by law whilst management accountants are used to provide information to assist decision-making.

c) Internal Auditors may be employed to monitor accounts, whilst external auditors provide independent checks.

d) To ensure consistency in accounts, the Accounting Standards Board issues Statements of Standard Accountancy Practice.

e) A set of Final Accounts are prepared at the end of each trading period.

f) The Trading and Profit and Loss Account shows the gross and net profit (or loss) for the period concerned.

g) The Balance Sheet shows the assets and liabilities of a business at a particular time. That is, what it owns and what owes.

h) Stock can be valued using either FIFO, LIFO, Replacement Price, Standard Price or the Average Cost System.

i) The depreciation of assets can be calculated using the straight-line or reducing instalment methods.

j) Final accounts can be analysed to provide information on capital owned, capital employed and working capital in a business.

k) Ratio analysis can also be used to assess the performance, profitability and solvency of a business.

l) Key performance indicators include the return on capital employed, profit on turnover and capital turnover.

m) Other performance ratios include rate of turnover, creditors ratio and debtors ratio.

n) The current and acid test liquidity ratios are used to measure a firm's ability to meet its debts.

o) A cash flow statement shows the sources from which a business has derived its cash and the uses to which it has been put in a trading period.

## Review questions *(answers can be found in the paragraphs indicated)*

1. Why is it necessary for organisations to keep accounts? (1)
2. Distinguish between the role of financial and management accountants. (2-7)
3. What are auditors and why are they necessary? (8-10)
4. Briefly explain some of the main concepts used when preparing accounts. (11-19)
5. Use a simple example to explain the double-entry system of accounting. (20-21)
6. What is the difference between gross and net profit? (22-23)
7. Why is a Balance Sheet often described as a 'Statement of Affairs'? (24-25)
8. Use examples to distinguish between the assets and liabilities in a business. (26-31)
9. Briefly explain 4 different methods for valuing stock. (32-39)
10. Explain the difference between the straight-line and reducing investment methods of depreciation. (40-43)
11. What is the difference between capital owned, capital employed and working capital? (45-50)
12. Distinguish between the return on capital employed, profit on turnover and capital turnover. (53-60)
13. Why is the rate of turnover important in a business? (62-65)
14. What is the difference between the creditors ratio and debtors ratio? (66-67)
15. What do the current and acid test ratios reveal about a business? (69-72)
16. Why is a cash flow statement included in a company's published accounts? (73-76)

## 11. Financial record-keeping

*Asterisks indicate those questions for which there are answers in Outline Answers (page 439)*

### Essay-style questions

1.* a) Explain what you understand by the term 'liquidity' in a business.
   b) How might a firm predict potential future liquidity problems?
   c) Can liquidity problems be avoided and if so, how?

2. Discuss and explain the records which a business needs to keep in order to determine whether or not it is trading profitably.

3. Why is ratio analysis used to assess the performance of a business? What key accounting ratios would indicate whether or not a business is operating efficiently?

### Short answer

1.* a) How is depreciation dealt with in the accounts of a business.
   b) Using the straight-line and reducing instalment methods, calculate the difference in value at the end of 5 years of an asset which originally cost £100,000 and estimated to depreciate at 20% per annum.

2.* a) Give **four** reasons why it is important for a business to keep accounts.
   b) Distinguish between financial and management accounting.

3. a) Give at least 2 reasons why a business may take stock throughout and at the end of a financial year.
   b) Explain 2 methods which might be used to value stock for accounting purposes.

### Multiple choice/completion

1.* Which of the following would not be taken into account in calculating working capital?
   a) Cash
   b) Debtors
   c) Creditors
   d) Premises

2.* Which of the following is the least liquid asset?
   a) Stock
   b) Bank
   c) Land
   d) Fixtures and fittings

3.* A fixed asset costing £13,000 has a scrap value of £2,000. Its life is 5 years. What amount should be set aside for depreciation each year if the straight-line method is used?
   a) £13,000
   b) £11,000
   c) £2,000
   d) £2,200

4.* Which of the following is a liability of a business?
   a) Company car
   b) Bank loan
   c) Petty cash
   d) Stock of finished goods

## 11. Financial record-keeping

5. During a trading period, the rate of stockturn in a business is best defined as the:
   a) cost of goods sold.
   b) average amount of stock at any particular time
   c) total sales
   d) number of times that average stock is sold

6. A business has a gross profit of £30,000, sales of £120,000, expenses of £12,000 and an average stock turn of 4. Therefore its net profit to turnover is:
   a) 20%
   b) 15%
   c) 25%
   d) Cannot be calculated from the above information.

*In each of the following questions, one or more of the responses is/are correct. Choose the appropriate letter which indicates the correct version.*

   A   if 1 only is correct
   B   if 3 only is correct
   C   if 1 and 2 only are correct
   D   if 1, 2 and 3 are correct

7. Which of the following is/are intangible assets in a business?
   1. Goodwill
   2. Patents
   3. Trademarks

8. Which of the following statements is/are correct?
   1. A funds flow statement shows the cash flow in a business.
   2. The debtors ratio indicates the average time taken by a business to pay its debts.
   3. The acid test ratio is a measure of liquidity in a business.

## Assignment

P. Conner runs a mobile snackbar and has just completed his first year of trading. Answer the following questions based on his accounts.

1. **Account for year ended 30. 9. 199 .**

|  | £ | £ |  | £ |
|---|---|---|---|---|
| Cost of Goods Sold: |  |  | Sales | 30,000 |
| Purchases | 15,600 |  |  |  |
|  | 15,600 |  |  |  |
| Less Closing Stock | 600 | 15,000 |  |  |
| Gross Profit |  | 15,000 |  |  |
|  |  | 30,000 |  | 30,000 |

Answer the following questions in connection with the account above.
   a) What is the name of the account and the trading period involved?
   b) What percentage gross profit is the business making on its turnover?
   c) If the business continues next year to sell the same types of goods in the same proportions, and sales increase to £40,000, what would you expect the gross profit to be?
   d) If, when stock was taken on 30 Sept 199.., a batch of stock which had cost £300 was omitted, what effect would that have in the account given above?
   e) If the mistake is not put right, what effect will it have on next year's figures for the same account?
   f) Why is the profit called 'gross' profit?
   g) How would 'net' profit be calculated?

2. **P Conner Balance Sheet as at 30 Sept 199...**

|  | £ | £ |  | £ |
|---|---|---|---|---|
| Capital | 5,000 |  | Mobile Van | 8,600 |
| Add Net Profit | 6,000 |  | Fixtures & Fittings | 2,050 |
|  | 11,000 |  | Stocks | 600 |
| Less Drawings | 6,500 | 4,500 | Debtors | 50 |
| Loan (for 5 yrs) |  | 6,000 | Cash & Bank | 500 |
| Creditors |  | 1,000 |  |  |
| Unpaid expenses |  | 300 |  |  |
|  |  | 11,800 |  | 11,800 |

Answer the following questions in connection with the Balance Sheet above:
   a) What is the total value of the fixed assets?
   b) What is the total value of the current assets?
   c) What percentage profit is P Conner making on his capital at the beginning of the year?
   d) Why has P Conner's capital fallen in value by the end of the year?
   e) Explain the difference between debtors and creditors.
   f) What percentage profit has the business made on the total funds it is using?
   g) Can the business pay its short-term debts in full? Give reasons for your answer.

3. Why are the above accounts needed?
4. What other useful information, if any, can be extracted from the Accounts?
5. P Conner has prepared the Accounts with the help of his father. Both attended college over 25 years ago. Show the Accounts in a more modern format.

# 12. Human Resources in an Organisation

1. This Chapter looks at the importance of people in an organisation and covers:
   * Personnel Management
   * Manpower Planning
   * Personnel Functions
   * Recruitment
   * Selection
   * Interviews
   * Training and Development
   * Staff Appraisal
   * Employment Legislation
   * Termination of Employment
   * Dismissal procedures
   * Unfair Dismissal
   * Redundancy Payments
   * Monitoring Personnel Policies

## People and Business

2. People are an essential and very valuable resource in any organisation. But they are also expensive to employ and in some 'people intensive' organisations like schools and hospitals, can represent over 70% of the total operational costs. People are also individuals and everybody is different in terms of personality and needs. Since a large part of each day is spent at work, it should be both interesting and enjoyable if employees are to be motivated to always give of their best. A business's success can very often depend upon the quality of the staff it employs. Their efficiency, loyalty, attitude and enthusiasm can make the difference between a firm making a profit or a loss.

## Personnel Management

3. The **management of human resources** in an organisation is referred to as personnel management. In small firms this function may be carried out by the owner or a manager whilst many large organisations have a specialist Personnel Officer or Department with the responsibility of developing policies to find the right people for particular jobs and to help staff to work efficiently and happily. A Personnel Officer has both a 'line' responsibility for his own department and a 'staff' relationship with other departments.

## Manpower Planning

4. This is the main function of the Personnel Department and **involves forecasting the future demand for labour in the organisation and planning to meet it**. This plan will be related to the overall development of the organisation and the anticipated future demand for its products or services.

5. Manpower planning requires a **skills audit** involving an assessment of all staff, including management, to determine their current capabilities and matching this against future needs. Arrangements then need to be made for training and development as appropriate and if necessary, for the recruitment of new staff where skills shortages exist. Skills are what an employee needs to be capable of doing in order to achieve results and operate effectively. Most jobs require a variety of skills which can be built up from experience or by repeated training. In broad terms skills can be classified as

   - **Manual** e.g. a gardener must be able to dig and lift objects.
   - **Intellectual** or mental e.g. a statistician must be able to make calculations.
   - **Perceptual** e.g. a manager must be able to understand data and make decisions.
   - **Social** e.g. a salesman must be able to get on with people.

   Another way of classifying skills is in terms of job roles, for example:
   - **Manual** or operative, using the hands e.g. labourer, machine operator.
   - **Administrative** or clerical e.g. office worker, receptionist.
   - **Technical** or vocational specialist e.g. computer technician, electrician, plumber.
   - **Managerial** or supervisory e.g. sales manager, factory supervisor.
   - **Professional** or specialist requiring extensive training e.g. doctor, teacher, accountant.

> **Task 12.1**
>
> Consider any job which you have done or would like to do in an organisation which you know well such as your school, college or place of work.
>
> Identify what you feel are the skills necessary to carry out the job successfully. Then list any of those skills which you feel you did not, or do not possess and explain the effect you think it might have (if any) on your job performance.

6. Manpower planning is likely to be both a short-term and long-term process:

   **Short-term** (1-2 years ahead) to cover situations such as training for new and existing staff and also replacing people who retire.

   **Long-term** (2-5 years ahead) when planning is less certain but geared to the organisation's corporate objectives and proposed future development eg closing down a particular factory site and opening another elsewhere.

7. The manpower plan will also need updating regularly to take account of external factors which can affect an organisation such as:

   - the development of new technology – requiring new skills, for example, word processing in offices and computer aided manufacture in factories.
   - Government legislation – particularly European changes such as the Health & Safety directives.
   - the state of the economy – like the recession of the early 1990's which has forced many firms to make staff redundant.
   - social changes – for example the demand for environmental friendly products such as recycled paper and CFC free aerosol sprays.

   All of these factors represent opportunities for growth or threat of decline to an organisation depending upon how they are managed.

> **Task 12.2**
>
> 1. Consider the following news headlines and indicate how such factors are likely to impact on an organisation's future manpower planning.
>    - £500,000 expansion for City firm.
>    - Demand for more opportunities for women and ethnic minorities.
>    - 37pc of North West firms working below half capacity.
>    - Relocation plans revealed.
> 2. Now examine a number of different newspapers. From them identify one or more current examples of such factors and explain how they might affect manpower planning for the organisation(s) concerned.

## Personnel Functions

8. Effective personnel management and manpower planning involves the co-ordination of a range of specialist functions which can be summarised as:-

   - **Recruitment and Selection.** To obtain the 'right' staff see (9-14)
   - **Staff Welfare.** This is anything which affects the well-being of staff, for example the provision of canteens, social facilities, sporting facilities, medical and safety matters and pensions.
   - **Recommending promotions and keeping confidential staff records**

     All firms need certain information about their staff for example name, age, address, date of joining company, departments worked in, wages and any changes, various jobs performed, details of any training courses attended, examinations passed or progress made, educational qualifications and sickness records. References for future jobs or positions will then be based on this information.

- **Discussing staff problems.** This may be something to do with domestic problems at home such as housing, or financial worries, or it may be some personal matter which is affecting an individual's work.
- **Industrial relations.** Many staff will probably be members of a trade union and frequently it is the Personnel Officer will negotiate with the union(s) on matters relating to wages, working conditions or staff problems. (see Chapter 14).
- **Health and Safety** may also be a personnel function. Under the 1974 Health and Safety at Work Act, employers are legally obliged to maintain a safe working environment. An employer may be liable to prosecution if he does not fulfil this responsibility. Industrial accidents and sickness are also costly if people are absent from work for long periods of time.
- **Training and Development.** Unless there is a separate training department this is usually the role of the Personnel Department.

    Training is important for all employees to enable them to perform their jobs to the best of their ability. This involves giving instruction in order to develop their knowledge and skills.

- **Termination of Employment** It may also be the role of the personnel manager to dismiss staff for misconduct or incompetence and deal with necessary redundancies when workers are surplus to requirements.

---

### Task 12.3
**Worthy of Promotion?**

```
                    Supervisor Financial Services
                           Mrs Lawrence
        ┌──────────────┬──────────────┬──────────────┐
   Miss Wilcox (29)  Mrs Nichols (36)  Ms Harris (45)  Miss Boot (32)
      3 years           9 years          5 years         10 years
```

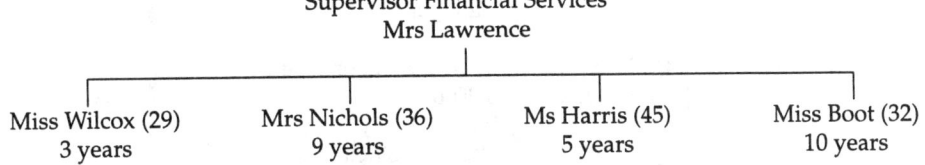

Mrs Lawrence, Supervisor (Financial Services Department), has been promoted to Office Manager of another department. She was asked to give her opinion of the four section heads to help decide the most suitable candidate for promotion. Her comments are summarised below.

**Miss Wilcox** – A satisfactory worker, but lacking personality and communication skills.

**Mrs Nichols** – A poor time keeper, often away sick, but an excellent worker when present. Potential to take on more responsibility.

**Ms Harris** – A reliable person, well-liked by everyone and suitable for the job in mind. Self-control could be improved.

**Miss Boot** – Considered 'narrow' in outlook, but career oriented and believed to have considerable interest in the vacant post.

As an employee in the Personnel Section, on the basis of this information:

1. State with reasons whether or not you would promote one of these people.
2. What other points (if any) would you draw to the attention of the Personnel Manager for further consideration.

## Recruitment

9. Before recruiting staff an employer must first of all decide:
   - What skills and personal qualities are needed.
   - How to attract suitable applicants.
   - Whether the post can be filled internally by existing staff or whether it requires new staff external to the organisation.
   - Whether full or part-time staff are required and
   - Whether the post is permenant or temporary.

10. **Job Description**

    When considering appointing or changing the role of staff an employer usually prepares a simple description of the job skills concerned. This will give the title of the job, an outline of the main purpose followed by a more detailed list of the main duties and responsibilities which it involves. It may also identify the section or site where the job is located.

11. **Examples**

    | TITLE | TRAINEE SALES ASSISTANT |
    |---|---|
    | PURPOSE | To perform a range of general duties as specified by the store manager |
    | DUTIES will include | Dealing with customers<br>Selling<br>Taking money<br>Checking stock<br>Filling shelves<br>Moving stock |

    | TITLE | JUNIOR OFFICE CLERK |
    |---|---|
    | PURPOSE | To undertake general clerical duties. Responsible to the office manager. |
    | DUTIES will include | Completing relevant paperwork<br>Filing<br>Answering the telephone<br>Some word processing<br>General reception duties |

12. **Job or Person Specification**

    From the job description an employer can draw up a job specification. This is a checklist of the personal qualities, education, qualifications, experience and skills which are needed in order to be able to do the job.

**13. Examples**

| JOB TITLE | TRAINEE SALES ASSISTANT |
|---|---|
| QUALITIES/ SKILLS | Good appearance<br>Ability to get on with people<br>Good general education<br>Honest<br>Numerate<br>Physically strong<br>Age 16–17 |

| JOB TITLE | JUNIOR OFFICE CLERK |
|---|---|
| QUALITIES/ SKILLS | RSA 1 Typewriting/Word Processing<br>3 GCSEs grade C, including English<br>Good appearance<br>Good telephone manner<br>Reliable<br>Age 16–18 |

### Task 12.4

If you are working either full or part-time, consider your own job. If not, consider a job that a member of your family or a friend has or any job with which you are reasonably familiar, for example, teacher, caretaker, bus conductor or cleaner.

Prepare a job description and person specification, including as much detail as possible.

## Selection

14. The employers next task is to attract and select suitable applicants for the job. Where the vacancy is at supervisory or middle-manager level, existing staff may well be promoted.

15. Places where job vacancies may be advertised include:

    - Local careers offices
    - Newspapers
    - Trade magazines
    - Job Centres
    - Private employment agencies
    - Local schools and colleges
    - Local radio or television
    - Vacancy boards or windows
    - In-house magazines
    - Internal memo/bulletin
    - Notice boards
    - Notices 'at the factory gate'

16. Many firms use advertisements in the national or local newspapers to fill job vacancies. The advertisement gives details about the job itself and usually asks people to reply in writing either by letter, by requesting an application form or by sending in a curriculum vitae (CV) i.e. summary of their education and career to date.

17. Whichever method is used the employer wants to find out as much as possible about the people who are applying for the job. This information is then matched against the job specification to select a shortlist of suitable candidates for interview. Applicants who do not meet the criteria on grounds of qualifications, experience or other factors such as poor presentation will be rejected at this stage.

*12. Human resources in an organisation*

### Task 12.5

External recruitment allows organisations to select staff with the qualities and skills required which may not exist within it, and to avoid jealousy often caused by internal appointments, particularly promotion. It also introduces 'fresh blood' with different experience and new ideas. On the other hand, it costs less to make internal appointments, the staff are already known and they know the organisation and how it operates. It also helps to motivate staff, particularly where opportunities for promotion exist.

1. Summarise the advantages of both internal and external recruitment.
2. Suggest some possible disadvantages of both the internal and external recruitment of staff to fill vacant posts.

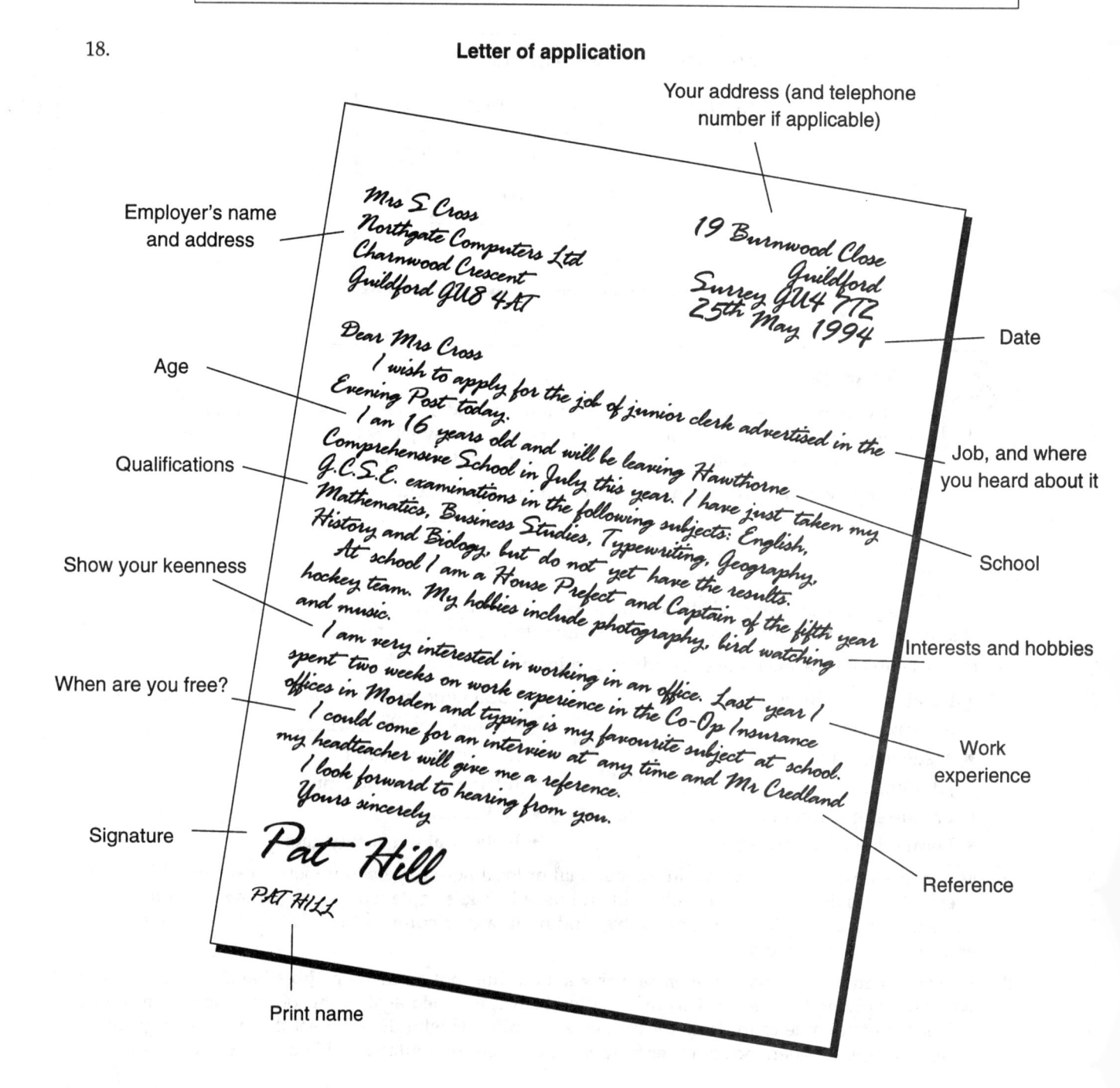

18. **Letter of application**

A handwritten letter of application with the following annotations pointing to its parts:

- Employer's name and address
- Age
- Qualifications
- Show your keenness
- When are you free?
- Signature
- Print name
- Your address (and telephone number if applicable)
- Date
- Job, and where you heard about it
- School
- Interests and hobbies
- Work experience
- Reference

Letter content:

Mrs S Cross
Northgate Computers Ltd
Charnwood Crescent
Guildford GU8 4AT

19 Burnwood Close
Guildford
Surrey GU4 7TZ
25th May 1994

Dear Mrs Cross

I wish to apply for the job of junior clerk advertised in the Evening Post today.

I am 16 years old and will be leaving Hawthorne Comprehensive School in July this year. I have just taken my G.C.S.E. examinations in the following subjects: English, Mathematics, Business Studies, Typewriting, Geography, History and Biology, but do not yet have the results.

At school I am a House Prefect and Captain of the fifth year hockey team. My hobbies include photography, bird watching and music.

I am very interested in working in an office. Last year I spent two weeks on work experience in the Co-Op Insurance offices in Morden and typing is my favourite subject at school.

I could come for an interview at any time and Mr Credland my headteacher will give me a reference.

I look forward to hearing from you.

Yours sincerely

Pat Hill

PAT HILL

19. **Application form**

| Annotation | Form content |
|---|---|
| | **HENLEY ENGINEERING LTD    APPLICATION FORM** |
| Name (print in capitals) | Surname: HUSSAIN    Christian name(s): SAJID |
| In full with post code | Home address: 19 EDGWICK CLOSE, BINLEY WOOD, COVENTRY CV6 4ED |
| | Telephone no: (0203) 616477 |
| | Nationality: BRITISH    Date and place of birth: 12/8/74 BIRMINGHAM |
| | Name and address of parent or guardian: MR K HUSSEIN, 19 EDGWICK CLOSE, BINLEY WOOD, COVENTRY CV6 4ED |
| Primary and secondary | Schools attended and dates: COUNDON COMPREHENSIVE SCHOOL COVENTRY 1986-1991; BINLEY PRIMARY SCHOOL 1979-1985 |
| If not yet taken say so | Exams taken and passes: GCSE MATHEMATICS, ENGLISH LANGUAGE, BUSINESS STUDIES, HISTORY, BIOLOGY, SPANISH, ART & DESIGN |
| | Other: ESB SENIOR GRADE ONE |
| Give full details, including dates | Previous employment (including part-time and holiday jobs): SATURDAY JOB ON FATHERS MARKET STALL SELLING CARPETS - SINCE 1989. YOUTH TRAINING - HARGREAVES ENGINEERING 1992-1993 |
| Cross out yes or no | Are you willing to travel if necessary? YES/~~NO~~ |
| | Have you a current driving license? ~~YES~~/NO |
| | Reason for applying: ALWAYS WANTED TO WORK IN AN OFFICE |
| | Name and address of two referees: MR J SMITH (HEADMASTER), COUNDON COMPREHENSIVE, COVENTRY CV6 3LJ; MR T JONES (YOUTH LEADER), 30 WESTVIEW, ATTON HILL, COVENTRY |
| Are you fit to do the job? | Details of serious illnesses: CHICKEN POX 1980 |
| | Any special skills — |
| Spare-time activities | Interests: SPORT: CRICKET, RUGBY, YOUTH CLUB, CYCLING |
| | Signature: Sajid Hussain    Date: 24 May 1994 |

There are many different types of application form, some requesting four or more pages of information. Each organisation which uses them will design one to suit its own recruitment and selection procedures.

*12. Human resources in an organisation*

20.

## Curriculum vitae

**Curriculum Vitae**

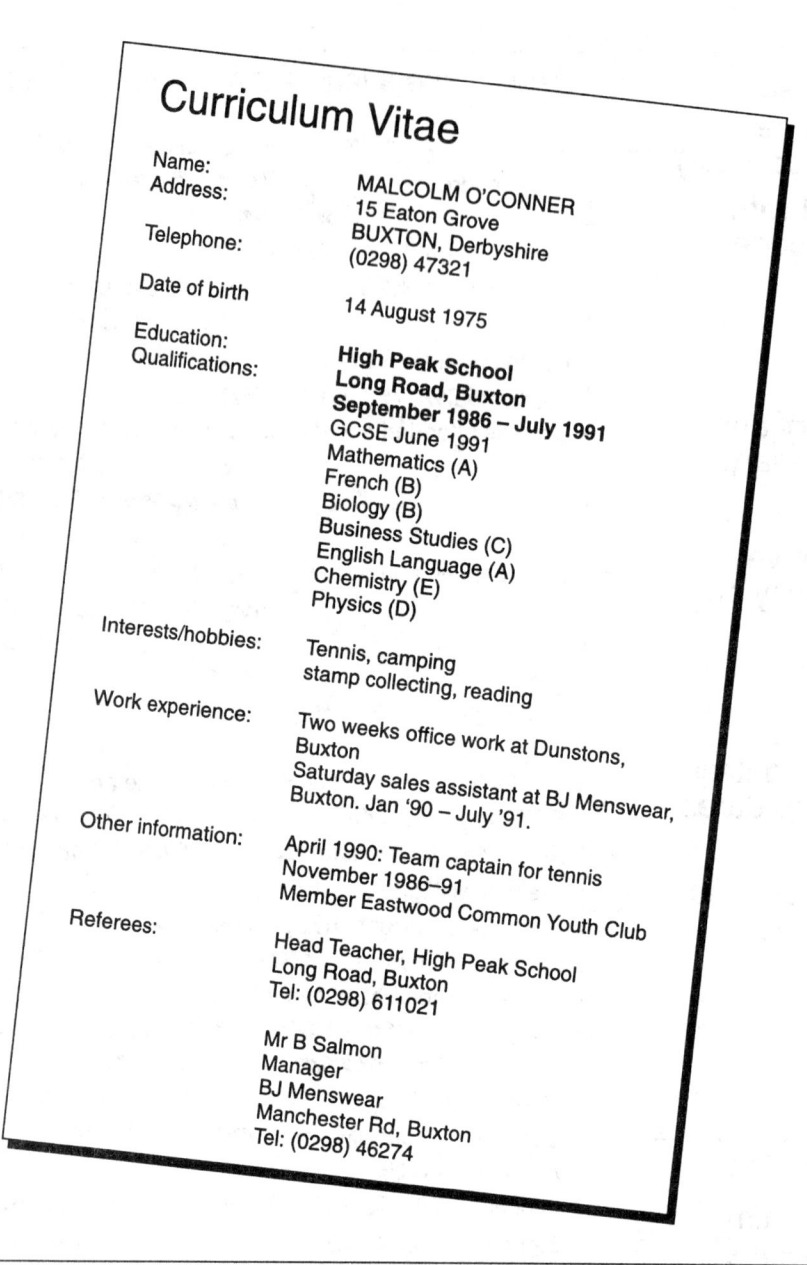

Name: MALCOLM O'CONNER
Address: 15 Eaton Grove
BUXTON, Derbyshire
Telephone: (0298) 47321

Date of birth: 14 August 1975

Education:
Qualifications:
**High Peak School
Long Road, Buxton
September 1986 – July 1991**
GCSE June 1991
Mathematics (A)
French (B)
Biology (B)
Business Studies (C)
English Language (A)
Chemistry (E)
Physics (D)

Interests/hobbies: Tennis, camping
stamp collecting, reading

Work experience: Two weeks office work at Dunstons, Buxton
Saturday sales assistant at BJ Menswear, Buxton. Jan '90 – July '91.

Other information: April 1990: Team captain for tennis
November 1986–91
Member Eastwood Common Youth Club

Referees: Head Teacher, High Peak School
Long Road, Buxton
Tel: (0298) 611021

Mr B Salmon
Manager
BJ Menswear
Manchester Rd, Buxton
Tel: (0298) 46274

### Task 12.6

Prepare your own curriculum vitae, if possible using a word processor. Include in it as much information about yourself as possible. It could be like the example shown above, or more detailed including comments if appropriate. Ask two colleagues to comment on its clarity and quality of presentation.

21. **NB**

- **References.** Most employers will require anyone applying for a job to give the names of two people who know them well to act as referees. For example, teacher, youth leader, vicar or former employer. The firm will then ask them for a confidential opinion on the character, attendance, punctuality and suitability of the applicant for the job.

- Some employers also accept **testimonials**. These are not confidential, and are usually headed 'To whom it may concern'. Copies can be given to any employer when applying for a job.

## Interviews

22. An interview is the last stage before getting a job. Many people may apply for a job, but only a small number will be interviewed. Many employers also ask candidates to take an aptitude test so that they can assess whether or not someone is suitable for the type of work: for example, police cadets, nurses, apprentice engineers.

23. The interview is important for the employer, who wants to find the best person for the job. It is also an opportunity for the candidate to find out more about the job and whether it is what they want. Therefore, it is very important to prepare for it.

## How to prepare for an interview

24. **Before you go**

    - Find out as much as possible about the firm.
    - Be prepared to answer questions.
    - Make sure you know the time and place of the interview.
    - Work out what you need to ask the employer.

25. **The Big Day**

    - Dress sensibly – look neat and tidy.
    - Be punctual.
    - Take your interview letter with you.
    - Remember and *use* the interviewer's name.
    - Be pleasant and polite. Shake hands, wait to be asked to sit down, say thank you. Smile.
    - Don't smoke, unless invited to.
    - Speak clearly and answer questions fully – *not* just 'yes' and 'no'.
    - Show that you are interested in the job – be enthusiastic and confident, but not too assertive.
    - Have some questions to ask – take a list with you if you wish.
    - Try not to oversell yourself by talking too much.
    - Don't forget the importance of body language (see Chapter 16).

## 12. Human resources in an organisation

### 26. Some questions you could ask

If an employer has not already told you, the following are examples of possible questions:

- What training will I be given?
- Will I be paid weekly or monthly?
- What are the prospects for promotion?
- Who will I be working with?
- When will I be expected to start?
- When will I know the outcome?

### 27. What questions might you be asked?

- Why do you want to work here?
- How did you hear about the job?
- What are your interests and hobbies?
- What were your favourite/best subjects at school?
- What appeals to you about the job?
- What kind of books or newspapers do you read?

---

**Task 12.7**

1. From a newspaper advertisement, select any job for which you would like to apply.
2. Prepare a letter of application which could be sent along with the CV that you prepared for Task 12.6.
3. Assuming that you have an interview, describe how you would prepare for it.
4. Carry out a mock interview with one or more of your colleagues. They will need to prepare some questions for this. Comment on whether or not you found it useful in preparing for the job.
5. Ask your colleague(s) to appraise your performance in the interview, stating with reasons whether or not you would have got the job.
6. Finally, repeat 4. and 5. by reversing roles with your colleagues.

---

## Training and Development

28. Most training takes place **'on-the-job'**, i.e. people learn at work either from other people or by themselves, often from experience. However, **'off-the-job'** training, either inside or outside a firm, is also important. For example a course in a firm's own training school or a day release or evening class at a local college.

29. There are five main types of training which firms may carry out.

- **Induction** – that is, all new staff should be introduced to the firm generally and told about the business, for example the goods which it makes and sells, the general organisation and what their particular job involves.
- **Basic skills** – whilst all new staff should receive induction training, junior staff in particular should also undertake an organised training programme. This should be designed to teach them basic skills required in their job and thus to develop them into more efficient and effective employees.
- **Re-training** – regular refresher or updating courses should take place for all staff. For example when new technology, Health and Safety measures or new products are introduced.
- **Management trainees** – many larger companies run special management trainee courses, for example ICI and Marks and Spencer. Often people with a University degree or GCE 'A' levels are recruited to undertake an intensive training programme. Potential managers who join the firm from school at 16 can usually join the scheme after a few years basic training.

- **Management** – regular training for executives in the latest management techniques should form an essential part of any firm's overall training plan to ensure that its business operates efficiently.

## Possible Benefits From Training

30. **For the employee:**

    - Feel valued by the organisation.
    - Opportunity to develop skills and knowledge.
    - May improve promotion prospects.
    - May improve job satisfaction because they are more confident and competent to do their job.
    - Makes them better able to cope with change by increasing understanding of, reasons for, and providing the knowledge and skills to adjust.

31. **For the employer:**

    - Improves quality and motivation of staff.
    - Brings in new ideas and skills that could improve efficiency, productivity and profitability.
    - Better health and safety helping to reduce accidents and raise standards.
    - More effective use of staff, more quickly and at less cost.
    - Helps to develop individual, team and corporate competence and improve performance in terms of output, quality and speed of operation.
    - Helps to develop a positive culture in the organisation, e.g. employees oriented towards quality and improved performance.
    - Provides higher levels of service to customers.
    - May increase commitment to the organisation if employees are better able to identify with its mission and objectives. **Investors in People** is a government scheme to encourage training by linking it to business development.

> **Task 12.8**
> 
> Consider, with reasons, what training is likely to be necessary in a small engineering company which is planning to introduce new technology in its factory and offices. It is well established and currently employs 50 people (40 in the factory), many of whom have been with the firm for 5 years or more.

## Staff Appraisal

32. Staff appraisal is the process of reviewing an individual's performance at work. It is important for manpower planning in all organisations for several reasons including:

    - To identify people worthy of **promotion** or in some cases redeployment or transfer.
    - To identify **training needs** which will help individuals to do their job better.
    - To **motivate** staff by discussing and recognising their achievements plus providing an opportunity for them to discuss prospects and/or problems.
    - To make individuals aware of the **culture and objectives** of the organisation.
    - In some organisations to help **management** to make **decisions** on pay increases or merit awards.
    - To check the **efficiency** of the organisations recruitment, selection and training.
    - To agree on future **performance targets**.

## Formal and Informal Appraisal

33. **Informal appraisal** is a an ongoing process carried out by anyone who is responsible for the work of other people. It takes place whenever they check on work or discuss how it could be improved.

34. Many larger organisations also have more **formal appraisal** systems often involving standardised forms which are completed by employees and managers combined with regular interviews. The outcomes are usually agreed by both parties and include drawing up a personal action plan.

35. Appraisal can be **closed,** where the individual does not see the report, or **open** where they are invited to read and comment on their assessment.

## Problems with Appraisal

36 Many staff dislike formal appraisal systems because they fear it may be critical and expose their weaknesses and thus may become resentful. Appraisal is also more difficult with complex jobs, whilst badly designed forms or poorly conducted interviews may result in subjective rather than objective appraisal.

> **Task 12.9**
> Draw up a list of factors which you feel could be used to appraise a teacher or college lecturer.

## Employment Legislation

37 The relationship between employers and employees is defined by law. This gives certain statutory rights to anyone in more than two years continuous full-time employment (i.e. working 16+ hours per week) or where they have been employed part-time (i.e. 8+ hours per week) for more than 5 years. Under European legislation these will increasingly apply to all employees after 2 years.

38 Summarised below these are the right to:
- A written statement of Terms and Conditions of Employment.
- An itemised pay slip.
- Notice of Termination of Employment.
- The guaranteed payment of wages.
- A safe working environment.
- Be treated fairly and without discrimination.
- Not to be unfairly dismissed. (All employees regardless of hours worked.)
- Time off for public duties.
- Reasonable time off for trade union duties.
- Statutory Sick Pay.
- Compensation if made redundant. (All employees regardless of hours worked.)
- Maternity benefit and the right to return to work for female employees.

The legislation in which these rights are contained is considered below:

## Terms of Employment

39. When an employer makes an offer of a job and the employee accepts it in return for a consideration (payment of wages/salary), then a legal agreement called a contract exists.

40. **The Trade Union Reform and Employment Rights Act 1993** states that an employee must be given a written statement of the main terms and conditions of their employment within two months of starting a new job.

41. This should include details of the following:
- Job Title
- Date the job started
- Rate of pay
- Frequency of payment, for example weekly, monthly
- Hours of work and holidays

- Sickness benefits
- Grievance procedure i.e. dealing with problems at work
- Rights concerning Trade Union Membership
- Disciplinary rules
- Period of notice required to leave

42. Sometimes not all this information is given directly to employees but instead is kept in a 'conditions of service' booklet to which they must be able to refer at any time.

43. Other legislation which has been introduced to protect employees and improve their conditions of employment includes the Health and Safety at Work Act 1974, Equal Pay Acts 1970 and 1983, Sex Discrimination Act 1975 and Race Relations Act 1976. The European Commission has also introduced a number of directives which affect employees at work.

44. **Health and Safety at Work Act 1974** The purpose of this Act is to protect employees or members of the public from health and safety hazards at work. The Act makes everyone concerned with work activities responsible for health and safety, including:
    - Employers, the self-employed, employees
    - Manufacturers, designers, suppliers and importers of articles and substances for use at work
    - Those in control of premises, for example Headteacher in a school.

45. The Act requires employers to:
    - Maintain safe plant equipment and systems of work
    - Provide safety training and
    - Produce a Safety Policy Statement of which all employees must be made aware.

    Employees are responsible for taking reasonable care at all times and for co-operating with the employer on safety matters.

46. The **Health and Safety Commission** was set up to enforce the Act. It employs Health and Safety Inspectors who visit firms. They may make recommendations to help firms or, where hazards are found, issue improvement orders (requiring an unsafe system to be altered within a specified period of time, usually 21 days), or prohibition orders (stopping the use of unsafe practices immediately). Anyone who breaks the law may be prosecuted and could be fined up to £20,000 or face a 6 month prison sentence. In Northern Ireland the Health and Safety Agency performs a similar function.

47. **Enforcement of Health and Safety Legislation**

---

### ACTION AGAINST BLAZE FIRM

A Castleford chemical company is to be prosecuted by the Health & Safety Executive in connection with a fire earlier this year which killed 5 workers.

---

### SAFETY CHARGE

The Royal Ordnance Company in Waltham Abbey, Essex is to be prosecuted for failing to ensure employees' safety after an explosion at the plant in January when toxic fumes were released over a wide area.

---

### Task 12.10

Describe what you think is your own responsibility for the health and safety of both yourself and the people with whom you attend school/college or work.

## Health and Safety (General Regulations) 1993

48. Sweeping changes to Health & Safety legislation were introduced in January 1993 when 6 new EU Directives came into force affecting virtually all employers, employees and the self-employed.

49. The regulations which are discussed below cover:
    - Health and Safety management.
    - Work equipment safety.
    - Manual handling of loads.
    - Workplace conditions.
    - Personal protective equipment.
    - Display screen equipment.

### Health and safety management

50. Designed to encourage a more systematic and better organised approach to dealing with health and safety, the Regulations require
    - a recorded assessment of the risks to employees.
    - arrangements to manage health and safety covering planning, organisation, control, monitoring and review.
    - the provision of health surveillance where necessary.
    - specialist staff to ensure compliance with the law and to deal with problems.
    - the setting up of emergency procedures.
    - the provision of easily understood information to staff.

### Work equipment safety

51. These Regulations govern the use of equipment at work which can be anything from a simple hand tool like a hammer, to complex plant such as an oil refinery.

    They aim to ensure that:
    - equipment is suitable and safe to use.
    - maintained in good working order and
    - staff are properly trained to use it.

### Manual handling of loads

52. These Regulations apply to any manual handling operations which may cause injury at work including lifting, pushing, pulling, carrying or moving loads by hand or other bodily force.

53. They require the following 4 key steps:
    - avoidance of hazardous operations where practicable.
    - adequate assessment of hazardous operations. that cannot be avoided.
    - measures taken to reduce the risk of injury to the lowest level possible.
    - information about loads for employees with additional training if necessary.

### Workplace conditions

54. These Regulations replace previous legislation including parts of the Offices, Shops and Railway Premises Act 1963 and the Factories Act 1961.

55. They apply to all workplaces and define specific standards in 4 broad areas covering the
    - working environment, eg ventilation, temperature, lighting and room dimensions.
    - safety, eg floors, ability to open and clean windows, doors, falling objects and passage of pedestrians and vehicles.

- housekeeping, eg maintenance of equipment, cleanliness and removal of waste.
- facilities, eg toilets, washing, eating, changing, clothing storage and rest areas.

### Personal protective equipment (PPE)

56. These Regulations set out the principles for selecting, providing, maintaining and using PPE. They cover all clothing and equipment designed to be worn or held to protect against a hazard. PPE should be a last resort where risks cannot be controlled by other means.

57. The Regulations require that:
    - risks are assessed to ensure PPE is suitable.
    - PPE must always be used, maintained in working order and stored correctly.
    - employees must be provided with information, instructions and training about PPE.

### Display screen equipment

58. These Regulations only apply to employees who regularly use display screen equipment as a significant part of their normal work, e.g. typists who use a word processor.

59. The main provisions are:
    - all workstations must be assessed for risk.
    - risks identified must be reduced.
    - workstations must comply with minimum standards.
    - work must be planned so that there are breaks or changes of activity.
    - users have the right to free eye-tests and special glasses if needed.
    - users must receive information and training about the risks.

> **Task 12.11**
>
> The 1993 Health & Safety legislation will clearly have a major impact on organisations.
> 1. Re-read the section and identify the key measures which organisations must implement.
> 2. What potential costs could an organisation face?
> 3. Comment on why you feel such legislation is needed.

60. **Equal Pay Acts 1970 and 1983** (and corresponding legislation in Northern Ireland). Under these Acts, women are entitled to receive equal pay with men when doing the same or broadly similar work.

61. **Sex Discrimination Acts 1975 and 1986.** These Acts make it unlawful to discriminate between men and women in employment, education and training, and the provision of housing, goods, facilities and services, and in advertising. Northern Ireland has similar legislation.

62. The **Equal Opportunities Commission** was set up in 1975 (1976 in Northern Ireland). It advises people of their legal rights and may give financial help when a case goes to a Court or Tribunal.

63. **Race Relations Act 1976.** This Act makes in unlawful to discriminate against someone on the grounds of colour, race or ethnic or national origin in employment, education and training, and the provision of housing, goods, facilities and services and in advertising. The **Commission for Racial Equality** was set up to investigate and eliminate discrimination and to promote racial harmony. It also provides advice and may assist individuals who have complaints.

## 12. Human resources in an organisation

*Reproduced by kind permission of the Commission for Racial Equality.*

### Task 12.12

From the following 5 situations, identify those which may represent some form of discrimination (ie adversely affect one particular group of people) at work and explain why in each case.

1. An Asian owned company making ladies clothing has an entirely Asian workforce. Notice of vacancies in the company is spread by 'word of mouth' i.e. existing employees tell people they know such as family and friends.

2. A male Afro-Caribbean trainee working on a Youth Training programme has opted to learn motor vehicle skills. He is told that whilst working in the workshop he will have to have his hair, which is a long Rastafarian style, tied back or enclosed in a hat. He claims this is racial discrimination.

3. A large organisation runs a crèche for the benefit of its female employees. A male employee is told that he cannot put his child in the crèche.

4. A canteen in an organisation has stringent Health & Safety rules and does not allow anyone with a beard to work in the kitchens.

5. A company employs both full-time and part-time staff. The part-time staff, mostly females, are employed on 10 hours a week contracts, but they are told that they must be available, if the company needs them, for up to 30 hours a week.

## Termination of Employment

64. The vast majority of jobs are full-time, but the recent rapid growth of temporary and part-time posts now means that employees often do not acquire any employment rights such as protection against unfair dismissal. This is because such rights are usually acquired on the basis of continued employment of at least 2 years.

    A contract of employment will terminate naturally when someone dies or retires from a job, whilst some contracts are only made for a fixed period (eg 12 months) and therefore automatically end at the agreed time. A contract of employment may also be legally terminated by giving a period of notice, which usually depends on seniority and length of service, as will happen when someone leaves for another job. Minimum periods of notice are laid down by law but can be varied by mutual agreement.

65. There will, however, be occasions when employers seek to summarily (ie without notice) terminate an employee's contract and dismiss them. Since the **Industrial Relations Act 1971**, employees have had statutory protection against arbitrary (unfair) dismissal by an employer. These provisions are included in the **Employment Protection (Consolidation) Act 1978** as amended by the **Employment Act 1980**.

66. Under this legislation there are 5 reasons for dismissal that are considered 'fair':

    - **Gross Misconduct** – i.e. dishonesty, negligence or wilful disobedience which represent a breach of contract.
    - **Redundancy** – i.e. where workers are surplus to requirements, possibly due to reorganisation or a decline in business.
    - **Incompetence** – i.e. unsatisfactory work demonstrating an incapacity to do the job. To be fair, the employer must be able to show that suitable written warnings have been given.
    - **Continued employment would break the law** e.g. a chauffeur who has lost his driving licence could not continue working.
    - **Some other substantial reason** e.g. refusal to accept a change in duties, particularly if this makes a worker surplus to requirements.

---

### Task 12.13

#### MARCONI JOBS CUT

Marconi Radar Systems has announced 540 redundancies because of a fall in orders. The Gateshead factory will close with loss of 450 jobs and another 90 will go at Chelmsford.

#### REDUNDANCY CARE

Employers are showing a more caring approach to redundant workers, according to a survey carried out for the Institute of Directors. It reveals that companies are realising that, with redundancy playing a prominent part of corporate life, severance pay is no longer enough, and employees need practical help. There are clear signs that many companies and organisations now have a formal policy for counselling and training to help employees find new jobs.

#### PILKINGTON JOB LOSSES

Recession-hit glass giant Pilkington shed 3,000 UK jobs last year – part of a worldwide cut of 12,400 in its workforce. Accounted for by redundancies and business sell-offs in a drive to reduce costs in the operating companies and at the centre. Market conditions in the flat and safety glass industry during what has become the longest recession since the Second World War have been the worst anyone can remember. The major users of the group's products – the building and automotive industries – have been particularly hard hit. No improvement in trading conditions is yet apparent.

From the above newspaper articles:

1. Identify the reasons for the redundancies.
2. What can firms do to help employees to cope with redundancy?
3. Discuss what action a firm could take which might possibly help to avoid making employees redundant.

## Dismissal Procedures

67. The ACAS Code of Practice on dismissal states
    - that all firms should have a clear dismissal procedure (such as that shown below) including the opportunity to appeal and
    - all employees should be made aware of it.

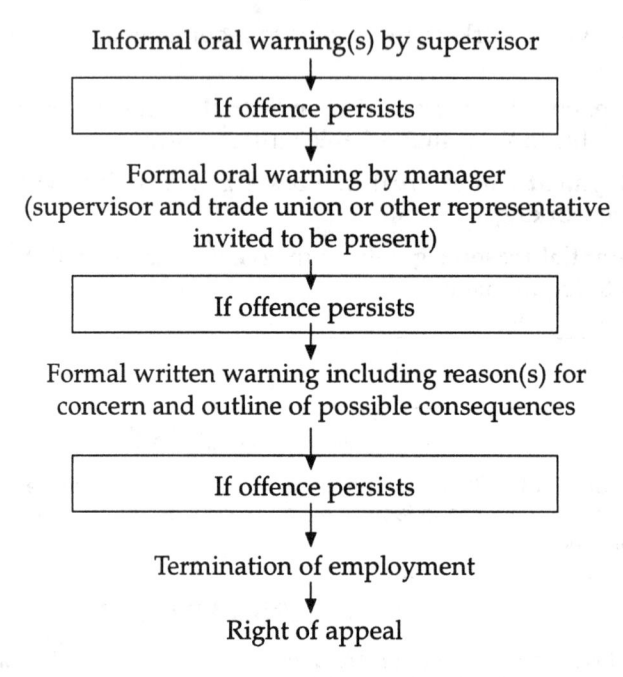

68.

**Dismissal procedure**

Informal oral warning(s) by supervisor
↓
| If offence persists |
↓
Formal oral warning by manager
(supervisor and trade union or other representative
invited to be present)
↓
| If offence persists |
↓
Formal written warning including reason(s) for
concern and outline of possible consequences
↓
| If offence persists |
↓
Termination of employment
↓
Right of appeal

## Unfair Dismissal

69. If someone feels that they have been unfairly dismissed they can appeal to an Industrial Tribunal and, if successful, get their job back or receive compensation. **Industrial Tribunals** are independent judicial bodies set up to deal with complaints from employees on infringements of their rights under a number of Acts, including Contracts of Employment, Equal Pay, Unfair Dismissal, Sex Discrimination and Redundancy Payments.

As an alternative to appealing to an Industrial Tribunal an individual may decide to seek compensation for unfair dismissal by taking the employer to court. This may be expensive because it will involve using a solicitor to prepare the case and possibly a barrister to represent it in court. It is usual, however, for costs to be awarded in successful cases.

To save time, and to reduce costs and possible bad publicity, employers may sometimes try to prevent a case reaching the courts. Instead, they may offer an 'out of court' settlement, or alternatively, suggest arbitration whereby an independent person or body will determine an outcome which both parties agree to accept.

## Redundancy Payments

70. Anyone made redundant after continuous employment for more than 2 years (working 16+ hours per week) or 5 years (working 8+ hours per week) is legally entitled to receive compensation. This is based on the employees age, length of service and final remuneration.

However, compensation may not be paid if the worker unreasonably refuses alternative employment in the firm.

> **Task 12.14**
>
> ### GAS BOSS BACK AT WORK AFTER SEX CASE WIN
>
> A sacked British Gas executive who won her job back after claiming sex discrimination returned to work for the first time yesterday.
>
> Miss Hilary Williams, 48, was awarded £8,000 damages by an industrial tribunal, for being unfairly removed from her £45,000 a year post as one of the company's top women employees.
>
> ### RACE CLAIM IS SETTLED
>
> A race discrimination claim by a Nigerian woman against the Legal Aid Board, was settled on undisclosed terms at a Manchester Industrial tribunal.
>
> Mrs Christianah Obasaju, Wadhurst Walk, Brunswick, an administration assistant, complained after she failed to win a promotion.
>
> ### SACKED STAFF VICTORY
>
> Eight workers who lost their jobs with the Bollin Cafe in Prestbury, Macclesfield, were awarded a total of over £11,000 by a Manchester industrial tribunal after claiming redundancy money and holiday pay.
>
> Reports of Industrial Tribunal cases like these regularly appear in both national and local newspapers. Try to find examples to illustrate complaints under at least 3 different Acts of Parliament and discuss what impact (if any) you feel the case could have on the organisation concerned.

## Monitoring Personnel Policy

71. The effectiveness of an organisation's personnel policy can be assessed in a number of ways. A problem in any of the following areas will indicate a personnel problem which must be addressed:

    - the rate of labour turnover (see Chapter 14)
    - the level of absenteeism eg sickness, stress, domestic problems, job dissatisfaction
    - the level of productivity and quality of work produced (see Chapters 15 and 19)
    - the level of wastage eg careless work, lack of motivation, inadequate training or management
    - the safety record eg industrial accidents, inadequate policy or standards.

## Summary

72. a) People represent an important resource and cost to a business.

    b) Manpower planning is the main function of personnel management and includes recruitment; selection; record-keeping; industrial relations; health, safety and welfare; and training and development.

    c) A job description gives details of the main duties involved in a job, whilst a job specification outlines the skills and experience needed to do the work.

    d) Information about job vacancies can be found in many places, including newspapers, careers offices, job centres, and private employment agencies.

    e) Applications for jobs may be made using a letter, an application form or a curriculum vitae.

    f) To find out more about applicants for jobs, employers usually ask for references.

    g) Short-listed candidates are usually invited to an interview.

    h) It is important to prepare for interviews both beforehand and on the 'big day'.

    i) Training is important for all employees from induction for new staff, to up-dating for managers.

j) The process of reviewing people's performance at work is called appraisal and may take place formally or informally.

k) Employees have certain statutory rights at work including the right to a contract outlining the main terms and conditions of their employment.

l) A number of Acts provide protection for employees covering Health and Safety; Equal Pay; Sex Discrimination; Race Relations; Unfair Dismissal and Redundancy.

m) Six new Health and Safety Regulations introduced in 1993 all require the assessment of risks, introduction of controls and monitoring procedures.

n) The fair termination of an employee's contract may be due to misconduct, redundancy, incompetence, where continued employment would break the law or some other substantial reason.

**Review questions** *(answers can be found in the paragraphs indicated)*

1. Why is it important that an organisation recruits good staff? (2)
2. What is manpower planning and why is it needed? (4-7)
3. Outline the main functions of a personnel department (3,8)
4. Explain the difference between a job description and a job specification (10-11)
5. Briefly outline the procedure which a firm may use to attract and select applicants for a job (12-17)
6. List 6 pieces of information which should be included in a letter of application for a job. (18)
7. What is the purpose of an interview and how should a candidate prepare for one? (22-27)
8. What is training and why is it needed? (28-31)
9. Why is staff appraisal important in an organisation? (32)
10. Explain the difference between formal and informal staff appraisal. (33-34)
11. What are the statutory rights of employees? (37-38)
12. What is a contract of employment and what does it include? (36-42)
13. Outline the Health & Safety (General Regulations) 1993. (48-59)
14. Give brief details of three laws which protect employees at work (43-63)
15. In what circumstances can a contract of employment be terminated? (64-66)
16. Describe the ACAS Code of Practice on dismissal of employees. (67-68)
17. If someone feels that they have been unfairly dismissed, what action can they take? (69)
18. How can an organisation's personnel policy be monitored? (71)

*Asterisks indicate those questions for which there are answers in Outline Answers (page 439)*

**Essay-style questions**

1.* Discuss the ways in which the Personnel function can contribute to the efficiency and success of a business.
2. Health and Safety at work is now the subject of important legislation covering a wide range of issues. Discuss the impact of this legislation and the implications for UK organisations.
3. In what circumstances can an organisation dismiss an employee under current legislation? Why therefore, do employees sometimes claim for unfair dismissal?

**Short answer**

1.* Explain each of the following terms:
   a) Manpower planning
   b) Sex discrimination
   c) Redundancy payments

2.* a) Distinguish between a job description and a job specification.
   b) What role do they play in the recruitment and selection of an organisation's employees?
3. a) What is staff appraisal?
   b) Why is it used by organisations?
   c) Distinguish between formal and informal methods of appraisal.
   d) What are the main problems of appraisal systems?

## Multiple choice/completion

1.* Who, under current legislation is responsible for health and safety in an organisation?
   a) Management
   b) Employees
   c) The employer
   d) Everyone

2.* The personnel function in an organisation usually includes all except
   a) manpower planning
   b) staff welfare
   c) promotion of staff
   d) recruitment and selection

3.* The Health & Safety (General Regulation) 1993 cover all except
   a) Workplace conditions
   b) Food hygiene
   c) Manual handling
   d) Protective equipment

4.* Manpower planning can best be defined as
   a) undertaking an audit and assessment of staff skills.
   b) forecasting the future demand for labour
   c) planning to meet the future demand for labour
   d) forecasting and planning future labour needs

5. A job description includes all except
   a) a checklist of the guidelines and skills required
   b) an outline of the main purpose involved
   c) a detailed list of the main duties and responsibilities
   d) the title of the job concerned

6. The purpose of staff appraisal in an organisation includes all except
   a) identifying training needs
   b) motivating staff
   c) changing attitudes
   d) identifying problems

*In each of the following questions, one or more of the responses is/are correct. Choose the appropriate letter which indicates the correct version.*

   A   if 1 only is correct
   B   if 3 only is correct
   C   if 1 and 2 are correct
   D   if 1, 2 and 3 are correct

7. By Law, which of the following must be written into a Contract of Employment?
   1. An itemised pay slip
   2. Time off for pubic duties
   3. Sickness benefits

## 12. Human resources in an organisation

8. Which of the following statements is/are correct?
    1. The Race Relations Act 1976 makes discrimination unlawful on the grounds of colour, race, ethnic or national origin.
    2. The Sex Discrimination Acts 1975 and 1986 make discrimination lawful in certain circumstances, in particular the provision of housing.
    3. The Equal Pay Acts 1970 & 1983 make it lawful for men to receive more pay than women for most but not all jobs.

### Assignment

The following article is based on newspaper reports. Read it carefully and then complete the following tasks:

#### CATHAY'S £1BN BOOST FOR ROLLS-ROYCE

ROLLS-ROYCE has just won a contract worth almost £1 billion to supply Trent 884 engines for 11 Cathay Pacific passenger jets. In addition, the Hong Kong based airline has taken an option on engines for 11 more Boeing 777s. This 44-engine contract was won against stiff competition from US giant General Electric and will help to guard hundreds of jobs in the Derby Plant. Rolls-Royce is now producing 100 of its engines for the Boeing jet. Thai and Emirates airlines have already ordered 28 engines each, worth more than £2 billion. A Rolls-Royce spokesman said: 'It will take 4 to 5 years to actually produce all these engines. So the order will help to secure the workload and workforce for the second half of the decade.' Deliveries of the Cathay 777s will begin in Spring 1996 and continue to 1998. Cathay chairman David Gledhill said the British company was chosen because its engine had undergone a longer test period than the General Electric rival, the GE90. Rolls-Royce Derby also produces Trent engines for the Airbus A330. More than 250 of these engines have now been ordered. Last year British Airways aroused controversy when it ordered 15 Boeing 777s and 15 on option with General Electric engines instead of Airbus, in which UK industry has a 20 per cent stake. If BA had bought the British-made engines, the order would have brought in well over £2 billion.

#### Tasks

1. What is meant by the '£1bn boost' for Rolls-Royce?
2. Why is this new order important to the Company?
3. Who was Rolls-Royce's main competitor for the business and why was it unsuccessful?
4. Explain what you understand by
    a) manpower planning and
    b) a contract
5. Consider in detail the manpower planning issues for the Company now that it has successfully obtained this contract.
6. Assume that the following are being proposed and a decision is to be made in the near future. In each situation, discuss the possible implications for the company and the issues which the management need to consider.
    a) The introduction of new technology which could result in the need to make up to 10% of the workforce redundant.
    b) The introduction of a new staff appraisal scheme on a pilot basis.
7. Finally, re-read the last paragraph of the article. What significant implications, if any, do you feel it has for the company?

# 13. Organisational Behaviour

This Chapter is about the internal structures which organisations adopt in order to achieve their objectives and covers:

* Why People Work
* Line and Staff Organisation
* Authority, Responsibility and Delegation
* Leadership
* Span of Control
* Centralisation and Decentralisation
* Formal and Informal Organisation
* Organisational Culture
* Organisational Management Theory
* Scientific Management
* Administrative Management
* Human Relations
* Expectancy Theory
* Systems Approach
* Contingency Approach

## Why Do People Work?

1. The first answer which most people would probably give to this question is 'for money'. But as we saw in Chapter 12, this is too simplistic since there are many other factors which are important to people at work such as status, responsibility, friendship and self-fulfilment. It is important to understand some of these factors since they influence individual behaviour and performance at work and have an impact on the way in which organisations are structured and managed.

> **Task 13.1**
>
> Consider what factors, other than money, are or would be most important to you in a job.

2. People are an expensive but vital resource in any organisation. In Chapter 1 we defined management as the personnel who run an organisation taking decisions on the use of its resources to achieve defined objectives. Managers who take account of employees' needs will improve job satisfaction, increase motivation and morale, and therefore the effectiveness of the organisation, enabling it to better achieve its objectives.

3. **Line and Staff Organisation**

   We saw in Chapter 1 that a business needs to be organised in a way which will enable it to meet its objectives. The most common form of organisation has a pyramid structure which involves what is called **line management** or a 'chain of command'. This is commonly shown on an **organisation chart** which is used to indicate the formal position of each person. Various job roles can also be identified including the different levels of management. The number of levels in the management hierarchy varies considerably usually with the size of the organisation. Generally, the fewer the number of levels, the easier is communication, and the more responsible are particular jobs. Instructions in the organisation are passed along lines in the hierarchy (usually downwards) as shown in the following diagram.

*13. Organisational behaviour*

4.  **An Organisation Chart**

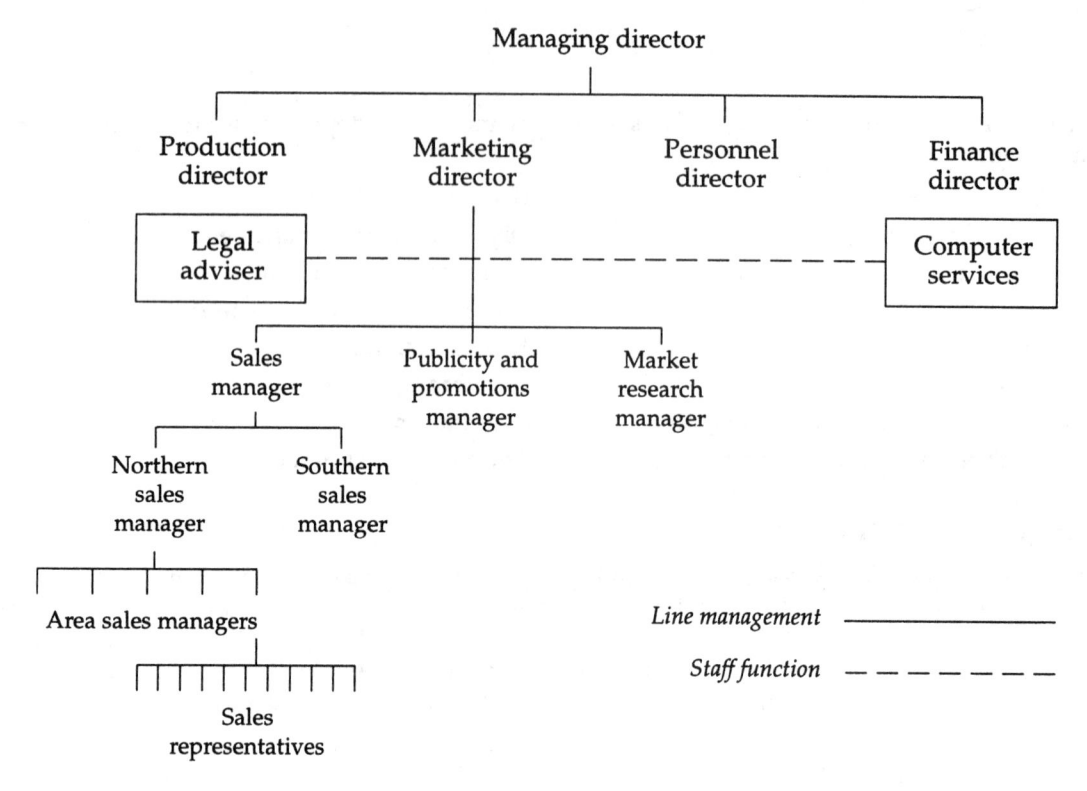

```
                         Managing director
                                │
        ┌───────────────┬───────┴───────┬───────────────┐
    Production      Marketing       Personnel        Finance
     director       director        director        director
  ┌─────────┐          │                          ┌──────────┐
  │  Legal  │----------┼--------------------------│ Computer │
  │ adviser │          │                          │ services │
  └─────────┘          │                          └──────────┘
              ┌────────┼────────┐
            Sales   Publicity    Market
           manager   and         research
                     promotions  manager
                     manager
         ┌─────┴─────┐
     Northern    Southern
      sales       sales
     manager     manager
         │
   Area sales managers
   ┌┬┬┬┬┬┬┬┐
     Sales
  representatives
```

Line management ─────────

Staff function  ─ ─ ─ ─ ─

5. • **First-line managers**, sometimes called supervisors or foremen (particularly in factories) have no subordinate managers and are directly concerned with getting the job done.

   • **Middle or senior level managers** are less involved with operational details and more concerned with what jobs should be performed and how.

   • Whilst at **top level management** the chief executive is concerned with setting long-term plans and policies and checking that managers carry these out. Chief executives usually delegate to functional specialists typically covering marketing, production, finance and personnel management.

6. Within an organisation structure, there may also be specialist advisory or support services, such as legal advice or computer services which are outside the line management structure. Frequently these service several departments and therefore are referred to as **staff functions**.

> **Task 13.2**
>
> From the organisational chart (4) above, identify examples of first-line, middle, senior and top level management.

## Authority, Responsibility and Delegation

7. The managing director or chief executive of an organisation needs to tell his managers what is expected of them in order to enable specific tasks to be achieved. The managers in turn will also pass instructions 'down the line' to their subordinates. This is known as **delegation** and is essential because it is impossible for one manager to maintain direct control over staff, especially in a large organisation.

8. To enable instructions to be carried out, managers must also be given **authority** over their subordinates. That is, they must have the power to make decisions such as telling staff what to do and then expecting them to do it. However, a manager is still ultimately **responsible** for the actions of his subordinates. So although he may delegate the task, he is still accountable to the organisation for ensuring that it is properly completed.

## Effective Delegation

9. A number of conditions are necessary for successful delegation including the following:
   - Tasks must be clearly communicated so that subordinates understand the type and limits of authority.
   - Delegated work should be understood and checked or authority might be undermined.
   - Managers must be prepared to let subordinates make mistakes (within reason and carefully controlled).
   - They must also be willing to trust subordinates. A manager is judged by the work of his team and must delegate to obtain results.
   - Managers must also be approachable, willing to listen to subordinates and discuss their ideas with them.

> **Task 13.3**
>
> A firm is reviewing its management structure. The Board of Directors is concerned that some managers are doing too much routine work themselves rather than creating time for planning, co-ordination and more effective control. Some are reluctant to delegate tasks partly because they think that they can do jobs better themselves. Others do not plan properly, fear the ability of their subordinates or have insufficient staff.
>
> 1. Identify in the above some of the main advantages and disadvantages of delegation.
> 2. Can you add any others not mentioned?

## Authority and Leadership

10. It is important to understand the difference between authority and leadership. **Authority** is connected with acceptance by subordinates and therefore closely related to leadership. It is concerned with the issuing of orders.

    Whilst **leadership** is the art of organising the work to be done, and motivating people to achieve objectives. The better the leadership, the greater is personal authority.

## Types of Authority

11. Authority can come about in several different ways:
    - **Legal** authority – from the internal rules and regulations laid down by the organisation. For example, a manager has authority over others because of their position in an organisation.
    - **Personal** authority – which is connected with the personality of a superior who in the eyes of subordinates is seen as having authority, even though this is not necessarily acknowledged by management.
    - **Authority by reputation** – usually based on knowledge. For example, people who become authorities on particular subjects such as economics, law or North Sea oil.
    - **Economic** authority – a right conferred by economic circumstances. For example a shopper deciding whether or not to buy a particular product.

> **Task 13.4**
>
> Discuss the importance of leadership and authority in a school, college or any other organisation with which you are familiar. Identify why you think they are necessary and how they could be made more effective.

## Types of Leaders

12. Studies of leaders' behaviour have identified 5 main styles of leadership – autocratic, democratic, bureaucratic, paternalistic and laissez-faire.

13. **Autocratic leaders** are authoritative and expect unquestioning obedience to orders with no opportunity for employees to be involved in the decision-making process. The group is dependent upon the leader and usually unable to operate independently. This can cause frustration because it stifles people's initiative and relies upon the qualities of the leader to work successfully.

14. **Democratic leaders** believe in consulting employees and allowing them to share in decision-making. This participation helps to increase workers' job satisfaction, morale and commitment to the organisation's objectives. It relies, however, on good communications, is usually time-consuming and can lead to the undermining of management control.

15. **Bureaucratic or constitutional leaders** manage by acting in accordance with the 'rule book'. Thus there is little opportunity for workers' initiative and flexibility but what is expected of them is always clear and consistent.

16. **Paternalistic leaders** are common in Japan. They manage by showing concern for workers' welfare in return for loyalty and hard work.

17. **Laissez-faire leaders** set clear objectives for subordinates and then allow them, within very broad parameters, the freedom and responsibility to achieve the objectives. This style of leadership motivates enthusiastic workers but its success is dependent upon the competence and integrity of employees.

### Task 13.5

Can you give examples from your own experience of each of the 5 types of leader identified above. State your reasons in each for:

1) why you think they operate in this way.
2) If you think they are successful and
3) whether or not it is the most appropriate form of leadership.

## Span of Control

18. Beyond a certain size it is impossible for one person to control all the activities of a business properly. Therefore, as noted earlier, some tasks must be delegated. The principle of the **span of control** states that no superior can directly supervise the work of more than five or six subordinates. In practice, the span of control will vary considerably from one organisation to another. However, if it is too wide, it can cause problems due to lack of proper control whilst too narrow a span is likely to be wasteful and costly because more supervisors are employed.

19. **Example**

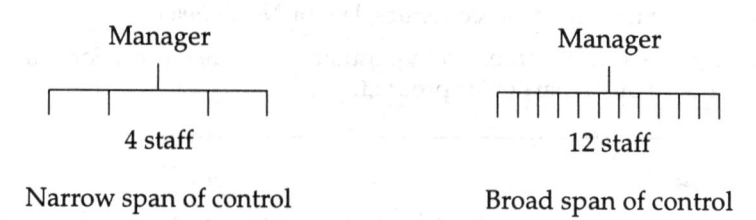

Manager — 4 staff — Narrow span of control

Manager — 12 staff — Broad span of control

## Centralisation and Decentralisation

20. Centralisation and decentralisation are other terms used when referring to the way in which businesses are organised. If a business is **centralised**, its activities are grouped together to enable it to operate more efficiently and effectively. Purchasing, advertising, personnel, typing and other func-

tions are all carried out centrally rather than in different parts of the organisation. Management may also be centralised so that the business is run and controlled from one place. Centralisation limits authority and delegation which can slow down decision making and also frustrate the initiative of junior managers.

21. Alternatively, a business may be **decentralised** whereby authority is delegated to enable work to be carried out in a number of different places. This may mean each department is managed separately, organising its own services such as typing, purchasing and advertising. Often firms with a number of branches or locations operate on a decentralised basis with managers in charge of each place. This enables decisions to be made faster and gives staff more responsibility.

22. In practice many firms often have some activities centralised and others decentralised. For example a supermarket chain may have its advertising centralised at Head Office whilst allowing each store manager to recruit their own staff.

## Formal and Informal Organisation

23. **Formal** relationships between people in any organisation are those shown on an **organisation chart**. However, most businesses also tend to have an **informal** organisation which operates at the same time. This results from the **personal relationships** which exist between individuals and groups of people in one department or several departments who have similar interests and ideas. These so called **primary groups** are important because through them, individuals develop attitudes, opinions, goals and ideals which can conflict with an organisation's objectives. If for example, a group does not agree with a particular policy, then it may deliberately try to obstruct it or make it difficult to implement.

### Task 13.6
You have just been appointed office supervisor in a rapidly growing company. You are immediately responsible to a well-liked, long- serving office manager. He has 10 years to go before he retires. Because of his old-fashioned ideas and resistance to change, he is a major stumbling block to increased efficiency and productivity. Because of your qualifications, knowledge and recent experience, you have been brought in to get things moving. How would you do this from a position of less authority?

## Organisational Culture

24. Everyone in an organisation is affected by its 'culture'. That is the **basic assumptions, attitudes and standards** which determine the systems, structure and rules in an organisation and hence the way things are done.

25. 'Culture' is important because it influences patterns of behaviour, attitudes to change and the motivation, morale and performance of employees. It can also have a significant impact on both business development and staff recruitment because the 'cultural reputation' can attract people to, or deter them away from, an organisation.

26. An organisation's culture is affected by a number of factors including:

    - The **environment** in which the organisation operates. Internally, this is often conveyed by its physical layout which can, for example, reflect warm friendliness or cold efficiency.
    - The **beliefs, values and norms** of employees within the organisation, particularly those communicated by top management, eg the way customers and staff are treated, even the way people dress.
    - The formal and informal **leaders** who personify the organisation's culture.
    - The **procedures** that have to be followed and the behaviour expected of people within the organisation, eg the structure and reporting arrangements.
    - The network of **communications** which disseminates the corporate image and culture. This might include, for example, high-profile publicity and advertising, staff magazines, social events, briefing meetings, pep-talks and employee participation in decision-making.
    - **Other factors** could include the organisation's size, history, ownership and technology; all of which can influence the development of its culture.

*13. Organisational behaviour*

27. It is important that management communicates and encourages all staff to follow the desired culture, even though many employees' attitudes will obviously come from outside the organisation. New employees are introduced to the culture either formally through induction and training or informally through the people they work with. This process of **socialisation** is important because it affects the individual's future attitudes, thoughts and behaviour.

28. Some people may not readily accept an organisation's culture. Where this **individualisation** takes place, it may be disruptive and lead to a lack of co-ordination and integration. This in turn may affect the corporate image, long-term objectives and ultimate success of the organisation.

---

**Task 13.7**

Think about the culture of an organisation such as Marks and Spencer, Sainsburys, or any other in which you have worked or studied.

1) How would you describe the culture?
2) What affect(s) does it have on their staff and customers/clients? Use examples to illustrate your answer.
3) How are you personally influenced by the culture?
4) How is the culture communicated?

---

## Organisational Management Theory

29. There have been many writers on the principles and practices of management each concerned with how to manage workers more efficiently and effectively. The five major schools of thought and their recognised 'pioneers' are as follows:

   - Scientific Management (Taylor, Gantt, Gilbreth) ⎫ Together often referred to
   - Administrative Management (Fayol) ⎬ as the Classical School
   - Human Relations (Maslow, Aldefer, McGregor, Mayo and Hertzberg) and Expectancy Theory (Vroom and Porter, Lawler)
   - Systems Approach (Trist, Bamforth)
   - Contingency Approach (Woodward, Burns & Stalker)

30. 
**Development of Management Theory**

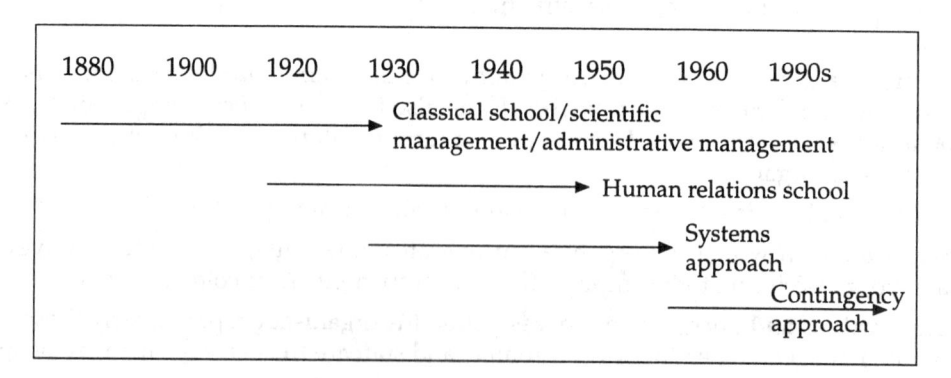

```
1880    1900    1920    1930    1940    1950    1960    1990s
─────────────────────────▶ Classical school/scientific
                           management/administrative management
         ──────────────────────────────▶ Human relations school
                   ──────────────────▶ Systems
                                       approach
                                       ──────── Contingency
                                                approach
```

## Scientific Management

31. Some of the earliest thinking on management theory was that of **Frederick W Taylor** (1856-1915). an American engineer who pioneered work study and spent years researching ways of increasing productivity in factories by making work easier to perform. He advocated the breaking down of jobs into small elements so that people could specialise and become very competent in particular tasks.

32. Taylor suggested that people worked simply to earn money and that nothing else was important. He therefore devised financial incentives offering large bonuses to workers if they increased output.

33. The main problem he found was in devising a scheme which was seen as 'fair' by both workers and management. Many incentive schemes today are based on Taylor's work study techniques.

> **Task 13.8**
>
> The first industrialist to link Taylor's principles to serve a mass market was Henry Ford in the early 1900's. He based standardised production of the famous Model T cars on the extensive use of the division of labour and specialist machinery which required minimum job-learning times. The major drawbacks were the costs of supervision and co-ordination as work becomes fragmented and workers get bored. It also requires specialist indirect labour such as quality inspectors and work study engineers.
>
> 1. Identify the main advantages and disadvantages of 'scientific management'.
> 2. Give at least 5 examples of other markets where these principles have been applied.
> 3. Can you suggest markets not suited to the principles?

34. **Henry Gantt**

    Gantt, a colleague of Taylor, helped to humanise scientific management by replacing the piece-rate system of pay with a day-rate, with bonuses for each worker who met and exceeded their set targets. Workers were also given greater responsibility for the tasks which they were performing.

35. Gantt is probably best remembered for developing a bar chart to show the relationship between the sequence of events in the production process and how far a task had been achieved in comparison with the optimum targets set. A Gantt chart shows the planned amount, the actual amount achieved each week and the cumulative amount over successive weeks.

36. **Example of a Gantt chart**

    **Assembly shop output control**

    Four weeks commencing 1.9.19..

    | Operator | | Week 1 | Week 2 | Week 3 | Week 4 |
    |---|---|---|---|---|---|
    | B Read | Standard | 300 | 300 | 300 | 300 |
    |  | Actual | 240 | 300 | 300 | 315 |
    |  | % | 80 | 100 | 100 | 105 |
    | S Tool | Standard | 450 | 450 | 450 | 450 |
    |  | Actual | 338 | 450 | 360 | 450 |
    |  | % | 75 | 100 | 80 | 100 |
    | R Winter | Standard | 400 | 400 | 400 | 400 |
    |  | Actual | 200 | 400 | 400 | 400 |
    |  | % | 50 | 100 | 100 | 100 |

    **KEY**
    ——  Standard output to be achieved
    – –  Actual output produced
    %    Percentage of actual to standard

This chart shows the performance of 3 shopfloor workers and, in particular, draws attention to exceptional circumstances. The low output of all three workers simultaneously in week 1 indicates some common problem which if not addressed would continue in future weeks.

37. **Frank and Lillian Gilbreth**

    The Gilbreths made significant contributions in the fields of time and motion study. Frank Gilbreth (1917) divided work into fundamental elements which were then timed. Operations were studied and resources using **flow process charts** with symbols for

    | Symbol | Name | Meaning |
    |---|---|---|
    | Operation | ○ | When an activity takes place |
    | Inspection | □ | To measure or test in some way |
    | Storage | ▽ | An object kept before further use eg parts in stock |
    | Transportation | ⇨ | Movement from one place to another |
    | Delay | D | If something doesn't happen when it should |

38. Motion Study was carried out to find the best way of doing jobs thereby improving production and reducing fatigue among workers. Using these symbols the number of times each particular type of function occurs in a process is recorded and used as a basis for analysing the process to try and improve it.

# Administrative Management School

39. Paralleling the growth of scientific management thinking, which was concerned mainly with first-line management, was administrative management particularly the studies of **Henri Fayol** (1841-1925) who analysed the work of chief executives into the following 5 principal components:
    - **Planning** – determining objectives and developing strategies to achieve them.
    - **Organising** – determining the tasks which need to be performed, grouping them into jobs and delegating the authority to individuals to enable them to carry them out.
    - **Commanding** – giving instructions to subordinates
    - **Co-ordinating** the groups in the organisation so that they are all working towards the overall objectives.
    - **Controlling** – monitoring and correcting the performance to ensure that it meets the requirements of the plan.

40. Fayol saw the task of management as being to steer the organisation to achieve its agreed objectives. He believed that if these 5 functions were applied, it would enable managers to run businesses positively and make clear decisions which they could then communicate to workers. Clear objectives for workers would then increase motivation and output.

41. **Fayol's Principles of Management**

    From the 5 functions, Fayol then developed the following 14 principles of management as a guide to management action. Subsequent writers including **Lyndall Urwick** have also developed very similar analyses of the job of management.

42. - **Division of work** – that is the specialisation of tasks to increase efficiency and output.
    - **Authority and responsibility** – managers with responsibility to carry out a task must be given the authority necessary to complete it.
    - **Discipline** – to get things done which requires good managers at all levels in an organisation.
    - **Unity of command** – this means that subordinates should report to and receive orders from one supervisor only.

- **Unity of direction** – each group of activities should have one plan and one manager so that everyone works towards the same objectives.
- **Subordination** – of the individual to the general interest of the organisation.
- **Remuneration** – and methods of payment should be fair and give satisfaction to both employees and employers.
- **Centralisation** – the extent to which authority is concentrated or dispersed which will vary with the organisation's circumstances.
- **Scalar chain** – an organisational hierarchy is necessary for unity of direction. Fayol suggested that the span of control should not normally exceed 7 or 8.
- **Order** – essentially this is a principle of organisation, requiring all resources, including people, to be properly structured and arranged.
- **Equity** – management should treat people fairly if they want loyalty and hard work.
- **Stability of tenure** – high labour turnover is a sign of bad management therefore workers need training and the opportunity to prove themselves to gain job satisfaction.
- **Initiative** – which managers should encourage to the full with all subordinates.
- **Esprit de corps** – the need to develop good team spirit and morale between workers and management.

### Task 13.9

In the organisation in which you work or study or any other organisation which you know well, try to identify an example of each of Fayol's principles of management.

## Human Relations School

43. We are all different in the way that we think and behave and each of us is motivated by varying needs which change frequently. There have been many studies of human behaviour and motivation covering, in particular, the factors which influence people's performance at work. Some of the most influential writers on this include:

    - **Maslow** – Hierarchy of needs
    - **Alderfer** – Hierarchy of needs
    - **McGregor** – Theory X and Theory Y
    - **Mayo** – Hawthorne experiments and
    - **Herzberg** – Motivators and Hygiene factors

## Hierarchy of Needs

44. In 1968 **A Maslow**, an American psychologist, produced what he called a hierarchy of human needs using the 5 categories shown on the next page.

45. **Maslow's Hierarchy of Needs**

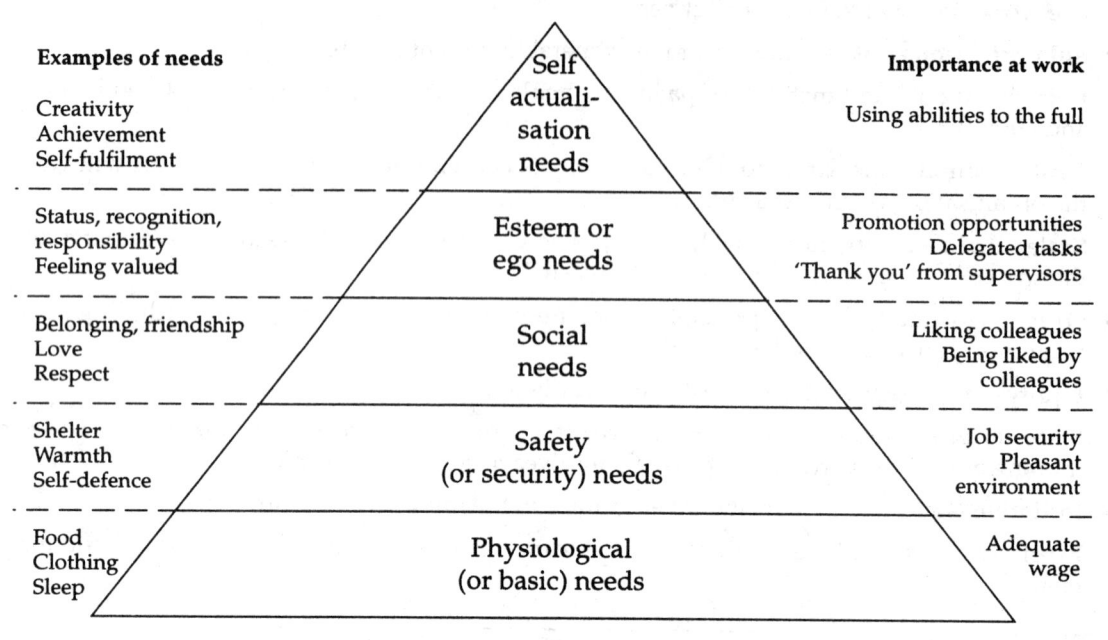

| Examples of needs | | Importance at work |
|---|---|---|
| Creativity<br>Achievement<br>Self-fulfilment | Self actualisation needs | Using abilities to the full |
| Status, recognition, responsibility<br>Feeling valued | Esteem or ego needs | Promotion opportunities<br>Delegated tasks<br>'Thank you' from supervisors |
| Belonging, friendship<br>Love<br>Respect | Social needs | Liking colleagues<br>Being liked by colleagues |
| Shelter<br>Warmth<br>Self-defence | Safety (or security) needs | Job security<br>Pleasant environment |
| Food<br>Clothing<br>Sleep | Physiological (or basic) needs | Adequate wage |

46. Maslow believed that people initially worked to satisfy their physiological needs which were met by employers paying an adequate wage. Once these were satisfied, individuals were motivated by safety needs, then social needs, esteem needs and if all these are satisfied, by self-actualisation needs. But, if while trying to satisfy a higher need a more basic need returns, an individual will turn their attention to it until it is satisfied.

### Task 13.10

As people progress in their career, they are more likely to seek to satisfy the higher needs in Maslow's hierarchy.

Suggest at least 3 reasons why this might happen.

47. **Alderfer (1972)** disagreed with Maslow and put forward a simpler model based on only 3 factors E.R.G. where:

   E = Existence – physiological and safety needs
   R = Relatedness – the need for social relationships
   G = Growth – the need to develop and fulfil personal potential

48. Whichever theory is preferred, it is important that managers recognise that employees basic needs must be met if they are to function effectively and concentrate on the job itself rather than worrying where the next meal is coming from.

## Theory X and Theory Y

49. **D. McGregor** in 1960 suggested that many managers adopt a particular style due to their basic beliefs concerning human nature.

50. **Theory X** – managers assume that:
   - people dislike work and will avoid it.
   - people must be coerced, controlled, directed and threatened in order to get them to work.
   - the average person prefers to be directed, has little ambition and avoids responsibility.

51. **Theory Y** managers assume that:
   - work is as natural as play.
   - people can exercise self-direction.

- people seek responsibility.
- the potential in people is not fully exploited by managers.

52. McGregor believed that people-centred management (Theory Y) was more effective for motivation than work-centred management (Theory X). In practice management styles vary considerably between these two extremes.

## Hawthorne Experiments

53. **Elton Mayo** conducted experiments into group behaviour between 1924 and 1932 at the Western Electric Company's (WEC) Hawthorne plant in Chicago, where over 30,000 employees assembled telephone equipment. WEC wanted to increase productivity and job satisfaction by improving working conditions.

54. Mayo and his colleagues varied lighting levels and discovered that social pressure within formal groups at work could increase output even when the working environment was made worse. Conversely, output could be restricted by informal group attitudes even when individuals were offered financial incentives to increase it.

55. After the Hawthorne experiment it was clear that people are **social** animals who work better when they are organised into small groups, feel appreciated for their efforts, are consulted on decisions and enjoy the company of the people they work with.

56. It was also recognised that the beliefs, objectives and aspirations within informal groups at work frequently produce pressures which can exceed the strength of the formal rules and regulations and thus conflict with an organisation's objectives.

### Task 13.11

Discuss possible situations in any organisation well known to you where informal group pressures could influence decision taking and outweigh formal business arrangements.

## Motivation and Hygiene Factors

57. Following Mayo, **Frederick Herzberg** (1966) developed the idea of **motivators** which lead to job satisfaction and **hygiene factors** which reduce job dissatisfaction.

58. **Motivators** include:
    - Recognition for work done
    - Promotion prospects
    - Sense of achievement
    - Responsibility for tasks
    - The job itself – when it is challenging and rewarding

59. **Hygiene (or maintenance) Factors** include:
    - Relationships within the organisation
    - Rules and regulations
    - Fringe benefits and social facilities
    - Wages and salaries
    - Working environment
    - Style of supervision and management control
    - Status and security

60. Herzberg argued that people do not work any harder if the hygiene factors are present at work, but that their output can decline if conditions deteriorate and poor hygiene factors can cause job dissatisfaction. Motivators on the other hand, which are all related to the intrinsic nature of the work itself, produce job satisfaction and higher output.

### Task 13.12

1. Consider what you feel are the most important ideas in the Human Relations School of thinking and why.
2. What factors do you think are or would be most important to you in terms of performance at work?

61. The work of the Human Relations School has lead to organisations adopting new, more 'democratic' or 'participative' management styles and methods of motivation including job enlargement, job enrichment, job rotation and group working.

62. **Job Enlargement**

This involves giving workers a number of tasks to perform rather than just one simple task to increase job enrichment. It is commonly used in mass production environments.

63. **Job Enrichment**

This is the process of making tasks more interesting and satisfying to workers. It involves giving individuals more responsibility and recognition for their own work.

64. **Job Rotation**

To overcome potential boredom a worker's tasks can be regularly changed so that they spend a certain amount of time on one task before being moved on to another.

65. **Group Working**

This involves workers completing a whole task in teams rather than just one small part of it, thus increasing motivation, job satisfaction and output. The Volvo car company in Sweden is an example of an organisation which has moved from an assembly line method of production to group working.

### Task 13.13

So far we have considered the simplistic view that people at work are motivated merely by money, moving to the idea of people as social animals who work better in social groupings, to the view that they seek self-fulfilment benefiting from job enrichment. More recent research has developed the further idea of **complex man** who is motivated by a variety of factors depending on the circumstances prevailing at the time.

Using this outline and referring back to Tasks 13.1 and 13.10, give some examples from your own experience to support the idea of complex man. Indicate the significance of your answers for managers in terms of motivating workers.

## Expectancy Theory

66. The theories of motivation considered so far have been based on the **content** or features of jobs and how they affect individuals at work. There are, however, also **process** theories which are concerned with how motivation works.

67. An example is the **expectancy (or path-goal) theory** developed by **Vroom and Porter** and **Lawler**. In expectancy theory, effort and performance is seen as linked not just to the desire of individuals to achieve a particular goal but also by their expectation of achieving that goal. The problem with this theory is that the goal or satisfaction the individual is seeking may not necessarily be found within the organisation.

68. Other process theories are based on rewarding employees who work to achieve business objectives with prompt praise, or possibly pay increases or promotion. Employees are not rewarded if their behaviour does not contribute to the objectives of the organisation. Examples of the application of this theory are prisoners gaining remission for good behaviour and footballers receiving bonuses for winning matches.

> **Task 13.14**
> Can you suggest other situations which you have experienced or are aware of where people are rewarded for good or bad performance or behaviour.

## Systems Approach

69. Since the Second World War, methods of structuring organisations so that they can be managed efficiently have been influenced by the development of the systems approach based on the work of, among others, **Galbraith and Likert**. This considers an organisation as a total system consisting of interconnected and interactive sub-systems, all mutually dependent upon each other. An organisation is structured to achieve its objectives through the system.

70. The systems approach is based on the processing or conversion of inputs from the environment (eg premises, labour, machinery, materials) by economic, technical and psychological forces in the organisation into outputs as illustrated below.

71.  **A Simple Business System**

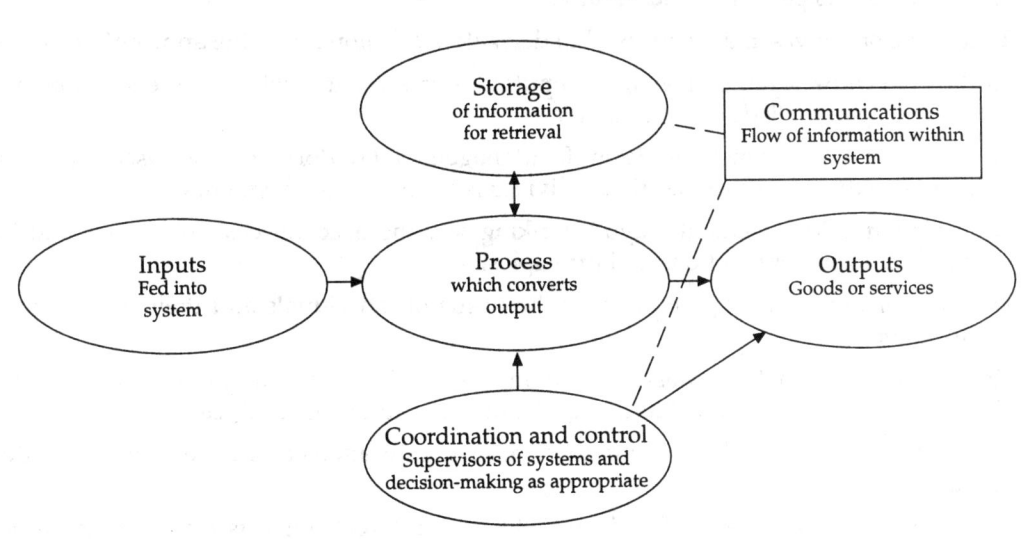

```
                    Storage
                 of information          Communications
                  for retrieval          Flow of information within
                                                system
                         ↕
    Inputs           Process                Outputs
    Fed into    →   which converts    →    Goods or services
    system            output
                         ↑
              Coordination and control
              Supervisors of systems and
             decision-making as appropriate
```

72. A business as a whole is a complete system structured on the basis of functions (eg administration, personnel, finance, sales) each of which can be classed as a sub-system. Each function operates within the framework of the corporate objectives. The functional activities are monitored and controlled by managers or directors and the Chief executive acts as the overall co-ordinator.

73. The significance of the systems approach is that the failure of one sub-system affects the other sub-systems dependent upon it and thus can prevent the organisation from achieving its basic objective of producing goods and/or providing services.

74. This was illustrated, for example, by the work of **Trist and Bamforth (1951)** who studied the relationship between technology and people in organisations. They found that new technology often led to absenteeism, disputes and low morale because it changed the previous social structure. They concluded that if new technical systems are introduced, they must be linked to social systems or the benefits may be lost or considerably reduced.

*13. Organisational behaviour*

> **Task 13.15**
> 1. Identify the main inputs and outputs of any system with which you are familiar.
> 2. What other parts make up the system?
> 3. Can you identify any sub-systems.
> 4. Discuss the ways in which they are dependent upon each other.,
> 5. Compare this with the interdependence between marketing and production in a business.

## Contingency Approach

75. Developed during the 1950's and early 1960's by **Joan Woodward** and **Burns and Stalker** contingency theory is based on the belief that there is no one best method applicable to all situations. Instead, the most appropriate organisational structure and its effectiveness is seen as dependent upon a number of factors including the size, history, environment and level of technology in the organisation.

## Summary

76. a) People, who are a vital resource in any organisation, are motivated by many different factors during their working life.

   b) Many businesses are organised with a line management structure which includes specialist staff functions such as personnel and finance.

   c) To achieve objectives, managers need to delegate work along with the appropriate authority.

   d) Authority can be legal, personal, by reputation or economic whilst leaders can be autocratic, democratic, paternalistic or bureaucratic.

   e) Organisational theory includes Scientific Management (Taylor) which is based on specialisation to increase output and assumes that individuals are motivated by money.

   f) Administrative Management (Fayol) thinking saw the need for clear objectives and identified specific management functions and principles.

   g) Human Relations thinking emphasises the needs of individuals and their social interaction in organisations.

   h) Key contributors include Maslow – Hierarchy of Needs; McGregor X & Y Theory; Mayo – Hawthorne Experiments and Herzberg – Motivators and Hygiene Factors.

   i) The systems approach (Trist & Bamforth) uses organisations as a collection of interdependent sub-units.

   j) The Contingency approach (Woodward, Burns & Stalker) suggests that there is no one single structure applicable to all organisations.

**Review questions** *(answers can be found in the paragraphs indicated)*

1. Why should managers have an understanding and awareness of employees' personal needs? (1-2)
2. What is the difference between line management and staff functions? (3-6)
3. Briefly, explain the terms 'authority', 'responsibility' and 'delegation'. (7-9)
4. What is the difference between authority and leadership? (10-17)
5. With examples, distinguish between formal and informal organisation. (23)
6. What do you understand by 'organisational culture'? (24-28)
7. List the 5 main schools of thinking on organisational management. (29-30)
8. Outline the work of Frederick Taylor. (31-33)

9. List Fayol's 5 functions of management. (39)
10. Describe Maslow's hierarchy of needs. (44-46)
11. Distinguish between McGregor's Theory X and Theory Y. (49-52)
12. Discuss the significance of Mayo's Hawthorne experiments. (53-56)
13. Describe Herzberg's thinking on 'motivators' and 'hygiene factors' at work. (57-60)
14. Explain, with examples, the difference between content and process theories of motivation. (66-68)
15. Outline the significance of the systems approach in organisational management. (69-74).
16. What is the key idea in the contingency approach? (75)

*Asterisks indicate those questions for which there are answers in Outline Answers (page 439)*

## Essay-style questions

1.* 'A fundamental principle of organisation is that anyone given responsibility should also be given the appropriate authority to go with it'.

   Discuss this statement giving reasons as to why you agree or disagree with it.

2. What factors do you feel should be taken into account in the delegation of duties and responsibilities.

3. Management is often described as a 'social process' because managers have to obtain action through other people. What do you consider to be the basic principles of motivation of people by the manager?

## Short answer

1.* Explain the difference between the following:

   Job enlargement, job enrichment,
   Job rotation and Group working

2.* a) What information would an organisation chart tell you about a business?
    b) Is it essential for organisations to have such charts?

3. a) Explain, with examples, the principle of the span of control.
   b) What could the effects on any organisation whose span of control is either too narrow or too wide?

## Multiple choice/completion

1.* An organisation chart in a business shows the
    a) Location of its different functions or departments.
    b) Type of work to be carried out by its employees.
    c) Order in which work should be carried out.
    d) Relative positions of its various employees.

2.* Delegation is best defined as
    a) telling staff what to do and expecting them to do it.
    b) being accountable for the actions of subordinates.
    c) being prepared to let subordinates make mistakes.
    d) giving instructions on specific tasks to be achieved.

3.* Autocratic leaders believe
    a) in showing concern for workers in return for hard work.
    b) that instructions should be followed without question.
    c) subordinates should have freedom to achieve objectives.
    d) in adhering strictly to rules and regulations.

## 13. Organisational behaviour

4.* A primary group usually results from
   a) the formal relationships between people in an organisation.
   b) the personal relationships which exist in organisations.
   c) the management style of an organisation.
   d) the line and staff structure of an organisation.

5. Which one of the following statements in respect of an organisation's culture is incorrect?
   a) the internal environment of an organisation often conveys its culture.
   b) individualisation means that some people may not readily accept it.
   c) most people in an organisation are affected by its culture.
   d) socialisation is important for communicating the culture.

6. The principles and practices of management associated with Henri Fayol were known as
   a) Hierarchy of needs
   b) Scientific Management
   c) Work Study
   d) Administrative management

*In each of the following questions, one or more of the responses is/are correct. Choose the appropriate letter which indicates the correct version.*

   A   if 1 only is correct
   B   if 3 only is correct
   C   if 1 and 2 only are correct
   D   if 1, 2 and 3 are correct

7. According to McGregor's Theory X and Theory Y, which of the following would relate to Theory X?
   1. people dislike work and will avoid it.
   2. the potential in people is not fully exploited by managers.
   3. work is as natural as play.

8. Which of the following are 'hygiene' factors in an organisation according to Frederick Herzberg?
   1. Rules and regulations
   2. Wages and salaries
   3. Working environment

---

### Assignment

Choosing an organisation well known to you, perhaps one of those chosen for the assignment in Chapter One, analyse it in terms of its organisation. Prepare a report covering relevant information including, for example:

1. An organisation chart to illustrate its line and staff organisation.
2. Local, regional and national structures as appropriate.
3. Identify, if possible, examples of the types of authority and leadership.
4. Describe the organisational culture and how it is communicated.
5. Explain how, if at all, you feel that the structure and management of the organisation demonstrates the application of the idea of organisational theorists.

# 14. Employer and Employee Relations

1. This chapter is about people as employees and covers:
   * Motivation and Job Satisfaction
   * Determination of Wage Rates
   * Methods of Payment
   * Fringe Benefits
   * Industrial Relations
   * Trade Unions
   * Collective Bargaining
   * Employers Associations
   * Industrial Action
   * Joint Consultation
   * ACAS
   * The Government and Industrial Relations
   * Labour Turnover

## Motivation and Job Satisfaction

2. It is important in running a business to understand what motivates workers and gives them job satisfaction. The more people enjoy their job and working environment, the more likely they are to work harder and take a pride in what they do. If workers are bored then they may be unhappy and therefore gain little job satisfaction.

3. We saw in Chapter 12 that most people go to work because they need to earn money to pay for their food, clothing and housing, but that there are also many other non-money factors which are important in giving people job satisfaction, for example:
   - Good working conditions
   - Prospects for promotion
   - Job Security
   - Responsibility to make decisions
   - Sense of Challenge
   - Involvement in decision-taking

> **Task 14.1**
>
> List at least 4 other non-monetary factors which may be important in giving workers job satisfaction.

## Determination of Wage Rates

4. The wages which workers receive for different jobs will vary for a number of reasons. As a general rule, wage rates are determined by **supply and demand**. That is where there are a lot of workers who are able to do a particular job, wages are likely to remain low. Where there is a shortage of workers, wages are likely to be higher.

5. The following examples explain this in more detail and also include other reasons for what are called **wage differentials.**
   - Certain types of work require **highly specialised skills** for which people may need to study or train for many years. Therefore, once qualified they receive higher rates of pay, for example, doctors, solicitors and accountants. Likewise, where **skill shortages** exist, as for example in catering, textiles, sales and technology, wages may be higher to attract labour.
   - **Unskilled workers** receive lower rates of pay because very little knowledge or training is needed to do the job, for example, cleaners and labourers.
   - Managers, supervisors and foremen are usually paid more than workers because they have a **responsible** job.

*14. Employer and employee relations*

- **A high level of unemployment** in an area like Northern Ireland or the North East of England is likely to keep wages lower because there will be more workers available for each job.
- From time to time the **government** also controls wages, particularly in the public sector industries.
- The **power of the trade unions** in an industry can also affect the wages of workers, for example, car and print workers get higher wages because the unions are well organised, whilst in retailing and catering, unions are weak and therefore wages relatively low.

> **Task 14.2**
> Consider the following list of occupations: Chauffeur, Gardener, Finance Director, Dentist, Road Sweeper, Coalminer. State with reasons, in which you would expect to receive the highest and in which the lowest wages.

## Hours of Work

6. Most workers in the UK now work for five days a week, although the actual hours and days of work depend upon the type of job, for example, most shop workers are expected to work on Saturdays, with a day off during the week. Teachers, on the other hand, work Mondays to Fridays.

## Flexitime

7. In recent years, many firms have started to introduce a system which allows flexible hours of work. Employees, particularly those in office jobs, are allowed to vary the time at which they start and finish work. Usually everyone must work a 'core time' perhaps from 10.00am – 4.00pm each day with an hour for lunch. They can then choose the rest of their hours to suit themselves.

8. The great advantage of flexitime to firms is that it **reduces absenteeism and leads to happier, better motivated workers**. Employees benefit because it enables them to avoid rush hour travel and fit in appointments, for example dentists, doctors or hairdressers. Married women with children find flexitime particularly useful. However, it also means that firms must keep strict records and could have some problems, for example, it may prove difficult to arrange staff meetings at a convenient time and staying open longer hours may incur extra costs such as heating and lighting.

9. **Shiftwork**

   To enable a firm to operate its machinery for longer periods, often 24 hours a day, it will use different groups of workers in rotation. This is known as shift work. For example workers operating a three shift system might work 2.00pm-10.00pm 10.00pm-6.00am or 6.00am-2.00pm. In return for this they are usually paid an extra shift allowance.

## Methods of Payment

10. There are a number of different ways in which workers may be paid:
    - **Hourly or time rates.** Often wages are paid on the basis of so much per hour, for example £4.00 This method is often used to pay factory workers.
    - **Flat rate.** This is a fixed amount per week or month, for example £850 per month. Most office workers are paid in this way.
    - **Overtime.** If an employee works more than the usual hours, they may be paid overtime, which for example, may be paid at time-and-a-half or double-time (perhaps for working Sunday).

| Example | Wages |
|---|---|
| Basic £5.00 per hour for 38 hours | £190.00 |
| 3 hours at time-and-a-half (£7.50 per hour) | 22.50 |
| 3 hours at double-time (£10.00 per hour) | 30.00 |
| | **£242.50** |

- **Piece-Work rates.** This is another common method of payment in factories. The work is broken down into 'pieces' and a worker is paid for each 'piece' produced. The more they produce, the more they are paid. For example a sewing machine operator may be paid 25p for each sleeve sewn on a coat. If she sews 500 sleeves in a week, she would earn £125.00.
- **Commission.** People who work in selling are often paid only for what they sell. This is usually a percentage of the value of the total sales, for example, a person might be paid commission at 10%. If they sell £1500 worth of goods in a week, they would receive £150.
- **Fees.** Professional people like dentists, solicitors and accountants charge a fee for their services, for example, £45 per hour or per visit.
- **Bonus.** Often employees are paid an additional amount for completing a particular job on time, for example, motorway workers. Other forms of bonus include extra payment to workers at Christmas or holiday times as a reward for hard work or loyalty (for staying with a firm).
- **Profit Sharing.** Sometimes at the end of the financial year, a firm will give employees a share of its profits. This may be given in cash or in the form of a number of the company's shares.

### Task 14.3

Consider which method of payment you feel is most appropriate and state why in each of the following situations:

1. A door-to-door salesman
2. The Chief Executive of a large public limited company.
3. A shop assistant required to work alternate weekends.
4. A long distance lorry driver.
5. A shop floor operative working on a 3 shift system

## Fringe Benefits

11. In addition to money, many firms offer other incentives to their workers. These are called **'fringe benefits'** or **'perks of the job'**, some examples of which include:
    - Company cars – sales staff, senior managers and directors often have the use of a car.
    - Luncheon Vouchers (LVs) – which can be used to help pay for meals in cafes and restaurants which accept them.
    - Canteens – large firms often provide subsidised low-priced meals for employees.
    - Transport – many firms provide free coaches or cheap transport for their employees.
    - Pension Schemes
    - Help with house purchase, for example low interest loans.
    - Medical facilities, for example nurse on premises.
    - Life Assurance.
    - Sports facilities
    - Good Holidays
    - Discounts on firm's products or services.
12. Fringe benefits can often be of more value to an employee than an increase in pay. This is because most are usually tax free. They may also be used to indicate a person's status in an organisation. A director, for example, would have a higher value car than a Sales Representative.

*14. Employer and employee relations*

### Task 14.4
Fringe benefits are sometimes referred to as the 'carrots' used by employers to encourage staff to work harder. On the other hand, an employer may also use 'sticks' or punishment such as demotion, transfers, redundancy or withholding performance related pay. Consider a firm which you worked for or one well known to you. Make a list of the important 'carrots' and 'sticks'. Say briefly with reasons, which of each you think is most important.

## Industrial Relations

13. The term **'Industrial Relations'** covers every aspect of the relationship between a firm's management and its workers. People are crucial to the successful running of any business and therefore it is important that workers are happy in their job. Industrial Relations then is about preventing conflict (disagreements) at work. It is largely concerned with employees conditions of service, working environment and pay.

## Trade Unions

14. A trade union is a **group of workers who have joined together** to bargain with their employers about pay and conditions of work. If one man in a firm tries to negotiate his own wages, he will have little power, and if he goes on strike it will have little effect on the firm. However, if 1,000 workers join together in a union then they are in a much stronger bargaining position.

15. The early trade unions developed in the 18th and 19th Century and there are about 300 in Britain today, with a total membership of nearly 10 million people. In 1979 trade union membership reached a peak of 13.2 million. 80% of the current membership is in the largest 23 unions.

16. In recent years, the number of trade unions has been declining mainly because a lot of smaller unions have joined with others to form larger unions. The number of union members has also fallen because of the increase in unemployment and move away from manufacturing and public service industries where traditionally membership was usually high.

17.

**Trade Union Membership 1900-1990**

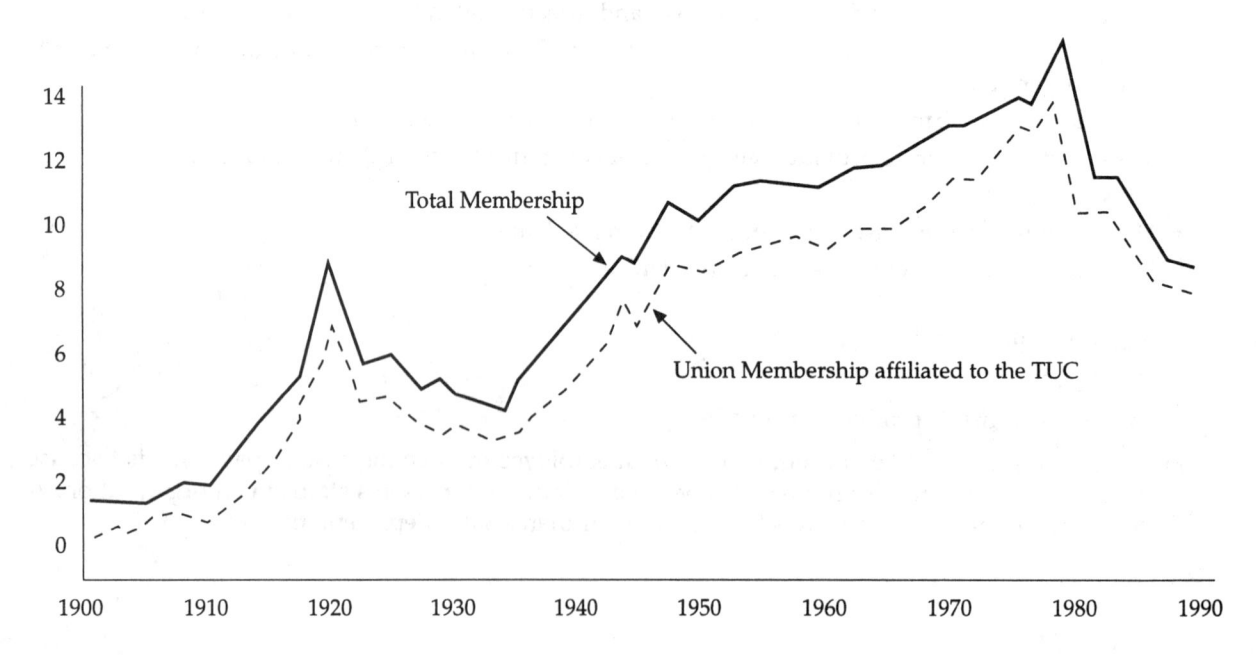

## Types of Trade Unions

18. The four main types of trade unions are craft, industrial, general and white collar.

- **Craft Unions**.
  These are the oldest type of union and tend to be quite small. They represent workers in particular skilled crafts or trades, for example, Society of Shuttlemakers, National Graphical Association (NGA) and Associated Society of Locomotive Engineers and Firemen (ASLEF). As traditional skills have been replaced by new technology the number of craft unions has declined.

- **Industrial Unions**
  These unions represent any workers in a particular industry, for example National Union of Mineworkers (NUM) and National Union of Seamen. Because they frequently represent all workers in an industry, these unions can often be very powerful.

- **General Unions**
  These are the largest type of union and represent groups of unskilled workers in many different jobs and industries, for example TGWU (Transport and General Workers Union) which has over 1 million members and GMB (General Municipal, Boilermakers and Allied Union) with 860,000 members. In 1993 public sector unions NUPE (National Union of Public Employees), NALGO (National And Local Government Officers' Association) and COHSE (Confederation of Health Service Employees) merged to form UNISON, with nearly $1\frac{1}{2}$ million members.

- **White Collar Workers**
  This is the most recent and rapidly growing type of union. They represent professional and clerical workers in a wide range of commercial and service industries, for example, National Union of Teachers (NUT) and National Union of Journalists (NUJ).

19. **The Growth of Trade Unions**

---

### MERGER AGREED

Public sector unions NUPE, NALGO and COHSE are to join forces to create an organisation with nearly $1\frac{1}{2}$ million members.

Called Unison, it will link workers in local government, health care, further and higher education, gas, electricity, water, transport and the voluntary sector. Each group will have its own identity.

The TGWU is also talking, tentatively, about merging with the GMB, a move which would also encompass $1\frac{1}{2}$ million members.

---

## Aims of Trade Unions

20. The following is a list of some of the **main aims** which unions seek to achieve for their members:
    - Better pay and working conditions
    - Shorter working hours
    - Longer holidays
    - Improved Health and Safety at work
    - Better Education and Training
    - Job security
    - Worker involvement in decision making
    - Equal pay and equal opportunities

### Task 14.5
Discuss what you feel are the main advantages and any possible disadvantages of joining a trade union. Ask friends and colleagues whether in a union or not, to ascertain their views.

## Collective Bargaining

21. To achieve their aims, trade unions negotiate with employers by a process known as collective bargaining. Each side seeks to get the best deal and reach a collective agreement which they both find acceptable.

22. **Example**

    - The trade union demands a wage increase of £20 per week for all members.
    - The employers offer £10 per week
    - Further bargaining takes place between the two sides.
    - Both the trade union and the employers agree to an increase of £15 per week.

23. Sometimes a settlement may also include a productivity agreement or points about changes in conditions or hours of work. A **productivity agreement** is a wage increase in return for workers producing more. This enables workers to get higher wages without increasing the costs to the employer.

## Employers Associations

24. Just as workers may be members of trade unions so employers can belong to an employers association. These are formed by firms in the same industry and represent them in negotiations with trade unions.

    They also provide other services for members, for example statistical information, and advice or help with recruitment, training, health, safety and industrial relations problems.

25. **Examples**

    - Engineering Employers Federation; British Decorators Association
    - Road Haulage Association; Building Employers Confederation

> **Task 14.6**
>
> At the top of the trade union movement is the Trades Union Congress (TUC) to which most unions belong. It represents trade unions generally and speaks for the common interests of all its members. The employers equivalent of the TUC is the Confederation of British Industry (CBI) whose members include both companies and employers associations. Both the TUC and CBI are powerful pressure groups representing millions of people. Find out all you can about the role and functions of each of these organisations.

## Industrial Action

26. If trade unions and employers cannot reach an agreement, either side can take industrial action to put pressure on the other. The main types of industrial action are outlined below.

    - **Work-to-Rule.** This involves following every single rule and regulation in such a way as to slow down work and add to the employers costs, for example, a bus driver may cause problems by refusing to drive a bus with a faulty petrol gauge.
    - **Go Slow.** This occurs when workers deliberately work slowly.
    - **Overtime Ban.** Workers may also refuse to work more than their normal hours which may delay an urgent order.
    - **Sabotage.** Sometimes workers will deliberately damage machinery and equipment thus delaying work.
    - **Sit-Ins.** This happens when workers refuse to leave their place of work in protest at some action by their employer. Sit-ins are often used to delay or stop a firm selling or closing down a factory.
    - **Boycott.** This occurs when union members refuse to handle certain goods or materials or refuse to work with other employees.

## Strikes

27. If everything else fails then as a 'last resort' workers may decide to strike, i.e. withdraw their labour and refuse to work.

    - An **official** strike is called by a union which sometimes also provides strike pay for workers. However, some strikes are **unofficial** because they take place without the backing of the union. Unions can be liable for damages if an industrial dispute is deemed unlawful.
    - A **'lightning'** or **'wild cat'** strike is a sudden walk-out as an expression of workers anger.
    - Union members who refuse to join a strike are known as **'scabs'**.

28. Workers on strike usually **picket** their firm which means that they stand outside the gates trying to persuade people, not in the union, from going to work. By law only 6 persons may picket at any one entrance to a work place.

### Task 14.7

In the place where you work or study find out:

1. what trade unions, if any, represent the employees;
2. if there is a staff association and, if so, what its main functions are;
3. what the arrangements are for joint consultation in the organisation;
4. if there have been any industrial disputes in the past two years and, if so, the reasons for them, any action taken and the outcome.

29. **Lock-Out.** This is the employers version of a strike. A firm may literally lock the gates to prevent its employees from getting to work.

30. 

**UK Working Days Lost Through Industrial Disputes 1980–1993**

working days lost in 12 months to March (in millions)

## 14. Employer and employee relations

### Reasons for Disputes

31. Some of the main reasons why workers take industrial action are summarised below:

    - **Pay and working conditions**
    - **Demarcation** – these are disputes between unions over which workers should do which jobs. For example, if a plumber fills a hole in a wall, the union may be annoyed because it is a plasterer's job. The problem is often caused because there are different rates of pay for different jobs and unions want to protect the jobs and wage rates of their members. To overcome this problem, multi-skilling has now become a common feature negotiated into many recent union agreements. Multi-skilling involves training employees to do a range of different tasks in the workplace instead of just one narrow task.
    - **Victimisation** – when a worker feels that they are being 'got at' by the firm.
    - **Threat of redundancy** – where employees may lose their jobs because there is no work for them.
    - **New technology** and how it is introduced, for example computers, robots – particularly where this may result in the loss of jobs.

---

**Task 14.8**

**200 IN 'SLEEP-IN'**

More than 200 workers at the Temperatures factory at Sandown, Isle of Wight, staged a 'sleep-in' at the plant in a dispute over 10 sacked colleagues.

**STRIKE REVOLT**

Hundreds of postmen in the South East said they would ignore their union's call for industrial action over local recruitment bonuses.

**WORK TO RULE THREAT**

Angry nurses yesterday took a major step towards industrial action over their pay claim. The move at the Royal College of Nursing Congress could result in nurses working to rule, causing chaos in the Health Service.

Headlines and articles such as those above are common. Find examples in the local or national press to illustrate 5 different types of industrial action. Identify in each situation the main reason(s) for the action taken.

---

32. **Joint Consultation**

    To help avoid labour problems or concerns leading to a dispute many organisations have regular meetings with unions. This enables any grievances to be aired and provides an opportunity for issues surrounding wages and salaries or working conditions to be discussed. It also enables employment issues such as potential redundancies or growth to be discussed.

33. Overall, such meetings can lead to a spirit of co-operation and understanding between unions and employers, thus producing a positive approach to industrial relations.

34. In addition to union meetings, many organisations also have laid down **grievance procedures** which individual employees can use if they have a problem. This enables them to discuss it with management in order to reach a solution.

### Advisory, Conciliation and Arbitration Service (ACAS)

35. Where unions and employers cannot agree in a dispute they may request the help of ACAS. This is an independent body set up by the government with a general duty to help promote and improve industrial relations. ACAS is run by a council consisting of a chairman and nine members – three nominated by the TUC, three by the CBI and three independent members.

36. ACAS provides four main services:
    - It gives free **advice** to unions and employers on any industrial relations issues.
    - It offers a **conciliation** service. This involves trying to persuade the two sides in a dispute to start talking to each other again.
    - If both sides agree ACAS can offer **arbitration**. An independent third party listens to all the arguments and then makes a decision which both sides agree to accept.
    - If both sides do not want a binding agreement ACAS can arrange **mediation**. This involves getting the two sides together with a third party who puts forward proposals for a solution. It is then up to the two sides to decide whether to accept or ignore it.

### Task 14.9

**ACAS Statistics**

|  | 1990 | 1991 |
|---|---|---|
| Requests for collective conciliation received | 1,260 | 1,386 |
| Conciliation successful or progress achieved | 964 | 1,056 |
| **Completed conciliation cases by cause of dispute:** | | |
| Pay and terms and conditions | 570 | 496 |
| Recognition | 159 | 174 |
| Changes in working practices | 67 | 46 |
| Other trade union matters | 50 | 91 |
| Redundancy | 109 | 233 |
| Dismissal and discipline | 147 | 144 |
| Others | 38 | 42 |
| **Total** | **1,140** | **1,226** |
| **Individual conciliation – cases received:** | | |
| Unfair dismissal | 37,564 | 39,234 |
| All discrimination cases | 3,516 | 6,214 |
| Wages Act | 8,114 | 11,763 |
| Other employment protection provisions | 2,877 | 3,394 |
| **All jurisdictions** | **52,071** | **60,605** |

1. Comment on the trends in the above figures.
2. What do they reveal about the role of ACAS?
3. Try to obtain the most recent figures and comment on whether or not the use/role of ACAS has changed.

## The Government and Industrial Relations

37. The government also plays an important part in industrial relations.
    - It is a **large employer of labour**. The government pays the wages of workers in the public sector and in recent years it has issued 'guidelines' saying that their pay increases should not be in excess of a certain percentage, for example 5%.
    - **Wages Councils** have been set up to decide minimum wages and working conditions in some areas of work where unions are weak, for example, catering, retailing, clothing and agriculture. These were abolished in the 1992 Employment Rights Bill.
    - It can introduce **prices and incomes policies** which attempt to limit price increases and prevent large pay increases. The present Conservative government has not used this policy.
    - It may pass **new laws** which affect both workers and employers. For example the Employment Protection Act 1975 which set up ACAS, the Health & Safety at Work Act 1974, and the Trade Union Act 1984 which states that before taking industrial action, a union must first obtain the support of its members through a secret ballot (vote).

*14. Employer and employee relations*

38. **The Trade Union Reform and Employment Rights Act 1993 (TURER)**

This Act, which brings together much existing employment legislation, was introduced with 2 main objectives:

- to strengthen the rights of individuals at work and the democratic rights of trade union members, and
- to increase the competitiveness of the economy and remove obstacles to the creation of new jobs. It made significant changes to several areas of employment law and introduced new rights for employees.

It covers a wide range of issues including health and safety protection, employment particulars, itemised pay statements, ACAS services, industrial tribunals, notice of industrial action, maternity rights, redundancy consultation, union membership, abolition of Wages Councils and changes in the management of the Careers Service.

> **Task 14.10**
>
> Modern governments have tended to get more involved in the whole structure of industrial relations. No government wants industrial disputes which slow down production thus damaging the economy. Equally, workers do not want to lose wages, whilst employers do not want to lose profits. As consumers, we do not want to suffer the inconvenience of a bus or electricity strike or of not being able to buy goods because of industrial action. Therefore, peaceful, industrial relations are of benefit to everyone.
>
> From the above statement and your own knowledge and experience:
>
> 1. Identify the possible consequences of industrial action for employers, employees and consumers.
> 2. Consider what effects you think it might have on other firms and on the economy as a whole.

## Labour Turnover

39. **Labour turnover** is the term used to describe the movement of people into and out of an organisation. This can be an important indication of job satisfaction, which we considered at the beginning of this Chapter.

## Reasons for Labour Turnover

40. Some of the most common reasons why employees leave an organisation include:

- **Voluntary** or avoidable reasons such as better pay, better prospects or job dissatisfaction. This can be a key indicator of discontent in an organisation.
- **Involuntary** or unavoidable reasons such as retirement, ill-health or death. Many women leave employment because of pregnancy or a change in their partner's career.
- **Management action**, for example, redundancy or dismissal due to poor performance or indiscipline

> **Task 14.11**
>
> Choose any organisation well known to you and try to discover information about its labour turnover. Consider the number of people it employs, make comparisons with previous years and if possible identify the main reasons for any changes.

## Measuring Labour Turnover

41. One method of measuring the rate of labour turnover over a period of time is the **wastage or separation rate** which can be expressed as:

$$\frac{\text{number of employees leaving during a period}}{\text{*average number employed during the period}} \times 100$$

42. **NB *** The average number can be calculated by taking the average of the number employed at the beginning and end of the period. The figure can be calculated to include or exclude the unavoidable turnover.

43. **Example**

$$\frac{700}{3,500} \times 100 = 20\% \text{ labour turnover}$$

A 20% per annum figure means that a firm would have to plan to replace its workforce over a 5 year period. It may also be a cause of concern as to why so many people are leaving

44. Another statistic which can be used is the **stability index**:

$$\frac{\text{number with 12 months' service}}{\text{Total number of employees 12 months ago}} \times 100$$

This indicates the extent to which a firm is losing or retaining its experienced staff.

45. Whilst statistics should be treated with caution, a high labour turnover may indicate trends which identify problems in the organisation overall or in particular departments or areas of work. It may also be an indicator of poor staff morale.

## Importance of Labour Turnover

46. A certain amount of turnover is healthy for an organisation because it can create **promotion opportunities** and may help to **reduce an ageing workforce** Whilst new staff can inject **new life, new ideas** and may respond better to **change.**

47. On the other hand, if the turnover is very high, it can cause **instability**, of lead to a **loss of experienced and skilled staff**, and impose **increased costs** on an organisation. This is because the recruitment, selection and training of staff is expensive and time-consuming and when staff leave it can result in reduced efficiency, lost production and higher costs of temporary overtime until new appointments are made. Therefore personnel managers need to devise policies which aim to keep turnover to an acceptable level.

### Task 14.12

Calculate the labour turnover and stability index from the following information and **comment** on the figures

| | |
|---|---|
| Number of employees beginning Jan 1992: | 5,000 |
| Number of employees end Dec 1992 | 4,600 |
| Number of employees leaving during the year: | |
|     Voluntary: | 500 |
|     Involuntary: | 100 |
|     Redundant: | 120 |
| Number of employees with more than 12 months service: | 3,900 |

*14. Employer and employee relations*

## Personnel Policies to Control Labour Turnover

48. Suitable policies to recruit and retain good staff by increasing morale and job satisfaction could include:
    - Improving recruitment and selection processes
    - Improving working conditions
    - Introducing or improving training programmes
    - Job enrichment, enlargement and rotation
    - Introducing career structures to provide promotion prospects
    - Reviewing pay structures or methods e.g. introducing bonuses.
    - Promoting a corporate feeling e.g. worker participation
    - Strategies for improving industrial relations and raising morale e.g. better communication.
    - 'Exit' interviews to discover why people are leaving and thus identify particular problems.

## Summary

49. a) Most people work for money but non-monetary factors are important for job satisfaction.
    b) The methods of paying workers include by hourly rates, flat rates, overtime, piece-work, commission, fees, bonus or profit-sharing.
    c) Many firms provide fringe benefits for workers, for example cheap canteen meals or free travel.
    d) Workers usually receive higher wages in jobs requiring greater skills or carrying more responsibility.
    e) A trade union is a group of workers who have joined together to protect and improve their pay and other working conditions.
    f) The four main types of union are craft, industrial, general and white collar.
    g) Negotiations between unions and employers are known as collective bargaining.
    h) Employers may also join together by becoming members of an employers association.
    i) Industrial action by workers may include a work-to-rule, go-slow, overtime ban, sabotage, sit-in, boycott or strikes.
    j) Employers may lock-out their workers in a dispute.
    k) The main reasons for disputes include pay, working conditions and demarcation issues.
    l) ACAS is an independent body which can offer help when unions and employers cannot agree in a dispute.
    m) The government also influences industrial relations through its policies and legislation.
    n) Labour turnover measures the movement of workers into and out of an organisation over a period of time.
    o) Whether it is voluntary, involuntary or due to management action, it is important that personnel policies are devised to control it.

## Review questions *(answers can be found in the paragraphs indicated)*

1. Why are some workers paid higher wages than others? (4,5)
2. What is flexitime and how does it operate? (6-8)
3. Name 4 methods of paying wages to employees. (10)
4. Use examples to explain the meaning of fringe benefits. (11,12)
5. Explain the term 'industrial relations'. (13)
6. List the 4 main types of union and give an example of each. (18)
7. List the main aims of trade unions. (20)
8. Who takes part in collective bargaining? (21-23)

9. What is the employers equivalent of a trade union? (24,25)
10. List 6 different types of industrial action. (26-29)
11. List 4 main reasons for industrial disputes. (31)
12. Briefly describe the functions of ACAS. (35-36)
13. Explain the role of the government in industrial relations (37-38)
14. Using examples, explain the main reasons for labour turnover. (39-40)
15. Outline the significance of labour turnover in an organisation and how it can be controlled. (36,48)

*Asterisks indicate those questions for which there are answers in Outline Answers (page 439)*

## Essay-style questions

1.* 'The objectives of trade unions can often be considered as being in direct conflict with those of the organisation hence the need for arbitration to settle industrial disputes.

    Discuss this statement explaining why you agree or disagree with it.

2. Discuss the importance of labour turnover in a business and how it might be controlled.

3. How can an organisation reward its employees? Discuss the various options available to it and the likely impact on the motivation of its employees.

## Short answer

1.*

### WORKERS SHARE SUCCESS

Managements find that employee share ownership plans make staff more productive and better motivated, according to a recent survey. Two out of three managements believe their share ownership plans make their company more competitive.

   a) Explain the statement in the above article.
   b) Why might share ownership make a company more competitive?

2.*

### FORD STRIKE THREAT

Ford's 21 British plants face the threat of an all-out strike over compulsory redundancies – the first for 30 years.

More than 10,000 white collar staff belonging to the giant transport union and the technician's union MSF ballot today on strike action.

The unions are confident of a large majority in favour of a stoppage when the result is announced later in the week.

Union leaders of 25,000 manual workers meet the company on Thursday to demand a guarantee of no compulsory redundancies.

If this is refused, they will also be balloted on an all-out strike.

   a) Explain the term 'compulsory redundancy'.
   b) What would an all-out strike mean and why is a ballot proposed?
   c) What are the white collar staff and which union are they likely to belong to?
   d) What is another term for the manual workers in a factory?
   e) Why do you think Ford needs to reduce its staffing levels?

3. a) Explain why a solicitor is likely to be paid more highly than a bus conductor.
   b) Why do workers in some industries like retailing and catering receive relatively low wages?

*14. Employer and employee relations*

## Multiple choice/completion

1.* Demarcation disputes are concerned with:
   a) Workers' fringe benefits
   b) The hours per week which people work
   c) Which union members should do which job
   d) Which trade union workers should join

2.* Which one of the following statements about trade unions in the past 20 years is correct?
   a) The number of unions and membership has decreased.
   b) The number of unions has decreased and membership increased.
   c) The number of unions and membership has increased.
   d) The number of unions is about the same but membership increased.

3.* Collective bargaining usually takes place between:
   a) Trade unions and the TUC
   b) Union Officials and employers
   c) Shop Stewards and their members
   d) The government and the employers

4.* The NUM is an example of:
   a) a white collar union
   b) a craft union
   c) a general union
   d) an industrial union

5. An additional payment for completing a particular job on time is known as:
   a) profit sharing
   b) bonus
   c) overtime
   d) piece-work rate

6. Wage rates are determined by the supply of and demand for labour. Which of the following is most likely to keep the general level of wages in an industry down?
   a) government intervention
   b) trade union power
   c) high unemployment
   d) demand for skilled workers

*In each of the following questions, one or more of the responses is/are correct. Choose the appropriate letter which indicates the correct version.*

   A   if 1 only is correct
   B   if 3 only is correct
   C   if 1 and 2 only are correct
   D   if 1, 2 and 3 are correct

7. Which of the following services is/are provided by ACAS?
   1. A conciliation service to persuade parties in a dispute to negotiate.
   2. Mediation resulting in proposals for settling a dispute.
   3. Free industrial relations advice to employers and unions.

8. Fringe benefits in an organisation would usually include which of the following?
   1. Sports facilities
   2. Good management
   3. Trade union membership

## Assignment

Read the case study below and complete the tasks that follow.

### IN THE PIPELINE

Ducket Conduits Ltd is a small specialist engineering company based in Shellfield. Ducket sells its products throughout the United Kingdom. However, approximately half of its output is exported, mainly to Europe and the Middle East. The company currently employs a total of 60 workers: 48 on the shop floor, 2 in the warehouse, 6 in the office and 4 to drive the company's delivery vehicles. The factory's normal output is 4000 conduits per week at an ex-works cost of £3.00 each.

During a recent dispute, the factory was closed for three weeks. The dispute involved the shop floor workers who receive an average weekly wage of £140 plus bonuses worth another £6 for a five day week.

They were seeking a wage increase of £7.50 per week plus a reduction from 40 to 38 hours in the working week. The workers claimed that they had maintained production at a high level, order books were full, the company was making good profits and that their basic working week was longer than most other engineering firms in the area. Management, on the other hand, was very concerned about increasing competition from the Far East. It felt that a settlement at this level would have to result in higher prices and this would affect sales. Anxious not to lose further production, the company therefore suggested that a productivity agreement might be a sensible way to resolve the dispute. This was rejected outright by the workers.

To settle the dispute quickly, and to avoid further action, the company suggested to the union's officials that the matter be referred to ACAS. Both parties agreed, the management insisting that this was subject to an immediate return to work.

### Tasks

1. 
   a. Identify the type of industrial action taken by the workers.
   b. Briefly describe three other types of action which they could have taken.

2. 
   a. Explain where in the company 'shop floor' employees would expect to work.
   b. Calculate the percentage of the total workforce employed on the shop floor.
   c. Draw a simple diagram to show the breakdown of where people are employed in the company.

3. 
   a. Calculate the number of conduits that were 'lost' during the dispute.
   b. Calculate the cost of the dispute to the company in terms of lost production.

4. Suggest the name of a trade union to which the shop floor workers might belong.

5. Assuming that the workers received their full claim, calculate the total weekly wage cost to the company.

6. Assuming that the working week is reduced as demanded, calculate the number of production hours that the company would lose each week.

7. Assuming that a productivity agreement is not reached:
   a. How many conduits would be produced weekly if the working week is reduced?
   b. Calculate the weekly cost of the 'lost' production;
   c. Discuss the effects which it could have on the company.

8. 
   a. Explain the basis of the workers' case and the reasons behind the company's attitude to it.
   b. Explain why the company suggested a productivity agreement and was anxious to settle the dispute quickly.

9. Describe the role of ACAS and how it might assist in resolving the dispute.

10. Draw conclusions and explain what you feel would be a fair outcome to the dispute on the basis of the facts given.

# 15. Production Processes and Control

This Chapter is about the function of production in a business and the way in which it is organised and controlled. It also covers business location and the factors which influence the size of firms. It includes:

* Production & Operations Management
* Production & Marketing
* Production Planning & Control
* Costs of Production
* Product Design Strategy
* Value Analysis
* Purchasing
* Stock Control
* Economic Order Quantity
* Organisation of Production
* Job Production
* Flow Production
* Batch Production
* Just-In-Time Production
* Productivity
* Work Study
* Organisation & Methods
* Business Location
* Economies of Scale
* Diseconomies of Scale
* Size & Growth of Firms
* Monopolies & Restrictive Practices

## Production and Operations Management

1. The **production function** in a business involves the planning and co-ordination of work to ensure that goods (or services) of the right quality are produced on time, in the required quantities and at minimum cost. In recent years, the growth of service industries and increasing use of new technology to replace labour in the manufacturing sector has lead to the term **operations management** often being preferred to that of **production management**.

## Production and Marketing

2. Depending on the type of organisation involved, production can be initiated from one of 3 key sources:
   * to meet demand anticipated in response to the marketing effort.
   * to replenish low stock levels.
   * to complete an individual customer's order.

3. Like many business functions, marketing and production are closely linked. A business must decide on the type and quality of product it wishes to make and sell and then invest in the resources needed, including equipment of the appropriate capacity and labour with the necessary skills, to produce it. If either of these are a problem then they will restrict the marketing effort.

4. There would, for example, be no point in promoting demand for a product which a business cannot supply. Whilst new products or changes to existing ones must be developed in response not just to identified market needs but also in relation to the production capacity and capability of the organisation.

## Production Planning and Control

5. If an organisation operates in a stable market where sales do not fluctuate widely then production can operate at a fairly steady level. Manufacturers of consumer products, for example, such as tea, sugar or soap powder are likely to experience a relatively regular demand. Some markets, however, are less stable and therefore close liaison with the marketing function is necessary so that production levels can be adjusted in response to changes in demand. Seasonal items, for example, such as ice cream and refrigerators where sales rise rapidly in warm weather and fashion items such as clothing and compact discs are subject to potentially quite erratic fluctuations in demand.

6. Therefore, for effective operations management, production must be planned, co-ordinated and controlled. Progress must be monitored to check that production schedules are being met and corrective action taken when necessary. This is essential to ensure that sufficient raw materials, equipment and labour are available when required so that production can run smoothly and costs are kept to a minimum. To achieve this involves establishing and implementing appropriate policies and systems for key factors such as:-

- Product design
- Purchasing
- Stock Control
- Organisation of production
- Quality control (see Chapter 19)
- Supervision and motivation of employees (see Chapter 12)

### Task 15.1

#### NO SUNSHINE FOR BREWING GROUP

Poor summer weather deterred drinkers from visiting riverside and garden pubs of London brewer Young.

The bleak economic climate also hit beer sales in the City, leading to a fall in half-year profits from £3.1m to £2.5m. Chairman John Young tells shareholders: 'These results take into account the very difficult economic times in which we live.'

#### FAIR-PLAY CHARTER AT XEROX

Photocopying giant Rank Xerox is hoping to set new standards in the industry with the introduction of its own version of the Citizen's Charter – the Rank Xerox Commitment.

The move is in response to the recent consumer initiative, the Campaign for Clear Copier Contracts.

It is an attempt to woo the customer back. Over the past year total UK market sales have fallen by a quarter. Rank has a third of the UK market.

#### PROFIT WARNING

Chocolate and confectionery group Thorntons warned today that annual profits will marginally under-perform current market estimates. It blames lower sales on the election and the hot weather.

Comment on how the above articles illustrate the importance of the need for the production and marketing functions of a business to work together.

## Costs of Production

7. The costs of production in a business involve those of:
   - **initial production** which uses materials, equipment and labour.
   - **waste** from scrap and faulty products.
   - **maintenance** of equipment which should be preventative by means of regular servicing rather than reactive to breakdowns. This helps to ensure that machines are normally only out of operation as part of the overall production plan.
   - **inspection** which is necessary for quality control.
   - **prevention** costs which may include, for example, staff training, extra maintenance or investment in new equipment.

*15. Production processes and control*

8. Additional costs may include those related to the:
   - **investigation and servicing** of complaints.
   - **loss of sales** and **customer goodwill**.
   - **replacement or repair** of faulty goods.
   - **rework** where this is undertaken

## Product Design Strategy

9. In Chapters 7 & 8 on Marketing, we considered the importance in business of market research and the need for a product strategy. An important stage in the creation of new products or the development of existing ones is that of design. The purpose of a **design strategy** in a business is to regularly review the features of all products in the range to ensure that they both meet customers requirements and are also cost effective to produce. This is particularly important in markets where technology is changing rapidly as, for example, with computers.

10. The main design factors which need to be considered can be summarised as performance, appearance, economy, and legal and environmental requirements.

11. **Performance.** To be successful, a product needs to be functionally efficient so that it does what it claims to do and what customers expect of it. Depending on the product, it may also need to be reliable, safe and easy and economical to operate and maintain.

12. **Appearance.** For many consumer products, for example, cars, houses and clothing, this is a very important factor. Essentially, unless a product looks appealing, even through the functional aspects may be good, it is unlikely to be successful. On the other hand, an attractive product is unlikely to be successful unless it functions well.

13. **Economy in production, distribution and storage.** If a business is to be competitive, then it must be able to manufacture its products at a reasonable cost. This may be affected by such factors as the raw materials, components and type of packaging used. For example, a manufacturer of soft drinks can use a variety of packaging techniques including glass bottles, plastic bottles, wax cartons and aluminium cans. Each of these is functionally sound but very different in terms of customer appeal, transport and storage. This is illustrated by considering the fact that glass is the heaviest and most fragile, although often favoured by customers because the product is visible inside. Wax cartons, on the other hand, are lighter, compact and easy to store and transport but generally less attractive to the eye.

14. **Legal requirements**. Nowadays, as discussed in Chapters 3 and 12 there is a wealth of Health and Safety and Consumer Protection Legislation which has to be taken into account when designing products. Examples include seat belts in cars, safety foam in furniture and accurate descriptions about holiday accommodation.

15. **Environmental factors.** Apart from the recent introduction of environmental legislation, there is also a growing public concern about the effect of many products and manufacturing processes on the environment. This has to be taken into account in design if an organisation is to avoid losing out to its competitors. Well known examples include the switch to unleaded petrol, ozone friendly aerosol sprays, smokeless fuels and recycled products.

---

**Task 15.2**

1. Consider the design features which you would regard as important to you when 'purchasing' each of the following.
   a) A consumer durable such as: A Television Set, Washing Machine or Table.
   b) A consumable such as: A convenience food or a fresh product
   c) A service such as an insurance policy, bank account or form of transport.

2. Using a recent example from your own experience, discuss and comment on how what you 'purchased' differed from the design features identified.

3. From your answers, what are the implications, if any, for each business concerned?

## Value Analysis

16. A technique widely used to aid decision-making in product design is that of value analysis. It is used to help businesses to improve efficiency and reduce production costs by evaluating whether all the materials or components in a product have a value commensurate with its cost. If, for example, complex expensive components are used it may be possible to replace them with simpler lower cost items without impairing the product's safety, quality or performance. Value analysis is particularly useful for mass produced items where a small saving on each part can result in a substantial reduction in overall costs.

## Purchasing

17. An important function in any organisation, is purchasing, but particularly in a manufacturing business where the cost of raw materials and components often constitutes a large proportion of the total costs of production. In a service industry, purchasing will be more concerned with consumables including paper, stationery and office equipment such as computers and photocopiers. These form a relatively small proportion of total costs but are nonetheless important.

18. A successful buyer aims to get the right goods, at the right price, in the right place, at the right time. If this is achieved then it should lead to increased sales and profits. Very large firms may employ a number of specialist buyers each dealing with the purchase of different goods or materials. A supermarket, for example, might have buyers for fashion goods, hardware and fresh foods.

19. The chief buyer, merchandise director, or purchasing manager is responsible for supervising the purchase of all supplies, materials and equipment for the organisation. This will include:

   - **Finding the best sources of supply**, reliable suppliers, the 'right' quality, styles, sizes and prices.
   - **Bulk-buying** ie buying in large quantities to save time and money.
   - **Controlling the ordering process** to ensure that orders are efficiently progressed for delivery when needed.
   - **Handling purchase requisitions** which are written requests from other departments or branches to the purchasing department specifying particular items which they require for example stationery, cleaning materials or merchandise.
   - **Rationalising** the range of materials purchased in conjunction with the design and quality control managers.
   - **Providing Reports** to the Management Accountant about price movements and, where appropriate, the availability of new materials for standard costing purposes.
   - The purchasing department may also be responsible for maintaining a store or warehouse and an efficient system of **stock control.**

## Vendor Appraisal

20. The importance of good purchasing to a business has led to the development of **vendor appraisal** techniques which can be used to identify and assess potential suppliers. Key factors such as price, reliability, quality, and delivery times are used and weighted according to their importance to the firm. Each potential supplier is given scores for each factor which are then added together to give an overall rating.

21. The score may not be the only basis for selection of suppliers and a more detailed evaluation may be necessary, particularly if inputs are purchased from abroad and therefore foreign exchange and exchange rates are significant. It is, however, nonetheless useful in helping to narrow down the choice.

## 15. Production processes and control

> **Task 15.3**
>
> Choose any product or service which you use on a regular basis. Carry out a vendor appraisal by identifying at least 4 places (including your usual one) where you could purchase the item concerned and assessing them under a range of 5-10 factors such as opening hours, price, accessibility and availability.
>
> Weight each factor according to its importance to you. Present your findings in a tabular form and comment accordingly.

## Buying Methods

22. An organisation will need to make decisions about how it wants to make purchases. Essentially, this will usually be done in one or a combination of 3 main ways.

    - **Regular contracts** to ensure that supplies are available continuously when required and at a known price which is particularly important where flow production techniques are used.
    - **Hand-to-mouth buying** whereby supplies are only purchased when needed which reduces storage costs and avoids tying up large amounts of capital. Unit costs, however, are likely to be higher because smaller quantities are being bought and at current prices (see paragraph 44).
    - **Speculative buying.** Sometimes a business may decide to buy stock in excess of its normal requirements in order to take advantage of anticipated future price rises.

## Stock Control

23. Most organisations need to carry stocks whether it be raw materials, components, work-in-progress, finished goods or stationery. If too much stock is held this takes up storage space and ties up cash, whilst a shortage of stock can cause delays in production and possible loss of sales.

24. Very often stocks constitute a high proportion of working capital and therefore must be controlled to ensure that they do not exceed an optimum level. Proper stock control should ensure that stock is always available when needed. The amount of stock required will clearly depend upon the type of product and the rate of stockturn. Fruit and flowers, for example, which are perishable but sell quickly will be kept in different quantities to durable items such as toys or jewellery.

25. Therefore stock records need to be kept which record the movement of stock into and out of an organisation. It is also necessary to set maximum stock levels and a re-order level at which an order will be placed with a supplier. These levels will depend upon how frequently the item is used or sold, and how quickly stock can be replaced.

26. **Stock Record Card**

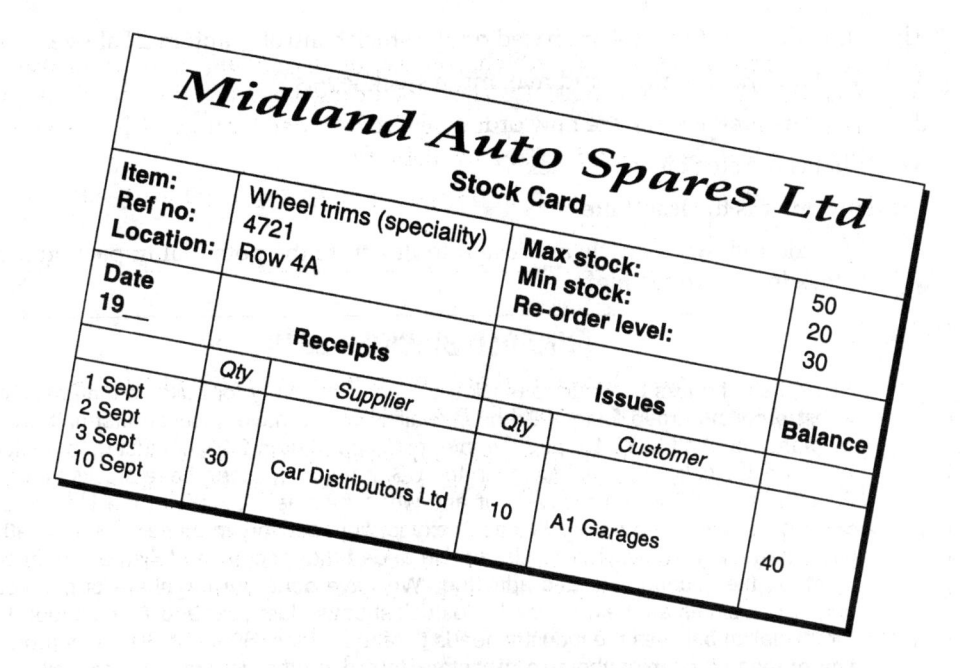

**Midland Auto Spares Ltd**
**Stock Card**

| Item: | Wheel trims (speciality) | Max stock: | 50 |
| Ref no: | 4721 | Min stock: | 20 |
| Location: | Row 4A | Re-order level: | 30 |

| Date 19__ | Receipts | | Issues | | Balance |
|---|---|---|---|---|---|
| | Qty | Supplier | Qty | Customer | |
| 1 Sept | | | | | |
| 2 Sept | | | | | |
| 3 Sept | | | | | |
| 10 Sept | 30 | Car Distributors Ltd | 10 | A1 Garages | 40 |

27. **Stock Control Graph**

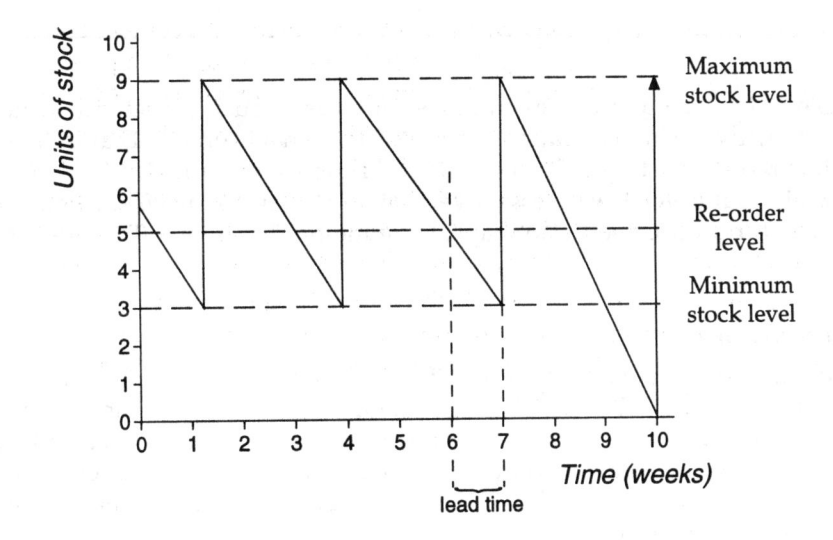

A graph showing units of stock (0-10) against time in weeks (0-10). Dashed horizontal lines mark the Maximum stock level (at 9), Re-order level (at 5), and Minimum stock level (at 3). Sawtooth pattern shows stock being used up and replenished. The lead time is shown between weeks 6 and 7.

28. A simple stock control graph like that shown above can be used to illustrate when ordering should take place and how much should be ordered.
    - Each vertical line represents a new delivery of stock.
    - The slanting lines represent the using up of stock.
    - A new order is placed when stock falls to the re-order level.
    - The delay between placing an order and the stock being delivered is called the **lead time**.
    - The minimum level is the buffer or amount of stock kept in reserve.

## Task 15.4

The following questions 1-4 are based on the stock control graph in 27 above.

1. What are the minimum and maximum stock levels?
2. At what level of stock are new orders placed?
3. What is the stock level at week 5?
4. How long is the lead time?
5. Read the following article and use it to illustrate the potential impact on a company if stock levels are too high.

---

### UNSOLD BRICKS PILE UP

Stockpiles of bricks continue to block the road to recovery for building materials and forest products group Ibstock Johnsen. Falling prices have knocked first-half profits by more than half to £3.1m and the interim dividend from 2.25p to just 0.5p. Ibstock has a brick stockpile of six months in the US. It needs to clear these stocks before it benefits from a housing recovery, if and when it comes. Stocks in the UK are still running at over four months. 'We don't expect any recovery in demand during 1993'. says managing director Ian Maclellan. He added that prices had fallen a further two points in the second half, and admitted: 'We have done our fair share of price-cutting.' Brick plants are being closed – Ibstock shut two last year and Tarmac four. But Mr Maclellan believes the industry needs to take a further 500m bricks out of production or 'two companies the size of Ibstock to reduce the general over-capacity.' He said Ibstock had reduced production and stock levels were 10m lower than last year's at 87m bricks or 17 weeks' sales.

---

29. **Pareto Rule**

    The Pareto Rule or Law is important in a number of areas of business activity including stock control. It states that many business situations have an 80/20 characteristic. That is, 80% of the value of items in stock is represented by 20% of the items. Thus stock control should concentrate on the important 20% high value items with less concern about the remaining 80%. Another example is that often 80% of sales turnover comes from only 20% of the product range. This again has implications for stock control.

## Economic Order Quantity

30. In order to minimise total costs, supplies are often purchased on the basis of the optimum or **economic order quantity** (EOQ). That is, the **cost of storage** such as warehousing – security – insurance – deterioration – obsolescence – pilferage and interest on capital tied up **balanced against the costs of ordering** including – administration – transport – handling – inspection and accounting. Generally, the larger the order is, the lower will be the unit costs due to quantity discounts but the higher are the costs of storage and vice versa.

31. It is possible, using a simple mathematical formula, to calculate the quantity which minimises total costs.

$$EOQ = \sqrt{\frac{2CD}{H}}$$

    Where   C = Cost of placing an order (Order costs)
            D = Annual rate of demand (Quantity)
            H = Cost of holding one unit of stock for a year. (Average unit stock value)

32. **Example**

    The annual demand for an item is 10,000 units. The cost of holding one unit in stock for a year is 15p and an order costs £30 to deliver.

$$EOQ = \sqrt{\frac{2(30)(10,000)}{0.15}} = 2,000 \text{ units}$$

Many businesses now use computerised record systems which automatically control stock and can be used to calculate EOQ

> **Task 15.5**
>
> From the following information, calculate the EOQ. A supermarket sells 60,000 packets of sugar annually. Delivery costs are £25 per order and the cost of holding a unit in stock is 12% of the total cost.

33. **Costs of Stockholding**

The EOQ can also be shown graphically as follows:

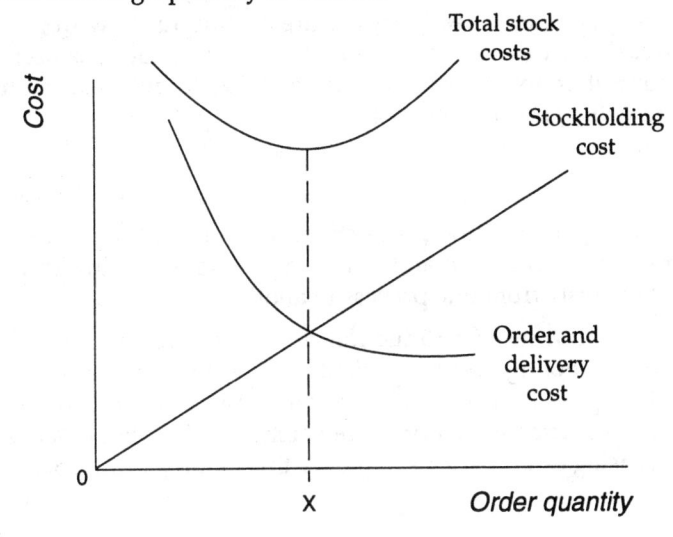

This illustrates how order and delivery costs fall as larger and less frequent deliveries are made. But this increases the average length stock is held and therefore the costs involved. The EOQ shown as OX occurs at the minimum point on the total cost curve.

34. Whilst the EOQ is a useful method it ignores the lead time needed for stock replacement and therefore 'buffer stocks' may need to be kept which will represent a further cost. Without this, there is a risk of a 'stock-out' situation which could lead to lost production or sales.

## Organisation of Production

35. The scheduling of production involves organising the activities in a manufacturing plant or service industry to ensure that the product or service is completed at the expected time. In order to achieve this, production can be organised in 3 basic ways – using job, batch or flow production. In practice, however, more than one method may be used.

36. The method chosen will depend upon a number of factors such as
    - **the type of product,** for example whether it is durable or perishable.
    - **the size of the business,** thus for example many small firms may never have sufficient demand or the capital investment required to operate on a large scale.
    - **the size and location of the market** and therefore the volume of production required.
    - **the frequency of demand,** that is whether the product is a regular purchase such as toothpaste or infrequent such as central heating equipment.

## Job Production

37. This method is used when a single product or small 'one-off' orders are made from start to finish to a customers own individual requirements. Generally, there is no repetition of products or tasks and each order must be planned and controlled separately.

## 15. Production processes and control

38. Because products are non-standard this is invariably the most expensive form of production, often very labour intensive and requiring considerable flexibility and technical skills. Examples could include exclusive luxury goods like jewellery, houses, ships, racing cars, and closer to home, birthday cakes at a local bakers.

## Flow Production

39. This method uses a series of repetitive processes and is common where mass produced standardised products pass along a conveyor belt or assembly line. Flow production makes maximum use of the division of labour and is particularly cost effective for large scale production. The longer the production run, the lower will be the unit cost due to the wider spread of fixed costs. Nowadays, assembly lines are usually highly automated as businesses make increasing use of robots and other forms of computerised technology.

40. Careful organisation and planning is needed to ensure continuous flow from one process to the next and to avoid 'bottlenecks'. That is, problems and delays which can be caused when machines have differing production capacities. Examples of goods produced by this method include cars, television sets, chocolates and many tinned and packeted goods.

## Batch Production

41. This method falls between job and flow production. Some repetition is involved so that complete batches or units of production can be made at any one time according to demand. All items in a batch will move simultaneously from one process to another.

42. Careful planning and monitoring of production is required to reduce the costs of changeover, including any necessary re-tooling and to prevent staff and machines lying idle for long periods. Units costs are slightly higher than with continuous flow because production runs are shorter. Examples include wallpaper firms which produce batches of different designs, paint manufacturers make colour batches, housing estates are also built by this method whilst bakery firms produce fresh batches of bread daily.

43.  **Example – Flow and Batch Production**

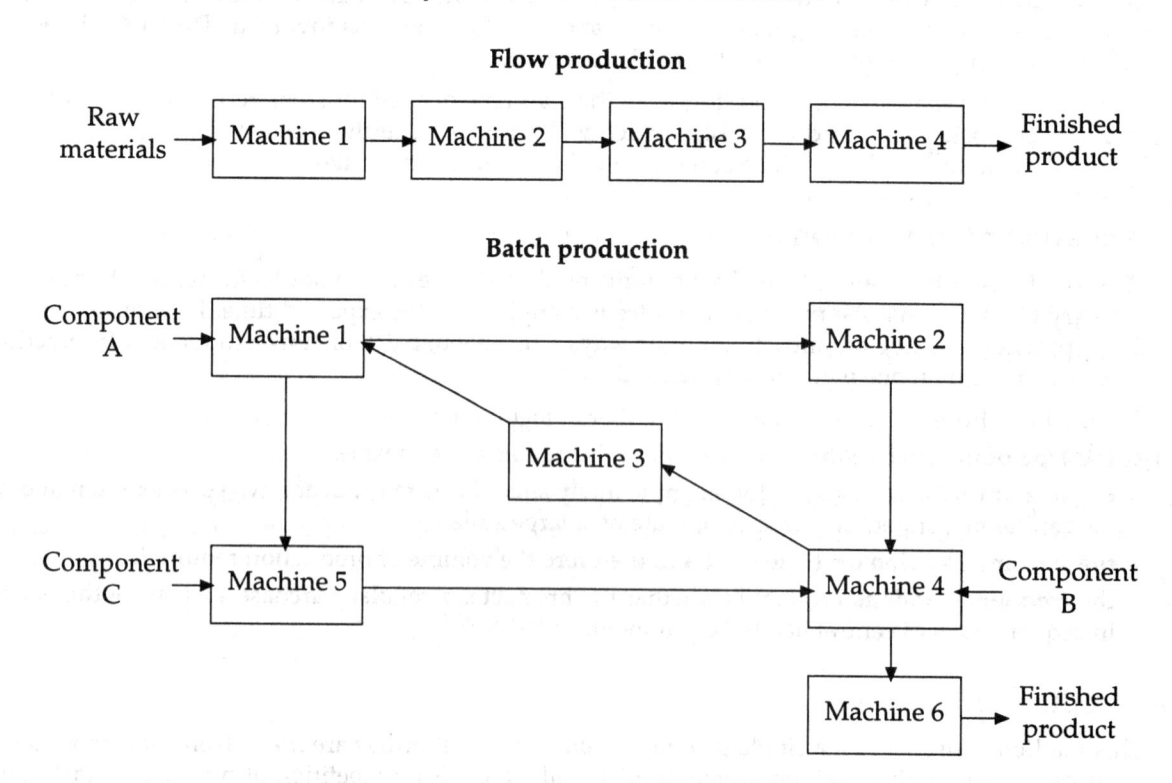

**Flow production**

Raw materials → Machine 1 → Machine 2 → Machine 3 → Machine 4 → Finished product

**Batch production**

Component A → Machine 1 → Machine 2
Machine 1 → Machine 3 → Machine 4
Component C → Machine 5 → Machine 4 ← Component B
Machine 4 → Machine 6 → Finished product

> **Task 15.6**
>
> From the items in your own home and place of study or work, try to identify at least 5 examples of goods or services which have been produced using:
>
> 1. job production
> 2. flow production
> 3. batch production
> 4. Now select one item from each list and discuss the factors which the supplier would take into account to determine the choice of production method.

## Just-In-Time Production

44. A recent development in production methods is that of **just in-time** (JIT) which originated in Japan. It has proved to be so successful in increasing productivity that it is now being adopted by many UK businesses. Although it is often referred to as **supply chain management**, based on working with suppliers to achieve quality and efficiency. The idea behind JIT is to reduce production costs by always keeping stocks of components, materials and work-in-progress to an absolute minimum.

45. JIT means that:
    - finished goods are produced just-in-time for them to be sold.
    - the components or raw materials needed to produce finished goods arrive just when required for use.

46. To work effectively JIT, sometimes called stockless production, requires 3 conditions to be met:
    - All sources of uncertainty must be removed from the manufacturing system in order to remove the need to keep buffer stocks. This means, for example, that unreliable suppliers or equipment cannot be tolerated.
    - The time needed to set up machines must be drastically reduced so that products can be produced in smaller batches which also has the effect of reducing lead times. This might be achieved by simplifying the production process.
    - Bottlenecks must be eliminated to prevent production holdups.

## Benefits of Just-In-Time

47. The major benefits of introducing JIT are that:
    - **lower stock levels require less working capital** and therefore release resources for use elsewhere.
    - **it forces an organisation to address problems.** Bottlenecks, for example, or problems with equipment and suppliers must be tackled for JIT to work.
    - **production is easier to control.** Since products are sold immediately rather than stored, any problems such as quality, will quickly come to light and can be rectified.

## Organising Just-In-Time

48. JIT is dependent upon a smooth flow of production and success through people and therefore work is usually organised by grouping workers in teams around the product they make. In practice this means that each worker is multi-skilled and trained to perform a number of operations. The Japanese car company, Nissan, set up its new factory in Sunderland on this basis with just 3 job classifications in order to overcome potential demarcation problems.

## Task 15.7

Mary Carter is production manager at Holcombe Products Ltd, a manufacturer of pet foods. She is planning a new automated production line which requires 3 different types of machine. The capacity of each machine is as follows:

Machine X processes 40 units per minute

Machine Y processes 60 units per minute

Machine Z processes 80 units per minute

1. Which machine will limit the production capacity of the line.
2. Discuss the potential bottlenecks, and/or under-utilisation which could arise, which need to be considered in the planning process.
3. Suggest the proportion of each type of machine which could be installed to achieve an efficient production run.

## Productivity

49. An important measure of the efficiency of production is referred to as productivity. It shows the relationship between the output of a system and the factor inputs – in terms of materials, labour and capital – used to produce it, taken either individually or together.

$$\text{Productivity} = \frac{\text{Outputs}}{\text{inputs}}$$

50. The most commonly used factor for productivity calculations is labour, that is, output per employee. Essentially, this is because in most cases it is easy to quantify by simply counting the number of workers engaged in a particular process. Another reason is that in the past, labour has tended to be the major factor input. Thus, for example, the weekly, monthly or annual productivity of a car assembly plant could be measured as:

$$\text{Productivity} = \frac{\text{Number of cars produced}}{\text{Average number employed}}$$

An increase in productivity occurs when the output per employee is raised. This is usually achieved by making better use of, or increasing the amount of capital.

51. It has been found that labour is a good measure of productivity showing in particular the benefits of technological improvements as they have increasingly been used to displace workers in the production process. It has to be remembered, however, that an increase in the productivity of labour may be due to other factors such as better organisation of production or increased efforts or skills, as well as the introduction of new techniques. Also, the relative importance of labour is declining with the growth of new technology.

52. Improvements in productivity, which are important not just for individual organisations but for raising a country's standard of living and promoting its economic growth, can come about in 2 main ways:

- **Increasing output as costs remain constant.** That is, boosting output without using additional resources.
- **Reducing costs whilst maintaining output.** Possibly by using less and/or cheaper labour or materials.

## Task 15.8

1. Compare the output per shift of the following 3 coal mines and identify the most efficient pit on the basis of the information given.

   A which employs 70 workers produces 250 tons per shift

   B which employs 48 workers produces 200 tons per shift

   C which employs 50 workers produces 210 tons per shift

2. The figures relate to the coal face workers only. Comment on whether or not you feel all employees, including management and administrative support staff, should be included in the productivity calculations.

## Work Study

53. Work study is the name given to the techniques used to determine the most efficient use of labour in relation to the other factor inputs in an organisation. It developed from the work of **Taylor** and **Gilbreth** who were pioneers of the 'Scientific Management School' of organisation theory (see Chapter 13) and consists of 2 parts, namely method study and work measurement.

54. **Method Study**

This is used to analyse how jobs are performed with a view to improving them. The basic steps involved can be remembered by the mnemonic SREDIM.

- **Select** the job to be studied.
- **Record** the details of the job and method used. This is done systematically using a flow chart or similar technique.
- **Examine** the details critically to eliminate any duplicated effort.
- **Develop** a revised and improved method which might involve, for example, changes to the layout of a workplace, the sequence of operations or improvements in product or equipment design.
- **Install** the new method.
- **Maintain** the method by reviewing it on a regular basis to ensure that it is operating as planned and modify if necessary.

55. **Work Measurement (or Time Study)**

This is used to measure and compare the time required to perform jobs by various methods. The basic steps involved can be remembered by the mnemonic SDMOE.

- **Select** the work to be measured.
- **Define** the method to be used for measurement.
- **Measure** the work to see how long it takes.
- **Obtain** details of the work, content and make allowances for factors including personal needs and fatigue. A rating is also given based on the 'normal' pace of workers.
- **Establish** a standard time for the defined method.

56. **Standard time** is a measure of work. It is the amount of work which can reasonably be expected to be achieved in one (clock) hour by a qualified worker without over-exertion and over a working day provided that they are motivated and follow the specified method.

## Timing

57. The method used for timing will depend on the volume and frequency of the task, the length of the production cycle and the cost of measurement. Common methods used are:

- **Observation** which usually involves the use of a stop-watch to record the time taken by workers to perform tasks over a specified period, perhaps several hours, days or weeks.

- Alternatively, workers may be asked to **record in a log** the time taken to perform tasks.
- or **work sampling** may take place where observations are spread over a period rather than concentrated.

58. The latter methods are generally less threatening to workers, particularly those whose performance is affected by being watched or fear that the object of the study is to reduce the workforce.

## Benefits from Work Study

59. The application of Work Study to a manufacturing process can lead to a number of benefits including:

- An improved flow of work and avoidance of 'bottlenecks'.
- Closer control of operations.
- Improved employee performance, particularly those engaged in repetitive tasks.
- Better utilisation of space, equipment and materials.
- Provision of a basis for incentive pay such as piece-work rates, which reward workers for the amount they produce.
- An overall increase in efficiency and productivity and therefore ultimately profit.

## Organisation & Methods (O&M)

60. The application of work study techniques to the administrative functions of a business is called organisation and methods. It uses the same systematic analysis in order to improve the efficiency, effectiveness and control of clerical and administrative procedures and systems.

61. The benefits of using O&M include:

- **Identification** and **elimination** of problems and waste.
- **Cost reductions** from improved methods.
- **Improved flow of work** from more efficient procedures.
- **Closer control of operations** enabling easier access to information and a faster response rate to internal and external customers.
- **Improved security procedures**, for example, from better cash handling procedures or control of confidential documents.
- It may also be used as the **basis of** a **job evaluation** exercise because jobs are systematically analysed and can be ranked in order of importance to determine their position in the pay structure.

### Task 15.9

Consider an organisation well known to you such as your place of study or work.

1. Your task is to examine how work study and/or organisation and methods techniques could be used to improve the efficiency of the organisation. Try to identify 3 different areas of its activities which you feel are in need of improvement and explain why this is needed.
2. Discuss any possible improvements which you feel could be made and what is required to bring them about.
3. If feasible, carry out some practical method study and work measurement and write a brief report on your findings and recommendations.

## Business Location

62. There are many reasons why firms or industries are located in a particular place.

- A firm will usually seek a site which offers it the lowest costs of production and distribution.

- Some of the more important factors which will influence these costs include historical development, natural resources and raw materials, nearness to markets, transport costs, availability of labour and government intervention.
- It is important to note that because of the development of new and improved sources of power, transport and raw materials, many businesses today are referred to as being **'footloose'**. That is they no longer have to locate near to raw material supplies or their market but instead they can choose to go where they like.
- Many industries have remained in their original locations even though the initial advantages have now declined. This is known as **'industrial inertia'**.

63. **Factors Influencing the Location of a Business**

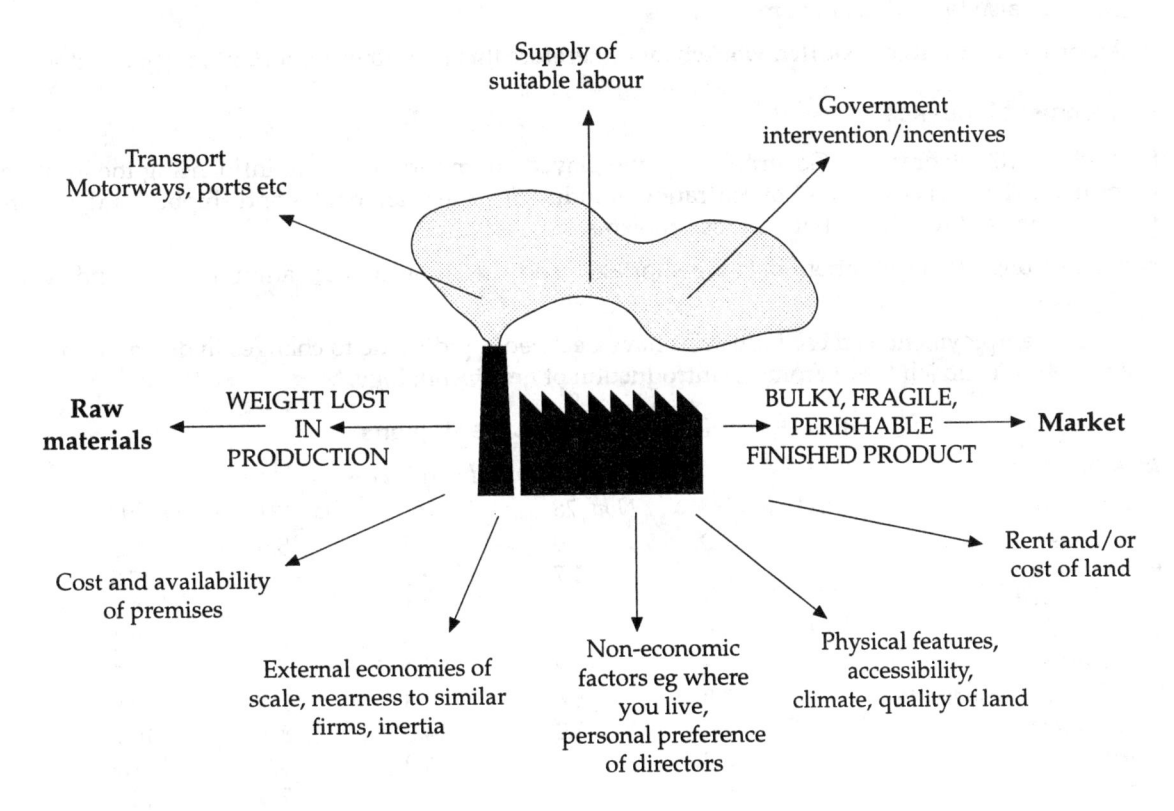

- Supply of suitable labour
- Government intervention/incentives
- Transport Motorways, ports etc
- Raw materials ← WEIGHT LOST IN PRODUCTION
- BULKY, FRAGILE, PERISHABLE FINISHED PRODUCT → Market
- Rent and/or cost of land
- Cost and availability of premises
- External economies of scale, nearness to similar firms, inertia
- Non-economic factors eg where you live, personal preference of directors
- Physical features, accessibility, climate, quality of land

64. **Historical Reasons**

Many industries became established in particular areas because of the nearness of power and raw materials. This can be illustrated by the following examples:
- Wool – originally developed in Yorkshire because of the availability of sheep and water power in the Pennie valleys.
- Engineering developed in the Midlands because iron ore and coal were readily available.
- Steel production was located in Sheffield because of the availability of coal, iron ore and limestone.
- Cotton was imported from America into Lancashire where the damp atmosphere helped the spinning and weaving processes.

65. **Natural Resources and Raw Materials**
- **Primary industries** have little choice in their location. Hence coal mining, quarrying and oil drilling must take place where the raw material is found. Agriculture where the land and climate is suitable and fishing near to fishing grounds and harbours.

- The location of **manufacturing industries** may also be influenced by the availability of raw materials. Usually a firm will locate near to its source of raw materials if they are difficult or expensive to transport, for example bulky goods. Thus a steel firm would locate near to sources of coal, limestone and iron ore because the weight of these raw materials is far greater than that of the finished product, ie steel is weight-reducing.

## 66. Nearness to Markets and Labour

- **Service industries** are usually located where the demand exists. Hence, for example, hairdressers, garages, retail outlets, banks are all found near to centres of population.
- If a firm manufactures **bulky or heavy goods** like furniture or bricks, then it is likely to be located near to the market. Firms which sell perishable goods like bread and milk, or fragile items like glass are also located near the market.
- All firms need **suitably skilled workers** and therefore this is another important location factor.

## 68. Government Influence

Since the 1930's depression, Governments have played an important role in influencing the location of industry. This is because the concentration of industries like coal, textiles and shipbuilding in particular areas has brought with it various problems, such as:

- Traffic congestion, pollution, housing shortages and the strain on education, medical and social services.
- High unemployment as these industries have declined rapidly due to changes in demand, foreign competition and job losses from the introduction of new technology.

69.

**How Unemployment Affects the Regions**

| Region | % of all employees | | | | |
|---|---|---|---|---|---|
| | Jan '73 | Nov '78 | Jan '87 | Jan '91 | Jan '94 |
| South East | 2.0 | 3.9 | 8.5 | 5.0 | 9.6 |
| East Anglia | 2.6 | 4.7 | 9.3 | 4.8 | 7.8 |
| South West | 3.4 | 6.4 | 10.4 | 5.7 | 9.1 |
| West Midlands | 3.0 | 5.4 | 13.8 | 6.7 | 10.2 |
| East Midlands | 2.8 | 4.8 | 11.4 | 5.9 | 9.1 |
| Yorks and Humberside | 3.8 | 5.8 | 130.8 | 7.6 | 9.9 |
| North West | 4.6 | 7.2 | 14.3 | 8.1 | 10.2 |
| North | 6.0 | 8.6 | 16.9 | 9.2 | 11.8 |
| Wales | 4.9 | 8.3 | 14.3 | 7.3 | 10.0 |
| Scotland | 6.1 | 7.8 | 15.1 | 8.0 | 9.3 |
| Northern Ireland | 7.5 | 10.9 | 19.3 | 14.0 | 11.8 |
| Average | 4.1 | 6.7 | 13.4 | 7.5 | 10.0 |

As can be seen from the table, unemployment is very high in some regions of the UK, like the North and Northern Ireland. Whilst in the South East and East Anglia, it is considerably lower. It is this problem of imbalance which the Government is trying to solve. Hence governments have tried to attract new and expanding industries to so called depressed areas. That is, those with high and persistent unemployment which are classified as either **assisted areas, development areas** or **intermediate areas**. The Government reassessed these areas in July 1993 to include those facing structural unemployment following major coal mine closures.

70. Some of the measures used to influence the location of industry and attract new industry which are aimed at both UK and overseas firms include:

- **Financial incentives** to firms, for example grants for buildings and equipment, loans at special low rates of interest and special tax allowances.
- **Ready built factories** for sale or rent on favourable terms, for example rent free for twelve months.
- **Subsidies** to train workers taken on.

- **Prevention of industrial development** in other areas.
- **Building of New Towns**, for example Stevenage, Milton Keynes, Peterlee.
- **Government Departments** have been moved into assisted areas, eg DVLC (Driver and Vehicle Licencing Centre) is now located in Swansea and the DHSS (Department of Health & Social Security) in Newcastle.

## 71. Urban Policy Initiatives

The economic recovery of inner city areas is being encouraged by improving the environment, developing new and existing businesses and better training to improve job prospects. This is being achieved via a number of co-ordinated Government initiatives including:

- **Inner Urban Programme (IUP) Grants** – (Through 57 'target' local authorities eg Aberdeen, Newcastle, Nottingham and Leeds) to support capital investment projects for rebuilding. These are being phased out to end in 1995.
- **City Challenge** – Introduced in 1993 whereby local authorities were invited to bid, competitively, for £20m of resources previously allocated within IUP. Among those successful were Bolton, Blackburn, Wigan and Sefton.
- **Enterprise Initiative** – Which offers assistance for between 5-15 days of consultancy for small firms (less than 500 employees) in key areas of marketing, design, quality, manufacturing systems, business planning and financial and information systems.
- **Urban Development Corporations** – set up to use grants to reverse large scale urban decline, eg London Docklands, Merseyside and Cardiff Bay.
- **Enterprise Zones** – 26 set up offering tax incentives and easy planning permission for firms who locate there eg Belfast, Tyneside, Telford and Swansea Valley.

---

### Task 15.10

#### FOREIGN FIRMS FLOCK TO THE VALLEYS

The Welsh Development Agency is delighted because despite the recession, overseas firms are descending on Wales after voting it the best place in Europe for a new factory. The legendary 'welcome in the valleys' helped to attract a record 71 new businesses over the last 12 months, official figures show. As a result 10,678 jobs were created or safeguarded, says the Department of Trade and Industry. Britain generally is attracting more foreign companies than anywhere else in the EU. In the 11 industrial development regions, including Wales, there were 332 new projects in 1991-92, bringing in 51,357 jobs. But Wales, with 30,000 steel and 28,000 coal mining jobs to replace after the decline of its traditional industries, is top of the league. It took 21 per cent of all foreign investment in the UK. Britain has proved more attractive than other EU countries because of a number of factors. One is the new era of industrial harmony, brought about by Government curbs on union power. Another is the fact that craftsmen from the old smokestack industries can be readily trained in new skills. Whilst major investors like the Japanese prefer English-speaking countries because it is their main second language. Recent big developments in Wales include a decision by Japanese electronics giant Sony to build a £147 million television plant at Bridgend, Mid Glamorgan. US chemicals firm Dow Corning is setting up a £150 million methyl silicone factory at Barry, South Glamorgan, and the Dutch food packaging firm Tedeco has announced that it is to open a factory at Port Talbot, West Glamorgan, employing 55 people.

The following questions are based on the above article which is taken from newspaper reports.

1. Why are overseas companies descending on Wales?
2. Why has Britain proved to be more attractive to companies than other EU countries?
3. How important is the attraction of new industry to the UK economy?

*15. Production processes and control*

## Economies of scale

72. As firms expand, they can gain the advantages of operating on a large scale. That is the cost per unit falls as output increases because of what are called economies of scale. These are of two types:

    - **Internal economies** – including production, finance, marketing, managerial and risk-bearing, which a firm gains directly as it increases the size of its own operations, and
    - **External economies** – which arise indirectly from the growth of the size of an industry and its concentration in a particular area.

## Internal Economies of Scale

73. **Production Economies**

    - Mass production makes it possible for firms to install larger and better technical equipment such as the use of computers and robots.
    - More use can be made of the division of labour.
    - Buildings and equipment can be used more intensively and economically.
    - Research and development – large firms are likely to have more money to spend on developing new or improved products.

74. **Financial Economies**

    - Large firms find it cheaper and easier to borrow money.
    - Large well known firms can raise capital more easily which may include access to the Stock Market for funds.

75. **Marketing Economies**

    - Bulk buying – large firms can negotiate lower prices, for materials and equipment.
    - Advertising and other costs can be spread over a wider range of products.
    - Transport – either more efficient use can be made of a firm's own vehicles or better rates obtained from outside carriers.
    - Packaging and administration costs – the average cost per unit will be lower for a large firm.

76. **Managerial Economies**

    - Organisation into departments and the use of specialist staff, for example purchasing, sales, accounts, marketing.
    - Ability to pay higher salaries to attract good staff.
    - Use of computers to provide management information.

77. **Risk-Bearing Economies**

    - Markets and demand – large firms can diversify and offer a wider range of products so that if demand for one falls it is possible that this can be offset by increased sales of another. For example, Walls sell both ice-cream and sausages. Therefore total demand is more stable or predictable.
    - Supplies and production – as a firm increases in size, it can buy from a wider range of suppliers and produce in a number of different locations. This helps to guard against the risks for example, of raw material shortages and strikes.

## Task 15.11

1. Define in your own words the meaning of production, financial marketing, managerial and risk-bearing economies of scale.
2. Give at least one example of each, other than those quoted in paragraphs 73-77.
3. Identify some potential internal economies of scale in an organisation which you know well such as a school, college or place of work.

## Diseconomies of Scale

78. We have seen that as a firm expands, it may be able to benefit from economies of scale. The optimum size to which it should grow being the point at which its average cost of production is at its lowest. However, it is possible for a firm to grow too large because an increase in size can bring problems as well as advantages. Problems which reduce efficiency and increase the cost per unit of output are called **diseconomies of scale**.

79.

**Costs of Production**

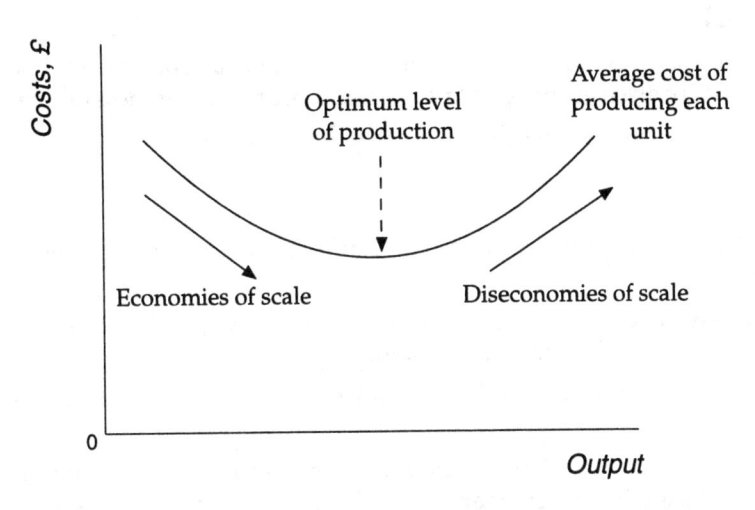

*(Graph showing a U-shaped average cost curve. Y-axis: Costs, £. X-axis: Output. The downward-sloping portion is labelled "Economies of scale"; the upward-sloping portion is labelled "Diseconomies of scale"; the minimum point is labelled "Optimum level of production"; the curve itself is labelled "Average cost of producing each unit".)*

80. Diseconomies of scale usually result from the difficulties of managing larger organisations and include:

   - **Co-ordination and control** – communications and management become much more complex and difficult to organise.
   - **Industrial relations** – problems caused because workers feel unimportant or out-of-touch with management; problems of boredom because work is repetitive.
   - **Technical limitations** – the inability to produce more with existing equipment or adapt quickly to new production methods.

## Task 15.12

Identify and compare the problems of running a large secondary school or college with over seventy staff which operates on more than one site, with a small primary school with perhaps four or five staff.

## External Economies

81. Once an industry becomes established in a particular area, it can benefit from certain advantages known as external economies of scale. These are factors which keep firms in an area or attract new firms and include:

- **Labour** – a supply of suitably skilled labour is available.
- **Ancillary/Support Industry** – for example, firms supplying specialist machinery, collecting by-products and producing components.
- **Marketing and distribution facilities** – for example specialist delivery services and warehousing.
- **Commercial services** – for example information provided by Trade Associations, Chamber of Commerce, or specialist College training courses.
- **Disintegration** may take place as individual firms specialise in single processes thus reducing costs, for example specialist spinning, weaving, dyeing and finishing firms in the Lancashire cotton industry.
- **Industrial Inertia** that it, many industries have remained in their original locations even though the initial advantages have declined.

**Task 15.13**

Identify an industry which has become established in your area or one nearby. Briefly describe the external economies of scale which firms in that industry benefit from.

## The Size of Firms

82. The size of a firm can be measured in a number of different ways, each of which could give different results including:

- **The number of employees.** However, a firm can still be 'big' without employing many people, particularly if it uses a lot of computer technology.
- **Profits.** Although small firms are unlikely to make very large profits, large firms can and do make losses.
- **Number of places of business.** A firm with branches or factories throughout the UK and overseas will obviously be large. However, many large firms produce a lot in a small number of workplaces.
- **Market Share.** This is the percentage of the total volume or value of sales which a firm has in a particular market. For example, IBM and Amstrad both have about 30% each of the business in micro-computer markets. However, this does not say how big the market is.
- **Capital employed.** The more capital invested in a business, then the bigger it is likely to be. However, although this is a good measure of size, it is not always easy to calculate the value of a firm's assets.
- **Turnover.** A firm doing a lot of business is likely to be larger than another doing very little. Therefore, measuring the value of a firm's sales probably gives the best indication of its size. This is particularly true if the number employed and capital are also considered.

## The Growth of Firms

83. There are many reasons why firms wish to grow in size but at least three important ones should be noted:

- To achieve economies of scale and reduce costs.
- To increase market share, possibly to gain a monopoly position.
- To reduce risks and obtain greater security by extending the range of products, or controlling supplies of raw materials or sales outlets.

84. **Methods of Growth**

Growth can be achieved by three methods:

- **Internal (Organic) Growth** – that is by making more of existing products or extending the range by making new products. This may need extra capital which can be obtained by 'ploughing-back' profits, issuing further shares or by borrowing.
- **Merger or Take-over.** – expansion may also take place by:

  Merger – where two or more firms agree to amalgamate together, or

  Take-over – where one firm, not necessarily with the consent of the other, gains a controlling interest. This is possible because shares can be freely bought and sold on the stock market.
- **Joint Ventures** – where firms agree to work together, eg Honda and Rover, Thorn-EMI and JVC. Other examples include Franchising, Licensing and Agency Agreements.

85. **Holding Companies**

We noted above that one firm usually merges with or takes over another by buying all of the others' shares. However, sometimes a firm does not actually own another completely, but still controls it by buying over 50% of its shares. A **holding company** is a company specifically formed to take a controlling interest in other firms. The firms controlled are called **subsidiaries**.

86. **Conglomerates**

Many large companies also hold such controlling interests which enables them to diversify into a wide range of completely different product areas. Such companies are called **conglomerates**, examples of which include Great Universal Stores (which has a controlling interest in many companies including Kays, Lennards, Home Charm, Times Furnishing, Burberrys and Scotch House) and Sears (Freemans [mail order], Adams [childrens' wear], Shoe Express, Shoe City, Hush Puppies, Miss Selfridge, Wallis, Richards, Olympus and Selfridges).

### Task 15.14

#### ICE CREAM YOGHURT

International food businesses BSN and Unilever have formed a joint venture to develop and market worldwide new yoghurt and ice cream combinations. BSN, with the Danone brand, and Unilever are the worlds leading producers of yoghurt and ice cream, respectively. Joining each partner's specific expertise offers the opportunity to develop products of unique quality they say.

Actual joint product development has reached such a stage that the joint venture can introduce its first yoghurt ice cream combination in France and Spain in the near future. Following this, extension to other countries will take place.

BSN and Unilever will each have a 50 per cent interest in the joint venture.

#### SWEET PROSPECTS

Cadbury Schweppes has won an important toehold in the huge German confectionery market by agreeing to buy 70% of Bavarian chocolate liqueurs and sugar products maker Piasten for about £20m. Piasten (sales £43m) has 2% of the market and its own sales force, which should help other Cadbury products. Germans eat 1m tonnes of confectionery a year and the total is growing as East Germans get their teeth into Western treats. Cadbury has an option on the remaining 30%.

continued...

*15. Production processes and control*

> **Task 15.14** continued
>
> ### BA BUYS GERMAN LINE
>
> British Airways has bought a German airline in a first step towards establishing a Continental operating base. Delta Air, based in Frederikshaven, flies 19 routes in Germany and to several European cities. It will be renamed Deutsche BA. The takeover, for an undisclosed sum, comes after the Bonn government required BA to withdraw from domestic German flights in favour of home companies. BA joined forces with three German banks to buy Delta Air and now has a 49 per cent stake in the airline and its ten twin-prop commuter planes.
>
> ### BREWER IN BID
>
> Brewer Greene King launched a £101.3m takeover bid today for the small independent brewer Morland.
>
> Greene King, based in Bury St Edmunds, Suffolk, said the deal would enhance its position as the largest regional brewer in the south of England. The bid is worth 477p a share.
>
> ### SCHOLL GOES HERBAL
>
> SCHOLL, the personal care products group best known for its comfort footwear, is moving into herbal medicines with the acquisition of Gerard House. Gerard markets 30 licenced herbal medicine products.
>
> ### BISCUITS IN SPAIN
>
> United Biscuits subsidiary McVitie's is to form a joint sales company with Spanish food group Royal Brands to distribute their products throughout Spain.
>
> Read the above newspaper extracts and from them:
> 1. Identify with examples, the different methods of business expansion mentioned.
> 2. The reasons and/or benefits which they are expected to bring to the organisations concerned.

## Integration

87. When two or more firms combine together to form a larger unit it is called **integration**. This can be horizontal, vertical or lateral.

    - **Horizontal Integration** takes place when firms at the same stage of production combine together under the same management. For example Dixons and Curry's, GEC and Ferranti, Ikea and Habitat, Clarke Foods and Lyons Maid ice cream.

    - **Vertical Integration** is the amalgamation of firms in the same industry but at different stages of production. This may take place either **'backward'** towards the source of the raw materials, or **'forward'** towards the market. For example, hop farms and public houses are all concerned at different stages with the supply of beer. Thus a brewery which acquires its own hop farms is said to be integrating backward. If it acquires its own public houses it is integrating forward.

    - **Lateral Integration** occurs when firms with similar, but not competing products, merge together. This enables firms to diversify and offer a wider range of related products, for example Cadbury-Schweppes (Food and Drink).

88.                              **Integration**

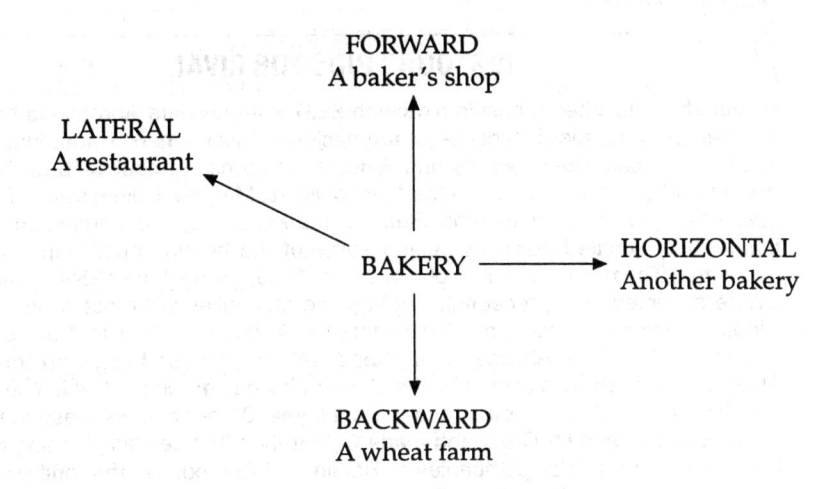

```
                    FORWARD
                    A baker's shop
                         ↑
    LATERAL              │
    A restaurant  ←      │
                         │                  HORIZONTAL
                      BAKERY  ──────→       Another bakery
                         │
                         ↓
                    BACKWARD
                    A wheat farm
```

## Monopolies and Restrictive Practices

89. The growth of firms can lead to monopoly situations. If monopolies are likely to operate against the public interest, then the Director General of Fair Trading can prevent them being formed (or break-up existing ones). For example, when a firm buys up other firms because this reduces competition it may lead to higher prices.

90. The **Monopolies and Mergers Act 1965** set up the Monopolies and Mergers Commission to investigate any mergers which might be against consumers interests. Under the **1973 Fair Trading Act** if a proposed merger would result in 25% or more of a market being controlled by one supplier (or the total assets from the merger would exceed £30 million), then it can be referred to the Commission which decides whether or not it can go ahead.

### Task 15.15

#### CONSUMER GROUP FIGHTS BID

The Consumers' Association has declared its formal opposition to north-west based Airtours' hostile £237m bid for rival holiday company Owners Abroad. It is writing to the Office of Fair Trading urging for the bid to be referred to the Monopolies and Mergers Commission on the grounds that Airtours would have between 27 and 30 per cent of the holiday tour market if successful. This, it considers to be too high, particularly given the fact that Thomson, the Number One operator, has itself about 30 per cent of the market. Airtours and the Consumers' Association clashed earlier this week over the group's criticism of the holiday company's operating standards. Owners Abroad was also criticised.

continued...

## Task 15.15 continued

### AIRTOURS BIDS FOR RIVAL

Airtours has launched a hostile bid worth £237m for Owners Abroad, its big rival, in an attempt to wrestle dominance of the package holiday market from industry giant Thomson. A combined Owners and Airtours would have about 29% of the holiday market and could be referred to the Monopolies & Mergers Commission. That would postpone everything for months. But that market share, it is suggested, could be comfortably whittled down by selling some of the holiday operations. There are hopes that Thomson's takeover of Horizon in 1989, giving it over 35% of the market, will be accepted as a precedent. But how the authorities will react is uncertain. But Airtours chairman David Crossland immediately made it clear that the bid will be withdrawn if Owners Abroad goes ahead with its proposed link with travel agent Thomas Cook, which is owned by the German holiday group LTU which bought 90% last year. Last month, Airtours reported a full-year 32 per cent increase in profit to a record £36.5m, and Mr Crossland made it clear then that he was planning to expand by buying more holiday companies in Britain and Europe. Three months earlier the company had bought Pickfords Travel from NFC. Owners profit for the year to last October was down from £2.5m to £31.6m mainly because of the old story of last minute discounting. Airtours is the third biggest operator after Owners Abroad and Thomson. It started its own airline last year. Owners owns Enterprise, Sovereign, SunMed and Falcon, and also has its own airline, Air 2000. It has about 19 per cent of the UK travel market, compared with Airtours' 17 per cent. Owners' immediate response to the bid was to urge shareholders to take no action and not to sell. Chairman of Owners, Howard Klein says: 'Owners Abroad is seeking to create a group with a strong presence throughout the European market. 'This contrasts with the defensive proposal by Airtours, which is clearly designed to protect its position in the United Kingdom in a way which we believe will work against the interests of both the industry and the consumer,' he added. Profits of holiday companies are notoriously fickle. There would undoubtedly be big savings to come out of either deal but they are some way down the road. In the meantime it would be no surprise if Thomson tightened the screw while its two competitors slug it out.

Read the above articles and answer the questions which are based on it.

1. Why is Airtours' bid considered 'hostile' and what does this mean?
2. What are the main reasons for the bid?
3. Why is the Consumers Association opposed to it?
4. If the bid is referred to the Monopolies Commission, what factors will it need to investigate?
5. From the information available and your own knowledge, comment on whether or not you feel the bid should be allowed to go ahead. Consider in your answer the interests of shareholders, consumers and the two companies.

## 91. Arguments Against Monopoly

The lack of competition and therefore potential abuse of the market power of monopolies often leads to a number of arguments being put forward against them including the following:

- **Slow innovation** because without competitive pressures, it is not essential to produce new goods or services in order to survive and prosper.
- **Reduced choice** because new firms can be prevented from entering a market.
- **Inefficiency** because without the incentive to compete, costs may rise which can result in increased prices and/or falling standards.
- **Reduced supply** resulting from a desire to create shortages in order to raise prices and profits, particularly where demand is inelastic.

92. **Collusion**

Sometimes instead of merging, firms may come to an agreement with each other to restrict competition. For example, two large bread manufacturers may agree to restrict production in order to create a shortage of bread and therefore keep prices at a high level. An extreme form of collusion would be a **cartel** such as OPEC. Such practices can be illegal in the UK. Under the **Restrictive Trade Practices Acts 1956-1968**, the Director General of Fair Trading can refer restrictive practices to the Restrictive Practices Court for investigation, whilst anti-competitive practices are controlled by the **Competition Act 1980**. In both situations firms can be ordered to discontinue practices found to be against the public interest.

## Survival of the Small Firm

93. Despite the advantages enjoyed by large firms, small firms still predominate in most forms of businesses. Small firms are especially important in certain industries such as agriculture, building, retailing and personal and professional services. It is also important to note that even within the same industry firms often vary considerably in size.

94. **Size of Manufacturing Units in the UK 1991**

| Employees | Number of businesses | % of total businesses | Number of employees (000's) | % of total employed |
|---|---|---|---|---|
| 1–19 | 121,077 | 77.4 | 532 | 11.2 |
| 20–99 | 25,886 | 16.5 | 1103 | 23.3 |
| 100–999 | 9,078 | 5.8 | 2298 | 48.5 |
| Over 1,000 | 408 | 0.3 | 806 | 17.0 |

NB Figures based on Annual Abstract of Statistics 1992 edition.

The above diagram shows two important features:

- Small firms are typical of UK manufacturing. Nearly 94% employ less than one hundred people.
- Those small units employ over a third of the total labour force and therefore make a major contribution to the economy.

95. **Why Small Firms Survive**

Below are some of the reasons why small firms are able to survive.

- **Professional and specialist services or products**, for example accountants, solicitors, racing cars where demand is local or limited.
- **Sub-contracting** or making components for large firms. Many small firms produce goods for other large firms.
- **Personal services**, for example hairdressing, plumbing, window cleaning can be more easily supplied by small firms.
- **Limited markets**, for example 'corner shops' provide a local service.
- **Banding together**, for example Spar and Mace group together to gain the benefits of economies of scale such as bulk buying.
- **'Being one's own boss'**. Some entrepreneurs may accept smaller profits in order to enjoy the satisfaction of working for themselves.
- **Government assistance** or advice is offered to prospective and established small businesses on a wide range of problems.

## Summary

96. a) Operations management is concerned with the planning and co-ordination of production in conjunction with the other business functions.

b) A product design strategy is needed for the creation of new products or development of existing ones.

## 15. Production processes and control

c) Important design factors include performance, appearance, economy and legal and environmental requirements.
d) Value analysis is used to improve efficiency and reduce production costs.
e) Materials or components can represent a major cost of production and therefore the buying function is very important.
f) Vendor appraisal techniques can be used to select suppliers.
g) Proper stock control is vital to avoid supply shortages or the tying up of large amounts of capital.
h) Total costs of stockholding can be reduced by calculating the economic order quality.
i) Production can be organised using job, batch, flow or just-in-time methods.
j) The productivity of labour is an important measure of efficiency.
k) Work study is the use of method and time study techniques to evaluate and improve the way jobs are performed.
l) The location of industry is influenced by historical factors, natural resources and raw materials, nearness to markets, transport costs and the availability of labour.
m) The government tries to influence location by offering incentives to firms who move into areas of high unemployment.
n) As a firm grows in size its costs per unit of output are likely to fall because it can benefit from economies of scale.
o) Internal economies result from the growth of the firm, external economies from the growth and concentration of an industry in a particular area.
p) Internal savings include production, financial, marketing, managerial and risk-bearing economies.
q) If a firm grows too large it may encounter problems leading to diseconomies of scale.
r) External economies include the availability of labour, ancillary/support industries, marketing and distribution facilities, commercial services and 'disintegration'.
s) Firms can grow either internally by expansion or externally by integration, which can be horizontal, vertical or lateral.
t) Despite the benefits from economies of scale, small firms continue to survive.

## Review questions *(answers can be found in the paragraphs indicated)*

1. In what sense are the production and marketing functions dependent upon each other in a business? (2-5)
2. What are the costs of production in a business? (7-8)
3. Outline the key factors to be considered in a product design strategy. (9-15)
4. Discuss the roles of the chief buyer in an organisation. (17-22)
5. How can a business control its stock levels? (23-28)
6. With the use of an example, explain the concept of an economic order quantity. (30-34).
7. Distinguish between job, batch and flow methods of production. (35-43)
8. Explain the main features and benefits of just-in-time production. (44-48)
9. Why is productivity an important measure of efficiency? (49-52)
10. Briefly explain the main features and benefits of work study and organisation and methods. (53-61)
11. List at least 5 factors which a firm is likely to consider when locating a new factory. (62-63)
12. Give 2 examples of measures which the government has used to try to influence the location of industry. (70-71)

13. Explain with the use of examples, the difference between internal and external economies of scale. (72-77, 81)
14. What are diseconomies of scale? (78-80)
15. In what ways can the size of firms be measured? (82)
16. Give 3 reasons why firms may wish to expand. (83)
17. Explain the difference between a merger, a take-over and a joint-venture. (84)
18. With the use of a diagram, briefly explain the difference between horizontal, vertical and lateral integration. (88-89).
19. What is a monopoly and why might it be against the public interest? (89-93)
20. Give 4 reasons why small firms are able to survive. (93-95)

*Asterisks indicate those questions for which there are answers in Outline Answers (page 439)*

## Essay-style questions

1.* If a Japanese manufacturer wanted to open a factory in Britain, what factors would influence the location of the business?
2. An investigator is charged with the task of studying the existing method in a manufacturing business prior to evolving a new and improved system. List at least a dozen questions which he might usefully ask, and outline the procedure he will adopt after considering those questions.
3. What problems would you envisage in trying to introduce Organisation and Methods into an office? How would you try to overcome these problems?

## Short answer

1.* Corley-Parker plc, is a specialist manufacturer of industrial machinery based in the West Midlands. The company is currently experiencing a growth in sales throughout new markets in Europe. The Board of Directors has decided to look for a new location because the existing site lacks space for expansion and the current plant is both old and nearing its production capacity. It is proposed that the new factory will be purpose built and highly automated with an integrated spare parts distribution centre.
    a) Why does the company need to relocate?
    b) Discuss the key factors which the Board will need to consider in choosing a new site.
    c) Explain why the Government may try to influence the Board's decision and describe 3 ways in which it might do this.
    d) What are the likely implications on the demand for labour of the proposed development?
    e) Outline some potential benefits from a new location.
2.* a) Distinguish between vertical, horizontal and lateral integration.
    b) Why do firms join together in these ways?
3. With the use of examples, explain each of the following terms:
    i) Job production.
    ii) Just-in-Time production
    iii) Productivity

## Multiple-choice/completion

1.* Which of the following is the kind of manufacturing which is often called the production line method?
    A. Batch production
    B. Job production
    C. Flow production
    D. Just-in-time production

## 15. Production processes and control

2.* Which of the following is an example of horizontal integration?
   A. A restaurant chain acquires a mushroom farm.
   B. Two restaurant chains merge.
   C. A wholesale firm acquires retail outlets.
   D. A firm doubles its output of existing products.

3.* A government wishes to encourage the development of industry in a particular area. Which of the following measures is LEAST likely to attract industry to the area?
   A. Special redundancy payments.
   B. Building advance factories in the area.
   C. Special training facilities in the area.
   D. Preferential tax treatment in favour of the area.

4.* Which of the following would you expect when a manufacturer introduces new equipment?
   A. Higher costs of production.
   B. Increased output per worker.
   C. An increase in job satisfaction.
   D. The work becomes less repetitive.

5. Internal economies of scale refers to the:
   A. Fall in unit costs as an industry grows larger.
   B. Fall in unit costs as a firm grows larger.
   C. Take-over of a small firm by a large firm
   D. Greater market power enjoyed by large firms.

6. All of the following reasons for a merger would be of advantage to both consumers and the economy except:
   A. Economies of Scale.
   B. Diversification.
   C. Rationalisation.
   D. Monopoly power.

*In each of the following questions, one or more of the responses is/are correct. Choose the appropriate letter which indicates the correct version.*

   A   if 1 only is correct.
   B   if 2 only is correct.
   C   if 1 and 2 are correct.
   D   if 1, 2 and 3 are correct

7. Which of the following represent economies of scale?
   1. In order to increase its output a firm runs a night shift on which workers are paid 50% above the day rate.
   2. A large firm is able to raise loan capital at an interest rate of 9% while in order to raise the same amount, a small firm pays 9[fraction]%.
   3. In order to accommodate additional employees, a firm moves to a new larger office block whose rent is £10 per square foot against £5 per square foot previously.

8. Which of the following would be likely to present obstacles which might hinder the growth of business units?
   1. The range and complexity of management problems.
   2. The difficulty of obtaining finance.
   3. A market too small for large scale production.

## Assignment

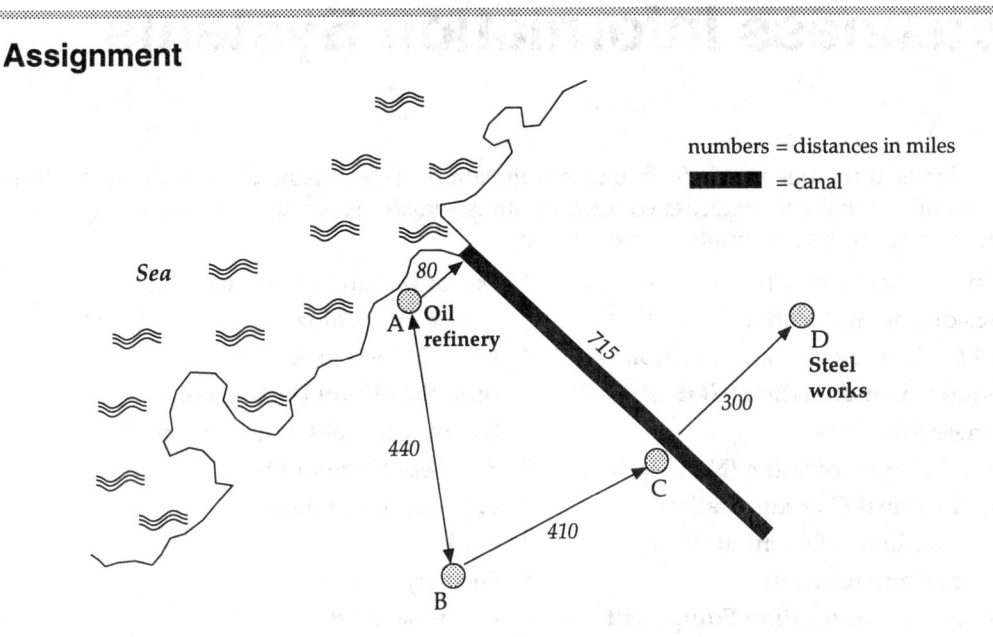

*[Map showing: Sea to the west with coastline. Point A (Oil refinery) on the coast. A canal runs from A southeast, passing through C to D (Steel works). Distances shown: A to canal entry 80, along canal A to C 715, C to D 300, A to B 440, B to C 410.]*

numbers = distances in miles
▬▬▬ = canal

A metal tube manufacturer wants to evaluate the comparative costs of locating its factory nearer to its source of raw materials, markets and labour supply. Costs of production are constant wherever the location. The following information is available about the 4 possible sites, A, B, C, D. There is no market for metal tubes at A so if the factory was located there, workers would have to commute from B.

A labour force therefore is only available at B, C & D.

The costs of producing each 100 tubes are summarised below:

1. It costs 30p per mile to transport the required labour from B to A.
2. Transporting oil from the refinery at A costs £12.00 per mile by road and 35p per mile by canal.
3. The cost of transporting metal tubes is £8.00 per mile by road and 25p per mile by canal.
4. Transporting steel from the steelworks at D costs £14.00 per mile by road and 45p by canal.

You are asked:

1. to calculate the transport costs involved for each location. Present your answers in the form of a table and show your working.
2. to make a recommendation to the Board on the cheapest location but include a comment on the other factors which it should consider in addition to the lowest cost.

# 16. Business Information Systems

This Chapter looks at the need for effective communication in the business world. It gives details of the main methods of internal and external communications which are used today including the important impact of new computerised technology and covers:

* Business Communication
* Types of Communication
* Need for Effective Communication
* Internal Communication (Verbal)
* Business Meetings
* Internal Communication (Non-Verbal)
* Other Informal Communication
* Visual Methods of Communication
* External Communication
* Internal Communication Equipment
* Storage and Retrieval of Information
* Hardware and Software

* Use of Business Systems
* Office Technology
* Data Protection Act
* Impact of IT on Businesses
* Organisational Benefits from IT
* Business Documents
* Payment Documents
* Banking
* Security
* Postal Services
* Future Developments
* Barriers to Effective Communication

## Business Communication

1. The ways in which businesses communicate with each other have changed dramatically in recent years. The impact of new computer technology has greatly increased the speed of communications in the UK. The use of satellites has enabled communication, by both sound and vision, to be made throughout the world in a matter of minutes.

2. Nowadays we receive news almost as soon as it happens via television, radio and newspapers. Modern businesses therefore also expect their methods of communication to be fast and effective. The speed with which suppliers, customers, staff and other business providers, such as banks, are contacted is important to ensure that a firm operates efficiently. There are many different forms of communication which a business may choose and it is important to select the most effective in any particular situation.

## Communication Defined

3. Communication is a two-way process to enable information to be passed from one person or organisation to another, or in the case of automatic systems, from one process to another. It involves the basic skills of listening, speaking, reading and writing in order to receive, interpret and understand messages and then respond to them accordingly. The rapid growth in the use of computerised equipment makes the need to develop information technology skills increasingly important. To be effective, communication must be understood by and acceptable to all parties, both those giving the information and those receiving it. Unfortunately, it is often very easy to misunderstand or misinterpret what is meant as the cartoon illustrates.

4. **Getting the Message**

*[Cartoon: A person at a doorway asks "WHAT WOULD YOU LIKE FOR SUPPER, DAD?" and a figure reading a newspaper in an armchair replies "ABOUT HALF PAST NINE AFTER THE FOOTBALL"]*

## Types of Communication

5. Communication in a business may take place in many different ways. It may be:
   - **Verbal** ie spoken by someone, for example face to face or on the telephone.
   - **Non-verbal** ie written, for example letters, memos, reports and diagrams. Body language such as facial expressions, the use of the hands, and how people sit or stand can also represent an important form of non-verbal communication, often revealing a lot about how people feel or think.
   - **Formal** ie following correct laid down procedures of which records are usually kept, for example committees, recruitment interviews, safety notices.
   - **Informal** ie as and when appropriate without the need to follow procedures or keep records, for example meeting or telephoning someone to discuss a particular problem as it arises.
   - **Internal** ie takes place within a business organisation, for example between the sales and personnel departments.
   - **External** ie outside an organisation or between organisations, for example with a customer or supplier.

### Task 16.1

1. Briefly describe the main forms of body language which you personally use.
2. Can you identify any situations where body language is, or might be, particularly important for communication in the place where you work or study?

## Need for Effective Communication

6. To be successful, a business needs to communicate effectively with a wide range of people both internally and externally. Imagine, for example, the chaos which could be caused if British Rail or your local bus company issued inaccurate timetables. Think about what might happen if this type of communication problem occurred in your school, college or place of work.

7. Effective communication then, is important for a number of reasons in an organisation including to:-
   - **enable decisions to be taken** based on appropriate information.
   - **issue instructions to its staff** to tell them what to do and thus enable the business to operate. This is referred to as vertical communication.
   - **enable people at the same level within the organisation to communicate with each other.** Different departments such as sales and production, for example, or employees who work in the same department. This is called horizontal communication.

## 16. Business information systems

- **communicate with its suppliers, customers, banks and other contacts** in carrying out its business. It must send information about its products, receive orders, supply goods, deal with documents and arrange payments.
- **keep staff informed of what is going on** so that they are able to perform their work better and enjoy what they are doing. It must transmit information about the firm's organisation, products, safety regulations and training.
- **provide essential information to staff** on pay, pensions, holidays, other benefits and general working conditions.

> ### Task 16.2
> An urgent order has just been taken at the main branch of Exclusive Tailoring Ltd, a company which produces high quality made-to-measure suits.
> 1. List all the possible ways which you can think of to get the order to Head Office for processing.
> 2. What do you think might happen if the order does not reach Head Office quickly and accurately?
> 3. Which method of communication would you choose and why, in this situation?

8. **Effective Communication** involves four elements:

   a) **The Transmitter** ie the sender or source of the communication.

   b) **The Message** or content of what is being communicated.

   c) **The Medium** or method through which the communication travels, for example a letter, by telephone, or leaflet

   d) **The Receiver** ie the audience or people to whom the communication is being sent.

9. **The Elements of Communication**

## Internal Communication – Verbal Methods

10. - **Spoken** communications are the most common way of passing information within an organisation. This involves seeing people face to face, for example the holding of meetings or contacting them by telephone.

- **Telephone** extensions are frequently used in an organisation to enable communication to take place between various sections or departments. This saves time if it is not possible to meet someone to speak to them personally.
- **Interviews** or individual discussions with staff are common in all organisations. They are used not only to select staff but also, for example, to deal with particular problems or disciplinary matters or to assess staff performance.
- **Business meetings** may take place where a number of people need to be involved in discussions. These may be formal or informal.

## Business Meetings

11. At any level in an organisation, employees may find themselves involved in attending meetings and as they move further up the promotional ladder, they are likely to find themselves attending an increasing number of them.
    - **Informal meetings** may be called at short notice to discuss matters which arise suddenly. Usually there is no agenda and often no record is kept of what happened.
    - **Formal meetings** are usually held after the people involved have been notified in advance, usually in writing and often with an accompanying **Agenda** which lists the items to be discussed. This may also involve preparing reports or documents, speaking to them and possibly notetaking.

## Reasons for Meetings

12. Although meetings can be time-consuming and sometimes ineffective, nonetheless, they are widely used in organisations for
    - setting objectives,
    - monitoring progress,
    - sharing views,
    - discussing ideas,
    - planning and
    - decision-making.

13. **Example of an Agenda:**

---

### ABC ELECTRICAL SUPPLIERS LTD

Meeting of Marketing Co-Ordination Committee
On Friday 14th January 1994 at 10am
To be held in the Boardroom

**Agenda**

1. Apologies for absence
2. Minutes of previous Meeting
3. Matters arising:
   - Item 21    Sales Training
   - Item 22    Promotion of New Products
   - Item 25    Advertising Budget
4. Marketing Department staffing
5. Report on Sales Enquiry Forms
6. Exhibition Plan
7. Any other business
8. Date and time of next meeting

---

14. Most organisations, whether a Youth Club, School, College or Company have committees which meet to discuss and make policy decisions. Often these consist of people elected to represent the views of members. Formal bodies usually have an Annual General Meeting (AGM) held once a year to elect officials, receive reports and to give members an opportunity to speak; for example, a limited company will hold an Annual General Meeting to which all its shareholders are invited.

15. A formal meeting is controlled by a chairman and minutes are taken by a secretary. **Minutes** are a record of a meeting and serve as a reminder of the issues discussed and decisions taken. All members of the committee will receive a copy of the minutes and any matters arising will be discussed at the next meeting. The most important committee in a company is the Board of Directors.

> **Task 16.3**
>
> You are employed as one of 20 staff in the offices of a local insurance company. The office supervisor has been concerned for sometime about poor staff morale following the closure of a small nearby branch and redundancies in 2 others.
>
> Reporting her concerns to the personnel manager, she is given assurances that your office will not suffer. He also recommends the setting up of a small committee to discuss the problems and come up with some positive suggestions for raising morale. He indicates that the company might also be able to find £200 from the personnel budget to assist in this matter.
>
> 1. As a group, form a committee(s) and decide on an appropriate chairperson, secretary and other positions which you feel are necessary.
> 2. Identify the reasons for each person being on the committee and the role they will be expected to undertake.
> 3. Decide when your meeting is to take place and draw up a suitable agenda.
> 4. Hold the meeting and from it, draw up a firm set of proposals, including the allocation of any expenditure. Ensure that minutes are taken.
> 5. Assuming you are the office supervisor, write a memo to the personnel manager, setting out the proposals. Include as much detail as possible and any potential benefits to the company.

## Internal Communication – Non Verbal Methods

16. Earlier, we considered the main verbal methods of communication in an organisation. The non verbal (written) methods used include memos, minutes, letters, notices, house journals and reports.

    - **Memorandum** (memos) are the method of written communication most commonly used within an organisation. They can be sent in a firm's internal post, are usually short and deal with only one or two specific points.
    - **Minutes** are used to provide a summary of the main points which are discussed at a meeting and are filed for future reference.
    - **Letters** are not normally used within a business. However, they are sent in some formal situations for example, to confirm the promotion of staff or to accept their resignation.
    - **Notices** are often used to display matters of interest to staff. However, unfortunately there is no way of ensuring that these are either read or understood.
    - **House Bulletins/House Journals.** In some organisations notices are circulated by means of a weekly or monthly staff bulletin. Some larger organisations also have a glossy house magazine or journal which includes information on a wide range of work-related and social topics, for example new products, new employees, births, deaths and marriages, or sports activities.
    - **Reports** are formal written communications required to cover a certain business topic. They may be provided for a number of reasons. For example, many firms have a standard accident or sick-

ness report form. Periodic reports may be needed to assess a firm's budget or sales performance. Technical reports may be prepared on new products and processes of production.

17. **Example of a Memorandum**

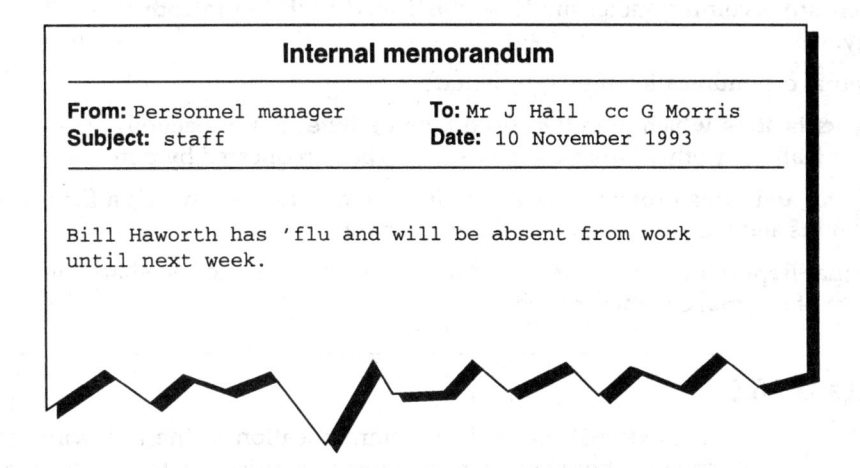

> **Internal memorandum**
>
> **From:** Personnel manager   **To:** Mr J Hall   cc G Morris
> **Subject:** staff   **Date:** 10 November 1993
>
> Bill Haworth has 'flu and will be absent from work until next week.

## Other Informal Communication

15. Communication may also take place in other ways in particular via the 'grapevine', over lunch and on social occasions.
    - **The 'grapevine'** or jungle telegraph is the term used to describe the rumours and general gossip which staff often use as a source of information in an organisation.
    - Informal **lunchtime** conversations are often used for both internal and external communication. They may involve casual discussion between staff or be working lunches often with visitors to an organisation.
    - **Social occasions** of all types provide a further opportunity for both internal and external communication to take place. Examples might include a Christmas Dinner, cricket match or annual outings where a number of staff will mix and talk together.

## Visual Methods of Communication

19. Another important means of communication, both internal and external is the use of charts, graphs and diagrams. The use of visual presentation enables complicated information, particularly statistical data, to be more easily understood. (see Chapter 18)

> **Task 16.4**
>
> Consider the place where you work or study or any other organisation which you know well.
>
> Give examples of situations where each of the following types of communication are used:
>
> Spoken (face-to-face)
> Telephone calls
> Hand – written
> Printed – forms
> Electronic Transmission (other than telephones)
> Social gatherings
> Reports

## 16. Business information systems

### External Communication

20. The most common forms of external communication are **letters** and **telephone.** In the UK the major suppliers of these and other external communication services are the Post Office and British Telecom (BT). These organisations provide a wide range of national and international communication systems which are becoming increasingly sophisticated with the introduction of new computerised technology.

21. Other external communication methods include

    - **compliments slips** which are often used when a letter is not needed; for example when a firm sends out leaflets or other information which has been requested by potential customers whilst
    - **advertising and sales promotion** are very important means by which a firm communicates with its customers and these are dealt with fully in Chapter 8.
    - the **Annual Report and Accounts** which in a company, is issued to shareholders is another common form of external communication.

---

**Task 16.5**

1. Identify the external methods of communication in the following list: Newspaper advertisement, letter post, managers meeting, price list, memorandum.
2. State 2 methods of external communication and 2 methods of internal communication which a major soap powder manufacturer might use.

---

22. **A Summary of the Main Methods of Business Communication**

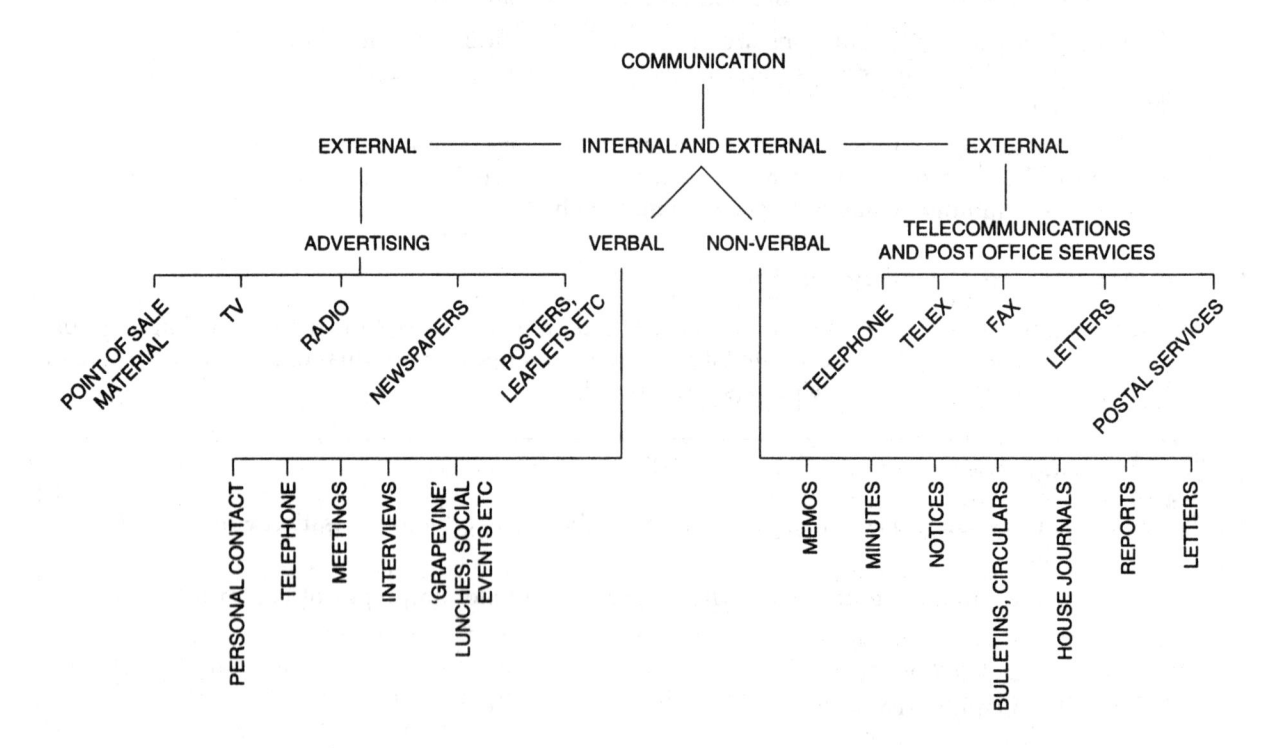

```
                          COMMUNICATION
                               |
        EXTERNAL —— INTERNAL AND EXTERNAL —— EXTERNAL
           |                  / \                |
                                             TELECOMMUNICATIONS
        ADVERTISING      VERBAL  NON-VERBAL   AND POST OFFICE SERVICES
```

External / Advertising: POINT OF SALE MATERIAL, TV, RADIO, NEWSPAPERS, POSTERS, LEAFLETS ETC

Verbal: PERSONAL CONTACT, TELEPHONE, MEETINGS, INTERVIEWS, 'GRAPEVINE' LUNCHES, SOCIAL EVENTS ETC

Non-verbal / Telecommunications and Post Office Services: MEMOS, MINUTES, NOTICES, BULLETINS, CIRCULARS, HOUSE JOURNALS, REPORTS, LETTERS

External / Telecommunications and Post Office Services: TELEPHONE, TELEX, FAX, LETTERS, POSTAL SERVICES

## Task 16.6

The best choice of medium for any particular message will depend upon a number of factors, including the urgency: who is to receive it; its length, complexity and confidentiality; the potential cost of sending it and whether or not a permanent record is required.

1. Suggest three possible methods of communication which could be appropriate in each of the following situations and
2. Decide on the best medium for each giving reasons for your choice.

   a) To invite a job applicant for an interview.
   b) To give an official warning to an employee for persistent lateness.
   c) To arrange an urgent internal meeting.
   d) To organise the annual staff dinner/dance.
   e) To present complicated statistical data to the Board of Directors.
   f) To inform all staff that the hours of work are to be altered.
   g) To confirm an offer of a job to a new employee.
   h) To provide the Managing Director with technical details of a new product.

## Postal Services

23. Postal Services in the UK are provided by the Post Office which is a Public Corporation owned and controlled by the Government. Every working day it delivers over 50 million letters and 600,000 parcels.

24. Letter services include first and second class post, recorded delivery, registered post, freepost and the business reply service, whilst Overseas mail can be sent by ordinary post, Airmail or Swiftair if faster delivery is needed. A similar range of options are offered for parcel deliveries. Up-to-date information about all services can be found in the Post Office Guide which is published annually.

## Telecommunications

25. The main telecommunications services which are summarised below are run in the UK by British Telecom (BT) which was government owned until 1986. It has now been privatised and operates in the private sector as a public limited company. In the 1990's, Mercury, run by Cable and Wireless plc, has developed as a competitor to BT. When BT was privatised, the **Office of Telecommunications (OFTEL)** was set up. OFTEL is an independent body which monitors and regulates BT's prices, the services provided and gives advice and assistance to telecommunication users.

26. **Telephone.** This is the main method of communication used by businesses because it is very quick and relatively cheap. Anyone who has a telephone is called a subscriber and they are able to make use of a wide variety of services offered by BT. The Freephone facility for example, is used by many firms whereby they pay for the cost of calls made by customers, whilst mobile radio phones, which enable calls to be made from anywhere in the UK, are also increasingly being used in business.

27. **Telex.** This service uses a special teleprinter machine which can send and receive messages from similar machines in the UK and throughout the world. Providing the machine is switched on it will automatically receive messages at any time of the day or night. This is very useful when contacting businesses overseas where time differences exist. The system is very similar to using the telephone except that the message is typed in and is then printed out at the other end. Each subscriber has a telex number and is issued with a UK Telex Directory. The cost of telex messages is based on the time it takes to transmit (send) the message and the distance involved.

28. **Electronic mail.** This is an alternative to sending letters by post, which involves the use of computer terminals linked via the telephone network. Subscribers who have a password enter the system and are able to send messages to a 'mailbox' where they are stored until 'opened' by the recipient. BT's Telecom Gold is a well known example.

29. **Telemessages.** These are accepted by telephone or telex and are delivered the next day by first class post. Telemessages replaced inland telegrams but **International telegrams** still exist.

## 16. Business information systems

30. **Facsimile Transmission (FAX).** A fax machine is rapidly becoming an essential piece of office equipment in business today.
    - The Post Office's system for sending facsimile (exact) copies of letters, documents and other information is called **Intelpost**.
    - British Telecom also has a facsimile service called **Bureaufax**. This enables firms with their own facsimile machine to send copies to other firms with similar machines either in the UK or overseas. The machines are linked by telephone and operate automatically once the contact is made.

31. **Contravision.** This service links individuals or groups of people in different places by sound and vision. This can be quicker and cheaper than trying to get a group of people together. For example, sales staff throughout the country can be linked in this way for a conference thus saving travelling costs and hotel bills. Contravision links can now be made, via satellites, to many countries throughout the world.

32. **An advertisement by the American company AT&T illustrating the use of contravision.**

> Next time, instead of flying to America, take the satellite.
> VIDEOCONFERENCE CENTRE
> AT&T

### Task 16.7

**OFFICES RUSH FOR FACSIMILE MACHINES AND MOBILE PHONES**

More small companies are joining the communications revolution. About one in three now have facsimile machines, while 22% are equipped with mobile telephones, 13% have telex facilities and 11% have pagers. The new figures emerge from a recent small business survey which also underlines growing worries about high interest rates. The report says the biggest expansion in business telecommunications over the next year will be in facsimile. Only 3% of companies have electronic mail links and 5% on-line database services.

1. Briefly explain the following terms in the above article: 'communications revolution', 'telex', 'pagers', 'electronic mail', 'on-line database services'.
2. Discuss the potential for the use of new communication technology in small businesses.
3. What significance if any do the 'growing worries about high interest rates' have on small firms?

## Other Telecommunication Services

33. Other important telecommunications services include teletext, prestel and datel.

    - **Teletext** is used to describe any computerised information displayed on a television screen which is broadcast by a TV company. It includes **Ceefax** the teletex system provided by the BBC and **Teletext** (formerly Oracle) on the ITV channels. Over 4000 pages of information are available on what in effect is a very comprehensive electronic newspaper. Where telephone lines are used to transmit data it is called **Viewdata,** examples of which are British Telecom's Prestel and Datel Services.

    - **Prestel.** This is a computerised system which provides a database of both general and business information on a wide variety of topics, for example share prices, financial statistics and sports results. To use the system a specially adapted television set is needed which is connected to a telephone line linked to the Prestel computer.

      Prestel is what is referred to as an interactive or two-way system because as well as receiving information, users can also send messages both to each other and to information providers. The system can be used to order goods from a supermarket, book a holiday or hotel room or reserve a theatre seat.

    - **Datel.** This telecommunication service operates using the telephone lines and can link a computer in one place with computers in other parts of the country and in many overseas countries.

      This service is particularly useful, for example, where a firm has a number of branches but needs to process orders centrally. It can have its main computer at Head Office with links in each branch.

### Task 16.8

#### BT GOES GLOBAL

British Telecom is poised to launch a £500m worldwide telecommunications service for multinational companies. BT intends to build a network of computerised exchanges in major cities around the world dedicated to handling voice, data and video transmission services for large corporations. The first four will be installed in London, New York, Frankfurt and Sydney by the mid 1990's with 32 others in operation by 2002. The attraction for corporate customers would be cheaper bills. The new service could reduce existing charges by between 5% and 15%. BT is keen to get underway in the US before its rivals secure a foothold. There, the telecommunications market is worth more than $1bn a year. US analysts are understood to be impressed with BT's determination to press ahead with the network. One said: 'It is taking the most aggressive step towards becoming a global carrier. A UK analyst said: 'It seems a logical expansion for the company. BT wants to be a world player and this looks a way of doing that and generating more profits.'

1. From the article, identify the main reasons why BT is launching a worldwide telecommunications service.
2. Why is the service targeted at multinational companies?
3. How and why is the service being well received by analysts?

## Internal Communication Equipment

34. We have already mentioned a range of typical equipment used in business today including the telephone, telex and fax. Other equipment in general use is summarised below.

    - **Telephone Switchboard.** Most businesses have a telephone switchboard which, depending on the size of the firm, can vary from one main line with use of a few extensions to hundreds of lines and thousands of extensions.

## 16. Business information systems

- **Telephone Answering Machines.** These make it possible to leave messages for people when they are out. A tape recorder is attached to the telephone receiver which automatically switches itself on to receive incoming calls. This enables messages of all kinds to be left after business hours.
- **Intercom.** In addition to telephone extensions, many firms also use an intercom system. This is a small microphone and loudspeaker which enables two or more people to speak to each other. For example, a manager may communicate with his secretary in this way or with staff in other offices or departments.
- **Paging.** The use of a pager enables businessmen to be contacted when they are out of the office. The pager bleeps to indicate when people are required who then go to the nearest telephone to take the call.
- **Public Address Systems (Tannoy).** This is a loudspeaker system which is often used for calling people or playing music in factories and warehouses. They are also used at football matches and other sporting events.

### Task 16.9

John Smith, a small local printer is considering various ways of developing his business. A friend has suggested that he should take a close look at the range of modern telecommunications services available which he says can be very profitable if used correctly. John obviously has a telephone but he is not keen on what he calls all this new complicated equipment.

1. From your own knowledge and with the help of a local Yellow Pages and Thomson Telephone Directory, suggest at least 6 services which might be of use to John in his business, giving reasons for your choice.
2. Is John right to consider any of the services suggested as being 'complicated'?
3. Compare a Yellow Pages and Thomson Directory. List the main features of each and state, with reasons, whether or not you feel that John should advertise in either or both of these publications.

## Storage and Retrieval of Information

35. All businesses need a system whereby records, letters, documents and other information can be filed or stored. It is important for good communication that this data is kept clean and safe and can be quickly and easily retrieved when required. However, there is no one correct method of filing and consequently each firm must set up a system most suited to its own needs. Traditionally, various types of filing cabinets have been used, but nowadays an increasing number of organisations are making use of computerised systems, that is, Information Technology (IT).

36. **Computers** are simply electronic machines which are able to store, retrieve and sort data at great speed. Information can be retrieved either directly onto a screen, printing out a hard copy on paper or on microfilm. Many firms need a lot of space for filing and this problem is reduced by microfilming, which involves taking miniature photographs of data. A special 'microfiche' viewer or reader is then used which enlarges the film so that it can be read easily. An example of the use of microfilm or microfiche can probably be seen in your local library which may store book lists or telephone directories in this way. **Optical disk systems** may also be used which can store vast amounts of data on a compact disk.

37.                               **Networking**

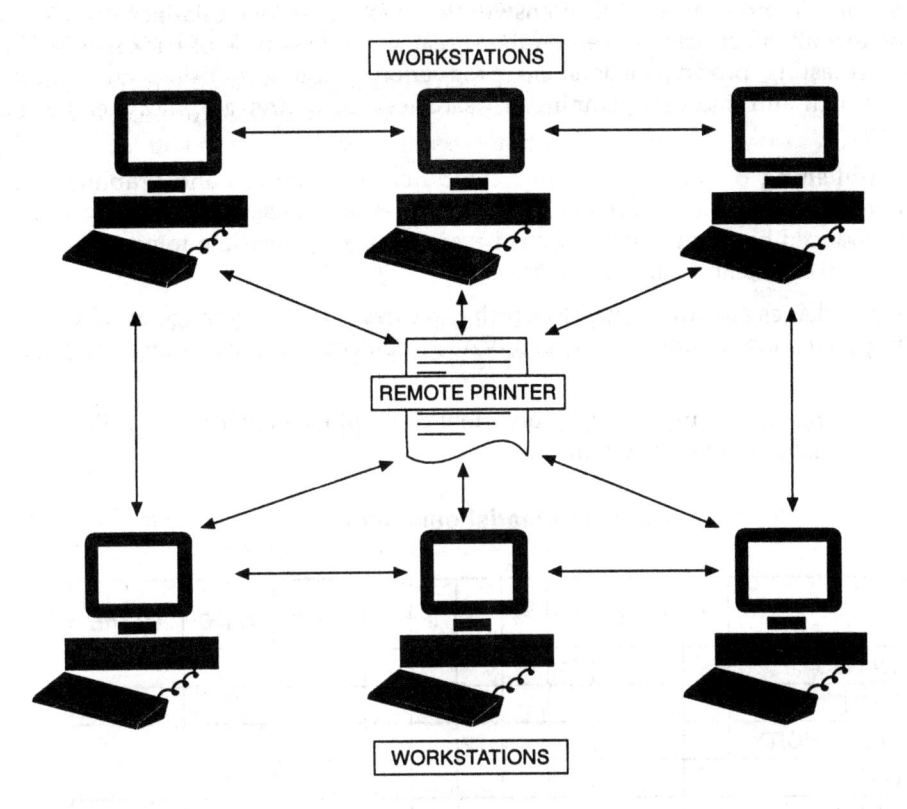

```
                    WORKSTATIONS
    [workstation] ↔ [workstation] ↔ [workstation]
              ↘        ↕        ↙
                [REMOTE PRINTER]
              ↗        ↕        ↖
    [workstation] ↔ [workstation] ↔ [workstation]
                    WORKSTATIONS
```

A feature of modern offices is the networking (linking) of free-standing computers to other machines within the same office or building. Wide Area Networks can be used to link different buildings or sites.

> **Task 16.10**
>
> Carry out some research in your place of study or work.
> 1. List as many different methods of storing data that you can find.
> 2. Identify the different types of data stored, why and how long it is stored for.
> 3. If possible, try to establish how much space, as a proportion of the total available, is used for storage.
> 4. Suggest ways in which the amount of data stored could be reduced.
> 5. Present your answers in the form of a chart(s) or diagram(s) and comment on your findings.

## Hardware and Software

38. The equipment used in a computerised system is called the **hardware.** It includes the Visual Display Unit (monitor), keyboard, printer and electronic components. The programs which tell the computer what to do are called the **software.**

39. Software programs can be linked together to create packages which can handle a range of needs. Typical business uses include databases, spreadsheets, desk top publishing, accounting and personnel packages.

    - **Databases** are a store of information which has been inputted into a computer so that it is ready to be processed and made available as required. They may be used for a wide variety of purposes and store vast amounts of data, for example addresses, receipts, payments and other records.

- **Spreadsheets.** provide a matrix on which calculations can be performed. They show data in an easy to read format and can be used to answer 'what if' questions. Changes can be made to the data and the overall effects can be seen on the spreadsheet. This type of package is often used for budgeting, forecasting, project management, production planning, statistical analysis of data such as market research and financial planning. Spreadsheets also offer graphics facilities such as pie and bar charts.
- **Desk Top Publishing** packages allow text, computer aided design and graphics to be merged together to produce high quality documents. This has revolutionised the publicity and promotional material produced by many organisations because it is now possible to produce them quickly, cheaply and to an excellent quality in-house.
- **Accountancy** packages are now available which can carry out a wide range of functions including book-keeping, invoicing, customer accounts, VAT, stock control, payroll and for producing final accounts.
- **Personnel packages** can be used to keep a variety of employee records, including training, sickness and absenteeism, holidays and pensions.

40. **A Basic Spreadsheet Layout**

|  | J | F | M | A | M | J | J | A | S | O | N | D | TOTAL |
|---|---|---|---|---|---|---|---|---|---|---|---|---|---|
| WAGES |  |  |  |  |  |  |  |  |  |  |  |  |  |
| RENT |  |  |  |  |  |  |  |  |  |  |  |  |  |
| ELECTRICITY |  |  |  |  |  |  |  |  |  |  |  |  |  |
| GAS |  |  |  |  |  |  |  |  |  |  |  |  |  |
| TOTAL |  |  |  |  |  |  |  |  |  |  |  |  |  |

This simple spreadsheet to illustrate a firm's expenditure could also be developed to include anticipated income. Potential changes such as a fall in sales or wage increases can also be entered and the impact on costs and profits immediately calculated.

## Use of Business Systems

41. The use of business software packages can readily be seen every day. If, for example you visit a travel agency to book a holiday, the details such as the place, dates, hotel and costs are entered directly into a computer. Most building societies now enter data directly into a computer and bank statements, gas, electricity and telephone bills are also prepared by computers. Companies usually keep a register of their shareholders on computer so that it can be kept up-to-date as shares are bought and sold. Whilst multiple retailers like Sainsbury's use optical character reader (OCR) scanners at check-outs which read bar-codes on products. These are linked to computers which not only produce customer till receipts but also act as a stock control and re-ordering system. Customers can then use a Connect or Switch card to pay for purchases and through EFTPOS (Electronic Transfer of Funds at the Point of Sale) computer technology, their account is debited immediately and the store's account credited. Thus what we have there is a very fast and efficient business communication tool performing tasks which were previously carried out manually.

42. **Office Technology**

Over a half of workers in the UK are employed in offices where one of the most significant developments in information technology has been **word processing** which is now used by many firms instead of typewriters. A word processor consists of an electronic keyboard with a built-in computer memory linked to a visual display unit (VDU). It can be used to insert, delete or move text and will automatically design page layouts, including margins, and carry out a spell check. Thus material can be quickly and easily corrected or altered on the screen before it is printed. When completed, the information can be filed (stored) away on magnetic tape or on a floppy or hard disc until it is needed again.

43. Word processors have many uses and can produce a vast range of material including letters, graphs, charts and diagrams. They are particularly useful for repetitive typewriting tasks such as standard letters which only require the name and address, date and time, or other simple information to be changed. Other uses might include the preparation of invoices, accounts, memos and reports.

> **Task 16.11**
>
> ### INSURANCE TECHNOLOGY
>
> Insurers are clamping down on phoney claims by tourists which cost the industry some £300 million a year. Firms say that fraudulent claims are seen as a 'legitimate crime' by many people and this has forced up premiums by as much as 25 per cent in recent years. Now the first computer database covering travel insurance has been set up to help trace fraudsters. All premiums and claims will now be logged on it, making it possible to see whether the same people, or people from the same address are claiming each year. As a result, anyone making regular claims or who has submitted fraudulent claims in the past will be more easily identified. Claims for non-existent cameras, jewellery or luggage are the insurers' biggest cause of concern.
>
> Another concern is the problem of bogus medical claims by travellers to the US who find they can get a full medical check-up costing £2,600 by putting it down as some sort of medical emergency. Doctors collude in the exercise because they make a tidy sum, which is a complete abuse of the system.
>
> The industry suspects that a third of all claims are fraudulent.
>
> Read the above article and from it identify, and with examples illustrate, how the use of IT databases can benefit both business and consumers.

## Data Protection Act 1984

44. Nowadays, most large organisations keep detailed computer records which include, for example, customers' names and addresses, staff records which may contain information on previous employment and any disciplinary or other action. To control the possible misuse of this type of information and in order to prevent it causing harm to individuals, the **Data Protection Act** was introduced in 1984.

45. The main provisions of the Act are that:
    - All organisations and individuals who hold personal records on computers must register with the Data Protection Registrar (the government's watchdog). Failure to do so can result in fines of up to £2,000.
    - They must tell the registrar
        - what type of information they hold
        - what use is made of it
        - to whom the information may be disclosed
        - how it was collected.
    - The Registrar has a duty to see that the data conforms to certain principles, namely:
        - it must have been obtained openly and fairly
        - it shall be held only for lawful purposes
        - its uses and possible disclosure must be declared to the Registrar.
        - it must be relevant to the purpose for which it is held
        - it must be accurate and up-to-date
        - it must be destroyed when it is no longer needed
        - individuals are entitled to know what information is held about them and to challenge inaccuracies.
        - it must be treated as confidential and protected against access by unauthorised persons.

- Organisations that do not comply may be liable to compensate individuals who may suffer as a consequence.
- There are, however, exceptions to the right to receive compensation, including:
  - data that has been supplied by individuals themselves.
  - data that has been acquired with 'reasonable care'
  - data held for payroll or pension purposes.
  - data held for statistical purposes, from which it is impossible to identify individuals.

## Impact of Information Technology on Businesses

46. The ability offered by information technology (IT) to gather, record, organise and act upon information quickly is vital in organisations. To gain maximum benefit however, IT needs to be properly managed and controlled. It should be seen as a dynamic and crucial resource supporting the organisation and helping it to achieve its objectives in the market place.

47. A properly managed IT system requires a clear organisation strategy with a number of key features.
    - **That all managers can gain access** to information as and when required. This means that users and providers of technological expertise need to be linked by placing information systems staff alongside other key business functions like finance, production, personnel and marketing.
    - **Information systems should be flexible** and able to adapt to the individual needs of the organisation in order to facilitate and control what goes on. They should also be fully tried and tested before being introduced to ensure that they work effectively.
    - **Management styles must be receptive** to the opportunities offered by IT including the creation of a shared information culture and a willingness to use the specialist skills available.
    - **All employees should have a broad overview of the business**, and made to feel part of it. This helps everyone to both better understand the business and also the use of IT in it.
    - **Information systems personnel need to act as change agents** assisting management and meeting the needs of end users.
    - **An IT action plan should be developed** with clear objectives, eg, to improve customer response time by 50% or maximise the return achieved on overnight cash balances. Such objectives should be clearly linked to the organisation's overall mission and business strategy.

48. **Organisational Benefits from IT and Effects on Individuals**

    If IT is properly managed in an organisation, it is likely to result in a number of important benefits, including:
    - Increased efficiency and effectiveness.
    - More stimulating and satisfying work for employees who can be freed from routine, less interesting tasks.
    - Increased autonomy, responsibility and feedback for individuals. Greater innovation. Better customer service.
    - Increased flexibility and the ability to respond to change and market requirements.
    - The highlighting of poor areas of work or employee performance.
    - Improved communication and relationships.
    - Better information and control over workflow and operations. Peaks, troughs, congestion and delays, for example, can be quickly identified.

49. Together the above benefits should lead to reduced staff absenteeism and labour turnover, increased productivity and a competitive advantage for the business. New technology can, however, bring problems. For example, it can cause stress if information cannot be easily accessed or is 'lost' instead of stored. Learning to cope with change and developing the skills to use new equipment can also prove stressful for some people. In addition, VDUs are potentially harmful to health, hence the European regulations introduced in 1993 to reduce the effects on individuals of prolonged use.

## Task 16.12

In large firms today, virtually every junior and middle manager has a personal computer on their desk. This is often networked locally with the machines of colleagues, frequently with a modem installed to enable public electronic mail service and databases to be accessed. This helps to facilitate immediate and better control of business operations. It is important however, to ensure that back-ups are made to prevent a possible disaster should any of the files get corrupted. If managers want information about stock, sales, production or budgets, it is now usually available to them on screen within seconds. If they require up-to-date information about share prices or exchange rates, this can be readily obtained through the Prestel database. The time saved from using such electronic technology can make managers more effective, freeing them to concentrate on planning and decision-making.

Read the above article and from it:

1. Explain the meaning of the following terms 'networked', 'modem' 'Prestel database', 'public electronic mail', 'electronic technology'.

2. Identify the benefits to a manager of using computer technology.

3. From the article and your own knowledge and experience, can you suggest any possible disadvantages of using new technology.

4. If possible, use a word processing program to type and print your own answer. Include a brief summary of the main advantages of using a word processor instead of a typewriter.

## Business Documents

50. The buying and selling of goods is called a transaction. This often involves considerable paperwork. Therefore, special **documents** are frequently used in order to make the process as quick and efficient as possible. They provide a record of each transaction and make communication easier. Each of these documents has a particular purpose in passing information between buyers and sellers and although they may vary from firm to firm, the basic principles are the same.

51. In a typical business transaction some or all of the following documents could be used:

    - **Enquiry.** When a business wishes to buy goods it will frequently make an enquiry to several firms asking them if they can supply the goods. It will also ask for details of the price, quality and delivery dates. This enquiry may take the form of a letter or a standard printed form.

    - **Quotation or tender.** In reply, the firms approached will send a letter, catalogue or price list. This will quote details of the price, delivery and any terms such as Trade and Cash Discount.

    - **Estimate.** Where no standard prices exist, a firm usually sends an estimate of how much the goods are likely to cost.

    - **Order.** When a firm decides to purchase goods, it will place an order.

    - **Acknowledgement of order.** Many firms will confirm an order by writing to say that it is receiving attention.

    - **Advice note.** This is sometimes sent to tell a customer that the goods are on the way. Goods sent in the suppliers own vehicle are usually accompanied by a **delivery note**. The customer can use this to check that they have received what was ordered.

    - **Consignment note.** This is used when a firm does not deliver goods itself but sends them by road or rail transport.

    - **Goods received note.** This may be used to provide a record of goods received. A copy will be kept by the warehouse or goods inward department with copies sent to notify the ordering department and to accounts for checking against the invoice.

    - **Invoice.** An invoice is sent by the supplier to the customer when goods have been bought on credit. It includes a description of the goods, the quantity supplied, the price charged and the total cost.

## 16. Business information systems

- **Pro forma invoice.** This is similar to an invoice but is not charged to a customer's account. They are often used when goods have already been paid for, or are sent on approval or sale or return. Mail order catalogue firms use this type of invoice.
- **Statement of account.** This is a request for payment of a customer's account and is usually sent monthly. It includes details of that month's invoices plus any credit or debit notes. The balance at the end is the amount owed.
- **Credit note.** A credit note is sent to a customer to correct an overcharge or to give a refund, for example, when faulty or damaged goods are returned. It has the effect of reducing the amount owed.
- **Debit note.** A debit note is sent to correct an undercharge, for example, when a mistake has been made on an invoice. It has the effect of increasing the amount owed.
- **Value Added Tax (VAT).** VAT is a tax by the government on sales and is usually added to the selling price of most goods and services. Therefore, a trader may well add VAT to an invoice thus increasing the cost of the goods purchased. The current rate of VAT is 17.5%.
- **Trade and Cash Discount.** Businesses buying goods from another firm for resale are usually given a percentage trade discount. This is deducted from invoices and may vary with the quantity bought. Cash discount may also be offered to encourage prompt payment.

### Task 16.13

1. Copy and complete the flow chart by filling in the words from the list below in the correct order.

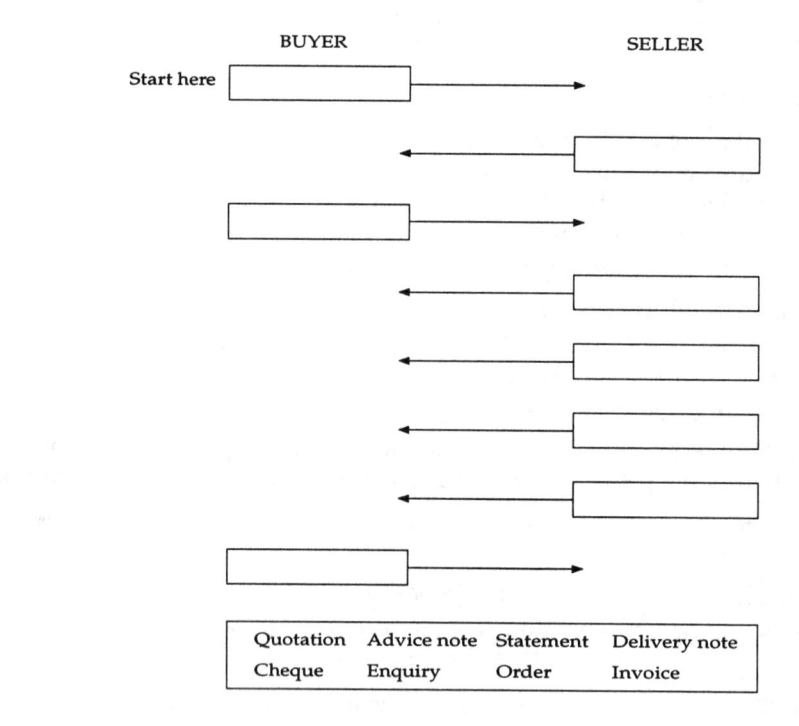

   BUYER → SELLER (flow chart with alternating boxes)

   | Quotation | Advice note | Statement | Delivery note |
   | Cheque | Enquiry | Order | Invoice |

2. Calculate the total cost of the following order. £1000 worth of goods delivered on 4th August 19..

   Terms are 20% trade discount and 5% within 30 days.

3. The firm had a debit note for £50 and a credit note for £125. What would be the balance shown on the August statement?

4. If the firm settled in full by 5th September, what would be the amount paid?

## Export Documents

52. It should be noted that some or all of the following additional documents may be used by firms which are involved in overseas trade. Export documents are necessary for the movement of goods, for invoicing the customer, for receiving payment for the goods delivered, and to satisfy various government regulations, both in the United Kingdom and overseas.

    - **The Bill of Lading.** This is used when goods are sent by sea. The shipping company provides a printed form which the cargo owner completes giving details of the:

        i)   Name of the ship and port of loading

        ii)  Description of the cargo and its destination

        iii) Charges payable

        At the destination, a copy of the Bill of Lading is presented by the importer to claim the goods at the dockside. It provides a 'document of title' (ie proof of ownership) which is important because the goods may have been sold whilst at sea.

    - **The Air Consignment Note or Air Waybill.** This is used as a receipt for goods sent by air. However, it is not a 'document of title' like a Bill of Lading.

    - **The Customs Declaration.** This is used for statistical purposes. It gives details of the type and value of the goods. This information is used in compiling the monthly trade figures.

    - **The Shipping Note.** This document is sent to the Port Authorities when goods are delivered to the docks. It gives details of the goods, name of ship and destination port, and acts as a docks receipt.

    - **The Certificate of Origin.** This provides evidence of where the goods were made. It is important because goods from some countries (for example outside the EU) will be subject to customs duties.

    - **The Insurance Certificate.** This provides proof that goods have been insured against loss or damage during transit.

    - **Consular Invoice.** Some countries require a copy of an export invoice which must be signed by the Consul in the importing country. This helps to speed up the customs procedures.

    - **Import Licence.** Often this is required from the importing government before the goods are allowed into the country. It can be used to enforce quotas.

    - **Export Licence.** This must be obtained before certain types of goods are allowed out of the country, for example, works of art or firearms.

53. Business documents are therefore a very important means of communication between an organisation and its customers. The developments in computer technology discussed earlier have made the issuing, monitoring and recording of such documents and transactions much quicker and easier for firms.

## Payment Documents

54. The most common methods used by businesses and individuals to pay for goods and services are cheques and cash. Other methods include standing orders, direct debits, bank giro and credit cards.

55. **Cheques**

    A cheque is simply a written instruction to a bank by a person with a current account to transfer money from their account to someone else's. The name of the company or the person to whom the money is to be paid is called the **payee**. The **drawee** is the name of the bank, whilst the customer writing and signing the cheque is called the **drawer**. Each cheque has a serial number, sorting code and the customer's account number to help the bank in identification and sorting.

    There is also a counterfoil on which to record the date and amount of the cheque and to whom it is made payable.

## 16. Business information systems

56. **Example of a cheque**

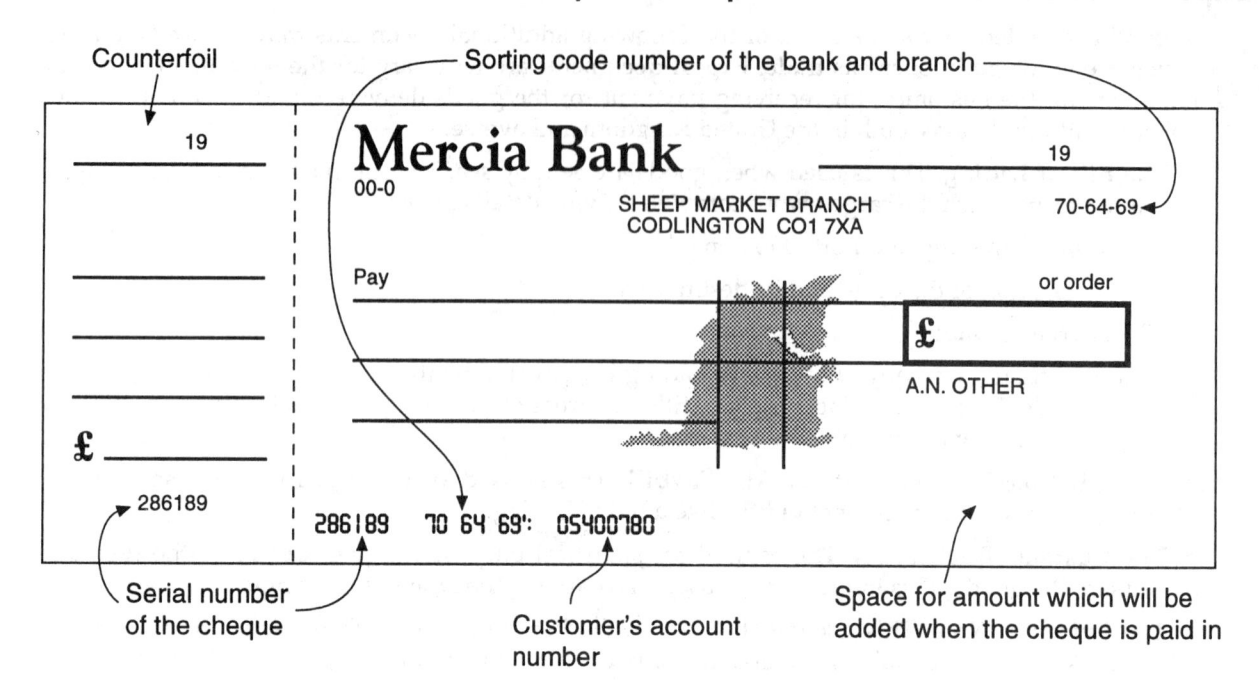

*Labels on the cheque diagram:*
- Counterfoil
- Sorting code number of the bank and branch
- Serial number of the cheque
- Customer's account number
- Space for amount which will be added when the cheque is paid in

*Cheque shows:* Mercia Bank, SHEEP MARKET BRANCH, CODLINGTON CO1 7XA, 00-0, 70-64-69, Pay ... or order, A.N. OTHER, 286189, 286189 70 64 69 05400780

57. An important feature of cheques is that they may be open or crossed. A crossed cheque is so called because it has two parallel lines across it. Crossing a cheque makes it much safer because it means that it must be paid into a bank account. Thus, if stolen it can be traced. On the other hand, an open cheque can be cashed over the counter. It will be paid to whoever presents it at the bank on which it is drawn.

58. **Cheque cards**

These are issued by banks to reliable customers, and guarantee that their cheques will not 'bounce', provided that:

- they are not made out for more than the limit printed on the card – usually £50 or £100
- they are signed in the presence of the payee and the signature matches that on the card
- the card number is written on the back.

59. Therefore, it is not possible to 'stop payment' on any cheque given with a cheque card. Most businesses, including shops, garages, hotels and restaurants, will not accept cheques unless they are backed by a cheque card.

60. **Example of a cheque card**

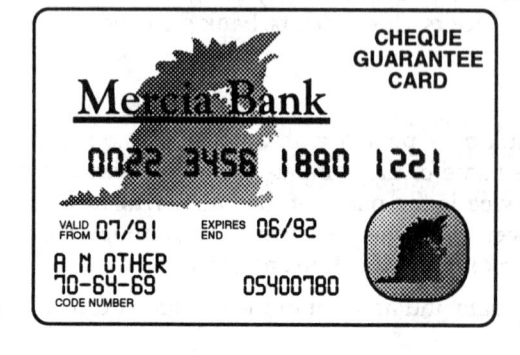

*Front:* CHEQUE GUARANTEE CARD, Mercia Bank, 0022 3456 1890 1221, VALID FROM 07/91, EXPIRES END 06/92, A N OTHER, 70-64-69 CODE NUMBER, 05400780

*Reverse:* SIGNATURE A N Other, Please keep this Cheque card in the wallet provided. If this card is found please hand it to a branch of the Mercia Bank plc., £50

Front         Reverse

328

> **Task 16.14**
>
> Working in groups of two or three, visit a local shopping area and complete the following. You will need to make rough notes which can be copied up later.
>
> 1. List the commercial banks in the area.
> 2. Obtain leaflets from at least one of them on the services offered.
> 3. Make a list of five or six services which you and/or a business might use. Briefly explain each one.
> 4. Name the two most common types of bank account and explain the differences between them.
> 5. Find out what you would need to do to open a bank account.

61. **Standing orders**

A customer can request their bank to make regular payments on their behalf. These are known as standing orders which the bank will carry out until they are cancelled. They are used for paying rates, mortgages, insurance premiumss, hire purchase instalments and other regular bills. If the amount to be paid by standing order changes, the customer must instruct the bank to pay the new amount.

62. **Direct debits**

These are similar to a standing order but, instead of instructing the bank to make regular payments on their behalf, the customer gives permission for a payee to withdraw money from their account. Direct debits are used when the amount is likely to vary – for example, trade union subscriptions which increase each year, or credit payments which might alter if the interest rate changes.

63. Standing orders and direct debits avoid the need to write cheques and mean that the account holder does not have to remember to make payments.

64. **Bank Giro or Credit Transfer**

The use of this service enables money to be transferred within the banking system. Payments can be transferred directly into the bank account of a payee at a branch of any bank anywhere in the UK.

A form is filled in for each payment, and the payer gives the bank a cheque or cash to cover the amount involved. Rent, gas, electricity and telephone bills are examples of payments which can be made by Bank Giro. People who do not have a bank account can also use the Giro service.

Bank Giro is most useful when several payments are made at the same time, because it is cheaper and easier than sending lots of cheques. By writing one cheque, a customer is able to have any number of payments transferred. For example, this is very often used when a company pays its employees wages directly into their bank accounts. It provides a very safe and simple method of payment with less chance of a mistake, since wage packets do not have to be made up.

65. **Petty Cash**

Businesses usually keep an amount of ready or 'petty cash' to pay immediately for small items of expenditure such as window cleaning, stamps, bus or taxi fares. The details are usually recorded on a petty cash voucher, to which receipts are attached, and entered in a petty cash book.

## 16. Business information systems

**66. Bank Giro Credit being used to pay an electricity Budget Account**

### 67. Credit cards

These are issued by most banks and some building societies eg ACCESS (Lloyds, Midland, NatWest, Royal Bank of Scotland) and VISA (Barclays, TSB, GiroBank, Leeds). Some are issued free of charge whilst others incur a small annual fee.

68. Credit cards enable the holder to buy goods or services at any shop, restaurant, garage etc which has joined the scheme. Each cardholder is given an overall personal limit, for example £750, which cannot be exceeded. Each organisation in the scheme is given a 'floor limit', for example £100, beyond which it cannot accept a credit card payment without first seeking authorisation from the credit card company. This is done either by telephoning the credit card company or by using a special machine with a direct computer link. The business receives payments from the credit card company. A small charge is made for this service (usually between 3% and 6%).

## Paying into a bank account

69. To pay into a bank account, a paying-in slip is completed and this is handed, together with the cheques, notes and coins, to the cashier. When the items have been checked, the cashier will stamp and initial the paying-in slip and the counterfoil (which acts as the customer's receipt).

70.

**Paying-in slip**

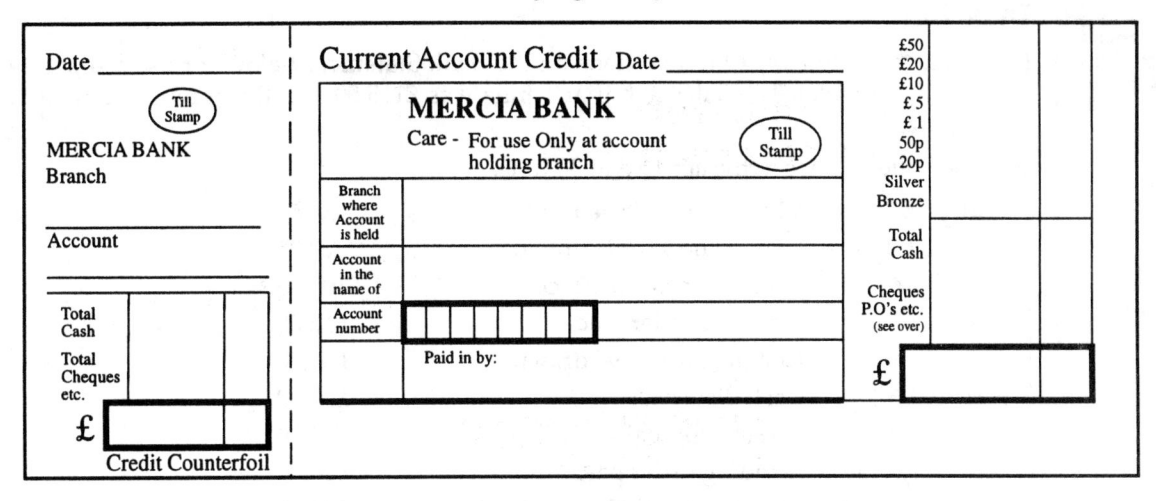

## Bank charges

71. Banks usually charge customers for the use of the current account. The charges will vary according to the number of cheques written, regular balance in the account and the other services which the bank provides. The charges are shown on a bank statement.

## The bank statement and bank reconciliation statement

72. The bank keeps a record of every payment made into and every withdrawal out of a current account. At regular intervals, or on request, it sends a bank statement to customers which lists this information. The statement can be checked against the entries on cheque and paying-in slip counterfoils, to reconcile any differences. These may be due to errors, cheques not yet presented or cleared or payments not yet entered in the cash book.

73. **Bank statement**

SPECIMEN ONLY Issued by Banking Information Service

TITLE OF ACCOUNT: D K ARMSTRONG
ACCOUNT NUMBER: 22963714
IN ACCOUNT WITH
BANK: MOSS BANK LIMITED
BRANCH: MANCHESTER
STATEMENT NUMBER: 4

| DATE | PARTICULARS | | PAYMENTS | RECEIPTS | BALANCE |
|---|---|---|---|---|---|
| | Balance Forward | | | | |
| 11 NOV | Balance forward | | | | 55.17 |
| | | 226352 | 0.54 | | |
| | | CD | 25.00 | | |
| 17 NOV | | 226351 | 6.86 | | 22.77 |
| | | 226354 | 8.93 | | |
| 26 NOV | | 226350 | 21.50 | | 7.66 DR |
| 30 NOV | CITY OF MANCHESTER 321206 422631 | BGC | | 216.97 | 209.31 |
| | | 226356 | 30.00 | | |
| 1 DEC | 2 A/C | SO | 75.00 | | 104.31 |
| | STANDARD LIFE MC 101062 X21 | DD | 15.19 | | |
| 2 DEC | 66917325116 | SO | 65.13 | | 23.99 |
| | | 226357 | 41.50 | | |
| | | 226355 | 60.00 | | |
| 10 DEC | BGC | | | 33.72 | 43.79 DR |
| | | 226358 | 1.89 | | |
| | | 226359 | 5.99 | | |
| 19 DEC | REMITTANCE | | | 63.10 | 11.43 DR |
| | CHS | | 2.84 | | |
| | INTEREST | | 3.12 | | 5.47 |

ABBREVIATIONS

BGC  Bank Giro Credit
DO   Direct Debit
CD   Cash Dispenser
DIV  Dividend
CHS  Charges
ADV  Separately Advised
O/D or DR  Overdrawn Balance
SO   Standing Order
TFR  Inter-Account Transfer

## 16. Business information systems

### Task 16.15

1. Enter the following 10 transactions on the Bank Statement below (or use a separate one if available). The balance b/f at 1 June was £115.50 and the account number is 07534217.

2. Show the balance in the account at 30 June.

| | | | |
|---|---|---|---|
| a) | 6.6.199 | Cheque no 117594 drawn | £4.50 |
| b) | 8.6.199 | Cheque no 117597 drawn | £22.95 |
| c) | 10.6.199 | Credit transfer received | £101.95 |
| d) | 11.6.199 | Standing order paid | £12.00 |
| e) | 14.6.199 | Cheque no 117596 drawn | £34.00 |
| f) | 14.6.199 | Cash dispenser | £50.00 |
| g) | 18.6.199 | Direct debit paid | £25.00 |
| h) | 19.6.199 | Standing order paid | £20.00 |
| i) | 22.6.199 | Cheque no 0907546 received | £13.90 |
| j) | 28.6.199 | Bank charges | £3.70 |

MINSTER BANK  
14 High Street  
ASHWORTH Notts

STATEMENT OF ACCOUNT

R Jones Esq  
A/c No ..................  
Date ..................

| DATE | DETAILS | DEBIT | CREDIT | BALANCE |
|---|---|---|---|---|
| | | | | |

### Payments in the future

74. In the future, banks will have less branches and make increasing use of post, telephones and automatic machines. Individuals and businesses will use cash and cheques to a lesser degree as more transactions are settled by credit cards and new methods of payment using computer technology, examples of which are CONNECT, SWITCH and home banking. Building societies will compete with banks by offering a wider range of financial services including current accounts with cheque books, personal loans and overdrafts.

75. CONNECT (Barclays, Lloyds) and SWITCH (Midland, National Westminster, Yorkshire) are systems of EFTPOS. Customers can use their Connect or Switch card to pay for purchases in shops and other organisations which are members of the scheme.

76. This is much quicker and simpler than using cheques because the cardholder's current account is debited immediately. Retailers have to pay a fixed charge for transactions accepted on a Switch or Connect card but their account is instantly credited with the money.

77. **Home banking** involves the use of a special device which provides a link via a television set with the bank's computer. A customer can key into the computer to make transfers direct from their account to pay bills or to obtain up-to-date information. Business customers can also use this service which is now offered by several organisations eg Nottingham Building Society, the Royal Bank of Scotland and Girobank.

## Security

78. Whatever methods are used to purchase and pay for goods and services, attention to security systems and procedures is essential to reduce the risk of theft and/or fraud.

79. Examples of measures which might be taken by a business include:

    - **Authorisation of orders.** Usually orders can only be signed by specific people in an organisation. Sometimes they must be signed by more than one person and depending on the value of the order may require authorisation by a senior manager.
    - **Checking procedures.** Deliveries, for example, are usually checked against the delivery note and likewise invoices checked against orders to ensure that the business only pays for what it receives.
    - **Authorised cheque signatories.** Only a small number of people in an organisation are usually allowed to sign cheques and the need for two signatories is quite common.
    - **Crossed cheques** are now the norm which helps to protect against fraud.
    - **Physical devices** such as video cameras, screens and safes are used in many organisations to reduce the risk of theft, particularly of cash and goods.
    - **Strict procedures** are usually laid down for the acceptance of cash, cheques and credit cards.

## Future Developments

80. As information technology becomes even more sophisticated, businesses will continue to make use of new and improved methods of communication. A few examples of how this might affect all of us in the future include:

    - All staff will find themselves working increasingly with **computer based new technology.**
    - More people will **work from home**, or from remote sites, contacting their offices and other businesses through view-data and other links.
    - **Videophone.** This is a facility being developed which links a small TV screen to a telephone to enable two people to see each other as they talk.
    - **Shopping from home** using Prestel could become quite common. It will soon be possible to **talk to computers** instead of operating them by keying in information.
    - The use of **electronic mail** systems like Prestel, Datel and Fax could develop so that they are used not just by businesses but by all of us. This might eventually result in newspapers and postal services being replaced by viewdata systems.

## Open Systems

81. Currently, one of the biggest problems of IT is the incompatibility of different manufacturers' products. The growth, however, of IT generally and the development of large international markets like the European Union has lead to pressure on manufacturers to develop products to homogeneous standards so that systems and applications work more freely across trading and operational barriers. In 1992, the DTI introduced a 3 year Open Systems Technology Transfer programme to help progress what is certain to be one of the most significant developments in recent years and likely to have considerable impact on all business in the future.

82. The greater IT compatibility from the development of 'Open Systems' will result in a number of important benefits for organisations including:
    - the freedom to choose suppliers and products which best suit the needs of the business.
    - better value for money from buying the most appropriate products at more competitive prices in the first place.
    - the reduction of development and operational costs.
    - easier handling and exchange of information both within and between organisations thus improving the overall efficiency of business operations.

## Barriers to Effective Communication

83. No matter how good the communication system in an organisation is, unfortunately barriers can and do often occur. This may be caused by a number of factors which can usually be summarised as being due to physical barriers, system design faults or attitudinal barriers.

84. **Physical barriers** are often due to the nature of the environment. Thus, for example, the natural barrier which exists, if staff are located in different buildings or on different sites. Likewise, poor or outdated equipment, particularly the failure of management to introduce new technology, may also cause problems. Staff shortages are another factor which frequently causes communication difficulties for an organisation. Whilst distractions like background noise, poor lighting or an environment which is too hot or cold can all affect people's morale and concentration, which in turn interfere with effective communication.

85. **System design faults** refer to problems with the structures or systems in place in an organisation. Examples might include an organisational structure which is unclear and therefore makes it confusing to know who to communicate with. Other examples could be inefficient or inappropriate information systems, a lack of supervision or training, and a lack of clarity in roles and responsibilities which can lead to staff being uncertain about what is expected of them.

86. **Attitudinal barriers** come about as a result of problems with staff in an organisation. These may be brought about, for example, by such factors as poor management, lack of consultation with employees, personality conflicts which can result in people delaying or refusing to communicate, the personal attitudes of individual employees which may be due to lack of motivation or dissatisfaction at work, brought about by insufficient training to enable them to carry out particular tasks, or just resistance to change due to entrenched attitudes and ideas.

87. Other common barriers to effective communication include:
    - **psychological factors** such as people's state of mind. We all tend to feel happier and more receptive to information when the sun shines. Equally, if someone has personal problems like worries about their health or marriage, then this will probably affect them.
    - **different languages** and cultures represent a national barrier which is particularly important for organisations involved in overseas business.
    - **individual linguistic ability** is also important. The use of difficult or inappropriate words in communication can prevent people from understanding the message, particularly if it is complicated.
    - **poorly explained** or misunderstood messages can also result in confusion. We can all think of situations where we have listened to something explained which we just could not grasp.
    - **physiological barriers** may result from individuals' personal discomfort, caused, for example, by ill health, poor eye sight or hearing difficulties.
    - **presentation** of information is also important to aid understanding as you will see in Chapter 18.

### Task 16.16
1. Identify the main barriers to communication in your place of work or study.
2. Consider the type of problems which they cause and whether or not you feel they can be easily solved with minimum expenditure.

## Summary

88. a) Communication may be verbal, non-verbal, formal or informal and may take place inside an organisation (internal) or between organisations (external).

   b) Effective communication is essential if a firm is to be successful. Staff need clear instructions whilst customers and other business contacts require a flow of information.

   c) The main verbal (spoken) methods of communication are personal contact with people either face to face, in interviews, in meetings or by telephone. The 'grapevine', working lunches and social events are others.

   d) The main non-verbal (written) methods of communication include memos, minutes, notices, staff bulletins, house journals and reports. Visual communication includes the use of charts and diagrams.

   e) Letters are not usually sent within an organisation but are the main method of external communication. The telephone, other telecommunications and postal services are also important, as are the various forms of advertising and sales promotion.

   f) The telephone is the main method of telecommunication whilst other BT services include telex, telemessages, FAX and contravision.

   g) Teletex is provided by Ceefax and Teletex whilst Prestel and Datel are forms of viewdata.

   h) Other internal communication equipment includes telephone switchboards and answering machines, intercoms, paging and public address systems.

   i) Increasingly firms are now using computers for preparing and storing (filing) data.

   j) Important business software includes databases, spreadsheets, desk top publishing, accounting and personnel packages.

   k) Word processing is one major application of computer technology in offices.

   l) To gain maximum benefit from IT it must be properly managed as an integral part of a businesses functions.

   m) In a typical business transaction, a range of special documents are used to make it as quick and effective as possible.

   n) Goods and services may be paid for in many ways including cash, cheques, standing order, direct debit, bank giro, credit card and EFTPOS.

   o) A bank statement is sent to customers at regular intervals giving details of all payments into and out of their bank account.

   n) Physical barriers, attitudual barriers and system design faults can all lead to breakdowns in communications.

## Review questions *(answers can be found in the paragraphs indicated)*

1. Briefly define 'communication'. (3)
2. Explain the need for effective communication in business. (6-7)
3. List the main verbal and non-verbal methods of internal communication. (5, 10-19)
4. What information is given in an Agenda? (11,13)
5. Why are minutes taken in a meeting? (15,16)
6. Give 2 examples of visual means of communication (19)
7. List 4 main methods of external business communication (20-30)

## 16. Business information systems

8. Briefly describe why a facsimile transmission service is important in business. (30)
9. How might contravision help an international company? (31-32)
10. What are Ceefax and Oracle examples of? (33)
11. Explain why Prestel is described as 'inter-active'. (33)
12. Briefly explain Datel. (33)
13. How can a telephone answering machine assist a business? (34)
14. Distinguish between computer hardware and software. (38,39)
15. Explain the main uses of word processing and at least 3 other business software programs. (39-43)
16. Outline the main features of the Data Protection Act. (44-45)
17. Describe the potential impact of IT on a business and the benefits which open systems could bring. (46,47,55,56)
18. What benefits can a business gain from the effective management of its IT systems? (47)
19. Briefly describe all the business documents which would be passed between a manufacturer (or wholesaler) buying goods on credit from the time the order is placed, to when the account is settled. (50-52)
20. Outline the main methods of payment which are likely to be used in a business. (54-77)
21. How can a business reduce the risks involved in its buying and selling procedures? (78-79)
22. Outline the main barriers to communication in an organisation (57-61)

*Asterisks indicate those questions for which there are answers in Outline Answers (page 439)*

### Essay-style questions

1.* 'Information Technology is an integral part of business today, but frequently it fails to achieve the expected results'.

   Explain what you understand by this statement. What could a firm faced with this situation do to improve matters?

2. Discuss the view that effective communication is the key element in a successful business.

3. Reply, in detail, to the following memo from the Office Manager of a small manufacturing company located on one site in the North of England. Although small, it is currently investigating the possibility of exporting to Europe and the USA.

---

### MEMO

**To:** R Chapman  **Date:** 19/11/9–
**From:** J Brown  **Subject:** Telecommunications

I have recently been reading an article on telecommunications which seemed to contain a lot of 'jargon'. Can you please find out the meaning of the following terms, and the potential benefits to the company.

Contravision, viewdata systems and facsimile transmission.

Do you think we should give serious consideration to introducing or using any of them?

---

## Short answer (A level)

1.* 'What's in a Name'

# What's in a name?

*by Adrian Day of Siegel & Gale, London, corporate identity and communications consultants*

■ A British household name can be an unknown quantity across the Channel; equally, would you buy an insurance policy from Munchener Lebensversicherung and what would German consumers make of the National Westminster Bank? As Europe opens its doors for business these questions become increasingly important.

For the consumer, a yet wider choice of broadly similar products is a daunting prospect and very often, selection is based on our perception of the organisation. For companies with a strong corporate identity, such as Body Shop or BMW, the company name is an essential part of this identity. However, many names which are strong and memorable in the home market may actually mislead, confuse or even alienate foreign audiences.

For example, a corporate name which is unique and distinctive in a national market may already be in use in another European country. Société Générale, for instance, is Belgium's largest conglomerate. But how is the perception of its business affected by the French bank of exactly the same name? The situation is further confused by the Swiss Société Générale and the Italian organisation Generali.

### Initials

Using initials rather than names may seem like a good way to overcome some of these problems. Customers can, however, find meaningless letters equally confusing. Although a few notable exceptions like IBM, BMW and ICI have made a success of initials, this has been achieved only through heavy exposure over a very lengthy period.

It is difficult and expensive to build awareness for fabricated company names such as Matra or Cegelec as neither have any obvious meaning. By contrast, real words, or combinations of real words such as Eurotunnel and Aerospatiale, give a clear impression of the organisation's business activities.

### The ideal name

The most effective European names are those which are easy to spell and pronounce and give an immediate impression of what the company does. Some companies have recognised and addressed this problem. Turkey's leading corporate bank was called Uluslararasi Interbank; with the pan-European audience in mind, it has rationalised its name to Interbank.

The new name has many of the features of the 'ideal' corporate name for a pan-European company. It is short, unique, memorable, free of national associations and pronounceable in all major European languages.

*Reproduced from DTI's quarterly publication 'Single Market News' Autumn 1992.*

    a) From the above article, identify, with examples, some potential barriers to communication.

    b) What action would you advise a company to take to overcome these barriers

2.* In what circumstances are each of the following documents used in business?

    a) Pro-forma invoice

    b) Credit note

    c) Statement of Account

    d) Estimate

    e) Bill of Lading

3. **COMPUTER LISTS 'MAY BREAK LAW'**

Thousands of computer users could be breaking the law without knowing it, a court was told. Because there seems to be a conception that if you use computers in a small way or the data you hold is not particularly sensitive, there is no need to register – but this is not the case. The warning came after a hotel boss was fined £100 for keeping details of names, addresses and bill details on a computer without being registered under the Data Protection Act

The article refers to the Data Protection Act.

    a) Why do businesses keep data on computer?

    b) Outline its main provisions

    c) Why is such legislation needed?

## 16. Business information systems

## Multiple choice/completion

1.* A database is
   a) A store of useful information
   b) A centre for sending telephone messages
   c) A computer programme with figures in rows and columns
   d) A record of a firm's turnover

2.* Which of the following documents has the sole aim of obtaining payment from a debtor?
   a) Credit note
   b) Debit note
   c) Invoice
   d) Statement of Account

3.* A 'Thomson Directory' is:
   a) Another name for a firm's Accounts Ledger
   b) A book listing all UK limited companies
   c) A local telephone directory
   d) A directory in which local businesses advertise

4.* An Agenda for a meeting is:
   a) A record of what takes place
   b) A statement of a company's policy
   c) A director's report
   d) A list of items for discussion

5. Trade discount is a discount given to which of the following?
   a) Customers who can pay cash for their goods
   b) Most customers who request it
   c) A firm's customers who are also in business
   d) Business customers who are involved in foreign trade.

6. Which of the following is a formal method of communication?
   a) Social gatherings
   b) House magazine
   c) Lunchtime discussions
   d) Team Briefing

*In each of the following questions, one or more of the response(s) is/are correct. Choose the appropriate letter which indicates the correct version.*

   A  if 1 only is correct
   B  if 3 only is correct
   C  if 1 and 2 only are correct
   D  if 1, 2 and 3 are correct

7. The 1984 Data Protection Act states that computerised data
   1  Must be destroyed when no longer needed.
   2. Can only be held for payroll purposes
   3. Should be sent to the Data Protection Registrar

8. Which of the following is/are always used by firms involved in export business?
   1. Certificate of origin
   2. Invoice
   3. Export licence

## Assignment

Consider, if possible by practical research, how each of the following types of organisation have been affected by developments in communication technology – Banks – Supermarkets – Police – Schools/Colleges.

Present your findings in a word processed report.

1. Identify the main internal and external methods of communication in each.
2. Identify the main applications of IT in each.
3. Suggest what you think were the main objectives behind each application.
4. Discuss how each application has affected:
    i) the organisation as a whole
    ii) its employees
    iii) its suppliers and
    iv) its customers/clients
5. Indentify the effects of the Data Protection Act on the use of and security of computer processed information in any 2 of the organisations.
6. Compare and contrast the different uses of IT in any 2 of the above types of organisation. Include a summary of the main advantages and disadvantages found.

# 17. Innovation and Change

In Chapter 3 we used the PEST analysis to consider the external influences which can affect the success or failure of organisations and therefore need to be considered in strategic planning. This chapter is about the introduction and management of innovation and change in organisations and covers:

* Concept of Change
* Internal Forces
* External Forces
* Challenge of Change
* Barriers to Change
* Conflict
* Resistance to Change
* Managing Change
* Innovation
* Research and Development
* Change – Opportunity or Threat
* Predicting Change
* Changing Lifestyles
* Environmental Change
* Environmental Strategies
* Recycling
* Employment and Change
* Community Impact

## Concept of Change

1. We live in a dynamic, exciting world where change is always taking place and affects both individuals and organisations. As individuals, we regularly experience change in our everyday lives as just a few examples help to illustrate. In recent years, our lives have been changed by the impact of the European Community and technological developments such as computers, satellite communications and lasers, whilst in the future, Sunday trading and the Channel Tunnel are likely to have dramatic effects on us.

2. Our concern, however, is with the impact of change on business organisations. In order to survive and prosper in a competitive and rapidly changing environment, organisations also need to change. This may be brought about by many factors which may be internal or external to the organisation.

3. **Internal Change** may include:
   * **new products or services** which require changes in order to introduce them.
   * **management** changes, due perhaps to a merger, take-over or the appointment of new staff. This may affect the management style and culture of the organisation.
   * **quality assurance** systems which are becoming increasingly important in organisations in order to meet changing customer expectations. This puts new demands on workers to achieve the required standards.
   * **productivity and profitability** improvements which often require changes in systems or procedures in order to control or reduce costs and/or increase output.
   * **customer service** is now more crucial than ever for organisations in competitive markets because they can only survive and prosper if they satisfy consumers. The impact of change on our lifestyles means that consumers now have higher expectations of the level of service and satisfaction from what they buy.

### Task 17.1
1. In the organisation in which you work or study or one well known to you, identify any changes which have taken place during the past 12 months.
2. Comment on how, if at all, they have affected you.

5. **External Change** may include:
   * **political** factors including legislation or other government measures. Organisations are forced to change in order to meet, for example, health and safety, environmental or consumer protection requirements.

- **economic** factors such as changes in levels of unemployment and interest rates which can have a major impact on demand.
- **social** factors including changes in lifestyles and environmental issues which organisations must respond to if they are not to lose out to competitors.
- **technological** progress such as word processing in the office or robots in the factory can change working materials, methods and practices.
- **competition** and changes in consumer tastes and demand all impact on business organisations, making change necessary in order to respond.

## Challenge of Change

6. To meet these challenges of change in a flexible and responsive way requires organisations to redefine their objectives, develop and invest in new products and services and introduce new systems and techniques of production and marketing. Change can therefore be expensive, particularly where it involves the cost of buying and installing new technology and training staff to use it.

7. Change will inevitably have a major impact on an organisation's workforce which can cause problems for management. Whilst change is necessary for progress and can often bring new life and vitality into an organisation, it is often feared, frequently resisted and therefore also represents a potential source of conflict.

### Task 17.2

#### FORD LOOK EAST

In response to the global success of companies such as Hitachi, Nissan and Sanyo, UK companies are beginning to show an increasing interest in Japanese management practices.

American owned Ford is actually introducing Japanese-style working in a drive for efficiency.

Employees will in future work in assembly line groups, eat in classless cafeterias and be encouraged to join in daily keep-fit workouts.

It is hoped that this will increase output, reduce costs, including those for supervision, and also help to overcome problems of boredom and job dissatisfaction. The move comes as part of a major cost-cutting reorganisation at the company's 14 British plants, which employ 38,000 people.

To keep the production lines moving, the multi-skilled work groups have already taken over repairs from maintenance staff at Dagenham, Essex, and Halewood, Merseyside. Rising unemployment and Conservative government legislation have weakened the trade union movement, making the fear of long strikes a thing of the past. Stockpiles of large parts have therefore been run down and suppliers are being signed up on ten-year rather than one-year contracts.

With the closure of executive and management dining rooms, even Ford UK chairman Ian McAllister now must queue in a self-service cafeteria with the rest of the staff.

Rover have already followed the lead of Sunderland-based Nissan by adopting Japanese- style work practices.

The following questions are based on the above information.
1. Why have Ford introduced Japanese working practices?
2. What changes will it bring for their employees?
3. What potential benefits will it produce?
4. Identify the type of production method which Ford has introduced.
5. Comment on the environmental conditions which helped to bring about the need for and implementation of the new working methods.

## Barriers to Change

8. Most individuals and groups are basically fairly traditional and conservative in their outlook and therefore do not generally welcome change. There are various reasons for this which can broadly be defined as behavioural, psychological and social and economic.

9. **Behavioural factors** relate to people's reactions to physical routines, for example:
   - **individuals become set in their ways** and used to established patterns and conventions.
   - **training may have to be undertaken** to adjust to new situations. Staff may have new tasks or jobs which they have to learn.

10. **Psychological factors** are those which affect the way people feel about their jobs, for example:
    - **even minor change can be seen as threatening** and produce stress and frustration. This is because its effects are generally unknown, uncertain and unpredictable. Therefore, people often fear that change will mean more work, less jobs or reduced job security.
    - **innovation often takes place so rapidly** that individuals feel unable to cope and adjust to new events. Older workers in particular may be psychologically incapable of accepting radical change.
    - **status, authority and power are often overturned.** Reorganisations, for example may result in managers being redeployed in less senior posts, leading to loss of self-esteem.

11. **Social and economic** factors include the relationships with other workers and fear of unemployment, for example:
    - **social structures and relationships may be disrupted** if redundancies, reorganisations or relocations take place.
    - **the consequences may be quite devastating** both for individuals and the local community, particularly if change leads to job losses.

> **Task 17.3**
>
> Referring back to Task 17.1, discuss the likely behavioural, psychological, social and economic effects of the changes which you identified.

## Conflict

12. Conflict is possible in all walks of like whether it be disagreements between friends, parents, relatives or workmates, a complaint about a faulty product or service or at the extreme, war between nations. The potential for conflict in organisations comes about because they consist of various 'stakeholders' – namely owners, managers, employees and society – each of which has a number of different objectives which are not always compatible with each other.

13. **Owners** including shareholders in a business are interested in protecting and increasing the value of their investment, and the return in the form of profits.

14. **Managers** have a responsibility to run the business efficiently and to ensure its survival, growth and profitability. This may lead to conflict with shareholders who may want higher dividends rather than retained profits and employees who want higher wages.

15. **Employees** are interested in job security, better wages, holidays and working conditions and improved promotion prospects which may lead to conflict with management trying to control costs and increase efficiency.

16. **Consumers and society** where the interests may be in consumer satisfaction from lower prices and/or better quality products. Whilst higher standards of living require increased productivity and economic growth. But other factors are also important such as a better environment, less pollution, safer products and equal opportunities.

17. Other sources of conflict may result from:
    - Proposed change
    - Breakdowns in communication
    - Poor organisation or
    - Bad management

18. Whilst some conflict in an organisation may be a good thing because it can lead to the generation of new ideas, serious or prolonged conflict is likely to be damaging and lead to inefficiency. Therefore conflict must be managed in order to achieve consensus, that is, a broad agreement which minimises the problem and enables the organisation to function effectively.

### Task 17.4

In the organisation in which you work or study:
1. Identify the 'stakeholders'.
2. Discuss any potential sources of conflict between them.

## Resistance to Change

19. The fear of change can bring about considerable resistance in organisations, even though employees may actually recognise the need for change. This resistance can result in conflict which can be shown in a number of different ways, in particular industrial action and low morale.

20. **Industrial action** may include working-to-rule, strikes, go-slows or essentially refusing to accept new working practices. Even if it does not lead to industrial action, discontented employees are likely to be more disagreeable and may clash with management or even each other, making control and smooth operation difficult.

21. **Low morale** can lead to increased labour turnover, low productivity and a general feeling of dissatisfaction amongst staff. Consequently, customers may suffer due to shortages, inefficiency and poor service or reduced quality, all of which could ultimately lead to lost business.

### Task 17.5

**PLASTIC PAY STOP**

Leading retailers may stop accepting debit and credit cards as banks threaten to charge more for processing transactions.

They have warned that they may insist on shoppers paying with cash or cheques unless the banks back down.

Tesco said yesterday it was 'very close' to refusing to accept cards, Sainsbury's said it was 'considering what steps to take' and W H Smith said action was being considered. The Office of Fair Trading confirmed that it was investigating complaints from retailers about the increases in card fees. The British Retail Consortium says stores will either have to stop accepting plastic, absorb the extra costs or pass them on to customers at a time when they are struggling to attract more shoppers.

Stores say they have invested millions of pounds in the new technology needed to accept cards because the banks assured them plastic payments would be no dearer to process than cheques. But planned increases could make the handling charges twice as expensive. The banks say they have been operating the service at a loss and need to put up their charges simply to cover costs.

They point out stores have also benefited from the new technology, which means guaranteed payments, reduced paperwork and is popular with shoppers.

continued...

### Task 17.5 continued

### TEACHERS BOYCOTT

Teachers fed up with too much testing and not enough teaching could wreck the government's new testing arrangements.

The 180,000-strong National Union of Teachers will shortly announce the results of voting on a boycott of this summer's English tests for 14 year olds.

Whilst leaders of the 127,000-member NASUWT will decide soon whether to ballot members on a boycott of national curriculum tests.

NAS-UWT general secretary Nigel de Gruchy said pupils faced tests at 7, 11, 14 and 16, plus the GCSE which was 'far too many' and overloaded teachers with work. The Government's determined to press ahead with nationwide testing of pupils despite criticism of a lack of preparation time and insufficient classroom trials.

The two articles illustrate some of the problems associated with change. In each situation:

1. Identify the nature of the change(s) and the main reason(s) for it being resisted.
2. Explain how the resistance is being demonstrated.
3. Comment on whether you feel that the proposed change(s) is a 'good thing' and whether or not it should be implemented.

## Managing Change

22. The fear of change can be exacerbated by:
    - poor communication which leads to ill-informed rumour and gossip and
    - authoritarian management with formal hierarchical chains of command which people often find intimidating. Therefore in order to successfully implement change, managers need to be aware of the reasons for any likely opposition and develop a strategy to overcome them.

23. The strategy should include:
    - **identifying the likely effects** of change and planning for it well in advance.
    - **adapting a flexible, democratic management style** even though this may be within a formal organisation structure, in order to create a climate where change is easier to achieve.
    - **establishing genuine consultation and participation** in advance of impending change and agreeing a programme for introduction. Trade unions should be involved where appropriate and **negotiation** of change in return for incentives such as more pay, holidays or conditions may sometimes be necessary.
    - **selling the benefits** of change, for example, better working conditions, a more profitable and therefore financially sound and secure business and the opportunity to use new technologically advanced equipment.
    - **practical support** for staff including, for example, training or re-training, and new work or counselling for those being made redundant or asked to take early retirement.

24. Even following the above strategy, change may still take time to implement fully but nonetheless should be achievable with minimum disruption and still retaining staff morale. The alternative strategy of simply 'pushing' change on people often with threats and coercion is likely to prove to be self-defeating and could have disastrous consequences for the organisation.

*17. Innovation and change*

> **Task 17.6**
>
> ### GRANADA STAFF AXED
>
> In December 1992, Granada announced a restructuring plan which included a reduction in its 1,300 workforce by approximately 200 and tried to tempt staff with voluntary redundancy cash packages.
>
> After consultation with unions, most of this reduction (120) was achieved through this and by the integration of management responsibilities. But unfortunately, 80 people had to be made redundant.
>
> Staff cutbacks were across the board and had come about because of a need to tighten management structures and preserve the company's programme-making base. Granada's chief executive Charles Allen had warned staff earlier that the rules were about to change as the company moved from monopoly to competition. The redundancy package on offer to those who volunteered also applied to those made redundant.
>
> Counselling and a job-search programme was made available to those staff who had been affected.
>
> In December the Granada group, which includes the Manchester-based TV company, announced a 129 per cent rise in profits to £130m.
>
> Answer the following based on the above case study.
> 1. Why did Granada need to make 200 staff redundant?
> 2. How were most of the redundancies achieved?
> 3. Comment on how the company managed the change.

## Innovation

25. The practical refinement and development of an original invention into a usable technique or product, is called innovation. It can be a lengthy and expensive process but is nonetheless an important means of improving an organisation's market performance, for example, by reducing costs or improving quality. Innovation is also a key contributor to a nation's economic growth. Consider, for example, the success of Japan through innovation in its electrical and photographic consumer products such as videos, camcorders, computers and cameras.

> **Task 17.7**
>
> Consider the following products in terms of your own knowledge and experience of innovation. Take each in turn and discuss the extent to which they have changed over the past 10-20 years.
> 1. Breakfast cereals
> 2. Cars
> 3. Building materials
> 4. Packaging materials for food and drink
> 5. Computers.

## Research and Development (R&D)

26. An important factor in bringing about innovation and change is that of research and development (R&D). The extent to which organisations develop and introduce new and improved products, production processes and distribution techniques, often depends upon the level of investment in pure and applied scientific research.

27. **Pure research** is often undertaken by Universities and government agencies (eg Medical Research Council, Economic & Social Research Council) to add to the general level of scientific knowledge and understanding. The important point is that it often has no practical application and therefore no

## 17. Innovation and change

financial return is expected from the investment. Despite this, business organisations often contribute to University research and also undertake some pure research themselves in their own laboratories.

28. **Applied research** on the other hand is concerned with developments which should have some commercial value. Therefore, it is used to meet particular needs and/or to share problems. As such it should at the very least pay for itself over a period of time. If successful, a major breakthrough can very quickly change the whole nature of a business. Radical innovations may result in lower manufacturing and distribution costs and thus either increase profits and/or reduce the price to the consumer. Whilst new or improved products may lead to an increase in market share.

29.

**Savings from Innovation**

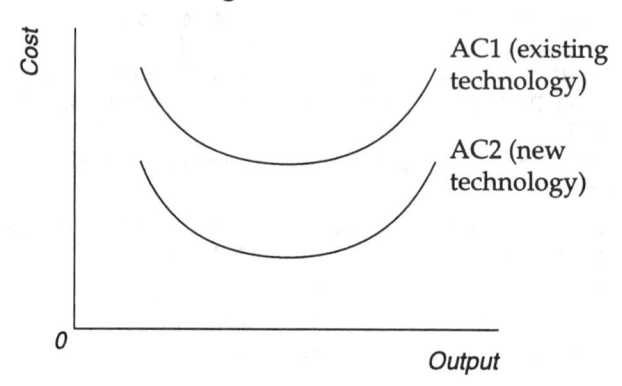

(Graph showing two U-shaped average cost curves: AC1 (existing technology) above AC2 (new technology), with Cost on vertical axis and Output on horizontal axis)

---

### Task 17.8

#### NO MORE SPECS

Wearing glasses or contact lenses could become obsolete for anyone under 45 within ten years, say doctors.

Research into eye surgery in Britain is advancing so fast that it will soon be possible to use lasers to treat millions suffering from vision defects.

Surgeons are achieving a 95 per cent success rate with laser surgery to correct short-sightedness (myopia) and are confident they will be able to cure long-sightedness (hyperopia).

Surgery normally costs around £1,000 an eye and is available at some private clinics. Clinical trials on more advanced techniques to treat astigmatism are described as 'extremely promising'.

Around 25 million Britons currently wear glasses. About three million have contact lenses. An estimated 12 million people suffer from myopia and nine million from astigmatism.

---

#### SECRET TAG THAT COULD COST SHOPLIFTERS £1BN

A revolutionary anti-theft tag could save retailers £1 billion a year, it is claimed. The slim magnetic strips – described as a 'quantum leap' in security technology – can be inserted into packaging or hidden behind bar codes on any goods, including basic food items. They are automatically deactivated as goods are paid for at the checkout. The tags, developed by the Centre for the Exploitation of Science and Technology, cannot be detected by shoplifters.

A spokesman for the Co-operative Wholesale Society, which plans to use them in a pilot scheme in Slough said: 'Our security people estimate these could deter 75 per cent of shoplifting offences.'

---

Read the articles and from them:
1. Identify the benefits from investing in research.
2. Explain who will gain most from the research and why.

30. Large organisations are often better able to afford to invest in R&D because their monopoly profits provide the necessary resources. Often they will have a specialist R&D department run by a senior manager. Although the amount of investment will depend upon an organisation's objectives and strategy, it should be related to profit forecasts resulting from the commercial potential if successful. Pharmaceutical companies, for example, often spend millions of pounds to develop new drugs.

31. In Britain, the highest level of R&D spending in relation to their gross output takes place in the high-technology manufacturing industries of aerospace, chemicals, instrument engineering and electrical and electronic engineering. The latter includes office machinery, telecommunications and data processing equipment.

32. **Development**

    Successful research will lead to the need for development into a practical application. In the case of new or improved products, organisations will clearly want to launch them as quickly as possible in order to give them a competitive edge. The time scale involved will depend upon the type of product, the costs involved and the amount of testing necessary for health and safety purposes. New drugs, for example, often have to be tested over several years to ensure that they do not have any harmful side effects.

33. **Problems of R&D**

    The following factors are important for organisations which invest in R&D.
    - **provision of finance** which will depend upon the type of product(s), the size of the organisation and its financial strength and the rate of technological change in the industry concerned.
    - **budgetary control** to try to ensure that resources are not wasted. But unfortunately there is no direct correlation between expenditure and results because the time required and eventual outcomes are usually unpredictable.
    - **personal involvement** and interest of researchers which is often so intense that it makes control and direction to a commercial end difficult.
    - **prioritising** may be difficult where a number of projects are being undertaken at the same time and the resources for some must be stopped or reduced.
    - **management decisions** about the potential of any particular project, whether to continue it and for how long, or alternatively to stop it, even though considerable resources may have already been invested.

### Task 17.9

Read the following comment by a manager on his approach to change.
1. From it, draw up a possible checklist of factors which may be of help to other managers facing the challenges of change.
2. Give your views on this approach to change and mention any other factors which you feel could be usefully added to the checklist.

> 'We operate in the fast moving world of telecommunications where the management of change is critical. Apart from our own extensive R&D, I find reading the main trade journals helps me to keep abreast of the latest thinking and developments. I also regularly attend seminars and exhibitions which I regard as important to find out about the latest products and processes on the market. The company invests heavily in staff training which helps to change attitudes and remove some of the fears. However, I think sometimes that it is important to experiment and innovate even if there's a slight risk of failure and also to be prepared to discard relatively young systems and equipment if they become obsolete. After a while it actually becomes a way of life to look at products, services, routines and systems, in fact everything we do, with a critical eye'.

## Change – Opportunity or Threat

34. We have seen that an organisation needs to plan to meet the challenges of change within its environment. Management must be alert to the unexpected so that it can take advantage of the opportunities which change offers and minimise any potential threats.

*17. Innovation and change*

35. The availability of new technology, for example, or withdrawal of a competitor from the market might represent opportunities. On the other hand, the introduction of new technology or new products by competitors may represent threats.

## Predicting Change

36. It is important if organisations are to take full advantage of the opportunities offered by change that managers are able to anticipate when it is likely to take place and plan to meet it. Trends need to be identified and analysed and acted upon.

37. Management must be alert to the unexpected so that it can take advantage of the opportunities which change offers and minimise any potential threats. Once the trends are identified, decisions must be made and plans adjusted accordingly in order to respond effectively. This is likely to impact on all business functions. Personnel, for example, will need to develop a revised manpower plan, whilst finance and production will need to consider future investment needs.

38. If firms do not change in order to respond to market needs, then they are likely to go out of business. Consequently, there are large numbers of both individual bankruptcies and company liquidations every year.

---

**Task 17.10**

### BUSINESS FAILURES ROCKET

Business failures in England and Wales in 1992 reached their highest level since the recession started more than 3 years ago. Over 63,000 businesses collapsed, a rate of over 100 a day and an increase of 44% on 1991. Larger companies were also badly hit – over 24,000 failing – an average 67 a day, a 12% increase. DTI figures show that there were nearly 40,000 bankruptcies of firms run by one person or a partnership in 1992. But although 6,028 businesses collapsed in the 3 months to the end of December, this was substantially less than the record number of 6,699 in the previous quarter. Falling markets and bad debts, however, means that 1 in 38 companies was still going to the wall and only 1 in 5 was working to full capacity

### MANAGEMENT BUYOUT

BP Chemicals has sold its Croydon-based foams business to its management in a £20 million deal backed by 3i, the investment capital group, Prudential Venture Managers and Barclays Bank. The new company, Zoetfoams, employs some 158 people

### MORE BUY-OUTS

The first quarter of 1992 saw the second highest start to a year in the UK management buy-out market, according to accountants KPMG Peat Marwick. There were 12 large MBOs totalling £570m Only the record year of 1989 was higher in terms of total funds raised for MBOs over £10m.

### BUTE BUYOUT

A Management buyout of the UK's largest dedicated flexible printed circuit manufacturer will secure 80 jobs on the isle of Bute and may create another 30 over the next three years. Graseby Flexible Technology, based in Rothesay, is returning to local ownership in a £1.4m project assisted by the Highlands and Islands Enterprise network.

From the above articles:

1. Discuss the extent of the problem of business failure and the reasons for it.
2. Why are management buy-outs on the increase?
3. Currently around 400,000 new businesses are starting up each year, 1 in 3 run by women. From the articles, discuss their prospects for survival and how they might be affected by future change.

*17. Innovation and change*

## Changing Lifestyles

39. In Chapter 3 we discussed some examples of the rapid social changes which have taken place in the second half of the twentieth century. These factors together have had a dramatic impact on all our lifestyles. The underlying reasons for these changes include a lower birth rate, longer life expectancy, a higher divorce rate, wider educational opportunities, technological progress, and higher standards of living.

40. **Lower Birth Rate**

13.8 live births per thousand in 1991 compared with 28.7 in 1901 and 15.9 in 1971. The projected rate for the year 2001 is 13.0.

41. **Longer Life Expectancy**

Death rates have fallen considerably in the 20th century from 17.3 per thousand in 1901 to 11.4 in 1993. This is due largely to better food, housing, clothing, sanitation and working conditions. Life expectancy therefore is now about 73 years for men and 78 for women compared with 49 and 52 respectively in 1901 and 68 and 74 in 1951.

42. **Higher Divorce Rate**

Currently almost 1 in 2 marriages end in divorce, although over a third of people remarry again.

43. **Wider Educational Opportunities**

The government has introduced measures to make further and higher education more accessible and responsive to the needs of the UK economy. Thus more people will have the opportunity to participate in education and training and therefore to improve their qualifications and skill levels.

44. The number of young people entering higher education, for example, rose from 1 in 8 in 1980 to 1 in 5 in 1990 and is expected to reach 1 in 3 by the year 2000. Whilst National Vocational Qualifications (NVQs) and General National Vocational Qualifications (GNVQs) are designed to make qualifications more relevant to the needs of employment by basing them on standards of competence set by industry.

45. **Technological Progress**

Since the second world war the so called information technology revolution has brought about many rapid changes in business and society. The major changes can be summarised as:

- **Communication** is much quicker and more accurate using television, satellite links, word processing, facsimile and electronic mail.
- **Information processing.** The use of microcomputers to store, retrieve, transmit and process data on discs or tapes.
- **Computer aided design** (CAD) is used to design new products.
- **Computer aided manufacture** (CAM). Much equipment is now automatically controlled by computers. Robots have been introduced making work faster and more accurate.
- **New materials** are now used, which are often lighter or stronger than those they replaced, such as carbon fibre composites in the Aerospace industry, new plastics in cars and high-fibre, cholesterol free protein in foods.

46. The resulting effects of technological progress include:

- More goods can be produced and of a higher quality.
- Reduced production costs possibly leading to lower prices for consumers.
- Stock records, payrolls, accounts and other data can be prepared and processed on computers.
- Men have been replaced by machines leading to increased unemployment in many industries.
- New range of services, for example banking from home, cash-points and a general growth of tertiary industries.
- New technology makes jobs cleaner, easier and safer for workers.
- Increased leisure time because more work can be done in less time.

*17. Innovation and change*

## Task 17.11

### NEW PRINTING TECHNOLOGY

Computer technology is now widely used in the production of national and provincial newspapers.

Journalists, for example, can type and edit articles directly into computer terminals where colour pictures or graphics can also be added. Where production plants are some distance from editorial offices, pages are transmitted by facsimile. Other technological developments include full-colour printing and the use of plastic-plate processes. London Docklands has become an important location for printing plants. The Financial Times moved there in 1988 with about 200 production workers compared with 650 at its former City of London facility. News International which publishes 3 daily and 2 Sunday newspapers has over 500 computer terminals, one of the largest systems in the world.

1. From the above information, discuss the impact of new technology on the printing industry.
2. Find the names of the newspapers published by News International.
3. Comment, if possible from a site visit, on how newspapers in your locality are now produced and how their format has changed in recent years. Also, describe how new technology has altered the type of work which is now performed.

### 47. Higher Standards of Living

This is due to rapid economic growth. In the 1980's, for example, Britain had eight successive years of growth at an annual rate of over 3 per cent, the highest in the European Community. Although like most other industrialised nations, this fell at the end of the decade and was only 0.5 per cent in 1990.

## Task 17.12

### Changing Lifestyles of Britain's Families

| % of households with... | | | | Family types | | | Average household size | | | Married women with jobs | | |
|---|---|---|---|---|---|---|---|---|---|---|---|---|
| Item | 1964 | 1971 | 1990 | | 1971 | 1990 | | 1971 | 1990 | Age | 1971 | 1990 |
| Telephone | 42 | 75 | 89 | Married/ cohabiting couple | 92% | 81% | Six or more | 6% | 2% | 20-24 | 57% | 65% |
| Colour television | – | 74 | 97 | | | | Five | 8% | 5% | 25-34 | 40% | 63% |
| Video Recorder | – | – | 70 | Lone mother | 7% | 17.5% | Four | 18% | 15% | 35-44 | 45% | 75% |
| Home computer | – | – | 21 | | | | Three | 19% | 17% | 45-54 | 57% | 70% |
| Compact disk player | – | – | 27 | Lone father | 1% | 1.5% | Two | 31% | 35% | 55-59 | 47% | 51% |
| Washing machine | 66 | 78 | 90 | | | | One | 18% | 26% | | | |
| Dishwasher | – | 4 | 15 | | | | | | | | | |
| Central Heating | 37 | 59 | 84 | | | | | | | | | |
| Car (one or more) | 52 | 59 | 68 | | | | | | | | | |

The above data is based on figures from the Government's Office of Population Censuses and Surveys. From it:

1. Identify the key trends
2. With reasons, state which household items you feel could now be described as necessities rather than luxuries.
3. What evidence, if any, is there to suggest that society is becoming much more consumer oriented?
4. What are the implications for businesses and the economy if the key trends continue in the future?

## Environmental change

48. Concern about the environment has become an increasingly important issue in recent years to such an extent that both the Government and European Community have introduced important strategies covering protection, preservation and pollution. These measures are of major importance to business organisations because they must alter their trading practices in order to meet them. BS7750 is an official British Standard against which environmental management systems can now be assessed.

## Environmental strategies

49. The **Environmental Protection Act 1990** is a significant legislative measure which sets out a wide range of powers and duties for central and local government including control over litter and waste, air pollution, noise and emissions to water.

50. **Litter and waste.** Local authorities how have a duty to control litter and make plans for the recycling of waste. The dumping of litter can result in fines up to £1,000.

51. **Air quality and pollution.** Local authorities are given powers to deal with statutory nuisances including smoke, dust and smells. The 3 main air pollutants are ozone, nitrogen dioxide and sulphur dioxide which must now be controlled in both existing and new industrial plants.

52. **Water.** In general it is against the law to allow any polluting matter to enter water in Britain without legal authorisation. Businesses who break the law face fines of up to £20,000.

53. **Noise.** Local authorities have a duty to inspect their areas for noise nuisance and to investigate complaints about it.

### Task 17.13

#### SHETLAND OIL DISASTER

The oil boom of the 1970's and 1980's brought great wealth to the Shetland Isles. But in January 1993, the area was hit by a major disaster when the engines of the oil tanker Braer failed in a fierce storm. It broke up spilling up to 80,000 gallons of crude oil into the sea and killing thousands of birds, otters and seals. It also caused extensive pollution to the environment as oil blown by the gales contaminated land affecting sheep and cattle farming. Crops were condemned as unfit for human or animal use.

Salmon farming, the island's second largest industry was affected by toxic chemicals used to disperse the oil. Marks and Spencer and other retailers quickly decided to stop buying fish from the area.

Many people faced financial ruin with the economic, environmental and social effects expected to last for years.

Much concern was expressed that the area had no radar to give early warning when ships were in trouble. Also, the tanker was sailing under a flag of convenience and therefore not subject to any stringent UK or other government safety standards. 60% of losses at sea are accounted for by such merchant vessels which are often poorly maintained. The Braer itself was 17 years old, in good condition for its age but with some leaking pipes which the owner could not afford to replace.

Complete the following which are based on the Braer disaster.

1. Identify the main industries of the area.
2. Who, if anybody, was to blame for the disaster?
3. What were the main economic, social and environmental consequences of the disaster?
4. What do you feel could be done to prevent such a disaster in the future and who should be responsible for it?

## 17. Innovation and change

### Other Environmental Strategies

54. Other government strategies include those covering land use, the countryside, conservation, wildlife and global warming.

55. **The regulation of land use** and planning restrictions include the protection of 'green belts' which are areas intended to be left open and free to prevent the sprawl of large build-up areas.

56. **Encouraging open-air recreation** takes place through the provision and improvement of country parks and picnic sites. This role is the responsibility of the Countryside Commission.

57. **Heritage conservation** covers the protection of historic buildings, ancient monuments and areas of special interest.

58. **Protection of wildlife** includes, for example, banning the import of seal pup skins, whale products and ivory from the African elephant.

59. **Global warming.** The so-called 'greenhouse effect' is a natural phenomenon which keeps the earth at a temperature which can sustain life. In recent years, there has been considerable concern about the emission of man-made gases which are leading to additional warming of the earth and could cause serious changes in the world's climate.

60. To help combat this problem, in 1991 the government introduced a number of measures, including:
    - a pledge to achieve a 15% improvement in the efficiency of its buildings over the next 5 years.
    - a major 3 year publicity campaign on the greenhouse effect and use of energy in the home.
    - tighter building regulations to promote energy efficiency in new houses.
    - a commitment to phase out all ozone-damaging substances by the year 2000, including CFCs (Chlorofluorcarbons) which are artificial gases used in the manufacture of foams, as solvents, in refrigeration and as aerosol propellants.
    - to reduce exhaust pollution from the 24 million vehicles on Britain's roads. Strict European Community standards for all new cars are now in force including the requirement to run on unleaded petrol which by October 1994 accounted for over 60% of all sales.

> **Task 17.14**
>
> In the area where you live or work, identify examples of environmental problems and any action which is being taken to tackle them.

### Recycling

61. Sometimes called material salvage, recycling is the recovery and re-use of materials from spent products. It has become an important issue in recent years for two main reasons:
    - On the one hand, the increasing scarcity and cost of natural resources such as oil, gas, coal, mineral ores and trees,
    - whilst on the other hand, the increasing pollution of air, water and land by waste materials such as plastics and chemicals, many of which do not decompose and/or can emit harmful gases.

62. There are two basic types of recycling.
    - **Internal salvage** is the re-use in a manufacturing process of materials which are a waste of that process. For example, re-melting and re-casting metal cuttings such as iron, copper or steel.
    - **External salvage** is the reclaiming of materials from a product which is worn out or obsolete. For example, the collection of old newspapers for the manufacture of new paper products; bottles for glass; drink cans for aluminium or electric storage batteries for lead. Whilst bark, wood chippings and lignin from wood and paper mills are often used as animal bedding or returned to the soil as fertiliser.

63. The importance of recycling, whether internal or external, is that it helps to save scarce economic resources. To make this worthwhile, however, the cost of reprocessing must be less than the costs involved in processing new materials.

*17. Innovation and change*

64. The Government encourages the reclamation of recycling of waste materials wherever this is practicable and has set a target that by 2000 half of all recyclable household waste will be re-used. To collect materials for recycling, there are currently some 5,000 'bottle banks' in Britain as well as 'can banks', 'paper banks' and in some places 'plastics' or 'textile banks'.

### Task 17.15

#### MONEY FROM RUBBISH

Plans to increase recycled household rubbish by the turn of the century have been announced by Derbyshire County Council.

The scheme will boost the amount of recycled domestic waste from the present 2.5 per cent to 25 per cent – or 1,000,000 tonnes – by the year 2000.

Recent changes in the law mean that the council can now pay a subsidy to rubbish collectors, provided the materials are to be recycled.

It has agreed to pay £6.40 per tonne to all waste collectors – including district councils and voluntary or non-profit making organisations – who will still be able to claim the full salvage value of the materials from the recycler. Among the items that could be reclaimed are glass, paper, metal cans, oil, textiles and scrap metal.

#### RECYCLED CARDS

A full circle will be completed with the launch of a Christmas card recycling scheme by the Countryside Commission in conjunction with Boots.

The money raised will be ploughed back into the development of the country's twelve community forests which are a joint initiative between the Countryside Commission and Forestry Commission in partnership with local authorities and communities. They will create wooded landscapes for wildlife, employment, recreation and education. Local schools have been invited to take part in the scheme.

A recycling point will be made available at Boots stores from January 4 and customers will be able to return unwanted Christmas and other greetings cards until the end of March.

In another scheme, some local councils have been shredding Christmas trees.

#### CANNY CASH

A new aluminium can recycling service, aimed at schools and voluntary groups and organised by Alcan Aluminium Can Recycling enables people to trade aluminium drink cans for cash at the rate of 45p a kilo. Alcan reckon that millions of cans are thrown away every year. The cans are taken to a £28 million recycling plant in Warrington: Europe's largest. There they are melted down to use again as future drinks cans.

Articles like those above regularly appear in local and national media. From these and others which you can collect yourselves, complete the following:

1. Identify, with the use of examples, at least 5 benefits from recycling.
2. Are there any potential drawbacks?
3. Who and why do you think stand to gain most from recycling – consumers, local authorities, businesses, other groups?
4. Suggest ways in which the organisation in which you work or study could benefit from introducing a recycling campaign.

*continued...*

*17. Innovation and change*

> **Task 17.15** continued
>
> 5. Finally, draw up outline plans for a recycling compaign and include in it how you would address the following issues:
>    - how to encourage people to sort their waste for recycling.
>    - where the nearest 'banks' are or could be located.
>    - how to inform people about the campaign and where to find the banks which may involve carrying out research before and after the campaign.
>    - how to evaluate the success of the campaign which may involve carrying out research before and after the campaign.

## Employment and Change

65. In the past two decades, jobs have changed substantially and this trend is expected to continue as increasing competition, particularly from Europe, and technological advance bring about more sophisticated products and methods of production leading to the need for new skills. The impact of these changes on the working population includes de-skilling, unemployment, new jobs/skills and new working patterns.

66. **De-skilling**

    This has come about because many traditional crafts, for example, printing, tailoring and joinery, have declined or been eliminated as machines have taken over from people. Nowadays, most clothing, publications and furniture no longer rely on the skills of highly trained workers. Whilst robots and computer-aided machines are being used on manufacturing production lines to perform many lower level skills.

67. **Unemployment**

    This is a key problem not just in the UK but throughout Europe. New technology increases productivity and leads to the need for less workers. Machines are replacing people and redundancy is becoming more common and socially acceptable. The growth in unemployment has lead to the development of a range of government education and training programmes aimed at helping unemployed people to get back to work.

68. **New jobs/skills**

    The rapid development and application of electronic and micro-electronic technologies has created the need for highly skilled specialists, scientists and technicians to develop and maintain computer hardware and software. At the same time, the leisure and tourism industries have also developed as hours of work have been reduced and paid holidays increased. Manual workers' holidays, for example, have increased on average from 2 weeks in 1961 to 4 weeks in 1990.

69. **Work patterns**

    Perhaps the most significant developments taking place are in the patterns of work.
    - new technology has lead to completely new methods of work and in the 1990's the development of working from home.
    - people now need to be more flexible and ready and willing to adapt to changes. The concept of the traditional working week is becoming more difficult to define. It is estimated that three quarters of the UK workforce now operate flexibly.

- In the past, it was common for people to have only one or perhaps two jobs in their working life. Increasingly, now and in the future, people have many different jobs often requiring re-training or an updating of skills and probably with some periods of unemployment in-between jobs.
- The early retirement of people from work in their 50's is another factor likely to continue.
- more women are joining the workforce. Modern domestic appliances have changed the role of women in the home, whilst the changing nature of work away from heavy manual tasks, the introduction of equal opportunities legislation and the desire to achieve higher standards of living have added further impetus.

### Task 17.16

#### STAY AT HOME COMMUTERS

Commuters could soon be a thing of the past. Up to 4 million office workers, roughly 1 in 6 of the working population are expected to plug into their computer terminals by 1995. Companies leading the way in introducing teleworking for staff include telecommunications giant BT, computer firms IBM and ICL, photocopier manufacturer Rank Xerox, chemical company ICI and Prudential Insurance.

BT has announced that junior managers, potentially 8,000 people, will have the right to apply to work from home, and reckons that as many as 1,000 will opt for the deal by the end of 1993. The company calculates that productivity per worker could rise by an average of 45 per cent. Although teleworkers find that household bills for heating, electricity and phones tend to rise, they are still well in pocket because they don't have to pay travel costs. On average, they could be almost £15 a week better off working at home for four days a week and the environmental benefits to the nation would be worth £10.3 billion a year. Some staff miss the companionship of fellow workers so BT has started providing videophones for discussing problems and removing the feeling of isolation. IBM says one in ten of its staff work from home using computer terminals, alongside their work in the office. It is considering introducing telecommuting on a more widespread basis, as it is time-efficient and gives staff more flexibility.

Rank Xerox found the cost of keeping workers in an office, commuting costs and other expenses came to two-and-a-half times their salaries. Sixty were re-employed as freelances and now work from a terminal at home.

National Westminster is very keen on the concept and has several thousand staff members working mainly or wholly from home. It is happy to consider introducing teleworking 'where it fits in and works'.

For staff who cannot work at home, the CBI suggest high technology 'neighbourhood offices' where staff from different firms share resources like telephones, fax machines and video conferencing. The idea being that 'they could drive in with their neighbour each morning and use shared facilities, enjoy meeting people while working for their own respective company. The CBI is also convinced that ending the wear and tear on workers' nerves caused by commuting will give companies better employees in the long run.

BT which is a world leader in piloting 'Teleworking' believes that it can be applied to many jobs, especially where work is highly structured and easily monitored, including those in mail order, ticket agencies, credit checking.

With the help of the above article and by carrying out research in your own area, answer the following. If possible, present your findings in the form of a word processed report. Use examples throughout to illustrate the points which you make.

1. Explain in full the meaning of teleworking.
2. Identify its potential benefits and drawbacks.
3. Teleworking potentially represents the most dramatic change in working practices ever. Consider the likely impact on both individuals and businesses in your locality and on the economy as a whole, assuming it develops as anticipated.

## 17. Innovation and change

**70. Future Industry Structure**

Notable trends include:

- the proportion of jobs in the **service sector** which now accounts for over 60% of jobs in the UK is continuing to rise, whilst those in manufacturing declines.
- it is likely that the **growth of private sector** output and employment will continue to increase at the expense of the public sector, particularly with the increase in privatisation.
- the number of **part-time jobs** which have increased by 35% in the past 10 years, and now at 6.6 million total over a quarter of the UK workforce, are likely to continue to rise.
- the number of **self-employed** is also expected to keep rising. In 1992 it was 3 million compared with 1.2 million in 1979.

71. **A Changing Industrial Structure**

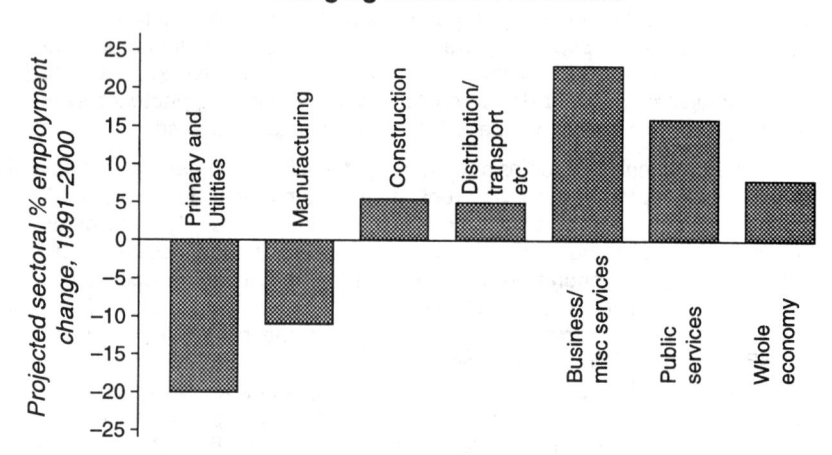

[Bar chart: Projected sectoral % employment change, 1991–2000. Primary and Utilities: –20; Manufacturing: –11; Construction: +5; Distribution/transport etc: +5; Business/misc services: +23; Public services: +15; Whole economy: +7]

*Source: IER*

72. **An Ageing Workforce**

**Projected labour force change: 1991–2000**

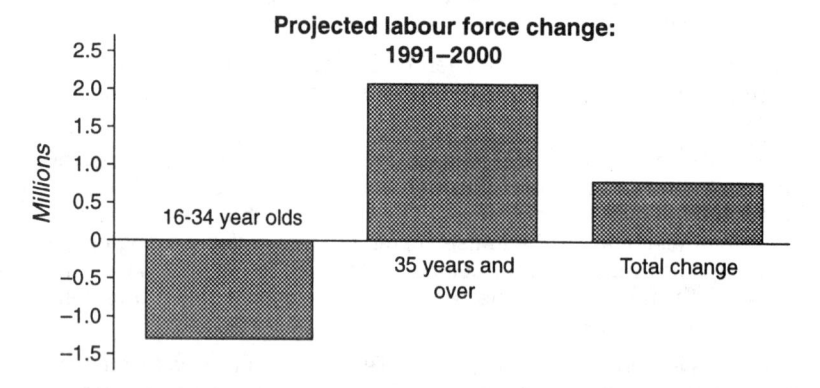

[Bar chart, Millions: 16-34 year olds: –1.3; 35 years and over: +2.0; Total change: +0.7]

*Source: Labour Market and Skills Trends 1993/4 Department of Employment*

73. Projected changes by 2001 include:

- a **growing labour force** to 28.8 million, an increase of 700,000 compared with 1992.
- an **ageing workforce** with 1.8 million more people in the 35-54 age group but 1.2 million fewer aged 16-34.
- an **increasing number of women** in the workforce, up to 45% of the total by 2001. In 1991 the government launched Opportunity 2000, an initiative to promote equal career opportunities for women in employment. It tries to encourage employers to demonstrate a commitment to a more balanced workforce by, for example, introducing flexible working arrangements and training.
- a **growth** in the number of **higher education** students by about 50% to 1.5 million.

## Community Impact

74. As you will have realised, change is wide reaching and endless, affecting every part of our daily lives. The aspects of change discussed in this chapter will impact on communities in different ways. Where, for example, large organisations in an area make thousands of employees redundant this can create not just economic problems from unemployment and therefore reduced business activity, but also social problems which in turn can impact on the environment.

75. Examples may include:
    - poor housing and social amenities.
    - pressures on health and other services.
    - widespread and lasting poverty if unemployment is long-term as families are unable to support themselves adequately.
    - social humiliation because people are 'forced' to seek financial help in the form of benefits.
    - demoralised people who feel useless and unwanted if out of work for a long time.
    - resentment, frustration and deprivation which can lead to increased crime and vandalism.

76. On the other hand, if the change comes about from a new firm moving into an area, this may create jobs, thereby increasing business activity and building confidence which can lead to further investment and regeneration.

## Summary

77. a) Change is always taking place and affects both individuals and organisations.
    b) Organisational change may be internal brought about by factors such as new products or management, or external resulting from environmental forces.
    c) The fear of change can lead to barriers which can be due to behavioural, psychological, social and economic factors.
    d) The potential for conflict in an organisation comes about because they consist of various stakeholders who may have incompatible objectives.
    e) Resistance to change may be demonstrated by industrial action or low morale.
    f) To successfully implement change, managers need to develop appropriate strategies.
    g) Research and development is important for bringing about innovation.
    h) Change can represent either an opportunity or threat in organisations.
    i) Lifestyles have changed for many reasons including a lower birth rate, longer life expectancy, higher divorce rate, wider educational opportunities, technological progress and higher standards of living.
    j) Increasing concern about the environment has lead to government legislation and strategies to protect it, including recycling.
    k) Employment trends resulting from change include de-skilling, unemployment, new jobs and work patterns.
    l) The structure of industry has also changed, in particular the rapid growth of the service sector.
    m) Further predictions include a growing but ageing workforce, with an increasing number of women in employment.
    n) Change in a community is likely to have economic, social and environmental implications.

## Review questions *(answers can be found in the paragraphs indicated)*

1. Explain what you understand by the concept of change. (1-2)
2. Distinguish between the internal and external forces for change. (3-5)
3. Briefly describe the main barriers to change. (8-11)
4. Why does potential conflict exist in an organisation? (12-18)

5. How do employees demonstrate resistance to change? (19-21)
6. Outline a possible strategy for managing change. (22-24)
7. Why is research and development important for innovation and what problems does it bring? (25-33)
8. Why do managers need to be able to anticipate potential change? (34-38)
9. Discuss the underlying factors behind the change in lifestyles since the Second World War. (39-47)
10. Outline the government's strategy for protecting the environment. (48-64)
11. Briefly describe the effect on the working population of industrial change. (65-69)
12. In what ways is the structure of industry affected by change. (70-72)
13. Outline some of the major changes predicted to take place in the workforce by 2001. (73)
14. How can change in business activity impact on a community? (74-76)

*Asterisks indicate those questions for which there are answers in Outline Answers (page 439)*

## Essay-style questions

1.* Outline the changes in the pattern of employment in the UK in recent years. Why have these come about?
2. How can an organisation which is struggling to survive, justify expenditure on research and development?
3. The government is planning to raise the retirement age for women from 60 to 65 by 2000. The new age which will be phased in will save £3-£4 billion when fully introduced. Comment on the likely impact of this change.

## Short answer

1.*

**Populations of United Kingdom Standard Regions (Millions)**

| Mid Year Estimates | Projections (1975 Based) | | | | |
|---|---|---|---|---|---|
| | 1961 | 1976 | 1981 | 1986 | 1991 |
| North | 3.1 | 3.1 | 3.1 | 3.1 | 3.1 |
| Yorkshire and Humberside | 4.7 | 4.9 | 4.9 | 4.9 | 4.9 |
| East Midlands | 3.3 | 3.7 | 3.8 | 3.9 | 4.0 |
| East Anglia | 1.5 | 1.8 | 1.9 | 2.0 | 2.1 |
| South East | 16.1 | 16.9 | 16.7 | 16.7 | 16.9 |
| Greater London | 8.0 | 7.0 | 6.6 | 6.2 | 6.0 |
| Outer Metropolitan Area | 4.4 | 5.3 | 5.4 | 5.6 | 5.8 |
| Outer South East | 3.7 | 4.6 | 4.7 | 4.9 | 5.1 |
| South West | 3.7 | 4.3 | 4.3 | 4.9 | 5.1 |
| West Midlands | 4.8 | 5.2 | 5.2 | 5.2 | 5.3 |
| North West | 6.4 | 6.6 | 6.5 | 6.5 | 6.5 |
| England | 43.6 | 46.4 | 46.4 | 46.9 | 47.6 |
| Wales | 2.6 | 2.8 | 2.8 | 2.8 | 2.9 |
| England and Wales | 46.2 | 49.2 | 49.2 | 49.7 | 50.5 |
| Scotland | 5.2 | 5.2 | 5.2 | 5.2 | 5.2 |
| Great Britain | 51.4 | 54.4 | 54.3 | 54.9 | 55.7 |
| Northern Ireland | 1.4 | 1.5 | 1.5 | 1.5 | 1.5 |
| United Kingdom | 52.8 | 55.9 | 55.8 | 56.4 | 57.2 |

*SOURCE: Social Trends. Central Statistical Office (HMSO)*

a) Identify the key trends in the above data.

b) How can information about changes in the population assist business organisations in their planning?

2.* Distinguish between the following recycling terms, using examples to illustrate your answer.
   a) Internal salvage
   b) External salvage
   c) Identify key ways in which the Government encourages recycling
3. The Environmental Protection Act 1990 sets out a wide range of powers for central and local government.
   a) Identify 4 key features of the Act.
   b) Outline at least 3 other ways in which the Government tackles environmental issues.

## Multiple choice/completion

1.* The government is most likely to contribute to research in all except which one of the following areas?
   a) Defence
   b) Chemicals
   c) Health
   d) Education

2.* The Environmental Protection Act 1990 sets out a range of powers and duties covering all except which one of the following?
   a) Air quality
   b) Health & Safety
   c) Water
   d) Noise

3.* Recycling is becoming increasingly important for businesses because
   a) It increases their profits
   b) It is a legal requirement
   c) It is encouraged by the government
   d) It helps to save economic resources

4.* The Government's environmental strategy does not include
   a) Lifting restrictions on green belt areas
   b) Protecting historic buildings and monuments
   c) Controlling the import of wildlife products
   d) Measures to control global warming

5. The impact of change on employment in the past 2 decades includes all except
   a) De-skilling of workers and increased unemployment
   b) New skills and methods of work
   c) An increase in the number of working women
   d) Workers changing their jobs less frequently

6. Conflict may exist in an organisation because of all except the
   a) Differing objectives of its various stakeholders
   b) Fear of and resistance to proposed change
   c) Adoption of a democratic management style
   d) Methods of communication and organisation

## 17. Innovation and change

*In the following questions, one or more of the responses is/are correct. Choose the appropriate letter which indicates the correct version.*

A  if 1 only is correct
B  if 3 only is correct
C  if 1 and 2 only are correct
D  if 1, 2 and 3 are correct

7. Which of the following is/are underlying reasons for changing lifestyles in the second half of the twentieth century?
    1. Higher birth rates
    2. Lower divorce rates
    3. Longer life expectancy

8. Which of the following statements is/are correct?
    1. The proportion of service sector jobs is increasing.
    2. Innovation is a key contributor to economic growth.
    3. Change is always a threat to organisations.

---

**Assignment**

### THE DAY A TOWN ALMOST DIED

Over 15,000 jobs came under threat when the Dutch owned truck and van maker Leyland-DAF fell into receivership in February 1993. Administrators moved onto plant sites to try to save its UK operation after banks refused to approve a £100m three-year restructuring plan for the parent company. More than 5,500 Leyland-DAF jobs in Birmingham, Glasgow and Leyland, near Preston were at risk, plus 10,000 more in UK component suppliers. In Leyland, where 2,200 are employed, shopkeepers were steeling themselves for a shutdown.

Greengrocer Barbara Smith said: 'If the factory closes it will turn this into a ghost town. Many businesses will go to the wall.'

DIY shop boss Gordon Watson said: 'Men who are paid off won't have much to spend. I heard the maximum even a long-server will get is £4,000.

The Leyland plant, is the UK's most modern truck assembly line.

But from booming world sales of around 69,000 heavy trucks in 1989, the market has slumped to about 30,000 a year as recession-hit firms hang on to ageing fleets. Last year was the worst since the war, even though Leyland DAF captured a quarter of the UK market.

Although the Dutch company is the major shareholder of Leyland DAF, 30 per cent is in the hands of private investors and institutions. The BAe-owned Rover Cars group has 10.9 per cent.

If Leyland sinks it will hand over a massive sales opportunity to Germany's Mercedes-Benz. An industry expert said: 'There are signs that the UK business is picking up, so for Leyland to die now would be tragic.

An Amalgamated Engineering and Electrical Union spokesman said: 'A campaign of action will be launched which will probably include a march through Leyland and the lobbying of Parliament. We also aim to get local MPs involved.

With unemployment nudging 3 million, a fierce political row erupted in the Commons over whether the Government should intervene. Trade President Michael Heseltine said he was 'ready to work closely' with DAF to save some of the business, but rejected Labour calls for direct aid.

'If there was to be some sort of restructuring involving capital injection in the company within the assisted areas, then there might be a possibility of Government capital grant. But that would have to be explored.'

*continued...*

## Assignment continued

> Whitehall feels a significant part of Leyland's UK business can survive and be sold – despite its Dutch parent company being close to collapse.
>
> A key question will be whether the UK factories can be protected from the Continental creditors of the parent firm, which took over Leyland Vehicles in 1987 but has suffered losses of £301 million in the past three years.
>
> Lancashire County Council leader Louise Ellman urged Mr Heseltine to work with the authority and its economic development agency, Lancashire Enterprises, in mounting a rescue package.
>
> She said: 'This is a major manufacturing concern. If it is allowed to die it will devastate a major part of Lancashire.
>
> After lengthy negotiation, the receivers revealed management buyout plans which involved the loss of some 1500 jobs at Leyland and 1000 at Birmingham. Twelve months later LDV (formerly Leyland Daf Vans) at Birmingham, bought for £40m, announced profits of £8.6m on a turnover of £80m, plus 100 new jobs, whilst Leyland Trucks at Leyland where 45 temporary workers had been recruited, was still in profit and expecting a turnover of £150m. Production was up by 20%.

From the article and your own knowledge of Leyland-DAF or similar local situations, complete the following:

1. Identify the element of change which caused the collapse of Leyland DAF.
2. Describe the economic impact on the Community of Leyland as a result of the collapse.
3. Discuss the likely social impact.
4. Assess the potential environmental impact.
5. Could the situation have been prevented?
6. Do pressure groups have a valid role to play in such situations?
7. Does any group stand to gain from the situation?
8. Prepare the case for and against 'letting Leyland die' and comment on which key factors and why, should determine the final decision in such situations.
9. Now carry out some practical research in your local area to identify a recent major change. Briefly describe the situation and how it came about.
10. Finally, analyse the problems associated with it and what action was or is being taken to alleviate them.

# 18. Data Analysis and Presentation

This Chapter is about the interpretation and use of statistical data in business. It provides an introduction to some key concepts, including how they are calculated and presented and covers:

* Sources of Data
* Statistics
* Statistical Presentation
* Statistical Trends
* Samples
* Probability
* Frequency Distributions
* Data Descriptions
* Measures of Central Tendency
* Mean, Median, Mode
* Measures of Dispersion
* Range/Interquartile Range
* Standard Deviation
* Normal Distribution
* Skewness
* Business Forecasting
* Time Series
* Causal Modelling
* Qualitative Approaches
* Index Numbers

## Sources of Data

1. Businesses today have ready access to vast amounts of data from both inside and outside the organisation. Much of this data is available on computers and therefore with the use of databases and spreadsheets can be very quickly and easily manipulated to assist with decision-taking.

2. Internal information, for example, about sales, price, costs, exports, stock levels, can be analysed in such a way that they enable conclusions to be drawn and better informed decisions taken about such issues as capital investment, production and marketing. This process is assisted by external information from, for example, the local and national press, government publications and trade associations.

## Statistics

3. The collection, recording and analysis of numercial data is called statistics. Thus, for example, we speak of economic statistics, population statistics and business statistics.

4. Statistical methods help people to identify, study and solve many problems and to take better informed decisions about uncertain situations, hence they are widely used throughout government, industry and commerce.

5. Studying a problem through the use of statistics involves at least 4 basic steps.
   - Defining the problem
   - Collecting data
   - Analysing data
   - Presenting the results

6. Much commonly used statistical data consists of simple counts of objects or monetary transactions. It is used to answer simple questions like:

   How many people are there in the country?
   How many are aged 0-16 or over 65?
   What was the value of imports in 1992?

## Task 18.1

1. Using a local library, identify in the reference section at least 6 key sources of statistical data.
2. State the source of the data and briefly explain why it is likely to be of interest to any local or national government or business organisation well known to you.
3. In what ways could it help them in planning to meet likely future economic conditions?

## Statistical Presentation

7. In order to make sense of data it is important that it is presented in such a way that it is easy to understand and makes the desired point(s) quickly and effectively.

8. The four main methods used to present statistical data are:
   - Tables of figures
   - Graphs
   - Charts – Pie charts and Bar charts
   - Diagrams such as Pictograms and Cartograms

9. **Tables of Figures**

   You will doubtless be familiar with information presented in tables like the one below. The problem with these is that the data may be difficult to interpret, absorb and retain. Hence, whilst statistical tables are useful, particularly when a lot of detailed information has to be presented, in general more visually interesting methods are to be preferred.

10. **Example of a Table of Figures**

**Manpower in Britain 1980–90**

*Thousands (as at June), seasonally adjusted*

|  | 1980 | 1985 | 1986 | 1987 | 1988 | 1989 | 1990 |
|---|---|---|---|---|---|---|---|
| Employees in employment [a] | 22.965 | 21,414 | 21,379 | 21,586 | 22,266 | 22,670 | 22,864 |
| Self-employed | 2,103 | 2,614 | 2,633 | 2,869 | 2,988 | 3,253 | 3,298 |
| Unemployed [b] | 1,274 | 3,019 | 3,121 | 2,839 | 2,299 | 1,791 | 1,618 |
| Armed forces | 323 | 326 | 322 | 319 | 316 | 308 | 303 |
| Work-related govt training programmes [c] | – | 176 | 226 | 311 | 343 | 462 | 424 |
| Workforce [d] | 26,759 | 27,743 | 27,877 | 28,077 | 28,347 | 28,486 | 28,509 |

Sources: Dept of Employment and Northern Ireland Dept of Economic Development
a Part-time workers are counted as full units
b Figures are adjusted for discontinuities and exclude school-leavers
c Not seasonally adjusted
d Comprises employees in employment, the self-employed, the armed forces, particpiants in work related government training programmes and the unemployed (including school leavers)

11. The key points which can be identified from this table include:
    - In 1990 the total workforce had increased to 28.5 million.
    - A substantial increase in self-employment to nearly 3.3 million.
    - Wide fluctuations in unemployment during the period.

*18. Data analysis and presentation*

12. **Graphs**

    Graphs are suitable for the clear presentation of rapidly changing figures such as the movements in share prices. They are often used to illustrate changes over a period of time or to make comparisons between, for example, different organisations, countries or age groups.

13. The examples below are of simple **line graphs** but there are other types of graphs beyond the scope of this text such as:

    - Lorenz curves
    - Semi-Logarithmic and
    - Layer Graphs

14. **Examples of Line Graphs**

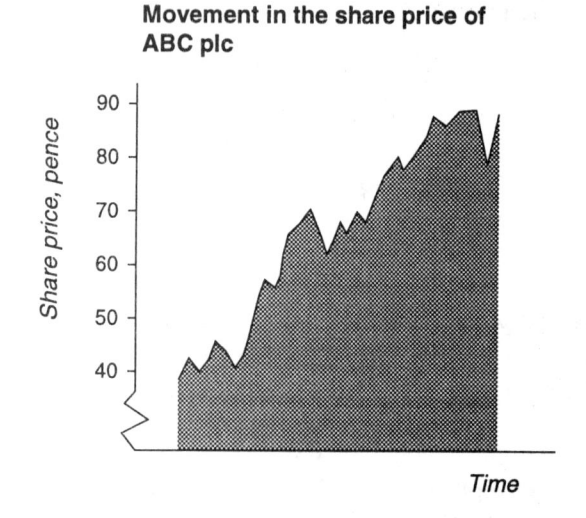

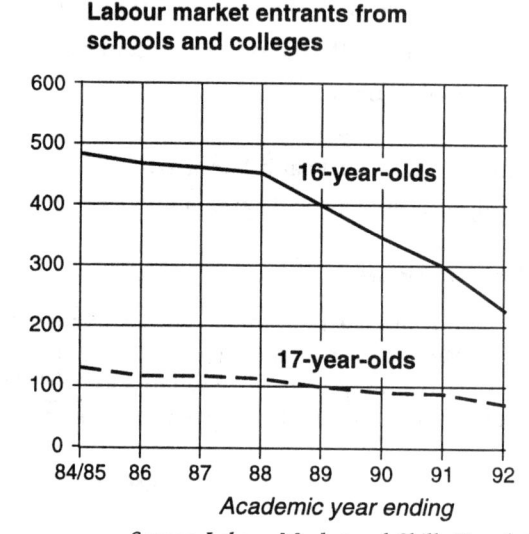

    **Movement in the share price of ABC plc**

    (Share price, pence vs Time)

    **Labour market entrants from schools and colleges**

    16-year-olds / 17-year-olds, academic year ending 84/85 to 92

    *Source: Labour Market and Skills Trends 1993/4*

    **Task 18.2**

    Study the share prices of any two companies over a time period of 1-4 weeks.
    1. Plot the prices on a graph.
    2. Comment on the trends and the reason(s) for any significant changes which have taken place
    3. Identify and describe the trends in the 2 graphs in the example above.

15. **Charts**

    The most common types of chart are pie charts, 'Z' charts and bar charts.

    - **Pie Charts** are useful to illustrate in a circle divided into segments, how a total is made up, such as the breakdown of exports shown on the following page.
    - **'Z' Charts**, so called because of their shape, are used to show 3 sets of data together. Current data, a cumulative total to show the position to date and the moving annual total which shows the trend. The latter is obtained by continually replacing a month from the previous year with the current month's data.

16. **Examples of Pie Charts and 'Z' Charts**

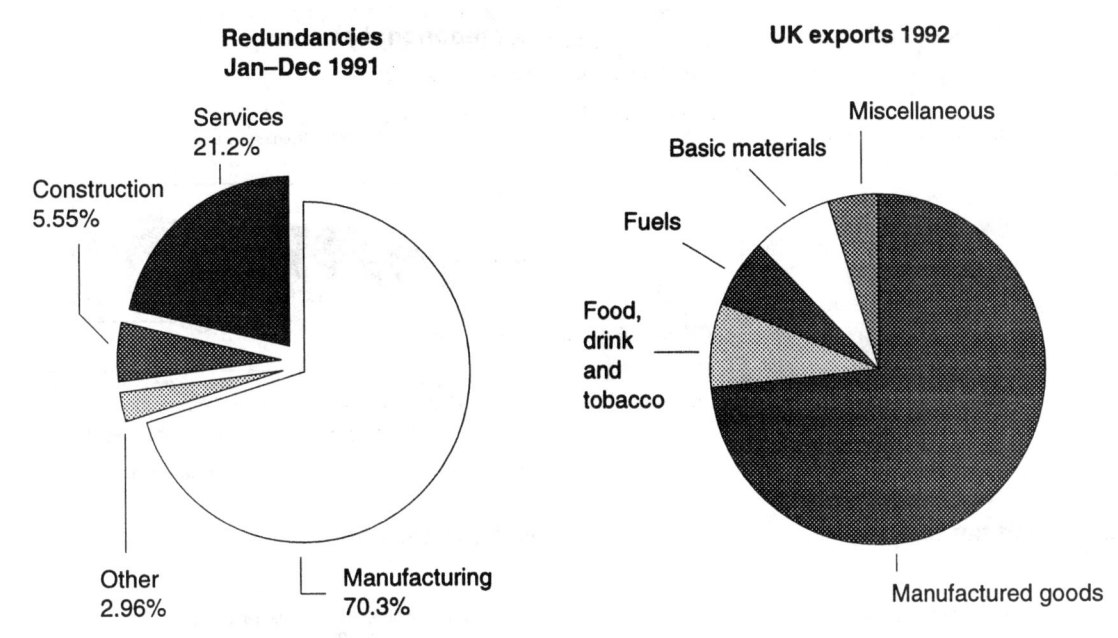

**Redundancies Jan–Dec 1991**
- Services 21.2%
- Construction 5.55%
- Other 2.96%
- Manufacturing 70.3%

*Source: Labour Market Review Spring 1992*

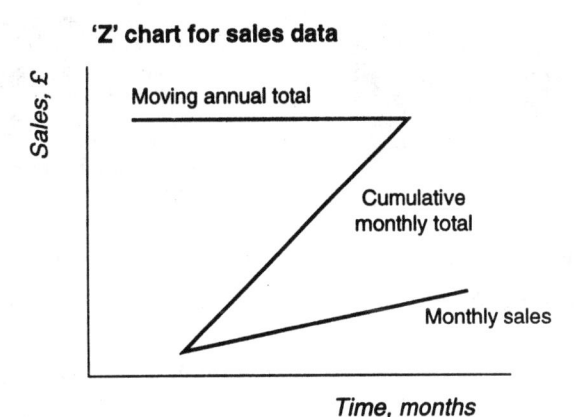

**UK exports 1992**
- Miscellaneous
- Basic materials
- Fuels
- Food, drink and tobacco
- Manufactured goods

**'Z' chart for sales data**

Sales, £ (vertical axis); Time, months (horizontal axis)
- Moving annual total
- Cumulative monthly total
- Monthly sales

### Task 18.3

The age distribution of the population in 1991 was estimated as follows:

* 20% under 16 years of age
* 64% between 16 and 64 years
* 16% aged 65 years and over

In 1951 the figures were 23%, 67% and 10% respectively.

Show this information in the form of pie charts and comment on the figures.

17. • **Bar Charts** are useful for summarising and comparing figures over a period of time or between items. Bar charts may also be presented in a number of different ways as the following examples illustrate. Here different formats are being used either simply to compare multiple data or to show the breakdown of a total into its component parts.

*18. Data analysis and presentation*

18. ## Examples of Bar Charts

**Multiple bar chart**

Occupational employment forecasts 1987–1995

**Component bar chart**

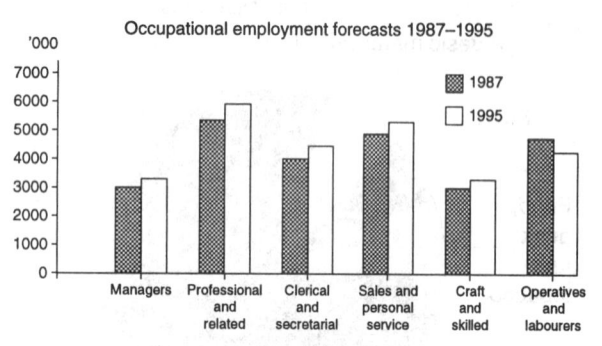

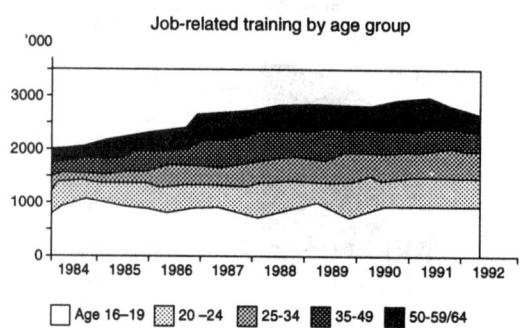

Job-related training by age group

*Source: Labour Force Survey*

**Component bar chart**

Fewer young people, but more staying on

**Multiple bar chart**

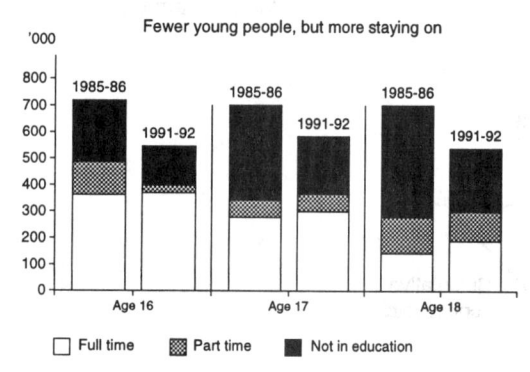

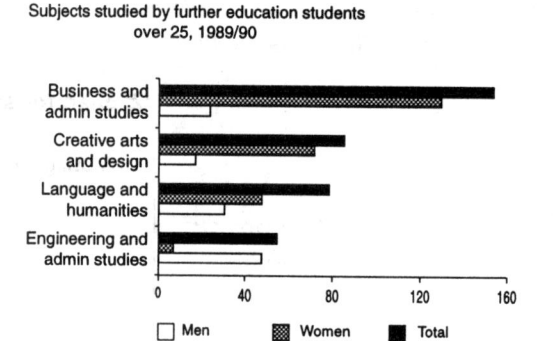

Subjects studied by further education students over 25, 1989/90

*Source: DFE Statistical Bulletin 14/92 July 1992*

*Source: Labour Market and Skill Trends 1993/4*

The multiple bar chart shows the breakdown of a total figure into its component parts.

### Task 18.4
Select any two of the bar chart examples in 18 and identify from each the key points which the data is illustrating.

## Pictograms and Cartograms

19. **Pictograms** are similar to bar charts but use small signs or symbols to illustrate data. Ideally, these have some resemblence to the subject of the data and hence tend to be more visually appealing.

20.
**Example of A Pictogram**
**Comparative Populations of Some Main Urban Areas – mid 1991**

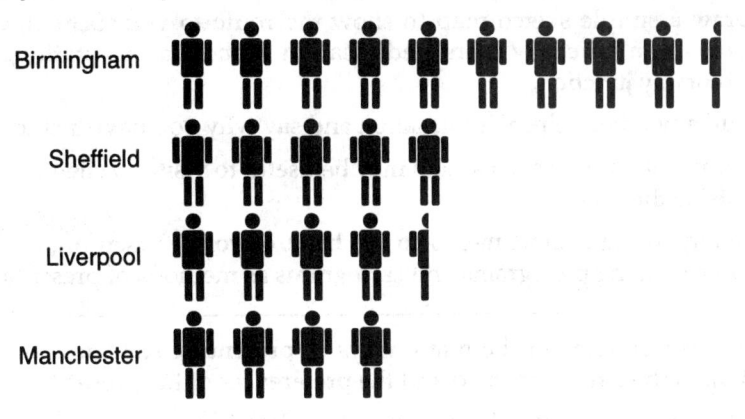

Birmingham

Sheffield

Liverpool

Manchester

Based on preliminary figures from 1991 Census

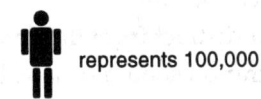

represents 100,000

21. **Cartograms** use maps to illustrate data. These are useful because they help us to put things in perspective. Many organisations, for example, use location maps to help clients to find them or to illustrate their spread of activities across the country or the world. The cartogram below is useful for illustrating the spread of some of Ford's multinational operations.

22.
**Example of a Cartogram**

**FORD OPERATIONS IN EUROPE**

1 Belfast
2 Cork
3 Halewood
4 Treforest
5 Swansea
6 Bridgend
7 Langley
8 Leamington
9 Daventry
10 Southampton
11 Dagenham
　Warley
　Aveley
12 Enfield
13 Woolwich
　Croydon
14 Basildon
　Dunton
　Boreham
15 Oslo
16 Stockholm
17 Helsinki
18 Copenhagen
19 Amsterdam
20 Antwerp
21 Lommel
22 Brussels
23 Wuefrath
24 Cologne
25 Genk
26 Dueren
27 Charleville
28 Paris
29 Saarlouis
30 Zurich
31 Bordeaux
32 Madrid
33 Lisbon
34 Valencia
35 Vienna
36 Salzburg
37 Rome
38 Berlin

Ford is one of Europe's leading organisations, employing some 110,000 people in 15 separate national companies. Its products are sold through 2,520 main dealers and 1,460 sub-dealers across Europe. In addition there are 2,150 Ford customer service and repair centres.

*18. Data analysis and presentation*

### Task 18.5

1. Draw a simple sketch map to show the route to your School, College or place of work from an easily identified location such as a bus station, railway station or motorway junction.
2. Add any other helpful information and say why you have included it.
3. Comment on why such a map may be useful to visitors/clients both from inside and outside the area.
4. Finally, write a short memo to the head of your chosen organisation outlining the value of using pictograms and cartograms as methods of presentation.

23. We have considered just some of the many ways of presenting statistics. The method chosen will usually depend upon the data concerned and the preferences of the presenter.

24. The most important points to remember in presenting data are:
    - The method chosen should be clear, concise and visually appealing.
    - Complex or over-fancy illustrations can confuse and/or distract from the data presented.
    - A clear title is essential and all components of the illustration should be labelled.
    - If secondary data is used the source should be quoted.
    - The units used should be indicated, for example, tonnes, thousands, £'s, hours.

### Task 18.6

**Employees in Employment** [a]

| Industry or service (1980 standard industrial classification) | Thousands (as at June) | | | | Per cent |
|---|---|---|---|---|---|
| | 1980 | 1985 | 1989 | 1990 | 1990 |
| **Primary sector** | **1,099** | **932** | **765** | **749** | **3.3** |
| Agriculture, forestry and fishing | 373 | 341 | 300 | 298 | 1.3 |
| Energy and water supply | 727 | 591 | 465 | 451 | 2.0 |
| **Manufacturing** [b] | **6,937** | **5,362** | **5,187** | **5,151** | **22.5** |
| **Construction** | **1,243** | **1,021** | **1,082** | **1,087** | **4.8** |
| **Services** | **13,712** | **14,108** | **15,627** | **15,868** | **69.4** |
| Wholesale distribution and repairs | 1,173 | 1,173 | 1,231 | 1,253 | 5.5 |
| Retail distribution | 2,177 | 2,080 | 2,283 | 2,299 | 10.1 |
| Hotels and catering | 972 | 1,042 | 1,217 | 1,272 | 5.6 |
| Transport | 1,049 | 900 | 915 | 940 | 4.1 |
| Postal services and communications | 437 | 427 | 447 | 434 | 1.9 |
| Banking, finance, insurance | 1,695 | 2,068 | 2,627 | 2,734 | 12.0 |
| Public administration | 1,980 | 1,921 | 1,931 | 1,949 | 8.5 |
| Education | 1,642 | 1,616 | 1,778 | 1,802 | 7.9 |
| Health | 1,258 | 1,347 | 1,465 | 1,466 | 6.4 |
| Other services | 1,327 | 1,533 | 1,734 | 1,718 | 7.5 |
| **Total** | **22,991** | **21,423** | **22,661** | **22,855** | **100.0** |

Sources: Dept of Employment and Northern Ireland Dept of Economic Development
a Figures are not seasonally adjusted
b In June 1990 employment in the main sectors of manufacturing industry included 752,000 in mechanical engineering; 645,000 in office machinery, electrical engineering and instruments; 540,000 in food, drink and tobacco; 518,000 in textiles, footwear and clothing; 476,000 in paper products, printing and publishing; 475,000 in timber, wooden furniture, rubber and plastics; 330,000 in chemicals and man-made fibres; and 248,000 in motor vehicles and parts.
Note: Differences between totals and the sums of their component parts are due to rounding.

continued...

> **Task 18.6** continued
> 1. Analyse the above data or selected parts of it and illustrate it using at least 3 different methods of presentation.
> 2. Justify why you have used each method chosen.
> 3. Comment on your diagrams and state the main point(s) which each is illustrating.

## Statistical Terms

25. In order to understand statistics it is important to be aware of some of the basic terms which are used. These include trends, samples, probability and data descriptions, in particular frequency distributions.

## Trends

26. These refer to the **general direction** in which a measured variable is moving. Data may show a 'rising' or 'falling' trend depending on whether there is an increase or decrease over time. For example, current trends show a continuing decline in employment in manufacturing industries. Trends are particularly important for business forecasting which is discussed in paragraph 77.

## Samples

27. Demographic and economic statistics are concerned with establishing total values such as the size of the working population or level of unemployment. But much statistical theory is concerned with summarising and analysing information about individuals for example why they buy particular products.

28. Since it is impractical, due to the difficulty and expense, to obtain data relating to every individual in a 'population', **a representative cross-section** called a sample is usually chosen from which the characteristics of the whole population can be inferred. A population in statistics means the complete set of variables being studied in any particular situation. Statistical theory can be used to calculate the minimum size of sample necessary to give the required degree of accuracy. Although generally the larger the sample, the greater the accuracy, this also increases the cost and therefore a balance between the two must be struck.

29. For practical purposes it is the selection of the sample which is more important than the size. The sample must be fully representative of the entire population, being studied. If, for example, a firm is carrying out market research to discover information about consumers of its products, it is important that the sample is balanced in terms of age, sex, type of occupation, social class and so on.

    Sampling techniques are discussed in Chapter 7.

> **Task 18.7**
> What would be the 'population' and what factors would you need to consider if you wanted to find out what influences the choice of brand or model for car owners in the UK?

## Probability

30. Probability is one of the most important statistical concepts. It refers to the **likelihood of a particular uncertain event or outcome occurring.** For example, we speak of the probability of rain tomorrow, the probability of something breaking down or the probability of a business being successful. Likewise we tend to say that it is highly improbable that we shall win our fortune on the football pools.

*18. Data analysis and presentation*

31. Probability is usually measured on a scale from 0.0, such an event will never occur, to 1.0 such an event is certain to occur, for example death.

32. Probabilities are usually structured on the basis of the relative frequency with which an event has occurred in the past. Thus all events have a probability between 0 and 1, although we do not know precisely what it is because we cannot be certain about the outcome of any course of action which we choose.

33. However, by means of statistical analysis, it is often possible to assess the likely probability of an event occurring. This is important for business because it is this which enables possible outcomes from events or decisions to be structured on a 'calculated risk' basis rather than pure guesswork.

34. There are two probability theories:

   - **Subjective theory** which essentially is based simply on what someone believes will happen.
   - **Frequency theory** which is applied to events which happen 'regularly' or that can be repeated over and over again under the same conditions. For example, insurance companies, calculate premiums based on the probability of events such as fire, theft or accidents taking place.

### Task 18.8

With some events it is possible to calculate the exact probability of it occurring.

Calculate the probability of:

1. A tossed coin landing as a 'head' or 'tail'.
2. Two six-sided dice thrown simultaneously, landing with a total score of 3.
3. Test your calculations by recording 50 occurrences of each.
4. Comment on your findings.

35. To get a better idea of what a set of probabilities look like, statisticians often present the information in a graphic form known as a **frequency (probability) distribution**. A set of data is called a distribution and the frequency is the number of times which any variable occurs in a distribution.

## Data Descriptions

36. The term '**raw data**' is used to describe data which has been collected but not organised or analysed in any way.

37. The summary or grouping of raw data into 'classes or categories' and determination of the number of individuals in each class is called the **class distribution**.

38. This information can be converted into a **histogram** which is constructed with rectangular blocks in such a way that their area (not heights) represent the total value.

39. The graph obtained by joining the mid-points of the top of each rectangle is called a **frequency polygon**.

40. The same data can also be converted into a **cumulative frequency distribution** which when drawn graphically is called an ogive.

41. **Example**

   The following table is a frequency distribution of the heights of 100 male students in a College.

   | Height | Number of Students |
   |---|---|
   | 4'6" – 4'10" | 3 |
   | 4'11" – 5'3" | 16 |
   | 5'4" – 5'8" | 39 |
   | 5'9" – 6'1" | 34 |
   | 6'2" – 6'6" | 8 |

42. This can be converted into a histogram and frequency polygon as follows:

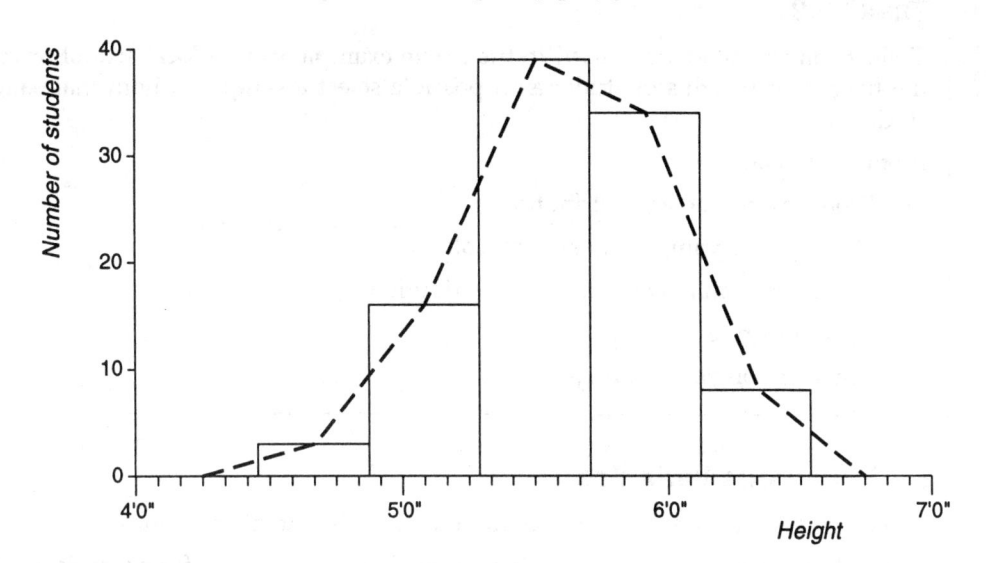

43. The same information could be shown as a cumulative frequency distribution.

| Height | Number of Students |
|---|---|
| Less than 4"6' | 0 |
| Less than 4"11' | 3 |
| Less than 5"4' | 19 |
| Less than 5"9' | 58 |
| Less than 6"2' | 92 |
| Less than 6"6' | 100 |

44. Drawn as an ogive it would appear as follows:

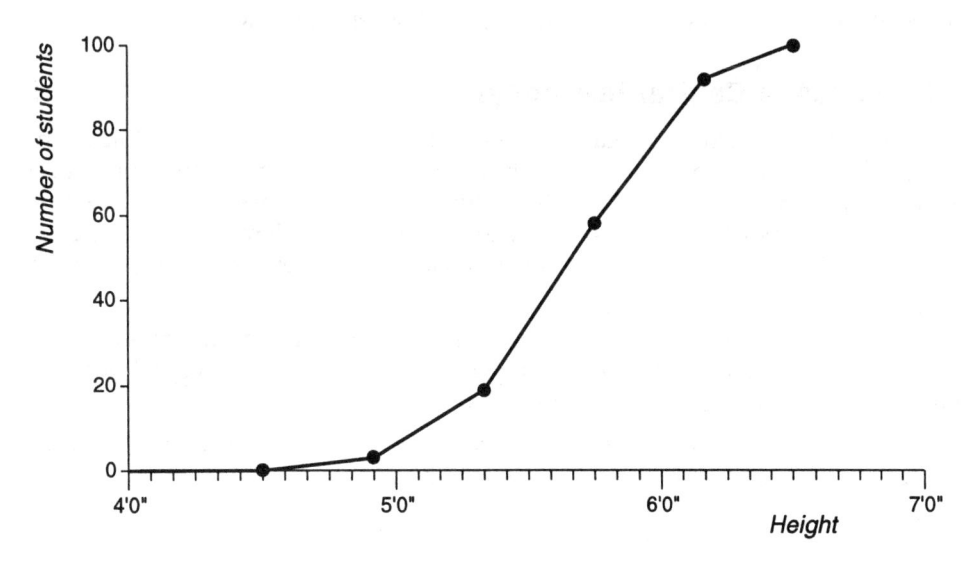

*18. Data analysis and presentation*

> **Task 18.9**
> Collect similar data to that used in the above example from a local school or college on the heights or weights of students. If possible select a sample of both male and female students.
>
> From your data:
>
> 1) Produce a frequency distribution.
> 2) Draw a histogram and frequency polygram.
> 3) Prepare a cumulative frequency distribution.
> 4) Draw an ogive.
> 5) Comment on your findings.

## Discrete and Continuous Variables

45. In statistics, a distinction is made between continuous and discrete distributions.

46. In **discrete distributions** the variable can only be a whole number. Thus, for example, the number of goals scored per team in a set of football results, the number of accidents per month in an office, or the number of visitors to an exhibition.

47. In **continuous distributions**, on the other hand, the measured variable can assume any value along a continuous scale. Examples of continuous variables include height, time, temperature, volume and weight.

## Analysing Frequency Distributions

48. There are 3 important features of any frequency distribution which we shall now consider.

    - **Averages** (or measure of central tendency)
    - The **spread of the data** (or the measure of dispersion)
    - **Degree of skewness** (or how distribution deviates from the 'normal')

## Averages (Measures of Central Tendency)

49. An average is a value which is typical and representative of a set of data. Although it should be noted that an average is not necessarily identical with any of the numbers which it represents. For example, the average number of individuals per household in an area may be 3.5 but clearly in reality it is a whole number such as 1, 2, 3, 4 or 5. There are several different types of averages which can be calculated from any set of data, the most frequently used measures being the arithmetic mean, median and mode.

50. **Arithmetic Mean.** This is the total of all individual values divided by the number of them. It is the most frequently used average, often abbreviated simply to mean, and useful because it takes into account all values and therefore can be used for further analysis.

51. Its main problem is that it can be distorted by extremes and therefore comparisons can be misleading. Consider, for example, the following two sets of numbers:

    - 16, 20, 14, 24, 21
    - 69, -47, 99, -2, -24

    Both have a mean of 19 but are clearly very different in their nature.

52. **Median.** This is found by taking the middle value of data arranged in order of magnitude (if there is an odd number of items in the set), or by the mean of the 2 middle numbers if there is an even number of items. It is a useful figure in that it helps to avoid the distortion by extremes. Consider, for example, the effect of an exam mark of 10 when all the others are between 45-65.

53. **Mode.** This is the value which occurs most frequently in a set of data. It is useful in that it can be used to represent data grouped in the form of a qualitative frequency distribution. Thus, for example, manufacturers interested in clothes sizes or shoe sizes could identify the numbers required for each size.

54. However, although the mode represents a typical value and is not affected by extremes, it does not use all of the values and therefore is not capable of further processing.

55. **Example – Mean, Median, Mode**

In the following set of numbers:

10, 14, 12, 13, 18, 14, 15, 10, 13, 10

the mode is 10 because it is the value which occurs most frequently.

If this data is rearranged in size order it would be

10, 10, 10, 12, 13, 14, 14 , 15, 18

hence the median is 13 because it is the middle value.

Whilst the mean is calculated from the sum of the values, that is,

$$10 + 14 + 12 + 13 + 18 + 14 + 15 + 10 + 13 + 10 = \frac{129}{10} = 12.9$$

> **Task 18.10**
> 
> 6 employees had weekly incomes of £250, £150, £350, £400, £150 and £200 what would be the mean, median and mode incomes?

## Measures of Dispersion

56. Whilst averages identify the middle value in a distribution they do not indicate how the values are distributed about the middle. Therefore, various measures of dispersion can be used to measure the degree which values are scattered about their mean. These include the range, interquartile range, standard deviation and the variance.

57. **Range**

This is simply the difference between the highest and lowest value in a set of data. It provides a very quick indication of the variability of data. For example, if the price of a tin of Heinz soup in 7 shops is 34p, 30p, 32p, 28p, 31p, 35p and 29p, the range is 35 minus 28 ie 7p.

58. However, because the range only considers the 2 extreme values, it ignores the other values and therefore is not a particularly accurate indicator of dispersion.

59. The **Interquartile Range** is a way of splitting data into four equal parts called **quartiles** and then finding the range between the first ($Q^1$) and third ($Q^3$) quartile.

$Q^1$ the lower quartile is the value which exceeds one quarter of the observations, ie

$$\frac{n+1}{4} \text{ value, where n = total frequency}$$

$Q^3$ the upper quartile is the value which exceeds three quarters of the observations, ie

$$\frac{n+1}{4} \times 3 \text{ value, where n = total frequency}$$

Quartiles are usually calculated from frequency distributions rather than raw data.

## 60. Example

If we take the frequency distribution of the heights of the students in 41.

$$Q^1 = \frac{n+1}{4} = 25.25$$

Since the first 2 groups contain only 19 we must take 6.25 (25.25 – 19) of the 39 cases from the third class. Thus:

$$Q^1 = 5'3'' + \frac{6.25}{39} (4'') = 5'3\tfrac{1}{2}''$$

$$Q^3 = \frac{n+1}{4} \times 3 = 75.75$$

Since the first three classes comprise only 58 cases we must take 75.75 – 58 = 17.75 of the 34 cases in the 4th class, thus:

$$Q^2 = 5'8'' + \frac{17.75}{34} (4'') = 5'10''$$

Thus the interquartile range = 5'10" – 5'3½" = 6½".

Hence, 25% of the students are less than 5'3½" in height whilst 75% are less than 5'10".

61. Thus the interquartile range measures the spread of the middle 50% of the observations and therefore is not distorted by extreme values.

### Task 18.11

Calculate the range and interquartile range of the weekly wages of the 60 manual employees of ABC Limited.

| Wages (£) | Number of Employees |
|---|---|
| 60 – 69.99 | 2 |
| 70 – 79.99 | 5 |
| 80 – 89.99 | 12 |
| 90 – 99.99 | 16 |
| 100 – 109.99 | 14 |
| 110 – 119.99 | 8 |
| 120 – 129.99 | 3 |

62. **Standard Deviation.** This is the most useful and important of all the measures of dispersion because it takes into account all the values in a set of data. The standard deviation measures the average dispersion of data around its mean value. The wider the distribution is spread around the mean, the larger will be the standard deviation.

63. It is calculated using the following formula:

$$S = \sqrt{\frac{\Sigma (X - \overline{X})^2}{n}}$$

where  $X$ = an observation
$\overline{X}$ = the mean
$n$ = the number of observations or items in a population σ means sum of

64. If 5 products had prices of £1, £2, £3, £4, £5

   then: X = $\frac{1+2+3+4+5}{5} = \frac{15}{5}$ = £3

   hence:

   | X | X − X̄ | Squared deviation | |
   |---|---|---|---|
   | 1 | −2 | −2 × −2 | = 4 |
   | 2 | −1 | −1 × −1 | = 1 |
   | 3 | 0 | 0 × 0 | = 0 |
   | 4 | +1 | 1 × 1 | = 1 |
   | 5 | +2 | 2 × 2 | = 4 |
   | 15 | £0 | | £10 |

   Thus, the sum of the squared deviations = £10 and their average = £10 ÷ 5 = £2, which represents the variance of the group of observations. To compensate for the squaring of the deviations, the square root of the average is taken, so that the standard deviation in the above =

   $\sqrt{2}$ = £1.41

65. The standard deviation, however, is usually calculated from grouped data ie from a frequency distribution. The formula for this is

   $$SD = C\sqrt{\frac{\Sigma fu^2}{\Sigma f} - \left(\frac{\Sigma fu}{\Sigma f}\right)^2}$$

   Where:
   C = the class interval (ie distance between class mid points)
   f = the frequency of an observation
   u = the number of classes away from the mean

66. **Example**

   XYZ Ltd operate an assembly line production system. The following are the times in minutes per day during which the cutting machine was not used. Calculate the average time the machine was idle during the period and its standard deviation.

   | 22 | 13 | 16 | 17 | 17 | 16 | 15 | 15 | 13 | 10 |
   |---|---|---|---|---|---|---|---|---|---|
   | 20 | 12 | 23 | 16 | 15 | 16 | 17 | 19 | 18 | 17 |
   | 15 | 12 | 17 | 19 | 14 | 14 | 15 | 14 | 17 | 16 |
   | 21 | 19 | 17 | 19 | 16 | 13 | 16 | 15 | 14 | 19 |

   Mean = X̄ = $\frac{\text{Total time}}{\text{No of observations}} = \frac{648}{40}$ = 16.2 minutes

*18. Data analysis and presentation*

| Time | Class mid-point | f | u | fu | fu² |
|---|---|---|---|---|---|
| 10-11 | | 1 | −3 | −3 | 0 |
| 12-13 | | 5 | −2 | −10 | 20 |
| 14-15 | | 10 | −1 | −10 | 10 |
| 16-17 | 16.5 | 14 | 0 | 0 | 0 |
| 18-19 | | 6 | +1 | 6 | 6 |
| 20-21 | | 2 | +2 | 4 | 8 |
| 22-23 | | 2 | +3 | 6 | 18 |
| | | $\Sigma f = 40$ | | $\Sigma fu = -7$ | $\Sigma fu^2 = 71$ |

$$SD = C\sqrt{\frac{\Sigma fu^2}{\Sigma f} - \left(\frac{\Sigma fu}{\Sigma f}\right)^2}$$

$$SD = 2\sqrt{\frac{71}{40} - \left(\frac{-7}{40}\right)^2}$$

$$SD = 2\sqrt{1.775 - 0.031} = 2.64$$

### Task 18.12

Calculate the standard deviation of the height of the male college students in the cumulative frequency distribution in paragraph 43.

## Normal Distribution

67. The dispersion of the values in a sample of a 'population' normally distribute themselves around a mean value. The greater the amount of data the more likely this is. This frequency distribution when plotted on a chart forms a bell shaped curve called a normal distribution.

68.

**Normal Distribution Curve**

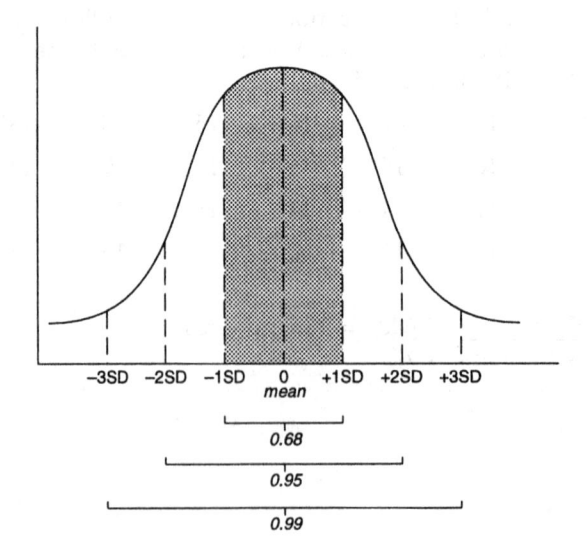

−3SD  −2SD  −1SD  0  +1SD  +2SD  +3SD
                    mean

0.68
0.95
0.99

69. All normal distribution curves have several important characteristics although the exact shape depends upon the mean and standard deviation.
    - They are always symmetrical and therefore have zero skewness.
    - The mean, median and mode all have the same value and therefore pass through the peak.
    - The width of the base is equal to 6 standard deviations.
    - 68% of values are within one standard deviation of the mean.
    - 95% are within two standard deviations of the mean.
    - 99% are within three standard deviations of the mean.
    - The curve extends infinitely at both ends.

70. The normal distribution is very important because it is the pattern most frequently encountered in the real world. The areas under the curve represent probabilities which are available ready calculated in a Z score table (see 74). Hence, it can be used to help make statistical inferences – either estimation or hypothesis testing – which can then be applied to the entire population.

71. **Estimation** involves calculating the unknown value of a population characteristic such as the average value of numerical data or a proportion having particular attributes. For example, the mean height of all adult females in Birmingham can be estimated by calculating the average height of a sample of adult females in Birmingham.

72. **Hypothesis testing** involves making a reasoned assumption, usually on the basis of observation and testing it. For example, the hypothesis that women are smaller than men or that salaries are determined by company size. These can be tested using the normal distribution curve, sample data or other statistical techniques before being accepted or rejected. A statistical hypothesis under test is referred to as the **null hypothesis.**

73. **Example**

    Z = the number of standard deviation of a variable from the mean

    $$Z = \frac{X - \mu}{\sigma}$$

    where:

    X = the value of the variable

    μ = the mean of the distribution

    σ = the standard deviation

    A manufacturer of long-life light bulbs knows that on average, they last for 2,500 hours with a standard deviation of 300 hours. The company wishes to discover the likelihood of the bulbs lasting for more than 3,000 hours.

    $$Z = \frac{3{,}000 - 2{,}500}{300} = 1.66$$

    From the tables where Z = 1.66 the probability is 0.4515. That it, there is a 45.15% chance that any bulb will last for more than 3,000 hours.

> **Task 18.13**
>
> A manufacturer of shoes is planning to introduce a new range for men. Research has revealed that 9 is the mean shoe size for men with a standard deviation of ½. Initially the company plans to produce 1000 pairs.
>
> Advise the company on the number of pairs which should be made between sizes 8½ – 9½.

## 74. Z Scores

| z | .00 | .01 | .02 | .03 | .04 | .05 | .06 | .07 | .08 | .09 |
|---|---|---|---|---|---|---|---|---|---|---|
| 0.0 | 0.0000 | 0.0040 | 0.0080 | 0.0120 | 0.0160 | 0.0199 | 0.0239 | 0.0279 | 0.0319 | 0.0359 |
| 0.1 | 0.0398 | 0.0438 | 0.0478 | 0.0517 | 0.0557 | 0.0596 | 0.0636 | 0.0675 | 0.0714 | 0.0754 |
| 0.2 | 0.0793 | 0.0832 | 0.0871 | 0.0910 | 0.0948 | 0.0987 | 0.1026 | 0.1064 | 0.1103 | 0.1141 |
| 0.3 | 0.1179 | 0.1217 | 0.1255 | 0.1293 | 0.1331 | 0.1368 | 0.1406 | 0.1443 | 0.1480 | 0.1517 |
| 0.4 | 0.1554 | 0.1591 | 0.1628 | 0.1664 | 0.1700 | 0.1736 | 0.1772 | 0.1808 | 0.1844 | 0.1879 |
| 0.5 | 0.1915 | 0.1950 | 0.1985 | 0.2019 | 0.2054 | 0.2088 | 0.2123 | 0.2157 | 0.2190 | 0.2224 |
| 0.6 | 0.2258 | 0.2291 | 0.2324 | 0.2357 | 0.2389 | 0.2422 | 0.2454 | 0.2486 | 0.2518 | 0.2549 |
| 0.7 | 0.2580 | 0.2612 | 0.2642 | 0.2673 | 0.2704 | 0.2734 | 0.2764 | 0.2794 | 0.2823 | 0.2852 |
| 0.8 | 0.2881 | 0.2910 | 0.2939 | 0.2967 | 0.2996 | 0.3023 | 0.3051 | 0.3078 | 0.3106 | 0.3133 |
| 0.9 | 0.3159 | 0.3186 | 0.3212 | 0.3238 | 0.3264 | 0.3289 | 0.3315 | 0.3340 | 0.3365 | 0.3389 |
| 1.0 | 0.3413 | 0.3438 | 0.3461 | 0.3485 | 0.3508 | 0.3531 | 0.3554 | 0.3577 | 0.3599 | 0.3621 |
| 1.1 | 0.3643 | 0.3665 | 0.3686 | 0.3708 | 0.3729 | 0.3749 | 0.3770 | 0.3790 | 0.3810 | 0.3830 |
| 1.2 | 0.3849 | 0.3869 | 0.3888 | 0.3907 | 0.3925 | 0.3944 | 0.3962 | 0.3980 | 0.3997 | 0.4015 |
| 1.3 | 0.4032 | 0.4049 | 0.4066 | 0.4082 | 0.4099 | 0.4115 | 0.4131 | 0.4147 | 0.4162 | 0.4177 |
| 1.4 | 0.4192 | 0.4207 | 0.4222 | 0.4236 | 0.4251 | 0.4265 | 0.4279 | 0.4292 | 0.4306 | 0.4319 |
| 1.5 | 0.4332 | 0.4345 | 0.4357 | 0.4370 | 0.4382 | 0.4394 | 0.4406 | 0.4418 | 0.4429 | 0.4441 |
| 1.6 | 0.4452 | 0.4463 | 0.4474 | 0.4484 | 0.4495 | 0.4505 | 0.4515 | 0.4525 | 0.4535 | 0.4545 |
| 1.7 | 0.4554 | 0.4564 | 0.4573 | 0.4582 | 0.4591 | 0.4599 | 0.4608 | 0.4616 | 0.4625 | 0.4633 |
| 1.8 | 0.4641 | 0.4649 | 0.4656 | 0.4664 | 0.4671 | 0.4678 | 0.4686 | 0.4693 | 0.4699 | 0.4706 |
| 1.9 | 0.4713 | 0.4719 | 0.4726 | 0.4732 | 0.4738 | 0.4744 | 0.4750 | 0.4756 | 0.4761 | 0.4767 |
| 2.0 | 0.4772 | 0.4778 | 0.4783 | 0.4788 | 0.4793 | 0.4798 | 0.4803 | 0.4808 | 0.4812 | 0.4817 |
| 2.1 | 0.4821 | 0.4826 | 0.4830 | 0.4834 | 0.4838 | 0.4842 | 0.4846 | 0.4850 | 0.4854 | 0.4857 |
| 2.2 | 0.4861 | 0.4864 | 0.4868 | 0.4871 | 0.4875 | 0.4878 | 0.4881 | 0.4884 | 0.4887 | 0.4890 |
| 2.3 | 0.4893 | 0.4896 | 0.4898 | 0.4901 | 0.4904 | 0.4906 | 0.4909 | 0.4911 | 0.4913 | 0.4916 |
| 2.4 | 0.4918 | 0.4920 | 0.4922 | 0.4925 | 0.4927 | 0.4929 | 0.4931 | 0.4932 | 0.4934 | 0.4936 |
| 2.5 | 0.4938 | 0.4940 | 0.4941 | 0.4943 | 0.4945 | 0.4946 | 0.4948 | 0.4949 | 0.4951 | 0.4952 |
| 2.6 | 0.4953 | 0.4955 | 0.4956 | 0.4957 | 0.4959 | 0.4960 | 0.4961 | 0.4962 | 0.4963 | 0.4964 |
| 2.7 | 0.4965 | 0.4966 | 0.4967 | 0.4968 | 0.4969 | 0.4970 | 0.4971 | 0.4972 | 0.4973 | 0.4974 |
| 2.8 | 0.4974 | 0.4975 | 0.4976 | 0.4977 | 0.4977 | 0.4978 | 0.4979 | 0.4979 | 0.4980 | 0.4981 |
| 2.9 | 0.4981 | 0.4982 | 0.4982 | 0.4983 | 0.4984 | 0.4984 | 0.4985 | 0.4985 | 0.4986 | 0.4986 |
| 3.0 | 0.4987 | 0.4987 | 0.4987 | 0.4988 | 0.4988 | 0.4989 | 0.4989 | 0.4989 | 0.4990 | 0.4990 |
| 3.1 | 0.4990 | 0.4991 | 0.4991 | 0.4991 | 0.4992 | 0.4992 | 0.4992 | 0.4992 | 0.4993 | 0.4993 |
| 3.2 | 0.4993 | 0.4993 | 0.4994 | 0.4994 | 0.4994 | 0.4994 | 0.4994 | 0.4995 | 0.4995 | 0.4995 |
| 3.3 | 0.4995 | 0.4995 | 0.4995 | 0.4996 | 0.4996 | 0.4996 | 0.4996 | 0.4996 | 0.4996 | 0.4997 |
| 3.4 | 0.4997 | 0.4997 | 0.4997 | 0.4997 | 0.4997 | 0.4997 | 0.4997 | 0.4997 | 0.4997 | 0.4998 |

The table gives the area under the normal curve between the mean and a point Z standard deviations above the mean

## Skewness

75. When a distribution is not normal, that is the arithmetic mean does not fall in the middle, it is said to be skewed. This usually means that it is distorted by a few extreme values which is shown graphically as below.

76. **Examples of Skewed Frequency Distributions**

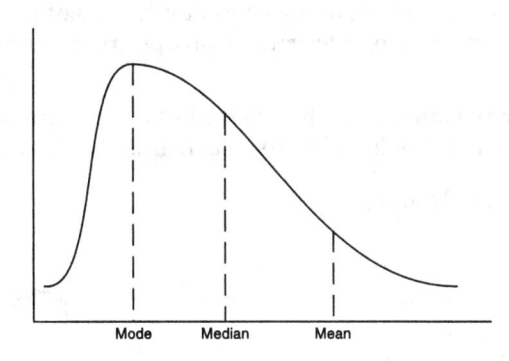

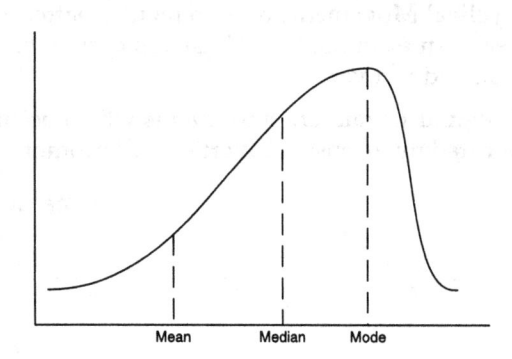

Positively skewed distribution  Negatively skewed distribution

### Task 18.14
Using the data collected for use in Task 18.9, draw a distribution curve. Comment on the reasons for its shape and whether it is normal or skewed.

## Business Forecasting

77. In order to assist planning and decision-taking, businesses need to be able to forecast (estimate) the likely future levels of such variables as sales, costs, stock and production.

78. There are a number of forecasting techniques available for this which can broadly be divided into the 3 categories of:

    - Time-series analysis  } quantitative methods
    - Causal modelling
    - Qualitative approaches

    The method chosen will depend upon the time period being forecast, degree of accuracy needed, the availability and relevance of appropriate data and cost involved. The more sophisticated the method used, the more accurate and expensive it is likely to be.

## Time Series

79. Economic and demographic statistics are usually presented as 'time series'. That is, a set of observations (measurements) which are made at regular intervals, for example, the level of inflation, production and exports which are measured monthly by the government.

80. A business, on the other hand, may produce this information for its production or sales figures. From a time series it is then possible to predict future values of a variable on the assumption that current patterns are likely to continue.

81. Time series contain 4 basic components – seasonal movements, long-term movements, cyclical movements and irregular movements.

82. **Seasonal Movements.** This refers to the pattern of upward and downward movements in data over a period of time due to recurring events which take place annually. Consequently, time series recorded at less than 3 monthly intervals are often presented **'seasonally adjusted'**.

83. For example, a sharp increase usually takes place in retail sales (which are measured in months) in December, prior to Christmas. From knowledge of what has happened in previous years, it is possible to calculate the expected rise. The seasonally adjusted figure is found by subtracting the expected

from the actual, which is useful in helping to identify any significant changes.

84. Seasonal movement can also be applied to daily, hourly or weekly situations depending on the data being analysed.

85. **Long-term movements or trends.** These refer to the general direction in which a graph of a time series appears to be moving over a long period.

86. **Cyclical Movements** refer to regular patterns which repeat themselves at intervals of more than one year. An example is the business cycle which represents intervals of prosperity, recession, depression and recovery.

87. **Irregular or random movements** which occur spasmodically, for example sales of a product may be boosted by extensive advertising or promotion, or by political factors such as an election or budget.

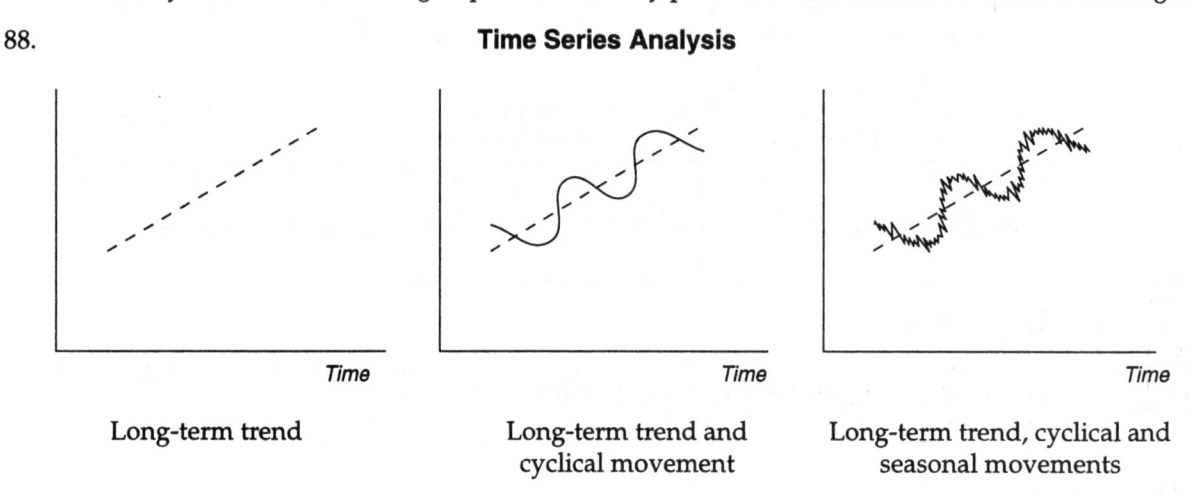

88. **Time Series Analysis**

Long-term trend | Long-term trend and cyclical movement | Long-term trend, cyclical and seasonal movements

## Causal Modelling

89. This involves identifying variables which are believed to affect or 'cause' changes in the variable to be forecast. For example, it may be considered that the most important variables which affect the sales of a product or service are its price, availability, level of advertising and promotion and consumers disposable income.

90. Once the statistical relationship (**correlation**) between the dependent variable (in this case, sales), and the associated independent variables is established, it is possible to forecast future sales from data about these variables. For example, it should be possible to forecast the level of sales for any given level of advertising expenditure, or level of demand at any given price. The statistical technique used to estimate the relationship between variables is called **regression analysis.**

## Qualitative Approaches

91. These may be used for forecasting where the data available is unsuitable or insufficient for quantitative analysis. For example, when records are incomplete or a market has changed so rapidly that historical sales data is of little use. There are a number of possible qualitative techniques available, two of which are the Delphi method and Scenario writing.

92. **Delphi Method.** This involves the use of a panel of experts selected from both inside and outside the organisation. They are presented with the forecasting problem and asked individually to give their written opinions of the likely future situation. To avoid bias, panel members are not allowed to communicate with each other. A Chairperson prepares a summary from which each member then makes a further forecast. This process is repeated until a consensus is reached known as the Delphi forecast. This is a useful technique for long-term forecasting.

93. **Scenario writing.** This involves making certain assumptions about the future from which a likely scenario is forecast. Uncertainty about the future means that there may be a range of possible outcomes and different sets of assumptions, each of which will produce different scenarios.

## Task 18.15

Business forecasting is difficult because different assumptions are likely to produce different outcomes. For example, a consumer market might be influenced by a number of variables which are difficult to predict such as interest rates, disposable incomes, the number of households and levels of unemployment. Whilst a supplier may also need to consider the level of competition, rate of technological development and product development. However, reliable, if not definitive, forecasts can be an important aid to decision-taking. Predicting the 'right' level of sales and therefore production, for example, can help to prevent over-stocking or loss of market share due to shortages both of which can be costly.

1. From the article, identify the main advantages and disadvantages of business forecasting.
2. Select 2 markets, for example DIY, insurance or house-building, and discuss what you would consider to be the main variables which influence them.
3. Now take each market in turn and consider the likely impact for a supplier of two different assumptions about 4 of the variables. For example, interest rates at 15% and 5%.

## Index numbers

94. Time series are often presented in the form of 'index numbers' instead of actual figures. The value for a base period is chosen and designated at 100. Subsequent figures are then expressed as percentages of the base.

95. **Example**

|  | 1988 | 1989 | 1990 | 1991 | 1992 |
|---|---|---|---|---|---|
| Observed | 200 | 210 | 220 | 230 | 250 |

If 1988 is chosen as the base year, then the index numbers would be calculated as follows:

1989: $\frac{210}{200} \times 100 = 105$

| Therefore | 1988 | 1989 | 1990 | 1991 | 1992 |
|---|---|---|---|---|---|
|  | 100 | 105 | 110 | 115 | 125 |

96. Thus, Index numbers measure simply and concisely the average percentage change in the price, volume or value of a variable from one period to another and are particularly useful for comparing trends in different time series. The variables in an index are often weighted to reflect their relative importance.

97. Some well known index numbers include the:
   - **Retail Price Index (RPI)** or cost of living index which measures the average price of a weighted sample of typical goods and services. The current base is January 1987 and in May 1994 it was 144.8 suggesting that retail prices have increased by 44% since 1987.
   - **Financial Times Industrial Ordinary Index** (FT-SE100) or 'Footsie' which measures price changes weighted by capitalisation in the shares of the 100 largest UK companies. It is calculated on a minute-by-minute basis.
   - **Index of Industrial Production** which measures changes in the volume of industrial output.
   - **Index of Consumers' Expenditure** which measures the overall net effect of both price and volume changes in the goods and services included in the index.
   - **Terms of Trade** which measures the relationship between the prices paid for exports and imports and whether they are moving in favour of or to the detriment of the UK calculated as:

$$\frac{\text{Index of export prices}}{\text{Index of import prices}} \times 100$$

## 18. Data analysis and presentation

98.

### Examples

| Indices of manufacturing output (1985 = 100) | | | | |
|---|---|---|---|---|
| | Share of output 1985 weight per 1,000 | 1984 | 1989 | 1990 |
| Metal manufacturing | 38 | 92.9 | 124.7 | 121.3 |
| Other minerals and mineral products | 50 | 100.4 | 120.1 | 113.4 |
| Chemicals and man-made fibres | 105 | 96.7 | 119.3 | 118.2 |
| Other metal goods | 55 | 104.4 | 113.5 | 110.9 |
| Mechanical engineering | 122 | 96.0 | 109.7 | 111.8 |
| Electrical and instrument engineering | 143 | 94.1 | 126.2 | 125.2 |
| Motor vehicles and parts | 55 | 93.5 | 125.3 | 121.0 |
| Aerospace and other transport equipment | 55 | 99.5 | 127.7 | 130.1 |
| Food, drink and tobacco | 130 | 100.4 | 105.6 | 106.1 |
| Textiles | 29 | 96.2 | 96.9 | 92.1 |
| Clothing, footwear and leather | 38 | 95.9 | 99.5 | 98.6 |
| Paper, printing and publishing | 101 | 97.8 | 132.0 | 133.8 |
| Other manufacturing | 80 | 99.1 | 132.6 | 132.4 |
| **Total** | **1,000** | **97.4** | **118.9** | **118.3** |

Source: Central Statistical Office

### Task 18.16

#### INDUSTRY RAW DEAL

Raw materials for industry have risen rapidly in price in the two months since sterling's ERM exit because suppliers have passed on price increases after devaluation faster than expected.

Provisional figures for November showed a rise of 2.4pc, much higher than expected and followed a 2.1pc October increase. Prices of materials and fuel bought by manufacturers, unchanged in the year to September, are now 4.1pc up on a year ago, the highest rate for 3 years. But the rise seems unlikely to be passed through in full to the High Street, where bargains abound. Manufacturers raised their output prices only 0.4pc in two months and 3.3pc over a year. Most forecasters see the retail price index – helped by mortgage cuts – falling below 3pc in April or May. More encouraging economic news is that total production rose 1pc in October with manufacturing up 0.3pc. Manufacturing output is now higher than a year ago, the first time in 26 months this has happened.

The above article is based on newspaper articles.

1. Identify the economic indices mentioned in the article.
2. What trends do they reveal?
3. In what sense has industry received a raw deal?
4. Why is the reference to the ERM significant?
5. What is the future economic outlook?

## Summary

99. a) The collection, recording and analysis of numerical data is called statistics.
    b) Statistical data can be presented as tables of figures, graphs, charts or diagrams.
    c) The method chosen will depend on the data concerned and preferences of the presenter but should be clear, concise and visually appealing.
    d) Important statistical concepts include trends, samples, probability and frequency distributions.
    e) Frequency distributions can be presented as tables, histograms or frequency polygons, whilst cumulative frequency distributions can be presented as frequency polygons or ogives.
    f) Measures of central tendency or averages can be calculated as the mean, median or mode.
    g) Key measures of dispersion include the range, inter-quartile range, standard deviation and the variance.
    h) The normal distribution curve is bell-shaped and shows the dispersion of data around the mean.
    i) When a distribution is not normal, it is said to be negatively or positively skewed.
    j) Statistical techniques used for business forecasting include time series analysis, causal modelling and qualitative approaches such as the delphi method and scenario writing.
    k) Time series are often presented as index numbers which show changes as a percentage of a base figure.

## Review questions *(answers can be found in the paragraphs indicated)*

1. Why are statistical techniques widely used throughout government, industry and commerce? (1-4)
2. Identify 4 different methods of presenting statistical data and give one key feature of each (7-22)
3. What are the important points to remember when presenting data? (23-24)
4. Briefly explain the statistical meaning of the terms trends, samples and probability. (25-34)
5. What is a frequency distribution? (35)
6. Distinguish between a histogram, a frequency polygon and an ogive. (38-44)
7. Using examples, explain the difference between the mean, median and mode. (49-55)
8. How and why are the range and inter-quartile range calculated? (56-61)
9. Why is the standard deviation the most useful measure of dispersion and how is it calculated? (62-66)
10. What are the characteristics of a normal distribution curve and why is it important? (67-73)
11. What do you understand by a skewed distribution? (75-76)
12. Describe the main features of a time series analysis. (78-88)
13. Explain the difference between a Delphi forecast and scenario writing as methods of business forecasting. (91-93)
14. Why are index numbers often used to present time series? (94-98)

*Asterisks indicate those questions for which there are answers in Outline Answers (page 439)*

## Essay-style questions

1.* A manager who mistrusts statistics, believes that they are not cost effective to collect and can be manipulated and presented to mislead. Prepare a response explaining how and why statistics are used and how their cost can be justified.
2. Discuss the importance of forecasting for a business and some of the methods which it could use for this purpose.
3. Describe 3 different ways in which a set of numerical data might be presented. Identify the advantages and any disadvantages of the methods chosen.

## 18. Data analysis and presentation

### Short answer

1.* Briefly explain each of the following statistical terms:
   a) Cumulative distribution
   b) histogram
   c) hypothesis
   d) frequency distribution

2.* With the use of examples, distinguish between:
   a) The mean
   b) The median
   c) The mode

3. a) What do you understand by an index number?
   b) Give 3 examples of index numbers and explain why each is of interest to businesses.

### Multiple choice

1.* The standard deviation is best defined as:
   a) The middle value in a set of data.
   b) The average dispersion of data around its mean.
   c) The measure of how a distribution is skewed.
   d) The method used to calculate the inter-quartile range.

2.* The following diagram represents:
   a) a histogram
   b) a bar chart
   c) a 'Z' chart
   d) a time series

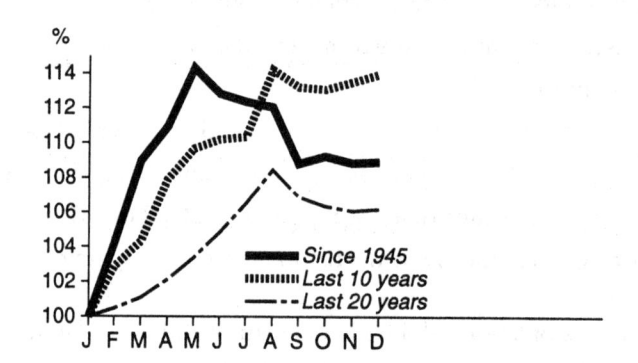

3.* Which, if any, of the following data about a football team represents a discrete variable?
   a) The result of a game.
   b) The heights of the players.
   c) The weights of the players.
   d) None of the above.

4.* What is the mean price in the following set of data?
   £1.85, £2.50, £2.65, £2.75, £2.90, £3.25
   a) £2.50
   b) £2.65
   c) £2.75
   d) £11.00

5. What is the range in the following data which relates to the price of compact discs?

   £3.99, £4.99, £7.99, £14.99, £12.99, £5.99, £11.99

   a) £7.99
   b) £8.00
   c) £11.00
   d) £9.98

6. A statistical hypothesis under test is called a

   a) Probability
   b) Normal Distribution
   c) Causal Model
   d) Null Hypothesis

*In each of the following questions, one or more of the responses is/are correct. Choose the appropriate letter which indicates the correct version.*

   A   if 1 only is correct
   B   if 3 only is correct
   C   if 1 and 2 are correct
   D   if 1, 2 and 3 are correct.

7. Which of the following are measures of central tendency?

   1. Arithmetic Mean
   2. Standard Deviation
   3. Inter-quartile Range

8. Which of the following components are included in time series analysis?

   1. Seasonal adjustments
   2. Cyclical movements
   3. Causal modelling

---

**Assignment**

Visit a library where you will find detailed statistics in government publications such as Regional Trends, Social Trends and the Annual Abstract of Statistics.

1. Your task is, using the latest available data, to carry out research into employment trends in **your region** of the UK.

   In particular, you are asked to investigate the following claims and to present data in a visually attractive way which, in your opinion, best illustrates whether or not they can be substantiated.

   a) That employment is on the increase in all industries, particularly manufacturing.
   b) That the number of industrial disputes is on the increase.
   c) That workers, on average, are the best paid in the UK.
   d) That the absentee rate from work due to sickness is one of the highest in the UK.
   e) That women are discriminated against in the field of employment.

2. Draw conclusions from the data about employment trends in your region. Include comments on any difficulties experienced or other significant factors such as the impact of seasonally adjusted figures.

# 19. Monitoring Business Performance

In Chapter One we referred to the importance of monitoring and controlling the performance of an organisation to ensure that it is achieving its objectives. In this chapter, we are considering some of the methods used to do this including:

- Cost Control
- Budgets
- Types of Budgets
- Budgetary Control
- Current and Capital Budgets
- Cash Flow Budgets
- Master Budget
- Standard Costing
- Variance Analysis
- Break-Even Point
- Importance of Quality
- Quality Control
- Quality Assurance
- Production Engineering
- Quality Standards
- Statistical Process Control
- Total Quality Management
- Operational Research
- Simulation
- Queueing Theory
- Linear Programming
- Network Analysis

## Monitoring and Measuring Performance

1. A measure of performance in an organisation is essentially a quantitative statement which is used to evaluate progress and to assist management in decision taking. Owners or managers must know what is going on if they are to be in a position to take action to ensure that objectives are achieved. Such information may also be of interest to other people who wish to assess performance such as shareholders, potential investors, suppliers, customers or the government.

2. There are a large number of different ways of monitoring and measuring performance. Some of those most commonly used include:

    - **financial controls** in particular keeping costs and budgets within agreed targets. Budgeting is an important part of an organisation's planning processes.

    - **performance ratios** based on an analysis of the accounts, in particular the balance sheet (see Chapter 11).

    - **productivity measurement** which defines performance as a ratio of output to input (see Chapter 15).

    - **quality control** which can help to increase customer satisfaction and therefore sales and also reduce costs such as those of wastage and returns.

## Cost Control

3. In order to operate efficiently and maximise profits, a business must ensure that it controls its costs. Direct costs, particularly in a manufacturing environment, are often controlled by the use of **standard costing**. Whilst **budgetary control** is used for indirect costs whereby budgets are allocated to cost centres. These control techniques are now widely used in both the public and private sectors.

4. **A cost centre** is any area of a business's activities to which costs can be ascribed. This may be to a department, a person, a geographical location or an item of equipment such as a photocopier.

## Budgets

5. A **budget** is a financial or quantitative statement relating to the use of resources to achieve specific objectives or targets over a given period of time.

6. As individuals, we all need to budget so that our income matches our expenditure. If we overspend this must be financed by using our savings, or borrowing possibly by having a bank loan or overdraft or maybe buying goods on credit and paying for them over a period of time. Alternatively, we may simply have to cut-back our expenditure and adjust our life-style accordingly, perhaps going out less or buying cheaper food and clothes.

7. To help reduce the commercial risks and in order to survive and prosper, a business must also undertake a similar exercise. This involves careful planning to produce budget forecasts for an agreed period, usually a financial year. The annual budget is then often broken down into shorter monthly or quarterly operating budgets for easier control. The use of computer-generated spreadsheets has greatly extended the scope for budgetary control.

> ### Task 19.1
> 1. Prepare two budgets, one to cover a month and another to cover 12 months, based on your own personal or family circumstances. List all the expected income and planned expenditure.
> 2. Comment on any differences between the two totals in each budget.
> 3. Identify the main cost centres and any factors which could cause costs to exceed your planned budgets. Distinguish between the fixed and variable costs.
> 4. Outline your plans to deal with any surplus or deficiency.

## Types of Budget

8. Organisations may choose to use different types of budgets depending on their needs and circumstances.

   - A **fixed budget** remains the same even if activity levels are different from those predicted.
   - A **flexible budget** is one which is adjusted in response to changes in variable costs or levels of business activity.
   - A **zero-based budget** is one which is calculated in relation to the needs of each activity rather than, as with many firms, on the basis of past spending with an adjustment for inflation. Before budgets are allocated, each activity is evaluated against its relevance to the business and perceived value-for-money.

## Budgetary Control

9. In order to monitor and control their activities, many firms set targets of achievement in line with their objectives and limits on spending for the various aspects of the business. The most common form of financial regulation is an accounting technique called budgetary control, which includes two broad stages – preparation and monitoring.

10. **Budget preparation**

    This involves:
    - identifying the objectives from which targets are set, for example in terms of output, sales volume and profits. In a large business organisation these targets will be sub-divided so that there is an individual target to achieve for each factory, office, branch, geographical area or product.
    - preparing initial budgets in line with these objectives. Thus, for example, budgets will be set for purchasing, production, distribution, personnel, administration and capital expenditure.
    - reviewing and co-ordinating these budgets with adjustments for any anomalies, before
    - final co-ordination and preparation. Thus, for example, if a firm has a production and sales target of 100,000 units it might allocate a budget for capital spending of £20,000 to achieve it.

## 19. Monitoring business performance

11. Thus budgetary control involves the planning of expenditure on the basis of a business's expected income.

12. **Continuous monitoring**

    Once a budget is allocated to a cost centre, actual performance must then be regularly checked by managers against targets to ensure that spending is within the limits set. Each department or section must be provided with information which it can use to assess progress against its budget. Any problems can then be identified and corrective action taken where necessary.

### Current and Capital Expenditure Budgets

13. Current expenditure requires the allocation of a budget which is sufficient for the coming year's planned level of operation to be achieved efficiently in line with objectives. But a budget will also be necessary for capital expenditure on equipment or other resources needed to ensure the future development of the organisation.

14. Whilst the current budget is likely to be based on the organisation's projected cash flow for the financial year, the capital budget also often involves additional funding in the form of loans, for example from banks or other external sources (see Chapter 9).

### Cash Flow Budgets

15. Money flows both into and out of a business. When it sells goods or services, it receives income but it also has a flow of money out in order to meet its fixed and variable costs such as payments to suppliers and workers. It is essential for success that there is a regular **cash flow** into a business. Therefore a system of control is important to ensure that a firm is able to pay its expenses and earn sufficient additional income to make a profit. Therefore a budget for cash flow is also prepared.

16. When cash shortfalls are predicted it will be necessary to negotiate bank loans or overdrafts. Whilst when cash surpluses are likely, arrangements can be made to utilise the cash by investing it.

17. A firm which suffers from cash deficiencies can quickly find itself unable to meet its current liabilities which could ultimately lead to liquidation. (see Chapter 2).

> **Task 19.2**
>
> Wholesale wine merchants, Sudlow's, have been experiencing excellent sales and the promise of profits well in excess of those forecast. The company approaches its bank for an overdraft to tide it through the current operating period.
>
> The bank is concerned at the size of the overdraft requested because it feels that it may indicate a cash flow problem. However, after further discussion with the company, it agrees to lend half the amount requested and recommends the introduction of tighter credit and stock controls as a matter or urgency.
>
> 1. Why do you think that the bank was concerned in this situation?
> 2. How might the bank's recommendations be implemented and how will they assist with the cash flow problem?

### Master Budget

18. The individual budgets for budgetary control, capital expenditure and cash flow are all incorporated into a master budget which includes a statement of the anticipated future profit and loss account and balance sheet.

## Task 19.3

From the following statement by a company executive, identify the potential advantages of using budgetary control in a business. Does this statement suggest any possible disadvantages?

'In line with the strategic plan and operational objectives, we ask each departmental manager to prepare a forecast of the likely expenditure needs for their area of responsibility. After adjustment, the agreed functional budgets are then co-ordinated into the master budget. Close monitoring provides regular information for managers which is so essential for the efficient control of activities and achievement of objectives because problems can be anticipated in advance. It also helps to ensure that resources are used in the most efficient and profitable way.'

## Standard Costing

19. Standard costing is the calculation of how much costs should be under defined working conditions and is best suited to repetitive manufacturing processes. Standard costs are usually based on the time (in standard hours or minutes) required to complete a certain volume of work. Thus, for example, standard costs would be established for labour, materials, production and sales. A proportion of indirect costs or overheads will then be added to these costs.

20. Costing is important because it provides an analysis of data which a business can then use for decision taking. For example, deciding whether to make products itself or to buy from someone else, or whether or not it can make sufficient profit to enable it to enter particular market segments.

## Variance Analysis

21. The differences between the actual results achieved and the planned budget or standard cost are called variances. These are used to prepare **exception reports** for management which are used to quickly focus attention on potential problem areas in the business so that corrective action can be taken.

22. Variances can be:
    - **negative (adverse)** which occurs when actual revenues fall short of the budget or standard, or when actual costs exceed budget or standard.
    - **positive (favourable)** which occurs when actual revenues exceed budget or standard, or when actual costs are less than budget or standard.

23. The main variances cover Direct-Materials, Direct-Labour, Overheads and Sales-Revenue. Each of these is now considered in more detail including possible reasons for the variances.

## Direct-Material Variances

24. • **Material-price variances.** If the prices paid for materials are higher or lower than the standard, it could mean that the market price has changed or that the firms' buying policy needs attention.

25. • **Material-useage variances.** If more materials have been used than the standard, this could reflect inefficiency, high wastage, theft or poor quality.

## Direct-Labour Variances

26. • **Labour-rate variances.** The most usual problem in a business is that there has been an increase in the rates paid. This may be due to excessive overtime or because higher paid labour is being used. If the changed rates are to be the norm in the future, then the standard will need revising.

## 19. Monitoring business performance

27. • **Labour-efficiency variances.** This shows whether more or less time has been spent on production than the standard allows. This may necessitate remedial action to sort out problems which may be due to worker inefficiency, machine breakdowns, poor planning or material shortages.

### Overhead Variances

28. • **Overhead expenditure variances.** If expenditure is higher than the standard it could mean that the full-cost of overheads is not being **absorbed** (covered) in the price. Any inaccuracy must therefore be rectified and any permanent change in the overhead costs would require the standard to be changed. **Over-absorption** would take place if the actual overhead costs are less than the standard.

29. • **Overhead volume variances.** If actual output is less than planned, this will produce a variance because the fixed overheads will not then be fully absorbed. On the other hand, over-absorption of overheads occurs when more is produced than planned.

### Sales-Revenue Variances

30. • **Sales price variances.** If the actual sales, based on the costs of production, are less than the standard cost, then this will be of concern to a business because it is likely to reduce profits. It may indicate that the cost of sales is higher than expected.

31. • **Sales volume variances.** If the actual volume of sales are less than the standard or budgeted volume, then a firm will need to identify why and take action to correct it. Reasons might include increased competition, or problems with some element of the marketing mix.

> **Task 19.4**
>
> A company has production and sales targets of 10,000 items for the current year. Its production levels are usually fairly even throughout the year but sales are subject to wide fluctuations with most taking place in the first half of the trading period.
>
> After 6 months, its actual production is running at 6,000 units with sales of 4,500 units. The Board had recently decided to raise prices to cover the rising cost of raw materials.
>
> 1. What variances, if any, should be brought to the attention of the Board?
> 2. What are the implications for the Company and what action would you recommend?

### Break-Even Point

32. Linked with the concept of planning through budgetary control is the use of break-even charts. These enable firms to analyse changes in sales volume, prices and costs as shown below.

| A<br>Output<br>(no of units)<br>produced) | B<br>Fixed<br>Costs<br>£ | C<br>Variable<br>Costs<br>£ | D<br>(B+C)<br>Total<br>Costs, £ | E<br>Sales<br>Revenue<br>£ | F<br>(E+D)<br>Profit<br>£ | G<br>(E+D)<br>Loss<br>£ |
|---|---|---|---|---|---|---|
| 0 | 2000 | 0 | 2000 | 0 | | 2000 |
| 100 | 2000 | 500 | 2500 | 1000 | | 1500 |
| 200 | 2000 | 1000 | 3000 | 2000 | | 1000 |
| 300 | 2000 | 1500 | 3500 | 3000 | | 500 |
| 400 | 2000 | 2000 | 4000 | 4000 | NIL | NIL |
| 500 | 2000 | 2500 | 4500 | 5000 | 500 | |
| 600 | 2000 | 3000 | 5000 | 6000 | 1000 | |
| 700 | 2000 | 3500 | 5500 | 7000 | 1500 | |

33. The above information shows a firm with variable costs of £5 per unit and a selling price of £10 per unit. In this situation the firm would need to sell 400 units before it reaches break-even point i.e. where total costs = total sales revenue. Beyond this point a profit can be made. However, if the firm sells less than 400 units it will be operating at a loss.

The break even point can be calculated using the following formula:

Break-even = $\dfrac{F}{S-V}$

Where F = total fixed costs

S = Selling price per unit

V = Variable costs per unit

Thus in the example above, we know that F = £2,000 S=£10 V=£5

Therefore break-even = $\dfrac{2,000}{10-5}$ = $\dfrac{2,000}{5}$ = 400 units

Variable costs at break-even point = 400 × £5 = £2,000

This information can also be shown graphically on a break-even chart.

34.

**Break Even Chart**

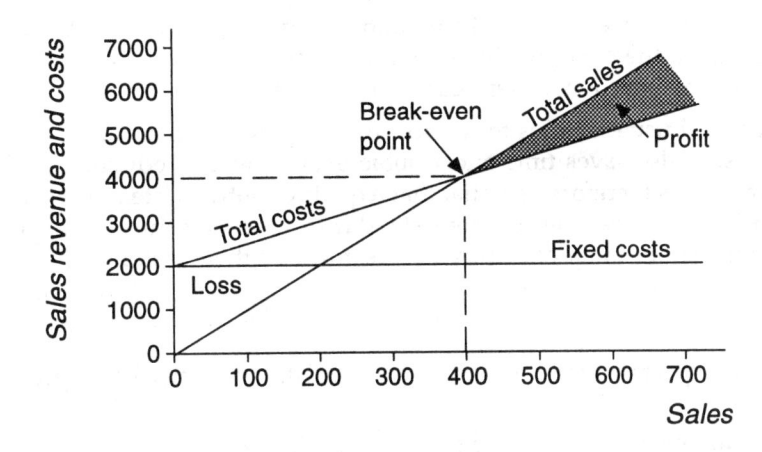

[Break-even chart showing Sales revenue and costs on y-axis (0 to 7000) and Sales on x-axis (0 to 700). Lines shown: Total sales, Total costs, Fixed costs. Break-even point at 400 units. Areas labelled Loss and Profit.]

A break-even chart illustrates the profit or loss at different levels of a firm's output.

35. In the illustration the sales revenue of £6,000 would represent the sale of 600 items sold for £10 each. From the chart, we can also see that it would cost £5,000 to make this number of items. Thus the cost of producing each item would be £5,000 divided by 600 = £8.33. Thus the profit per item sold was £1.67 (£10-£8.33).

36. On the other hand, if sales were only £3,000 ie 300 items, we can see that the total cost would be £3,500. Thus to produce each item it would cost £11.67 (£3,500 divided by 300). At this level of sales, the firm would be making a loss of £1.67 per item.

37. As the firm sells more so the average cost of producing each unit will fall. This is because the fixed costs do not change and therefore these costs are spread over a larger output.

Average or unit cost = $\dfrac{\text{Total Cost}}{\text{Output}}$

Using the figures in the above example

a) At an output of 100 Average cost = $\dfrac{2,500}{100}$ = £25 per unit

b) At an output of 500 Average cost = $\dfrac{4,500}{500}$ = £9 per unit

Thus, although the variable cost per unit is still £5, the fixed cost per unit has fallen from £20 (£25-£5) to £4 per unit (£9-£5).

## Task 19.5

Gary Carter owns a small garage where he services cars. Each week he usually has about 30 customers, the average bill being £100 per customer. Fixed costs are £400 per week, variable costs are about £60 per customer.

1. Give examples of possible fixed and variable costs which Gary will have in his business.
2. Construct a break-even chart and identify the break-even point.

## Importance of Quality

38. Quality is something which everyone recognises and is familiar with but a concept which is not always easy to define. Essentially it is about the way in which products or services are perceived by customers relative to the alternatives available. Some organisations, for example, like Sainsbury's and Marks and Spencer are immediately associated with quality because they have clearly identifiable standards which demonstrate a degree of excellence.

39. In a manufacturing situation, a widely used definition of quality is that of 'fitness for purpose' whilst in a service environment the 'best possible standard' is often used. But, however, it is defined quality is about the attributes of a product or service which are needed in order to satisfy a customer.

40. A quality approach to business helps to reduce costs of production because it results in less waste, re-work and delays. It also saves time and trouble dealing with production problems and/or customer dissatisfaction. It is therefore essential that a quality control system exists to ensure that goods and services consistently meet the required standards. Quality control is also necessary because firms have the legal responsibility of a 'duty of care' towards their customers.

## Aspects of Quality

41. Quality has several aspects which essentially distinguish between what a product is and what is does. These are:

    - **Quality of design.** This is the proposed standards in the design specification. A product will have been developed so that it meets consumer expectations, including those for quality.
    - **Quality of conformance.** This is the extent to which the goods produced meet the standards laid down. It is important that products are consistently produced to the required standards.
    - **Quality of performance.** This is the extent to which a product achieves what consumers expect from it which is particularly important for repeat business.
    - **Quality of reliability.** This is the extent to which a product consistently performs well over a period of time. Again this is important for future business.

## Task 19.6

Select 4 different products used in your own home, college, school or place of work.

Comment on

1. the extent to which they meet the various aspects of quality identified above, and
2. how, if at all, these aspects affect you as a user of the products.
3. how the products have changed in the past 5 years.

## Quality Control

42. The object of quality control is to prevent faulty components or finished goods being produced thereby reducing costs and helping to increase customer satisfaction. The value of quality control is that it actually reduces the costs of production. This usually involves both the systematic inspection of products during production and also the examination of any faulty goods returned so that corrective action can be taken and problems remedied.

## Methods of Quality Control

43. The way in which quality is controlled varies and can involve one or more of a number of different approaches including:-
    - Quality assurance
    - Production engineering
    - 'Zero-defects'
    - Quality circles
    - Quality standards
    - Statistical process control
    - Total quality management

> **Task 19.7**
> 1. Identify at least 6 organisations which you feel offer quality products and/or services.
> 2. Explain what they offer which determines this.
> 3. What standards do you personally look for or expect from such an organisation?
> 4. Who benefits from these standards and how?
> 5. Can you identify any areas for improvement in the products or services of the organisations concerned?

## Quality Assurance

44. Quality assurance is a term used to describe an approach to production and the checks and audits which are carried out to ensure that quality control procedures are followed.

45. This approach involves working with suppliers to ensure that materials and components meet the required standards of, for example, safety, reliability and performance. Some companies, for example, Marks and Spencer and Ford actually set their own very rigid standards for the quality of their products and then carefully select manufacturers who can meet them. They also insist that suppliers are organised in such a way as to ensure quality output and carry out regular checks to verify that standards are being maintained. They will also reject complete batches if just one item is found to be below standard.

## Production Engineering

46. The control of many modern manufacturing processes, particularly where highly automated or computerised technology is involved, is such a complex issue that it is now common practice for organisations to use specialist production engineers to assist with the selection, planning and installation of such equipment.

47. They will be involved in drawing up specifications for machines and equipment which will include defining the standards of quality to be achieved. They may also be used to monitor and evaluate manufacturing processes with a view to finding ways of improving them.

## Zero-Defects

48. Achieving quality is often as much to do with people as with machines. It has been recognised that human error can arise because of such factors as boredom, fatique, indifference to a job and lack of vigilance. The more automated is the production process, the more such factors are likely to exist.

49. Therefore, many organisations have adapted a positive approach to such potential problems by introducing a 'zero-defects' programme whereby workers are rewarded with financial and non-financial incentives if output of the desired quality is achieved. The cost of such rewards is often paid as a small percentage of the overall savings in production costs.

*19. Monitoring business performance*

## Quality Circles

50. Sometimes called quality control circles, these originated in the USA but are also widely used in Japan where they have been extensively applied in relation to just-in-time production methods. Quality circles consist of groups of shopfloor workers who meet regularly to discuss production problems, for example, rising costs or wastage, identifying their causes and looking for solutions.

51. This form of worker participation, with management support, has been found not only to raise quality awareness but also to improve employee motivation. This results from a greater recognition, responsibility and involvement in decisions about the business which in some organisations has been extended to include other important issues such as health, safety and environmental issues.

## Quality Standards

52. **British Standards Institution (BSI).** This is an independent organisation, although it receives financial support from the Government, which is important for the development of quality control in the UK. BSI's purpose is to set minimum standards for a whole range of products in terms of quality, safety and reliability.

53. It also works closely with the **International Standards Organisation (ISO)** to promote the use of internationally agreed terms, definitions and standards. Products which reach the specifications laid down are awarded the BSI kitemark as a symbol of quality provided that the manufacturers agree to regular inspection and control.

### Task 19.8

1. In your home, college, school or place of work, identify at least 6 items which have a British Standard.
2. Comment on the importance of BSI to you as a consumer.

54. **BS 5750** (which equates to ISO 9000 Series). The BSI also has a general purpose standard against which an organisation's overall quality management system can be assessed. BS 5750 sets out how activities should be operated and controlled to ensure that products conform to the specifications laid down.

55. If an organisation wishes to be registered as having achieved BS 5750, it must undergo a detailed analysis and assessment of each step in the production process. This covers, for example, management responsibility, design control, document control, purchasing, production, inspection and testing, quality records, quality audits and training. BS 5750 can now be adapted by any type of organisation including those in the service sector.

56. The BS 5750 registration mark is not a product quality kitemark or specification but rather confirmation that an organisation has **quality systems** and procedures in place. This, however, is very important and nowadays many large organisations will only deal with suppliers who have achieved this standard.

## Statistical Process Control

57. The best and surest check of quality is of course 100% inspection and/or testing of products. This, however, would be very expensive and generally speaking neither practical or cost effective. Therefore, it is only likely where very small quantities are being produced or where a product could represent a major health or safety risk.

58. It is more usual for spot checks to be made from time to time, either ad hoc or on a regular basis using statistical sampling techniques. Where large scale flow production is used, it is possible to calculate the number and frequency of checks needed to maintain the required quality standards.

## Task 19.9

1. Find out how quality is controlled in your place of work or study.
2. Compare this with another organisation well known to you. Perhaps one of those chosen in the Assignment in Chapter One.
3. Comment with reasons, on any significant differences in the approach used.

## Total Quality Management (TQM)

59. Seen by some people as an alternative to BS 5750, particularly in the non-manufacturing sector, TQM originated in the USA and is widely used both there and in Japan. TQM is the term used to describe the process and management of change in pursuit of quality. It involves an organisation's mission, culture and working practices being directed towards the continuous pursuit of improvement.

60. A TQM culture requires:
    - creation of a climate where people are not satisfied with current inputs, processes, performance or outcomes.
    - a commitment by everyone in the organisation to customers and their interests, needs, requirements and expectations.
    - management support and positive promotion of a commitment to quality
    - training throughout an organisation to achieve this culture and commitment.

61. The basic philosophy behind TQM is that anything can be improved. To do this successfully requires:
    - **involvement and consultation with customers** in the pursuit of improvements – both internal and external customers.
    - **overcoming internal obstacles** and solving problems which prevent people from doing the best that they can.
    - **possible investment** in equipment, facilities and training to improve the skills of the workforce.
    - **management by targets** so that everyone knows clearly what is required and what progress is being made.
    - **people-based management** whereby participation in decision-making is encouraged and people work together to identify and solve problems in the pursuit of improvement. It is also important that people's efforts are recognised and acknowledged.
    - **implementation of systems and procedures** which regularly review and evaluate all aspects of the organisation's work

62. TQM may take several years to achieve in an organisation because of a reluctance to change 'the way things have always been done', but once established, it provides a sound basis for continued quality and excellence. Many High Street banks, insurance companies, building societies and retail organisations have implemented TQM.

63. The benefits of TQM for the organisation and its employees include:
    - **Provision of a competitive edge** – most people will pay for quality and seek-out a supplier who offers it.
    - **Job enrichment** – work can become more interesting by involving people in the way things are done and giving them more responsibility for getting it done.
    - **Job satisfaction** because it is about doing things better.
    - **Job security** because it overcomes the cost of poor quality and helps an organisation to stay in business.

## BS 5750 or TQM

64. BS 5750 and TQM are both methods available to managers seeking to implement quality assurance and control. BS 5750 is about systems and procedures which organisations should follow to achieve quality, whereas TQM is a process for managing and measuring the continuous quality improvement of everything that an organisation does. Some organisations have introduced one or the other whilst others have chosen to introduce both methods. The important issue is what best meets the needs of an organisation.

---

**Task 19.10**

### QUALITY CONTROL MANAGER
#### Competitive Salary + Car + Benefits

We are one of the country's leading 'Own Label' convertors of toilet rolls, kitchen rolls, facial tissues, cling film and aluminium foil. Our high speed, automated, rewinding and packaging lines are amongst the best in the industry, and represent our commitment to high quality, value for money products. As a prominent member of our management team, you will lead and motivate a small department responsible for quality assurance with 3 key tasks.

* Investigating and eliminating service quality failures
* Assessing and monitoring service quality to develop and enhance current levels
* Installing and maintaining BS 5750

The position carries overall control of quality systems company wide, and you will carry out systems audits and improvements, cost reduction programmes and supplier assessments. The role is vital to our company's continued progress, and will provide an exciting opportunity for a Quality specialist, who has a proven track record within a high volume production environment.

Qualified to degree level or equivalent, you will currently be providing a QA service through the implementation of TQM or BS 5750 in a small to medium size company. The successful applicant will be able to communicate at all levels within our company, and be confident in dealing with customers and suppliers.

Further details from _____

1. Explain the role of the quality control manager in the above post.
2. In what ways are TQM and BS 5750 important for quality control?
3. From your knowledge of quality control suggest ways in which the 3 key tasks can help to improve quality.

---

## Operational Research

65. There are a number of statistical techniques available to assist managers in the process of decision-taking as they strive to achieve the best use of resources. Together these techniques are referred to as operations or operational research (O.R.) and they can be applied in many areas of business activity including production, marketing, distribution, finance and stock control.

66. O.R. involves:
   - **defining** the problem
   - **formulating** a model to represent the system
   - **manipulating** the model in order to develop decisions or strategies in respect of the cost, quality control and direction of the variables.
   - **identifying the best solution** which after testing is then applied to the real problem.

> **Task 19.11**
> 
> Identify a recent problem which you have faced at work, home, college or school.
> 1. Define the problem and the approach you adopted to solve it.
> 2. Comment on how, if at all, your approach to the problem compares with the OR approach outlined above.

67. The main O.R. techniques are:
    - simulation
    - queueing theory
    - linear programming
    - network analysis often referred to as critical path analysis
    - net present value calculations which are used to evaluate investment projects are discussed in Chapter 10.

## Simulation

68. Simulation techniques involve studying the problems of real-life systems by building and analysing statistical models which contain all the relevant variables, constraints and probabilities.

69. Simulation programs are usually run on a computer which enables the model to be varied and the effects of different decisions or circumstances, over several months or years, to be quickly analysed. From the predictions, management decisions can be made to improve efficiency by changing the existing system or introducing new ones.

70. Where a system cannot be specified precisely, a **Monte Carlo** simulation is used which is a model based on historical data or estimated values regarding the likely frequency of events.

71. The different types of simulation techniques used can range from simple spreadsheets to complex mathematical formulas or models such as those used for training pilots and astronauts. Such techniques offer a very quick and relatively cheap method of business analysis and are frequently used to help solve stock control and queueing problems.

## Queueing Theory

72. This is a simulation technique used specifically to analyse business operations where queues are involved. Examples might include:
    - customers waiting to pay at supermarket checkouts.
    - the flow of a production line to prevent bottlenecks.
    - trains waiting to enter or leave stations or planes taking-off or landing at airports.
    - customers waiting for service in banks.

73. The technique involves studying the features of the situation such as average waiting times, peaks and troughs and idle periods. The cost of resources needed to reduce queueing or service times is then assessed against the cost of time lost by waiting.

> **Task 19.12**
> 
> Study and analyse a queueing situation with which you are familiar, for example, in a canteen or bus queue and suggest ways in which it might be improved.

## Linear Programming

74. This is another complex statistical planning technique used to determine how to produce the highest output from a given set of machines and equipment, taking account of any constraints such as production time. It can be extended to deal with more than one product, and can also provide a mea-

## 19. Monitoring business performance

sure of the opportunity costs of different combinations of inputs and outputs, provided they are expressed in physical terms and all the relationships involved are linear.

75. Linear programming came to prominence when it was widely used in World War II to deal with the transportation, scheduling and allocation of resources subject to certain restrictions such as cost and availability. It is now used in many industries including, for example, the scheduling of iron and steel production, in the oil and paper industries and in transport (to minimise freight costs).

## Network Analysis

76. A common technique used for planning and co-ordinating complex projects is called Network Analysis. You may also see it referred to as:
    - **Critical Path Analysis (CPA)** which is used to identify the time which a project should take to complete.
    - **Critical Path Networks (CPN)** which assumes that the time required to complete an activity can be calculated precisely.
    - **Programme Evaluation Review Technique (PERT)** which recognises that the time to complete an activity cannot be predicted with certainty and is therefore based on probability.

77. Network analysis can be used with commercial, industrial and administrative processes to identify the critical activities in a sequence of operations or procedures and thus to determine the shortest possible time for completion. The activities are shown diagramatically as a network which is then analysed to determine the critical path. Some activities will be performed simultaneously in parallel, whilst others are performed sequentially, one after another. The time needed to complete each activity can then be added together to give the minimum completion time.

78. The **critical path** is that path through the network which takes longest to complete. Thus, if any activity on the critical path is delayed, then the final completion time of the project will also be delayed.

79. As shown in the example below, a network analysis chart consists of a series of circles (called nodes), each of which is numbered to represent a particular part of the project; and lines representing the activities which link the parts together.

80. Where an activity depends on two or more activities to finish before it can begin, a dotted line called a **dummy** is used to indicate the link and also that it requires no time or resources.

81.
**A simple network**

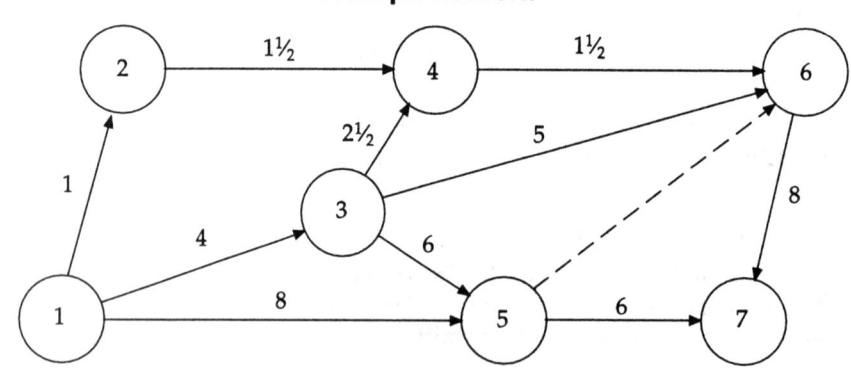

82. Each activity is numbered, in this case 1-7, together with the number of days it should take to complete. Activities not on the critical path will be completed in a shorter time and thus it is possible for free time (called the **float**) to exist. This will create resources which can possibly be switched to the critical path.

83. The float is calculated from the difference between the earliest start time (EST) and latest finish time (LFT) of each activity and is important because it shows how long the start of an activity can be delayed before it affects the start time of the next activity.

84. The total float for the whole project can also be calculated to show how long the start can be delayed before the overall length of the project is affected. Critical activities do not have any float. The float is often shown by splitting the node as follows:

85.

Node number → ⊕ ← Earliest start time (EST)
           ← Latest finish time (LFT)

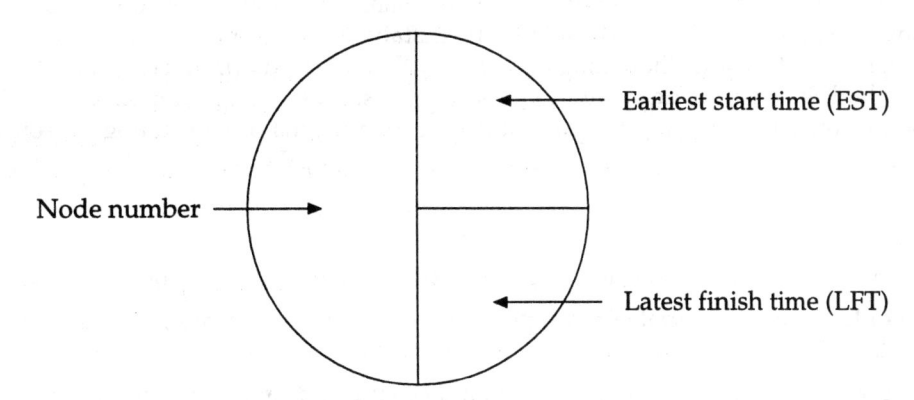

86. The EFT for the project can be calculated by totalling the activity times. Some activities have different times depending on how they are approached through the network. Activity 4, for example, could take 6½ or 2½ days. But since it depends on the completion of both activity 1 to 2 and 1 to 3, the earliest completion date must be the longer time path.

87. The critical path can be found by working backwards so that the LFT of each activity is determined. This is calculated by subtracting each activity time from the total project time, again taking the longest path as shown below.

88.

| Event No. | Earliest Start Time (Days) | Latest Finish Time (Days) |
| --- | --- | --- |
| 1 (start) | 0 | 0 |
| 2 | 1 (1 2) | 7 (7 6 4 2) |
| 3 | 4 (1 3) | 5 (7 6 3) |
| 4 | 6½ (1 3 4) | 8½ (7 6 4) |
| 5 | 10 (1 3 5) | 10 (7 6 5) |
| 6 | 10 (1 3 5 6) | 10 (7 6) |
| 7 (end) | 18 (1 3 5 6 7) | 18 (7) |

89. **A simple network showing the EST and LFT and critical path**

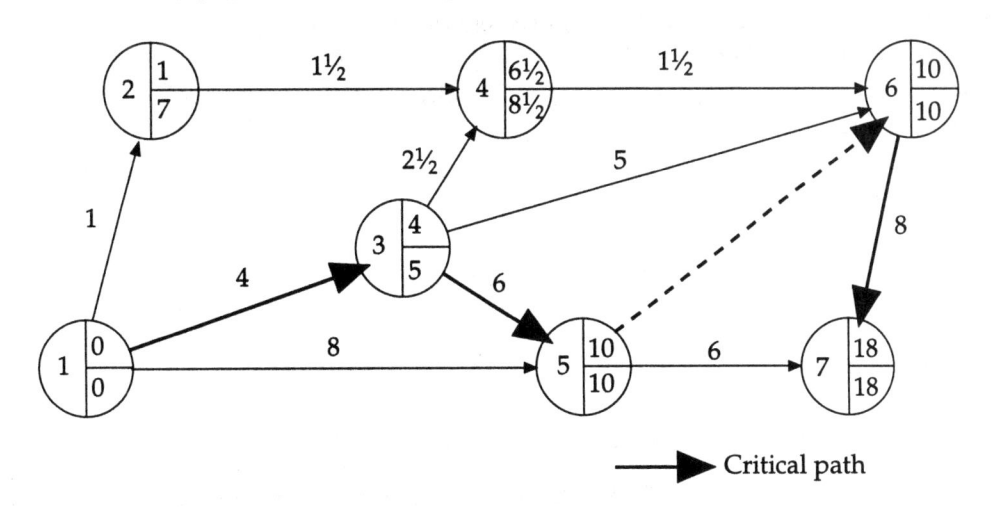

→ Critical path

### Task 19.13

On Thursday, you decide to invite 4 friends round for a meal on Saturday evening at 8.00pm. Consider the activities involved in preparing the meal and also being ready on time. List the activities and prepare a critical path analysis.

*19. Monitoring business performance*

90. Network analysis techniques are widely used for planning the construction of buildings, bridges, ships, motorways and aircraft and also for the installation of computer systems. In practice, it is difficult to accurately predict how long activities will take because they are affected by such factors as good or bad weather, or delays in material supplies. Nonetheless, network analysis is a useful technique not only for planning purposes but also as a means of controlling a project through to completion.

## Summary

91. a) The monitoring of performance is important to ensure that organisations meet their objectives.

   b) This could include financial control, performance ratios, production, measurement and quality control.

   c) Costs can be controlled by the use of standard costing and/or budgetary control.

   d) Budgetary control involves the allocation of finance to cost centres and monitoring the way in which it is used.

   e) Budgets can be fixed, flexible or zero-based.

   f) Budgets can be prepared for current expenditure, capital expenditure, and cash flow. Together these provide a summary on master budgets.

   g) Standard costing is the calculation of how much costs should be under defined working conditions.

   h) Differences between the actual results achieved and the planned budget or standards are called variances.

   i) Variances, which can be negative or positive, are used to prepare exception reports for management.

   j) The main variances cover direct-material, direct-labour, overheads and sales-revenue.

   k) Break-even point is the level of sales at which total costs are equal to total revenue.

   l) This information can be shown graphically on a break-even chart.

   m) A quality approach to business helps to reduce the costs of production.

   n) Quality control can be achieved by using one or more of the techniques of quality assurance, production engineering, zero-defects, quality circles, quality standards, statistical process control or total quality management.

   o) Operational research is one of the main statistical techniques available to assist managers in making decisions.

   p) The main O.R. techniques are simulation, queueing theory, linear programming, network analysis and net present value.

## Review questions *(answers can be found in the paragraphs indicated)*

1. Why and how can an organisation measure and monitor its performance? (1-2)
2. Why do businesses need to control costs? (3)
3. What is a budget? (5-7)
4. Distinguish between fixed, flexible and zero-based budgets. (8)
5. How does a system of budgetary control help a firm to monitor its activities? (9-17)
6. What is a master budget? (18)
7. Explain why standard costing is particularly suited for use in repetitive manufacturing processes. (19-20)
8. With the use of examples, explain how variance analysis can assist managers. (21-31)
9. At what point does a firm break even? (32-37)
10. Outline the meaning of and importance of quality in a business organisation. (38-41)

11. Describe 4 different methods of quality control. (43-64)
12. Describe some of the main techniques of operational research and state why an organisation might choose to use them. (65-85)

*Asterisks indicate those questions for which there are answers in Outline Answers (page 439)*

## Essay-style questions

1.* A large U.K. company with world-wide markets is experiencing difficulty in achieving its budgeted sales for the first quarter of the current year.

   Budgeted and actual sales for this quarter are as follows:

   | PRODUCT | \multicolumn{2}{c}{UK} | \multicolumn{2}{c}{EU} | \multicolumn{2}{c}{N America} | \multicolumn{2}{c}{Others} |
   |---|---|---|---|---|---|---|---|---|
   | | \multicolumn{8}{c}{Sales (thousands)} |
   | | Bud | Act | Bud | Act | Bud | Act | Bud | Act |
   | A | 20 | 18.6 | 8 | 6.4 | 6 | 3.9 | 4 | 2.7 |
   | B | 16 | 14.0 | 6 | 5.6 | 5 | 4.8 | 3 | 3.2 |
   | C | 12 | 12.2 | 8 | 8.4 | 7 | 7.2 | 8 | 5.1 |
   | D | 10 | 6.5 | 4 | 2.8 | 6 | 3.7 | 8 | 5.6 |

   a) Present these figures in a suitable form to senior management.

   b) Write a report to the managing director, explaining these figures together with reasons for the budgeted sales not being generally achieved.

   c) Assume that the present trend continues. Suggest possible action that can be taken.

2. Discuss the importance of quality in a business organisation and how this might be achieved.

3. Discuss the meaning of operational research and the main techniques which a business organisation might use.

## Short answer

1.* a) Distinguish between standard costing and budgetary control in a business.
    b) How are budgets prepared?
    c) Outline 3 methods which may be used to calculate budgets.

2.* a) Explain the term 'variance analysis'.
    b) With the use of examples, explain the difference between a negative and positive variance in respect of materials, labour, overheads and sales revenue.

3. Peter Townsend runs a small garden shed business. The following graph shows his costs and sales for the month of July.

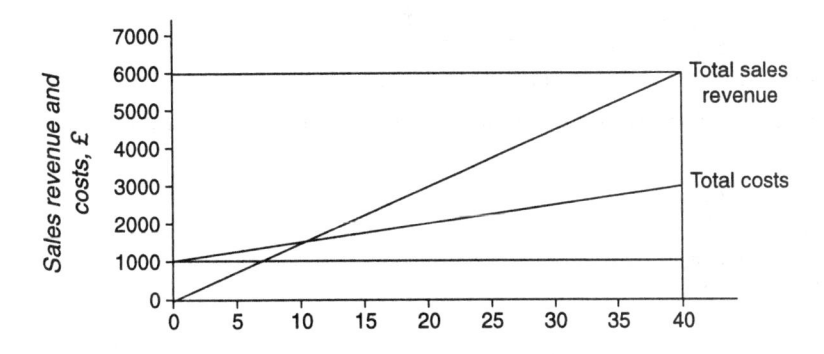

## 19. Monitoring business performance

Identify the following values from the graph:
a) the fixed costs in the business
b) the variable costs when 10 sheds are sold
c) the total revenue when 10 sheds are sold
d) the average price of a shed
e) how is the graph useful to Peter?
f) how and why would you expect the total sales revenue on the graph to change if it showed data for December.

## Multiple choice/completion

1.* A firm which produces video recorders has fixed costs of £30,000. If the selling price is £350 each and variable costs are £100 per unit, the break-even point will be at an output of:
   a) 80
   b) 120
   c) 250
   d) 300

2.* The level of production at which a firm's total costs equal its total revenue is referred to as the:
   a) Average cost
   b) Maximum profit point
   c) Break-even point
   d) Variable cost

3.* Total cost divided by output equals:
   a) Average cost
   b) Variable cost
   c) Average fixed cost
   d) Average total cost

4.* A budget which is calculated in relation to the needs of each activity in a business and its perceived value for money is called a:
   a) fixed budget
   b) flexible budget
   c) zero-based budget
   d) master budget

5. The quality control method which involves groups of shopfloor workers in regular meetings to address problems is referred to as:
   a) production engineering
   b) zero-defects
   c) quality assurance
   d) quality circles

6. A material-usage variance may come about because:
   a) Material prices are higher than the standard.
   b) More materials have been used than the standard.
   c) Excessive overtime has increased the cost of labour.
   d) The full-cost of overheads is not being absorbed.

*In the following questions, one or more of the responses is/are correct. Choose the appropriate letter which indicates the correct version.*

   A if 1 only is correct
   B if 3 only is correct
   C if 1 and 2 are correct
   D if 1, 2 and 3 are correct

7. Which of the following statements is/are correct?
   1) The British Standards Institution is a government body which promotes quality.
   2) BS 5750 is a product quality kitemark.
   3) The International Standards Organisation promotes the use of common terms, definitions and standards.
8. Which of the following are necessary for a total quality management culture in an organisation?
   1) Training for all employees.
   2) Commitment by everyone except management.
   3) Satisfaction with current performance.

## Assignment

Birchall Enterprises Ltd is a manufacturer of high quality wooden doors which it supplies mainly to the building trade. Currently the company produces 4,500 doors per year which it sells for £100 each. Fixed costs are £165,000 per annum and variable costs £45 per door.

At a recent meeting of the board of directors, managing director John Clark said that the company must improve its present output and profits. Marketing director Bob Moss stated that he believed that the company could increase its current selling price by 10 per cent and still remain competitive. Production director Jill Bennett estimated that to double current production would increase the firm's variable costs by a third although fixed costs should remain the same.

The directors feel that before reaching a final decision they would like to see some break-even details at the next meeting.

Complete the following tasks which are based on the above situation.

1. Is Birchall's a public or private limited company? How can you tell from the information provided?
2. a) What is a 'board of directors'?
   b) Briefly describe the main functions of the managing director in a company.
   c) Name two other directors who might be on the Board at Birchall's and outline their likely responsibilities.
3. a) With the use of examples, explain the terms fixed and variable costs.
   b) What are the company's current fixed costs?
   c) What are the company's current variable costs per door?
4. Suggest ways in which the company could reduce its fixed and variable costs.
5. Calculate the following for the current year:
   a) Total variable costs
   b) Total costs
   c) Total revenue
   d) The average cost of producing: 500 doors; 4,000 doors
6. a) Draw a break-even chart and show on it Birchall's current break-even point.
   b) What is the break-even output?
7. Assuming that the company achieves its revised targets, calculate the new break-even point.
8. a) What is the company's new sales target?
   b) Suggest reasons why the firm might not achieve its sales targets at the new selling price.
   c) What action could the firm take if sales do not meet their target?
   d) Advise the company whether, in your opinion, it should go ahead with the proposed new product and pricing structures.

# 20. Starting and Running Your Own Business

The final Chapter in this text takes you through the essential stages involved in setting up in business. It is specially written to enable you to apply the knowledge acquired throughout your business studies course and to demonstrate your understanding in a practical and meaningful way. Much of what is covered is revision and therefore may require you to refer back to earlier chapters for help. The tasks can be completed on an individual or group basis. It covers:

* Why Bother?
* Self Assessment
* Professional Advisers
* Insurance
* Business Planning
* Markets and Marketing
* Price
* Promotion and Advertising
* Place
* Legal Form
* Obtaining Finance
* Record-keeping and Accounts
* Simple Accounting Systems
* Budgeting & Cash Flow
* Legal Basics
* Law of Contract
* Taxation
* Tax and National Insurance
* Employing People
* Business Training
* Monitoring Performance

## Why Bother?

1. More and more people are considering the option of self-employment. Setting up your own business is both exciting and challenging and if successful can be rewarding both financially and in terms of personal satisfaction. The idea of being one's own boss is appealing to many people especially to those who may have suffered from redundancy and unemployment.

2. But going into business is not an easy matter. There is no such thing as a guarantee of success and it can mean long hours of hard work with few holidays. It also involves taking a financial risk because, no matter how well you have researched your idea, you could lose money.

### Task 20.1
1. List at least 4 reasons why people may want to start their own business.
2. What problems or drawbacks might there be?

3. Whatever the reasons for starting up, it is important for success to have clear business and personal objectives and to set goals which you want to achieve. A mission statement is also needed to indicate the clear direction of the business.

### Task 20.2
1. List 5 ideas which you believe would make a successful business venture.
2. Select one which you would like to run and write down the likely business and personal objectives associated with it. You will be asked to use your chosen business to complete the other tasks in this chapter.
3. Write a mission statement for the business.

## Self-Assessment

4. Before getting started it is also important to assess your own personal characteristics against those required to succeed in business. By assessing your strengths and weaknesses, it will help you to decide if you have got what it takes. Weaknesses may not necessarily hold you back but you may need help or advice to compensate.

5. The following is a list of 20 factors to help you to assess your suitability for running your own business.

   - ☐ I am self disciplined, able to keep control and not let things drift.
   - ☐ I have the full support of my family
   - ☐ I am ready to work 7 days a week, if necessary
   - ☐ I can get on with and communicate well with people
   - ☐ I can make considered decisions
   - ☐ I can cope under stress
   - ☐ I do not give in when the going gets tough
   - ☐ I can learn from mistakes and take advice
   - ☐ I have the skills and knowledge needed for my business idea
   - ☐ I am patient and prepared to work for success
   - ☐ I can lead and motivate people
   - ☐ I am in good health
   - ☐ I am enthusiastic, determined and committed
   - ☐ I am aware of the risks involved
   - ☐ I have specific personal and business aims
   - ☐ I am innovative and resourceful
   - ☐ I am good at planning
   - ☐ I would enjoy doing bookwork
   - ☐ I am good at controlling my finances
   - ☐ I am prepared to risk everything if necessary

> **Task 20.3**
> 1. Try the above self-assessment, first for yourself and then ask someone who knows you well to carry out the same assessment on you.
> 2. Compare the results and comment on any differences.
> 3. Identify which you feel are the most important factors and why.

## Professional Advisers

6. Whether starting from scratch with your idea, buying an existing business or entering into a franchise, professional advice may be essential in order to raise the necessary finance and to assist with the negotiation of the price. It is important to assess key areas of the business, consider all factors involved and seek as much advice as possible to ensure that the idea is a sound proposition. Once trading, professional advisers can save you time and money, freeing you to run your business.

7. Professional advisers you will probably need include:
   - **An accountant** to help prepare the initial cash flow forms, a set of accounts and to complete tax returns including allowable expenses.

- **A bank manager** possibly for a loan but also to discuss your business idea. They have good local business knowledge and can direct you to specialist organisations for help and support. You will also need a separate bank account for your business.

- **A solicitor** to handle any legal issues such as the formation of your business, particularly if it is a company or partnership, but also if you buy or lease premises, have to sue a customer for non-payment or indeed if for any reason someone sues your business. Also for preparing employee and other contracts.

## Insurance

8. Insurance is essential from the start for almost all kinds of business, to give protection against some of the risks involved. Because premiums vary from company to company as does the promptness with which they pay up on claims, it is often worthwhile to use an **insurance broker** to advise you. They can check premiums and have knowledge of how efficiently claims are usually handled.

9. The main kinds of business insurance are

   - **Premises, contents and stock** against fire, theft or damage. These should also be covered for 'consequential loss' caused by the interruption to business. If, for example, a bookshop's stock is destroyed in a fire, then it not only loses the value of the books, but also the loss of business until they can be replaced. This can be covered as can the cost of renting temporary premises if necessary.
   - **Employer's liability** which is compulsory by law. This provides protection against claims for compensation from staff who have accidents at work.
   - **Public liability** which is needed to compensate anyone else who may have an accident whilst visiting a firm's premises

10. Other important types of business insurance include:

    - **Fidelity Guarantee** to protect against the possible dishonesty of employees such as the stealing of goods and money.
    - **Bad debt** and risks of losses due to customers not paying for goods bought on credit.
    - **Motor vehicle**, for which third party insurance is compulsory by law to protect passengers or pedestrians injured in accidents.
    - **Legal insurance** to protect against prosecution under Acts of Parliament, for example unfair dismissal and unfair trading.
    - **Professional liability** insurance is needed in some professions such as surveyors and architects to protect against the consequences of mistakes.

11. Some business risks, however, cannot be insured against. For example, you cannot insure against making a trading loss or going out of business. This is because these may be caused by inefficiency, out-of-date stock, changes in fashion or even how hard someone works. These are factors which it is impossible for an insurance company to calculate and therefore are uninsurable risks.

12. Although insurance is expensive, it is a vital precaution because on the one hand you could pay out thousands of pounds in premiums without making a claim. On the other hand, a fire or legal action could wipe out your business overnight and the many years of hard work spent building it up.

### Task 20.4

An accountant and solicitor will charge you a fee for their services. Operating a bank account also usually involves charges although advice is generally free. An insurance broker, however, does not charge you but instead receives commission from insurance companies on the policies sold.

Suggest how you might go about choosing each of these as your professional adviser and identify what you feel are the most important factors to consider.

## Business Planning

13. Approximately 500,000 new businesses start up each year, but two out of five fail within three years. Those that survive are the firms that have thought their concept through, have worked out all the eventualities and are 100 per cent committed to their new business. Drawing up a business plan is a crucial factor in all this. This simply sets out your expectations and forecasts on paper.

14. It is needed for 3 main reasons:
    - to clarify your own thoughts by writing them down.
    - to obtain finance. You cannot get a bank loan without a plan. Even if you do not need finance, a plan will help you to focus on the main issues that are likely to determine the success of your venture, including indentifying the resources needed and the costs involved.
    - to measure success by assessing progress against the plan, including sales and profit targets.

15. A business plan should:
    - explain your idea and why you think there is a market for your product or service, its size and potential. Evidence of market research will help you here. One of the surest routes to business failure is to set up on the basis you think that there ought to be a demand when, in fact, no such demand exists.
    - give details of any competition, its strengths and weaknesses and how you intend to counter it, for example by price or service.
    - an outline of how you intend to market your product or service and the costs involved.
    - include plans for premises and any capital equipment which is needed. A potential lender will want to see evidence that you know your way around the business. Include where you intend to obtain supplies, production plans (if appropriate) and reasons for your choices.
    - give details of your own background and business experience and that of any others involved.
    - state how much of your own money you are proposing to put in.
    - state the amount of financial backing required and what return an investor could expect.
    - outline the security which you are able to offer.
    - finally, you will need some fairly detailed financial forecasts, including a monthly cash flow and a profit and loss forecast for the first 12 months. The figures given for anticipated sales are absolutely critical because time and again people overestimate what these will be.

16. Preparing a business plan sounds a chore, but it is absolutely essential that you do it. Assumptions based on market research should underlie every figure. On the basis of this information, a bank manager or other financier will decide what form of help they are able to offer. And remember that preparing a plan is a continuing process. It should be regularly updated to keep lenders informed of your progress.

### Task 20.5

1. For the idea which you chose to pursue in Task 20.2: Identify what essentials you will need to start up in business. Include for example, premises, machinery, secretarial facilities or other support services such as telex, fax, wordprocessing, reception and mail boxes.

2. An alternative to starting up yourself would be to buy an existing business. What factors would you need to consider in this situation?

NB When you have completed all the tasks in this chapter, in the Assignment you will be asked to prepare a Business Plan.

## Markets and Marketing

17. Once you have decided on your business idea and objectives, it is time to consider the likely market potential. Some simple **market research** will enable you to assess the viability of your idea. It is better to try and find out at this stage if it is likely to be successful rather than failing in the market place. Remember, if people don't want your idea, it is doomed to failure.

18. In order to assess the likely consumer appeal
    - discuss your idea with family, friends and potential customers,
    - seek advice from your local Training and Enterprise Council, Enterprise Agency or Chamber of Commerce and
    - study trade journals which are available from local libraries.

19. Try to assess the likely **demand** and identify key trends in the market for your product or service. Gardening products, DIY and health and vegetarian foods, for example are growth markets, whereas records and motor bikes are declining. Clearly it may be unwise to enter a declining market.

20. Other factors to consider are
    - whether or not the market is big enough,
    - can the potential customers pay a price that will enable you to make a profit and
    - what quality standards are required.

21. It is also important to study the strengths and weaknesses of likely competitors from the point of view of image, price, design, quality, reliability, delivery dates and any other factor which might give them a competitive edge.

22. From research, identify the people who are likely to buy your product or service by age, sex, income, occupation and geographical location. Then consider whether what you are offering has a **Unique Selling Point (USP)** which differentiates it from competitors and which through advertising and promotion will persuade people to buy.

23. In markets where products are very similar, depending on what is being sold, examples of USP's might be better service, better prices, faster delivery, wider range, after-sales service, car parking, convenience of location or longer opening hours.

## Task 20.6

1. Taking the 5 business ideas listed in Task 20.2, list a possible USP for each.
2. For your chosen business, identify the potential competition.

24. You will also need to consider the likely **product life cycle** and your ideas for extending it or bringing in new products or services in order to secure your long-term future. Fashion items, for example, are often high profit but have a relatively short life cycle with limited opportunities for repeat sales. Looking ahead is therefore essential to determine where the business will be in 12 months time and what changes are likely to affect it.

25. Other important factors to consider include
    - **any legal constraints**, particularly the increasing impact of European legislation, which might affect your business. Safety, labelling, descriptions, packaging and transport, for example, are all subject to legislation, as is planning permission.
    - **the state of the economy** both locally and nationally and how it affects your business. For example, are you setting up in an area of high unemployment and if so, how is this likely to affect sales.

## Task 20.7

1. From your own knowledge and experience identify 5 growing and 5 declining markets.
2. Evaluate and compare the ideas identified in Task 20.2 in terms of likely consumer appeal, competition, life cycle, legal constraints and current economic conditions.

## Price

26. Having considered the product, it is then necessary to consider the other elements of the marketing mix – price, promotion and place.

27. Price, to a large extent, will be determined by 'what the market will bear' and the costs which you have to cover. If price is too low, profits may be low and the product could look cheap and inferior to its competitors. On the other hand, too high a price could mean that people will not want to buy. Therefore, it is important to establish a fair price which provides a reasonable profit and retains customer goodwill and future business.

28. **Calculating Prices**

    A simple five step approach to calculating prices is to
    1. Determine your annual salary, which should be at least sufficient to cover your personal and household expenses.
    2. Calculate your business costs for the same period.
    3. Total your salary and business costs.
    4. Divide the total by the estimated number of sales over the year. This gives the cost per item.
    5. To the unit cost, add a margin of profit to give the price charged.

29. In many businesses, an **estimate or quotation** may be requested before a firm order is placed. Examples include builders, decorators, electrical repairs, carpets and office services. Calculating prices here involves ascertaining the costs of materials involved, estimating how long the job is likely to take to complete, relating this time to a proportion of your fixed costs, then adding your wages and a margin for profit.

30. Quotations should express clearly what work is to be carried out and include the terms of payment. They should also have a time limit (eg 30 days) so that the price can be adjusted if additional work is requested or to protect against increases in material or other costs due, for example, to inflation or higher wages.

> **Task 20.8**
> 1. Using the following information, calculate the price per item for a product. The desired profit is 50% on cost.
>    Personal salary, £20,000, Wages £30,000, Materials £10,000
>    Interest on Bank Loan £12,000, Stationery £400,
>    Advertising £1,000, Rent and Rates £6,000. Heat & Light £1,600
>    Insurance £2,000, Professional fees (Accountant and Solicitors) £2,000.
> 2. Consider some of the other factors which in practice may influence the price charged for a product or service and in particular the idea which you selected in Task 20.2.

## Promotion and Advertising

31. It is essential that people know about your business and what it offers. Promotional activities are used by businesses to maintain and increase sales. This may involve, for example, special offers, after-sales service, quality, price, gimmicks and other features which together offer customers a 'good deal'.

32. Advertising is then used to tell people and to persuade them to buy from you. You can arrange this yourself or through an advertising agency. What is important is choosing which media or mixture will attract most customers at least cost. Examples include newspapers, word-of-mouth, Yellow Pages, sides of vehicles, local radio and even television, depending on the success of the business. Whilst press releases are an important form of free advertising.

## Task 20.9

1. List and briefly describe at least 6 different methods of sales promotion and 6 different advertising media.
2. Decide on a 3 month promotional campaign for your business idea.
3. Choose appropriate media in which to advertise the campaign.
4. Prepare an advertisement for one of the chosen media.
5. State how you intend to measure and evaluate the success of the campaign.

## Place

33. Many small businesses are **run from home**. Examples, might include driving instructors, builders, insurance agents, mail order, office cleaners, sandwich suppliers, toy makers and childminders. However, whilst this is probably the cheapest, most convenient and quickest way to set up a business, it is nonetheless important that appropriate legal advice is taken in order to avoid potential pitfalls.

34. Examples might include
    - the need for planning permission from the Local Authority
    - the conditions in your mortgage or property deeds which restrict or forbid business activities.
    - any local by-laws in existence which might restrict your trade.

35. A **town centre site**, on the other hand, may be easier to find and more accessible for customers but will incur higher overheads, such as rent and rates and involve time travelling to work. Clearly, the choice of location will also depend upon the type of business concerned. A shop, for example, must be well located from the point of view of attracting the type of trade you are looking for and parking may be a major consideration. Whilst a factory may be better located near to a motorway for distribution and supplies.

36. When leasing property, it is important that
    - a formal agreement is drawn up and checked by a solicitor,
    - your proposed use for the premises is within the terms of the lease and allowed by the local authority,
    - you know your rights as a lessee,
    - you carefully consider the length of the lease in relation to the potential of your business.

## Task 20.10

Briefly describe where you would choose to locate your business and why. Are there any restrictions which may affect your choice?

## Legal Form

37. Your business can be structured in a number of ways. You may operate as a
    - sole trader
    - partnership
    - limited company
    - co-operative or
    - franchise

38. Deciding which is best again requires good professional advice which can be obtained from accountants, solicitors, banks or other agencies. Before you start trading, you must decide on the legal form because it affects taxation and the accounting records which you are required to keep. Even if you

are considering running your business from home, it may be advantageous to form a partnership or limited company.

> **Task 20.11**
> 1. List the main features of operating as a sole trader, partnership, co-operative and limited company.
> 2. How does a franchise differ from the other legal forms of business?
> 3. State, with reasons, which form you would choose for your business idea.

## Obtaining Finance

39. For the new and expanding business, getting enough money at the right time is often the biggest problem. There are many ways to raise business finance but all routes benefit from a properly presented business plan.

    Potential sources of finance include:

    - own funds
    - Venture capital
    - Government grants, for example a DTI Regional Selective Assistance grant; Business-Start-Up Scheme run by TECs.
    - local authorities
    - equity capital
    - business development loans are usually available for new and small businesses from banks and other sources
    - overdrafts
    - credit from suppliers

40. There is also a Small Firms Loan Guarantee Scheme. In return for a quarterly 'insurance' premium the Government will guarantee a proportion of a loan up to £250,000 over 2 to 7 years and allow capital repayments to be deferred for two years in certain circumstances. This is used where a loan is justified but not supported by a track record or sufficient security.

> **Task 20.12**
> Identify and describe 2 sources of short-term, medium-term and long-term finance and state how each might assist your business idea.

## Record-Keeping and Accounts

41. It is estimated that at least 80% of **all** business failures are caused by inadequate record-keeping. Unfortunately, it is often neglected in small businesses where other tasks often take priority. A methodical approach to financial record-keeping is, however, essential. An effective book-keeping system is needed not just to meet tax requirements but also to have vital information readily available about the business, including its:

    - Liquidity
    - Profitability
    - Fixed costs
    - Variable costs
    - Debtors
    - Creditors

- Working capital
- Stock levels

> **Task 20.13**
>
> Define each of the terms listed in 41 and state why they are important in a business.

## Simple Accounting Systems

42. There are various systems available on the market ranging from simple manual record-keeping to computerised based systems which may be needed as the business grows. The essential records which are required include:
    - Cash Book
    - Sales Day Book
    - Purchase Day Book
    - Ledger
    - Petty Cash Book

> **Task 20.14**
>
> Define each of the above terms and briefly explain why they are needed in a business.

43. The books described above will provide the necessary information from which an accountant can prepare the annual Trading and Profit and Loss Account and Balance Sheet.

> **Task 20.15**
>
> Identify and explain the main information which a Trading and Profit and Loss Account and Balance Sheet gives about a business.

## Budgeting and Cash Flow

44. 'Cash Flow' refers to the money which flows into and out of a business over a period. It is important to understand the difference between this and profit. A business may be operating profitably but still unable to meet its day-to-day expenses because its resources are tied up in stock, or even worse, equipment.

45. Part of this problem comes about because for many businesses sales and payments are not made by cash but instead involve credit. For example, an invoice for a sale made in July may not be paid until August or even September. These delays in making and receiving payments can have a significant effect on a business's cash flow. Therefore it is important to plan the cash requirements in a business by preparing a cash-flow budget, revising it at three or six-monthly intervals and checking back against what actually happened. It should be possible to explain any variances and take remedial action if necessary.

46. **Example of a Cash Flow Forecast**

**Cashflow forecast**

| Enter Month | | | | | | | | | | | | | |
|---|---|---|---|---|---|---|---|---|---|---|---|---|---|
| Figures rounded to £'s | | Budget | Actual | Budget | Actual | Budget | Actual | Budget | Actual | Budget | Actual | Budget | Actual |
| 1 | Receipts<br>Sales (inc VAT) – Cash | | | | | | | | | | | | |
| 2 | – Debtors | | | | | | | | | | | | |
| 3 | Other Trading Income | | | | | | | | | | | | |
| 4 | Loans Received | | | | | | | | | | | | |
| 5 | Capital Introduced | | | | | | | | | | | | |
| 6 | Disposal of Assets | | | | | | | | | | | | |
| 7 | Other Receipts | | | | | | | | | | | | |
| a | Total Receipts | | | | | | | | | | | | |
| 8 | Payment<br>Cash Purchases | | | | | | | | | | | | |
| 9 | Payments to Creditors | | | | | | | | | | | | |
| 10 | Principals Remuneration | | | | | | | | | | | | |
| 11 | Wages/Salaries (net) | | | | | | | | | | | | |
| 12 | PAYE/NI | | | | | | | | | | | | |
| 13 | Capital Items | | | | | | | | | | | | |
| 14 | Transport/Packaging | | | | | | | | | | | | |
| 15 | Rent/Rates | | | | | | | | | | | | |
| 16 | Services | | | | | | | | | | | | |
| 17 | Loan Repayments | | | | | | | | | | | | |
| 18 | HP/Leasing Repayments | | | | | | | | | | | | |
| 19 | Interest | | | | | | | | | | | | |
| 20 | Bank/Finance Charges | | | | | | | | | | | | |
| 21 | Professional Fees | | | | | | | | | | | | |
| 22 | Advertising | | | | | | | | | | | | |
| 23 | Insurance | | | | | | | | | | | | |
| 24 | | | | | | | | | | | | | |
| 25 | | | | | | | | | | | | | |
| 26 | VAT | | | | | | | | | | | | |
| 27 | Corporation Tax etc | | | | | | | | | | | | |
| 28 | Dividends | | | | | | | | | | | | |
| b | Total Payments | | | | | | | | | | | | |
| c | Net Cashflow (a-b) | | | | | | | | | | | | |
| 29 | Opening Bank Balance | | | | | | | | | | | | |
| d | Closing Bank Balance (c ± Line 29) | | | | | | | | | | | | |

Basic Assumptions – Please specify the following assumptions in completing this form and list any other relevant ones overleaf:
Credit Taken – the average period taken from creditors    Days
Credit Given – the average period given to debtors    Days

47. Certain regular **expenses** can be readily identified such as wages, rent, PAYE, National Insurance Contributions, telephone, insurance and repayments for loans or leasing arrangements. All other expenses should also be included.

48. In order to meet these commitments, you will then need to identify a **sales target** for the business. Whether based on firm orders or just expectations, it is important that the target is realistic. Having calculated the cost of materials and additional overheads to achieve your sales target, all these figures can then be included in your forecast. It should also be remembered that there may be a cash flow time lag between actually completing work and being paid for it. Hence, you may well have to meet the costs of materials and wages in advance.

49. Cash flow forecasting can help you to identify potential difficulties in advance, particularly deficient months and thus take appropriate action. During trading, actual and projected performance can be compared and if different, help can be sought from your bank or financial adviser. This is important because they may spot a basic error which can be put right or recommend practical measures to help overcome the problem. An example might be, reducing the time you allow customers to pay and/or asking suppliers for longer credit time, whilst a short-term overdraft may be needed to get through a difficult period or to provide additional working capital if the business is expanding.

50. Thus, the essential points about a cashflow forecast are that:
    - it identifies cash shortfalls before they happen.
    - it enables potential surplus cash to be identified and used efficiently, for example, invested.
    - it emphasises the importance of getting maximum credit and allowing the minimum.
    - it encourages more efficient use of resources and control of costs.
    - it helps to determine decisions about when to buy stock and materials.
    - it helps to determine priorities between spending time obtaining work and actually doing it.
    - it ensures sufficient cash is available for any necessary capital expenditure.

51. **Profit and Loss Forecast**

    Finally, it is important to distinguish between a cash flow and an operating budget. Cash flow is about when money which comes into or out of a business and when it is likely to occur whilst an operating budget is concerned with profit and loss. A budget is used to plan the use of resources to achieve objectives. It is important for helping to control costs. Thus, for example, if you allocate £2,000 per month for wages and £100 for advertising, it is important to compare the actual against the budget to ensure that you do not overspend. The operating budget therefore provides a profit and loss forecast as the following example illustrates.

52. **Example of an operating budget**

| **Operating budget** | | | | | | | | | | | | | |
|---|---|---|---|---|---|---|---|---|---|---|---|---|---|
| | Enter Month | | | | | | | | | | | | |
| | Figures rounded to £'s | Budget | Actual | Budget | Actual | Budget | Actual | Budget | Actual | Budget | Actual | Budget | Actual |
| 1 | Sales<br>Home | | | | | | | | | | | | |
| 2 | Export | | | | | | | | | | | | |
| a | Total Sales | | | | | | | | | | | | |
| 3 | Direct Costs<br>Materials – purchases | | | | | | | | | | | | |
| 4 | Wages and Salaries | | | | | | | | | | | | |
| 5 | Stock Change<br>(Increase)/Decrease | | | | | | | | | | | | |
| b | Cost of Goods Sold | | | | | | | | | | | | |
| c | Gross Profit [a-b=c] | | | | | | | | | | | | |
| d | Gross Profit as % of Sales [c÷a×100=d] | | | | | | | | | | | | |
| 6 | Overheads<br>Production | | | | | | | | | | | | |
| 7 | | | | | | | | | | | | | |
| 8 | | | | | | | | | | | | | |
| 9 | | | | | | | | | | | | | |
| 10 | | | | | | | | | | | | | |
| 11 | | | | | | | | | | | | | |
| 12 | Selling & Distribution | | | | | | | | | | | | |
| 13 | | | | | | | | | | | | | |
| 14 | | | | | | | | | | | | | |
| 15 | | | | | | | | | | | | | |
| 16 | | | | | | | | | | | | | |
| 17 | | | | | | | | | | | | | |
| 18 | Administration | | | | | | | | | | | | |
| 19 | | | | | | | | | | | | | |
| 20 | | | | | | | | | | | | | |
| 21 | | | | | | | | | | | | | |
| 22 | | | | | | | | | | | | | |
| 23 | | | | | | | | | | | | | |
| 24 | Other Expenses | | | | | | | | | | | | |
| 25 | | | | | | | | | | | | | |
| 26 | | | | | | | | | | | | | |
| 27 | | | | | | | | | | | | | |
| 28 | | | | | | | | | | | | | |
| 29 | | | | | | | | | | | | | |
| 30 | Finance Charges | | | | | | | | | | | | |
| 31 | Depreciation | | | | | | | | | | | | |
| e | Total Overheads | | | | | | | | | | | | |
| f | Net Profit before Tax [c-e=f] | | | | | | | | | | | | |
| g | Sales required to break-even [c÷d×100=g] | | | | | | | | | | | | |

## Task 20.16

For your chosen business idea, prepare a potential cash flow forecast and operating budget for a 12-month period.

## Legal Basics

53. A wide range of legislation exists which is designed to protect consumers, employees, the general public and businesses themselves. It is therefore important that you have at least a basic understanding of the legislation and how it affects you and your business.

54. Examples, all covered elsewhere in this text, include:

    Consumer Protection Act 1987
    Trade Descriptions Acts 1968 and 1972
    Data Protection Act 1984
    Employment Protection (Consolidation) Act 1978
    Employment Act 1980
    Health & Safety at Work Act 1974
    European Safety Directives 1993
    Environmental Protection Act 1990
    Monopolies and Mergers Act 1965
    Restrictive Trade Practices Acts 1956 to 1968
    Companies Acts 1948 to 1989
    Insolvency Act 1986
    Business Names Act 1985
    Copyright Act 1956
    Patents Act 1977

## Task 20.17

1. Briefly describe how each piece of legislation above might affect your proposed business.
2. Is there any other legislation which you feel could be important? State which and in what ways.

## Law of Contract

55. It is also very important to have a basic understanding of the law of contract. A contract is a legally binding agreement between two or more parties which if 'broken', gives the 'injured' party the right to claim some form of redress. A contract, which is usually written but may be oral, is valid as long as it has the essential features of offer and acceptance, consideration, intention, capacity and validity.

56. **Offer and Acceptance.** The offer is the terms under which a person is willing to sell or supply something. It will usually include the price, quantity, quality and also any delivery and payment terms. The offer must be accepted to form a contract.

57. **Consideration.** Both parties to a contract must show consideration which means that one must give a profit or benefit in exchange for a promise made by the other. In business, this usually means one party supplying goods or services in return for payment.

58. **Intention** to create a legally binding relationship. This is usually assumed to be the case in business agreements unless a contract states specifically that it is 'binding in honour only'. An example of this would be property bought 'subject to contract'.

59. **Capacity to contract.** For a contract to be binding, the parties to it must have legal capacity. For example, contracts signed by anyone who is under 18 (minors), mentally ill or drunk come into this category and are likely therefore to be declared void.

60. **Validity.** If a contract meets all of the above essential requirements, it is said to be valid and therefore legally enforceable. The only exceptions to this could be where a genuine mistake has been made, some material fact has been withheld (for example, not describing details of previous claims on an insurance proposal), deliberate misrepresentation has taken place (under, for example, a breach of the Trade Descriptions Act 1968) or where an unlawful act is intended, such as fraud.

> **Task 20.18**
> State, with reasons, whether or not each of the following situations represents a legal contract.
> 1. A bank manager agrees to invest money in your business.
> 2. She also agrees to introduce you to a local accountant.
> 3. A taxi driver agrees to take you to the nearby station.
> 4. The rail travel clerk agrees to sell you a ticket.
> 5. A friend agrees to collect you at the station.

## Taxation

61. Just about everyone pays tax on income, whether it be PAYE from employment, dividends or interest from investments or an income from self employment or other sources, or some combination of them all.

62. For business purposes, sole traders and partnerships pay income tax. A company pays corporation tax on profits, whilst employees' wages and salaries are subject to income tax. You may also be involved with capital gains tax on the disposal of capital assets.

63. If your business exceeds a turnover of £46,000 (1995–6) for the supply of certain goods and services, you are obliged to charge VAT and pay it over to the Customs and Excise Department, less any VAT on goods and services supplied to you (materials, telephone etc), in the course of business. This has to be paid every month or quarter.

## Allowable Business Expenses

64. In your business you are allowed to deduct from earnings any revenue expenditure which is 'wholly and exclusively incurred' in carrying on your trade or profession.

65. This includes business expenses which principally cover:
    - **Cost of raw materials or goods bought for resale.**
    - **Running costs** such as light, heat, rent, rates, advertising, cleaning and insurance. If you use your home as an office, you can claim up to two thirds of the running costs as a business expense, if your tax office agrees. But this may mean having to pay capital gains tax on the 'business' part if the house is sold.
    - **Packing, delivery and carriage costs.**
    - **Wages and salaries.** You cannot count anything taken out by a proprietor but it is possible to reduce tax by paying a salary to your spouse.
    - **Entertaining.** Costs of entertaining staff or overseas visitors are allowed.
    - **Travel.** Costs of business travel and a proportion of the costs of running a car can be claimed.
    - **Interest.** This is allowed on loans and overdrafts for the business, as are any hire purchase or leasing charges.
    - **Business Insurance,** including any taken out on behalf of employees, is allowable.

- The **VAT element** in allowable business expenses, such as VAT on petrol can also be claimed.
- **Professional fees** such as legal or audit fees.
- **Subscription to professional or trade bodies.**
- **Bad Debts** actually incurred are also allowable.
- **Business gifts** to employees may also be allowable.

## Tax and National Insurance Contributions

66. If you employ full or part-time staff on a regular basis, you are legally obliged to deduct tax and National Insurance Contributions (NIC) from their wages. You are also liable to pay employer's NIC. The local tax office will notify you of the amount of tax to deduct for each employee and where to send the money. You are also required to keep a record of each employee's earnings and deductions and to inform your tax office annually of the amounts.

### Task 20.19
1. Outline the ways in which taxation and national insurance can affect a business.
2. Find out what would be the current rates of each payable by a small business?

## Employing People

67. Initially, it may be possible to run your business by yourself or with limited family help, but if not, or as it expands, it may be necessary to employ staff. Before doing this, it may be worthwhile considering sub-contracting some work which may be more cost effective, especially to iron out short-term trading peaks and troughs.

68. If you do employ staff, it is important to be aware of the legal responsibilities involved, including the payment of wages, tax and national insurance contributions and protection such as unfair dismissal, statutory sick pay, trade unions, health and safety and redundancy.

69. Other issues to address include:
    - determining the exact skills required and wage to be offered.
    - preparing a job description and contract, including terms and conditions of employment.
    - recruitment using an advertisement, Job Centre, Careers Office or private Employment Agency.
    - devising an application form, interviewing and checking references.
    - personnel record-keeping, including a system of review or appraisal.

70. Once staff are appointed, it is important to keep them happy and motivated so that they give of their best.
    - Treat people as you would wish to be treated and set an example of the standards you expect such as punctuality, good manners and commitment.
    - Involve them as much as possible in the business and ask for their ideas and suggestions.
    - Delegate where possible, praise them for work well done and
    - express care and consideration by showing an interest in their domestic circumstances and personal well-being which may have an important effect on their performance at work.
    - Always try to sort any problems quickly and establish a 'grievance procedure' so that an employee knows what to do if they have a complaint.
    - Training is necessary to ensure that staff know why and how a job has to be done. It can also make them more efficient and help to increase productivity.
    - Targets and bonuses are also useful for motivation, leading to greater purpose and productivity.

> **Task 20.20**
> 1. Determine the staffing needs of your proposed business. Discuss the role which each employee would undertake.
> 2. Prepare at least one job description and a draft advertisement and outline how you would undertake recruitment.
> 3. Discuss the main legislation which would influence your recruitment strategy and conditions of employment.

## Business Training

71. It is essential for anyone starting up or running a business that they develop the necessary knowledge and skills required such as:
    - marketing and selling
    - sources of finance
    - book-keeping and basic accounting
    - financial control and preparation of business plans
    - employing people and training skills analysis
    - taxation
    - opportunities for exporting
    - managing growth
    - keeping abreast of new developments in the market place

72. In all businesses, of whatever size, performance is fundamentally linked to management capability. In small businesses, the business consists of the owner-manager who develop their capability as they develop their business. Training therefore can help to develop their skills and ability to succeed.

## Monitoring Performance

73. All businesses, from the largest conglomerate to the smallest, one-man-concern, have one thing in common. The overall objective of making profits, without which no business can survive.

74. As you know, the 2 key elements involved in producing profits are:
    - **generation of sales**, thus marketing is vital to success.
    - **keeping costs down**, and within budget is essential

75. It is necessary therefore to monitor the actual performance of the business against the Business Plan, cash flow and operating budget forecasts. This should take place on a regular basis in that problems can be identified and remedial action can be taken where necessary.

76. If, for example, sales are not meeting targets, then it will be necessary both to try and obtain more business and also to look for ways of reducing costs such as overheads or possibly cutting back on staff.

77. If, on the other hand, problems are being caused by slow paying creditors, then tougher credit control measures may be needed. This is vital if cash is tight because later payment makes you late in paying your own debts. This might not only damage your reputation but is also likely to increase your overdraft which in turn costs more in interest, thus reducing the overall profitability of the business. Therefore, it is important to monitor the **aged debtors** list, analysing it to identify the slow payers on the basis of how much they owe and how long the debts have been outstanding. **Aged creditors** are also important to ensure they are paid on time thus avoiding breach of contract and the risk of legal action and/or loss of future credit.

78. You may find the use of computers helpful for monitoring and controlling your business. The use of new technology is now widespread in businesses of all sizes and ranges from record-keeping to word processing to robots and other forms of computer aided manufacturing.

## 20. Starting and running your own business

79. Technology can help to save time and money and increase efficiency and productivity as well as giving a competitive edge. Technology, of course, costs money both for installation and maintenance but should be seen as an investment which is worthwhile it is offers an appropriate profit return to the business.

> **Task 20.21**
>
> As a final task in this chapter you are asked:
>
> 1. To write a **summary** of the key factors to consider in starting your own business.
> 2. To list the 20 key questions/factors which you feel should be considered before making a decision to start up.
> 3. To discuss the importance of monitoring performance and how this could be done with your chosen business idea.

*Asterisks indicate those questions for which there are answers in Outline Answers (page 439)*

### Essay-style questions

1.* Describe the kind of small business which you would like to own and say how you would control it and make it successful.

2. Discuss the role of professional advisers and how they might offer assistance to a new or developing business.

### Short answer

1. Read the following article and answer the questions based on it.

---

#### RAGS TO RICHES WITH JOE BLOGGS

Shami Ahmed, the teenager who left school at 16 with just two O-levels is now one of the country's wealthiest businessmen.

As managing director of The Legendary Joe Bloggs Jeans Company, he boasts an annual turnover of £40 million and, at 32, a personal fortune of more than £25 million.

Shami left school in 1976 and went to work in the family's wholesale business, buying and selling major brand names like Levis. But by 1986, when he was only 26, he was bored. So, backed by his father, he started up the Joe Bloggs label, deciding on the name because it is 'truly British and common-sounding'.

Shami took on the major manufacturers and soon started antagonising them – mainly with his audacious successes. First he went against the jeans trade's traditional habit of turning out two ranges a year, in the spring and autumn. Joe Bloggs started producing a new range every month. The other companies laughed, said it wasn't feasible. But soon they were forced to imitate him.

Some of his ideas were immediate successes, others controversial and doomed to failure. One such was his revolutionary unisex 'one size' jeans which would be baggy on the thin and snug on the obese. But the style was dropped after a few months. Far more successful was the deal Joe Bloggs clinched with Warner Brothers to produce the clothes for the movie New Jack City – and even better, the deal to produce all Prince's clothes for his Sign of The Times tour.

Perhaps his greatest talent lies in his ability to hype everything he does. He has sponsored the Milton Keynes Bowl, featuring names such as 808 State and The Shamen. He paid a still undisclosed sum to Tottenham Football Club in 1991 for the FA Cup players to wear his clothes (Paul Gascoigne refused, putting the entire deal under threat). Now he is confidently stating the he can twist Michael Jackson's arm to wear his diamond-encrusted denims.

Today Shami Ahmed is understandably proud of his achievements. But more than anything he is proud, as the label of his jeans company emphasises, to be 'truly British'.

---

*Based on an article in The Daily Mail, August 1992*

1. Explain the term 'brand name'.
2. What was Shami Ahmed's USP?
3. What evidence is there of a successful business?
4. How did he set about making his business a success?
5. What obstacles did he have to overcome to be successful?
6. What lessons are there for anyone considering starting their own business?

2.* The following list contains the 10 factors which are usually regarded as being the main reasons why firms go out of business.

- Lack of professional advice.
- Inadequate financial resources.
- Wrong location.
- Poor management.
- Poor marketing and market research.
- Poor decision making and planning.
- Poor quality control.
- Lack of technical skills.
- Expansion without planning.
- Lack of financial management and discipline.

Select any 5 and comment on why they are so vital to running a successful business.

3. 'The Fire Precautions (Places of Work) Regulations 1992 and Associated Guidance – apply at first only to new or modified premises. Existing premises will have a period of grace until January 1996.

- **Employers** must carry out an assessment of the risk in case of fire, using technical guidance from the fire authorities.
- **Premises** must have emergency plans prepared and kept up to date.
- **Premises** must have proper and well-maintained fire escapes.
- **Fire-fighting** and fire-warning systems must be provided, and written records kept of maintenance work carried out on them.
- **All** staff must be given instruction and training in fire precautions, with written records kept of any instructions and training given.

Small business insists it cannot afford these extra costs. Yet can Britain as a nation afford the high toll of workplace deaths – 538 in 1991 – and accidents – 30,684?

Health and safety rules will become considerably tighter in 1993.'

This extract illustrates just one example of recent Health and Safety at Work legislation.

Outline the main legislation. Explain why it is needed and why small businesses are concerned about the costs involved.

## Assignment

Having completed all the tasks in this chapter you are now asked:

1. To complete a Business Plan for your business idea. Include clear aims, objectives and targets, plus sales and marketing plans, production plans, resource requirements and financial support data. You may find it helpful to ask a bank for a specimen form.

2. Include all the necessary documentation to support your plan. This, for example, may include some actual market research findings, location or layout plan (if appropriate) and a prototype of your idea.

3. Outline when and how you would review the plan.

4. Identify at least 5 factors which may cause you to make changes to your plan and describe the action you would take or need to take.

5. Calculate your break-even point.

6. If possible, present your plan to a bank manager and write a report on their reaction to it. If this is not possible, present it to a group of colleagues, teacher(s) or other appropriate person(s).

7. Identify other possible sources of funding for small businesses. You may need to contact your local TEC, Enterprise Agency or library for this information.

8. Finally, an issue for anyone starting their own business is that of a future pension. Discuss why this is important and how you would go about securing your finances beyond retirement.

# Business update

This section has been added in specific response to the excellent feedback received to the first edition. It covers a number of key business terms and government initiatives, some of which are not mentioned elsewhere in the text, plus sources of information.

It should be used in conjunction with the index and is intended both to add to your overall level of knowledge and to help you to gain a better understanding of important concepts and developments.

It includes

- some current/recent government initiatives
- glossary of business terms
- some key computing terms
- a list of useful addresses

## Some Current/Recent Government Initiatives

This section provides a summary of the main measures which the government and European Union has introduced in recent times to help combat the high levels of unemployment and develop the skills of the workforce for the future.
It includes

1. 'Competitiveness' Helping Business to Win
2. European Community Aid
3. Growth, Competitiveness and Employment
4. Investors In People (IIP)
5. Modern Apprenticeships
6. National Advisory Council for Education and Training Targets (NACETT)
7. National targets for education and training
8. Training and Enterprise Councils
9. Training for young people
10. Training for unemployed adults
11. Trade Union Reform and Employment Rights Act 1983
12. Reform of vocational qualifications
13. Single Regeneration Budget
14. Sunday Trading Act 1994.

### 1. 'Competitiveness' Helping Business to Win

A White Paper issued in May 1994 which sets out what the UK needs to do to compete successfully in world markets as we approach the 21st Century. It includes a range of important initiatives aimed at raising the skill levels of the workforce, including:

- improving education and training
- increasing labour market flexibility
- ensuring better use of public funds to combat unemployment
- providing training for young school leavers
- simplifying Single Market legislation affecting small businesses.

### 2. European Union Aid

Whilst the principal responsibility for regional problems rests with the UK Government, the EU has a number of schemes which may be used to attract additional aid.

These include the:

- **European Regional Development Fund (ERDF)** which aims to stimulate economic development in the least prosperous EU regions. Britain was allocated £571 million in 1993. ERDF is used to help finance initiatives such as environmental and infrastructure improvements, tourism and industry developments, R & D and vocational training.

- **European Investment Bank (EIB)** which helps to finance projects of common interest to several member states e.g. the Channel Tunnel.
- **European Social Fund (ESF)** which is targeted at helping young people joining the labour market, the long-term unemployed, people with particular disadvantages in finding and keeping work and promoting equal opportunities at work. The UK is to receive £2.5 billion from ESF between 1994 and 1999.

### 3. Growth, Competitiveness and Employment

A **European Commission White Paper** presented to the European Council Summit in December 1993 proposed a series of measures to stimulate economic growth and jobs in response to current low growth and high levels of unemployment (17 million). It recommended that the European Commission set itself a target of creating 15 million new jobs by the end of the century and achieve an annual growth rate of 3 per cent until the year 2000.

The White Paper suggested possible ways of meeting these targets. In the spirit of subsidiary, however, it did not prescribe actions to be taken. Instead, it offered member states a choice of options to be selected according to prevailing national conditions.

The commitment to create 15 million new jobs by the year 2000 was removed at the UK's request.

The UK's initiatives are outlined in the white paper 'Competitiveness' Helping Business to Win.

### 4. Investors in People (IIP)

IIP was launched by the Government in 1990 to encourage employers of all sizes to improve their business performance by linking the training and development of their employees to business objectives. It is run on behalf of the Employment Department by local TEC's and LEC's who help organisations to work towards the standard and award it.

To achieve the IIP standard employers training provision is accessed to ensure that it involves all employees, is linked to business objectives and meets specific quality standards.

### 5. Modern Apprenticeships

See Training for Young People.

### 6. National Advisory Council for Education and Training Targets (NACETT)

Set up by the Government in 1993. It is an independent employer-led body and includes members from education and trade unions. It monitors and reports publicly on progress towards the targets which includes identifying barriers and ways to overcome them. It will also regularly review and update them.

### 7. National Targets for Education and Training (NTET's)

NTET's which were launched in 1991 by the CBI in its document 'World Class Targets', came about from the recognised need for action to fill the skills gap brought about by the challenge of technological change and need for flexible working necessary to meet global competition and more sophisticated consumer demand.

Four Foundation Learning and Four Lifetime Learning Targets which set goals for business, education and Government.

**Foundation Learning**

1. By 1997, 80% of young people to reach NVQ11 (or equivalent.)
2. Training and Education to NVQ 111 (or equivalent) available to all young people who can benefit

3. By 2000 50% of young people to reach NVQ 111 (or equivalent)
4. Education and Training provision to develop self-reliance, flexibility and breadth.

**Lifetime Learning**
1. By 1996, all employees should take part in training or development activities.
2. By 1996, 50% of the workforce aiming for NVQ's or the units towards them
3. By 2000, 50% of the workforce qualified to at least NVQ 111 (or equivalent)
4. By 1996, 50% of medium to larger organisations to be 'Investors in People'

The Government has asked TEC's to take the lead locally in maintaining the commitment of employers and education in working to achieve the NTET's which are currently being reviewed by NACETT.

## 8. Training and Enterprise Councils (TEC's)

See Index

## 9. Training for Young People

- About 70% of 16 and 17 year olds who leave school to enter the labour market go into **Youth Training (YT)**. A weekly training allowance is paid whilst trainees in a job receive a full wage. YT is run by TEC's through a range of training providers who are responsible for arranging the trainees pay, work placement, training programme and for looking after their general welfare. All schemes provide the opportunity to obtain specific job skills and qualifications to a minimum of NVQ level II.

- A **Modern Apprenticeship Scheme** will replace YT from 1995-6. The intention is to have 150,000 young people on the scheme at any one time and for around 40,000 to achieve NVQ's at level 3. They are expected to cost £1250m over three years (compared to £700m per year expenditure on YT.) The Apprenticeships will be piloted in 1994-5. One major difference from the old style apprenticeships is the abolition of 'time serving' to be replaced by the achievement of work based competence. The scheme will be funded through Youth Credits and the Youth Training programme phased out.

- **Youth Credits** or **Training Vouchers** give young people who have left full-time education to join the labour market an entitlement to train to approved standards. They carry a monetary face value and can be presented to an employer or training provider in exchange for training.

- **Workfare schemes** for young unemployed are being piloted in 2 areas from April '94. 20,000 people aged 18-24 and unemployed for more than one year are likely to be involved. Workfare schemes oblige the jobless to work in return for benefit, and the Employment Department has indicated that those refusing to participate in proposed trials would have their benefit withheld.

## 10. Training for unemployed adults

- Through the TEC's and Employment Services the Government provides a **range of training programmes and support** for the unemployed. Examples include Training for Work, Learning for Work, Community Action, Job Centres, Job Clubs and the Restart Programme. The schemes are usually run by approved training organisations such as further education colleges, private training providers and voluntary organisations.

- **Training for Work** was introduced in April 1993 to replace the Employment Training and Employment Action programmes. It aims to help long-term unemployed people to find jobs and improve their work-related skills. Each participant receives an individually adapted package of training and/or structured work activities based on an assessment of their needs. The programme is expected to help up to 320,000 people. In April '94 the age limit was increased from 59 to 63.

- **Learning for Work** aims to equip 30,000 long-term unemployed with marketable skills and recognised qualifications by following full-time vocational courses of up to one year without loss of benefit.

- **Community Action** is a scheme to provide 95,000 long-term unemployed people with part-time voluntary work and effective help with jobsearch. Placements last for up to six months and priority is given to the disabled and people aged under 25 who have never worked.
- **Work Trials** allow people unemployed for more than six months to try out a job for up to three weeks while claiming benefits and travel expenses.
- **Information and advice** about job hunting and training opportunities is provided for example by:

    **Job Centres** – which exist in most towns to help people to find jobs. They also offer a comprehensive service to employers recruiting staff including advice, assessment and short-listing.

    **Job-Clubs** – which offer help with job search including access to telephones and newspapers.

    **Restart Programme** – which offers job search advice and training opportunities.

### 11. Trade Union Reform and Employment Rights Act 1993 (TURER)

This was introduced with 2 main objectives:

- to strengthen the rights of individuals at work and the democratic rights of trade union members and
- to increase the competitiveness of the economy and remove obstacles to the creation of new jobs. It made significant changes to several areas of employment law and introduced new rights for employees.

**The main features of the Act** are summarised below:

**Health and Safety Protection** – anyone victimised or dismissed because of a health and safety issue is entitled to claim compensation.

**Unfair dismissal** – if an employee has made a claim against an employer under current legislation and is subsequently dismissed or made redundant it will automatically be considered as unfair.

**Compensation for failure to re-employ** – if an employer ignores a Tribunal order to re-employ someone unfairly dismissed additional compensation can be awarded.

**Transfer of undertakings** – this incorporates EU Directives which protect the existing rights and conditions of employment for staff who transfer from one employer to another e.g. following a merger or takeover.

**Redundancy consultation** – in an effort to gain their agreement employers must inform and consult trade unions in relation to any proposed redundancies.

**Maternity rights** – all pregnant employees are entitled to 14 weeks maternity leave and protection against dismissal because of it.

**Industrial action** – unions must hold a postal ballot before taking industrial action, inform the employer in writing that it is taking place and of the result, and give 7 days notice of any impending action.

**'Citizen's Right'** – any individual deprived of goods or services by unlawful industrial action has the right to bring proceedings to stop it happening. Help is available from the Commissioner for Protection Against Unlawful Industrial Action.

**Employment particulars** – all employees working more than 8 hours per week must receive a written statement of their main conditions of employment, including pay, hours and holidays within 2 months of starting a job.

**Itemised pay statements** – these should be given to anyone working over 8 hours per week. In firms employing less than 20 there is a 5 year qualifying period.

**Tribunal matters** – an agreement in a dispute between an employer and employee can be enforceable where the employee has received appropriate independent legal advice. Tribunals have been made more informal to speed up cases.

**ACAS** – is now able to charge for some services (see Chapter 14.)

**Union members' rights** – individuals have the right to join a union of their choice. An employer cannot automatically deduct trade union subscriptions (under 'check-off' arrangements) without an employee's written consent within the last 3 years.

**Internal trade union affairs** – unions must provide members with an annual written statement about its financial affairs. The annual return to the Certification Officer must contain details of pay and benefits given to union leaders.

Two other important measures in the Act were:

- the **abolition of Wages Councils** which set statutory minimum hourly rates of pay. The government considered these to be outdated by the move away from traditional, industry-wide collective bargaining where pay was fixed without any regard to the skills and performance of employees and the need to contain costs in order to create jobs.

- **changes in the management of the Careers Service** which is being opened up to local education authorities, TEC's and other private organisations to enable it to offer a more flexible, responsive service for local communities. Quality standards and performance indicators are to be set for guidance in consultation with employers.

## 12. Reform of vocational qualifications

- **National Vocational Qualifications** (NVQ's) were introduced in 1988 and more than 600 are now available. NVQ's are based on real work standards which have been set by industry indicating what an individual is actually competent to do in a job. There are initially 5 levels ranging from basic tasks at Level 1 to higher technician and management skills at Level IV and professional jobs at level V.

- **General National Vocational Qualifications** (GNVQ's) were introduced in 1993. They are designed to lead on to work and higher education by developing knowledge and skills in broad vocational areas such as business studies and engineering.

- The new qualifications have been developed by industry lead bodies often **Industry Training Organisations** (ITO's). These are independent bodies covering sectors which employ about 85% of the workforce. They act as the focal point for training matters in their sector and have a role of ensuring that standards are established and maintained and skill needs met.

## 13. Single Regeneration Budget

- In April 1994 the Government created 10 new **Integrated Regional Offices** bringing together the existing regional offices of the Departments of Transport, Trade and Industry, Employment (Training, Enterprise and Education Directorate) and Environment.

- It also introduced a **Single Regeneration Budget** (SRB) to replace the budgets of the various departments. The aim is to encourage local initiatives and partnership to overcome disadvantage and promote regeneration in employment, education and skills, economic development, housing, environment, crime prevention and aid to ethnic minorities. Local authorities, TEC's and Business Leadership Teams will be key partners, together with voluntary groups, schools, police, health authorities, small firms and others.

- The new offices will co-ordinate UK and EU funds and provide business with a key focal point for comprehensive and easy access to government services in the regions. Senior Regional Directors are accountable to the relevant Secretary of State for the programmes their offices carry out.

## 14. Sunday Trading Act 1994.

Updated 1950 Shops Act making Sunday trading legal. Big department stores and supermarkets may now open for six hours while small shops can open when they like. Wines and spirits can still only be sold between 12.00 and 3.00.

# Glossary of business terms

**Appraisal:** the process of reviewing an individual's performance at work.

**Appropriation Account:** shows how a company's net profit is divided between corporation tax, dividend payments and reserves. In a partnership profits are appropriated between the partners.

**Arbitration:** settlement of an industrial dispute by an independent person or body.

**Articles of Association:** set of rules which regulate the internal management of a company including voting rights and how profits are shared.

**Assets:** anything owned by a business.
- **Current** assets (or circulating capital) those which are constantly changing from day-to-day e.g. stock of goods, debtors, cash and bank balances.
- **Fixed** assets (or fixed capital) those which remain the same over a period of time and are held for use in the business rather than for resale e.g. land, buildings, fittings, furniture and equipment.

**Authority:** power given by managers to subordinates to enable them to carry out instructions.

**Automation:** use of machinery to replace labour in performing industrial and administrative processes and operations.

**Average or unit costs:** Total costs divided by total output.

**Average revenue** (AR): the amount which a firm receives for each unit of output sold, in other words, the price.

**Balance of payments:** A nation's account of its financial dealings with the rest of the world.

**Bank draft:** cheque drawn on a bank.

**Bank Giro:** method used by clearing banks to transfer money rapidly from one account to another.

**Bankrupt:** person or business unable to meet its debts.

**Bank statement:** written statement from a bank giving details of credits, debits and balance of an account.

**Basic pay:** minimum amount of pay for a normal working week.

**Bill of exchange:** document which tells a bank to pay a person, mainly used for foreign trade payments.

**Bill of lading:** 'document of title' used when goods are transported by sea; it gives details of cargo and provides proof of ownership.

**Birth rate:** number of births per thousand of the population.

**Bonus:** extra sum of money paid to employees as a reward for hard work or improved efficiency.

**'Bounced' cheque:** cheque on which the bank refuses payment because there is insufficient money in the account to cover it.

**Branch:** local part of a trade union to which members belong.

**Branding:** giving a name to a product to distinguish it from others.

**Break-even point:** the level of output at which a firm's revenue is just sufficient to cover its costs.

**Budget:** plan of expected income and expenditure, usually over one year.

**Budget account:** bank account into which a set amount is paid each month. Payments are made to meet expenses as they arise.

**Business cycle:** regular (cyclical) fluctuations in overall economic activity ranging from boom to slump.

**Cadbury Report:** Published December '92. Recommended that the Board of all listed companies should say in their annual report that they are complying with a code of best practice, and if not why not, which contains a system of checks and balances intended to safeguard against the concentration of power in executive directors.

**Capital:** value of assets (wealth) owned by a business and used to create further capital. May include money, machinery, stock and premises.

**Authorised:** total amount of money that a limited company may obtain by issuing shares

**Issued:** the value of shares actually issued to shareholders in return for cash

**Capital Gearing:** simply a measure of the degree to which a business is financed by loans rather than equity capital.

**Cartel:** an agreement between firms to regulate prices and/or output, thereby effectively creating a monopoly. The best known example being the Organisation of Petroleum Exporting Countries (OPEC).

**Cash discount:** percentage deduction from the price of goods or services to encourage prompt payment

**Cash flow:** refers to the money which comes into and goes out of business over a period.

**Cash flow forecast:** a budget or estimate which identifies the anticipated income and expenditure and the time when it is likely to take place, usually, over a six or twelve-month period.

**Certificate of Incorporation:** issued by the Registrar of Companies to a new company, which meets the legal requirements, allowing it to begin trading.

**Cheque:** written instruction to a bank asking them to pay a certain amount of money to someone else.

**Closed Shop:** where all employees in a firm must be members of a trade union.

**Codes of Practice:** rules drawn up by an association which members agree to follow in the course of their business.

**Collective bargaining:** employees or trade unions negotiating with employers to get the best deal and reach a collective agreement which they both find acceptable.

**Communication:** process of passing information from one person to another.

**Competition:** the amount of rivalry between organisations and their products or services or market.

**Cut-throat competition:** a situation where prices in a market are so low that no one is likely to make a profit.

**Conglomerates:** companies which diversify into a wide range of completely different product areas.

**Contravision:** telecommunication service which links different places by sound and vision.

**Consequential loss:** additional financial loss resulting from an insured risk, e.g. extra expense following a fire.

**Consumer:** individual or organisation which purchases goods and/or services.

**Contract:** legal agreement used in business between two or more people stating the terms of a transaction.

**Contribution:** if a risk is insured with more than one insurance company then any loss would be shared between them, i.e. each would contribute.

**Conurbation:** continuous built-up area linking several towns or cities, e.g. Greater London.

**Council Tax:** set and collected by local authorities to help their expenditure, based on the value of domestic property and the number of people living there. Introduced in 1993 to replace the Community Charge (Poll Tax) which itself replaced domestic rates in 1990. (see UBR)

**Credit:** being allowed to pay for goods or services over a period of time.

**Credit card:** plastic card which allows goods to be purchased without immediate payment.

**Creditor:** someone to whom a business owes money, e.g. a supplier of stock who has not been paid.

**Credit note:** sent by a supplier to a customer to make an allowance which is deducted from the original invoice.

**Culture:** the basic assumptions, attitudes and standards which determine the systems, structure and rules in an organisation and hence the way things are done.

**Current account:** bank account used for day-to-day transactions.

**Death rate:** number of deaths per thousand of the population.

**Debentures:** long-term stock issued by companies to raise capital. Debentures usually carry a fixed rate of interest and guaranteed payment at a future date.

**Debit note:** sent to customers to notify them of an increase in the amount owed.

**Debtor:** someone who owes money to a business, e.g. for goods which they have bought.

**Delegation:** term used to describe instructions given by managers to their subordinates.

**Demand:** the amount of goods or services which consumers are willing to buy, at a given price, over a period of time, e.g. 400 units @ £5 each per week.

**Deregulation:** a form of privatisation where the government removes official barriers to competition such as quality standards or special licensing.

**Derived demand:** products wanted for their use as a factor of production e.g. sugar for jam.

**Joint demand:** complementary products that are needed together, e.g. petrol and cars.

**Primary demand:** products wanted for their own sake, e.g. a video or carpet.

**Deposit account:** bank account used for savings on which interest is paid.

**Depreciation:** amount by which assets lose their value over a period of time.

**Direct debit:** when a customer instructs their bank to allow a payee to withdraw money from their account, often used for regular payments.

**Direct tax:** tax which is paid directly to the government, e.g. income tax.

**Director:** person appointed by shareholders to help run a company on their behalf.

**Discretionary income:** the amount left over after essential spending on food, clothing and housing.

**Diseconomies of scale:** reduced efficiency and rising costs per unit resulting from a firm growing too large.

**Disintegration:** individual firms specialising in one part of the production process.

**Disposable income:** amount left over after deductions from wages such as tax and national insurance, in other words, 'take-home pay.'

**Downsizing:** when a company reduces costs by restructuring to concentrate on its core business, usually results in job losses.

**Drawee:** the name of the bank on which a cheque is drawn.

**Drawer:** person who writes and signs a cheque.

**Dumping:** term used to refer to 'surplus' foreign goods which are sold ('dumped') abroad at a lower price than in the home market. This creates unfair competition.

**E and OE (Errors and Omissions Excepted):** this is shown on many invoices and enables firms to correct any mistakes.

**Earning:** payments received in the form of wages or salaries, profits, dividends or interest.

**Economic growth:** annual increase in the national income.

**Economies of scale:** advantages gained from operating on a larger scale, e.g. by producing goods in larger quantities.

**Elasticity of Demand:** the degree of responsiveness of demand to changes in demand conditions. There are three common forms:
- **price elasticity** which is the effect on demand of a change in price,
- **income elasticity** which is the effect on demand of a change in income levels and
- **cross elasticity** which is the effect on demand of a change in the price of other goods or services.

**Elasticity of supply:** the degree of responsiveness of supply to changes in price.

**Endowment policy:** a life policy which pays out benefit on an agreed date or on death, if earlier.

**Entrepreneur:** someone who brings together the factors of production, (land, labour, capital) and organises them into a 'business', taking risks in anticipation of making a profit.

**Environment:** the surroundings and circumstances which affect the way in which an organisation operates.

**European Currency Unit (ECU):** a hypothetical exchange rate, based on a basket of EU currencies..

- **European Monetary Co-operation Fund (EMCF):** used by EU Central Banks, including the Bank of England, for borrowing to balance their books after intervening in the foreign exchange markets to adjust supply and demand.
- **Exchange Rate Mechanism (ERM):** EU system of semi-fixed exchange rates within agreed bands. It limits how far member currencies can fluctuate against the ECU and between each other before intervention is demanded. (see VSTF).

**Ex-works:** factory price of goods excluding the cost of transport and delivery.

**Facsimile:** an exact copy of a letter or document.

**Factoring:** buying of business debts at a discount.

**Factors of production:** essential resources needed for production, consisting of land, labour, capital and enterprise.

**Financial Times Industrial Ordinary Index (FT-SE100) or 'Footsie':** measures price changes weighted by capitalisation in the shares of the 100 largest UK companies. It is calculated on a minute-by-minute basis.

**Fiscal policy:** government policies based on the use of taxation and public expenditure.

**Fixed costs or overheads:** those costs which do not vary in direct proportion to a firm's output and must be paid regardless of the level of output e.g. rent, rates, heating, lighting.

**Franchise company:** a company which sets people up in business and allows them to use its name and products in return for a fee.

**Free trade:** trade between countries free of any tariffs, quotas or other protective measures.

**'Futures' market:** trading situation where a price is agreed now for goods which will be delivered at some future date, perhaps in three or six months time. Foreign exchange is frequently bought in this way, as are sugar, grains and metals.

**Game Theory:** statistical technique used to analyse situations of conflict. It is based on the use of strategies to achieve gains or losses in anticipation of what others may do in response. It can be applied to business situations such as those relating to competitive strategies and oligopolistic markets.

**General Agreement on Tariffs and Trade (GATT):** organisation of almost 120 member countries working together to reduce tariffs and other barriers to trade. (See World Trade Organisation.)

**Gilt-edged securities:** very safe investment issued when the government borrows money. Variously called 'treasury' stock, 'exchequer' stock, 'funding' and 'TAP'.

**Goods:** physical items which can be purchased. **Consumable** goods are quickly consumed, eg. food, drinks, make-up, soap powder, stationery. **Durable** goods last much longer, eg. cars, houses, washing machines, furniture.

**Goodwill:** established custom of a business. Measured when sold by the difference between the price paid and its net asset value.

**Hire purchase:** purchasing of goods on credit. Payments are made by regular instalments, e.g. £20 per month for two years.

**Holding company:** a company specifically formed to take a controlling interest in other firms called subsidiaries.

**Hypermarket:** very large supermarket located on the outskirts of large towns or cities, eg. Carrefour.

**Impulse buying:** unplanned spending, goods bought on the spur of the moment.

**Index numbers:** measure the average percentage change in the price, volume or value of a variable from one period to another. The variables in an index are often weighted to reflect their relative importance.

*Glossary of business terms*

**Indirect tax:** tax which is not collected directly by the government, e.g. VAT.

**Industrial relations:** relations between management and its employees.

**'Infant industries':** young (or new) industries which may need protection from foreign competition to enable them to develop and grow.

**Inflation:** situation where prices are generally rising. Two figures published by government – **headline rate** and **underlying rate** which excludes mortgage interest payment.

**Innovation:** the bringing to the market of a new product or process.

**Insider dealing:** making profits from trading in the shares of a company on the basis of undisclosed information which is likely to affect their price. Eg. employees with privileged knowledge, such as a proposed merger or takeover. It is a criminal offence under the Company Securities (Insider Dealing) Act 1985. The Guiness-Distillers takeover in 1989 resulted in 10 prosecutions following a DTI investigation.

**Integration:** where businesses join together as a result of a takeover or merger.

**Interest:** charge made for the use of borrowed money.

**Investment:** money used to earn a financial return, e.g. buying shares or capital equipment.

**Investment appraisal:** financial analysis of the various ways of achieving business objectives to assess whether or not the return from an investment outweighs the costs.

**Investors in People:** a national standard for investing in employees which helps to link the development of people to achieving business objectives.

**Job evaluation:** a systematic comparison of jobs. It is used to compare the demands of different jobs and put them in rank order.

**Job description:** outline of main duties and responsibilities of a job.

**Job satisfaction:** combination of factors which motivate people and help them to enjoy their work.

**Joint ventures:** where firms agree to work together, e.g. Honda and Rover, Thorn-EMI and JVC.

**Labour:** total of human effort used in the production of goods or provision of services.

**Labour Force Survey (LFS):** conducted quarterly by the Office of Population Censuses and Surveys on behalf of the Employment Department. It covers a sample of 60,000 households in Britain and asks questions about employment, self-employment, hours of work, unemployment, education and training, qualifications and other information including age and ethnic origin.

**Labour turnover:** the term used to describe the movement of people into and out of an organisation.

**Land:** all the natural resources used by man, e.g. soil, coal, trees and fish.

**Leasing:** hiring or renting of assets rather than buying outright.

**Liabilities:** anything owed by a business
- **Fixed liabilities** which remain the same over a long period, e.g. capital and long-term loans.
- **Current liabilities** which change from day to day, e.g. creditors, bank overdrafts and short-term loans.

**Life expectancy:** average number of years a person can expect to live.

**Limited liability:** should a business fail, investors cannot lose any of their personal possessions, i.e. liability is limited to the amount invested.

**Liquidation:** term used for a company which becomes bankrupt.

**Listed company:** a public limited company whose shares are traded on the main stock exchange.

**Loan:** sum of money lent for a stated period of time. Interest is charged on the amount borrowed.

**Management:** a group of people who are appointed by the owners of a company to run it.

**Marginal costs (MC):** the additional cost of producing one more unit.

**Marginal revenue (MR):** the extra revenue from the sale of one more unit.

**Market:** any situation where buyers and sellers come into contact.

**Market niche:** a very clearly defined market segment which a business seeks to supply.

**Market research:** collecting, recording and analysing information to find out about markets, consumer needs and why they buy particular goods or services.

**Market segmentation:** dividing a market into parts in terms of similar consumer characteristics.

**Market share:** value of a firm's sales as a proportion of the total sales in a market.

**Marketing mix:** the four 'P's of product, price, promotion and place which together make up a marketing plan for a business.

**Mark-up:** amount added to the cost price of an item to arrive at its selling price.

**Mass media:** means of communication designed to reach large numbers of people, e.g. television, newspapers.

**Mass production:** manufacturing of goods in large quantities.

**Media:** different means of communication, e.g. advertising, telephone, letters.

**Memorandum of Association:** document giving details of the rules governing the external affairs of a company, including its name, address, objectives and capital.

**Merchandising:** the process of stocking retail and wholesale outlets to promote and facilitate additional or impulse purchases. Many firms employ special merchandisers to ensure that goods are well displayed.

**Merger:** where two or more firms agree to amalgamate together.

**Microfilming:** taking miniature photographs of data to make it easier to store (file).

**Mission statement:** states a clear view of the primary purpose of an organisation on which its strategic plan is then based.

**Monetary policy:** government's financial policy based on control of interest rates and bank lending.

**Monopoly:** strictly speaking a sole supplier in a market. By law where 25% or more of a market is controlled by one supplier.

**Morale:** general emotional feeling of a group or individual, e.g. enthusiasm or loyalty.

**Mortgage:** loan for the purchase of property.

**Motivation:** factors which encourage or discourage people at work, often linked with job satisfaction.

**Multi-national company:** one which owns and controls business operations outside the country in which it is based, e.g. EXXON (Esso), ICI, Nissan, Nestlé and Unilever.

**Multi-skilling:** when a worker is trained to perform a variety of different tasks.

**National Record of Achievement:** record of individual achievements, – completed by school leavers, to show in detail what they can do. Useful for interviews and to record and plan development throughout life.

**National debt:** accumulated amount owed by the government of a country.

**National income:** total annual output, in money terms, of all goods and services produced in a country.

**Night safe:** safe found on outside wall of banks which enables deposits of money and documents when bank is closed.

**Objectives:** what a business aims to achieve, e.g. profit, growth, market share.

**Oligopoly:** markets dominated by just a few large firms. Examples include cars, cigarettes, soap powders, cement, petrol and banking.

**Operating statement:** a detailed action plan which relates the short-term strategy (usually annual) to the longer-term objectives of an organisation.

**Optimum population:** level of population at which income per head is at its maximum.

**Opportunity cost:** the value of a choice in terms of the next best alternative forgone.

**Organisation:** a group of people who co-operate together for a common purpose, e.g. schools, colleges, libraries, charities, trade unions, political parties and businesses.

*Glossary of business terms*

**Overdraft:** being allowed to take more money out of a bank current account than there is in it, i.e. to overdraw.

**Overheads:** fixed expenses of running a business (see Fixed Costs).

**Overtime:** time spent at work in excess of normal working day or week for which additional money is usually paid.

**Payee:** person to whom a certain sum of money is to be paid.

**Performance related pay (PRP):** financial rewards such as a pay increase or bonus linked to the performance of an individual, team or organisation.

**Petty cash:** money available for the purchase of small items of expenditure e.g. stamps, window cleaning, stationery.

**Prestel:** two-way communication system which provides a data base of information via a specially adapted television set.

**Primary production:** the first stage of production involving extractive industries, e.g. agriculture, forestry, mining.

**Private sector:** term used to describe all businesses owned by individuals or groups that are run essentially for profit.

**Privatisation:** government policy of selling off public corporations to the private sector as public limited companies, e.g. British Telecom, British Gas.

**Production:** making or manufacturing of goods for sale.

**Productivity:** shows the relationship between the output of a system and the factor inputs – in terms of materials, labour and capital – used to produce it, taken either individually or together.

**Productivity agreement:** wage increases related directly to increases in output.

**Profit:** money left over after expenses have been paid.
- **Gross:** profit made from sales of goods or services before deduction of overheads.
- **Net:** profit after deduction of all expenses.

**Prospectus:** issued when a company offers its shares to the general public giving information (as per the Company's Acts) about its development, future prospects, and current financial situation.

**Public Relations (PR):** action by a business to keep the public informed about its activities e.g. press releases.

**Public sector:** businesses that are owned and controlled by the Government or local authority and run for the benefit of the community.

**Public sector borrowing requirement (PSBR):** borrowing by the Government when its expenditure exceeds its income from taxation.

**Quality control:** ensuring that a business's products/services reach a required standard, e.g. in terms of reliability, safety or appearance.

**Quoted company:** a public limited company whose shares are traded on the main Stock Exchange or the USM.

**Rate of exchange:** expresses the value of one currency in terms of another currency.

**Recession:** a period in which overall business activity is falling.

**Recycling:** the recovery and use of materials from spent products, eg. old newspapers.

**Redundancy:** when an employee is dismissed because the job they do is no longer needed.

**Reserves:** savings, profits or other money retained for future use.

**Resources:** premises and equipment (physical), people (human), and capital (financial) needed to start and run a business.

**Responsibility:** when a manager can delegate a task but is still ultimately accountable for the work carried out.

**Retail Price Index (RPI):** used to measure changes in the value of money i.e. inflation.

**Ring trading:** this is used, for example, on the London Metal Exchange. The dealers gather in a circle and shout out the price at which they are prepared to buy or sell a particular metal until a price is agreed.

**Sample:** used in market research to ask a representative group of people what they think about a product or service.

**Secondary production:** the manufacturing or construction stage of production, e.g. engineering, building.

**Services:** facilities which we use like the telephone, buses, education and entertainment.

**Share:** capital which represents part ownership of a company.

**Shareholder:** a person who owns shares in a company.

**Shop steward:** union member elected to represent others in their place of work.

**Skills gap:** difference between the total demand for a skill and the total supply.

**Social costs:** ways in which a business decision will affect a local community.

**Specialisation:** the dividing of work into particular jobs, functions, processes or areas so that individuals and /or organisations can concentrate on what they are best at doing.

**Spot trading:** trading situation where goods are sold at a cash price for immediate delivery. Examples might include tea, coffee and oil.

**Standing order:** written instruction by a customer to a bank to make regular payments on their behalf.

**Stock Exchange:** market where second-hand shares are bought and sold.

**Stockturn:** number of times average stock is sold during a trading period.

**Strategic plan:** based on an organisation's mission statement, develops clear intentions in terms of its major objectives and targets and a timescale by which these are expected to be achieved, often 3-5 years.

**Subsidiary:** see holding company.

**Superannuation:** amount deducted from employees' wages to pay for a pension on retirement.

**Supply:** the amount of goods or services which businesses are willing to offer for sale, at a given price over a period of time, e.g. 200 units per week @ £2 each.

**System:** a collection of inter-dependent parts organised to achieve a particular objective.

**Takeover:** buying of one company by another.

**Technology:** application of scientific processes to improve production and efficiency, e.g. computers and robots.

**Tertiary production:** distribution stage of production which also includes other service industries, e.g. transport, banking, insurance, retailing.

**Trade Association:** group of companies in a similar trade or profession.

**Trade credit:** when a trader sells goods to another trader and allows time for payment.

**Trade discount:** percentage reduction in price given to businesses in the same trade.

**Trade price:** price at which goods are bought by businesses.

**Trade union:** a group of workers who have joined together to bargain with their employers about pay and conditions of work.

**Turnover:** accounting term for the total sales of a business over a period of time, e.g. one year.

**Unemployment:** a situation where people are actively seeking to obtain work but are unable to do so because there are insufficient jobs.

**Uniform business rate (UBR):** tax collected by local authorities based on the rateable values of business properties. The UBR figure is set by the government.

**Unlisted Securities Market (USM):** known as 'second-tier' stock market and often used by young companies going public (i.e. offering their shares for sale to the public for the first time). Being replaced in 1995.

**Unique selling point (USP):** feature(s) of a product/service which distinguish it from competitors.

**Variable costs:** those costs which vary directly with output, e.g. if a firm produces more goods, it will need additional raw materials, labour, power and transport. Also known as direct or prime costs.

**Variance analysis:** the comparison between the actual results achieved and those planned.

**Very-short-term finance facility (VSTF):** gives ERM members unlimited credit facilities in their own currency. This can be used to finance intervention when currencies reach their ERM margins.

**Wage differentials:** the difference in wages which workers receive for different jobs in different occupations or areas.

**Wealth:** the quantity of money or assets possessed by individuals or organisations.

**Working capital:** the money which a business must have available to meet its day-to-day expenses such as staff wages, purchasing of stock and other overheads.

**Working population:** everyone with a job, those registered as unemployed and the self-employed.

**World Trade Organisation:** the tougher policing body which will replace GATT.

**Yield:** calculation to show the annual percentage return on capital.

# Some key computing terms

**Back up:** term used for making a copy of files held on disk. Important in case a disk crashes or becomes unreliable. Without it much information could be lost.

**Central processing unit:** the technical term for the 'brains' of a computer.

**Computer aided design (CAD):** can range from simple drawing programmes to very complex Desk Top Publishing packages. Allows the use and production of graphics on the computer e.g. plans of a building drawn by an architect.

**Computer aided manufacturing (CAM):** generally the automation of production lines.

**Cursor:** marker on a computer screen which indicates where next character will appear.

**Data:** the term for information inputted into a computer.

**Database:** a collection of information or data which the computer can handle in different ways for searching, sorting etc.

**CD-ROM:** stands for compact disc read only memory. Used to store masses of information such as large reference databases. Works in similar way to a conventional compact disc player.

**Disk:** a memory device used for recording information (see Floppy disk and Hard disk).

**Desk-top publishing (DTP):** use of computers to produce high quality publications by combining text and graphics.

**Disk drive:** a piece of hardware used to record and recover information on a disk.

**Disk operating system (DOS):** the programme which enables a user to operate a disk drive e.g. to tell the operating system to copy a file from one disk to another (see MS-DOS).

**Electronic mail:** an alternative to sending letters by post, which involves the use of computer terminals linked via the telephone network. Subscribers who have a password to enter the system are able to send messages to a 'mailbox' where they are stored until 'opened' by the recipient. BT's Telecom Gold is a well known example.

**File:** a collection of information usually stored on a disk.

**Floppy disk:** not actually floppy but small discs used in computers to store data. Standard size usually five and a quarter inches.

**Down-time:** the period when a computer is out of operation because of a technical fault.

**Hard disk:** used to store data.

**Hardware:** the equipment used in a computerised system.

**Interface:** used to enable a computer to communicate e.g. a keyboard interfaces between the computer and user and the Centronics interface between the computer and printer.

**Menu:** the range of options offered by a computer programme.

**Modem:** a device used to connect computers through the telephone network.

**Mouse:** an electronic pointer used to operate computers without using the keyboard.

**MS-DOS:** Microsoft Disc Operating System which has become the industry standard operating system.

**Network:** the linking of computers using a cable or internal telephone line to enable machines to share information and resources.

**Random Access Memory (RAM):** the memory or working space in a software package, usually a minimum of 640k. It is usually possible to upgrade to a bigger memory at a later date.

**Software:** the programmes which tell the computer what to do.

**Spreadsheet:** allows data to be entered and calculations made easily and quickly. Changing any of the data causes all the results to be recalculated. Looks like a table of figures when presented on the screen.

**Visual display unit (VDU):** screen on which computer data is displayed.

# A list of useful addresses

**ACAS**, 11-12 St James Square, LONDON SW1Y 4LA

**Access**, Priory Crescent, SOUTHEND ON SEA SS2 6QQ

**Advertising Standards Authority**, Brook House, 2-16 Torrington Place, LONDON WC1E 7HN

**Bank Education Service**, 10 Lombard Street, LONDON EC3V 9AT

**Bank of England**, Threadneedle Street, LONDON EC2R 8AH

**Barclaycard**, NORTHAMPTON NN1 1YU

**Board of Customs and Excise**, King's Beam House, Mark Lane, LONDON EC3R 3HE

**Board of Trade**, 1 Victoria Street, LONDON SW1

**British Electro-Technical Approvals Board (BEAB)**, 153 London Road, KINGSTON-UPON-THAMES, Surrey KT12 5NA

**British Gas plc**, 152 Grosvenor Road, LONDON SW1V 3JL

**British Insurance Brokers Association**, 10 Bevis Marks, LONDON EC3

**British Overseas Trade Board**, 1 Victoria Street, LONDON SW1H 0ET

**British Standards Institution**, 2 Park Street, LONDON W1A 2BS

**British Telecommunications plc**, 81 Newgate Street, LONDON EC1A 7AJ

**British Tourist Authority**, Thames Tower, Blacks Road, LONDON W6 9EL

**Building Societies Association**, 14 Park Street, LONDON W1X 4AL

**Central Office of Information**, Hercules Road, LONDON SE1 7DU

**Central Statistical Office**, Great George Street, LONDON SW1P 3AQ

**Confederation of British Industry**, Centre Point, 103 New Oxford Street, LONDON WC1A 1DU

**Consumers Association (Which?)**, 14 Buckingham Street, LONDON WC2N 6DS

**Department of National Savings**, 375 Kensington High Street, LONDON W14 8SD

**Department of Trade and Industry**, 1 Victoria Street, LONDON SW1H 0ET

**Design Centre**, 28 Haymarket, LONDON SW1Y 4SU

**Employment Department**, Caxton House, Tothill Street, LONDON SW1H 9NF

**European Commission**, 8 Storey's Gate, LONDON SW1P 3AT

**Good Housekeeping Institute**, Vauxhall Bridge Road, LONDON SW1V 1HF

**Heath and Safety Executive**, Information Centre, Broad Lane, SHEFFIELD S3 7HQ

**HMSO**, St Crispins, Duke Street, NORWICH NR3 1PD

**Independent Broadcasting Authority**, 70 Brompton Road, LONDON SW3 1EY

**Inland Revenue Press and Information Officer**, New Wing, Somerset House, LONDON WC2R 1LB

**Market Research Society**, 15 Belgrave Square, LONDON SW1X 8PF

**National Chamber of Trade**, Enterprise House HENLEY-ON-THAMES Oxon RG9 1TU

**National Council for Vocational Qualifications**, 222 Euston Road, LONDON NW1 2B2

**Northern Ireland Dept of Economic Development**, 176 Newtownbreda Road, BELFAST BT8 4QS

**Office of Fair Trading**, Bromyard Avenue, Acton, LONDON W3 7BB

**Port of London Authority**, Leslie Ford House, Tilbury Docks, ESSEX RM18 7EH

**Schools' Officer**, Postal Headquarters, St Martins-le-Grand, LONDON EC1A 1HQ

**The Stock Exchange Information Officer**, Throgmorton Street, LONDON EC2 1HP

**Trades Union Congress**, Great Russell Street, LONDON WC1B 3LS

**Training Education and Enterprise Directorate (TEED)**, Moorfoot, SHEFFIELD S1 4PQ

**Unit Trust Information Service**, Kingsway, LONDON WC2B 6TD

# Outline Answers

## Chapter 1: Business Environment

**Essay-style question – suggested plan**

- **Introduction:** Define entrepreneur, factor of production.
- **Main Part:** Explain role entrepreneur – risk taker who organises other factors to initiate production. Profit motive. Role other factors – land, labour, capital. Quantity/quality varies.
- **Conclusion:** Essential in that production cannot take place otherwise.

**Short Answer**

1. a) Able to meet own needs, eg growing own food.
   b) Specialising in particular jobs/functions, eg farmers, builders, teachers
   c) Exchange of goods for goods, eg potatoes for carrots, sheep for wine.
   d) Any generally accepted medium of exchange, eg notes, coins.
   e) Increased output, easier exchange, selling surplus, increased trade.
2. a) Land, Labour, Capital, Enterprise.
   b) Land – Natural Resources, eg land itself, trees, minerals.
   Labour – skills and efforts of people, eg operating machines, driving vehicles
   Capital – anything owned by a business and used for production, eg buildings, machinery, equipment.
   Enterprise – entrepreneur organises other factors, takes risks, motivated by profit, eg owner of local shop, Alan Sugar (Amstrad), Richard Branson (Virgin).

**Multiple Choice/Completion**

1. C    2. B    3. C    4. C

## Chapter 2: Business Enterprise

**Essay-style question – suggested plan**

- **Introduction:** Define Limited Liability, Companies, Capital.
- **Main Part:** Need for capital, how raised – public/private Ltd companies, why shares, main source.
- **Conclusion:** Not impossible but very difficult, could hinder growth, restrict business.

**Short Answer**

1. a) Second-hand market for securities, facilitates raising of capital for companies and government, imposes rules and regulations to protect investors.
   b) Introduced 1993 to replace Poll Tax, based on value of domestic property and number of people living there. Set by Local Councils, houses valued in one of 8 bands. Those in A pay lowest tax, those in H highest.
   c) Comparatively new and growing form of business ownership; involves an existing, usually well-known company allowing someone exclusive right to manufacture, service or sell its products in a particular area. Royalty paid, which may be lump sum and/or share of profits.
   d) Value of share capital which a company is allowed to have. For a company to go public it must issue at least a quarter of its authorised capital. Shown in Memorandum of Association.
2. a) Own boss, quickly/easily set up, personal contact with customers, receives all profits, job satisfaction, business affairs private.
   b) Unlimited liability, limited capital, no division of labour, lack of continuity, unable to benefit from bulk buying, problems if sick.
   c) Partnership, Franchising, Co-operative, Private Limited Company. Reasoned argument as to which is most suitable.

**Multiple Choice/Completion**

1. C    2. C    3. C    4. A

## Chapter 3: Business Planning

**Essay-style question – suggested plan**

- **Introduction:** Define: Population, Workforce
- **Main Part:** Trends, eg ageing population, decline in number school leavers, more working women, increase in part-time employment. Social and Technological changes have altered nature of jobs. Firms response: personnel policies to retain existing employees, attract new workers, may involve more training/retraining, discouraging retirement/ early retirement. Increasing job satisfaction by improving environment, or offering incentives such as private health schemes, social clubs and bonuses. Applicable to all age groups.

Appendix: outline answers

Some firms eg B&Q deliberate policy to employ over 50's.

☐ **Conclusion:** Less young people means they can choose, therefore must be attracted by good job with prospects. But all businesses in same position therefore plan essential since ultimately older employees have to retire. Further option might be to replace labour with new (computerised) capital equipment

**Short Answer**

1. a) Says what an organisation is about. Sets out clear view of primary purpose, values, distinctive features and provides rationale for Strategic Plan.

   b) Develops clear intentions for an organisation in terms of major objectives, targets and timescales.

   c) Detailed action plan which determines how strategic plan is to be implemented and achieved.

   d) Required to review progress towards objectives, in regular and systematic way, and update strategic plan.

2. a) i) Trade Descriptions Acts 1968/1972 make it a criminal offence to give a false or misleading description to goods, services, accommodation and facilities.

   ii) Consumer Credit Act 1974 requires licensing by OFT of all businesses offering credit. Borrowers must be given written statement of cost of loan including APR.

   iii) Food Safety Act 1990 requires all food handling businesses to take all reasonable precautions in the manufacture, transport, storage, preparation and sale of food, introduce appropriate hygiene controls and ensure food is safe.

   b) Examples include Office of Fair Trading which looks after consumer affairs; Monopolies and Mergers Commission which investigates proposed mergers. Environmental policies to reduce pollution and improve conservation and regulation of privatised industries.

**Multiple Choice/Completion**

1. B    2. D    3. C    4. C

---

## Chapter 4: The Market Mechanism

**Essay-style question – suggested plan**

☐ **Introduction:** Define – elasticity, demand

☐ **Main Part:** Types of elasticity, price, income, cross, elastic, inelastic, unitary demand, effects on business revenue. Diagrams to illustrate, plus use of examples. Factors determining elasticity – substitutes, proportion income, necessities/luxuries, habit.

☐ **Conclusion:** Important when making decisions, eg. misjudgement of price sensitivity could result in falling sales and profits.

**Short Answer**

1. a) True, no real substitute but demand for different brands may be elastic.

   b) False. But may be relatively inelastic in hot weather.

   c) False. It is inelastic because of the growing time involved (5-7 years per tree)

   d) True. More is now demanded at each and every price.

   e) True. An increase in the supply of beef results in an increase in the supply of hides.

2. a)

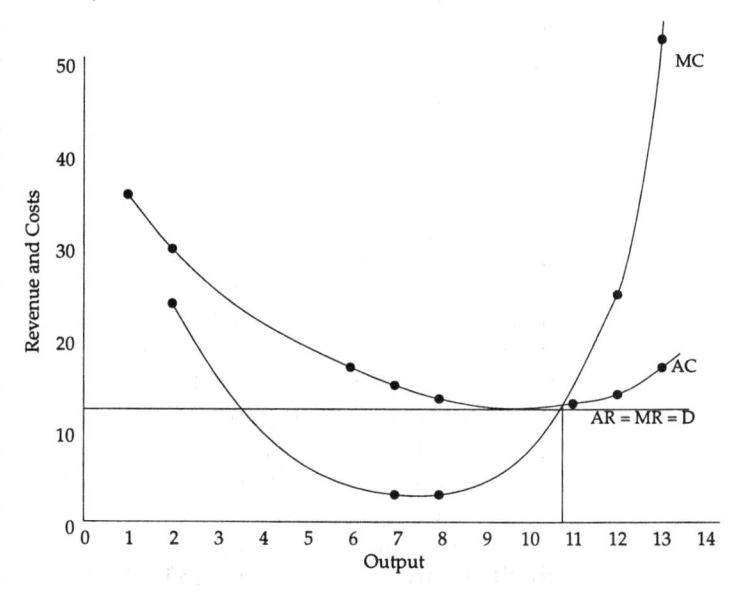

| Output | Average Cost | Total Cost | Marginal Cost |
|---|---|---|---|
| 1 | 36 | 36 | 36 |
| 2 | 30 | 60 | 24 |
| 6 | 17 | 102 | – |
| 7 | 15 | 105 | 3 |
| 8 | 13.5 | 108 | 3 |
| 11 | 13 | 143 | – |
| 12 | 14 | 168 | 25 |
| 13 | 17 | 221 | 53 |

b) 11 units, £12

**Multiple Choice/Completion**

1. D    2. C    3. A    4. B

## Chapter 5: Business and the Economy

**Essay-style question – suggested plan**

- **Introduction:** Define – Recession, British Economy
- **Main Part:** Governments main macro-economic aims – economic growth, full employment, low inflation, balance of payments stability. Achieved through Fiscal/Monetary policies. Can be used to encourage or discourage spending which in turn affects investment, the demand for goods/services, prices, employment and foreign trade. British Economy also affected by world economy. Effects recession – social – health, loss of status, crime/vandalism, work ethic; economic – waste of resources, cost to exchequer, inequality of income, lower standard of living.
- **Conclusion:** Recession affects everyone. Reduced demand, wages, employment, profit. Thus government economic policies aim to relieve recession and promote growth.

**Short Answer**

1. a) 'Injections' – additions to circular flow of income, eg government expenditure, exports, investment. 'Withdrawals' – leakages from the circular flow of income, eg savings, imports, taxation.

   b) Aggregate level of demand in economy depends upon level of injections and withdrawals. If injections greater will stimulate demand, if withdrawals greater, will reduce demand. Long-term affects could include employment, inflation, balance of payments.

2. a) Tax which takes a higher proportion of income as income rises, eg Income Tax.

   b) i) Basic rate 25%, Lower rate 20%, Higher Rate 40%, therefore progressive.

   ii) Basic rate $17\frac{1}{2}$% levied equally on everyone, therefore not progressive.

   iii) Levied according to value of house and number of people living there. Thus some progression involved but not related to income.

   c) Governments usually have objective to see wealth distributed fairly. Higher income may be due to many reasons, eg skills/nature work, investment income, and/or inherited wealth. Taxation used to redistribute – generally high earners pay more tax. If everyone received same income, would probably reduce incentives to work hard and also affect supply of workers for highly skilled and lowly skilled jobs.

**Multiple Choice Questions**

1. C    2. A    3. B    4. D

---

## Chapter 6: Business and the International Economy

**Essay-style question – suggested plan**

1. a) SEM – 12 countries including UK. Impact – eg political stability, increased trade and investment, wider choice goods/services, European Standards eg food, health – safety, opportunity to live/work abroad, more competition, new market opportunities, free movement goods/services. Increasing European impact as we move closer to political and monetary union.

   b) EEA made up of EU and former EFTA states (many likely to eventually join EU). Opens up wider markets. Aims to strengthen trade/economic relations. Creates world's largest trading alliance 43% world trade. Moving towards Confederal Europe of Nations.

**Short Answer**

1. a) Visible balance calculated from difference in value of physical goods which are imported and exported.

   b) From the value of services such as transport, banking, tourism, insurance.

   c) UK's account with rest of world. Balance of payments consists of:

   i) Visible Exports – Visible Imports = Balance of Trade

   ii) Balance of Trade + Invisible Balance = Current Balance

   iii) Current Balance + External Assets and Liabilities + Balancing Item = Total Currency Flow (TFC)

2. a) Government body part DTI to help reduce risks. Services include market assessment, market research, trade fairs/exhibitions, advice/information on trade restrictions/regulations, issue of export licences where required.

   b) Many provide information/advice, short/long-term loans, special payment facilities including discounting Bills of Exchange.

   c) 3 main ways – as merchants buying and selling on their own account; as agents handling all or part of a firm's overseas business; as agents for foreign buyers by making contact with UK suppliers.

Multiple Choice Questions

1. A    2. C    3. B    4. A

## Chapter 7: Marketing and Market Research

**Essay-style question – suggested plan**

- **Introduction:** Define – Consumer Products, Exporting, Marketing Research
- **Main Part:** Market Research used to find answers to questions – who? why? how? where? what? when? Can provide information about markets and consumers eg age, sex, occupation, habits, location. Need to find out which countries best to export to. Could involve desk and/or field research. Sources – eg banks, Chambers of Commerce, BOTB.
- **Conclusion:** Research helps identify what consumers want and then produce them. Overseas markets involve different tastes, cultures, language, legislation, buying habits. Thus successful domestic products cannot be assumed to sell abroad, research therefore helps reduce risks of failure.

**Short Answer**

1. a) All activities which are concerned with obtaining and keeping customers. A marketing-oriented company puts customers first in order to achieve its objectives and pays attention to the marketing mix.

    b) From market research can identify goods/services which consumers want and then produce them. Advertising and promotion then used to sell them. Operating this way does not remove business risks but greatly reduces them, thus improving a firm's chances of selling more and making a profit.

2. a) Where products are sold directly to the general public mainly through the retail trade, eg food, toiletries. Also consumer durables, eg TVs, cars.

    b) Goods sold to companies and manufacturers who use them to produce other goods and services, eg office equipment, raw materials.

    c) Tertiary Production. Not physical goods but commercial services/aids to trade. Can be consumer or industrial, eg Insurance, Banks, Garages, used by both. Some firms specialise, eg office cleaning, plant hire, travel agencies.

**Multiple Choice/Completion**

1. D    2. A    3. C    4. D

## Chapter 8: The Marketing Mix – Product and Price

**Essay-style question – suggested plan**

- **Introduction:** Define Marketing
- **Main Part:** Need for marketing – to achieve objectives (market share, return on investment, profit targets, growth) Research to identify markets, beat competition, reduce business risks. Costs/research involved – marketing mix – product, price, promotion, place.
- **Conclusion:** To be successful organisation must be market-oriented. Good product cannot sell if not available or wrongly priced. Better chance of repeat business if correctly marketed.

**Short Answer**

1. a) Diagram – development, introduction, growth, maturity, saturation, decline

    b) Extension strategy – more frequent use, new uses/markets, modifications, technical developments, wider range.

2. a) How it is perceived by consumers, which is often reflected in its name, eg First Direct Banking, Directline Insurance, Kwiksave, Betterware

    b) Distinct, easily recognisable; use of shape, size, colour, logos

**Multiple Choice/Completion**

1. C    2. B    3. D    4. B

## Chapter 9: Marketing – Promotion and Place

**Essay-style question – suggested plan**

- **Introduction:** Define – advertising media, advertisers
- **Main Part:** Main Media – newspapers/magazines, TV, cinema, commercial radio, outdoor, catalogues, circulars. Factors – cost, type goods/services, size of firm, market, objectives, budget Research – agencies, eg advertising; specialists eg ABC, BRAD, JICTAR, in-house eg Questionnaires.
- **Conclusion:** Advertising expensive therefore aim to find most effective combination at lowest cost and with most persuasive message possible Need to evaluate

**Short Answer**

1. a) Specialist firms who employ experts to find most effective way of advertising. Will plan and carry out campaigns on behalf of clients.

b) Usually on above-the-line basis where main income comes from commission received from media concerned. Sometime charge a fee for services known as below-the-line.

c) Agency offers complete range specialist services, eg P R., Brochure production; devises/implements campaigns Offers creativity; media selection/strategy/buying Can be cost-effective if used properly with clear briefs.

2. a) Unique Selling Proposition – distinctive feature(s) of a product/service which is used in advertising/promotion.

b) Public Relations – planned and sustained action to establish and maintain mutual understanding between an organisation and its public, eg Press releases, factory visits, house magazines.

c) British Rate and Data – provides up-to-date information on the unit costs of and size of audiences or circulation of all main media Published monthly.

d) Advertising Standards Authority – financed by the industry to provide list of guidelines. 'British Code of Advertising Practice' aimed at ensuring all advertising 'legal, decent, honest and truthful'.

**Multiple Choice/Completion**

1. D  2. C  3. C  4. B

## Chapter 10: Business Finance

Essay-style question – suggested plan

- **Introduction:** Define: Capital, Small Firms.
- **Main Part:** Sources – bank borrowing, retained profits, government grants/loans, financial institutions, factoring, trade credit, leasing/renting/hire purchase, venture capital companies, loans by organisations, shares
- **Conclusions:** Wide choice, depends on needs, security, growth prospects, interest rates, anticipated rate of return on investment.

**Short Answer**

1. a) If dividends not paid one year, then may be paid in following year, if sufficient profits.

b) Dividends paid out of current year only. No arrears paid.

c) Issued for a specific period. Company agrees to repay capital at some future date.

d) In addition to fixed dividend, receive an extra dividend depending on company profits.

2. a) Yield $= \dfrac{\text{Nominal share value}}{\text{Cost or market price}} \times \%$ dividend

e.g. a 5% dividend is paid on a share with a current market price of 75p and nominal value of 25p

Yield $= \dfrac{25}{75} \times 5 = 1.6\%$

b) Dividend cover

$= \dfrac{\text{Net profit after tax}}{\text{Declared dividend on ordinary shares}}$

e.g. company makes profit of £20,000 after tax. Dividend on preference shares is £5,000 leaving £15,000 for distribution. If £10,000 is paid out in dividends on its 25,000 ordinary shares.

Cover $= \dfrac{20{,}000}{10{,}000} = 2$

c) EPS $= \dfrac{\text{Net profit after tax}}{\text{Number ordinary shares}}$

e.g. company makes profit of £20,000 after tax. Dividend on preference shares is £5,000 leaving £15,000 for distribution. If £10,000 is paid out in dividends on its 25,000 ordinary shares.

$\dfrac{20{,}000}{25{,}000} = 0.8$p per share

d) P/E Ratio $= \dfrac{\text{Market price per share}}{\text{Earnings per share}}$

Thus a share with a market of 75p and an EPS of 0.8p P/E ratio $= \dfrac{75}{0.8} = 93.75$

**Multiple Choice/Completion**

1. D  2. A  3. D  4. C

## Chapter 11: Financial Record-Keeping

Essay-style question – suggested plan

1. a) Ease/speed with which assets can be converted into cash without loss of value, thus cash most liquid; land/buildings usually least.

b) Cash flow forecast, preparation of budgets, variance and control ratios Can plan for in short-term but could lead to bankruptcy/liquidation in long-term.

c) Yes, depends on cash flow, budgeted costs, sales need to be monitored and controlled. Plan overdraft/other borrowing if necessary.

**Short Answer**

1. a) Deducted as an expense in the Profit and Loss Accounts.

Reduces value of fixed assets in Balance Sheet.

b) Straight-line £100,000 ÷ 5 = £20,000 pa

Reducing instalment end year 1 worth £80,000 pa
£64,000
£51,200
£40,960
£32,770

Thus written-off after 5 years under straight-line but valued at £32,770 under reducing instalment.

2. a) Record financial transactions, provide management information, information for owners/shareholders, tax, legal requirements, business evaluation.

b) Financial – concerned with true and fair record of financial transactions as required by law. Responsible for planning, monitoring, controlling, accounts, assets.

Management – concerned with statistical analysis of accounts to supply management information.

Could include cash flow analysis, cost accounting, preparation of budgets, evaluation of projects, preparing variance and control ratios.

**Multiple Choice/Completion**

1. D  2. C  3. D  4. B

## Chapter 12: Human Resources in Organisations

**Essay-style question – suggested plan**

- Introduction: Define: Personnel Function, Efficiency
- Main Part: Describe functions – manpower planning, recruitment/selection, staff welfare, records/recommendations, industrial relations, health/safety, training/development, termination employment.
- Conclusion: Contribute to overall business development/success, which often depends on quality of staff employed, can represent up to 70% + total costs.

**Short Answer**

1. a) Short and long-term process which involves forecasting the future demand for labour in an organisation and planning to meet it.

b) Unlawful discrimination, under 1975 and 1986 Acts, between men and women in employment, education and training and the provision of housing, goods, facilities and services and in advertising.

c) Compensation to employees who are dismissed from their jobs because they are surplus to requirements, possibly due to re-organisation or a decline in business.

2. a) Job description describes skills required in a job. Includes title, outline of purpose and details of main duties/responsibilities involved. Job specification is prepared from this and is a checklist of the personal qualities, experience and skills needed to perform job.

b) Usually sent out with other details to job enquiries. Then used as basis to help short-list applicants.

**Multiple Choice/Completion**

1. D  2. C  3. B  4. D

## Chapter 13: Organisation Behaviour

**Essay-style question – suggested plan**

- Introduction: Define – Principle of Organisation, Responsibility, Authority.
- Main Part: Organisation needed to meet objectives. Usually pyramid with line management or 'Chain of Command'. Involves – authority, responsibility, delegation, leadership.
- Conclusion: Delegation with authority allows tasks to get done but manager still ultimately responsible for actions of subordinates.

**Short Answer**

1. Job enlargement – giving workers a number of tasks to perform rather than just one simple task to increase job enrichment.

Job enrichment – process of making tasks more interesting/satisfying to workers. Involves giving individuals more responsibility and recognition for own work.

Job rotation – changing workers' tasks on a regular basis to avoid boredom.

Group working – involves workers completing whole tasks as a team, rather that just parts of it.

2. a) Positions of authority/responsibility, functional areas, span of control, number of levels.

b) Important to have organisational structure to achieve objectives. Charts important graphical representation which enables people to identify their place in an organisation. Need/complexity depends very much on size of organisation. Usually essential in all but the smallest firms where position of authority/responsibility more easily identified and communicated.

**Multiple Choice/Completion**

1. D  2. D  3. B  4. B

# Chapter 14: Employer and Employee Relations

### Essay-style question – suggested plan

- **Introduction:** Define: Trade Unions, conflict, industrial disputes, arbitration.

- **Main Part:** Trade Union objectives – better pay/conditions/job security, holidays, shorter working hours, improved health and safety, better training, worker involvement, equal opportunities. Organisation objectives – profit, market share, return on investment, growth. Good industrial relations involves consultation, collective bargaining which should help develop mutual understanding of each sides problems. Objectives not incompatible since increased productivity will help finance better pay and other benefits.

- **Conclusion:** Reasoned argument e.g. no organisation wants conflict everyone loses – workers, business, customers. Therefore better to try to prevent if possible. Arbitration may be used as a last resort to prevent potential conflict.

### Short Answer

1. a) Many companies by way of 'bonus' give or sell at discount, shares to employees.

   b) This motivates because it gives them part-ownership and therefore encourages a greater interest/involvement in its success. Helps increase productivity and competitiveness.

2. a) Unemployment because job no longer exists and therefore workers are forced to leave.

   b) All workers would refuse to work in support of proposed redundancies. Ballot required by law if strike proposed, to determine whether or not supported by workers.

   c) Those who do not work on 'shop-floor' usually refers to clerical, administrative and management employees. Article suggests belong to TGWU.

   d) 'Shop-floor'

   e) Falling demand, sales and profits.

### Multiple Choice/Completion

1. C   2. A   3. B   4. D

---

# Chapter 15: Production Processes and Control

### Essay-style question – suggested plan

- **Introduction:** Define: Business Location, Manufacturer.

- **Main Part:** Important factors – supply raw materials, nearness to markets, transport costs, availability of labour, government intervention/support/incentives eg grants/ factories/subsidies.

- **Conclusion:** Other factors may include country's industrial relations record/reputation, education/training facilities and managerial preferences. Firm will usually seek site which offers lowest costs of production and distribution.

### Short Answer

1. a) Existing site lacks space required for expansion in Europe. Also current plant old and nearing its production capacity.

   b) Supply raw materials, nearness to markets, transport costs, availability/skills of labour, possible government assistance.

   c) To attract firm into area of high unemployment, to reduce problems in congested areas, to try to ensure stays in UK and does not relocate in Europe. May offer incentives – grants, subsidies, ready-built factories, planning restrictions in some areas.

   d) Would expect demand to increase particularly for employees with skills in new technology.

   e) Economies of scale – Internal – production, financial, marketing, risk-bearing, managerial. External – labour, ancilliary industries, markets, distribution, commercial.

2. a) Vertical – Amalgamation of firms in same industry at different stages of production. 'Backwards' towards source of supply, 'forwards' towards market.

   Horizontal When firms at same stage of production merge.

   Lateral – When firms with similar but not competing products merge together.

   b) Vertical – Security/control of supplies/markets, reduces costs.

   Horizontal – Economies of Scale, monopoly power, Increased market share.

   Lateral – To diversify, spread risks

### Multiple Choice/Completion

1. C   2. B   3. A   4. B

---

# Chapter 16: Business Information Systems

### Essay-style question – suggested plan

- **Introduction:** Define: Information Technology

- **Main Part:** Uses – information storage, retrieval, databases, spreadsheets, desk top publishing, packages, eg Accountancy, Personnel, Word Processing. Needs to be properly managed and controlled resource. Accessible, user friendly, flexible, need/uses understood. Can result in many benefits such as increased efficiency/service/information and control.

❏ **Conclusion:** Requires action plan with objectives to ensure integral part of business. Training to develop use and understanding and enable staff, including management, to see benefits.

**Short Answer**

1. a) Organisation's name or initials eg Munchener Lebensversicherunc Well known names/initials such as IBM, ICI, BMW are notable exceptions. Customers' perceptions of names are important.

   b) Recognising problem, ensure name is easy to spell and pronounce eg Interbank, particularly throughout Europe. From this, develop strong corporate identity.

2. a) When goods have already been paid for, or sent on approval or sale or return. Not charged to customers' account.

   b) Sent to correct an overcharge or to give a refund.

   c) Request for payment, usually sent monthly. Details invoices, credit/ debit notes and shows balance owed.

   d) Used where no standard price exists to indicate how much goods/job likely to cost.

   e) Used when goods sent by sea. Gives details of ship, port, cargo, destination and charges payable. Provides 'Document of Title'. (Proof of ownership).

**Multiple Choice/Completion**

1. A    2. D    3. D    4. D

## Chapter 17: Innovation and Change

**Essay-style question – suggested plan**

❏ **Introduction:** Define: Pattern of Employment.

❏ **Main Part:** Changes – de-skilling, unemployment, new jobs/skills, new working patterns. Reasons- increasing competition (particularly Europe) Technological advances, more sophisticated products and production methods.

❏ **Conclusion:** Technology and social change likely to have increasing impact. Future trends could include working from home, more self-employed, continued increase in service sector, growth private sector, increase part-time employment.

**Short Answer**

1. a) Growth in population in East Midlands, East Anglia, outer South East, outer Metropolitan areas, South West England. Decline in population Greater London. Fairly static population in North, Yorkshire and Humberside, West Midlands, North West, Scotland and Northern Ireland.

   b) Improves decision-taking, can identify trends, potential changes in demand.

2. a) Use of processed waste, eg, re-using metal cuttings such as iron, copper, steel.

   b) Reclaiming of materials from a worn-out or obsolete product, eg recycled newspaper into toilet rolls.

   c) Recycling centres with bottle banks, can banks, paper banks. Target by 2,000 half all recycling household waste will be reused.

**Multiple Choice/Completion**

1. B    2. B    3. D    4. A

## Chapter 18: Data Analysis and Presentation

**Essay-style question – suggested plan**

❏ **Introduction:** Define – Statistics

❏ **Main Part:** Sources Statistics – Internal eg sales, price, costs, exports, stock levels.

External – eg local/national press, government publications, Trade Associations, Chambers of Commerce.

Much available on computers and therefore with use of databases and spreadsheets can be very quickly and easily manipulated to assist decision-taking.

Costs can vary, sampling often used. Depends what is required. Can be presented in many ways eg tables, charts, graphs, diagrams.

Examples of statistics frequently used in business include – frequency distributions based on probability. Can be analysed to find mean, median, mode, range, inter-quartile range, standard deviation, normal distribution, estimation, hypothesis testing.

Business forecasting of sales, costs, stock, production – can use time-series analysis, causal modelling, qualitative approaches.

❏ **Conclusion:** Statistical methods help identify, study and solve many business problems and to take better informed decisions about uncertain situations. Modern computer technology makes them easier and more cost-effective to collect and analyse.

**Short Answer**

1. a) Data which has been collected but not organised or analysed in any way.

b) A graph of a frequency distribution. A histogram is constructed with a series of rectangular blocks representing the class frequencies in such a way that the areas (not the heights) of the blocks are proportional to the frequencies.

c) A reasoned assumption based on observation. Can be tested under a normal distribution curve. A statistical hypothesis under test is called a null hypothesis.

d) A set of data is called a distribution and the frequency is the number of times which any variable occurs in the distribution. This can be added to give the cumulative frequency distribution.

2. a) Total of all individual values divided by the number of them:

$$Eg: 5, 4, 2, 9 = \frac{20}{4} = 5$$

b) Middle value of data arranged in order of magnitude. Eg: 2, 4, 5, 9 = 4.5 (mean of middle 2)

c) Value which occurs most frequently in set of data: Eg: 2, 3, 5, 4, 5, 9, 7 = 5

## Multiple Choice/Completion

1. B    2. D    3. A    4. B

## Chapter 19: Monitoring Business Performance

### Essay-style question – suggested plan

1. a) For example, Bar Charts, graphs

   b) Report format – eg title/purpose, summary, introduction, body, conclusion. Include sales variance analysis – due to increased competition, problems with marketing mix.

### Short Answer

1. a) Standard costing – used to control direct costs. Calculation of how much costs should be under defined working conditions. Best suited to manufacturing processes. Budgetary control – used for indirect costs whereby budgets allocated to cost centres, involves preparation and monitoring.

   b) Identify objectives, targets, prepare initial budget in line with this, review and adjust, final co-ordination and preparation.

   c) Fixed – remains same even if activity levels change Flexible – adjust in response to changes in variable costs or levels business activity. Zero-based – calculated in relation to needs of each activity, evaluated against importance to business.

2. a) Differences between actual results achieved and planned budget or standard cost.

   b) Negative – revenues short and/or costs exceeded. Positive revenues exceed and/or costs are less. Materials – price, materials – labour, labour-rate, labour-efficiency, overhead expenditure, overhead volume, sales price, sales volume.

   c) Adjust budgets to more realistic levels. Increase marketing activity to generate sales. Concentrate on most successful products and/or markets.

## Multiple Choice/Completion

1. B    2. C    3. D    4. C

## Chapter 20: Starting and Running Your Own Business

### Essay-style question – suggested plan

☐ **Introduction:** Define – Small Business idea and why chosen, eg interest/research, USP.

☐ **Main Part:** Should consider objectives and elements of business plan including – legal form, markets/marketing, location, accounts/record-keeping, finance, legal requirements, tax/national insurance, staff, training. Monitoring/control performance – use technology, financial – budgeting/cash flow, variance analysis, break-even Performance – analysis accounts Productivity-inputs/outputs Quality – customer satisfaction, returns, waste, complaints.

☐ **Conclusion:** Success depends on a good business idea well researched and implemented. Many factors to be taken into account and managed. Many small businesses also depend partly upon skills/efforts of owner. As develop, can introduce division of labour.

### Short Answer

1. a) Name given to a product to differentiate it from others, eg, Levis, Joe Bloggs.

   b) Producing a new range of jeans every month.

   c) £40 million turnover, £25 million personal fortune of owner, 'legendary' name.

   d) Breaking with tradition in industry, introduced new ranges, promotion via links with 'pop' stars and sponsorship deals.

   e) Major manufacturers, setting up manufacturing plant, tradition.

   f) Do not be afraid of the competition, no matter how big; be determined; develop a USP; be prepared to try out new ideas; develop an innovative marketing plan; exploit strengths (eg British name).

2. Lack of professional advice – banks, solicitors, TEC's and others who can help to avoid obvious pitfalls, particularly when starting up.

Inadequate financial resources – capital investment which may involve loans and cash flow to provide working capital.

Wrong location – particularly in retailing or service industry. Cost of location must be evaluated against potential to attract customers or ability to achieve other objectives such as good distribution.

Poor management – lack of skills or particular skill can result in a business being mis-managed. Many people good at job, eg builder but lack skills to run business.

Poor marketing and market research – failure to identify markets and/or the wrong marketing mix – product, price, promotion and place.

Poor decision-making and planning. A proper business plan is needed to aid decision-taking and should be updated on a regular basis.

Poor quality control – can lead to poor quality products or services which affects customer satisfaction, sales, costs, waste.

Lack of technical skill – where a business is unable to meet its objectives. May be due to lack of resources and/or inadequate training.

Expansion without planning – particularly where this results in an over-commitment of finance or other resources. Expansion should take place within the framework of an overall strategic plan.

Lack of financial management and discipline – budgeting, proper record-keeping and cash flow forecasts are all necessary to enable a business to survive and prosper.

# Index *(by reference to chapter and paragraph)*

Accounting 1, 56
    Concepts 11, 11
    Financial 11, 2
    Management 11, 2
    Systems 20, 42
    Standards Board 11, 11
Accounts
    Dept 1, 56
    Final 11, 22; 11, 23; 11, 44
    Need for 11, 1
Absolute advantage 6, 2
ACAS 14, 35; 14, 38
Administration 1, 59
Administrative Management 13, 39
Advertising 9, 9; 9, 36; 20, 31
    Agencies 9, 22; 9, 25
    Benefits 9, 30
    Control 9, 32; 9, 36
    Criticisms 9, 31
    Effectiveness 9, 26; 9, 29
    Media 9, 12; 9, 13
    Standards Authority 9, 33
Adult Training ???
Agenda 16, 11; 16, 13
Agents 6, 69
Ansoff Matrix 8, 41
Application, letter of 12, 18
    form 12, 19
Appropriation Account 11, 77
Arbitration 12, 69; 14, 35; 14, 36
Articles of Association 2, 31
Assets 11, 24; 11, 27; 11, 30
Assisted Areas (see Development Areas)
Auditors 11, 8; 11, 10
Authority 13, 8; 13; 11

Balance of Payments 5, 38; 6, 9; 6, 14
    Tackling Problems 6, 19
Balance Sheet 11, 24
Balance of Trade 6, 10
Baltic Exchange 4, 6
Banking Acts 5, 65
Bank
    Charges 16, 71
    Giro 16, 64
    Reconciliation statement 16, 72
    Statement 16, 72
Bank of England – Authorised Institutions 5, 65
    Monetary Policy 5, 56
Banks 5, 67; 6, 75; 20, 6
Bankruptcy 11, 50
Barter 1, 2
Bill of Exchange 6, 76
Bill of Lading 16, 52
Black Economy 5, 13
Board of Directors 1, 49; 1, 61; 2, 18; 2, 26; 16, 15
Borrowing 10, 5
Boston Matrix 8, 37
BOTB 6, 72
BRAD 9, 20
Branding 8, 14
Break-Even Point/Chart 19, 32
Bretton Woods 6, 28
British Standards Institution 17, 48; 19, 52
Broadcasting Act 9, 34
BS 5750 19, 54; 19, 64
B.T. 5, 48; 16, 20; 1625
Budgetary Control 19, 3; 19, 9
Budget, The
    Operating 20, 52
Budgeting 17, 33; 19, 5; 19, 10; 20, 44
Budgets
    Promotional 9, 44
    Types of 19, 8; 19, 13
Building societies 10,3
Business
    and the Economy 5
    Communication 16, 1
    Constraints on 1, 71
    Documents 16, 50
    Environment 1; 1, 73
    Forecasting 18, 77
    Functions 1, 52; 1, 73; 13, 72
    Information Systems 16
    Location 15, 62
    Names Act 2, 5; 20, 54
    Objectives 1, 33
    Organisations 1, 20; 1, 44; 2
    People and 12, 2
    Planning 3; 20, 13
    Resources 1, 12
    Start Your Own 20
    Tax Implications 5, 47
    Training 20, 71

Capital 1, 12; 2, 4; 10, 11
    Authorised 2, 27
    Employed 13, 45; 13, 54; 15, 82
    Gains Tax 5, 44
    Gearing 10, 30
    Market 4, 6
    Social 5, 4
    Sources 10, 3
    Types of 10, 21; 11, 45
    Working 10, 2; 11, 48; 11, 73; 15, 47
Cash Flow 8, 6; 19, 15; 20, 44
    Forecast 20, 46
    Statement 11, 74
Cartel 4, 99
Causal Modelling 18, 89
CBI 6, 61
Centralisation 13, 20
Certificate of incorporation 2, 33
Chain of command 13, 3
Chamber of Commerce 6, 61
Chancellor of Exchequer (see Budget)
Change 17
    Barriers to 17, 8
    Community Impact 17, 74
    Concept of 17, 1
    Cultural 3, 53
    Employment and 17, 65
    External 17, 5
    Environmental 3, 57; 17, 48
    Internal 17, 3
    Lifestyles and 17, 39
    Managing 17, 22
    Predicting 17, 36
    Resistance to 17, 19
    Social 3, 52
    Technological 3, 58
Charities 1, 8; 9, 9; 9 ,31
Cheques 16, 55; 16, 79
Choice 1, 3; 15, 91
Circular Flow of Income 5, 16
City Challenge 15, 71
Collective bargaining 14, 21
Collusion 15, 92
Commercial Services (see Tertiary production)
Commission for Racial Equality 12, 53
Commodity markets 4, 6
Communication 1, 10; 16, 1; 16, 10
    Barriers to 16, 83
Companies 2, 16
    Acts 2.16; 3, 31; 20, 54
    Dissolution of 2, 34
    Multi-national 6, 78
    Single Member 2, 24
Company secretary 2, 18
Comparative advantage 6, 2
Competition 1, 7
    Act 15, 92

## Index

Imperfect 4, 88
Perfect 4, 73
Pricing and 8, 46
Service (utilities) Act 2, 76
Competitor Analysis 3, 62
Competitive Strategies 8, 34
Tendering 2, 71
Computers (see Technology, Word Processing and Information Technology)
Confederation of British Industry 14, 25
Conglomerates 15, 86
Conflict 17, 12
Consular officials 6, 61
Consumer 1, 7; 3, 60
Consumer Credit Act 3, 41; 9, 36
Consumer goods/durables 7, 18
Consumer Panels 7, 40
Consumer Protection Act 3, 45; 20, 54
Consumer Protection 1, 22; 3, 36; 3, 38; 15, 14
Contract, law of 20, 55
Contract of Employment Acts 12, 30
Contravision 16, 31
Contingency Approach 13, 75
Control Loop 1, 75
Co-operatives 2, 46; 20, 37
Co-operative Wholesale Society 9, 55
Copyright Act 11, 29; 20, 54
Corporate Gap 3, 65
Identity 7, 6; 9, 40
Corporation Tax 5, 44
Cost Centre 19, 4
Costs- Fixed and Variable 4, 59
Cost Benefit Analysis 10, 53
Council Tax 2, 66; 5, 42; 5, 46
Credit Cards 16, 67
Creditors 11, 26; 20, 77
Ratio 11, 66
Critical Path Analysis 19, 76
Networks 19, 76
Culture
Organisational 1, 10; 13; 24
Curriculum Vitae 12, 20
Customs and Excise Duties 5, 45

Data Analysis and Presentation 18
Data – Descriptions of 18, 36
Protection Act 16, 44
Sources of 18, 1
Datel 16, 33
Debentures 10, 20
Debtors 11, 26; 20, 77
Ratio 11, 67
Decentralisation 13, 21
Decision-Making 1, 64; 10, 35
Trees 10, 57
Deflation 5, 103
Deflationary Gap 5, 32
Delegation 13, 7
Delphi Forecast 18, 92
Demand 3, 56; 4, 8; 20, 19
Aggregate 1, 7; 5, 27
Kinked 4.96
Supply and 4, 49
Department of Trade and Industry 6, 70; 10, 3; 16, 55
Department Stores 9, 60
Depreciation 11, 12
Depressed areas (see Development Areas)
Deregulation 2, 71
Design Strategy 15, 9
Desk Top Publishing 16, 39
Development areas 15, 69
Direct Debits 16, 62
Direct Mail 9, 7
Discount Houses 5, 61; 5, 67
Discount Stores 9, 61
Diseconomies of Scale 15, 78
Dispersion, Measures of 18, 56
Disposable Income 3, 51
Distribution, chain of 9, 53
Management 9, 62
Objectives 9, 52

role of 9, 51
Dividends 2, 18; 10, 14; 10, 22
Division of Labour 1, 2
Door-to-door selling 9, 61
Double-entry Book-keeping 11, 20
Dumping 6, 18

Economic Analysis 3, 49
Growth 3, 50; 5, 33; 5, 68
Order Quantity 15, 30
Systems 1, 18; 1, 23
Economics Business and 4.1
Macro 5, 2
Micro 5, 1
Economies of Scale 15, 72
EFTA 6, 30
EFTPOS 16, 41
Elasticity of Demand 4, 15
Price 4, 16; 8.15
Income 4, 27
Cross 4, 30
Elasticity of Supply 4, 42
Electronic mail 16, 29
Embargo 6, 17
Employer and Employee Relations 14
Employers Associations 14, 24
Employment Legislation 1, 22; 12, 37; 14, 37
Employment, Terms of 12, 29
Employing People 20, 67
Employment
Termination of 12, 8; 12, 54
Trends 17, 70
Enterprise 1, 12
Scheme 5, 86
Zones 15, 71
Environment 1, 7
Environmental Protection 1, 22; 15, 14; 17, 49
Protection Act 3, 48
Environmental Scanning 3, 20
Equal Opportunities Commission 12, 52
Equal Pay Acts 12, 33
EU (see European Union)
European Economic Area 6, 30
European Monetary System 6, 39
European Union (EU) 6, 30
Benefits of 6, 57
Directives/Standards 3, 37
Impact on Business 6, 58
Legislation 6, 50
Organisation of 6, 41
Exchange Controls 6, 17
Equalisation Account 5, 63
Exchange Rates 3, 51; 5, 63, ; 6, 20
Fixed and Floating 6, 25
Importance of 6, 29
Expectancy Theory 13, 66
Expenses, business 20, 47; 20, 64
Export Houses 6, 69
Export Licence 16, 52
Exports 5, 1; 6, 7
Export Documentation 16, 52

Facsimile transmission 16, 30
Factors of Production 1, 12; 5, 16; 5, 69
Factoring 10, 3
Fair Trading Act 3, 40; 15, 90
Filing (see Information, Storage and Retrieval)
Finance 20, 39
Companies 10, 3
Financial Controls 19, 2
Financial Record-keeping 11
Financial Services Act 2, 42
Firms
Growth 15, 83
Size 15, 82
Survival of small 15, 93
Theory of 4, 53
Fiscal policy 3, 30; 5, 38; 5, 84; 5, 99
Fixed Assets 11, 24; 11, 27
Fixed Costs (see Costs)
Food Safety Acts 3, 46
Flexible working time 14, 7

# Index

Flow Process Charts *13, 37*
Footloose Industries *15, 62*
Foreign Exchange market *4, 6*
Foreign trade (see International Trade)
Franchising *2, 53*
Fringe Benefits *14, 11*
Frequency Distribution *18, 35; 18, 48*
Funds Flow Statement *11, 73*

GANTT Chart *13, 36*
GATT *6, 30*
GNVQs *17, 44*
Government
    and the Economy *5, 3; 5, 38*
    and Business *3, 30*
    Benefit payments *5, 4; 5, 54*
    Departments *2, 64; 5, 74; 15, 70*
    Employment and Training *3, 33*
    Environmental Strategies *17, 49*
    Expenditure *5, 19*
    Finance *2, 40; 10, 3; 2, 72*
    Industrial Relations *3, 34; 14, 37*
    Influence *3, 27*
    International Trade *3, 32*
    Location of Industry *3, 35; 15, 68*
    Marketing and Consumer
        Protection *3, 36; 3, 38*
    Policies *2, 39; 5, 39*
    Protection *3, 36*
    Securities *5, 64*
    Social objectives *5.40*
    Training Schemes *5, 75; 5, 86*
Goods *1, 7*
Goods received note (see Business documents)
Goodwill *11.29*
Grievance Procedures *14, 34*
Gross Domestic Product *5, 6*
Gross National Product *5, 9*
Group Working *13, 65*

Halo Effect *8, 18*
Hawthorne Experiments *13, 53*
Health & Safety *1, 22; 12, 8; 15, 14*
    at Work Act *12, 33; 14, 37*
    General Regulations *12, 38*
Hierarchy
    of Needs *13, 44*
    Organisational *1, 10*
Hire Purchase *10, 3*
Holding Companies *15, 85*
Hours of Work *14, 6*
Human Relation School *13, 43*
Hypermarkets *9.60*
Hygiene Factors *13, 57; 13, 59*
Hypothesis Testing *18, 72*

Import Licence *16, 52*
Imports *6, 7*
Income Tax (see PAYE)
Independent Traders *9, 60*
Index Numbers *18, 94*
Induction *12, 19*
Industrial Action *14, 26; 17, 20*
Industrial inertia *15, 62*
Industrial relations *3, 34; 5, 79; 12, 8; 14, 13; 15, 80*
Industrial tribunals *12, 59*
Inflation *3, 51; 5, 87*
    Causes of *5, 94*
    Effects of *5, 90*
    Policies to control *5, 96*
Inflationary Gap *5, 32*
Information Technology *3, 58; 16, 35; 16, 46; 16, 54; 17, 45*
Inheritance Tax *5, 44*
Innovation and Change *17*
    Innovation *15, 91; 17, 25*
Insolvency Act *2, 35*
Insurance *16, 52; 20, 8*
Integration *15, 87*
Interest Rates *3, 51; 5, 61*
International Monetary Fund *6, 30*
International Standards Organisation *19.53*
International Trade *6*
    Barriers to *6, 15*
    Benefits from *6, 6*
    Free Trade *6, 30*
Interquartile Range *18, 56*
Interviews *12, 22*
Investment Appraisal *10, 37*
    Average Rate of Return *20, 43*
    Discounted Cash Flow *10, 46*
    Payback Technique *10, 40*
Investors *2, 36; 10, 12; 10, 14*
    Institutional *4, 6*
Investors in People *12, 31*
Invisible trade *6, 10*
Invoice (see business documents)
Issuing Houses *4, 6; 10.13*
ITV Commission *9, 34*

Job Centres *5, 54; 5, 86*
    Description *12, 10*
    Enlargement *13, 62*
    Enrichment *13, 63; 19.63*
    Evaluation *15, 61*
    Roles *12, 5; 12, 10; 13, 3*
    Rotation *13, 64*
    Satisfaction *14, 2; 19.63*
    Specification *12, 2*
Joint Consultation *14, 32*
Joint Ventures *15, 84*

Labour *1, 12*
    Turnover *12, 61; 14, 39*
Land *1, 12*
Leadership *13, 10*
    Types of *13, 12*
Legislation *20, 54*
Leasing *10, 3*
Liabilities *11, 24; 11, 31*
Limited Company *2, 16*
Limited Liability *2, 17*
Line and Staff Organisation *13, 3*
Linear Programming *19, 67; 19, 74*
Liquidity *11, 30*
    Ratios *11, 69*
Liquidation *2, 34; 11.50*
Lloyd's of London *4.6*
Local Authorities *2, 65; 20, 34; 20, 36*
Local Authority Loans *10, 3*
Location of Industry *3, 35; 15, 62*
Loss Leaders *9.4*

Mail Order *9, 61*
Management *1, 7; 1, 61; 9, 62; 12, 13; 12, 19; 13, 5; 15, 1*
    by Objectives *1, 74*
    Principles of *13, 41*
Manpower Planning *12, 4*
Manufacturing Account *11, 77*
Market Characteristics *7, 52*
Market Research *1, 58; 3, 24; 7, 1; 7, 22; 7, 36; 9, 25; 20, 17*
    Agencies *7, 48*
    Evaluation of *7, 60*
Market Segmentation *7, 50*
Market Share *7, 4; 8, 46; 15, 82*
Markets and Marketing *20, 17*
Marketing *7; 8; 9*
    Budget *9, 44*
    Defined *7, 1*
    Function *1, 58*
    Industrial *9, 49*
    International *6, 67*
    Objectives *7, 3*
    Management *7, 7*
    Mix *1, 58; 7, 8; 7, 7*
    Test *7, 42*
    Types of *7, 18*
Markets, Retail *4, 6; 9, 59*
    Industrial *9, 49*
Mean, Median, Mode *18, 49*
Meetings *16, 11*
Memorandum *16, 16*
Memorandum of Association *2, 31*
Merchant Banks *5, 67*
Merger *15, 84*

451

# Index

Merit Goods 5, 4
Method Study 15, 54
Middlemen 4, 3
Minutes 16, 15
Mission 1, 10; 1, 73
    Statement 3, 5
Mixed economy 2, 1
Mobile shops 9, 61
Money 5, 58
Money Market 4, 6
Monetary policy 3, 30; 5, 39; 5, 56; 5, 84; 5, 97
Monetary Sector 5, 65
Money Supply 5, 59
Monitoring and Evaluation 3, 9
Monitoring and Measuring Performance 19
Monopolies and Mergers Act 15, 90
Monopoly 4, 81; 5, 4; 15, 89
    Arguments against 15, 91
Monte Carlo Simulation 19, 70
Motion Study 13, 38
Motivation 13, 57; 14, 2; 15, 6
Motivational Research 7, 47
Motivators 13, 58
Multiple Stores 9, 60
Multiplier 5, 27
Multinational Companies 6, 78
Multi-skilling 14, 31

National Debt 5, 51
National Income 5, 5; 5, 25; 5, 68; 6, 63
National Insurance 5, 46; 20, 66
Nationalised Industry (see Public Enterprise)
Needs 1, 3
Network Analysis 10, 36; 19, 67; 19, 76
Networking 16, 37
New Towns 15, 70
Normal Distribution Curve 18, 68
NVQs 17, 44

Objectives 1, 7; 1, 10; 1, 33; 1, 73; 7, 3; 8, 46; 19, 52
Office of Fair Trading 4, 100
OFTEL 16, 25
Oligopoly 4, 94
Omnibus survey 7, 39
Open Systems 16, 55
Operational Research 10, 36; 19, 65
Operating Statement 3, 8
Operations Management 15, 1
Opportunity Cost 1, 6
Organisation
    Definition 1, 8
    Chart 1, 50; 13, 4
    Components 1, 10
    Informal 13, 23
    of Production 15, 6
Organisational Behaviour 13
    Theory 13
Overdrafts 10, 3; 20, 39
Overheads 4, 59
Overseas Markets 6, 20

Packaging 8, 23
Partnerships 2, 9
Party Selling 9, 61
Pareto Rule 15, 29
PAYE 5, 18, 5, 44
Performance
    Measurement 1, 74; 19
    Monitoring 20, 73
    Ratios 13, 53
Personal Selling 9, 45
Personnel Department 1, 53
    Functions 12, 8
    Management 12, 3
    Policies 14, 48
PERT 19, 76
Petty cash 16, 65
Picketing 14, 28
Place 7, 15; 9, 51
Point-of-sale 9, 5; 16, 22
Poll Tax (see Council Tax)
Population 3, 54

Age Distribution 3, 54; 3, 55
Birthrate 3, 54; 17, 40
Deathrate 17, 41
Geographical distribution 3, 54
Mobility 3, 56
Sex distribution 3.54
Trends 3, 54; 17, 74; 17, 73
Working population 3, 56; 5, 79
Life expectancy 17, 41
Postal services 16, 23
Post Office 16, 20
Preference shares 10, 17
Pressure Groups 3, 57
Prestel 2, 41; 16, 33
Price 4, 7; 7, 13; 8, 44; 20, 26
Price/Earnings Ratio 10, 27
Price Leadership 4, 99
Pricing Objectives 8, 46
Pricing Policies 8, 47
Prices and Incomes Policies 5, 101
Primary Groups 13, 23
Primary Industry 1, 16; 15, 65
Private enterprise (sector) 1, 39; 2, 1; 17, 70
Private limited company 2, 19
Privatisation 2, 70
Probability 7, 28; 18, 30
Product Design 15, 6; 15, 9
    Development 8, 9
    Differentiation 8, 24
    Life Cycle 8, 3; 20, 24
    Mix (Range) 7, 10; 8, 1
    Segmentation 8, 19
    Strategy 8, 25
    Withdrawal 8, 12
Production 15; 1, 7; 1, 12; 1, 16
    and Marketing 15, 2
    Costs of 15, 7; 15, 79
    Department 1, 54
    Engineering 19, 43; 19, 46
    Job, Flow, Batch 15, 22; 15, 37
    Just-In-Time 15, 44; 19, 50
    Management 15, 1
    Organisation of 15, 35
    Planning and Control 15, 5
    Systems 3, 59
Productivity 12, 61; 15, 49; 19, 2
    Agreement 14, 23
Professional Advisers 20, 6
Profit 1, 15; 5, 47; 7, 4; 15, 82
    Gross and Net 11, 56
Promotion 7, 14
Prospectus 2, 26
Protection (see International Trade)
Public Corporation 2, 56
Public Enterprise 2, 55
    Advantages and disadvantages 2, 68
    Reasons for 2, 67
    Objectives 1, 40
Public expenditure 5, 52
Public limited company 2, 26
Public relations 9, 37
Public Sector Borrowing 5, 49
    Requirement
Purchasing 1, 55; 15, 6; 15, 17
    Methods 15, 22

Quality 19, 38
    Aspects of 19, 41
    Assurance 19, 43; 19, 44
    Circles 19, 43; 19, 50
    Control 15, 6; 19, 2; 19, 42
    Importance of 19, 38
    Standards 19, 43; 19, 52
    Systems 19, 56
    TQM 19, 43; 19, 59; 19, 64
Queueing Theory 19, 67; 19, 72
Quotas 6, 15; 6, 81
Questionnaires 7, 39

Race Relations Act 12, 33; 12, 53
Radio Authority 9, 34
Range 18, 57

Rate of Exchange (see Exchange Rates)
Ratio Analysis 10, 21; 11, 51
Recruitment, Selection and Training 12, 9
Recycling 17, 61
Redundancy 12, 56; 14, 21; 14, 31
    Payments 12, 60
Responsibility 13, 7
Restrictive Trade Practices 4, 100; 5, 4; 15, 92
Research and Development 17, 26
Retail Audits 7, 45
Retail Price Index 5, 87; 18, 97
Retail Trade 9, 59
Revenue 4, 57
Risk Analysis 10, 65
Retail Trade 9, 59
Revenue 4, 57
Risk Analysis 10, 65

Salaries (see under Wage Rates)
Sale of Goods Acts 3, 43
Sales Promotion 9, 2; 20, 31
    Targets 9, 50; 20, 48
Sampling 7, 26; 18, 27
Scientific Management 13, 31
Security 16, 78
Selection 12, 14
Sensitivity Analysis 10, 65
Services 1, 7
Sex Discrimination Act 12, 33
Scarcity 1, 4
Secondary Industries 1, 16; 15, 65
Securities and Investments Board 2, 43
Self Regulatory Organisations 2, 43
Self-service stores 9, 60
Self-Sufficiency 1.2
Service Industry (see Tertiary Production)
Shares 2, 17; 10, 11
Share Issue 10, 13
Share Prices 2, 33
Simulation 19, 68
Single European Act 6, 38
Single regeneration budget 5, 86
Skills 12, 5; 14, 5; 15, 66
Social Costs/Benefits 5, 4; 5, 71; 10, 53
Sole Trader 2, 4
Special Deposits 5, 64
Span of Control 13, 18
Sponsorship 9, 15
Spreadsheets 16, 39; 19, 7
Staff Appraisal 12, 32
Standard Deviation 18, 62
Standard Costing 19, 3; 19, 19
Standing Orders 16, 61
Statement of Account (see Business Documents)
Statistical Presentation 18, 7
    Process Control 19, 43; 19, 57
    Terms 18, 25
Statistics 18, 3
    National Income 5, 14
Stockturn 15, 24
Stock control 1, 55; 15, 6; 15, 19; 15, 23
Stock Exchange 2, 40; 5, 64
Stock Evaluation 11, 32
Strikes 14, 27
Subsidies 6, 17
Supermarkets 9, 60
Supply 4, 35; 15, 91
    Chain Management 15, 44
    And Demand 4, 49
SWOT Analysis 3, 11
Systems 1, 7
    Approach 13, 69

Takeover bid 15, 84
Tariffs 6, 15; 6, 81
Taxation 5, 42; 20, 61, 20, 66
Technology 14.12; 16, 46; 17, 45
TECs 5, 54; 5, 86; 10, 3; 20, 18
TEED 5.54
Telecommunications 3, 58
Telephone 16, 26
Teletext 16, 33
Telex 16, 22
Terms of Trade 18, 97
Tertiary production 1, 16; 5, 13; 15, 66; 17, 70
Theory X & Y 13, 49
Time Series Analysis 18, 79
Trade (see also International Trade) 1, 2; 6, 1
Trade Associations 7, 36
Trade Credit 10, 3
Trade Descriptions Acts 3, 39; 9, 35
Trade Discount 16, 51
Trade Union Reform and Employment Rights Act 14, 38
Trade Unions 1, 8; 5, 86; 14, 14
Trade Union Congress 14, 25
Trading, Profit and Loss Account 11, 22
Trading Standards Department 12, 8; 12, 18
Training (see also Recruitment) 5, 69; 5, 74; 20, 71
    Benefits 12, 30
    Types of 12, 28
Transfer Payments 5, 13
Transfer Pricing 6, 81
Trends 18, 26
Trial balance 11, 22
Turnover 15, 82

Unemployment 3, 50; 5, 72; 15, 69
    Effects of 5, 80
    Policies 5, 84
    Reasons for 5, 79
    Types of 5, 76
Unfair Contract Terms Act 3, 42
Unfair Dismissal 12, 59
Uninsurable risks 20, 11
Unique Selling Point 9, 1; 20, 22
Urban Policy 15, 71

Value Added Tax 5, 18; 5, 45; 6, 59; 16, 51
Value Added Statement 11, 77
Value Analysis 15, 16
Variable costs (see Costs)
Variance Analysis 19.21
Variety Chain Stores 9, 60
Vending machines 9, 61
Vendor Appraisal 15, 20
Venture Capital 10, 2; 10, 3
Visible Trade 6, 10

Wage Rates 14, 4
    Differentials 14, 5
Wages Council 14, 37
Wants 1, 3
Weights and Measures Act 3, 44
Wholesalers 4, 6; 9, 54
Word Processing 16, 42
Work To Rule 14, 26
Workstudy 10, 36; 15, 53
World Trade Organisation 3, 30

Youth Credits 5, 86
Youth Training 5, 75

'Z' Charts 18, 15
Z Scores 18, 74
Zero Defects 19, 43; 19, 48

## Index of names

Alderfer 13,47
Bamforth 13,74
Burns 13,75
Galbraith 13,69
Gantt, Henry 13,34
Gilbreth, Frank 13,37; 15,53
    Lillian 13,37

Fayol, Henri 13,39
Herzberg, F 13,57
Kahn 5,27
Keynes, J.M 5,23
Lawler 13,67
Likert 13,69
Maslow, A 13,44

Mayo, E 13,53
McGregor, D 13,49
Mills 5,24
Porter 8, 34; 13,67
Ricardo 5,24
Say 5,24
Smith, A 5,24

Stalker 13,75
Taylor, F.W 13,31; 15,53
Trist 13,74
Urwick, L 13,41
Vroom 13,67
Woodward, J 13,75